FUTURES GUIDE 2021

The Top Prospects For Every MLB Team and more

Edited by Collin Whitchurch and Nick Schaefer

Mark Barry, J.P. Breen, Ben Carsley, Spring Cullen, Mike Gianella, Steve Givarz, Nathan Graham, Keanan Lamb, Jeffrey Paternostro, Jen Ramos, Jesse Roche, Bret Sayre, Nick Schaefer, Jarrett Seidler, Ben Spanier, Forest Stulting, Brandon Williams, Kris Willis, Matt Winkelman

Bret Sayre, Consultant Editor
Robert Au, Harry Pavlidis and Amy Pircher, Statistics Editors

Library of Congress Cataloging-in-Publication Data:
paperback
ISBN-10: 1950716880
ISBN-13: 978-1950716883

Project Credits
Cover Design: Ginny Searle
Interior Design and Production: Amy Pircher, Robert Au
Layout: Amy Pircher, Robert Au

Cover Photos
Front Cover: Wander Franco. © Kim Klement-USA TODAY Sports

Baseball icon courtesy of Uberux, from https://www.shareicon.net/author/uberux

Manufactured in the United States of America
10 9 8 7 6 5 4 3 2 1

Table of Contents

Top 101 Prospects

by Jeffrey Paternostro, Jarrett Seidler and Keanan Lamb

1. Wander Franco, SS, Tampa Bay Rays

Franco remains the top prospect in baseball in large part because there's no new evidence to suggest he isn't. What is known about Franco's 2020: 1) He was at the alternate site, and even made the playoff taxi squad. 2) As part of said taxi squad he appeared on the field after Tampa Bay clinched the AL pennant, showing off bigger arms in a cutoff t-shirt. 3) He went to the Dominican Winter League and looked more or less like you'd expect before those swole biceps started barking. Franco was shut down as a precautionary measure, but it's considered a minor injury. He's on the verge of taking his place in the middle of the Rays lineup and infield, where he should challenge for batting titles—in a world without Nick Madrigal, he'd have the best contact ability on this list—and bop 20-plus home runs. Sometimes no news isn't the worst news.

2. Adley Rutschman, C, Baltimore Orioles

How many cold-weather catchers, lightly followed out of high school and with a meager beginning to their college career, end up garnering consideration for the top overall spot just a few years later? Not many. Despite the geographical biases, or the iffy historical success rate for catchers, Rutschman is a well-rounded player on both sides of the ball, and he may ascend to the top spot next year—if he doesn't graduate first, anyway. There is power in the bat, plenty of contact ability and the discipline of a professional approach. (He sees the ball incredibly well from both sides of the plate, which isn't always true with switch hitters.) On the defensive side, he's nimble and athletic with at least a plus arm, and he also collaborates well with his pitching staff. You can't really build a potential franchise player much better than this.

3. Julio Rodríguez, OF, Seattle Mariners

If you wanted to make an argument for Rodríguez as the top prospect in baseball you can start with this: He hits the ball incredibly hard. Exit velocity can be a bit of a fun fact, or merely an expression of the obvious, but when a teenager is regularly showing the kind of hard contact that would garner a tip of the cap from Giancarlo Stanton, take notice. The on-field performance got Rodríguez into the top 10 last year—he slugged .540 at two A-ball levels as an 18-year-old—and the reports from the alternate site in 2020 did nothing to dampen our enthusiasm. Unlike the two players ahead of him, though, we can point out minor quibbles. It's still unclear how good the hit tool is—it projects as above-average, which could allow the elite raw to play to 40 home runs—or where he will stand in the outfield. (Right field currently looks more likely than center.) Rodríguez should be a plus defender in a corner, and given the present (and voluble) offensive tools, he may have the highest ceiling of any prospect on this list.

4. Sixto Sánchez, RHP, Miami Marlins

Sánchez's ascension turned out to be worth waiting another year for. The uber-talented righty has long tantalized with ace potential: triple-digit heat from a free and easy delivery and nearly every offspeed in the book. In 2020, one of the offspeeds—his hard changeup—revealed itself to be a fully-operational out pitch. That was the last ingredient Sánchez needed for major-league success, and he was splendid down the stretch for the Marlins. There are minor nitpicks: his health record is not clean, his fastball shape doesn't lead to as many swings-and-misses as the velocity would indicate and his command occasionally deserts him (most notably in the NLDS). But make no mistake, it's absolutely elite stuff and pitchability, and he has the best chance to be an ace of anyone on this list by a good margin. That makes him the best pitching prospect in baseball...

5. Ian Anderson, RHP, Atlanta Braves

... but it was actually a razor-close call. While Sánchez does have a better chance of being an ace, we think Anderson's probably the better pitcher right now. His changeup progressed even more than Sánchez's, jumping from a pitch with average-to-above-average projection to a straight present plus-plus offering that was baffling hitters deep into the playoffs. His fastball and curveball are good enough to overcome mediocre spin rates, and the back of his baseball card has been nearly spotless since he was the third-overall pick in 2016. Sure, he could use another half-grade of command improvement, but who couldn't? Anderson is a very good major-league pitcher, right now.

6. Jarred Kelenic, OF, Seattle Mariners

Kelenic unlocked his full offensive potential following his trade to Seattle two years ago. With an improved swing path, he now projects for both plus-or-better hit and plus-or-better power potential. The Wisconsin native has excellent barrel control and the ball just jumps off his bat. He has a very good shot to remain in center field all the way up the chain, with above-average speed at present and strong outfield instincts, although he could move to a corner as the natural aging progression takes its course. He's poised for a call-up in the near future; if the Mariners were a little more aggressive he might've gotten there already.

7. Ke'Bryan Hayes, 3B, Pittsburgh Pirates

Last year's blurb noted Hayes' loud contact, good approach and Gold Glove-quality defense at the hot corner. It specified that "the wait continues to see if he can adjust the launch angle on those laser beams off his bat." As you might be able to intuit from his current ranking, he did. The power breakout we'd finally been waiting for happened, as he smashed 14 extra-base hits in 24 games, including five home runs that all landed somewhere between the power alleys. He still doesn't hit the ball in the air as often as a typical 30-homer hitter should, but when he does they go an awful long way, and he's capable of putting on a plus-plus raw power show in batting practice. Hayes only needs to scrape 20 to be an All-Star caliber player given the rest of the profile. There's always some danger in moving a prospect this much off such a small sample, but this doesn't seem like an outlier, merely an inevitability.

8. Marco Luciano, SS, San Francisco Giants

Like Rodríguez, Luciano hits the ball *extremely* hard. He mashed a monstrous homer off Ryan Rolison during fall instructs that registered a bonkers 119 mph off the bat, the product of a lightning-fast swing (which he pairs with an equally intense bat flip). Unlike Rodríguez, Luciano doesn't have the solid 2019 foundation of torching both full-season A-ball levels; his entire pro experience has been in the complex, save a nine-game cup of coffee in short-season last year. The lack of a 2020 season cost him the opportunity to prove that he could make consistent quality contact against more advanced pitching, and that's the only thing stopping him from vaulting to the very top of this list.

9. Bobby Witt Jr., SS, Kansas City Royals

It's only natural that kids are attracted to following in the footsteps of their fathers. It's rarer when the progeny plays the same sport as Dad, but excels in a completely different way. The elder Witt pitched for 16 years in the big leagues, and while Junior does have a cannon for a right arm, he'll be terrorizing pitchers instead. The physicality, body control, plus power and makeup all point towards a future star in the making. As one of the younger members at the Royals'

alternate site, he established himself as someone who not only belonged, but excelled against older competition. Every indication says he'll stay at shortstop, with the worst-case scenario being a plus defender at third base. Follow that up with good wheels, and the only question mark remaining will be whether the bat will make enough contact to become a true five-tool player.

10. C.J. Abrams, SS, San Diego Padres

Abrams went sixth overall to the Padres in 2019, and he immediately dispelled any pre-draft concerns about his offensive tools by brutalizing the Arizona League. Okay, that's complex ball played across a series of launching pads, but the reports only got louder at instructs this past fall, when he raked against a much older level of competition. Okay, that's instructional ball across a series of launching pads. But it's unfair to hold that missing 2020 season where he might've dominated full-season ball against him. All we can do is look at the available information. Abrams is a top-of-the-scale runner who will land at a premium defensive position—if he doesn't quite have the arm for shortstop, center field should make for a soft landing given his tool set. He may never hit for a ton of over-the-fence power, but he is already capable of loud contact against plus velocity, and he has room to get stronger without losing his speed. Abrams will be able to hurt opposing teams in a variety of ways. He's better than the sum of his parts, albeit with some uncertainty—for good and ill—about the individual parts until we see him in a more normal prospect environment.

11. MacKenzie Gore, LHP, San Diego Padres

We waited all season for Gore to get the call to The Show. And then, when the Padres needed a live arm the most in the playoffs, they went instead to Ryan Weathers. This decision made little sense on the surface; Weathers had never pitched above Low-A while Gore had Double-A experience, and Gore is a much better prospect. Combined with reports that he didn't look sharp at the alternate site, we're left to infer that this probably wasn't a great season of development for the talented southpaw. Our 2019 looks were splendid; a four-pitch starter led by a mid-90s fastball and a dazzling curveball. He certainly could come out throwing seeds in 2021 and make us look foolish for doubting, even a little, but for now Sánchez and Anderson have passed him as the top pitching prospect in baseball.

12. Nick Madrigal, 2B, Chicago White Sox

Madrigal became an even more extreme version of himself in 109 major-league plate appearances in 2020, hitting .340 by making an extraordinarily large amount of contact and shooting the ball where they ain't. He also showed off next-to-no power, even less than expected—of his three extra-base hits, only one was actually hit over an outfielder's head, and he didn't have a single batted ball all season which

Statcast rated as a barrel. It's possible that the complete lack of wattage was due to an early-season shoulder separation, which cost him just enough time to remain rookie-eligible, and that he had surgery after the season to fix. It's also possible that this is just who he is: a singles machine on par with The Beatles living in a world where Top 40 radio has given way to Spotify. That still has a lot of value, but it's not a superstar in the 2020s.

13. Spencer Torkelson, 3B/1B, Detroit Tigers

As ready-made as collegiate sluggers come, Torkelson toyed with the college ranks, biding his time before being selected first overall in the 2020 draft with little hesitation. While he may not be mentioned in the same breath as other recent slam-dunk college picks like Rutschman and Stephen Strasburg, there is a reasonable argument to make that he is one of the "safer" picks you can make in the amateur draft. So much is unknown at the time players are picked; Tork alleviates much of the guesswork. He has an above-average hit tool, a plus-plus eye to get on base, plus-or-better game power to all fields, a Statcast-friendly profile. Simply put: He is an offensive machine. So what if he's only a first baseman for a considerable amount of his career? The certainty he brings when dealing with probabilistic career outcomes for a franchise that can't mess around with missing on guys at the top of the draft is incalculable.

14. Andrew Vaughn, 1B, Chicago White Sox

Inevitably tied at the hip to Torkelson, Vaughn has a similar history and profile: a bat-first top-three pick that pummeled the Pac-12 and is likely to play mostly first base. The difference between the two is that Vaughn is shorter, and even a little undersized (6-feet tall) compared to what you'd expect out of a power hitter. Alas, his shorter stature does not give him an advantage in the athleticism department, where he is a below-average runner and lesser compared to Torkelson. Though there has been some experimentation with Vaughn, both in the outfield and at third base, in order to get his bat into an already stacked White Sox lineup, the fact remains that he will end up playing first base over the long haul. Regardless, Vaughn has a chance to hit for more average utilizing a line-drive swing that still produces a ton of power.

15. Kristian Robinson, OF, Arizona Diamondbacks

Let's Make a Deal, hosted by Hugh Everett

Behind Door #1: Robinson dominates the Midwest League in 2020, sending 400-plus foot shots through the frigid April night skies of Fort Wayne, Beloit and Lansing. He continues to mash in the Cal League after a midseason promotion and ranks up with the top outfield prospects in baseball. He certainly has that level of ceiling.

Behind Door #2: Robinson struggles to adjust to full-season arms as a 19-year-old. College pitchers who can spin a breaking ball when they're ahead give him fits, and a high strikeout rate eats into his game power, although it still shows up in flashes. He slashes something like .246/.304/.455, not bad given his age and experience level, but enough to knock him down the list a bit.

Behind Door #3: The 2020 minor league season is cancelled due to a pandemic. Robinson struggles at times at the alternate site against more advanced arms than he'd see in A-ball. The All-Star upside remains due to the power/speed combination. Likewise, the risk remains high given the swing-and-miss concerns. Nothing new is laid bare, nothing made obvious.

16. Dylan Carlson, OF, St. Louis Cardinals

After a 2019 breakout, Carlson got the call to St. Louis after the team's COVID-19 outbreak. He looked better than his .176/.233/.265 line in August, taking good at-bats and hitting a bunch of line drives right at some gloves. But as the team got healthy and found themselves in a playoff race, a sub-.500 OPS wasn't going to play. Perhaps Carlson found something back at the alternate site, perhaps he just had some better results on contact or perhaps he made those key secondary adjustments against major-league pitching. Back in The Show, he posted an .806 OPS in September and started all three games in the wild card round. There's little reason to think he isn't broadly the same prospect as last year, a plus hit/power/speed triple threat who can play all three outfield spots.

17. Deivi García, RHP, New York Yankees

García didn't get to prove he could handle a full starting workload given the abbreviated season and an August 30 call-up. He *did* get to prove that his stuff was plenty good enough to hang with the big boys. García's fastball is nothing special in terms of velocity or spin, but it plays extremely well off his go-to overhand curveball. The big, tumbling hook has been an obvious out-pitch for years, and he's developed better command to spot it where needed, often on the edges of the strike zone. He mixes in enough changeups and sliders to keep batters honest, and everything but his height (he's 5-foot-9) points to long-term success in the rotation. A couple decades ago, that almost certainly would've consigned him to the bullpen, but the Yankees are likely to give him every chance to start moving forward.

18. Cristian Pache, OF, Atlanta Braves

We got an appetizer portion's worth of Pache in late August during his brief call-up, followed by something closer to resembling an entrée during the Braves postseason run. Never in doubt were his elite fielding skills in center, featuring preternatural instincts off the bat with above-average speed and a 70-grade arm. Those traits alone would have him starting every day for most any team. The heights of his career arc will be determined by how much value comes from his offense. There is plus bat speed to go with an aggressive approach that hunts fastballs early in the count, showing there is some pop to go along with the glove. And during his 29 plate appearances there was some evidence of patience, something that had been lacking in previous years in the minors. If he can be a league-average hitter—the dessert of this 3-course meal—we're talking about 20-20 potential at a premium position.

19. Riley Greene, OF, Detroit Tigers

While the BP Prospect Team didn't get to see a lot of live baseball in 2020, among our handful of in-person looks was Tigers instructional league action. Taken one pick before C.J. Abrams in the 2019 draft, Greene has seen similar rapid maturation despite the atypical player development environs. If you would have predicted a Greene breakout last offseason, it would have looked a lot like this. He's added significant good weight and we're more confident the plus power part of the plus hit/power projection gets there. After looking tentative in the outfield in his first pro summer, additional reps on the grass have improved his center field defense. The reports from the alternate site—against better arms—back up our instructs looks. In a season where almost nothing went to plan in baseball, Greene's improvements seem comfortingly normal for a highly touted projectable prep outfielder.

20. Randy Arozarena, OF, Tampa Bay Rays

In a single shortened season, Arozarena advanced from an interesting-if-tweenerish outfield prospect with average pop to a true slugger with apparent plus-plus game power. If you're reading this book, you probably already know that he had one of the best postseasons in baseball history. He was quite difficult to rank on merit, because a two-grade jump in game power that has only shown up for a couple months is difficult to evaluate, and the new power came at the cost of significant swing-and-miss, especially within the zone. Some sources thought he should be in the top five of this list, and others wouldn't place him in the top half.

Arozarena was detained in Mexico in November after domestic violence allegations. His ex-partner declined to press charges.

21. Asa Lacy, LHP, Kansas City Royals

The power lefty out of Texas A&M dazzled during his limited spring season, striking out nearly two batters per inning and pairing improved strike-throwing ability with a tick in stuff. Lacy's fastball velocity comfortably sits in the mid 90s with an extra gear available when he needs it. There is effort to the delivery, which has caused control issues in the past, but the prominent head whack he had earlier in his college career was a touch more reserved of late. His nasty slider that is

effective against both righties and lefties, and his curve and change are in the vicinity of average. Add it all up and he's got a starter's repertoire, a starter's body and frontline potential.

22. Austin Martin, SS, Toronto Blue Jays

What is an "Austin Martin?" Try defining him, and you end up with a bunch of different player comps, none of which aptly describes what he does in the game. There is enough varied defensive ability to play just about anywhere in the field, but no obvious position where he fits best. He has a whippy, looping swing with plenty of energy and barrel control to collect hits of all varieties. The power is coming along, steadily advancing each year at Vanderbilt while maintaining his excellent control of the strike zone. He doesn't fit a particular cookie cutter profile, which shouldn't diminish anything he brings to the field each day. He is his own brand of player, one that should be a good regular in short order.

23. Nolan Gorman, 3B, St. Louis Cardinals

In a shade over a season's worth of plate appearances, Gorman has cracked 30-plus home runs and 40-plus doubles. He did this before turning 20 and with most of the games coming at full-season levels. Flash forward a few years, and a few levels, and that's what you are hoping to get from his bat in the majors. There's plus-plus raw power that might end up top of the scale as he gets stronger in his 20s. The swing has some stiffness and length, but there's plenty of bat speed and loft, and his hands work well enough to project an average hit tool. That's all he will need to be a middle-of-the-lineup force. He's not the rangiest third baseman, but he does enough there that he should stick at the hot corner, and his arm is strong enough to be an asset. Major League Equivalencies aren't as simple as made out above, and Double-A will be a stern test of the present profile. If he hits there, then Gorman could soon be bringing majestic dingers to a Cardinals game near you.

24. Shane Baz, RHP, Tampa Bay Rays

In *Kiss Me Deadly*, a rather loose adaptation of one of Mickey Spillane's Mike Hammer novels, our hard-boiled detective finds himself caught between a *femme fatale* and a bunch of hired goons, all searching for a mysterious box that his secretary (and occasional lover) Velda calls "the great whatsit." Baz is the great whatsit of this year's prospect list. Since being drafted 12th overall in 2017, he's been used awfully sparingly due to the conservative development proclivities of both the Pirates and Rays. When on the mound, he has routinely hit triple digits with his fastball and he can unleash a plus-plus slider as well. In *Kiss Me Deadly*, the mystery box is filled with radioactive material that immolates the *femme fatale*; in the movie version, the great whatsit is a metaphor for Cold War nihilism. In the prospect blurb version, one supposes it could be a metaphor for Baz's blazing fastball, or the control and command issues that keep him from being higher on the list. After all, any good film critic allows for the possibility of multiple meanings.

25. Luis Patiño, RHP, Tampa Bay Rays

It's easier to deal with a new, positive level of performance for prospects in the majors in 2020. There are more tools to identify what, if anything, changed in the profile and how sticky it might be going forward. But what about when a prospect struggles during our least favorite year? It's hard to hold Patiño's season against him. He had made a grand total of two starts above A-ball coming into the year and his role with the Padres would have been unfamiliar. He was asked to pitch out of the bullpen; to come in with runners on base. The stuff that made him the No. 15 prospect last year was still broadly present, with three potential plus offerings. He still missed plenty of bats swung by the best hitters in the world. Patiño's command and control weren't quite ready for the show, but was it fair to expect any different? Still, how a prospect fails can be useful information too, and Patiño clocks in at No. 24 this year, because those command and control issues—combined with his smaller frame—up the reliever risk in the profile. Is that fair? We're not sure. The Rays are betting on the 2019 version returning in force after making him the centerpiece of the Blake Snell deal.

26. Leody Taveras, OF, Texas Rangers

This marks Taveras' fifth consecutive entry on the 101, and he posted his best slugging percentage of his career in 2020.

"That's good!"

It was in the majors.

"That's even better!"

It was .395.

Tumbleweeds roll by as the BP Lead Prospect Writer stares off into the middle distance.

Taveras got handed the everyday center field job late in the season as the Rangers made their September roster into a mini-Arizona Fall League for many of their top prospects. He was as advertised defensively, looking like an immediate Gold Glove candidate. The plus-plus defense/speed combo makes him likely to have a long career, even if he only xeroxes his 2020 line going forward. But there's reason to be optimistic: He was jumping straight to the majors after only a half season of Double-A, and he's shown the ingredients for above-average hit and power tools while playing in some terrible home parks—including Globe Life Field which played like old school Petco in its debut season.

Okay, you may have noticed this also marks a fifth consecutive entry on the 101 handwaving Taveras posting a .700 OPS while ranking him in the Top 50, but he only has to hit a little bit more to be a plus regular.

27. Casey Mize, RHP, Detroit Tigers

Making a somewhat surprising debut in 2020 as the Tigers flirted with contention during a condensed season, Mize showed he was perhaps not quite ready for the bigs. The book on Mize since his draft year at Auburn, where he quickly pitched himself into the consensus first-overall pick, was one of a control pitcher who also happened to have plenty of juice on each of his four potential plus offerings. Often command is sacrificed for stuff—he had both. What was most surprising in his seven major-league starts was a dramatic uptick in walks. The mechanics appeared to be consistent; moreover, he seemed to be trying to be too fine with his locations, especially with his cutter and splitter that both move a fair amount. Instead of letting his pitches work for him, he was getting behind and unable to recover. Let him get that extra seasoning in the minors in 2021 so he can rediscover his dominant form from before his arm injury in 2019, and work up to the big leagues with less pressure.

28. Ryan Mountcastle, OF, Baltimore Orioles

This will be more coda than prospect projection, as Mountcastle was a mere four at-bats from exhausting his list eligibility. He's long been a confounding prospect, but we always thought he'd get to the majors and hit. Sure enough, he got to the majors and hit. Mountcastle is not a true talent .333 hitter, mind you; the strikeout rate and underlying swing rates don't support that, but he should have a plus hit tool going forward. We'd expect him to show more extra-base pop as well, something in the range of 25 home runs and 35 doubles. Drafted as a prep shortstop who was never going to stick, he's settled in as a decent enough left fielder. He'll likely see some time at first base and DH as well.

29. Joey Bart, C, San Francisco Giants

In a perfect world, Bart would've spent 2020 conquering the high-minors, making up for time lost to injuries in 2019 and perhaps coming up for a cameo as part of a long-term passing of the torch with Buster Posey. In this one, Posey opted out of the season and Bart was called up in mid-August when the Chadwick Tromp/Tyler Heineman catching tandem went about as well as you'd expect. Contact was always an ephemeral concern for Bart, and in 2020 it proved to be an insurmountable one; staying productive while striking out nearly 37 percent of the time is a feat only Joey Gallo seems to be able to pull off, and while Bart has real power, he doesn't have *that* kind of power. Luckily Posey is back, so Bart can return to his own developmental timetable.

30. Grayson Rodriguez, RHP, Baltimore Orioles

Rodriguez made steady improvements over the course of the 2019 season, showing markedly better by the end of the campaign than he did at the beginning: velocity up, changeup sharpening, curveball and slider both flashing, command improving. He was invited to the alternate site and continued to pump mid-90s gas with strong reports on the overall development track, and all arrows seem to still be pointing up. If he ever gets the chance to throw 100 innings with that heat, there's a pretty good chance he'll be one of the best pitching prospects in baseball by the end of it—if he's not in the majors first. When you draft a prep pitcher in the top of half of the first round, this is exactly where you hope he'll be two-plus years in … well, except for the whole cancelled season part.

31. Royce Lewis, IF/OF, Minnesota Twins

Let's start with what's good about Lewis: he's got explosive actions and great lateral quickness, along with plenty of thunder in a bat that can catch up to velocity. What is holding him back, and what obviously held him back at the team's alternate site, is a swing that is not ready for high-caliber pitching. We were among the first to note in 2019 how his mechanics had become disjointed following a strong introduction to pro ball. His upper body and lower half were out of sync, failing to work in concert with each other except for the occasional ambushed early count fastball, and his strikeout rate ballooned as a result. Even after earning MVP honors of the Arizona Fall League, the underlying concerns remained, and were exacerbated as he began to see less and less time at shortstop. There is only so much that can be done with elite bat speed alone, and until he can figure out a way to quiet his timing down to match good pitching, we will remain bearish on his future.

32. Heliot Ramos, OF, San Francisco Giants

In a year where time passed more slowly than the event horizon of a black hole, prospect fatigue conversely accelerated. We are only three years removed from Ramos announcing himself on the national prospect stage by mashing in Arizona as a 17-year-old. He's been on quite the *bildungsroman* as a player since, adding some bad weight and struggling at full-season ball as an 18-year-old, reshaping his body and reaffirming potential plus hit and power tools in the California and Eastern Leagues as a 19-year-old. As a 20-year-old his season was bookended by a pair of oblique strains, one that hampered him during spring training, and one that cut his time short at Giants instructs. In between he spent time at the alternate site, where he still looked like a quality major-leaguer, albeit one that will spend more time in right field than center.

33. JJ Bleday, OF, Miami Marlins

The Marlins boast one of the best farm systems in all of baseball. One piece of their embarrassment of riches is Bleday, the former Vandy standout and the fourth-overall pick in 2019, who is likely to make his big-league debut in 2021. He is well-rounded offensively, displaying power and contact to all fields with a keen eye of the strike zone. He's also the type of player who is nearly impervious to streaks, never too high or too low. He'll never wow you with his speed, which might be the only deficiency to his game, but he'll make up for it in right with a plus arm. Regardless, his track record of performance and proximity to a call-up make him one of the safer prospects on the list.

34. Corbin Carroll, OF, Arizona Diamondbacks

Every year we lament leaving a prospect off the list, only to see them break out during the season. Carroll served as that prospect in 2020, which is impressive given the whole lack of a season thing. There has to be a good reason to jump a prospect this much, especially without on-field performance to point to. There are two factors working in concert here: 1) We probably underrated Carroll coming off the draft last year because he's an undersized prep outfielder; despite how hard he hits the ball, there's limited physical projection in the offensive tools when you are listed at 5-foot-10. And, 2) Carroll, really, really mashed at the alternate site, doing so against significantly more advanced pitching. Some prospects make the leap every year, and Carroll sure seemed to amid tough circumstances. He's an above-average center fielder with a plus hit tool and at least average power. You could even argue he should be in the next tier of outfielders up with Taveras, Pache and Greene.

35. Nate Pearson, RHP, Toronto Blue Jays

More than 20 prospects on this list made their big-league debuts in 2020, including Pearson. Starting strong in his first game versus the Nats, he found a comfortable release point to amp up his 80-grade heat late in the outing. However, finding that release point wasn't always easy. He struggled in other starts, failing to land the fastball for strikes while his secondaries didn't fare much better. His entire game is predicated off velocity, speeding up the hitter's bats so he can break off his plus-plus power slider and other offspeed varieties. Pearson's frustration later turned to injury, and he missed a month with a strained elbow, only to return late in the season to produce better results in a bullpen role. Don't worry (yet) about a potential full-time move to the 'pen—as with most pitchers of his size and mechanics, he just needs to find a routine he can settle into and find his groove.

36. Garrett Crochet, LHP, Chicago White Sox

Tell me if you've read this script before: the White Sox drafted a spindly college lefty with questionable mechanics who throws a huge fastball and a hellacious slider, and then brought him to the majors the same year as a dominant reliever. Crochet has an enormous ceiling as a starting pitcher—if you saw him on the right day as an amateur, he looked like a potential ace—but he only made 13 collegiate starts at Tennessee between injuries, use as a reliever and the pandemic. Chicago brought him straight to the majors for its playoff run and he was sitting 100 mph, touching 102 out of the bullpen and generally looking unhittable … right up until his velocity tanked in the playoffs and he was diagnosed with a flexor strain. If this all works out, Crochet could turn into an ace, but there's a ton of bullpen risk evident with his command, changeup and arm health. At least the proof of concept for a dominant relief outcome is already there.

37. Michael Kopech, RHP, Chicago White Sox

After spending all of 2019 recovering from Tommy John surgery, Kopech opted out of the 2020 season; James Fegan of *The Athletic* reported he was concerned about the short ramp-up to game action and the uncertainty about his role and the pandemic season at large. He hasn't seen official game action since September 2018, although he has pitched in instructs and threw a spring inning before the league shut down. In that frame, he looked phenomenal, sitting 100-101 mph and mixing in his best breaking balls. Kopech's command was a work-in-progress before he got hurt, and this ranking is a pure dart throw given how much developmental time he's missed.

38. Logan Gilbert, RHP, Seattle Mariners

The first of a trio of right-handed Mariners pitchers on this list, you'll notice a pattern within the group. Gilbert separates himself from the pack as he is further along the developmental track. Although he's a strong-bodied 6-foot-5 hurler, he's not known for throwing gas. In fact, his fastball velocity has ebbed and flowed over the last several years, at times averaging in the mid 90s, and at other times a bit lower. Reports from camp have the fastball pendulum swinging back toward the positive side, to go along with a plus snapping curveball and advanced control.

39. Nick Gonzales, 2B, Pittsburgh Pirates

There are few instances of diminutive players surpassing all the obstacles and biases placed in front of them to be taken as high as Gonzales was in the most recent draft. While 5-foot-10 might be a generous listing, his work ethic and video-game numbers are unmistakable. He maximizes his height thanks to fast hands and sound lower-half mechanics, which adds loft to his swing path. Yes, the aforementioned stats may have been helped by extremely friendly home field conditions, but he also raked and earned MVP honors at the Cape in 2019. He's going to need to keep hitting, because he's likely to be limited to second base by so-so range and an arm that wouldn't play at shortstop.

40. Drew Waters, OF, Atlanta Braves

Twenty-year-olds who win batting titles in Double-A are to be celebrated, even as we await the arrival of their power and have concerns about an overly aggressive plate approach. The power was an area of focus at the alternate site this summer for Waters, with Atlanta hoping his hard-hit line drives would gain the carry needed to get over the fences. Even with an advanced hit tool from both sides of the plate,

he's a conundrum to predict based upon his pro performance thus far and the potential for the best pitchers in the world to better exploit the holes in his game. You want to believe in it, yet you remain hesitant because you haven't seen it with your own eyes.

41. Jordan Groshans, SS, Toronto Blue Jays

Good news: Groshans is fully recovered from the foot injury that cost him most of 2019, and the reports from the alternate site indicate the same strong offensive tools that propelled him up our rankings to begin with.

Bad news: He lost even more developmental time since his "season" didn't get going until summer camp commenced in July.

Groshans is a better prospect than he was two years ago, though he only has 96 real plate appearances in the time since, making this a real outlier situation, in a season filled with them. He hit the ball hard against good pitching at Toronto's alternate site, and that's promising given his general lack of professional experience. The bet here is that he's going to come out in 2021 and rip up Double-A, but that's still a gamble—not just that he'll reach that level and perform, but that there will be a Double-A season for him to tear up at all.

42. Ronny Mauricio, SS, New York Mets

Mauricio's gap year is a tricky one to evaluate. Signed as a switch-hitting shortstop out of the Dominican Republic in 2017, Mauricio has been pushed aggressively throughout his career. He kept his head above water for the most part, showcasing a potential plus hit/power combination—especially from the left side—though he'd go through periods where it was all he could do just to make contact. We ranked him as aggressively as he was pushed last year, slotting him into the Top 50, with the wager that he'd get stronger, gain experience and hit a bit more at a new level. Our bet never got a chance to play out, as Mauricio had only brief stints at the alternate site and instructs (Mets camp was shut down early due to a COVID-19 outbreak). We don't know what we don't know, so this has become a bit of a parlay on last year's gamble.

43. Matthew Liberatore, LHP, St. Louis Cardinals

When one franchise known for its player dev voodoo trades a prospect to another org also known for its developmental witchcraft, who ends up getting the better end of the deal? That's where we stand with Liberatore, a highly regarded prep pitching prospect who fell into Tampa Bay's lap thanks to pre-draft nitpicking, then proceeded to pitch well before being shipped to St. Louis. A tall lefty with a good frame and an easy arm action, he doesn't have the kind of backspin on his fastball that would pair well with his curveball. The breaker instead stands alone as an elite pitch, with his sinking fastball working independently. For someone his age and size, he's a surprisingly good strike-thrower, relying more on pitchability than the pure stuff potential he possesses. It's this dichotomy—command/control artist or swing-and-miss butcher—that has evaluators flummoxed.

44. Brandon Marsh, OF, Los Angeles Angels

Imagine an outfield with Mike Trout, Jo Adell and Marsh. Pretty good, right? That image in your head is close to becoming a reality. While Marsh's in-game power hasn't quite manifested to the point you'd expect from a 6-foot-4 23-year-old, he's played in some pitcher-friendly environments in the minors. One scout had predicted before the shutdown he could hit 30 homers in the Pacific Coast League with an improved ability to lift the ball. His is an impressive overall package, and he moves incredibly well despite his hulking frame. He would be a center fielder on most teams, but, given the current state of the Angels, he'll be repositioned as an above-average defender in one of the corner-outfield spots.

45. Edward Cabrera, RHP, Miami Marlins

The Marlins already feature a mononymous pitcher in their system, because when you're great and your name is uniquely memorable you can do that, like Cher or Madonna or Prince. Sliding under the radar, yet routinely referenced by sources as having stuff just as good as Sixto's, is Edward Cabrera. He hasn't received the hype that comes with being the centerpiece of a blockbuster deal, but with a fastball in the upper-90s and two secondary pitches that both flash plus, there is a palpable reason for excitement. Cabrera has a more ideal starter's body than Sixto does, and he has shown an ability to make adjustments to his mechanics at the request of pitching coaches. Minor injuries have dogged him the past two years, and the hope is that he can avoid those nicks as he approaches a role in Miami's rotation in 2021.

46. Matt Manning, RHP, Detroit Tigers

The Tigers called up two of their three notable pitching prospects in 2020—Casey Mize and Tarik Skubal. Both struggled to various degrees. You could argue that struggling in the majors is better than "dealing with a mild forearm strain," which caused Manning to be shut down at the alternate site. (On the other hand, we haven't seen Manning struggle yet.) Since overhauling his delivery in the low minors, he's routinely hit 95 with big extension and plane from his 6-foot-6 frame. He pairs it with a curve that flashes plus, or even better some starts, and an improving changeup that has a chance to be more than just a show-me pitch against lefties. It's never all come together for him, but he remains a good mid-rotation prospect. We'd say "safe" mid-rotation prospect, but there's really no such thing as a "mild" forearm strain.

47. Alek Thomas, CF, Arizona Diamondbacks

The third of three Diamondbacks center fielders in the Top 50, Thomas puts on a pretty good show himself. He is more likely to stick in center and be above-average there than Robinson, though perhaps less so than Carroll. While he doesn't have Robinson's projection and physicality, he's bigger than Carroll, and he arguably has the most advanced hit tool of the three. Thomas sprays hard line drives all over the field, showing plus bat speed despite noisy hands as he sets up. He doesn't lift the ball enough at present to get his plus raw power into games, and while Thomas is likely to be an above-average regular for a long time, he lacks the upside of his organization mates. There's no real shame in coming in third among this trio of prospects though.

48. George Valera, OF, Cleveland

Player value can be reduced to a simple sum of discrete parts. Offensive runs created + defensive runs prevented + positional value + replacement level. Valera has played mostly center field as a professional, but he's spent enough time in a corner in the low minors to suggest he's likely to operate there long term. He should be fine, but he won't be a real asset with the glove there. That means the lion's share of his value will have to come from his bat. His swing is even noisier than Thomas', and it's not the loose, rotational, aesthetically pleasing lefty swing prospect writers dream about. Even so, he has a ton of bat speed and is able to generate an impressive amount of in-game power. We think he's going to hit for average as well, making him one to watch.

49. Zac Veen, OF, Colorado Rockies

Veen provided about as much data as possible for a high school pick prior to the shutdown. After a solid summer where he entered first-round consideration, the early beginning to Florida baseball allowed scouts to see him against top competition. Lean and with long levers, he displayed a gliding-sort of athleticism rare for his 6-foot-4 size. The swing, like the rest of his movements, is smooth and effortless and packs plenty of power potential to go along with good contact skills. Unlike a lot of players of his age and ilk, he has an advanced approach at the plate and he is content with being patient, unafraid to take a pitch while he works the pitcher. It was moderately shocking to see a different high school outfielder (Robert Hassell III) taken ahead of him. Veen's ranking reflects the difference between the two.

50. Emerson Hancock, RHP, Seattle Mariners

Before the college season began, Hancock was among a select shortlist of players vying to be the first-overall pick. A rough first start short-circuited that argument, but his final three outings went more to plan: he threw 20 innings, allowing 13 hits and two walks while punching out 30. Like his other Mariners brethren found in the 101, he's blessed with an ideal starting pitcher's body. He has an advanced feel for, and command of, his arsenal. The fastball rests comfortably in the 94-96 mph range and at times he can dial it up into the upper 90s while working all quadrants of the zone. His best secondary is a hard-biting slider, with the changeup not far behind; a passable curve rounds out his repertoire. There may not be the unlimited ceiling so many scouting directors scour for in the draft, though the appeal of Hancock and the other M's recent high pitching picks is the elevated floors that offer plenty of mid-rotation depth.

51. Max Meyer, RHP, Miami Marlins

Meyer, listed at an even 6-feet tall, is a gifted athlete who maximizes every movement in his delivery to generate blistering velocity. He even eclipsed the 100-mph mark in some outings. His downward breaking slider, meanwhile, is one of the best out-pitches seen in years by amateur scouts. He's shown a propensity for using it as both a chase offering and a pitch that he can throw for strikes. Meyer may have two plus-plus pitches, but he needs the changeup to be at least a show-me pitch for him to stick in the rotation. At worst, his present traits profile to an elite closer; at best, if he can prove he can hold up against the rigors of a starter's schedule and develop that third pitch, it checks the boxes of a no. 2 starter, and perhaps even better.

52. Nolan Jones, 3B, Cleveland

Jones has plus-plus raw power and an excellent plate approach, producing elite offensive performance driven by walks and extra-base hits up and down the minor-league chain (he's posted a 150 DRC+ or better at every full-season stop so far). Of course, if you scratch a little deeper under the surface, there's some warts, too; otherwise, he'd be higher on this list. Jones has struck out a high clip, and we're concerned that his approach is too pull-heavy to maintain a decent average at the highest level. His defense at third base is rough despite a plus-plus arm, and he might end up at a corner-outfield spot or first base down the road (especially given José Ramírez's presence). Even if he doesn't totally iron out the defense or contact, Jones stands a pretty good chance to be a fun Three True Outcomes slugger regardless.

53. DL Hall, LHP, Baltimore Orioles

We've finally reached the mid-rotation starter or late-inning reliever tier, a Top 101 tradition like no other. A review of the ground rules: the pitcher must have a plus fastball, one plus secondary (it's most often a breaking ball) and questions about his command and third pitch (usually the *cambio*). This template isn't as cut and dry as it used to be, as teams figure out ways to maximize the best part of their arms' arsenals, but it's a useful descriptor for our purposes. Hall tops this group because the fastball isn't merely plus; a 2020 velocity jump had him sitting in the upper 90s and touching

99. He has the requisite plus breaker, and his changeup improved as well. He's not in the "number two starter" tier because the questions about his command are along the lines of "uh, didn't he walk six per nine in Advanced-A last we saw him?" Yes reader, yes he did.

54. Mick Abel, RHP, Philadelphia Phillies

It was a widely-held belief within the industry that with a shortage of both picks and information before the draft that teams would ration both to be more risk averse. This "go with what you know" rationale created a recency bias working against some prospects who had little-to-no game action. Abel, the presumptive best prep pitcher in the class and one of only two first-round selections from that group, was one such instance of that dynamic at play. Scouts weren't able to see him in the spring with Oregon's late start to games, so they instead turned to his social media and devoured workout videos of bullpen sessions where he was touching 99. In a normal year, he likely would have pitched his way into a higher pick than 15th overall. Reports out of Clearwater suggest he has already added strength to his highly projectable frame. He might be a monster in the making.

55. Josiah Gray, RHP, Los Angeles Dodgers

Gray went from a Division II college shortstop to a mid-rotation pitching prospect in the space of about three years. He's on the shorter side at only 6-foot-1, but his delivery is fluid and repeatable with only moderate effort. There's the issue of limited reps on the mound, but that cuts both ways, as there's limited wear and tear as well. The idea with position-player converts is often "they have big arm strength, try to teach them a slider and then let them rip." Gray was a full-time starter by his junior year at LeMoyne College, and he tossed 130 effective innings across three levels in 2019. He does have the big arm strength, sitting mid-90s, but he has also shown a feel for both a slider and change as a pro. Sure, everything might play up in short bursts, but perhaps Gray is just a mid-rotation starter, full stop.

56. Josh Jung, 3B, Texas Rangers

Calling Jung's scouting report dry is a little unfair, but it's not the most interesting nor the loudest collection of tools. He was a productive three-year starter at Texas Tech, torching the Big 12 his sophomore and junior years. But his tools don't pop as loud as his slash line. He's a solid third baseman, but one limited by fringy range and instincts. He's an above-average hitter, but he's unlikely to challenge for batting titles. He has plus raw strength, but a swing plane on the flatter side, which might make his power play merely to average. Jung also has a quality approach that makes the offensive side of his game play up. Reports from the alternate site rumor a swing change that has him unlocking more of his raw pop. If that's true, then it works contrary to what a different Jung proposed: there is linear evolution, not merely a circumambulation of the self.

57. Nick Lodolo, LHP, Cincinnati Reds

Nothing is flashy when it comes to Lodolo. You'd think that a big 6-foot-6 lefty with good downward plane on his fastball would be cruising in the mid-to-upper 90s with minimal effort. Instead, it's mostly 92-94 with some sink. His breaking ball and changeup don't serve as your typical "fool me" pitches, either, and he uses them to throw strikes and get ahead in the count. It sounds all too overly simplistic, but he's been able to strike out as many batters as he has and limit walks simply by pounding the zone using excellent command. Maybe there is more to coax out of the arm in the form of added spin, but it's hard to tamper with a good thing when you know you have a mid-rotation starter in hand.

58. Jazz Chisholm, SS, Miami Marlins

As recent, highly-anticipated Jazz debuts go, Chisholm's late season call-up for the Marlins failed to reach the critical heights of Kamasi Washington's *The Epic*, but the Christgaus on the BP Prospect Team still foresee a *Heaven-and-Earth*-quality follow-up in his near future. Jumping from Double-A—where he struck out 32 percent of the time in 2019—to the majors would be a heavy ask in normal circumstances; the Marlins did Chisholm no favors, as he received inconsistent playing time behind Jon Berti and Miguel Rojas. Despite tempering his aggressive approach some, he struggled badly against high-quality offspeed stuff. Chisholm still flashed his plus power and plus glove enough in 2020 to keep us on the hook. Elvis Costello once said "you have 20 years to write your first album and you have six months to write your second one." We'll see if that's enough time for Chisholm to find the right chord.

59. Jasson Dominguez, OF, New York Yankees

In the nature of full disclosure, we don't know much more about where Dominguez should be on this list than we did a year ago. He was briefly stateside for spring training, but the Yankees didn't invite him to the alternate site, and they were one of two teams who didn't hold domestic fall instructs. Dominguez spent his summer training in his native Dominican Republic. By reputation, he is one of the most hyped and talented prospects around, a potential five-tool center fielder, but he's never faced a real professional pitch and we do like seeing these things for ourselves (or, at least, talking to unbiased sources who have). Hopefully, the reality of Dominguez meets the hype, because he'll be a hell of a prospect if everything we've heard is true.

60. Dane Dunning, RHP, Texas Rangers

Dunning made his major-league debut opposite Casey Mize's, and frankly outshined the former no. 1 pick. He continued to play the part of a present mid-rotation arm throughout the season, looking like exactly the pitcher he looked to be *before* spring 2019 Tommy John surgery. Dunning is perfectly typecast for the role: he's a four-pitch starter with a low-90s fastball and solid command, yet he's missing an out-pitch. The White Sox flipped him to the Rangers for Lance Lynn this offseason, trading the likelihood of solid pitching for a year of potential greatness as they loaded up for a pennant run.

61. Luis Campusano, C, San Diego Padres

Campusano made an unexpected major-league debut in 2020, and homered in his first game. He was then scratched from his planned start a day later and missed the rest of the season with a sprained wrist. When right, he's an offense-first catching prospect with the potential to hit for both average and power. Defensively, he's got a big arm, but he remains a work-in-progress as a receiver.

In October, he was charged with felony marijuana possession after a traffic stop in Georgia. It is patently absurd that possession of slightly less than three ounces of weed constitutes a felony, to say nothing of broader systemic racial bias in the criminal justice system. At the time of publication, Campusano was still facing these ridiculous charges.

62. Kyle Muller, LHP, Atlanta Braves

The 2020 Braves had Josh Tomlin, Robbie Erlin and Tommy Milone toe the rubber, while Muller—a former second-round pick with a full-season of Double-A under his belt—hung out at the alternate site. The fact that he never made a start for a team struggling to find enough starting pitching while making a playoff push is a piece of actionable data, especially in a season where we'd have been happy to find a prospect's TikTok montage from instructs. Reports from Gwinnett suggested that while Muller's command and control were improving over his 2019—where he walked almost 15 percent of the batters he faced—it was still a bit of an issue. That's also actionable data. But so is the fact that Muller is regularly touching 100 now. Six-foot-seven lefties who throw that hard are rare commodities, and he isn't a mere arm-strength prospect either, as both his change and breaking ball should end up as above-average offerings.

63. Brailyn Marquez, LHP, Chicago Cubs

The Cubs called Marquez up at the very end of the season for a look-see, since it cost them next-to-nothing in service time and he had to be added to the 40-man roster this offseason anyway. He was absolutely dreadful, allowing five runs in less than an inning, and he had major trouble throwing strikes. But we did see the promising parts too: the easy upper-90s heat, the big-breaking slider. Marquez focused on nursing his changeup at the alternate site, and he reportedly made major strides there. That changeup development is going to be the key in whether he sticks as a starting pitcher over the longer term. There's big potential in his power arm regardless of role, provided he can throw enough strikes.

64. Robert Hassell III, OF, San Diego Padres

One of the best pure hitters in the class, Hassell made a late jump into the top 10 thanks to a sweet swing the Padres couldn't bear to pass on. (There was even a thought that he could be a two-way player with a fastball up to 93 off the mound.) His hit tool projection and present ability to play in center field are the focus, though he may end up in a corner spot where his plus arm can be featured. The swing itself is balanced and level, showing good barrel control that sacrifices outright power for line-drive hard contact. Not to worry, there's still plenty of juice in the bat and has been known to show off rare oppo power. With other young position players in their system, it will be interesting to see how aggressively he is pushed in his first year in the minors.

65. Spencer Howard, RHP, Philadelphia Phillies

Howard is the best example of a class of players that flummoxed this season: he wasn't just bad in the majors, but was bad in ways that didn't seem promising for the future. Ranked 36 last year under the expectation that he was a major-league-ready pitcher with substantial upside, he came up and it was just all a little less than anticipated—a tick or two less on the radar gun; a less-than-plus slider and changeup; homers by the bushel. Pitchers were especially compromised by having to ramp up twice this year, so it's quite possible some of this is not representative of the future. We're kind of middling it, dropping Howard a bit since the high-end stuff isn't there, but also recognizing there's a real chance his 2019 stuff shows back up with a more normal schedule.

66. Heston Kjerstad, OF, Baltimore Orioles

The first "wow" moment of the draft saw the Orioles selecting Kjerstad second overall. It's not as if he was a complete unknown, entering the night with a distinct possibility of going in the first dozen picks. It was a calculated tactic, as they chose to add an offensive-minded player with SEC pedigree in order to spread their bonus pool around to others. A perennial terror during his two years and change with Arkansas, he somehow found another gear during their abbreviated season. His innate barrel control allowed him to find the ball anywhere in the zone—oftentimes not in the zone at all—and suggests a potential above-average hit tool. There is plus power as well, and even when he's fooled on outside offerings he can keep the hands back with strong wrists to elevate to the opposite field. His defense and overall athleticism don't rise to the level his hitting prowess does, and that's fine, since the stick is largely where his value will be coming from.

67. Vidal Bruján, 2B, Tampa Bay Rays

Bruján is a much better fantasy prospect than real life one. Steals are far, far more valuable to your dynasty team than to a major-league team. Conversely your fantasy team doesn't care as much about position or defense. Bruján is a good real-life prospect, too. Those steals are borne of his plus-plus speed, and he has good feel for contact and a solid approach that should allow for something like a .280 average and a .350 OBP. As for slugging, Bruján is not going to hit for much power—he may scrape 10 or so homers at the Trop, limiting the upside of the offensive game. He's an above-average defender at second base, and played a little center field in winter ball, adding to his positional versatility. The total package is more above-average regular than star, but Bruján could reach that designation as soon as the 2021 season.

68. George Kirby, RHP, Seattle Mariners

The last of the Mariners pitchers on this list, Kirby might be the most unique of the trio. He also presents one of the most uncommon skill sets you'll find on the 101. Top-of-the-scale grades aren't thrown around often, and for good reason, as they measure something truly special. His individual pitch grades and velocity are average-to-better, but what is incredible is the level of command he bestows on each pitch. He has a strikeout-to-walk ratio exceeding 6.00 dating back to his college career, including stints in the Cape Cod League and his first 23 professional innings. Kirby arrived at spring training with added muscle that propelled his fastball velocity into the mid-90s and higher, and reports indicate the stuff may have gone up without requiring that he sacrifice his precious command. Watch out for Kirby in 2021; he's someone who could take a big leap forward.

69. Forrest Whitley, RHP, Houston Astros

2017: Establishes himself as one of the best pitching prospects in baseball, throwing 92 1/3 innings between Low-A, High-A and Double-A.

2018: Suspended for the first 50 games for a banned stimulant. Makes six great starts in Double-A, misses a month-and-a-half with an oblique strain, ramps back up to the Arizona Fall League and looks like the best pitching prospect in baseball again in front of half the scouts and prospect writers in the known universe.

2019: Posts an airplane ERA in the high-minors sandwiched around missed time for vague shoulder fatigue, repeatedly showing up without his best stuff. Once again looks great in the AFL.

2020: Feels arm discomfort ramping up at summer camp, never really gets going and doesn't officially pitch anywhere. (There's no AFL for him to star in, of course.)

Whitley needs to make 20 healthy starts at some level this year, badly.

70. Daniel Lynch, LHP, Kansas City Royals

The fastball now sits mid-nineties or more
Slider has always had plus two-plane bite
His pro career has been all you'd ask for
Changeup improved at the alternate site
His name should be in the prospect limelight
Command and injuries still leave some doubts
But lefties with stuff will always get chances
So Lynch will soon extract major-league outs
Worse comes to worst, your pen he enhances
But third-starter role, that's what our stance is

71. Alex Kirilloff, OF, Minnesota Twins

Kirilloff is now immortalized as the answer to a bit of trivia: Who was the first position player to make their major-league debut in the playoffs? His first big-league hit, after a 1-for-4 day at the plate, won't be recognized as his first official hit, since postseason stats are recorded separately from the regular season. We expect many more hits from the free-swinging lefty, who has been a tough one to evaluate during his minor-league career. Tommy John surgery caused him to lose what would have been his first full professional season, and nagging injuries affected his 2019 progression in Double-A. Kirilloff has plus hit potential, although he's altered his lower half to open up his hips on virtually every swing, pulling off to sell out for more power. This has caused an uptick in strikeouts since he's more vulnerable to pitches away. The physical traits are still there to be a well-above-average offensive player.

72. Taylor Trammell, OF, Seattle Mariners

How many top prospects have been dealt twice before reaching the majors?* We often say to watch what organizations do with a player, not what they say about them. That's going to be even more true until things return to normal. The Padres dealt Trammell to the Mariners at the deadline for a 30-year-old catcher with fewer than a season's worth of games under his belt (albeit one that showed signs of being a first-division starter). In an era where front offices hold their prospects close, two teams have seen Trammell as excess. (Conversely, you could argue two teams have made it a priority to acquire him.) He remains a divisive prospect for us as well, and it doesn't help that he didn't get to change our opinions last season. Some of us see Trammell as a bench outfielder with a swing that won't work consistently and an arm best suited for left field. Others see a potential five-tool center fielder. We don't feel too bad, since it seems major-league teams aren't even that confident either.

If you want to take the game of half-full/half-empty to its logical conclusion, the four prospects that jumped to mind immediately were Gio Gonzalez, Anthony Rizzo, Jake Odorizzi and Lewis Brinson.

73. Triston McKenzie, RHP, Cleveland

McKenzie dominated the minors off a low-90s fastball that played up due to the deception and extension in his delivery, and a plus curveball he could manipulate in and out of the zone. He then missed a chunk of 2018 with a forearm strain and all of 2019 with a back injury. We began to wonder if his projectable, but downright thin frame, was sturdy enough to handle the rigors of a starting pitcher's workload. He was healthy by 2020 spring training, but it was a surprise to see him make his first pro start in two years for Cleveland's big-league team. It was a shock to see him come out pumping 95 and showing a new slider with above-average projection. He had a dominant debut, making us wonder if the last two years weren't some sort of Mandela Effect we had all collectively imagined. His velocity backslid in subsequent starts, a reasonable result given he hadn't pitched in game conditions in two years. Still, it's fair to have the same concerns about his fastball and overall durability. Even back working in the low-90s, McKenzie might be a present mid-rotation starter.

74. Keibert Ruiz, C, Los Angeles Dodgers

Ruiz's evaluation has seen ups and downs thanks to inconsistent quality of contact. The underlying profile hasn't changed much—he's shown a strong feel for hitting, and there's always been above-average raw power and defensive abilities. He's been consistently young for the levels he's played at, but our live looks haven't always resulted in a strong hit tool projection. Ruiz debuted in 2020 and homered in his first at-bat, but it was only a two-game fill-in, leaving questions about his offensive consistency unanswered. He's currently stuck behind emerging star Will Smith, and the Dodgers have several notable catching prospects coming up behind him. Naturally, he has been rumored in trade talks, although that might not be necessary given Smith's positional versatility and how the org has tended to split catching playing time over the past few years.

75. Hunter Bishop, OF, San Francisco Giants

Bishop set perhaps unrealistic expectations for himself as a prospect by challenging Barry Bonds' junior-year triple crown stats at Arizona State. He further followed in Bonds' footsteps by donning the orange and black after getting popped 10th overall in 2019. There's little to be learned since, as Bishop generated pedestrian numbers with an elevated strikeout rate in 85 short-season at-bats following the draft and lost an entire minor-league season to COVID-19. The pressure, a bit unfairly, will be on Bishop to come out of the gates hitting the next chance he gets, given that he'll be 23 heading into next season. As it stands the 6-foot-5 outfielder remains a power/speed dual-threat outfielder with some risk in the hit tool due to his 6-foot-5 frame and lengthy swing.

76. Jordyn Adams, OF, Los Angeles Angels

Adams is a sure shot center fielder who could develop into one of the best outfield defenders in the game because of his plus speed and advanced route running (the reasons he was also a highly-regarded wide receiver recruit out of high school). His bat lags behind, especially in the power department, but both offensive tools project to be above-average at peak. His .704 OPS in Burlington in 2019 actually grades out as 22 percent better than average accounting for how tough that park and league is on offense. So, in a reversal of expectations, this prep outfielder might be the safer bet when compared to the collegiate prospect ranked directly ahead of him.

77. Miguel Vargas, 3B, Los Angeles Dodgers

Vargas tends to fly under the radar. He wasn't a big bonus recipient out of Cuba, signing for just $300,000 after defecting as a 16-year-old. He's a third baseman without notable physical tools, and there's some risk he grows off the position. But he's hit .300 each of his professional seasons while dealing with aggressive assignments for his age. His swing and approach both support a plus-or-better hit tool. If his current doubles power turns into home run power as Vargas moves through his early 20s, he will be an offensive force. And while the body might be high maintenance, he's presently a fine defender at third, with more than enough arm for the left side.

78. Brennen Davis, OF, Chicago Cubs

Limited to just 50 games in 2019 because of a broken finger, the stage seemed set for a 2020 breakout for the former second-round pick. Davis got stuck in a round of Q2Q rehearsals at the alternate site instead. There he showed off a stronger frame and harder contact against more advanced arms. We will have to wait for the curtain to rise in 2021 before we know for sure if an all-star is born. We won't tell him to "break a leg"— that idiom should probably stay in the theater world, since durability may be the only hurdle between Davis and the top half of this list.

79. Matthew Allan, RHP, New York Mets

Allan has a fine starting kit for a pitching prospect—mid-90s fastball with good shape, excellent feel for a curveball, developing changeup, you know the drill. Allan possesses the type of velocity and spin rate that tends to show up nicely on a TrackMan readout, which is how teams were doing the majority of their professional scouting in 2020. Correspondingly, reports from his alternate site work were

quite strong. We still need to see this in full-season ball, but Allan might shoot up this list pretty quickly with increased exposure.

80. Shane McClanahan, LHP, Tampa Bay Rays

McClanahan became the first pitcher to make his major-league debut in the postseason, as the Rays managed to get the benefit of his electric arm on their postseason roster without granting him any service time. The upper-90s fastball and mid-80s breaking ball both flashed huge in four outings. He was also wild, inconsistent with his mechanics (which haven't always been great) and barely threw his changeup. While the top two pitches are electric, nothing that we saw in the majors or heard about his work earlier in the summer increased our confidence that McClanahan has a great shot to remain in the rotation. With every year that passes without the necessary improvements to his command and changeup, the relief risk inches up.

81. Shea Langeliers, C, Atlanta Braves

Langeliers is in some ways a throwback catching prospect. He has a good arm and gets high marks for handling his pitching staff, and he's a switch-hitter with big raw power, although it's unclear how much of that will find its way into games against better velocity. You saw a lot of these types in the 90s: Todd Hundley, Darren Daulton, Mike Lieberthal, etc. Catcher evaluation has changed markedly since then with a focus on framing, but Langeliers also grades out well there. There's little doubt the glove will make him a major-leaguer, but the track record of non-elite catching prospects without a high offensive floor has just as many Dan Wilsons in the mix as well. Catchers are weird, so by extension catching prospects are weird.

82. Jeremy Peña, SS, Houston Astros

I had no choice but to bump you
You stated your case, time and again
I thought about it

You showed up late to Corpus Christi
I'm not used to scouting LIDOM tape
You flashed improved bat speed

You've already won me over, in spite of me
And don't be alarmed if I fall glove over cleats
I won't be surprised if you're big league, with all that you are
I couldn't help it, you could go far

83. Trevor Larnach, OF, Minnesota Twins

Larnach's bat has some of the easiest game power you'll find. Utilizing an up-the-middle approach, the power mostly manifests to the pull-side with a growing ability to distribute to all fields. This has been the case since his draft year at Oregon State. Hit the ball, hit the ball hard, get on base and try not to do anything too bad on defense. He's a big, lumbering guy that should be hidden in left field so the bat can be in the lineup on an everyday basis. There isn't much left to prove on the minor-league side of things.

84. Francisco Alvarez, C, New York Mets

Alvarez was sent stateside as soon as he was eligible and it took only a week in the Gulf Coast League to show that he was too good for complex ball. He then more than held his own in the Appalachian League as a 17-year-old. Alvarez spent a few weeks at the Mets alternate site in 2020, and then a few more in the St. Lucie and Dominican complexes, but the only trace of him you'll easily find this year was from a team-affiliated prospect account posting video of him at instructs. We can discern the Mets have tweaked his stance and setup, as he has a much wider base with minimal lower half engagement compared to 2019. What does this mean for his advanced contact ability and above-average power projection? How have his raw defensive skills progressed? Tune in next year to find out!

85. Triston Casas, 1B, Boston Red Sox

As the Red Sox begin the arduous task of rebuilding a depleted farm system following the closing of their championship window, Casas is the type of player that opens the next championship window when he's ready. Boasting one of the best raw power tools in the prep ranks over the last several years, he's been working to try and cut down on the amount of swing-and-miss to his game. Hitting instructors in the org noted their desire to get him to avoid being so pull-happy, believing the use of all fields will make him a more well-rounded hitter and assist with the strikeout numbers. He has seen time at third base thanks to an above-average arm, yet it seems like a forgone conclusion that the body will move him to exclusively first base, which is perfectly fine for a left-handed swinging slugger.

86. Reid Detmers, LHP, Los Angeles Angels

It has been no secret that the Angels have prioritized multi-sport athletes in recent drafts, hoping to plug holes in the pitching staff with rentals and cast-offs at discounted prices. Detmers' selection bucked that trend. A star lefty at Louisville who carries very little risk of becoming a reliever, his polished starter attributes include a fastball that lacks upper tier velocity but that can be commanded around the plate and a snapdragon curveball that was nearly untouchable in college. With fluid mechanics and feel to pitch, the one piece of polish that is noticeably missing is a clear third pitch. A changeup might be the obvious answer, although a short slider/cutter could also provide utility.

87. Gabriel Arias, SS, Cleveland

Arias was the prospect centerpiece sent to Cleveland in the Padres deadline deal for Mike Clevinger. There likely wasn't room for him on the left side of the San Diego infield for the next decade or so, and Cleveland might have a Francisco-Lindor-shaped hole at shortstop by the time this book is in your hands. It's not fair to ask any prospect to replace Lindor, but Arias is capable of making the kind of plays at shortstop that might make fans reminisce. He's a potential plus-plus defender whose bat broke out in High-A in 2019. Many prospects have shined in the launching pads of the California League and then taken a step back in more normal environs against advanced pitching—we raise a glass to you, Lars Anderson. Until it's clear the bat will play under typical conditions, we're going to say he's more steady than stratospheric.

88. Ed Howard, SS, Chicago Cubs

Widely considered the best prep shortstop in the draft, the South Side kid landed crosstown in what could amount to a steal. His game is built around elite hands that offer loose actions from the shortstop position and excellent bat-to-ball skills. Missing from the profile is a sense of where the power will eventually go, with the prevailing thought being that his projectable frame will add the needed muscle to get to at least average grades. He's a long ways away, but the Cubbies can afford to be patient.

89. Miguel Amaya, C, Chicago Cubs

Amaya remains a solid two-way catching prospect, where you can dream on above-average hit and power tools and a still-developing, but potentially solid defensive profile as well. His arm is ahead of his receiving, but both project to at least average. Amaya still needs to conquer the upper minors without the bat stagnating—a common malady for catchers first identified by John Sickels—but his overall balanced skill set should keep him on these lists until he arrives.

90. Geraldo Perdomo, SS, Arizona Diamondbacks

While we are in a bit of a golden era for major league shortstops, there still aren't that many players that do enough things well enough to stick at the 6. Perdomo will do more than stick, he has a chance to be a good defensive shortstop. Combine that with an advanced approach and a chance for double-digit home run power as he fills out in his 20s, and you will get a (relatively) safe future major leaguer.

91. Michael Busch, 2B, Los Angeles Dodgers

It's always wise to bet on the player you think is going to hit. Busch hit for average and power and walked more than he struck out his sophomore year at UNC, that summer on the Cape, and then again his junior year. Okay, he didn't hit in 10 games post-draft, but every report we got on him from the alternate site and instructs suggests he has above-average hit and power tools and a good approach. If that's the case, teams will find a place for you to stand in the field. Busch was primarily a first baseman and corner outfielder as an amateur, but so far he's primarily played second base. He's fringy but playable there. Also, being as it is the Dodgers, Busch will probably see time all over the diamond, because they'll want to get that bat in the lineup as much as possible.

92. Jordan Walker, 3B, St. Louis Cardinals

This placement might exaggerate the gap between Walker and Nolan Gorman at this point in time; there is just more of a track record on Gorman. After being drafted 21st overall in 2020, Walker immediately started matching his organization mate's prodigious power potential at the alternate site. A divisive draft prospect, who some thought might end up in the outfield due to his 6-foot-5 frame, Walker has quelled a lot of doubts with his post-draft performance. His upside matches Gorman's, and his OFP might soon as well. Just have that pesky need to see him in some games first to feel more confident that he's a .270, 30-home-run third baseman. Of course, if the bat gets there, it doesn't really matter whether he's a third baseman either.

93. Xavier Edwards, SS/2B, Tampa Bay Rays

Edwards' potential carrying weapon is his hit tool; he has strong bat-to-ball skills, an advanced plate approach and decent bat speed. Most of our live reports on Edwards point to a plus hit outcome, and he's going to leg out a few extra singles a year with his elite speed. He's going to need to hit for a high average, because his game power is currently negligible and it doesn't project out. He might have even less raw power than Nick Madrigal. He's not likely to stay at shortstop full-time, either, and long-term he might find his best fit as a slash-and-burn multi-positional type. He's certainly made his way to the right organization for that.

94. Trevor Rogers, LHP, Miami Marlins

Rogers showed better stuff in the majors than he'd ever shown as a prospect, continuing a gradual glow-up dating back to the 2017 draft. His fastball sat around 94 mph, up a few ticks from past readings, and it's a high-spin offering that induced good swing-and-miss. His diving changeup has developed into exactly the kind of out pitch that so many of the prospects you've read about here need to reach, and his slider is a solid pitch as well. The topline results in terms of runs allowed weren't there (owing to one disastrous outing), but the underlying rate metrics were quite promising. Rogers' development is why teams will constantly bet on projectable prep lefties high in the draft—he was the No. 13 overall pick because his frame portended velocity and secondary pitches would come—even though the house tends to win that particular game of chance.

95. Jackson Kowar, RHP, Kansas City Royals

Kowar is the third and final Royals pitcher on this year's 101. Last year's edition included Brady Singer and Kris Bubic, both of whom got just enough service time to graduate. That makes a full starting rotation of young, quality pitching prospects. It rarely works out so neatly in the end, but if you collect enough quality arms, one or two might break out past their mid-rotation projection. Kowar isn't a bad bet in that regard. He's continued to gain velocity as a pro, and now sits mid-90s and was touching 99 at the alternate site. His breaking ball has improved to the point that it's an average offering and his change remains a bat-misser he can throw with confidence to both lefties and righties. It would be nice to see him truly dominate a level in the minors given the stuff, and his command will need to improve another grade or so for that to happen, but everything is trending positively.

96. Clarke Schmidt, RHP, New York Yankees

Schmidt tore through the Grapefruit League with two distinct mid-90s fastballs and a hellacious breaking ball that has the best properties of a curve and slider. Though he pitched poorly in the majors, we now have some additional context on that breaking ball: The average spin rate was 3,085 rpm, which makes it one of the highest-spin breaking balls in the majors. It's likely to be an elite swing-and-miss pitch in any role, though he's going to need substantial development on his changeup and command to stay in the rotation.

97. Erick Peña, OF, Kansas City Royals

Peña's stock has been steadily rising as a pro—and he signed for the fourth-highest signing bonus in the 2019 international class, so he wasn't exactly a low-profile prospect to begin with. We started hearing impressive buzz from pro scouts when he came stateside for 2019 fall instructs (where he roomed with Bobby Witt Jr.), and that steam kept building last offseason. Instead of making his pro debut in the summer, the Royals sent him to both sets of fall camps they ran. While he struggled adjusting to the advanced pitching prospects who were at the alternate site, he later shined against more age-appropriate competition in Arizona. Like Jasson Dominguez, we're going to need to see Peña hit in real games to truly buy in, but we can already tell there's a sweet swing with hit and power potential present.

98. Sam Huff, C, Texas Rangers

If Shea Langeliers is one type of throwback catching prospect, Sam Huff is a different kind of throwback: a huge dude with light-tower power and a big arm. Huff had only 20 batted balls in the majors, but he absolutely murdered the ball when he made contact, with a superlative 95.7 mph average exit velocity. He arrived ahead of schedule, with no experience above High-A, and looked fine. There are approach contact issues here to be sure—he struck out 154 times in A-ball in 2019, and in the small sample in the majors he was still swinging at, and through, too many pitches. There's some risk he's going to have to move off catcher to a corner eventually. But there is also big upside if everything clicks and he stays behind the dish.

99. Tarik Skubal, LHP, Detroit Tigers

Skubal made eight appearances (seven starts) for the Tigers in 2020, and even that allows for a wealth of data on his arsenal and its relative effectiveness. The problem here is his pitch mix *wasn't* effective. Skubal's mid-90s fastball produced a .547 slugging against, and he threw his changeup—his clear third pitch—more often than his potential plus-plus slider. The heater is high-spin and comes from a deceptive angle, but can run a bit true, and Skubal wasn't fine enough with his command the first go-round against major-league hitters. So, when he wasn't missing bats, he got hit hard. The Tigers have every reason to keep giving him a chance to start, but given the health track record and early returns, he might be best suited as a late-inning multi-inning force where the fastball velocity might play up and he can throw the wipeout slider more.

100. Daniel Espino, RHP, Cleveland

High-school hurlers who touch 100, have advanced secondaries and an athletic body rarely make it to the tail-end of the first round, where Espino was selected. Of concern was an elongated arm action that whips through the delivery giving a less-than-pleasing visual. It is unorthodox, sure, but so is an 18-year-old who throws that hard. After entering the system, he has received high praise for his ability to retain information, being receptive to coaching on his mechanics and working hard in the weight room to fill out his thin frame. We received strong reports on his development this summer and fall, and with so many explosive qualities, file Espino under the category of players who we're dying to see take a big step in 2021.

101. Alejandro Kirk, C, Toronto Blue Jays

The short-and-stout backstop was one of the more surprising call-ups of the 2020 season. We were in on Kirk's hit tool and improving defense some coming into the season, but 21-year-old catchers who haven't played above A-ball aren't traditional call-ups. (Then again, 2020 wasn't a traditional season.) Kirk didn't look out of place in the majors, scorching the ball when he got into games and looking perfectly fine behind the dish. We still aren't sold on his ability to lift the ball for game power, but he sure seems like he's going to hit a bunch and be able to catch. That the Blue Jays thought he was one of their best options during a pennant chase—even DHing him in a playoff game against Blake Snell—is a vote of confidence, too.

Arizona Diamondbacks

The State of the System:

Another bumper crop of draft picks buoy an already-deep system, but the lost development year may affect the Diamondbacks org—or at least the variance and risk within—more than most.

The Top Ten:

──────────────────── ★ ★ ★ *2021 Top 101 Prospect* **#15** ★ ★ ★ ────────────────────

1 **Kristian Robinson** **CF**   OFP: 70   ETA: 2023

Born: 12/11/00   Age: 20   Bats: R   Throws: R   Height: 6'3"   Weight: 190   Origin: International Free Agent, 2017

YEAR	TEAM	LVL	AGE	PA	R	2B	3B	HR	RBI	BB	K	SB	CS	AVG/OBP/SLG	DRC+	BABIP	BRR	FRAA	WARP
2018	MIS	ROK	17	74	13	1	0	3	10	11	21	5	3	.300/.419/.467		.405			
2018	DIA	ROK	17	182	35	11	0	4	31	16	46	7	5	.272/.341/.414		.351			
2019	HIL	SS	18	189	29	10	1	9	35	23	47	14	3	.319/.407/.558	208	.398	-0.1	CF(22) 1.6, RF(18) 3.8	2.8
2019	KC	LO-A	18	102	14	3	1	5	16	8	29	3	2	.217/.294/.435	90	.259	-0.3	CF(18) 0.6, RF(5) 0.2, LF(2) -0.3	0.2
2021 FS	ARI	MLB	20	600	53	26	2	12	58	40	222	15	7	.216/.275/.342	68	.335	-3.6	CF 3, RF 3	-0.5

Comparables: Yorman Rodriguez, Domingo Santana, Nomar Mazara

The Report: We kick off our prospect lists with a teenager (at time of publication) who has one of the best power/speed combinations in the minors. The Baseball Prospectus Prospect Team is always on brand. Robinson is a plus runner with potential top-of-the-scale pop who has a good chance to be an above-average glove in center field. The other tools aren't as loud, but he potentially has all five; the hit tool is the thorniest, although that's not unusual given Robinson's limited pro experience. The swing-and-miss concerns do create a gap between the present and the projected and increase the out-and-out bust risk.

Development Track: There's an alternate history—hoo boy will this be a recurring theme in this section across all 30 lists—where Robinson torched both A-ball levels and established himself as one of the elite prospects in baseball. The tools are all there, and showed in enough flashes at the alternate site to more or less hold serve in the Top 101. Despite the lost year he will only be 20 on Opening Day. But in what will be another recurring theme this list cycle, it's still a lost year. And that inserts a bit more uncertainty into the profile.

Variance: High, bordering on extreme due to the lost developmental time and swing-and-miss concerns. He's a high ceiling/ low floor prospect, with a wide swath of outcomes in between. We'll know a lot more this time next year … hopefully (ominous orchestral stinger), after Robinson has spent a full season at … well, full-season, but his upside isn't that far off Julio Rodriguez's.

Mark Barry's Fantasy Take: First list, first prospect, first taste of hyperbole. There's a chance Robinson is what we thought Jo Adell might be. Obviously it's early on Adell, but his five-tool potential is seriously tainted by a case of the whiffs. Robinson has flashed better plate discipline than Adell on his rise through the minors, and he has stolen more bases. Pair those attributes with a career line of .281/.366/.474 and we're heading into top-prospect-in-the-game territory. It's upside with an absolute Capital "U". Nice little start here.

★ ★ ★ *2021 Top 101 Prospect* **#34** ★ ★ ★

2 **Corbin Carroll** **OF** OFP: 60 ETA: Late 2022/Early 2023
Born: 08/21/00 Age: 20 Bats: L Throws: L Height: 5'10" Weight: 165 Origin: Round 1, 2019 Draft (#16 overall)

YEAR	TEAM	LVL	AGE	PA	R	2B	3B	HR	RBI	BB	K	SB	CS	AVG/OBP/SLG	DRC+	BABIP	BRR	FRAA	WARP
2019	DIA	ROK	18	137	23	6	3	2	14	24	29	16	1	.288/.409/.450		.366			
2019	HIL	SS	18	49	13	3	4	0	6	5	12	2	0	.326/.408/.581	116	.452	0.8	CF(11) 0.0	0.3
2021 FS	ARI	MLB	20	600	48	26	5	6	51	43	203	24	3	.220/.281/.327	69	.335	16.9	CF -3, LF -1	0.9

Comparables: Ronald Acuña Jr., Aaron Hicks, Trent Grisham

The Report: "If he were two inches taller and 20 pounds heavier" is usually the introductory clause for a short right-handed pitcher we like more than we should. It applies to Carroll as well. If he were 6-foot—or at least tall enough to be listed at 6-foot—and a lean 185 or so, he wouldn't have slid to Arizona's 16th-overall pick last year. Everything else here points to a top-10 prep outfield pick, a potential plus speed/power combo for a likely major-league center fielder.

Development Track: There's an alternate history—are you sick of this yet—where Carroll torched both A-ball levels and made a jump from just off the 2020 Top 101 … well, into the meaty part where he will reside in the 2021 edition. A half dozen, maybe more, prospects make that jump every year. What would it have looked like? A .300 batting average, surprising power on contact given his frame, good defense in center field? There was enough of that present at Salt River Fields to justify the jump anyway, despite not having the Midwest and Cal League looks that would have laid that bare. And frankly, we were probably too low on Carroll last year due to his size. There's less upside than Robinson, but a bit more surety in the hit tool.

Variance: High. It's a collection of 55 or 60s on the scouting sheet, but when you line them all up in a center fielder, the overall profile should play up. On the other hand if it all falls a half grade short, there isn't a carrying tool and you just have an okay regular. And we are still a ways away from feeling too comfortable divining either of those outcomes.

Mark Barry's Fantasy Take: By now you're aware that steals are pretty hard to come by in fantasy circles, and Carroll offers a sweet, sweet blend of speed and a knack for getting on base that gives him a "Better Adam Eaton" upside. If that surprising power on contact holds, or dare I say, improves, he could be considerably more than that, but either way, Carroll is a top-20ish dynasty prospect for me.

★ ★ ★ *2021 Top 101 Prospect* **#47** ★ ★ ★

3 **Alek Thomas** **CF** OFP: 60 ETA: 2022
Born: 04/28/00 Age: 21 Bats: L Throws: L Height: 5'11" Weight: 175 Origin: Round 2, 2018 Draft (#63 overall)

YEAR	TEAM	LVL	AGE	PA	R	2B	3B	HR	RBI	BB	K	SB	CS	AVG/OBP/SLG	DRC+	BABIP	BRR	FRAA	WARP
2018	MIS	ROK	18	134	26	11	1	2	17	11	19	4	3	.341/.396/.496		.392			
2018	DIA	ROK	18	138	24	3	5	0	10	13	18	8	2	.325/.394/.431		.381			
2019	KC	LO-A	19	402	63	21	7	8	48	43	72	11	6	.312/.393/.479	153	.372	0.4	CF(76) -10.1, LF(7) 0.2, RF(7) 0.8	2.5
2019	VIS	HI-A	19	104	13	2	0	2	7	9	33	4	5	.255/.327/.340	89	.373	0.4	CF(23) 2.6	0.6
2021 FS	ARI	MLB	21	600	52	26	4	10	57	36	163	7	6	.238/.288/.359	76	.318	-4.5	CF -6, LF 0	-1.0

Comparables: Kyle Tucker, Albert Almora Jr., Manuel Margot

The Report: Hmm, perhaps the Diamondbacks have a type. Here's the third of the troika of center fielders who make loud contact. Thomas slots in between Carroll and Robinson in terms of physicality—although 99 percent of prospects are gonna slot behind Robinson in that respect—and his swing is geared more for the gaps than for over-the-fence power at present. It's plus raw though, and he's a plus athlete who might end up the center fielder of the group if all three find themselves on the same Diamondbacks roster.

Development Track: Thomas still has a very pretty left-handed swing with some power projection, and is the most likely of this group to be exactly a role-55 outfielder. That's not just because he's actually seen a fair bit of full-season ball. His is a more advanced game on both sides of the ball, and he's likely to be a passable regular even if the offensive profile plays more to averagish against better arms, but there is some hit-tool risk which isn't ideal for a profile that is also hit-tool driven. However, we think he will hit, and in a normal year, we might have seen him on the cusp of the majors by this point.

Variance: High. Thomas has more tangible pro experience than Robinson or Carroll, but it's not *a lot* of pro experience and it's a more batting-average-reliant profile, so you will want to see how the bat plays in the upper minors.

Mark Barry's Fantasy Take: You know, there's an alternate history where—oh you've heard that before? Fine.

His ceiling isn't quite as high as the other two ultra-talented center field prospects in this system, but that's akin to saying strawberry is the third-best Neapolitan ice cream flavor. That's still pretty good. I have a little less faith in Thomas's efficiency on the bases, which is the separator between him and Carroll for me, but Thomas is a no-doubt top-35 guy in my estimation.

★ ★ ★ *2021 Top 101 Prospect* **#90** ★ ★ ★

4 Geraldo Perdomo SS   OFP: 60   ETA: 2022. 2021 is in play though.
Born: 10/22/99   Age: 21   Bats: S   Throws: R   Height: 6'2"   Weight: 185   Origin: International Free Agent, 2016

YEAR	TEAM	LVL	AGE	PA	R	2B	3B	HR	RBI	BB	K	SB	CS	AVG/OBP/SLG	DRC+	BABIP	BRR	FRAA	WARP
2018	MIS	ROK	18	29	3	0	1	0	2	7	4	1	1	.455/.586/.545		.556			
2018	DIA	ROK	18	101	20	4	2	1	8	14	17	14	1	.314/.416/.442		.382			
2018	HIL	SS	18	127	20	3	2	3	14	18	23	9	4	.301/.421/.456	148	.359	1.4	SS(30) 3.9	1.3
2019	KC	LO-A	19	385	48	16	3	2	36	56	56	20	8	.268/.394/.357	126	.318	-2.2	SS(80) 2.1, 2B(11) -0.1	2.7
2019	VIS	HI-A	19	114	15	5	0	1	11	14	11	6	5	.301/.407/.387	128	.325	-0.2	SS(26) -1.0	0.6
2021 FS	ARI	MLB	21	600	61	25	3	7	54	56	148	17	9	.240/.320/.345	87	.317	-4.6	SS 6, 2B 0	1.1
2021 DC	ARI	MLB	21	33	3	1	0	0	2	3	8	0	0	.240/.320/.345	87	.317	-0.3	SS 0	0.1

Comparables: J.P. Crawford, Asdrúbal Cabrera, Hanser Alberto

The Report: Perdomo more than held his own as a teenager at two A-ball stops in 2019 and slotted toward the back of last year's 101 on the strength of his advanced two-way profile. The offensive performance was mostly approach-driven, which can become a problem when upper minors pitchers start to challenge you, but he should be able to sting the ball enough to keep better arms honest. And Perdomo doesn't have to hit a ton, as he's a slick fielding shortstop who does everything well, if nothing spectacularly.

Development Track: We don't really have reason to move Perdomo much one direction or the other. He has a fairly stable, high-floor profile even with the missing year of minor league baseball. Generally, I'd think we'd argue the few months off would be more deleterious to hitters than pitchers, but Perdomo will enter 2021 in High-A or Double-A as a 21-year-old with some track record of pro performance and solid enough alternate site reports. How much power comes next season and beyond will determine whether or not the modifier "glove-first" gets tagged to his profile going forward. That profile is still likely to be that of a useful regular, though.

Variance: Medium. The defensive tools give Perdomo a high floor, as even if he settles in as an OBP-driven 90 DRC+ type, the glove should be good enough to make him an average regular. There is upside in the bat if he fills out and adds a bit of power, but his ceiling is likely lower overall than the names above him.

Mark Barry's Fantasy Take: I love this system.

I also love high-contact dudes who also have a knack for getting on base. As a pro, all Perdomo has done is hit, and when he's not hitting, he's working walks. Even without the possibility of power, he's one of my favorite under-21 guys in the minor leagues, but if he matures into a little pop, we're looking at a legit, five-category contributor.

5 Bryce Jarvis RHP   OFP: 60   ETA: Second half 2022
Born: 12/26/97   Age: 23   Bats: L   Throws: R   Height: 6'2"   Weight: 195   Origin: Round 1, 2020 Draft (#18 overall)

The Report: Prior to 2020, Jarvis was a scrawny back-of-the-weekend pitcher for Duke with advanced secondary pitches and command. What was lacking was an at-least average fastball, as his was typically scraping 90 mph. Jarvis needed to add several extra ticks to help his off-speed pitches get further separation off each other. Fast forward to this past spring and the fastball is now 92-95 with movement, command, and control all paired with two breaking balls flashing above average and a changeup that is easily plus or better. The added arm strength is visible in the rest of his body, with a highly athletic frame and delivery.

Development Track: The jump between his first two years on campus to his draft-eligible year was seismic. College hitters always had trouble against his spin and arm speed, so taking that next great leap with the fastball is what got him into the first round. The question many evaluators have is whether the velo bump is real and sustainable. This next year of development will be pivotal—not only in regards to maintaining this year's gains, but also to determining how much more can be added on his projectable body.

Variance: Medium. With no history of arm trouble and fluid mechanics, there is no reason to assume there is an impending injury around the corner even when factoring in the spike on the heater. Still, it's always a baked-in concern in the background. The great separators are the unteachable traits of his secondary pitches which should keep him a starter long-term.

Mark Barry's Fantasy Take: OK, so maybe I jumped the gun on my unconditional love for this system. And that's not a knock on Jarvis, at least not really. The improvements during his stint in college are super intriguing, but a righty with middling velocity typically is just another translation for a mid-to-back-end starter, which is definitely not as exciting. I'll take a flyer with a late-first or early second-round FYPD pick, but Jarvis isn't someone I'm immediately targeting.

6 Blake Walston LHP   OFP: 60   ETA: 2023

Born: 06/28/01   Age: 20   Bats: L   Throws: L   Height: 6'5"   Weight: 175   Origin: Round 1, 2019 Draft (#26 overall)

YEAR	TEAM	LVL	AGE	W	L	SV	G	GS	IP	H	HR	BB/9	K/9	K	GB%	BABIP	WHIP	ERA	DRA-	WARP
2019	DIA	ROK	18	0	0	0	3	2	5	2	0	0.0	19.8	11	83.3%	.333	0.40	1.80		
2019	HIL	SS	18	0	0	0	3	3	6	6	0	3.0	9.0	6	41.2%	.353	1.33	3.00	122	-0.1
2021 FS	ARI	MLB	20	2	3	0	57	0	50	49	8	5.3	9.1	50	41.1%	.304	1.58	5.43	127	-0.6

Comparables: Hunter Harvey, Jenrry Mejia, Noah Syndergaard

The Report: I wasn't in the room for the Starling Marte trade discussions, but I can see why perhaps the D'backs may have been more willing to part with Brennan Malone than Walston. We preferred Malone over Walston a smidge last year on present stuff, but Walston had more upside due to his projectability and potential plus fastball/curve combo as a southpaw.

Development Track: Walston's velocity and changeup remain inconsistent. The frame remains projectable. He has reportedly added a slider to give a second breaking ball look. The lost development year still stings but, as noted in the Perdomo blurb, it stings less for pitchers and Walston still would have gotten his work in and received hands-on coaching in terms of stuff development. You'd have liked to see the slider in game action, and see how the fastball velocity held up across six innings on a cold night in the Midwest League, but the projection remains, and we remain bullish on a mid-rotation profile.

Variance: High. With all the added complexity in evaluation and ranking prospects in 2020, it's nice for one of these to just be able to fall back on "needs to consolidate plus fastball velocity and make change and command gains." It's like catching up with an old friend.

Mark Barry's Fantasy Take: Mid-rotation upside with high variance is not really the stuff of fantasy legend. Walston probably needs to be rostered in leagues of 200 prospects or more, but his present skill set should be fairly replicable on the waiver wire.

7 Corbin Martin RHP   OFP: 55   ETA: Debuted in 2019

Born: 12/28/95   Age: 25   Bats: R   Throws: R   Height: 6'2"   Weight: 228   Origin: Round 2, 2017 Draft (#56 overall)

YEAR	TEAM	LVL	AGE	W	L	SV	G	GS	IP	H	HR	BB/9	K/9	K	GB%	BABIP	WHIP	ERA	DRA-	WARP
2018	FAY	HI-A	22	2	0	1	4	3	19	4	0	3.3	12.3	26	63.9%	.111	0.58	0.00	65	0.5
2018	CC	AA	22	7	2	0	21	18	103	84	7	2.4	8.4	96	47.7%	.277	1.09	2.97	69	2.3
2019	RR	AAA	23	2	1	0	9	8	37¹	33	2	4.3	10.8	45	38.7%	.348	1.37	3.13	61	1.3
2019	HOU	MLB	23	1	1	0	5	5	19¹	23	8	5.6	8.8	19	42.6%	.283	1.81	5.59	147	-0.3
2021 FS	ARI	MLB	25	9	8	0	26	26	150	133	21	4.2	9.3	154	42.1%	.284	1.35	4.18	98	1.2
2021 DC	ARI	MLB	25	1	2	0	8	8	32	28	4	4.2	9.3	32	42.1%	.284	1.35	4.18	98	0.4

Comparables: Brandon Bielak, Mitch Keller, Wade LeBlanc

The Report: Martin is your standard polished, four-pitch college arm without obviously plus stuff. There is no weakness in the arsenal. He can run the fastball into the mid-90s, show you a couple different breaking ball looks, and has an advanced, above-average changeup. Martin cruised through the minors (although the performance probably stopped short of "dominant") but everything pointed to a safeish, mid-rotation arm, and he made it to the majors less than two years after he was drafted. Then Martin tore his UCL and needed Tommy John surgery. Then he was traded to the Diamondbacks as part of the Zack Greinke deal. "Safeish" doesn't mean safe.

Development Track: Martin was functionally on rehab at the alternate site and was throwing without restriction within those parameters. The fastball velocity is back to mid-90s and was there for multi-inning stints. Assuming no major setbacks this offseason or next spring, he should be ready to go for Opening Day, and while he may not break camp with the big club, a healthy Martin is a major-league ready starter.

Variance: Medium. Martin's recovery from Tommy John surgery hasn't had any real red flags yet. But recovery isn't "recovered" and until we see how the stuff plays in longer stints in real game action, there's going to be additional health and profile risk.

Mark Barry's Fantasy Take: For my money, I'll take Martin as the top fantasy hurler in this org. If mid-rotation is the upside, give me the guy who's the closest and has flashed the ability to look fairly decent against big-league hitters (minus giving up eight dingers in 19 1/3 innings—that's, uh, less than ideal). Factor in his return from Tommy John surgery, and you might have a guy who's flying a little below the radar this offseason. As an aside, if your league gives extra points for dudes named Corbin, this is the system for you.

8 Slade Cecconi RHP   OFP: 60   ETA: Late 2022 as a starter, early 2022 as a reliever
Born: 06/24/99   Age: 22   Bats: R   Throws: R   Height: 6'4"   Weight: 219   Origin: Round 1, 2020 Draft (#33 overall)

The Report: Cecconi ranked 30th on our pre-draft big board due to his prototypical starting pitcher's frame and big fastball/slider combo. As a draft-eligible sophomore he didn't have a long college track record, and might have been able to move into the top half of the first round with a full ACC campaign where he showed off a more complete arsenal along with the ability to log innings and throw good strikes. But all in all there's more upside with Cecconi than your median supplemental round college arm.

Development Track: Cecconi was up into the high-90s in short bursts at the alternate site. He paired the fastball with a potential plus slider and showed a full four-pitch mix. He's a potential breakout arm in 2021 if he continues to refine his secondaries and manages to log 100+ healthy innings as a starter.

Variance: Medium. Cecconi will have to show he can hold up under a starter's workload because he has had arm issues and was used fairly conservatively as a freshman at Miami. He will also need to develop the curve and/or change as well to avoid the fallback position of power fastball/slider reliever.

Mark Barry's Fantasy Take: On the one hand, pairing arm issues with a predominantly two-pitch mix sure screams reliever. On the other, those two pitches are good enough to give Cecconi a pretty exciting ceiling should the changeup or curve develop into legit offerings. Outside the top-100, I'm more likely to chase the upside on an arm like Cecconi than settle for a back-end starter.

9 Seth Beer 1B   OFP: 55   ETA: 2021
Born: 09/18/96   Age: 24   Bats: L   Throws: R   Height: 6'3"   Weight: 225   Origin: Round 1, 2018 Draft (#28 overall)

YEAR	TEAM	LVL	AGE	PA	R	2B	3B	HR	RBI	BB	K	SB	CS	AVG/OBP/SLG	DRC+	BABIP	BRR	FRAA	WARP
2018	TRI	SS	21	51	9	3	0	4	7	6	10	0	0	.293/.431/.659	177	.296	-0.8	LF(7) -1.0, 1B(4) -0.1	0.1
2018	QC	LO-A	21	132	15	7	0	3	16	15	17	1	0	.348/.443/.491	160	.391	-1.2	RF(10) -0.9, LF(9) -1.1, 1B(7) -0.5	0.6
2018	FAY	HI-A	21	114	15	4	0	5	19	4	22	0	1	.262/.307/.439	106	.287	-2.2	LF(13) -1.4, 1B(6) -0.2	-0.4
2019	FAY	HI-A	22	152	24	8	0	9	34	14	30	0	3	.328/.414/.602	188	.359	-1.6	1B(16) 0.0, LF(15) -0.7	1.3
2019	JXN	AA	22	101	8	7	0	1	17	8	25	0	1	.205/.297/.318	74	.270	0.0	1B(14) -0.7, LF(10) -0.4	-0.2
2019	CC	AA	22	280	40	9	0	16	52	24	58	0	0	.299/.407/.543	176	.333	-3.1	1B(46) 0.8, LF(8) -0.1	2.1
2021 FS	ARI	MLB	24	600	77	27	2	25	81	44	159	0	0	.259/.338/.461	121	.323	-0.1	1B -1, LF 0	2.7

Comparables: Anthony Santander, Michael Taylor, Greg Bird

The Report: Beer has been a well-known prospect since he was one of the best offensive players in college baseball as a true freshman at Clemson in 2016. That made him an early 1.1 candidate for the 2018 draft, and he's never quite lived up to it since. Still, he has a fantastic plate approach, and the potential for plus hit/plus power. There's more swing-and-miss than you'd hope for given the rest of the offensive profile. Defensively … well, he has "versatility" in the sense that he can stand at first or in the outfield and catch most of what's aimed directly at him, but the best fit here is at DH. He'll get as far as his bat carries him.

Development Track: We got surprisingly strong positive feedback on Beer from the alternate site. On the flip side, he didn't show up in the majors despite spending most of 2019 in Double-A and the unexpected availability of DH at-bats. We think the arrow is pointing up a little, and the likelihood of a permanent NL DH spot certainly helps the long-term value.

Variance: Medium. The hitting profile in and of itself is low variance. But the lack of secondary value past his bat means that even if Beer falls just a moderate amount short, he's more likely to be a Triple-A (or KBO) superstar than a major-league role player.

Mark Barry's Fantasy Take: If this were a pure fantasy list, Beer would probably check in at number five, just behind Perdomo. His power, plate discipline, and lack of defensive position is very Kyle Schwarber-y, even if all of Beer's offerings are a notch below. As a guy whose defensive role is "Lol, no thanks", he'll need the DH to stick in the NL or a trade to an American League team to reach his full potential, but he hits and has always hit. He's going to need to in order to be useful as a fantasy option, or else he might not get enough run to really matter.

10 Levi Kelly RHP OFP: 55 ETA: Late 2021 as a reliever, Late 2022 as a starter.

Born: 05/14/99   Age: 22   Bats: R   Throws: R   Height: 6'4"   Weight: 205   Origin: Round 8, 2018 Draft (#249 overall)

YEAR	TEAM	LVL	AGE	W	L	SV	G	GS	IP	H	HR	BB/9	K/9	K	GB%	BABIP	WHIP	ERA	DRA-	WARP
2018	DIA	ROK	19	0	0	0	4	4	6	3	0	3.0	9.0	6	46.7%	.200	0.83	0.00		
2019	KC	LO-A	20	5	1	0	22	22	100¹	72	4	3.5	11.3	126	46.0%	.293	1.11	2.15	65	2.4
2021 FS	ARI	MLB	22	2	3	0	57	0	50	46	7	5.3	9.0	49	42.2%	.287	1.52	4.97	116	-0.3

Comparables: Neftalí Feliz, Casey Crosby, Robert Stephenson

The Report: Kelly jumped as a pitching prospect in 2019 in full-season ball, showing a plus fastball/slider combo that usually overpowered Midwest League lineups. Improved mechanics gave him a better shot to start, while the two-pitch combo provided a solid relief fallback.

Development Track: Well, if anything the slider might be even better now, and Kelly's stuff played against much more advanced hitters at the alternate site. The rest of the arsenal still lags behind, but it's 2021 and your starting pitching projection is determined less by the quality of your third pitch than the quality of your best two.

Variance: Medium. Given the potential plus-plus slider, Kelly could break camp in the Diamondbacks' bullpen, spam that pitch 40 percent of the time, and find immediate major-league success. And major-league teams are much more willing to take a pitcher with two really good pitches and let them start than they were a decade ago. That all said, Kelly hasn't pitched above A-ball, and has the usual third pitch and command concerns. So I'm going to note there is significant reliever risk even considering the potential reliever impact.

Mark Barry's Fantasy Take: Kelly is probably a reliever, and it takes an awful lot to be fantasy relevant from the 'pen. That slider is going to need to be really, really good.

The Prospects You Meet Outside The Top Ten:

Prospects who might be Top Ten in a shallower system

Tommy Henry LHP Born: 07/29/97   Age: 23   Bats: L   Throws: L   Height: 6'3"   Weight: 205   Origin: Round 2, 2019 Draft (#74 overall)

YEAR	TEAM	LVL	AGE	W	L	SV	G	GS	IP	H	HR	BB/9	K/9	K	GB%	BABIP	WHIP	ERA	DRA-	WARP
2021 FS	ARI	MLB	23	2	3	0	57	0	50	51	8	4.9	7.9	43	39.8%	.298	1.58	5.49	128	-0.7

Comparables: Humberto Mejía, Cal Quantrill, Austin Voth

The former Michigan Man's velocity jumped a bit in the spring before everything shut down, scraping the mid-90s now, and he held it at the alternate site. The changeup was already above-average coming out of college, and the breaking balls are improving too. Combine that with his already strong command profile, and his stock is moving up. Even though his entire pro career is only three innings in short-season ball, Henry could be a rotation option as early as 2021.

Luis Frias   RHP   Born: 05/23/98   Age: 23   Bats: R   Throws: R   Height: 6'3"   Weight: 180   Origin: International Free Agent, 2015

YEAR	TEAM	LVL	AGE	W	L	SV	G	GS	IP	H	HR	BB/9	K/9	K	GB%	BABIP	WHIP	ERA	DRA-	WARP
2018	DIA	ROK	20	1	1	0	7	6	29	17	1	3.4	9.6	31	49.3%	.229	0.97	2.48		
2018	HIL	SS	20	0	4	0	7	7	25²	21	0	5.3	9.5	27	32.4%	.309	1.40	3.16	263	-2.2
2019	HIL	SS	21	3	3	0	10	10	49²	36	0	3.1	13.0	72	42.5%	.340	1.07	1.99	73	0.9
2019	KC	LO-A	21	3	1	0	6	6	26²	22	1	4.0	9.8	29	36.6%	.300	1.27	4.39	98	0.1
2021 FS	ARI	MLB	23	2	3	0	57	0	50	46	7	5.6	9.2	51	36.0%	.293	1.56	5.09	118	-0.4

Comparables: Gregory Infante, Victor Alcántara, Duane Underwood Jr.

Frias might end up in "major-league-ready arms, but probably relievers" group a year or so down the line, but given the size and plus fastball/curve combo, there's no reason to rush the transition. He also has feel for a developing split as the third pitch, but the bigger hurdle to starting might be the sheer length of limbs Frias has to corral in his delivery. The fastball could play in the upper-90s in relief though, and the curve is a nasty 12-6 downer to pair with it in short bursts.

Prospects to dream on a little

Wilderd Patino   CF   Born: 07/18/01   Age: 19   Bats: R   Throws: R   Height: 6'1"   Weight: 175   Origin: International Free Agent, 2017

YEAR	TEAM	LVL	AGE	PA	R	2B	3B	HR	RBI	BB	K	SB	CS	AVG/OBP/SLG	DRC+	BABIP	BRR	FRAA	WARP
2018	DSL DB2	ROK	16	111	10	5	0	0	7	14	19	2	3	.225/.360/.281		.278			
2018	DSL DB1	ROK	16	27	4	1	0	0	2	2	5	4	2	.409/.519/.455		.529			
2019	DIA	ROK	17	125	18	4	3	1	21	11	32	13	3	.349/.403/.472		.462			
2019	MIS	ROK+	17	40	6	1	2	0	4	2	14	1	1	.229/.300/.371		.364			
2021 FS	ARI	MLB	19	600	45	26	3	6	49	31	221	19	8	.212/.264/.308	57	.337	-0.7	CF 4, RF -1	-1.1

Comparables: Ronald Acuña Jr., Jahmai Jones, Aaron Hicks

Patino's upside isn't that far off Carroll and Thomas, due to big time raw power out of a frame that can stick in center field—at least for now. The lost developmental year hits hard here as he needs to make strides with his hit tool and general swing-and-miss, and that would have been best served by 140 games against age-appropriate competition.

Jeferson Espinal   CF   Born: 06/07/02   Age: 19   Bats: L   Throws: L   Height: 6'0"   Weight: 180   Origin: International Free Agent, 2018

YEAR	TEAM	LVL	AGE	PA	R	2B	3B	HR	RBI	BB	K	SB	CS	AVG/OBP/SLG	DRC+	BABIP	BRR	FRAA	WARP
2019	DIA	ROK	17	43	6	1	0	0	7	8	11	4	1	.286/.419/.314		.417			
2019	DSL DB1	ROK	17	206	36	9	2	2	14	15	45	22	9	.358/.412/.460		.464			
2021 FS	ARI	MLB	19	600	43	26	2	5	45	37	226	40	15	.203/.257/.287	50	.331	-0.3	CF -1, LF -1	-2.3

Comparables: Monte Harrison, Dalton Pompey, Michael Hermosillo

Espinal is a safe—and potential plus—center fielder, as he's a true top-of-the-scale burner. There is some potential at the plate as well, but it's mostly projection outside of an already-advanced-for-his-age approach, and the overall tool kit isn't as loud as Patino's.

Safe MLB bats, but less upside than you'd like

Pavin Smith 1B Born: 02/06/96 Age: 25 Bats: L Throws: L Height: 6'2" Weight: 210 Origin: Round 1, 2017 Draft (#7 overall)

YEAR	TEAM	LVL	AGE	PA	R	2B	3B	HR	RBI	BB	K	SB	CS	AVG/OBP/SLG	DRC+	BABIP	BRR	FRAA	WARP
2018	VIS	HI-A	22	504	63	25	1	11	54	57	65	3	2	.255/.343/.392	112	.275	-1.1	1B(109) 9.0, RF(1) -0.1	0.6
2019	JXN	AA	23	507	62	29	6	12	67	59	61	2	1	.291/.370/.466	142	.310	-5.9	1B(79) 2.5, RF(28) -2.6, LF(13) 1.0	2.5
2020	ARI	MLB	24	44	7	0	1	1	4	5	8	1	0	.270/.341/.405	90	.300	-0.2	1B(5) 0.2, LF(3) 0.1, RF(2) -0.3	-0.1
2021 FS	ARI	MLB	25	600	67	27	5	14	67	56	114	0	0	.255/.328/.406	100	.300	2.7	1B 4, RF -2	1.5
2021 DC	ARI	MLB	25	437	48	19	3	10	49	40	83	0	0	.255/.328/.406	100	.300	2.0	1B 3, RF -1	1.2

Comparables: Rangel Ravelo, Jordan Brown, Chris Parmelee

At this point, Smith is unlikely to reach the heights with the bat that would justify taking a college first baseman seventh overall, but he is a disciplined hitter who could give you .270 with plenty of walks and some pull side pop. He has started playing some corner outfield and runs well enough to handle it, although he's a bit awkward on the grass at present. He's an above-average first baseman. Smith is a useful lefty bench bat who could spend a few years as an average regular if he more consistently taps into the pull side power.

Stuart Fairchild OF Born: 03/17/96 Age: 25 Bats: R Throws: R Height: 6'0" Weight: 200 Origin: Round 2, 2017 Draft (#38 overall)

YEAR	TEAM	LVL	AGE	PA	R	2B	3B	HR	RBI	BB	K	SB	CS	AVG/OBP/SLG	DRC+	BABIP	BRR	FRAA	WARP
2018	DAY	LO-A	22	276	40	12	5	7	37	31	65	17	4	.277/.377/.460	135	.352	2.3	CF(30) -2.3, LF(26) -0.4, RF(6) -0.1	1.4
2018	DAY	HI-A	22	242	25	14	1	2	20	17	63	6	2	.250/.306/.350	98	.335	-4.4	LF(31) 0.1, CF(30) -2.4, RF(2) -0.3	-0.6
2019	DAY	HI-A	23	281	32	17	2	8	37	25	60	3	5	.258/.335/.440	148	.306	-1.1	CF(39) -3.3, LF(15) 3.5	1.9
2019	CHA	AA	23	179	25	12	1	4	17	19	23	3	2	.275/.380/.444	131	.302	-1.1	CF(29) 0.2, RF(10) 1.6, LF(4) 0.3	1.2
2021 FS	ARI	MLB	25	600	63	26	4	13	62	44	167	8	4	.230/.301/.372	87	.305	0.4	CF -5, LF 0	0.4
2021 DC	ARI	MLB	25	33	3	1	0	0	3	2	9	0	0	.230/.301/.372	87	.305	0.0	CF 0	0.0

Comparables: Tyler Colvin, Clint Frazier, Brad Snyder

Acquired from the Reds as part of the Archie Bradley trade, Fairchild is a pretty safe bet to get some major-league run due to his plus center field glove and ability to hit left-handed pitching, but the profile likely tops out as a good fourth outfielder.

Dominic Fletcher CF Born: 09/02/97 Age: 23 Bats: L Throws: L Height: 5'9" Weight: 185 Origin: Round 2, 2019 Draft (#75 overall)

YEAR	TEAM	LVL	AGE	PA	R	2B	3B	HR	RBI	BB	K	SB	CS	AVG/OBP/SLG	DRC+	BABIP	BRR	FRAA	WARP
2019	KC	LO-A	21	239	33	14	1	5	28	22	50	1	1	.318/.389/.463	144	.396	2.3	CF(25) -2.1, RF(22) 4.0, LF(6) 0.1	2.2
2021 FS	ARI	MLB	23	600	54	27	2	12	58	37	179	0	0	.234/.288/.357	76	.323	0.1	CF -1, RF 3	0.1

Comparables: Harrison Bader, Darren Ford, Cedric Mullins

Fletcher and Fairchild are a bit of a matched set. The likely outcome for both is fourth outfielder, and Fletcher is merely decent in center. But there's upside in the bat—and underrated pop—that is more likely to carry him to a regular role. He's also further away, so order the profiles how you like.

MLB-ready arms, but probably relievers

J.B. Bukauskas **RHP** Born: 10/11/96   Age: 24   Bats: R   Throws: R   Height: 6'0"   Weight: 210   Origin: Round 1, 2017 Draft (#15 overall)

YEAR	TEAM	LVL	AGE	W	L	SV	G	GS	IP	H	HR	BB/9	K/9	K	GB%	BABIP	WHIP	ERA	DRA-	WARP
2018	AST	ROK	21	0	0	0	1	1	1²	5	0	0.0	10.8	2	12.5%	.625	3.00	10.80		
2018	TRI	SS	21	0	0	0	3	3	8¹	8	0	2.2	9.7	9	45.5%	.364	1.20	0.00	235	-0.5
2018	QC	LO-A	21	1	2	0	4	4	15	15	0	4.2	12.6	21	50.0%	.405	1.47	4.20	33	0.6
2018	FAY	HI-A	21	3	0	0	5	5	28	13	1	4.2	10.0	31	58.7%	.194	0.93	1.61	67	0.7
2018	CC	AA	21	0	0	0	1	1	6	1	0	3.0	12.0	8	60.0%	.100	0.50	0.00	64	0.1
2019	JXN	AA	22	0	1	0	2	2	7	10	0	6.4	14.1	11	38.9%	.556	2.14	7.71	150	-0.2
2019	CC	AA	22	2	4	1	20	14	85²	81	8	5.7	10.3	98	46.1%	.332	1.58	5.25	125	-1.3
2021 FS	ARI	MLB	24	1	1	0	57	0	50	44	6	6.1	9.4	52	43.4%	.286	1.57	4.98	115	-0.3
2021 DC	ARI	MLB	24	1	1	0	31	0	33	29	4	6.1	9.4	34	43.4%	.286	1.57	4.98	115	-0.1

Comparables: Carson Fulmer, Duane Underwood Jr., Jorge Alcala

Bukauskas has had durability and command issues dating back to his college days at North Carolina. He's still likely to be a reliever, but he is healthy now and showing two plus secondaries (change and slider) to go with his plus-plus heat. It's potential closer stuff as soon as Opening Day 2021.

Jon Duplantier **RHP** Born: 07/11/94   Age: 26   Bats: L   Throws: R   Height: 6'4"   Weight: 240   Origin: Round 3, 2016 Draft (#89 overall)

YEAR	TEAM	LVL	AGE	W	L	SV	G	GS	IP	H	HR	BB/9	K/9	K	GB%	BABIP	WHIP	ERA	DRA-	WARP
2018	DIA	ROK	23	0	0	0	2	2	7	5	0	2.6	11.6	9	43.8%	.312	1.00	1.29		
2018	JXN	AA	23	5	1	0	14	14	67	52	4	3.8	9.1	68	54.0%	.284	1.19	2.69	99	0.5
2019	DIA	ROK	24	0	0	0	2	2	2	5	1	13.5	13.5	3	50.0%	.571	4.00	18.00		
2019	VIS	HI-A	24	0	0	0	1	1	3	2	0	0.0	9.0	3	50.0%	.333	0.67	0.00	103	0.0
2019	RNO	AAA	24	1	2	0	13	11	38	31	1	6.6	10.4	44	44.7%	.330	1.55	5.21	60	1.4
2019	ARI	MLB	24	1	1	1	15	3	36²	39	2	4.4	8.3	34	42.5%	.359	1.55	4.42	117	-0.1
2021 FS	ARI	MLB	26	1	1	0	57	0	50	46	6	4.8	9.3	51	45.4%	.297	1.47	4.75	107	-0.1
2021 DC	ARI	MLB	26	1	1	0	28	3	27	25	3	4.8	9.3	27	45.4%	.297	1.47	4.75	107	0.1

Comparables: Ryan Helsley, Yonny Chirinos, Jordan Montgomery

Duplantier has had durability and command issues dating back to his college days at Rice. He's still likely to be a reliever, but he is healthy now, and has a power fastball/breaker combo that could make him a late-inning reliever as soon as Opening Day 2021.

Taylor Widener **RHP** Born: 10/24/94   Age: 26   Bats: L   Throws: R   Height: 6'0"   Weight: 230   Origin: Round 12, 2016 Draft (#368 overall)

YEAR	TEAM	LVL	AGE	W	L	SV	G	GS	IP	H	HR	BB/9	K/9	K	GB%	BABIP	WHIP	ERA	DRA-	WARP
2018	JXN	AA	23	5	8	0	26	25	137¹	99	12	2.8	11.5	176	34.8%	.276	1.03	2.75	64	3.6
2019	RNO	AAA	24	6	7	0	23	23	100	133	23	3.7	9.8	109	30.8%	.383	1.74	8.10	138	0.0
2020	ARI	MLB	25	0	1	0	12	0	20	14	5	5.4	9.9	22	37.3%	.196	1.30	4.50	123	-0.1
2021 FS	ARI	MLB	26	2	2	0	57	0	50	45	8	4.2	9.6	53	34.2%	.288	1.38	4.51	104	0.0
2021 DC	ARI	MLB	26	2	2	0	51	0	54	49	8	4.2	9.6	57	34.2%	.288	1.38	4.51	104	0.2

Comparables: Nabil Crismatt, Tyler Thornburg, Ryan Helsley

Widener has not had recent durability issues, pitching more than 100 innings every year from 2017-2019. He hit a wall as a starter in the PCL West with Reno—happens to the best of us, especially with the 2019 Triple-A ball—and the Diamondbacks moved him to the 'pen where he was a (high spin) 95-and-a-slider reliever for the big club in 2020. It's late-inning stuff if he can refine his command and find more consistency with the razorblade, mid-80s breaker.

Humberto Mejía RHP Born: 03/03/97 Age: 24 Bats: R Throws: R Height: 6'4" Weight: 235 Origin: International Free Agent, 2013

YEAR	TEAM	LVL	AGE	W	L	SV	G	GS	IP	H	HR	BB/9	K/9	K	GB%	BABIP	WHIP	ERA	DRA-	WARP
2018	BAT	SS	21	1	6	0	15	12	62²	55	8	2.0	8.5	59	36.9%	.275	1.10	3.30	113	0.0
2019	CLI	LO-A	22	5	1	1	13	10	66²	42	4	2.6	9.2	68	32.7%	.229	0.92	2.02	55	1.9
2019	JUP	HI-A	22	0	1	0	5	4	23²	15	2	1.9	8.0	21	43.8%	.210	0.85	2.28	63	0.5
2020	MIA	MLB	23	0	2	0	3	3	10	13	3	5.4	9.9	11	29.0%	.357	1.90	5.40	115	0.0
2021 FS	ARI	MLB	24	2	3	0	57	0	50	50	8	3.4	8.0	44	36.1%	.291	1.38	4.75	111	-0.2
2021 DC	ARI	MLB	24	0	0	0	3	3	12	12	2	3.4	8.0	10	36.1%	.291	1.38	4.75	111	0.1

Comparables: Joe Musgrove, David Paulino, Beau Burrows

Mejía has a better chance to be a starter then the names above—and has already made MLB starts—but might fit best as a 95-and-a-curve reliever. He's going to be 24 and hadn't pitched in the upper minors yet when the Marlins called him up to soak up starts. The delivery is effortful enough I think he fits best maxing out in a setup role, but Mejía has a solid frame and will show you four pitches. You might develop a fourth starter with further minor league reps, but he doesn't have the same late-inning upside as the rest of this group if he does end up in the 'pen.

Top Talents 25 and Under (as of 4/1/2021):

1. Zac Gallen, RHP
2. Kristian Robinson, OF
3. Corbin Carroll, OF
4. Alex Thomas, OF
5. Daulton Varsho, C/OF
6. Geraldo Perdomo, SS
7. Bryce Jarvis, RHP
8. Blake Walston, LHP
9. Corbin Martin, RHP
10. Slade Cecconi, RHP

Once again, Zac Gallen was a very good major-league pitcher in 2020. His ERA has outshined his DRA since he's been called up, and between his 2019 midseason call-up and the shortened 2020 season, he's only done this for 152 innings. Yet it's 152 innings of a No. 2 starter, and nothing seems wildly unsustainable. Gallen throws four pitches, misses bats, and has been quite durable over his pro career. He might "only" be a No. 3 moving forward if he regresses a bit, but that's still a heck of a pitching talent, and we're pretty confident he's at least going to be that good.

Daulton Varsho is the first player we've mentioned who lost their rookie eligibility when MLB amended its own rules at the end of the season to include September service time for the 2020 season only. After internal discussion, we went with the MLB rule, and Varsho was 29 at-bats short of exhausting his eligibility but tipped over on service time when including September days. We still get to talk about him (and most of the rest of this cohort) in our 25U writeups, though.

Arizona used Varsho in a third catcher/superutility type role the first half of the season, playing once a week for Carson Kelly and Stephen Vogt behind the plate while also seeing time in the outfield and DH. After Starling Marte was traded to Miami, he slowly took over semi-regular center field duties, while also still catching once or twice a week. It was an unusual deployment for an unusually speedy catcher in an organization with a young major-league starter ahead of him. At the plate, he struggled to hit for average, though he came on late after settling into a more regular role. The long-term defensive home is still unsettled, and it might not be easy to define, but we think he'll bring value and versatility to a club for a long time to come.

Atlanta Braves

The State of the System:

There's still a few of the same names who have made this a perennial Top 10 system during their rebuild and contention cycle, but Atlanta is probably not long for the Top 10 of our org rankings. That doesn't really matter when you've won back-to-back division titles, and there are a few more bullets to fire here to get the big-league club over that last playoff hump.

The Top Ten:

★ ★ ★ *2021 Top 101 Prospect* **#5** ★ ★ ★

1 Ian Anderson RHP   OFP: 70   ETA: Debuted in 2020
Born: 05/02/98   Age: 23   Bats: R   Throws: R   Height: 6'3"   Weight: 170   Origin: Round 1, 2016 Draft (#3 overall)

YEAR	TEAM	LVL	AGE	W	L	SV	G	GS	IP	H	HR	BB/9	K/9	K	GB%	BABIP	WHIP	ERA	DRA-	WARP
2018	FLO	HI-A	20	2	6	0	20	20	100	73	2	3.6	10.6	118	44.9%	.285	1.13	2.52	68	2.3
2018	MIS	AA	20	2	1	0	4	4	19¹	14	0	4.2	11.2	24	43.5%	.311	1.19	2.33	67	0.5
2019	MIS	AA	21	7	5	0	21	21	111	82	8	3.8	11.9	147	44.4%	.290	1.16	2.68	78	1.6
2019	GWN	AAA	21	1	2	0	5	5	24²	23	5	6.6	9.1	25	37.1%	.277	1.66	6.57	100	0.4
2020	ATL	MLB	22	3	2	0	6	6	32¹	21	1	3.9	11.4	41	53.1%	.250	1.08	1.95	65	0.9
2021 FS	ATL	MLB	23	9	8	0	26	26	150	131	19	4.3	10.2	169	45.8%	.292	1.36	4.09	95	1.5
2021 DC	ATL	MLB	23	8	9	0	27	27	148	129	19	4.3	10.2	167	45.8%	.292	1.36	4.09	95	1.9

Comparables: Archie Bradley, Henry Owens, Dustin May

The Report: Entering 2020, Anderson was an extremely good pitching prospect, straddling the 70/60 OFP border for the previous few years. He had a plus fastball and a plus curveball dating back to the draft, coming out of a difficult arm angle that was tough for hitters to pick up. The changeup flashed but lacked consistency, and the command sometimes wobbled. The statistical track record was solid outside of a late-season Triple-A stumble, but a lot of pitchers struggled in the 2019 Triple-A offensive barrage. In last year's *Annual* we wrote he was "a touch less likely to hit a top-of-the-rotation outcome (perhaps 20 percent instead of 25 percent) since he hasn't taken a major step forward in stuff and the command hasn't sharpened out yet." That "yet" is a saving grace.

Development Track: Anderson showed up in the majors on August 31 with everything he already had in the minors—along with one of the best changeups in baseball, fully formed, and improved command. Welp.

You probably know how the rest of this all went already. He was one of the best starting pitchers in baseball from his debut right through until Game 7 of the NLCS. Armed with his easy plus-plus change, he's now one of the best prospects in baseball. He's frankly more of a "young major-league star" in profile than a "prospect."

Variance: About as low as you can get for a pitcher. Anderson showed every indication he was already a present No. 2 starter in the majors this year, and he has no specific health or durability concerns. He's a hard 7 now.

Mark Barry's Fantasy Take: Unless your name rhymes with Mixto, I can't think of another pitching prospect who boosted his stock with a breathtaking late-season run more than Anderson. Heading into the season, I liked the strikeout potential, but was concerned about the walks/WHIP. After this season, I'm still slightly troubled by the walks, but Anderson showed that his stuff certainly plays against big-league hitters, so we're still in a better spot. Anderson is an SP2, and he'll flirt with SP1 seasons, especially if he masters the command.

★ ★ ★ *2021 Top 101 Prospect* **#18** ★ ★ ★

2 Cristian Pache CF   OFP: 70   ETA: Debuted in 2020

Born: 11/19/98   Age: 22   Bats: R   Throws: R   Height: 6'2"   Weight: 215   Origin: International Free Agent, 2015

YEAR	TEAM	LVL	AGE	PA	R	2B	3B	HR	RBI	BB	K	SB	CS	AVG/OBP/SLG	DRC+	BABIP	BRR	FRAA	WARP
2018	FLO	HI-A	19	387	46	20	5	8	40	15	69	7	6	.285/.311/.431	113	.330	-1.1	CF(93) 3.9	1.3
2018	MIS	AA	19	109	10	3	1	1	7	5	28	0	2	.260/.294/.337	71	.347	-0.5	CF(28) 1.3	-0.1
2019	MIS	AA	20	433	50	28	8	11	53	34	104	8	11	.278/.340/.474	139	.351	-1.7	CF(58) 1.6, RF(23) 3.3, LF(22) 0.0	3.3
2019	GWN	AAA	20	105	13	8	1	1	8	9	18	0	0	.274/.337/.411	90	.329	-0.9	CF(23) -3.2, RF(3) 3.3	0.2
2020	ATL	MLB	21	4	0	0	0	0	0	0	2	0	0	.250/.250/.250	83	.500		LF(2) 0.2	0.0
2021 FS	ATL	MLB	22	600	57	19	5	11	56	35	160	11	5	.231/.279/.350	72	.302	1.2	CF 2, RF 4	0.5
2021 DC	ATL	MLB	22	535	50	17	5	10	50	31	142	9	5	.231/.279/.350	72	.302	1.1	CF 2, RF 4	0.3

Comparables: Felix Pie, Greg Halman, Anthony Gose

The Report: Pache is an elite defensive center field prospect; extremely rangy with a plus-plus arm. When you start off a prospect evaluation with the defense, though, that in and of itself says something about the bat. We've been concerned about the swing-and-miss and approach issues for several years now, and we remain concerned. His walk rate improved in 2019 but not to the point of being outright good, and his strikeout rate ticked up too, especially at Double-A. He's grown into some power, so even without a big hit tool improvement he should provide offensive value, and he's made improvements to his swing that hint the big hit tool improvement may yet be coming. If he gets there, there's superstar potential.

Development Track: Entering the playoffs, we were a bit perplexed as to why we hadn't seen a lot of Pache during the 2020 season. He'd been sparingly used, appearing in only two games and both times he was in left field. Before we got a chance to really drill down into why he wasn't being used much, he was added to the playoff roster. After spending the first two rounds as a corner defensive replacement, he was inserted into the regular lineup in center for the NLCS when Adam Duvall got hurt. It was only 25 plate appearances, but he didn't look out of place.

Variance: Medium. His glove is likely to carry the profile some even if he doesn't hit a whole lot, but we don't actually have anyone on staff who is completely sold that he's going to hit a *whole* lot.

Mark Barry's Fantasy Take: Please stand by for the first of many "Better IRL than in fantasy" tags. Pache might be better IRL than in fantasy. When your A1 calling card is defense, that tends to be the case. Still, there's a lot to dream on with Pache's offensive profile. He brought some new and improved plate discipline to his brief stint with the big club down the stretch, and there's definitely speed, even if it hasn't consistently manifested on the bases. There's stuff to like, but it's still projection. If things break right, we could see .280ish with 15 homers and 20 steals, which isn't too shabby.

★ ★ ★ *2021 Top 101 Prospect* **#40** ★ ★ ★

3 Drew Waters CF   OFP: 60   ETA: 2021

Born: 12/30/98   Age: 22   Bats: S   Throws: R   Height: 6'2"   Weight: 185   Origin: Round 2, 2017 Draft (#41 overall)

YEAR	TEAM	LVL	AGE	PA	R	2B	3B	HR	RBI	BB	K	SB	CS	AVG/OBP/SLG	DRC+	BABIP	BRR	FRAA	WARP
2018	ROM	LO-A	19	365	58	32	6	9	36	21	72	20	5	.303/.353/.513	139	.362	3.9	CF(83) -0.6	2.4
2018	FLO	HI-A	19	133	14	7	3	0	3	8	33	3	0	.268/.316/.374	92	.363	0.0	CF(30) -1.5, RF(1) -0.1	-0.1
2019	MIS	AA	20	454	63	35	9	5	41	28	121	13	6	.319/.366/.481	143	.436	-3.3	LF(55) 6.3, CF(38) 7.0, RF(18) -1.2	4.2
2019	GWN	AAA	20	119	17	5	0	2	11	11	43	3	0	.271/.336/.374	79	.429	0.7	RF(16) 2.1, LF(7) 0.4, CF(3) 0.8	0.3
2021 FS	ATL	MLB	22	600	58	26	5	11	58	37	210	9	3	.225/.280/.354	74	.338	4.1	LF 10, CF 1	1.5
2021 DC	ATL	MLB	22	468	45	20	4	9	45	29	163	7	2	.225/.280/.354	74	.338	3.2	LF 8, CF 0	0.9

Comparables: Cristian Pache, Felix Pie, Fernando Tatis Jr.

The Report: Waters has been on the fast track through the Braves' system since he was drafted in the second round in 2017. He has shown great offensive potential as a switch-hitter with above-average power potential, and has hit at every stop, capturing the Double-A Southern League batting title and MVP Award in 2019. Waters has a chance to be a perennial .300 hitter with 20-home run pop if his hyper-aggressive approach doesn't overwhelm his natural bat-to-ball abilities. He's a solid center fielder, but not good enough to displace Pache. Very few prospects would be, though.

Development Track: The lack of a minor league season in 2020 denied Waters an opportunity to further his offensive development against upper-level pitchers. He has just 119 plate appearances at the Triple-A level and the Braves have no need to rush him. Waters spent the 2020 season at the alternate site where he worked to improve his approach at the plate.

He has added strength and has a solid work ethic and makeup. If he can carry over the refinements he made at the alternate site, he could be knocking on the door of the majors early in 2021. Waters might have even made the postseason roster if the Braves didn't already have Pache and his excellent glove on the depth chart.

Variance: High. The offensive potential is there and Waters has yet to be challenged in the minors. He may always be a high strikeout player due to the approach, but if the power develops he could be a star regardless.

Mark Barry's Fantasy Take: If you're a gambler, Waters can provide a sizable return on investment. There's a path to no-doubt fantasy stardom for the switch-hitter as a true five-category contributor. That's obviously hard to find. I'm a little worried about all of the swing-and-miss—Waters has incrementally been striking out at a higher clip since a 2018 stint in A-ball, culminating in a strikeout rate a tick above 36 percent in a small Triple-A sample. If he's going to strike out that much (and not walk very much) the batting average is going to dip and he'll have fewer opportunities for base thievery. Personally, I'd be a little more comfortable with Waters in that 20-25ish range as opposed to flirting with the top-10 for dynasty prospects.

★ ★ ★ *2021 Top 101 Prospect* **#62** ★ ★ ★

4 Kyle Muller LHP OFP: 60 ETA: Late 2021

Born: 10/07/97 Age: 23 Bats: R Throws: L Height: 6'7" Weight: 250 Origin: Round 2, 2016 Draft (#44 overall)

YEAR	TEAM	LVL	AGE	W	L	SV	G	GS	IP	H	HR	BB/9	K/9	K	GB%	BABIP	WHIP	ERA	DRA-	WARP
2018	ROM	LO-A	20	3	0	0	6	6	30	24	3	2.4	6.9	23	50.0%	.256	1.07	2.40	99	0.2
2018	FLO	HI-A	20	4	2	0	14	14	80²	80	2	3.6	8.8	79	39.6%	.355	1.39	3.24	98	0.5
2018	DAY	HI-A	20	2	0	0	2	2	13	10	0	2.8	11.1	16		.357	1.08	0.00		
2018	MIS	AA	20	4	1	0	5	5	29	22	3	1.9	8.4	27	35.8%	.247	0.97	3.10	89	0.4
2019	MIS	AA	21	7	6	0	22	22	111²	81	5	5.5	9.7	120	39.2%	.286	1.33	3.14	99	0.1
2021 FS	ATL	MLB	23	1	1	0	57	0	50	47	8	5.3	8.6	48	38.3%	.289	1.55	5.22	121	-0.5
2021 DC	ATL	MLB	23	1	1	0	4	4	19	18	3	5.3	8.6	18	38.3%	.289	1.55	5.22	121	0.0

Comparables: Rony García, Luis Severino, Jayson Aquino

The Report: Muller has come a long way since making his pro debut in 2016 with a fastball that sat in the upper-80s. He spent that offseason working at Driveline, and it has paid off as his velocity quickly jumped and has continued to rise. That added velocity in 2019 did have a negative effect on Muller's command, however. Muller also throws a curveball and a changeup that can play above average when the command is there. Reports from the alternate site were that he showed improvement in his command but he will need to carry that into minor league games next season. He is a great athlete and can stick as a starter long term, but his stuff would also play well as a late-inning reliever.

Development Track: Muller was sitting in the upper 90s with quality spin and touched 100 with a potential plus changeup at the alternate site. He will be ticketed to begin the season at Gwinnett where the focus will again be on his command. There is no questioning the stuff, but he is going to have to show the ability to throw strikes and further refine the secondaries. Atlanta isn't going to rush him to the majors, but if he can show improvement with his strike throwing in Triple-A, a 2021 debut isn't out of the question.

Variance: High. Triple-digit velocity with one of the best fastball spin rates in the minors gets you to the majors, but the command issues could force him into a relief role.

Mark Barry's Fantasy Take: Muller flashing command improvements at the alternate site feels a little like my totally real, totally great middle school girlfriend who I met at camp who lives in Canada. Like, it would be incredible if it were real, but also the likelihood of that reality is unfortunately fairly slim. I think Muller is probably a reliever long term, and that's okay, as the Josh Haders and Dustin Mays have shown that there's still fantasy value in relief, even without saves.

★ ★ ★ *2021 Top 101 Prospect* **#81** ★ ★ ★

5 Shea Langeliers C   OFP: 60   ETA: 2022
Born: 11/18/97   Age: 23   Bats: R   Throws: R   Height: 6'0"   Weight: 205   Origin: Round 1, 2019 Draft (#9 overall)

YEAR	TEAM	LVL	AGE	PA	R	2B	3B	HR	RBI	BB	K	SB	CS	AVG/OBP/SLG	DRC+	BABIP	BRR	FRAA	WARP
2019	ROM	LO-A	21	239	27	13	0	2	34	17	55	0	0	.255/.310/.343	100	.325	-1.3	C(42) 0.8	0.9
2021 FS	ATL	MLB	23	600	54	25	2	9	52	37	190	1	0	.213/.267/.318	64	.305	0.2	C 1	-0.2

Comparables: Josh Phegley, José Briceño, Kyle Higashioka

The Report: The Braves used the ninth pick in the 2019 draft on Langeliers and quickly sent him to Low-A for his professional debut. He was a little slow to come around at the plate but there was no questioning his defensive skills. Langeliers is a plus defender with a good arm, solid footwork, and plus pop times. He handles pitchers well and displays excellent leadership qualities.

Development Track: Offensively, Langeliers has elite raw power with a well-balanced swing from the right side, and he showed improved power to the opposite field at the alternate site. Langeliers is likely to start 2021 at High-A or Double-A, and while there are few questions about his defense, how his bat improves and whether or not he taps into his raw power with more consistency will determine how quickly he moves.

Variance: Medium. Langeliers' defensive tools are good enough that he won't need to hit a ton. There is enough power potential that, if the bat develops, it could push him to another level.

Mark Barry's Fantasy Take: "If the bat develops" dynasty catchers are one of my least favorite things, right up there with when someone quickly changes lanes right in front of you on the freeway, and then slows way down.

6 William Contreras C   OFP: 55   ETA: Debuted in 2020
Born: 12/24/97   Age: 23   Bats: R   Throws: R   Height: 6'0"   Weight: 180   Origin: International Free Agent, 2015

YEAR	TEAM	LVL	AGE	PA	R	2B	3B	HR	RBI	BB	K	SB	CS	AVG/OBP/SLG	DRC+	BABIP	BRR	FRAA	WARP
2018	ROM	LO-A	20	342	54	17	1	11	39	29	73	1	1	.293/.360/.463	134	.351	-0.9	C(43) -0.3	1.6
2018	FLO	HI-A	20	90	3	7	0	0	10	6	16	0	0	.253/.300/.337	102	.309	-0.3	C(20) -0.4	0.1
2019	FLO	HI-A	21	207	26	11	0	3	22	14	44	0	0	.263/.324/.368	112	.329	-0.2	C(43) -0.8	1.0
2019	MIS	AA	21	209	24	9	0	3	17	15	40	0	0	.246/.306/.340	99	.295	0.8	C(53) -1.1	0.9
2020	ATL	MLB	22	10	0	1	0	0	1	0	4	0	0	.400/.400/.500	83	.667	-0.3	C(4) 0.2	0.0
2021 FS	ATL	MLB	23	600	59	22	1	14	58	38	167	0	0	.222/.278/.347	71	.291	-0.1	C -5	-0.3
2021 DC	ATL	MLB	23	133	13	4	0	3	13	8	37	0	0	.222/.278/.347	71	.291	0.0	C -1	-0.1

Comparables: Bryan Anderson, Austin Romine, Miguel Perez

The Report: Willson's younger brother has developed into a strong catching prospect himself, one quite distinct from his sibling in style. It's a bit of an all-or-nothing swing, meaning he will never have his older brother's batting average and on-base combo, but there's plus raw power waiting to be unleashed. He's made consistent strides behind the plate, and while he is athletic enough to perhaps have some positional flexibility, concerns he might have to move out from behind the plate have quieted down.

Development Track: Contreras broke summer camp with the Braves after both Tyler Flowers and Travis d'Arnaud were sidelined while in COVID-19 protocols. He was only up for the first few games, and tried to hit every fastball he saw—and some off-speed as well—to the moon. The swing is long even when he's not pressing, and he got beat consistently with velocity. He had 200 plate appearances above A-ball coming into 2020, so none of this is particularly concerning. He showed better hands behind the plate than expected which, combined with his plus arm and sound footwork, should make him an above-average overall catcher once the bat gets some more seasoning. It's not clear how much offensive upside is really in there, but .250 and 15 home runs is more than enough to start behind the plate, and he's got projection beyond that.

Variance: High. Contreras was overmatched by good fastballs too often in his major-league cameo. So the bat will need more seasoning in the minors, but the glove—especially receiving—has made enough strides that I think he will be back up sooner rather than later. While he's already been a major leaguer, the range of the ultimate outcomes is still pretty wide.

Mark Barry's Fantasy Take: Call me crazy (and absolutely DO NOT look at what I wrote last year), but I like Contreras more than Langeliers in a dynasty context. The bar at catcher is so low on offense that .250 with 15 homers and room for more is probably a back-end, mixed-league backstop, or a must-add in two-catcher leagues. It's not great, nor is it fun, but it's where we're at. Excitement!

7 Tucker Davidson LHP   OFP: 50   ETA: Debuted in 2020
Born: 03/25/96 Age: 25 Bats: L Throws: L Height: 6'2" Weight: 215 Origin: Round 19, 2016 Draft (#559 overall)

YEAR	TEAM	LVL	AGE	W	L	SV	G	GS	IP	H	HR	BB/9	K/9	K	GB%	BABIP	WHIP	ERA	DRA-	WARP
2018	FLO	HI-A	22	7	10	0	24	24	118¹	120	5	4.4	7.5	99	46.7%	.334	1.50	4.18	91	1.2
2019	MIS	AA	23	7	6	0	21	21	110²	88	5	3.7	9.9	122	48.6%	.311	1.20	2.03	91	0.7
2019	GWN	AAA	23	1	1	0	4	4	19	20	0	4.3	5.7	12	49.2%	.345	1.53	2.84	112	0.2
2020	ATL	MLB	24	0	1	0	1	1	1²	3	1	21.6	10.8	2	28.6%	.333	4.20	10.80	119	0.0
2021 FS	ATL	MLB	25	1	1	0	57	0	50	48	7	5.4	8.2	45	45.6%	.292	1.57	5.20	114	-0.3
2021 DC	ATL	MLB	25	1	1	0	4	4	19	18	2	5.4	8.2	17	45.6%	.292	1.57	5.20	114	0.1

Comparables: Bernardo Flores Jr., Robert Dugger, Ryan Helsley

The Report: Davidson took a big step forward in 2019, upping his velocity while improving his secondary offerings. He added a slider to go along with an average curveball and a changeup. The curveball has good spin, but the slider may be the bigger weapon at this point. The fastball is low-to-mid-90s with improved command. Davidson had a solid spring, but was a little behind some of the other pitchers when summer camp opened, which delayed his debut until the final series of the regular season.

Development Track: Another good showing in spring training could put Davidson in contention for a rotation spot as soon as next season. He still needs to improve the slider and change to give him enough of an arsenal to be a starter, but if he's a reliever, he should be a good one.

Variance: Medium. There are enough durability concerns to see a relief role as the most likely outcome.

Mark Barry's Fantasy Take: Against my better judgment, I kinda/sorta like Davidson. The upside is iffy, but there's SP4-5 potential there which is definitely useful in 20-plus team leagues. That sounds like damning with faint praise, but I promise I don't mean it to be.

8 Braden Shewmake SS   OFP: 50   ETA: Late 2021
Born: 11/19/97 Age: 23 Bats: L Throws: R Height: 6'4" Weight: 190 Origin: Round 1, 2019 Draft (#21 overall)

YEAR	TEAM	LVL	AGE	PA	R	2B	3B	HR	RBI	BB	K	SB	CS	AVG/OBP/SLG	DRC+	BABIP	BRR	FRAA	WARP
2019	ROM	LO-A	21	226	37	18	2	3	39	21	29	11	3	.318/.389/.473	162	.359	3.5	SS(39) -0.0	2.5
2019	MIS	AA	21	52	7	0	0	0	1	4	11	2	0	.217/.288/.217	58	.278	0.7	SS(14) 1.8	0.3
2021 FS	ATL	MLB	23	600	52	27	2	10	56	39	141	10	3	.230/.287/.345	74	.291	2.6	SS 7	0.9

Comparables: Max Schrock, Stephen Piscotty, Garin Cecchini

The Report: The Braves are famous for aggressively pushing their prospects with promotions and, in the span of six months, Shewmake went from the SEC to the Low-A Sally League to the Double-A Southern League. A big-framed shortstop—albeit on the lean side—he continued his hitting prowess that made him a first-round pick in 2019 out of Texas A&M. Even with a 6-foot-4 body, there is a significant question whether the power will ever manifest due to his swing mechanics, though the physicality is there to get the ball over the fence. The hands stay low and tend to lag behind, flattening out the bat-path and failing to provide a conducive launch angle. His contact rate is his calling card on offense, and with decent on-base numbers, it's more of a put-the-ball-in-play approach, keeping his strikeout numbers below average. Defensively, he is athletic and sure-handed enough to stick at short, with the belief he has the versatility to move around the diamond if asked.

Development Track: The advanced hit tool shown in 2019 would have likely landed him back in Mississippi for 2020, with clear areas to improve upon being strength gains and perhaps some swing tinkering without sacrificing too much contact. At Atlanta's alternate site there was talk of his natural power being put on display more regularly, which can only help the offensive-minded profile that features at least average-to-better defensive skills. The foundation of fundamentals could move him very quickly. However, with no clear path for playing time ahead of him in the majors, the Braves can slow-play Shewmake's development with no additional rush.

Variance: Medium. The thing about guys who hit for a lot of average and not much else is that they have to keep hitting for a lot of average to derive value.

Mark Barry's Fantasy Take: If you're not in a hurry, I like Shewmake as prospect depth. The Braves promoted him aggressively right out of the draft, and while he hasn't set the world ablaze, he has some big Chris Taylor/"Insert your favorite Rays utilityman here" vibes. With Dansby Swanson and Ozzie Albies in tow, they'll also be able to wait on moving Shewmake too quickly from here, which should help with his development. If you have a roster spot, there are worse ways to use it than waiting on Shewmake.

9 Jared Shuster LHP   OFP: 50   ETA: 2023
Born: 08/03/98   Age: 22   Bats: L   Throws: L   Height: 6'3"   Weight: 210   Origin: Round 1, 2020 Draft (#25 overall)

The Report: A minor surprise as a first-round selection, Shuster benefited from his eye-popping numbers and performance during the abbreviated spring evaluation period. He was able to dominate with just two pitches, having arrived on campus with a plus changeup in his back pocket. His draft year ascent was dependent on adding to his fastball and improving his command. Both got upgrades following a strong campaign at the Cape Cod League. Shuster went from upper-80s on this heater to touching mid-90s with regularity. The arm action is very short, but that makes the release on his changeup deceptive, and that pitch has good downward fade. What is missing from the toolbox is a breaking ball up to par with his fastball and change. Presently, it's a below-average, slurvy offering he'll need to improve to be effective against both lefties and righties as a starter.

Development Track: As is usually the concern when a player takes a big leap from one year to the next, you want to see them replicate that success to ensure whatever changes made have subsequently stuck. With Shuster in particular, the emphasis will be on his delivery and the maturation of his breaking ball. The delivery is repeatable thanks to a very short arm action—which is good—but kinetically it leaves less room for further improvement on his velocity gains, which isn't as good. It also makes it harder to tinker with the breaking ball. He should be able to further its consistency to spot it for strikes, but it may never be a true swing-and-miss pitch.

Variance: High. The pressure put on the elbow with the kind of short arm action he has, while also needing to develop a snappier breaking ball, increases the risk profile. Shuster could inevitably end up being a very good reverse-split lefty with how good his changeup is against right-handed hitters.

Mark Barry's Fantasy Take: If Shuster figures out the breaking-ball-of-it-all, he's eminently more interesting. As it stands, I'm passing unless you're in a league that has 250ish prospects.

10 Michael Harris OF   OFP: 55   ETA: 2023
Born: 03/07/01   Age: 20   Bats: L   Throws: L   Height: 6'0"   Weight: 195   Origin: Round 3, 2019 Draft (#98 overall)

YEAR	TEAM	LVL	AGE	PA	R	2B	3B	HR	RBI	BB	K	SB	CS	AVG/OBP/SLG	DRC+	BABIP	BRR	FRAA	WARP
2019	BRA	ROK	18	119	15	6	3	2	16	9	20	5	2	.349/.403/.514		.414			
2019	ROM	LO-A	18	93	11	2	1	0	11	9	22	3	0	.183/.269/.232	57	.246	-0.7	RF(18) 5.1, CF(4) 0.8	0.4
2021 FS	ATL	MLB	20	600	47	26	3	7	50	34	187	8	1	.220/.269/.321	61	.316	4.5	CF 3, RF 2	-0.3

Comparables: Jesús Sánchez, Byron Buxton, Oscar Taveras

The Report: The Braves went overslot in the third round to buy Harris out of a commitment to Texas Tech. He was a two-way player in high school, and a lot of teams preferred him on the mound. Atlanta liked him more as a hitter where he shows plus raw power as a switch-hitter with good bat-to-ball skills. He is a potential five-tool center fielder with a strong arm and plenty of upside.

Development Track: A return to Rome would seem to be in order for 2021 after Harris appeared in just 22 games in 2019. He spent time at the Braves' alternate training site this season.

Variance: Very High. Harris has all the tools and has been impressive during his short time as a professional. The swing can occasionally get long and he will need to refine his approach as he moves up through the system, but he is just at the beginning of his development. He struggled during his Low-A stint and needs to establish himself against more advanced pitching to jump past the safer names ahead of him.

Mark Barry's Fantasy Take: The top-shelf outcome is certainly exciting for Harris. The distance to the majors, however, keeps him on the watchlist for the next season, or so.

The Prospects You Meet Outside The Top Ten

MLB-ready, but probably relievers

Jasseel De La Cruz RHP Born: 06/26/97 Age: 24 Bats: R Throws: R Height: 6'1" Weight: 195 Origin: International Free Agent, 2015

YEAR	TEAM	LVL	AGE	W	L	SV	G	GS	IP	H	HR	BB/9	K/9	K	GB%	BABIP	WHIP	ERA	DRA-	WARP
2018	ROM	LO-A	21	3	4	0	15	13	69	65	6	4.4	8.5	65	62.4%	.309	1.43	4.83	88	0.8
2019	ROM	LO-A	22	0	1	0	4	4	18	19	1	2.5	11.0	22	51.1%	.391	1.33	2.50	96	0.1
2019	FLO	HI-A	22	3	1	0	4	4	28	12	0	2.2	8.4	26	52.2%	.174	0.68	1.93	50	0.9
2019	MIS	AA	22	4	7	0	17	16	87	71	7	3.8	7.6	73	45.4%	.263	1.24	3.83	96	0.3
2021 FS	ATL	MLB	24	2	3	0	57	0	50	50	8	5.4	7.9	44	42.4%	.291	1.60	5.64	127	-0.6
2021 DC	ATL	MLB	24	0	0	0	11	0	12	12	2	5.4	7.9	10	42.4%	.291	1.60	5.64	127	-0.1

Comparables: Chad Bettis, Braden Shipley, John Gant

De La Cruz more or less held serve as the same fourth-starter/power-reliever prospect that charted at No. 10 on the Braves' list last offseason. He's closer to the majors now—even spending two separate days on the big-league roster as an unused bullpen arm—yet we're no closer to knowing the ultimate outcome. But we'll place a small bet on a setup guy with high-90s heat, a plus slider, and not quite good enough command to close.

Patrick Weigel RHP Born: 07/08/94 Age: 26 Bats: R Throws: R Height: 6'6" Weight: 240 Origin: Round 7, 2015 Draft (#210 overall)

YEAR	TEAM	LVL	AGE	W	L	SV	G	GS	IP	H	HR	BB/9	K/9	K	GB%	BABIP	WHIP	ERA	DRA-	WARP
2018	BRA	ROK	23	0	0	0	4	3	4	2	0	0.0	13.5	6	33.3%	.333	0.50	0.00		
2019	MIS	AA	24	0	1	0	7	7	15^2	8	0	5.2	9.2	16	53.8%	.205	1.09	1.72	66	0.3
2019	GWN	AAA	24	6	1	0	21	11	63^1	42	9	4.5	7.8	55	36.3%	.214	1.17	2.98	62	2.2
2020	ATL	MLB	25	0	0	0	1	0	0^2	2	0	40.5	0.0	0	25.0%	.500	7.50	27.00	99	0.0
2021 FS	ATL	MLB	26	1	1	0	57	0	50	50	8	5.2	8.1	45	40.0%	.293	1.58	5.67	122	-0.5
2021 DC	ATL	MLB	26	1	1	0	18	1	24	24	4	5.2	8.1	21	40.0%	.293	1.58	5.67	122	-0.1

Comparables: Ryan Helsley, Chase De Jong, Brady Lail

Weigel has bounced around a deep Braves system the past few list cycles; sometimes personal cheeseball, sometimes legit back-end starting prospect, occasionally out with Tommy John. He's settled in as a major-league-ready 95-and-a-slider guy. His mid-90s heater has a bit of run and he works it around the zone well. The slider doesn't always get ideal depth from his lower slot, but it's sharp even when it's sweepy. How the breaker ultimately plays will determine whether Weigel is more of a middle reliever or a setup man.

Prospects to dream on a little

Bryce Ball 1B Born: 07/08/98 Age: 22 Bats: L Throws: R Height: 6'6" Weight: 235 Origin: Round 24, 2019 Draft (#727 overall)

YEAR	TEAM	LVL	AGE	PA	R	2B	3B	HR	RBI	BB	K	SB	CS	AVG/OBP/SLG	DRC+	BABIP	BRR	FRAA	WARP
2019	DAN	ROK+	20	173	37	12	0	13	38	22	30	0	0	.324/.410/.676		.321			
2019	ROM	LO-A	20	90	14	6	0	4	14	4	20	0	0	.337/.367/.547	153	.403	-0.7	1B(11) -1.3	0.4
2021 FS	ATL	MLB	22	600	54	27	2	13	59	36	177	0	0	.229/.281/.356	74	.311	-0.1	1B -5	-1.7

Comparables: Brandon Laird, Rowdy Tellez, Jacob Nottingham

Ball was a 2019 post-draft darling as a 24th-rounder out of Dallas Baptist who immediately looked like he should've been popped in the first two rounds when unleashed in pro ball. He's a 70-power guy with a better feel for hitting than you'd think, although the overall projection is limited by a first base-only profile and swing-and-miss concerns. He was in consideration for the last couple of spots on this year's list, but ultimately we heard stronger things about how Harris developed at the alternate site than we did for Ball. We remain cautiously optimistic that he'll hit upper-level pitching, and disappointed that he didn't get that chance in 2020.

Mahki Backstrom 1B Born: 10/10/01   Age: 19   Bats: L   Throws: L   Height: 6'5"   Weight: 220   Origin: Round 18, 2019 Draft (#547 overall)

YEAR	TEAM	LVL	AGE	PA	R	2B	3B	HR	RBI	BB	K	SB	CS	AVG/OBP/SLG	DRC+	BABIP	BRR	FRAA	WARP
2019	BRA	ROK	17	82	8	5	0	2	8	12	27	1	0	.300/.402/.457		.463			
2021 FS	ATL	MLB	19	600	45	26	2	6	48	37	257	2	0	.206/.260/.298	53	.369	0.7	1B 1	-2.6

Comparables: Matt Olson, Jay Bruce, Kennys Vargas

Backstrom was taken six rounds earlier than Ball and signed away from Fresno State for a hair under $400,000. As a prep first baseman he's going to be a much slower burn than Ball, but the power upside here is significant—the swing isn't short, but the ball jumps like it's a slow pitch home run derby—and he only just turned 19.

You always need catching

Alex Jackson C   Born: 12/25/95   Age: 25   Bats: R   Throws: R   Height: 6'2"   Weight: 215   Origin: Round 1, 2014 Draft (#6 overall)

YEAR	TEAM	LVL	AGE	PA	R	2B	3B	HR	RBI	BB	K	SB	CS	AVG/OBP/SLG	DRC+	BABIP	BRR	FRAA	WARP
2018	MIS	AA	22	252	27	12	1	5	24	20	78	0	0	.200/.282/.329	69	.280	-0.9	C(61) -2.1	-0.4
2018	GWN	AAA	22	125	15	11	2	3	17	12	42	0	0	.204/.296/.426	86	.292	0.2	C(29) 2.7	0.5
2019	GWN	AAA	23	345	52	9	0	28	65	20	118	1	0	.229/.313/.533	105	.261	-2.8	C(78) 17.9	3.1
2019	ATL	MLB	23	15	0	0	0	0	0	1	5	0	0	.000/.133/.000	76	.000		C(4) 0.5	0.1
2020	ATL	MLB	24	7	0	1	0	0	0	0	4	0	0	.286/.286/.429	68	.667	-0.2	C(4) -0.0	0.0
2021 FS	ATL	MLB	25	600	59	23	1	16	56	37	233	0	0	.190/.266/.331	66	.296	-0.2	C -2	-0.4
2021 DC	ATL	MLB	25	167	16	6	0	4	15	10	64	0	0	.190/.266/.331	66	.296	0.0	C -1	-0.1

Comparables: Kyle Skipworth, Greg Halman, Pete Alonso

Jackson probably deserved a shot to become the league's latest power-and-defense hidden secret catcher after bopping 28 homers and grading out as the best defensive catcher in Triple-A in 2019. But Atlanta went out and signed Travis d'Arnaud, another former top prospect turned power-and-defense hidden secret. That one became less hidden when d'Arnaud ended up hitting .321 with power and his usual excellent framing; Jackson mostly remained stuck on the taxi squad. We continued to get positive feedback on his defense this season, a surprising turn given that he didn't catch until his fourth professional season. Incumbent backup Tyler Flowers is a free agent and turns 35 in a couple months, so Jackson's shot could be coming in 2021, though Langeliers and especially Contreras are starting to look bigger in the rearview mirror.

Interesting draft follow

Spencer Strider   Born: 10/28/98   Age: 22   Bats: R   Throws: R   Height: 6'0"   Weight: 195   Origin: Round 4, 2020 Draft (#126 overall)

The Braves drafted Strider in the fourth round out of Clemson in 2020. He will need to prove himself after coming back from injury, but he offers a power arm with a chance to start. He was one of Atlanta's most impressive pitchers at fall instructs and touched 99 mph with a high-riding fastball. Strider also showed a plus curveball and is working to develop a changeup. The rotation is not out of the question, but he looks like he could be an impact arm out of the bullpen.

Top Talents 25 and Under (as of 4/1/2021):

1. Ronald Acuña Jr., OF
2. Ozzie Albies, 2B
3. Mike Soroka, RHP
4. Ian Anderson, RHP
5. Cristian Pache, OF
6. Austin Riley, 3B
7. Drew Waters, OF
8. Kyle Muller, LHP
9. Kyle Wright, RHP
10. Shea Langeliers, C

Ronald Acuña Jr. turns 23 in December and is one of the best baseball players in the universe. He was the first prospect we gave an 80 OFP to while I was on staff here at Baseball Prospectus. He's already lived up to it.

Ozzie Albies suffered through an injury-riddled 2020 season, hampered by a wrist injury. Yet going back to his major-league debut in 2017, he's never put up worse than a 106 DRC+, and he's a more-than-solid defender at second base. He was a four-plus win player in both 2018 and 2019, and the best could be yet to come if he puts it all together as he enters his mid-20s.

Soroka vs. Anderson was an extremely tough call. Soroka is only a year removed from being a Cy Young candidate, but he blew out his Achilles in his third start of 2020. In the end, he's just done it for longer than Anderson so far; if you want to go the other way because of the injury uncertainty or Anderson's more overpowering stuff, I certainly wouldn't begrudge you for it.

Austin Riley still hits the ball extremely hard and not enough. He made strides toward hitting it more in 2020, but his power dipped a little with the adjustments. The power potential here remains tantalizing if he can ever hit .270, and the whole package does play better at third base if he can stick at the hot corner. It's too many "if"s to rank higher in a loaded 25U list.

We've written what feels like books on Kyle Wright already. The short version is that he's perpetually one adjustment away from looking like a good major-league starter. The September 2020 flavor was repositioning him on the rubber; he ripped off four solid starts in a row down the stretch and in the NLDS and then completely imploded against the Dodgers in the NLCS. In his last year eligible for this list, I'm not sure we're truly any closer to figuring out whether he's going to get there than we were on the day he was drafted.

Baltimore Orioles

The State of the System:

The Orioles 2020 draft strategy didn't seem to quite come off, but it remains a deep system albeit lacking in high upside profiles. Also, Ryan Mountcastle is still here somehow.

The Top Ten:

★ ★ ★ *2021 Top 101 Prospect* **#2** ★ ★ ★

1 Adley Rutschman C   OFP: 70   ETA: Mid-to-late 2021

Born: 02/06/98   Age: 23   Bats: S   Throws: R   Height: 6'2"   Weight: 220   Origin: Round 1, 2019 Draft (#1 overall)

YEAR	TEAM	LVL	AGE	PA	R	2B	3B	HR	RBI	BB	K	SB	CS	AVG/OBP/SLG	DRC+	BABIP	BRR	FRAA	WARP
2019	ORI	ROK	21	16	3	0	0	1	3	2	2	1	0	.143/.250/.357		.091			
2019	ABD	SS	21	92	11	7	1	1	15	12	16	0	0	.325/.413/.481	177	.387	-0.1	C(8) -0.2	0.8
2019	DEL	LO-A	21	47	5	1	0	2	8	6	9	0	0	.154/.261/.333	84	.138	0.1	C(6) 0.1	0.1
2021 FS	BAL	MLB	23	600	60	26	2	14	60	42	168	2	0	.235/.294/.371	82	.312	0.4	C 0	1.1
2021 DC	BAL	MLB	23	65	6	2	0	1	6	4	18	0	0	.235/.294/.371	82	.312	0.0	C 0	0.1

Comparables: Lucas Duda, Stuart Turner, Trey Mancini

The Report: One of the best catching prospects in recent memory. Rutschman is a switch-hitter with a quick swing from both sides of the plate. His swing plane is made for the modern game. He controls the barrel. His plate approach is solid. His power is at least plus and we think he'll get it into games. He's an average runner, which is superb for a catcher. He projects as an above-average to excellent defender in all facets, including pitch framing. He has the potential to be a top-of-the-line two-way catcher with few weaknesses.

Development Track: Rutschman was brought to the alternate site midway through summer camp, essentially eliminating any chance he'd have to force his way onto the major-league roster. We suspect given their backgrounds that the new Orioles regime is going to be extremely aggressive with service time manipulation, so we aren't holding that against him developmentally. Everything is still on track here, and Rutschman remains one of the best prospects in the game.

Variance: Low. There's always going to be a certain amount of variance attached with the catching position, but we think there's an unusually high likelihood that he'll be at least a first-division starter.

Mark Barry's Fantasy Take: I'll be honest, I kinda thought Ben Carsley's love/hate/loathe relationship to catching prospects was a bit. But after writing fantasy analysis for said catching prospects for a little while now, I'm starting to wonder if our pal doesn't have a point. Catching prospect fatigue is REAL.

All that said, Rutschman is about as good a bet as any to be a successful fantasy contributor behind the dish. He can hit, hit for power, and he's so good defensively, there's no doubt he's staying behind the plate. He's one of the five or 10 best prospects in the game, and while I'd personally bump him down a few spots for the "catcher penalty" it's pretty much Rutschman and everyone else as far as fantasy catching prospects are concerned.

★ ★ ★ *2021 Top 101 Prospect* **#28** ★ ★ ★

2 Ryan Mountcastle 1B   OFP: 60   ETA: Debuted in 2020

Born: 02/18/97   Age: 24   Bats: R   Throws: R   Height: 6'3"   Weight: 210   Origin: Round 1, 2015 Draft (#36 overall)

YEAR	TEAM	LVL	AGE	PA	R	2B	3B	HR	RBI	BB	K	SB	CS	AVG/OBP/SLG	DRC+	BABIP	BRR	FRAA	WARP
2018	BOW	AA	21	428	63	19	4	13	59	26	79	2	0	.297/.341/.464	117	.339	-1.5	3B(81) -4.9	0.8
2019	NOR	AAA	22	553	81	35	1	25	83	24	130	2	1	.312/.344/.527	114	.370	-0.9	1B(84) -6.1, LF(26) 2.1, 3B(9) -0.1	1.3
2020	BAL	MLB	23	140	12	5	0	5	23	11	30	0	1	.333/.386/.492	104	.398	-0.9	LF(25) -1.7, 1B(10) 0.3	0.0
2021 FS	BAL	MLB	24	600	66	26	2	24	79	28	150	1	0	.262/.302/.445	97	.318	-0.3	1B -2, LF -4	0.4
2021 DC	BAL	MLB	24	558	61	24	1	22	74	26	140	1	0	.262/.302/.445	97	.318	-0.3	1B -2, LF -4	0.3

Comparables: Dayan Viciedo, Wes Bankston, Brett Wallace

The Report: Mountcastle was a consistent offensive force at the plate throughout his minor league career. He hit between .276 and .314 at all his full-season spots, turned doubles power into 20+ home run power as he filled out, and always did enough damage on contact to prop up an approach that even the most genteel and restrained among us would describe as "aggressive." There's always the risk that this type of slugger will get exposed against major-league pitching. Mountcastle's bat speed is above-average but not special, and there's some stomp and lift in the swing, some holes you might be able to exploit. As he's filled out and added that home run pop, he's also slid down the defensive spectrum and was handed a first base glove at the beginning of 2019 after being drafted as a shortstop four years earlier.

Development Track: Honestly, the fact that Mountcastle is still eligible for this list at all—by a mere four at-bats—is a testament to service time manipulation. His major-league debut was an unqualified success. He posted league-average-ish strikeout and walk rates, and if he can do that going forward … well he won't hit .330, but a perennial .300 hitter might be in play. That's unlikely to continue, though, as the underlying zone control and contact rates don't support it, nor does the minor league track record. All together, Mountcastle looks more or less like we expected, plus 50 points of batting average or so, which can happen in a quarter of a season. We're more confident he's a good major-league hitter now, but good remains .280 with 25 home runs and plenty of doubles. Maybe a few extra walks now, to boot. He did look perfectly serviceable in left field, despite only having playing there for 26 games in the minors. Mountcastle played some first base as well and don't be shocked to see him DH now and again. He's broadly fine wherever he stands, but it all looks a lot better when he's standing in the batter's box.

Variance: Low. There's enough of a chance there've been some real approach gains here that Mountcastle can get to a plus regular despite very limited defensive value and the absence of the kind of plus-plus pop you associate with your Role 6 corner mashers. He feels more like a safe 55 type. Maybe one season that looks better when he has a nice 150-game run of BABIP fortune. And then maybe one season that gets non-tendered after he hits .250 with a few too many Ks (and then goes to the Rays and rips off three more solid seasons, as long as we are reading the auguries).

Mark Barry's Fantasy Take: Look, it's going to be awfully hard for Mountcastle to maintain his pretty good strikeout rate (and in turn, batting average) with a swinging-strike rate five percentage points higher than league average. But despite (or maybe because of?) his uber-aggressiveness, Mountcastle was impressive in his debut. I would be remiss if I didn't drop a Nick Castellanos comp in this space for the third consecutive season because it still feels so right. I'd have Mountcastle among the top-30ish dynasty prospects in the game.

★ ★ ★ *2021 Top 101 Prospect* **#30** ★ ★ ★

3 Grayson Rodriguez RHP   OFP: 60   ETA: 2022

Born: 11/16/99   Age: 21   Bats: L   Throws: R   Height: 6'5"   Weight: 220   Origin: Round 1, 2018 Draft (#11 overall)

YEAR	TEAM	LVL	AGE	W	L	SV	G	GS	IP	H	HR	BB/9	K/9	K	GB%	BABIP	WHIP	ERA	DRA-	WARP
2018	ORI	ROK	18	0	2	0	9	8	19¹	17	0	3.3	9.3	20	43.4%	.321	1.24	1.40		
2019	DEL	LO-A	19	10	4	0	20	20	94	57	4	3.4	12.4	129	44.2%	.262	0.99	2.68	55	2.8
2021 FS	BAL	MLB	21	2	3	0	57	0	50	44	7	5.1	9.4	52	39.2%	.282	1.46	4.61	108	-0.1

Comparables: Hunter Harvey, Tyler Glasnow, Danny Duffy

The Report: I got three Rodriguez looks in the second half of 2019. Not only was he progressing compared to early-season looks from other BP prospect staff, he also progressed from when I saw him in early-July to when I saw him in late-August. By the end of the season, he was consistently sitting 94-97 and touching 98, up from sitting 91-93 and touching 95 in Ben

Spanier's April look. He's flashed both a plus slider and a plus changeup projection for us, along with a curveball that has a nice shape but tends to run together with the slider in the slurviness, as well as an occasional cutter. There's a lot of potential here, some of it already actualized, and a pretty good shot to stay in the rotation all the way up to the majors.

Development Track: Like Rutschman, Rodriguez wasn't brought to summer camp initially; he was added to the alternate site roster around the time the major-league team broke camp. His alternate site velocity was essentially identical to our late-summer 2019 looks, so he held the fastball gains, if not quite to a full season then at least to the next year. We probably need to see it over 100 innings to go truly hog wild with his projection, but he's on the cusp of the top pitching prospects in the game.

Variance: Medium. It's mostly all the generic good young pitcher risk, but if you want to start nitpicking he could use better separation of his offerings on the curve/slider/cutter continuum.

Mark Barry's Fantasy Take: I don't mean this to sound too hot take-y, but I'm not sure there are five pitching prospects I'd take over Rodriguez, and if there were, he'd surely be in the top six or seven. I love the fact that he brought his high-90s fastball velocity back with him to the alternative site, giving him three potentially plus pitches in his arsenal. It almost doesn't matter if the curveball ever fully gets there. Even better? You might not have to pay top-five prices to scoop him up.

★ ★ ★ *2021 Top 101 Prospect* **#53** ★ ★ ★

4 DL Hall LHP OFP: 60 ETA: 2022
Born: 09/19/98 Age: 22 Bats: L Throws: L Height: 6'2" Weight: 195 Origin: Round 1, 2017 Draft (#21 overall)

YEAR	TEAM	LVL	AGE	W	L	SV	G	GS	IP	H	HR	BB/9	K/9	K	GB%	BABIP	WHIP	ERA	DRA-	WARP
2018	DEL	LO-A	19	2	7	0	22	20	94¹	68	6	4.0	9.5	100	41.6%	.268	1.17	2.10	78	1.6
2019	FRE	HI-A	20	4	5	1	19	17	80²	53	3	6.0	12.9	116	34.1%	.301	1.33	3.46	76	1.3
2021 FS	BAL	MLB	22	2	3	0	57	0	50	45	7	7.2	10.2	56	38.0%	.294	1.70	5.67	127	-0.6

Comparables: Brailyn Marquez, Dustin May, Alex Reyes

The Report: The alternate site was good to Hall. The young lefty took full advantage of the opportunity to battle against higher-level hitters, and managed to upgrade his game all around. His fastball remains his top offering, regularly sitting 95-98 and flirting with 99. Exploding with late life, the added velocity only makes it more dangerous. Between the fastball and his two above-average secondaries—a curve with serious sharp bite and a vastly improved changeup—Hall's built up a solid arsenal. He isn't afraid to attack hitters. He's got impact stuff and he knows it. The potential here is obvious, and there's a reason Hall's been high on this list year after year, and he only continues to progress.

Development Track: Hall's high walk rate was his biggest hurdle coming into the season, a struggle to reliably master both control and command overshadowing his strikeout numbers. When he can find the zone, he can easily elicit big swings and misses, as well as weak contact, but it's the inability to find the zone that's been the problem. He's made great strides on the control front, and will likely spend the majority of the 2021 season refining his command. The ceiling is still high here.

Variance: Medium. There's been substantial improvement in his control, but he still hasn't fully developed his command quite yet. Consistency is key, and Hall's consistently shown reliever risk.

Mark Barry's Fantasy Take: Not to beat a dead horse (which btw I totally wouldn't recommend anyway, it just seems cruel), but I would've loved to see Hall pitch in 2020. The stuff is undeniable, and reports of increased velocity from the left side are tantalizing. But we mostly knew this last year, and still have the same concerns about ALL OF THOSE WALKS. Hall is still a top-100 name for me, but until we know that he's scaled back on the free passes, he's a pretty big relief risk.

★ ★ ★ *2021 Top 101 Prospect* **#66** ★ ★ ★

5 Heston Kjerstad OF OFP: 60 ETA: Early 2023 (under current CBA rules)
Born: 02/12/99 Age: 22 Bats: L Throws: R Height: 6'3" Weight: 220 Origin: Round 1, 2020 Draft (#2 overall)

The Report: We were all told to expect the unexpected when it came to this year's June draft, and the warnings proved true almost immediately as the Orioles popped Kjerstad second overall on an under-slot deal as they saw him among the best college hitters in the class. And indeed, he is. While sliding in at No. 7 on our pre-draft rankings, it wasn't that much a stretch to see him picked so high. The bat control and power shown in two-plus years at Arkansas were evident. Even with a slightly unorthodox stroke he is able to make contact in every quadrant in the zone with hands that can adjust to velocity mid-pitch. This ability is both a gift and a curse, as he tends to swing at a lot of pitches outside the zone, too.

Development Track: There is room for added mass on his 6-foot-3 frame, and maybe not the good kind, either. Keeping his body lean so he can stay in a corner outfield spot while maintaining at least average speed on the basepaths will help get his bat in the lineup sooner rather than later. He has dabbled at first base in the past, but there is far more value in his profile as an outfielder. Who knows if the O's will bother to attempt to refine his pitch selection; the kid has raked for nearly three years in the best college conference, needing refinement in other areas of his game instead of nit-picking his strengths.

Variance: Medium. Depending on which way the body goes the OFP could go a full grade up or down. The bat is likely to play regardless.

Mark Barry's Fantasy Take: Looking back, I was probably a little unfair to Kjerstad on draft day. Sure, the aggressive approach could require an overhaul against advanced pitching, but complaining about a 20ish percent strikeout rate and a walk rate under eight percent when you're hitting .340 and slugging nearly .600 in your college career is a little like being miffed that the $100 bill you found on the street wasn't also wrapped in $100 bills. There are still other bats from the 2020 draft I'd prefer, but Kjerstad is a top-60 guy for fantasy with the possibility of solid contributions in four categories.

6   Dean Kremer   RHP   OFP: 50   ETA: Debuted in 2020

Born: 01/07/96   Age: 25   Bats: R   Throws: R   Height: 6'3"   Weight: 185   Origin: Round 14, 2016 Draft (#431 overall)

YEAR	TEAM	LVL	AGE	W	L	SV	G	GS	IP	H	HR	BB/9	K/9	K	GB%	BABIP	WHIP	ERA	DRA-	WARP
2018	RC	HI-A	22	5	3	0	16	16	79	67	7	3.0	13.0	114	39.9%	.353	1.18	3.30	67	1.8
2018	BOW	AA	22	4	2	0	8	8	45^1	38	3	3.4	10.5	53	37.9%	.315	1.21	2.58	76	0.9
2018	TUL	AA	22	1	0	0	1	1	7	3	0	3.9	14.1	11	75.0%	.250	0.86	0.00	37	0.3
2019	FRE	HI-A	23	0	0	0	2	2	9^2	6	0	3.7	13.0	14	20.0%	.300	1.03	0.00	73	0.2
2019	BOW	AA	23	9	4	0	15	15	84^2	75	9	3.1	9.2	87	41.1%	.299	1.23	2.98	96	0.3
2019	NOR	AAA	23	0	2	0	4	4	19^1	30	2	1.9	9.8	21	36.5%	.467	1.76	8.84	156	-0.2
2020	BAL	MLB	24	1	1	0	4	4	18^2	15	0	5.8	10.6	22	30.6%	.306	1.45	4.82	96	0.2
2021 FS	BAL	MLB	25	9	8	0	26	26	150	135	27	3.3	9.4	156	37.0%	.279	1.26	4.13	93	1.6
2021 DC	BAL	MLB	25	6	8	0	25	25	116	104	21	3.3	9.4	121	37.0%	.279	1.26	4.13	93	1.6

Comparables: T.J. Zeuch, Ryan Helsley, Robert Dugger

The Report: Kremer was effective throughout his minor league career, consistently posting hefty strikeout numbers. We had him slated to debut this year, and he had all the stuff to back it up, so it was only a matter of time before he broke out of the alternate site and made his way to Baltimore. Three of his four starts were clear successes, with one unfortunate outing that ballooned his ERA to 4.82 for the season. Rough appearance aside, Kremer gave the O's a great look at what he can do. He threw his 92-94 fastball half of the time, as expected, and the offering topped out at 96. Paired with his equally impressive mid-70s curveball with serious drop, Kremer held his steady strikeout numbers, striking out 22 in 18 2/3 innings. He has the ability to pitch fairly deep into games by today's standards, only being pulled before completing five innings once.

Development Track: His fastball and curve remain high quality, above-average pitches, but the rest of his stuff lingers between barely average and just good enough. The slider is a self-proclaimed work in progress; there's not much break and while he can get it over for strikes, it's inconsistent. His mid-80s changeup exists, although sightings are rare. It's hard to gauge its true effectiveness, as he threw it fewer than a dozen times this season. He's still ramping up to a four-pitch mix; refining his third and fourth offerings would make him a potential middle-of-the-rotation guy. Kremer may slide back into a relief role at some point, but he's definitely solidified his role as a starter thus far.

Variance: Low. Kremer's proven he can handle the big stage.

Mark Barry's Fantasy Take: Do you ever comb through stat lines to find relatively unheralded prospects with fairly decent numbers, plant your flag early in their career, and then become unreasonably attached to them, inflating their value in your head and in your head only? That's me with Kremer. Nice guy. Probably an SP5/streamer, though.

7 Ryan McKenna CF   OFP: 50   ETA: 2021

Born: 02/14/97   Age: 24   Bats: R   Throws: R   Height: 5'11"   Weight: 185   Origin: Round 4, 2015 Draft (#133 overall)

YEAR	TEAM	LVL	AGE	PA	R	2B	3B	HR	RBI	BB	K	SB	CS	AVG/OBP/SLG	DRC+	BABIP	BRR	FRAA	WARP
2018	FRE	HI-A	21	301	60	18	2	8	37	37	45	5	6	.377/.467/.556	210	.436	2.5	CF(64) -6.2, LF(2) -0.2	3.4
2018	BOW	AA	21	250	35	8	2	3	16	29	56	4	1	.239/.341/.338	90	.312	2.6	CF(55) 3.4, RF(3) 2.1, LF(2) -0.4	0.9
2019	BOW	AA	22	567	78	26	6	9	54	59	121	25	11	.232/.321/.365	111	.287	1.9	CF(98) -4.1, LF(19) 0.6, RF(11) 0.9	2.3
2021 FS	BAL	MLB	24	600	63	25	2	14	59	52	174	10	3	.228/.306/.369	86	.309	0.8	CF -5, LF 0	0.5
2021 DC	BAL	MLB	24	32	3	1	0	0	3	2	9	0	0	.228/.306/.369	86	.309	0.0	CF 0	0.0

Comparables: Rey Fuentes, Michael Bourn, Brian Goodwin

The Report: You would never call McKenna a five-tool outfielder in the way we use that term as prospect writers, but you can put at least a 5 at every spot on the scouting sheet—well, maybe not his arm unless you want to give his below-average arm strength a bump for accuracy. The problem is you have to squint a little to get any of those 5s to 55s. He is a good enough defender in center, but above-average might be a stretch. His approach can make the hit tool play more to average The power is more average raw than average game at present. It all adds up to a major leaguer, and one who could end up greater than the sum of his tools, but one with little room to fall short and still carry a starter's profile.

Development Track: I expected McKenna to perhaps get a look at some point in 2020, but the Orioles outfield was actually pretty good, especially after Mountcastle took over left field. You could note that the bat hasn't really been amazing in the upper minors and he didn't force the issue at the alternate site. Really, nothing much has changed for McKenna, other than perhaps a tougher road to playing time if you believe in the Anthony Santander breakout.

Variance: Medium. The broad base of skills on both offense and defense should keep McKenna employed as a bench outfielder for most of his team control years even if the bat doesn't play enough to make him a starter.

Mark Barry's Fantasy Take: Like Jeffrey said, the Orioles' outfield was actually fairly decent this season. That said, it's also probably not a great sign that you couldn't wrestle away reps from anyone in the Orioles' outfield. McKenna hasn't really been an impact bat since his 2018 stint in High-A, so bench outfielder sounds right—which means you can probably pass unless your league carries 350 or so prospects.

8 Kyle Bradish RHP   OFP: 50   ETA: Mid-to-Late 2021

Born: 09/12/96   Age: 24   Bats: R   Throws: R   Height: 6'4"   Weight: 190   Origin: Round 4, 2018 Draft (#121 overall)

YEAR	TEAM	LVL	AGE	W	L	SV	G	GS	IP	H	HR	BB/9	K/9	K	GB%	BABIP	WHIP	ERA	DRA-	WARP
2019	IE	HI-A	22	6	7	0	24	18	101	90	9	4.7	10.7	120	43.9%	.314	1.42	4.28	99	0.1
2021 FS	BAL	MLB	24	2	3	0	57	0	50	46	7	6.0	8.7	48	41.2%	.284	1.60	5.22	122	-0.5

Comparables: Pierce Johnson, Dietrich Enns, Albert Abreu

The Report: The standout from the Dylan Bundy trade, Bradish turned the most heads at the alternate site, showing off a 3-4 mph uptick in velocity. His fastball, one of his strongest offerings, now sits in the mid 90s, touching as high as 97. He boasts a four-pitch mix, including a high quality top-spinning curveball and a high-80s slider; both effective put away pitches. His firm changeup isn't as polished as his other pitches, but it plays up because of his heater, and he has enough feel to pump it through the zone. Bradish's deceptive delivery serves him well, throwing off batters and keeping them unbalanced. The 6-foot-4 righty uses every inch of his large frame to his advantage.

Development Track: Previous issues with command of his secondaries aren't nearly as prominent as they once were, although there's always room for improvement there. He's aggressive on the mound, a more efficient delivery granting confidence and more pitches in the strike zone. The stuff is powerful, easily above average, and his fastball regularly flashes plus. The changeup is still only decent, but alongside the rest of his arsenal it's a solid weapon and he's learning how to utilize it. With no real experience at higher levels, the Orioles may be cautious with him, but I fully expect Bradish to make a case for himself and find a way to crack the starting rotation before the season ends, or appear in the bullpen, at the very least.

Variance: Low. Aside from the pitchers who have already made their debuts, Bradish is the closest to being major league ready. The stuff is great and he's incredibly poised; the opportunities from the big club will come sooner rather than later.

Mark Barry's Fantasy Take: Righty destined for middle relief adds four ticks to his fastball and all of his other pitches now play up?

<Kombucha Woman meme>

I hadn't given Bradish a second thought before now, but he's definitely heading to the watchlist after this write up. He may be a SP4-5, but he's relatively close and there's upside.

9 Keegan Akin LHP   OFP: 50   ETA: Debuted in 2020
Born: 04/01/95   Age: 26   Bats: L   Throws: L   Height: 6'0"   Weight: 225   Origin: Round 2, 2016 Draft (#54 overall)

YEAR	TEAM	LVL	AGE	W	L	SV	G	GS	IP	H	HR	BB/9	K/9	K	GB%	BABIP	WHIP	ERA	DRA-	WARP
2018	BOW	AA	23	14	7	0	25	25	137²	114	16	3.8	9.3	142	31.7%	.278	1.25	3.27	87	2.0
2019	NOR	AAA	24	6	7	0	25	24	112¹	109	10	4.9	10.5	131	32.4%	.333	1.51	4.73	89	2.6
2020	BAL	MLB	25	1	2	0	8	6	25²	27	3	3.5	12.3	35	34.3%	.358	1.44	4.56	85	0.4
2021 FS	BAL	MLB	26	8	9	0	26	26	150	140	29	4.4	10.0	166	32.7%	.292	1.43	4.93	106	0.5
2021 DC	BAL	MLB	26	6	9	0	25	25	114	106	22	4.4	10.0	126	32.7%	.292	1.43	4.93	106	0.8

Comparables: Conner Menez, Taylor Hearn, Anthony Misiewicz

The Report: The word "solid" takes a human form in Akin. The thick, stocky lefty has all the workings of a No. 5 starter, someone you can rely on, who has good, sometimes above-average stuff. He's regained full control and command of his low-to-mid-90s fastball, throwing it over 60 percent of the time. He holds velo well, touching as high as 96 this season, with the ability to overpower batters. His movements are clean and it's a standard, easily repeatable delivery with some deception. There's nothing particularly flashy about Akin, he gets into a rhythm and he gets the job done.

Development Track: Akin's developed his secondaries into genuine offerings, but the fastball is still the star of the show. While the change and slider appear average at best and still improving, they play up beside his fastball. The high-quality heater makes it easy for him to mix in the low-80s sinking changeup for swings and misses. His slurvy slider is the lesser of his off-speeds, but it induces weak contact and pop ups. He's still refining, but the changeup flashes above-average potential at times. It's a good sign. Like Kremer, Akin's bound to be part of the starting rotation next season and beyond.

Variance: Low. Akin was solid in his debut year, both as a starter and out of the bullpen. He's part of the O's future, one way or another.

Mark Barry's Fantasy Take: After a pair of middling relief appearances, Akin made six starts down the stretch for the O's and really was quite good, striking out a third of batters faced, with eight of his 10 earned runs coming from 3 2/3 innings in two ill-fated starts. The strikeouts are encouraging, and there's a good chance for positive regression thanks to a high BABIP and low strand rate. I am definitely talking myself into this system. Like Kremer, Akin might be a SP5/streamer-type, but the strikeouts lift the floor.

10 Terrin Vavra SS   OFP: 50   ETA: 2022
Born: 05/12/97   Age: 24   Bats: L   Throws: R   Height: 6'1"   Weight: 185   Origin: Round 3, 2018 Draft (#96 overall)

YEAR	TEAM	LVL	AGE	PA	R	2B	3B	HR	RBI	BB	K	SB	CS	AVG/OBP/SLG	DRC+	BABIP	BRR	FRAA	WARP
2018	BOI	SS	21	199	22	8	4	4	26	26	40	9	1	.302/.396/.467	142	.373	-0.5	SS(28) 0.8, 2B(16) -2.0	0.7
2019	ASH	LO-A	22	453	79	32	1	10	52	62	62	18	9	.318/.409/.489	151	.350	0.4	SS(53) -1.4, 2B(41) 2.7	4.0
2021 FS	BAL	MLB	24	600	55	27	3	12	59	41	151	11	5	.236/.292/.363	80	.303	-1.5	SS 0, 2B 2	0.7

Comparables: Cole Figueroa, Jurickson Profar, Chase d'Arnaud

The Report: If Akin is solid made flesh, they may have re-used the cast on Vavra. He hit .380 his junior year at Minnesota with more walks than strikeouts. There was a small power spike which continued in the friendly confines of Asheville in 2019. He's the kind of college shortstop who ends up playing mostly second base—and he already had almost an even split between the two in A-ball. He'll hit enough and control the zone well enough that even low-double-digit home run totals should make him a solid enough major league hitter, something in the 5-10 percent better than average range. Nothing is going to stand out on the scout sheet, but he does everything well enough.

Development Track: Vavra was handled fairly conservatively by the Rockies, spending all of 2019 in the South Atlantic League despite being a relatively polished college bat. His power numbers will no longer get a boost from the Rockies' spate of bandboxes and/or high altitudes throughout their minor league system, but Vavra offers enough advanced offensive skills that you could start him at Double-A in 2021—I'm sure MLB will let us all know where that will be soon enough—without him missing a beat. He did miss a year though, so variance creeps in here like it does with most of the prospect population.

Variance: Medium. Vavra can hit and play both middle infield spots, so he's likely to carve out a major-league role of some sort. But if there is such a thing as an infield tweener, he might fall into that camp. I suppose I am obligated to mention there's an underlying skillset here that could yield more game power with a swing adjustment, but oh, that way madness lies for both Kings and prospect writers.

Mark Barry's Fantasy Take: Vavra put up some good numbers in Ashville last year, stealing 18 bases in just over 100 games. That's good! He also got caught nine times, however, which is definitely less, uh, good. Using a lazy, new-teammate comp, he could be the heir apparent for Hanser Alberto, in other words a guy who seems good, but in reality is just a multi-positional guy for deep-flexibility.

The Prospects You Meet Outside The Top Ten

Recent draftees with upside

Gunnar Henderson **SS**   Born: 06/29/01   Age: 20   Bats: L   Throws: R   Height: 6'3"   Weight: 195   Origin: Round 2, 2019 Draft (#42 overall)

YEAR	TEAM	LVL	AGE	PA	R	2B	3B	HR	RBI	BB	K	SB	CS	AVG/OBP/SLG	DRC+	BABIP	BRR	FRAA	WARP
2019	ORI	ROK	18	121	21	5	2	1	11	11	28	2	2	.259/.331/.370		.338			
2021 FS	BAL	MLB	20	600	44	26	3	7	49	31	215	7	3	.206/.252/.304	52	.319	-1.1	SS -1	-2.0

Comparables: Rey Navarro, Isan Díaz, Gavin Cecchini

Henderson was a tricky rank. He was badly overmatched at the alternate site, but he was also facing a lot of the arms above him on this list, as well as a bunch more close-to-ready backend starter types. And this was functionally his pro debut. He looked more like the draft report at instructs against age-appropriate competition, a projectable power bat that should land somewhere on the left side of the infield, likely at third base. There's more upside here than the back half or so of the Orioles Top 10, but the issues with bat control at the alternate site have us tempering expectations a tad for now.

Hudson Haskin   Born: 12/31/98   Age: 22   Bats: R   Throws: R   Height: 6'2"   Weight: 200   Origin: Round 2, 2020 Draft (#39 overall)

As Hunter Pence rides off into the sunset after announcing his retirement, we already have a candidate for his likely reincarnated baseball kindred spirit: meet Hudson Haskin. Setting aside their eerily similar names, their bodies and movements are also awkwardly similar in the way they shouldn't work at all and yet produce a ton offensively. Haskin is a plus runner with a good arm, albeit funky, with an innate ability to make contact despite a weird setup—tall and upright to begin with a very large stride that keeps him low through impact.

Coby Mayo   Born: 12/10/01   Age: 19   Bats: R   Throws: R   Height: 6'5"   Weight: 215   Origin: Round 4, 2020 Draft (#103 overall)

It may not have been their initial strategy, but Mayo became one of two Orioles draftees who benefited from the Kjerstad under-slot deal, signing for $1.75 million dollars ($1.18 million over the fourth round pick value). He's a mountain of a kid out of the south Florida prep scene who is a good athlete for his size. Some tinkering is needed to clean up the swing mechanics, however there is no shortage of bat-speed that can produce plenty of power.

Infielders you will see in the majors at some point

Adam Hall **SS**   Born: 05/22/99   Age: 22   Bats: R   Throws: R   Height: 6'0"   Weight: 170   Origin: Round 2, 2017 Draft (#60 overall)

YEAR	TEAM	LVL	AGE	PA	R	2B	3B	HR	RBI	BB	K	SB	CS	AVG/OBP/SLG	DRC+	BABIP	BRR	FRAA	WARP
2018	ABD	SS	19	256	35	9	3	1	24	17	58	22	5	.293/.368/.374	133	.386	2.6	SS(59) -3.0, 2B(4) 0.4	1.0
2019	DEL	LO-A	20	534	78	22	4	5	45	45	117	33	9	.298/.385/.395	140	.387	3.1	SS(79) 0.4, 2B(39) 0.2	4.5
2021 FS	BAL	MLB	22	600	50	26	3	6	51	33	187	20	7	.238/.298/.334	76	.349	2.6	SS 2, 2B 0	0.7

Comparables: Eugenio Suárez, Rosell Herrera, Pete Kozma

We've been talking a lot about teams telling us things while preparing for these lists. One way teams leaked information about whom they *really* like was alternate site assignments. The Orioles didn't invite Hall to the alternate site, even though they invited Henderson, who has a broadly similar profile as a prep infielder but is two years behind Hall developmentally. Based on 2019 looks, he's a hit-tool driven middle infield prospect who lacks significant power.

Jordan Westburg   Born: 02/18/99   Age: 22   Bats: R   Throws: R   Height: 6'3"   Weight: 203   Origin: Round CBA, 2020 Draft (#30 overall)

There were rumors that the subsequent target for the Orioles after Kjerstad in the compensation round—30th overall—would be prep pitcher Nick Bitsko. The Rays thwarted that plan six picks earlier, leaving Westburg as their consolation prize. A solid player with average tools across the board, and a projectable athletic body, Westburg had been trending upward before the season cancellation. He will need to show positional versatility to up his value, as well as try to tap into more power from his contact-oriented approach.

Starterish Upper Minors Types

Michael Baumann   RHP   Born: 09/10/95   Age: 25   Bats: R   Throws: R   Height: 6'4"   Weight: 225   Origin: Round 3, 2017 Draft (#98 overall)

YEAR	TEAM	LVL	AGE	W	L	SV	G	GS	IP	H	HR	BB/9	K/9	K	GB%	BABIP	WHIP	ERA	DRA-	WARP
2018	DEL	LO-A	22	5	0	0	7	7	38	23	0	3.1	11.1	47	50.6%	.284	0.95	1.42	68	0.9
2018	FRE	HI-A	22	8	5	0	17	17	92²	82	9	3.9	5.7	59	32.9%	.263	1.32	3.88	171	-2.9
2019	FRE	HI-A	23	1	4	0	11	11	54	40	2	4.0	12.8	77	43.1%	.317	1.19	3.83	77	0.8
2019	BOW	AA	23	6	2	1	13	11	70	45	2	2.7	8.4	65	41.4%	.242	0.94	2.31	57	1.8
2021 FS	BAL	MLB	25	8	9	0	26	26	150	135	22	5.0	8.9	148	40.2%	.282	1.46	4.67	108	0.4
2021 DC	BAL	MLB	25	2	3	0	9	9	40	36	6	5.0	8.9	39	40.2%	.282	1.46	4.67	108	0.3

Comparables: Ryan Borucki, Patrick Murphy, Matt Hall

Baumann has gone from Prospect Staff meme to pretty good prospect. He got a bump into last year's top ten as his secondaries improved around a solid-average fastball and the performance in Double-A backed it up. He's not all that different in quality of stuff or likely profile from the Akins and Bradishes or the world, but the former got the call over him, and the latter has a clear above-average secondary. It's fine margins at this part of the list though, and we wouldn't put you through the ringer if you prefer Baumann.

Kevin Smith   LHP   Born: 05/13/97   Age: 24   Bats: R   Throws: L   Height: 6'5"   Weight: 200   Origin: Round 7, 2018 Draft (#200 overall)

YEAR	TEAM	LVL	AGE	W	L	SV	G	GS	IP	H	HR	BB/9	K/9	K	GB%	BABIP	WHIP	ERA	DRA-	WARP
2018	BRK	SS	21	4	1	0	12	3	23²	12	1	2.3	10.6	28	49.0%	.220	0.76	0.76	130	-0.3
2019	STL	HI-A	22	5	5	0	17	17	85²	83	5	2.5	10.7	102	44.1%	.359	1.25	3.05	88	0.7
2019	BNG	AA	22	3	2	0	6	6	31¹	25	1	4.3	8.0	28	39.3%	.289	1.28	3.45	115	-0.2
2021 FS	BAL	MLB	24	2	3	0	57	0	50	48	8	4.4	8.7	48	39.2%	.291	1.45	4.91	112	-0.2
2021 DC	BAL	MLB	24	0	0	0	3	3	13	12	2	4.4	8.7	12	39.2%	.291	1.45	4.91	112	0.1

Comparables: David Peterson, Bernardo Flores Jr., Mitch Keller

The Orioles got Smith from the Mets for Miguel Castro. The stuff is fringy—the fastball sits a tick either side of 90 and the slider flashes 50—but the extension, spin, and deception all help the arsenal play up. Whether it plays up enough to make him a back-end starter or merely a lefty middle reliever is yet to be seen.

Top Talents 25 and Under (as of 4/1/2021):

1. Adley Rutschman
2. Ryan Mountcastle
3. Grayson Rodriguez
4. Heston Kjerstad
5. DL Hall
6. Dean Kremer
7. Ryan McKenna
8. Kyle Bradish
9. Austin Hays
10. Terrin Vavra

This was, perhaps, the easiest 25-and-under list I'll ever have to deal with, outside of lists that exactly mirror the prospect list. Keegan Akin turns 26 on literally the day we set as the age cutoff for the list, so he drops off. The Orioles only have one eligible non-rookie on their 40-man, Austin Hays, and he just happens to slot in exactly where Akin does on the prospect list. Easy peasy, right?

Last year, Hays ranked 12th on the Baltimore prospect list. He was coming off a scorching September as Baltimore's regular center fielder, and frankly we took significant criticism for having him too low; we did not feel his level of offense was sustainable and weren't completely sold on his defense in center, either. A year later, I think *some* of our concerns have borne out. He was a slightly below-average hitter over the course of the season, and Baltimore chose to mostly play Cedric Mullins in center and Hays in a corner when Hays returned from a broken rib in September. He's neither as good as his 2019 cup of coffee suggested nor as bad as he was in 2017, and 2020's acceptable hitting and ability to play any outfield spot does represent a compromise between those outcomes.

Boston Red Sox

The State of the System:
The Red Sox system continues to improve, but it's more depth than top-end talent at present.

The Top Ten:

★ ★ ★ *2021 Top 101 Prospect* **#85** ★ ★ ★

1 **Triston Casas** **3B** OFP: 60 ETA: Late 2022/Early 2023
Born: 01/15/00 Age: 21 Bats: L Throws: R Height: 6'4" Weight: 238 Origin: Round 1, 2018 Draft (#26 overall)

YEAR	TEAM	LVL	AGE	PA	R	2B	3B	HR	RBI	BB	K	SB	CS	AVG/OBP/SLG	DRC+	BABIP	BRR	FRAA	WARP
2018	RSX	ROK	18	5	0	0	0	0	0	1	2	0	0	.000/.200/.000		.000			
2019	GVL	LO-A	19	493	64	25	5	19	78	58	116	3	2	.254/.349/.472	144	.300	-0.9	1B(94) -4.7, 3B(8) -1.2	2.1
2019	SAL	HI-A	19	7	2	1	0	1	3	0	2	0	0	.429/.429/1.000	158	.500	0.1	1B(2) -0.0	0.1
2021 FS	BOS	MLB	21	600	55	27	3	16	64	37	197	0	0	.212/.268/.363	71	.296	1.3	1B -4, 3B 0	-1.7

Comparables: Lars Anderson, Mike Carp, Anthony Rizzo

The Report: As a first-round prep first baseman, you'd expect Casas to have a big offensive projection. He does. The hit tool isn't quite as good as the elite cold-corner prospects, but Casas generates a lot of pop without a lot of length and approach improvements could get the hit tool to above-average. He played some third base in high school, but has solely played first in the pros, and while he should end up more than passable there, some defensive refinement will be necessary as the game speed increases up the organizational ladder. Even in his first pro season in 2019—and given a challenging full-season assignment—Casas showed improvements as the season wore on. So there could be a breakout looming once we all get back to a more normal minor league season.

Development Track: I have a pet theory that the prospects hit hardest by the lack of a 2020 campaign were young, high-ceiling prospects with one year in A-ball. Now this isn't based on anything scientific, and frankly the two major points of improvement we'd look for in games here—approach and defense—got positive reviews on the alternate site side. Would I be more confident Casas will hit enough to carry the first base profile if he did it in the Carolina League? Sure. But he's on the right track. We also got good reports on the power, but you already knew he'd crush dingers. We'll still have to wait another year for the potential breakout, but we've had to wait another year for a lot of things.

Variance: High. There are thin margins for the prep first base profile, so you'd like to see a long track record of mashing in the pros. Casas doesn't have that yet.

Mark Barry's Fantasy Take: Casas has emerged as one of the most "I Once Caught a Fish THIS Big" guys from alternative site reports, with tales of his raw power and newly developed physique growing more extravagant with each retelling. The ceiling feels Pete Alonso-ish, but the realistic outcome might come more in the Mitch Moreland aisle. Still good, but less exciting.

2 Jeter Downs SS

OFP: 60   ETA: Late 2021 maybe, likely 2022

Born: 07/27/98   Age: 22   Bats: R   Throws: R   Height: 5'11"   Weight: 195   Origin: Round 1, 2017 Draft (#32 overall)

YEAR	TEAM	LVL	AGE	PA	R	2B	3B	HR	RBI	BB	K	SB	CS	AVG/OBP/SLG	DRC+	BABIP	BRR	FRAA	WARP
2018	DAY	LO-A	19	524	63	23	2	13	47	52	103	37	10	.257/.351/.402	121	.306	-1.6	2B(73) -2.9, SS(43) -9.3	0.8
2019	RC	HI-A	20	475	76	32	4	19	75	53	96	22	8	.269/.353/.506	126	.302	4.1	SS(91) -4.0, 2B(10) -1.1	2.9
2019	TUL	AA	20	56	14	2	0	5	11	6	10	1	0	.333/.429/.688	166	.333	0.8	SS(11) -0.4, 2B(1) -0.0	0.6
2021 FS	BOS	MLB	22	600	67	27	2	23	77	47	162	16	7	.237/.306/.429	101	.293	-1.3	SS -11, 2B -2	0.6

Comparables: Addison Russell, Daniel Robertson, Lonnie Chisenhall

The Report: When the 32nd-overall pick bounces between three teams in four years after being selected, you do tend to wonder why a high draft pick would be traded that much. In the case of Downs, there is some debate where he ends up defensively and just how high the ceiling might be. Given his involvement in the Mookie Betts deal, the Red Sox seem to view his upside as quite high, especially with the bat. He has a naturally aggressive approach, but has shown an improved ability to be more selective at the plate and use the entire field. Downs isn't the fastest guy by the stopwatch, but has good instincts that help both his infield range and ability to steal bases.

Development Track: A highly touted high school shortstop making it to Double-A in his second full season of pro ball is very noteworthy, regardless of how many organizations he's been with. The original plan for 2020 was to continue his rapid matriculation while getting accustomed to yet another set of coaches and philosophies. By every estimation the development track continues upward with the likelihood he switches over to second base in 2021, making stops in Triple-A and a potential big-league call-up not out of the question.

Variance: High. It's no small feat having to listen to three sets of voices over three years. No one would fault him for some amount of stagnation as a result, but his success so far is very much to his credit.

Mark Barry's Fantasy Take: Huge Jeter Downs guy here. We're looking at an above-average hit tool paired with the ability to work walks and a knack for base thievery, not to mention enough power to the pull side to potentially turn into a 20/20 guy at the six. He's a top-50 dynasty guy for me and honestly, I think I prefer him to Casas in fantasy.

3 Noah Song RHP

OFP: 55   ETA: Around a year after his service commitment ends.

Born: 05/28/97   Age: 24   Bats: R   Throws: R   Height: 6'4"   Weight: 200   Origin: Round 4, 2019 Draft (#137 overall)

YEAR	TEAM	LVL	AGE	W	L	SV	G	GS	IP	H	HR	BB/9	K/9	K	GB%	BABIP	WHIP	ERA	DRA	WARP
2019	LOW	SS	22	0	0	0	7	7	17	10	0	2.6	10.1	19	41.5%	.244	0.88	1.06	51	0.5
2021 FS	BOS	MLB	24	2	3	0	57	0	50	49	8	5.0	8.0	44	37.9%	.291	1.55	5.26	125	-0.6

Comparables: Jesse Hahn, Hayden Penn, Josh Zeid

The Report: If Song had been allowed to transfer to the Navy Reserve after graduating, he'd be a Top 101 prospect. He's a four-pitch, advanced college arm of similar quality to the pitchers who rank around the middle of the 101 in any given year, and in some alternate world would've moved very quickly and been at the forefront of Boston's rebuild. Of course, the Red Sox never would've been able to take him as a below-slot fourth-rounder without the availability questions…

Development Track: Song would not have pitched in 2020 even if there were a season; he reported to naval flight school in June after he was denied a deferral waiver. He's eligible for early release from his service commitment as early as May 2021, but our sources with the Red Sox were unsure when he'd be able to resume his professional career, and the Secretary of Defense who was making these calls got fired by tweet last week. Song pitching in the 2021 Olympics makes way too much sense for everyone involved for it not to happen, not that political decisions are always based on making sense or anything.

Variance: High. On talent, he's better than this, but it's a unique level of uncertainty here. We would note, though, that many prospects ended up having a lost 2020 not all that unlike Song, so if he ends up pitching in 2021 he might not be as far behind the curve as you'd think.

Mark Barry's Fantasy Take: Before getting into the Song-of-it-all, I just wanted to reemphasize the majesty of this sentence:

"our sources with the Red Sox were unsure when he'd be able to resume his professional career, and the Secretary of Defense who was making these calls just got fired by tweet last week"

Anyway, there are a lot of questions surrounding Song's reemergence onto the prospect scene, but funny enough, lost development isn't really one of them, thanks to, uh, a global pandemic that kept all minor leaguers out of competitive games. Song was fairly advanced before his Naval service, so it's easy to envision the Red Sox moving him pretty quickly when he gets back in the fold. Still, I don't think you'd have to be too aggressive with him outside of leagues that roster 250+ prospects.

4 Jarren Duran OF   OFP: 55   ETA: 2022, could force his way into 2021 discussion
Born: 09/05/96   Age: 24   Bats: L   Throws: R   Height: 6'2"   Weight: 187   Origin: Round 7, 2018 Draft (#220 overall)

YEAR	TEAM	LVL	AGE	PA	R	2B	3B	HR	RBI	BB	K	SB	CS	AVG/OBP/SLG	DRC+	BABIP	BRR	FRAA	WARP
2018	LOW	SS	21	168	28	5	10	2	20	11	26	12	4	.348/.393/.548	168	.406	0.4	2B(20) 4.9, CF(15) 0.1	1.6
2018	GVL	LO-A	21	134	24	9	1	1	15	5	22	12	6	.367/.396/.477	163	.438	1.6	RF(30) -0.0	1.1
2019	SAL	HI-A	22	226	49	13	3	4	19	23	44	18	5	.387/.456/.543	200	.480	3.4	CF(50) 0.2	3.3
2019	POR	AA	22	352	41	11	5	1	19	23	84	28	8	.250/.309/.325	75	.335	5.1	CF(80) -3.3	0.5
2021 FS	BOS	MLB	24	600	60	29	7	8	59	33	163	28	9	.255/.304/.378	84	.348	7.6	CF -5, 2B 0	1.0
2021 DC	BOS	MLB	24	66	6	3	0	0	6	3	17	3	1	.255/.304/.378	84	.348	0.8	CF -1	0.1

Comparables: Engel Beltre, Gorkys Hernández, Noel Cuevas

The Report: You might not find another player in this system who invokes as wide a range of opinions. Finding a seventh-rounder who can potentially bring value to the major-league club is always a feather in the cap for the scouting department, no matter if he's a bench bat, defensive/baserunning sub, everyday guy, or star player. All are potential future outcomes for Duran, depending on whom you talk to. After playing the infield in college, he is adapting to life in the outfield where his plus-plus speed plays well in the gaps, even as his reads and angles improve with more reps at the new position. That speed is evident on the basepaths as well, as he uses it to his advantage to get on-base with his slap-contact approach. The power is still under development as he's adjusting to drive the ball more with authority to the pull-side.

Development Track: Duran burst onto the scene surpassing every expectation in his two seasons since being drafted. However, the buzzsaw who had carved up the lower levels met some resistance in Double-A and again in the 2019 Fall League against better competition. Reports from the Pawtucket alternate training site suggest he had acclimated to the environment and addressed many of the concerns associated with his profile. Progressing to a well-rounded hitter, with the raw athletic tools he possesses, puts him in line to be patrolling the Fenway outfield within the next year.

Variance: High. Simply because of the multitude of different opinions we received from scouts and front office types.

Mark Barry's Fantasy Take: Duran is very, very fast. And rumor has it that he got more compact with his swing, enabling him to lift more balls in the air. Had that development happened in actual games (and if it's real, I guess), he'd probably be garnering a lot more buzz in fantasy circles. The speed alone has him flirting with the top-100 with room for more if he can somehow muster 10-15 homers.

5 Bryan Mata RHP   OFP: 55   ETA: 2021
Born: 05/03/99   Age: 22   Bats: R   Throws: R   Height: 6'3"   Weight: 240   Origin: International Free Agent, 2016

YEAR	TEAM	LVL	AGE	W	L	SV	G	GS	IP	H	HR	BB/9	K/9	K	GB%	BABIP	WHIP	ERA	DRA-	WARP
2018	SAL	HI-A	19	6	3	0	17	17	72	58	1	7.2	7.6	61	56.6%	.297	1.61	3.50	106	0.3
2019	SAL	HI-A	20	3	1	0	10	10	51¹	38	1	3.2	9.1	52	64.0%	.270	1.09	1.75	75	0.8
2019	POR	AA	20	4	6	0	11	11	53²	54	6	4.0	9.9	59	50.3%	.350	1.45	5.03	111	-0.3
2021 FS	BOS	MLB	22	8	10	0	26	26	150	138	19	5.2	8.2	135	46.9%	.282	1.50	5.01	115	-0.2
2021 DC	BOS	MLB	22	2	4	0	12	12	53	48	6	5.2	8.2	47	46.9%	.282	1.50	5.01	115	0.1

Comparables: Sixto Sánchez, Lucas Sims, Deolis Guerra

The Report: Consistently praised by Red Sox brass throughout the minor league-less summer, Mata's body is finally maturing to match the big-time stuff he showed off as one of the youngest players in each of his stateside seasons. Always known as a hard thrower with fastball velocities in the mid-to-upper 90s, the issue was his ability to throw quality strikes given how much movement he generates on each of his pitches. Those within the org believe he has simplified his delivery which has allowed for more consistency locating the heater. He's also added a cutter that flashes plus. Paired with a curveball and change that are both at least average, the difference between being a frontline starter or perhaps back-end of the rotation type will wholly depend on keeping the walk rate down.

Development Track: Given the myriad directions a player of this type could go development-wise, Mata appears to be one of the few who has made substantial gains this year. Listed last year at 160 pounds, he's now well over 200 on a nearly filled out athletic frame. With the physical growth here instead of projected, maintaining his newly tweaked mechanics will be the cornerstone of his early 2021 focus.

Variance: Extreme. The news has all been positive regarding Mata, but two things stick out: 1) big physical gains can sometimes be troublesome for a pitcher's arm, and 2) once you've earned a reputation as a "thrower" with control issues, it's awfully hard to turn that around completely.

Mark Barry's Fantasy Take: If you like speculating for saves, in the minor leagues, then Mata could be your guy. If he stays in the rotation, though, you're looking at a right-handed Martín Pérez, which is extremely Not What You Want.

6   Bobby Dalbec   3B   OFP: 55   ETA: Debuted in 2020

Born: 06/29/95   Age: 26   Bats: R   Throws: R   Height: 6'4"   Weight: 227   Origin: Round 4, 2016 Draft (#118 overall)

YEAR	TEAM	LVL	AGE	PA	R	2B	3B	HR	RBI	BB	K	SB	CS	AVG/OBP/SLG	DRC+	BABIP	BRR	FRAA	WARP
2018	SAL	HI-A	23	419	59	27	2	26	85	60	130	3	1	.256/.372/.573	159	.318	0.9	3B(91) 5.2, SS(1) 0.0	3.8
2018	POR	AA	23	124	14	8	1	6	24	6	46	0	0	.261/.323/.514	96	.377	-0.1	3B(18) -3.9, 1B(2) -0.3	-0.4
2019	POR	AA	24	439	57	15	2	20	57	68	110	6	4	.234/.371/.454	150	.278	-2.2	3B(90) 7.2, 1B(13) 0.9	4.2
2019	WOR	AAA	24	123	12	4	0	7	16	5	29	0	2	.257/.301/.478	83	.278	0.3	3B(17) 2.0, 1B(11) -1.3	0.2
2020	BOS	MLB	25	92	13	3	0	8	16	10	39	0	0	.263/.359/.600	92	.394	-0.2	1B(21) 1.8, 3B(2) -0.2	0.2
2021 FS	BOS	MLB	26	600	73	26	1	28	81	55	238	1	0	.226/.310/.441	107	.344	-1.0	1B -9, 3B 0	0.8
2021 DC	BOS	MLB	26	568	69	24	1	26	77	52	226	1	0	.226/.310/.441	107	.344	-1.0	1B -8	0.5

Comparables: Mat Gamel, Matt Carpenter, Mike Olt

The Report: This will be Dalbec's fifth and final appearance on a Red Sox prospect list, and if we're honest, he hasn't changed a whole heckuva lot over the years. Now, it's been a good development track. There were quite a few outcomes where the swing-and-miss ate into his performance too much in the upper minors, while others saw him try his luck as a pitcher at 25 after another season hitting .220 in Portland. But his TTO style worked all the way up the ladder, and he even cut the Ks enough in 2019 where you could see enough of the power playing in games to make the profile work as an everyday player.

Development Track: He got his major-league shot in 2020 after the Red Sox sent Mitch Moreland to San Diego, and you got the full Bobby Dalbec experience. He hit a home run every 11.5 plate appearances, and struck out every 2.4 plate appearances. He's unlikely to sustain the former—although it's 30-home-run pop—and will need to improve the latter. It's not an approach issue, as he continues to rack up the free passes, but his in-zone contact rate was only a smidge better than Jo Adell's (that's bad). The overall line was buoyed by a .394 BABIP, and the profile remains quite boom-or-bust. He played mostly first base in deference to Rafael Devers, but that might get flipped soon, despite my remaining bullish on Devers' glove.

Variance: Medium. Yes, Dalbec made the majors and hit a bunch of dingers, but that batting average could end up closer to .220 than .260, and then the whole profile looks more like a bench bat.

Mark Barry's Fantasy Take: Pretty much every sample size was small this season, but only Jorge Alfaro and Luis Robert swung and missed more frequently than Dalbec this season. The Red Sox rookie also struck out more than 40 percent of the time. It's possible you could get a .260 average and a bunch of dingers from Dalbec (like you did this year), but that's like the absolute 90th percentile outcome if he's going to whiff this much. You're more likely looking at a batting average flirting with the Mendoza Line, at which point not even solid plate discipline will get him on base enough to be useful outside of the power department.

7   Nick Yorke   2B   OFP: 55   ETA: 2024

Born: 04/02/02   Age: 19   Bats: R   Throws: R   Height: 6'0"   Weight: 200   Origin: Round 1, 2020 Draft (#17 overall)

The Report: No player selected in the first round of this year's draft caused more head-scratching than the 17th-overall selection by Boston. An Arizona commit who seemed destined to make it onto campus because of his defensive limitations and overall athletic profile, the Sox believed he was the best hitter in the class without exception. Losing their second-round pick due to the sign-stealing scandal, they feared he wouldn't make it to their next pick at 89 and didn't want to leave it to chance. While puzzling at the time, Yorke demonstrated his advanced hit tool at the alternate training site, often facing grown men many years ahead of him in their development while still managing to compete. Likely destined for second base as a fringe-average defender, the term "carrying tool" has never been more applicable than it is here in reference to the offensive potential moving forward.

Development Track: As one of the youngest players at ANY alternate site this year, Yorke held his own. His development arc is still gauged in years despite the promising early signs, and he needs to shore up any and all defensive concerns that exist. Additionally, while all the talk has been about the bat—and rightfully so—there is still the need to grow into power which evaluators believe will eventually come thanks to a smooth stroke that creates natural loft. Look for him to follow a similar path to that of Casas.

Variance: Extreme. When you're known exceptionally for one thing, you better find other ways to diversify your toolset, lest you lose that defining quality, leaving you with nothing else to offer.

Mark Barry's Fantasy Take: Between Yorke likely being 2B-only and lacking much pop in the stick, he's a deep-league MI candidate or AL-only guy. Otherwise, he doesn't need to be on the radar right now.

8 Matthew Lugo SS   OFP: 55   ETA: Late 2023 or 2024
Born: 05/09/01 Age: 20 Bats: R Throws: R Height: 6'1" Weight: 185 Origin: Round 2, 2019 Draft (#69 overall)

YEAR	TEAM	LVL	AGE	PA	R	2B	3B	HR	RBI	BB	K	SB	CS	AVG/OBP/SLG	DRC+	BABIP	BRR	FRAA	WARP
2019	RSX	ROK	18	157	19	5	1	1	12	15	36	3	0	.257/.342/.331		.340			
2019	LOW	SS	18	8	0	0	0	0	1	0	2	0	0	.250/.250/.250	79	.333	-0.1	SS(2) -0.6	-0.1
2021 FS	BOS	MLB	20	600	46	26	2	8	50	31	213	3	1	.209/.257/.310	55	.320	0.6	SS -1	-1.6

Comparables: Tzu-Wei Lin, Gavin Lux, Luis Sardiñas

The Report: Lugo was a physically projectable shortstop who was young for his draft class. In his first pro summer he displayed a broad base of skills, but perhaps lacked a standout tool. He also looked a bit overmatched at the plate in his brief Penn League cameo against more experienced arms. It wasn't hard to see the outline of a solid everyday shortstop, though.

Development Track: Lugo has added some good, lean muscle to his frame and he already showed solid pull-side raw power. He hasn't given back the above-average speed or range at shortstop, but the glove remains ahead of the bat developmentally. All in all though, there continue to be positive markers on his offensive projection, and he will still be a teenager to start the 2021 season.

Variance: Extreme. The physical growth is a plus and the added power potential adds to the upside, but we are still talking about a 19-year-old who has played two games outside of the complex.

Mark Barry's Fantasy Take: Lugo's tools standing toe-to-toe in the ring, exhausted.

Plus speed *Crowd erupts "Yaaay"

Not much present power *Crowd erupts "Booooo"

Adding muscle, flashing pull-side pop "Yaaay"

No experience against advanced competition (and middling success in Complex League) "Booooo"

Projectable teenager "Yaaay", good mechanics "Yaaay", Potential for 4.5 category contribution "Yaaay".

9 Gilberto Jimenez CF   OFP: 50   ETA: 2023
Born: 07/08/00 Age: 20 Bats: S Throws: R Height: 5'11" Weight: 160 Origin: International Free Agent, 2017

YEAR	TEAM	LVL	AGE	PA	R	2B	3B	HR	RBI	BB	K	SB	CS	AVG/OBP/SLG	DRC+	BABIP	BRR	FRAA	WARP
2018	DSL RSB	ROK	17	284	42	10	8	0	22	19	40	16	14	.319/.384/.420		.378			
2019	LOW	SS	18	254	35	11	3	3	19	13	38	14	6	.359/.393/.470	190	.413	1.2	CF(57) -9.8, LF(1) -0.1, RF(1) -0.1	1.9
2021 FS	BOS	MLB	20	600	49	26	4	6	53	27	160	19	11	.251/.292/.351	76	.339	-6.5	CF -6, RF 0	-1.2

Comparables: Harold Ramirez, Franklin Barreto, Manuel Margot

The Report: Despite a meager five-figure bonus, Jimenez developed quickly with the lumber and was one of the best pure bat-to-ball guys in the New York-Penn League in 2019. The pure contact ability is easy plus, but there isn't much raw pop and the bat speed is fringy. He has the burn part of slash-and-burn down as he's a plus runner and aggressive on the bases. Jimenez should stick in center due to his foot speed and instincts although the arm is on the fringy side. He may have limited offensive upside due to the combination of a lack of physicality and an aggressive approach at the plate, but he's going to be a scout's favorite because of everything else.

Development Track: Jimenez should start 2021 in A-ball and the bat shouldn't really be challenged until Double-A.

Variance: High. The hit tool might be plus, but it's going to need to be, and we haven't seen it against better velocity or sequencing yet.

Mark Barry's Fantasy Take: This is the kind of guy who I think might be affected most by the lack of reps in 2020, unfortunately. He has tools (ie: those sweet, sweet wheels) and makes a ton of contact, but does lack experience. There's enough current promise to keep an eye on him, but I don't think you need to run out and make an immediate acquisition.

10 Tanner Houck RHP   OFP: 50   ETA: Debuted in 2020

Born: 06/29/96   Age: 25   Bats: R   Throws: R   Height: 6'5"   Weight: 230   Origin: Round 1, 2017 Draft (#24 overall)

YEAR	TEAM	LVL	AGE	W	L	SV	G	GS	IP	H	HR	BB/9	K/9	K	GB%	BABIP	WHIP	ERA	DRA-	WARP
2018	SAL	HI-A	22	7	11	0	23	23	119	110	11	4.5	8.4	111	49.3%	.299	1.43	4.24	119	-0.4
2019	POR	AA	23	8	6	0	17	15	82²	86	4	3.5	8.7	80	48.5%	.346	1.43	4.25	112	-0.5
2019	WOR	AAA	23	0	0	1	16	2	25	19	3	5.0	9.7	27	43.3%	.258	1.32	3.24	72	0.7
2020	BOS	MLB	24	3	0	0	3	3	17	6	1	4.8	11.1	21	46.9%	.161	0.88	0.53	85	0.3
2021 FS	BOS	MLB	25	8	9	0	26	26	150	137	19	5.2	9.3	155	45.4%	.294	1.50	4.89	108	0.4
2021 DC	BOS	MLB	25	7	9	0	25	25	137	125	17	5.2	9.3	141	45.4%	.294	1.50	4.89	108	0.8

Comparables: Jayson Aquino, Keury Mella, Cal Quantrill

The Report: Houck transitioned to the pen in 2019, but the Red Sox stretched him back out and used him as a starter for the big club towards the end of 2020. He still primarily deploys a sinker/slider mix. The fastball can hit the mid-90s in short bursts, but was more 91-94 as a starter. It has heavy sink with some run as well, but Houck can be a bit loose with his command of the pitch and will get erratic with his control as well. The slider is a big breaker in the low 80s. It can tend to have more sweep than depth, but there's enough two-plane action here to miss bats. Houck also throws the occasional split-change which doesn't really have enough velo, separation, or sink at present to even keep lefties honest.

Development Track: Houck was nothing short of dominant in his three starts for the 2020 Red Sox, but over the long haul the stuff and command might not be enough to stick in a rotation (the 2021 Red Sox rotation will give him plenty of opportunities, though). It's a good enough two-pitch combo to work in the seventh and eighth inning, although given his platoon issues over the years, he may need to deployed strategically.

Variance: Low. Houck looked more than ready to get major-league hitters out in his three start cameo. The lack of a weapon against lefties might limit him to the bullpen or some to a role as some sort of bulk guy role where you can leverage a plus two-pitch mix, but he's an asset to your pitching staff in 2021.

Mark Barry's Fantasy Take: I'd be a lot more interested in Houck if his splitter were more developed, as he was actually really good in a brief stint in Boston toward the end of the 2020 season. As it stands, though, he's probably a reliever, and not really a high-leverage one at that.

The Prospects You Meet Outside The Top Ten:

Solid pitching prospects, but limited upside

Thad Ward RHP Born: 01/16/97   Age: 24   Bats: R   Throws: R   Height: 6'3"   Weight: 182   Origin: Round 5, 2018 Draft (#160 overall)

YEAR	TEAM	LVL	AGE	W	L	SV	G	GS	IP	H	HR	BB/9	K/9	K	GB%	BABIP	WHIP	ERA	DRA-	WARP
2018	LOW	SS	21	0	3	0	11	11	31	33	2	3.5	7.8	27	54.3%	.337	1.45	3.77	159	-0.8
2019	GVL	LO-A	22	5	2	0	13	13	72¹	51	2	3.1	10.8	87	47.8%	.280	1.05	1.99	66	1.7
2019	SAL	HI-A	22	3	3	0	12	12	54	38	4	5.3	11.7	70	47.1%	.296	1.30	2.33	89	0.5
2021 FS	BOS	MLB	24	2	3	0	57	0	50	47	7	5.7	9.0	50	43.7%	.290	1.57	5.30	122	-0.5

Comparables: Albert Abreu, Justin Grimm, Tyler Thornburg

Ward isn't a markedly different pitcher now compared to when he ranked fifth in the system last year. There's just been improvement around him. He's more likely to stick as a starter than Houck, given the more rounded out arsenal with a plus slider/cutter and two other useable secondaries. Ward also has less experience as a starter—he was more of a multi-inning reliever at Central Florida—and the frame is on the slender side. There's a fourth starter projection, but he's a bit further away than Houck, and there's a little less upside than Mata and Murphy. So he slides out of the top ten this year. But there really isn't a significant difference from 7 to 15 in this system.

Connor Seabold **RHP** Born: 01/24/96 Age: 25 Bats: R Throws: R Height: 6'2" Weight: 190 Origin: Round 3, 2017 Draft (#83 overall)

YEAR	TEAM	LVL	AGE	W	L	SV	G	GS	IP	H	HR	BB/9	K/9	K	GB%	BABIP	WHIP	ERA	DRA-	WARP
2018	CLR	HI-A	22	4	4	0	12	12	71²	57	6	1.8	8.5	68	46.5%	.262	0.99	3.77	68	1.7
2018	REA	AA	22	1	4	0	11	11	58²	55	10	2.9	9.8	64	34.5%	.292	1.26	4.91	74	1.2
2019	PHE	ROK	23	0	1	0	1	1	2¹	6	0	0.0	7.7	2	54.5%	.545	2.57	11.57		
2019	PHW	ROK	23	0	0	0	2	2	5	1	0	0.0	18.0	10	83.3%	.167	0.20	0.00		
2019	CLR	HI-A	23	1	0	0	2	1	9	4	1	1.0	10.0	10	50.0%	.158	0.56	1.00	58	0.2
2019	REA	AA	23	3	1	0	7	7	40	35	2	2.2	8.1	36	45.5%	.303	1.12	2.25	84	0.4
2021 FS	BOS	MLB	25	2	3	0	57	0	50	46	7	3.2	8.5	47	39.5%	.284	1.28	4.09	103	0.0
2021 DC	BOS	MLB	25	0	0	0	3	3	13	12	1	3.2	8.5	12	39.5%	.284	1.28	4.09	103	0.1

Comparables: Marco Gonzales, Ryan Helsley, Tyler Wilson

A third-round pick for the Phillies in 2017, the Phillies sent Seabold (and Nick Pivetta) to Boston for Brandon Workman and Heath Hembree. Seabold is not overpowering; his fastball will touch the mid 90s, but sits lower. Seabold has three secondary pitches in a slider, curveball, and changeup, with his changeup the best of the bunch. He has above-average command and a good feel for pitching, making him a major-league-ready back-end starter. He has a strong enough foundation that he could take another step forward if any of his pitches makes an improvement.

Chris Murphy **LHP** Born: 06/05/98 Age: 23 Bats: L Throws: L Height: 6'1" Weight: 175 Origin: Round 6, 2019 Draft (#197 overall)

YEAR	TEAM	LVL	AGE	W	L	SV	G	GS	IP	H	HR	BB/9	K/9	K	GB%	BABIP	WHIP	ERA	DRA-	WARP
2019	LOW	SS	21	0	1	0	10	10	33¹	23	1	1.9	9.2	34	45.8%	.268	0.90	1.08	69	0.7
2021 FS	BOS	MLB	23	2	3	0	57	0	50	50	8	4.4	7.9	43	39.2%	.295	1.50	5.19	124	-0.5

Comparables: Humberto Mejía, Héctor Noesi, Caleb Cotham

Despite putting up gaudy strikeout numbers in college, Murphy put up equally bad walk totals as well, relegating him to the sixth round of the 2019 draft. It didn't take long for coaches to make adjustments to the delivery which not only cleared a path for more control, but also upped the velocity by a full grade. Now up to 95 with a four-pitch mix, Murphy knows how to get batters out with regularity and could move quickly up the system.

Good upside, but a ways away

Chih-Jung Liu **RHP** Born: 04/07/99 Age: 22 Bats: S Throws: R Height: 6'0" Weight: 185 Origin: International Free Agent, 2019

Signed out of Taiwan with a fastball reaching triple digits, Liu is still getting accustomed to life half a world away. While getting on a throwing program and training regimen traditional to major league orgs, Liu has worked on finishing his secondary pitches more consistently as the velocity hasn't quite flashed where it was when he was signed.

Bradley Blalock **RHP** Born: 12/25/00 Age: 20 Bats: R Throws: R Height: 6'2" Weight: 190 Origin: Round 32, 2019 Draft (#977 overall)

YEAR	TEAM	LVL	AGE	W	L	SV	G	GS	IP	H	HR	BB/9	K/9	K	GB%	BABIP	WHIP	ERA	DRA-	WARP
2019	RSX	ROK	18	0	2	0	4	3	6²	5	0	5.4	5.4	4	47.6%	.238	1.35	6.75		
2021 FS	BOS	MLB	20	2	3	0	57	0	50	54	8	6.2	7.0	39	39.1%	.303	1.79	6.58	145	-1.1

Comparables: José Torres, Elvis Luciano, Mauricio Cabrera

A relative unknown when selected late in the 2019 draft out of high school, Blalock impressed at instructs showing a four-pitch mix, projectable body, not to mention a heater that sat 94-95 with riding life. He's a long ways away, but it's easy to dream on this kind of player.

Interesting Draft Follow

Blaze Jordan **3B** Born: 12/19/02 Age: 18 Bats: R Throws: R Height: 6'2" Weight: 220 Origin: Round 3, 2020 Draft (#89 overall)

[extreme Southie voice] Blays hits balls wicked fah. We've seen this kind of player make headlines ever since Bryce Harper peppered the back wall of Tropicana Field at a high school showcase. Truth is, next to none present the total package anywhere remotely near where Harper was as a prep. On the plus side, Jordan is on the young side for his class, and his hit tool might be closer to average with his ability to make hard contact.

Jeremy Wu-Yelland   Born: 06/24/99   Age: 22   Bats: L   Throws: L   Height: 6'2"   Weight: 210   Origin: Round 4, 2020 Draft (#118 overall)

Part of Boston's draft strategy was leveraging under-slot deals (like Wu-Yelland) into higher priced, over-slot players in an effort to acquire higher ceiling talent. A southpaw with a funky delivery, Wu-Yelland had been relegated to almost exclusively coming out of the pen because of the mechanics. That funk plays up as a reliever, with radar readings at instructs ticking up to 97. So even though he may have been seen as an afterthought at draft time, the makings of a future dynamic reliever are in play.

You were going to ask about him in the comments

Jay Groome   LHP   Born: 08/23/98   Age: 22   Bats: L   Throws: L   Height: 6'6"   Weight: 220   Origin: Round 1, 2016 Draft (#12 overall)

YEAR	TEAM	LVL	AGE	W	L	SV	G	GS	IP	H	HR	BB/9	K/9	K	GB%	BABIP	WHIP	ERA	DRA-	WARP
2019	RSX	ROK	20	0	0	0	2	2	2	2	0	0.0	13.5	3	80.0%	.400	1.00	0.00		
2019	LOW	SS	20	0	0	0	1	1	2	3	0	4.5	13.5	3	28.6%	.429	2.00	4.50	85	0.0
2021 FS	BOS	MLB	22	2	3	0	57	0	50	45	7	6.2	9.2	51	45.1%	.283	1.59	5.20	122	-0.5

Comparables: Brusdar Graterol, Carl Edwards Jr., Mat Latos

Groome was finally back to full health in 2020. He looked fine at the alternate site—Boston was one of the teams which broadcast a lot of its action, so we've got a lot more video on Groome than for other prospects this year. Back when he was the 12th-overall pick in 2016, Groome's projection was enormous; he was one of the best prep pitching prospects I've ever seen. After years of arm injuries, there's still pieces of it here, but we're just not talking about a potential future ace anymore. The curveball still flashes but it's no longer a 70 projection, and the fastball and command haven't ended up getting all the way there either. His falling off the list is more due to the system getting much stronger around him, but we're talking about a mid-rotation or bullpen prospect with an injury history now, not a potential future ace.

Top Talents 25 and Under (as of 4/1/2021):

1. Rafael Devers, 3B
2. Alex Verdugo, OF
3. Triston Casas, 1B
4. Jeter Downs, SS
5. Noah Song, RHPF
6. Jarren Duran, OF
7. Bryan Mata, RHP
8. Bobby Dalbec, 3B
9. Nick Yorke, 2B
10. Michael Chavis, 1B

Rafael Devers had a down 2020 coming off a 2019 in which he got MVP votes. Offensively, he more or less just lost 50 points of average, and that type of thing happens over a short season. He did crater defensively, and that's not great considering his obvious spot to slide to is first base, the home of the best prospect in the system. Wherever he ends up over the long haul, we expect him to put up more 2019-quality seasons in the years ahead.

Alex Verdugo is not Mookie Betts. He will never be Mookie Betts. But if you're evaluating Verdugo solely on his individual on-the-field merits, he's still on the same track as when he was a top 25 prospect in baseball a few years ago. He hit .302 this year, and that's probably for real; we've long pegged him as a plus-plus hit tool type. He should be a good player on the next good Boston team.

Michael Chavis didn't hit at all this year, managing just a 70 DRC+. He's got some positional versatility—he played second and outfield in addition to first this year—but he's not hitting as much in the majors as we projected. He might be settling in as more of a utility type or second-division regular.

Darwinzon Hernandez missed most of this year with shoulder issues. The Red Sox have toyed with converting him back to starting, and if we had any confidence he could pull it off he'd have certainly made the list. Considering him as a reliever, he's a bit off the bottom in an improved system.

Chicago Cubs

The State of the System:

With the Cubs seemingly prepared to break up their championship core, you may be waiting a while for the farm to produce the next one. There's some interesting talent at the top though.

The Top Ten:

★ ★ ★ *2021 Top 101 Prospect* **#63** ★ ★ ★

1 **Brailyn Marquez** LHP   OFP: 60   ETA: Debuted in 2020
Born: 01/30/99 Age: 22 Bats: L Throws: L Height: 6'4" Weight: 185 Origin: International Free Agent, 2015

YEAR	TEAM	LVL	AGE	W	L	SV	G	GS	IP	H	HR	BB/9	K/9	K	GB%	BABIP	WHIP	ERA	DRA-	WARP
2018	EUG	SS	19	1	4	0	10	10	47²	46	5	2.6	9.8	52	50.8%	.333	1.26	3.21	272	-4.3
2018	SB	LO-A	19	0	0	0	2	2	7	7	0	2.6	9.0	7	33.3%	.333	1.29	2.57	75	0.1
2019	SB	LO-A	20	5	4	0	17	17	77¹	64	4	5.0	11.9	102	50.8%	.337	1.38	3.61	108	-0.1
2019	MB	HI-A	20	4	1	0	5	5	26¹	21	1	2.4	8.9	26	44.4%	.282	1.06	1.71	81	0.3
2020	CHC	MLB	21	0	0	0	1	0	0²	2	0	40.5	13.5	1	33.3%	.667	7.50	67.50	133	0.0
2021 FS	CHC	MLB	22	8	9	0	26	26	150	143	22	5.0	8.9	148	44.0%	.294	1.51	5.08	111	0.2
2021 DC	CHC	MLB	22	3	4	0	32	9	68	64	10	5.0	8.9	67	44.0%	.294	1.51	5.08	111	0.2

Comparables: Huascar Ynoa, Julio Teheran, Luis Severino

The Report: Marquez's September relief cameo pretty well summed up where things stand for him, honestly. His fastball sits in the upper 90s and touches 100, and comes backed by a big, biting slider and a developing changeup. He's battled significant mechanical inconsistencies and wildness during his pro career, and that manifested in his inability to command his fastball at all during his big-league debut. He wasn't ready for the majors, but it was worth a look.

Development Track: Marquez had to be added to the 40-man roster this offseason anyway, so his September appearance only came at the cost of a few days of service time. Although he did not throw it in the majors, he spent a lot of time at the alternate site working on a promising mid-90s sinker.

Variance: High. Marquez still has no real track record of consistently throwing strikes, and until he does there's major bullpen and downside risk.

Mark Barry's Fantasy Take: It's sorta weird that a pitcher who debuted in the majors is still pretty far away, but that's what 2020 will do to a dude like Marquez. All of the upside we loved last year is still there, and this time it's joined by a new sinker. I like the next guy on this list more for fantasy purposes, but Marquez is still a top-100 guy, with one of the most fun ceilings in dynasty.

★ ★ ★ *2021 Top 101 Prospect* **#78** ★ ★ ★

2 Brennen Davis CF OFP: 60   ETA: 2022
Born: 11/02/99   Age: 21   Bats: R   Throws: R   Height: 6'4"   Weight: 175   Origin: Round 2, 2018 Draft (#62 overall)

YEAR	TEAM	LVL	AGE	PA	R	2B	3B	HR	RBI	BB	K	SB	CS	AVG/OBP/SLG	DRC+	BABIP	BRR	FRAA	WARP
2018	CUBR	ROK	18	72	9	2	0	0	3	10	12	6	1	.298/.431/.333		.370			
2019	SB	LO-A	19	204	33	9	3	8	30	18	38	4	1	.305/.381/.525	154	.346	-0.6	LF(23) -1.2, CF(23) -2.1, RF(2) 0.7	1.4
2021 FS	CHC	MLB	21	600	58	26	3	14	63	40	169	8	2	.237/.299/.378	86	.315	1.8	CF 2, LF 0	1.2

Comparables: Jesse Winker, Christian Yelich, Alen Hanson

The Report: "A finger injury limited Davis to just 50 games in 2019, but he showed enough in that abbreviated season to be considered one of the rising stars of the organization. Despite his lack of pro experience, he showed an unexpected polish at the plate, combining contact with natural power. A former prep basketball star, he is built like a shooting guard, but could add good weight to bring more of the power forward. The Cubs will keep him in center as long as they can, and there is a chance he may be able to stick there. However, if a move to a corner spot is necessary, the bat might have enough plus tools in it to carry the load.

Development Track: The lost minor league season might have a silver lining for Davis. Instead of spending a summer in Myrtle Beach, which is extremely hostile to hitters, he faced a steady diet of close-to-major-league ready pitching at the alternate site. Reports out of South Bend tell of a bigger and stronger frame and the ball jumping off the bat. That type of progress in a normal season might have easily put him into the top half of our 101.

Variance: High. Davis still has fewer than 250 professional at bats. It's not a lock he sticks in center, putting a lot of pressure on the hit tool to continue to develop.

Mark Barry's Fantasy Take: You don't have to strain too hard to see a five-category contributor here, and as mentioned above, the lost year of competition might not have been as lost for Davis. He might not stick in center field, but that doesn't really concern me at all. He's a top-30 name for me and if you want to even go a little higher, I wouldn't really argue.

★ ★ ★ *2021 Top 101 Prospect* **#88** ★ ★ ★

3 Ed Howard SS OFP: 60   ETA: 2024
Born: 08/06/01   Age: 19   Bats: R   Throws: R   Height: 6'2"   Weight: 185   Origin: Round 1, 2020 Draft (#16 overall)

The Report: Last year's draft class skewed heavily to the college side, pushing the consensus top prep infielder in the class—and Chicago native—to the Cubs with the 16th pick. Howard has a projectable 6-foot-2 frame and loose hands that display ahead-of-the-curve contact skills, and there's a belief he will grow into power as the body fills out. There is no denying the glove is ahead of the bat—there's clear present defensive skills at the 6—but that is to be expected and totally fine at present. And even if his final outcome is a glove-first, plus-defender at shortstop, the stick should be more than good enough to justify his presence in the lineup as an everyday starter.

Development Track: While there are some present tools to be excited about, Howard is still very much a freshly-drafted prep bat. His senior spring season was canceled before it started, making it imperative he doesn't lose out on an entire year of much-needed development. Much of the focus for Howard in the next year will be adding strength without losing a step. From a skills standpoint, letting his natural ability play up to a refined pro plate approach won't happen overnight. Patience will be key here, but worth the wait.

Variance: Extreme. Inexperienced prep bats always have inherent risk. Add in the lost senior season and pro summer to COVID-19, and there is further risk of not fully reaching the potential.

Mark Barry's Fantasy Take: Oh hey, there's the cliff.

Admittedly, that's a little unfair to Howard, who I do like. It's just that we haven't seen him play real games since like, the Carter administration. While there are a ton of shortstops out there, Howard's defense will help him stay there long term, where you can expect some top-15 or so production at the six. Or, you know, he could show up as the second-coming of Barry Larkin and we wouldn't have ever known, you know, because of the no games thing.

★ ★ ★ *2021 Top 101 Prospect* **#89** ★ ★ ★

4 **Miguel Amaya** **C**   OFP: 60   ETA: Late 2021/Early 2022

Born: 03/09/99   Age: 22   Bats: R   Throws: R   Height: 6'2"   Weight: 230   Origin: International Free Agent, 2015

YEAR	TEAM	LVL	AGE	PA	R	2B	3B	HR	RBI	BB	K	SB	CS	AVG/OBP/SLG	DRC+	BABIP	BRR	FRAA	WARP
2018	SB	LO-A	19	479	54	21	2	12	52	50	91	1	0	.256/.349/.403	117	.298	0.6	C(95) 2.5, 1B(9) -0.7	2.5
2019	MB	HI-A	20	410	50	24	0	11	57	54	69	2	0	.235/.351/.402	124	.259	-3.6	C(91) 2.8	2.7
2021 FS	CHC	MLB	22	600	60	27	1	16	62	37	156	2	0	.216/.276/.364	74	.270	-0.1	C 1, 1B 0	0.5
2021 DC	CHC	MLB	22	136	13	6	0	3	14	8	35	0	0	.216/.276/.364	74	.270	0.0	C 0	0.1

Comparables: Austin Hedges, Alejandro Kirk, Luis Campusano

The Report: In 2019, 20 catchers were worth between 1.5 and 3.0 WARP. Broadly speaking that would be your Role 45-55 catcher tier. You'll find the odd over-performing backup or half-timer—a Will Smith breakout debut mixed in as well—but it's mostly full-time starters. And among that group there's no clear type. Danny Jansen was a defensive specialist with an 82 DRC+, a reverse of his prospect profile. Omar Narváez and Gary Sánchez carried big sticks, but struggled with the defensive load. Robinson Chirinos was pretty average at everything, which of course made him an above-average catcher.

We are writing Amaya as an OFP 60, which means he's likely to fall into that 1.5-3 win group more years than not. What type will he be? Oh, maybe like the good, but declining Yan Gomes seasons. Enough hit tool to get enough of the plus raw pop into play, a solid but not plus-level defender, OBPs that flirt with .300. Amaya does enough things well that you'd expect one of them to stand out enough to make him a solid everyday catcher, but catchers are weird and it's hard to say what that carrying tool will be yet. It's also easy to guess wrong. And there's a chance he stays pretty good at enough stuff to hit that OFP.

Development Track: Amaya spent the summer at the alternate site, mostly because he is quite a good prospect, but also because you always need extra catchers. The quality of arms he would have been facing was broadly Double-A quality or better, so he might be closer to the majors than you'd think for a prospect with no upper minors experience. The reports don't suggest a big move for the profile one way or the other.

Variance: High. Catchers are weird. We might have learned a fair bit about Amaya in Double-A this year instead here we are still writing "Catchers are weird."

Mark Barry's Fantasy Take: *takes a drag of a cigarette, somehow everything is in black and white*

I remember when I liked catching prospects. It was a couple of weeks ago. Amaya is a great real-life catching prospect, but the fantasy variance behind the plate and the ability to find average-ish production on the waiver wire keep him out of my top-200.

5 **Adbert Alzolay** **RHP**   OFP: 55   ETA: Debuted in 2019

Born: 03/01/95   Age: 26   Bats: R   Throws: R   Height: 6'1"   Weight: 208   Origin: International Free Agent, 2012

YEAR	TEAM	LVL	AGE	W	L	SV	G	GS	IP	H	HR	BB/9	K/9	K	GB%	BABIP	WHIP	ERA	DRA-	WARP
2018	IOW	AAA	23	2	4	0	8	8	39²	43	4	2.9	6.1	27	35.1%	.310	1.41	4.76	88	0.6
2019	IOW	AAA	24	2	4	0	15	15	65¹	53	10	4.3	12.5	91	32.1%	.295	1.29	4.41	55	2.5
2019	CHC	MLB	24	1	1	0	4	2	12¹	13	4	6.6	9.5	13	32.4%	.273	1.78	7.30	113	0.0
2020	CHC	MLB	25	1	1	0	6	4	21¹	12	1	5.5	12.2	29	43.2%	.256	1.17	2.95	85	0.4
2021 FS	CHC	MLB	26	9	9	0	26	26	150	132	24	4.5	10.3	171	36.7%	.287	1.37	4.42	99	1.1
2021 DC	CHC	MLB	26	7	7	0	22	22	113	99	18	4.5	10.3	129	36.7%	.287	1.37	4.42	99	1.2

Comparables: Alex Reyes, Walker Lockett, Jake Faria

The Report: Alzolay has bumped up and down these lists for a while, ranking as high as No. 1 in the system and No. 95 on the Top 101 three years ago. The report has never really changed much—plus mid-90s fastball, plus breaking ball (sometimes two), enough change to start—but we've wavered back and forth on whether injuries and command would ultimately limit him to the bullpen.

Development Track: I'm not actually sure 2020 answered those questions in the way we would've liked. Alzolay pitched well in the majors when called upon as an up-and-down swingman type. But he never made it through the order more than twice, and between the short season and his usage we didn't really get any more of an idea if he's a starter or not. The stuff will play in any role, at least.

Variance: Medium. It already looked right in The Show, he just needs to find the right role.

Mark Barry's Fantasy Take: I think Alzolay is probably that guy who gets called on to start games on short notice, but otherwise is a solid multi-inning reliever. He can definitely be useful in that role, but it's not a spot that I would spend a lot of roster capital to fill.

6 Christopher Morel 3B   OFP: 55   ETA: Late 2022/Early 2023

Born: 06/24/99 Age: 22 Bats: R Throws: R Height: 6'0" Weight: 140 Origin: International Free Agent, 2015

YEAR	TEAM	LVL	AGE	PA	R	2B	3B	HR	RBI	BB	K	SB	CS	AVG/OBP/SLG	DRC+	BABIP	BRR	FRAA	WARP
2018	CUBB	ROK	19	128	20	6	0	2	12	11	28	1	4	.257/.331/.363		.321			
2018	EUG	SS	19	93	7	2	0	1	8	0	29	0	1	.165/.172/.220	-5	.226	1.7	3B(17) -2.1, SS(6) -0.7	-1.1
2019	SB	LO-A	20	278	36	15	7	6	31	11	60	9	6	.284/.320/.467	112	.345	0.2	3B(72) 2.2, LF(1) 0.4	1.6
2021 FS	CHC	MLB	22	600	49	26	3	11	56	34	190	16	9	.211/.263/.333	61	.299	-6.9	3B 3, SS -1	-2.0

Comparables: Tyler Goeddel, Jesmuel Valentín, Dustin Fowler

The Report: Morel found his way onto the back end of our 2020 Cubs list based on his slick fielding ability and knack for barreling up pitches. He was beginning to catch fire at South Bend, slashing .364/.395/.584 in the second half of 2019, before being sidelined with a fractured knee. The glove is arguably the best in the organization, strong enough for short but potentially elite at third. Offensively, he's still a work in progress, but there's enough potential to project a future major league regular.

Development Track: It was somewhat surprising to see Morel included on the Cubs' alternative site roster due to his relative inexperience. However, the reports from South Bend were glowing about his development. Swing adjustments and physical growth reportedly made for some loud contact and big exit velocity numbers. If the bat is finally catching up, Morel could be on the fast track to Wrigley.

Variance: Medium. Even if the reported offensive strides are a mirage, the glove should be good enough to make him a major league regular.

Mark Barry's Fantasy Take: It would be lovely if Morel's bat caught up to his glove, as his glove is quite good. I wouldn't expect the market for him to be robust right now, so I'd toss him on your watchlist and keep an eye on his first few games. If he's raking, scoop him up before the rest of your league mates know what hit 'em.

7 Kohl Franklin RHP   OFP: 55   ETA: 2024

Born: 09/09/99 Age: 21 Bats: R Throws: R Height: 6'4" Weight: 190 Origin: Round 6, 2018 Draft (#188 overall)

YEAR	TEAM	LVL	AGE	W	L	SV	G	GS	IP	H	HR	BB/9	K/9	K	GB%	BABIP	WHIP	ERA	DRA-	WARP
2018	CUBR	ROK	18	0	1	0	5	3	8²	5	0	6.2	8.3	8	33.3%	.208	1.27	6.23		
2019	EUG	SS	19	1	3	0	10	10	39	31	2	3.2	11.3	49	46.9%	.305	1.15	2.31	68	0.9
2021 FS	CHC	MLB	21	2	3	0	57	0	50	48	8	6.2	8.6	47	38.6%	.291	1.66	5.73	130	-0.7

Comparables: Miguel Castro, Robert Gsellman, Edgar Olmos

The Report: Franklin had a small breakout in 2019, adding some good weight, some good velocity, and flashing a plus breaking ball. Everything was lined up well for him to have a bigger breakout in 2020 in full-season ball and perhaps move himself into 101 contention and the upper echelon of the system.

Development Track: Franklin wasn't included in the alternate site or instructional league roster. So we have little actionable info. He's hardly the only prospect in this boat, but it's particularly annoying given the shallowness of the Cubs' system.

Variance: High. 2020 is a lost developmental year and the risks here were already on the high side.

Mark Barry's Fantasy Take: Last season, Ben mentioned that we were a year away from really knowing Franklin's fantasy value. So, about that ... it's not ideal, but it also means we're all in the same boat as far as Franklin's development is concerned.

8 Ryan Jensen RHP

OFP: 55   ETA: 2022 as a reliever, 2023 as a starter

Born: 11/23/97   Age: 23   Bats: R   Throws: R   Height: 6'0"   Weight: 180   Origin: Round 1, 2019 Draft (#27 overall)

YEAR	TEAM	LVL	AGE	W	L	SV	G	GS	IP	H	HR	BB/9	K/9	K	GB%	BABIP	WHIP	ERA	DRA-	WARP
2019	EUG	SS	21	0	0	0	6	6	12	7	0	10.5	14.2	19	68.2%	.318	1.75	2.25	141	-0.2
2021 FS	CHC	MLB	23	2	3	0	57	0	50	48	8	8.6	9.2	51	44.9%	.292	1.92	6.82	146	-1.2

Comparables: Dillon Tate, Spencer Turnbull, Humberto Mejía

The Report: Jensen had a dominant junior season at Fresno State on the back of his explosive fastball/slider combo, but it was his only college season as a full-time starter and the only one where he was able to tame his high-effort mechanics from a command and control standpoint. There was significant reliever risk given the size and delivery—and the needed changeup development—but the Cubs appeared to see him as a starter, and the stuff should have dominated A-ball in 2020, but well, you know.

Development Track: Jensen wasn't included in the alternate site or instructional league roster. So we have little actionable info. He's hardly the only prospect in this boat, but it's particularly annoying given the shallowness of the Cubs system.

Variance: High. There was significant profile risk coming out of college, and you would have liked to have Jensen just work on his changeup in real games for a year. He could move quickly as a reliever but everything is an open-ended question until April 2021.

Mark Barry's Fantasy Take: What's the expression about square pegs in round holes? That you don't need to worry about them in a fantasy sense unless they turn into round pegs?

9 Yohendrick Pinango OF

OFP: 55   ETA: 2025

Born: 05/07/02   Age: 19   Bats: L   Throws: L   Height: 5'11"   Weight: 170   Origin: International Free Agent, 2018

YEAR	TEAM	LVL	AGE	PA	R	2B	3B	HR	RBI	BB	K	SB	CS	AVG/OBP/SLG	DRC+	BABIP	BRR	FRAA	WARP
2019	DSL CUBB	ROK	17	274	43	20	0	0	36	27	20	27	7	.358/.427/.442		.386			

The Report: Pinango wasn't the biggest name or biggest bonus out of the Cubs 2018 IFA class, but he may be the most advanced hitter at present.

Development Track: Pinango was one of the youngest Cubs in Mesa for instructs, and he acquitted himself well, showing advanced bat-to-ball skills and hard contact against higher-level arms, although the swing isn't currently geared for power. Pinango has played mostly corner outfield so far, although the team believes with more time in a pro strength and conditioning program he could work himself into a passable center fielder.

Variance: Extreme. He hasn't played outside of a complex and might be a corner outfielder who hasn't started lifting the ball yet. The hitting ability suggests he isn't a mere lottery ticket, but everything in the profile is a long way from actualizing.

Mark Barry's Fantasy Take: While his name might suggest a star Quidditch player for the Chudley Cannons, I'm intrigued by Pinango and his contact ability. He's one for the watchlist right now, but he's a teenage-J2 guy putting up gaudy stolen base numbers, so he'll be super trendy if he hits early. You'll need to move fast.

10 Burl Carraway LHP

OFP: 55   ETA: 2021

Born: 05/27/99   Age: 22   Bats: L   Throws: L   Height: 6'0"   Weight: 173   Origin: Round 2, 2020 Draft (#51 overall)

The Report: Prior to the 2020 draft, one Texas-area scout said Carraway would be the first player in the class to make it to the big leagues. Even though a different power lefty playing on the South Side of Chicago officially holds that title, Carraway is still viewed by many as a quick-moving reliever who should crack the Cubs' bullpen sooner rather than later. Not the biggest guy you see with a power fastball, he manages to get good plane on the mid-to-high 90s pitch thanks to an over-the-top slot. Paired with a big bending curveball, the two-pitch mix with plus grades should function well in high leverage situations provided the command improves.

Development Track: It certainly is swing-and-miss stuff, with the clear areas of improvement being command of the curveball and control of the fastball. He can get away with attacking hitters earlier in the count to get ahead, then finishing off the plate to get hitters to chase. Where he gets into trouble is getting behind in the count and having to make higher quality pitches. If he shows he can limit the free passes he will be knocking on the door of the Wrigley Field home clubhouse in no time.

Variance: High. The fastball/curve combo is so good you don't want to sacrifice too much of the dynamic nature of the pitches to shift a gear down for a better idea where it's going.

Mark Barry's Fantasy Take: The question with Carraway will be whether he can strike out enough guys to stay useful without saves, or multiple-inning outings. It's possible, but it's an awfully small needle to thread. I'll pass.

The Prospects You Meet Outside The Top Ten:

High upside, but a ways away

Rafael Morel SS   Born: 11/22/01   Age: 19   Bats: R   Throws: R   Height: 5'11"   Weight: 165   Origin: International Free Agent, 2018

YEAR	TEAM	LVL	AGE	PA	R	2B	3B	HR	RBI	BB	K	SB	CS	AVG/OBP/SLG	DRC+	BABIP	BRR	FRAA	WARP
2019	DSL CUBB	ROK	17	268	50	16	5	4	32	26	38	23	9	.283/.373/.448		.319			

The Cubs signed the younger Morel brother in the summer of 2018, out of the Dominican Republic for $850,000. Thinly built, Rafael mirrors older brother Chris' prowess on the left side of the diamond and with his ability to make contact. He currently lacks for pop offensively but his feel for hitting and ability to stick at short will buy him time for it to develop.

Interesting draft follows

Jordan Nwogu   Born: 03/10/99   Age: 22   Bats: R   Throws: R   Height: 6'3"   Weight: 235   Origin: Round 3, 2020 Draft (#88 overall)

Featuring the type of frame and strength you wish you could clone for every outfielder, Nwogu has first-round tools. He wasn't selected until the third round because his swing mechanics are a work-in-progress (to put it lightly) that were in a constant state of flux during his time at the University of Michigan. Once in the hitting lab with his new coaches, he'll need to find a comfortable setup that maximizes his ability to hit the ball hard, getting him shorter to the ball with better hand placement and no wasted movement.

Luke Little   Born: 08/30/00   Age: 20   Bats: L   Throws: L   Height: 6'8"   Weight: 225   Origin: Round 4, 2020 Draft (#117 overall)

Little was a little-known junior college pitcher committed to South Carolina when he hit 105 in May. Granted, it was an indoor bullpen session with a Pocket Radar, so not exactly game conditions, and he walked nearly a batter an inning during his junior college career, mostly out of the 'pen. But still, 105 is 105, and when it's coming from a 6-foot-8 left…

Top Talents 25 and Under (as of 4/1/2021):

1. Brailyn Marquez, LHP
2. Brennen Davis, OF
3. Nico Hoerner, 2B/SS
4. Ed Howard, SS
5. Miguel Amaya, C
6. Christopher Morel, 3B
7. Kohl Franklin, RHP
8. Ryan Jense, RHP
9. Yohendrick Pinango, OF
10. Burl Carraway, LHP

Just one shout here, but it's a pretty good one. Nico Hoerner was the top prospect in this system and No. 41 in baseball last year. He almost retained prospect eligibility this year, so we did some initial evaluation work on him. We're moderately concerned that his hit tool didn't show up much at all in 2020. We never expected big power out of the profile, but we did expect more than four extra-base hits in 126 plate appearances. It was a weird season where he didn't truly get regular playing time and bounced around the diamond, but we did think he was more ready than he looked and his stock is down a bit. We're still cautiously optimistic overall, though.

Chicago White Sox

The State of the System:

It's a good thing the White Sox have one of the best and most dynamic lineups in baseball, because this is a very pitching heavy system now.

The Top Ten:

1 | **Nick Madrigal 2B** OFP: 60 ETA: Debuted in 2020
Born: 03/05/97 Age: 24 Bats: R Throws: R Height: 5'8" Weight: 175 Origin: Round 1, 2018 Draft (#4 overall)

YEAR	TEAM	LVL	AGE	PA	R	2B	3B	HR	RBI	BB	K	SB	CS	AVG/OBP/SLG	DRC+	BABIP	BRR	FRAA	WARP
2018	WSX	ROK	21	17	2	0	0	0	1	1	0	0	1	.154/.353/.154		.154			
2018	KAN	LO-A	21	49	9	3	0	0	6	1	0	2	2	.341/.347/.409	143	.319	1.1	2B(12) 0.9	0.5
2018	WS	HI-A	21	107	14	4	0	0	9	5	5	6	3	.306/.355/.347	120	.319	0.0	2B(25) -1.8	0.1
2019	WS	HI-A	22	218	20	10	2	2	27	17	6	17	4	.272/.346/.377	114	.269	3.6	2B(41) 3.4	1.6
2019	BIR	AA	22	180	30	11	2	1	16	14	5	14	6	.341/.400/.451	154	.348	0.3	2B(39) 0.1	1.6
2019	CHA	AAA	22	134	26	6	1	1	12	13	5	4	3	.331/.398/.424	102	.336	0.5	2B(28) 1.5	0.6
2020	CHW	MLB	23	109	8	3	0	0	11	4	7	2	1	.340/.376/.369	101	.365	-1.5	2B(29) 1.7	0.4
2021 FS	CHW	MLB	24	600	66	26	2	7	60	34	50	19	8	.301/.352/.399	111	.320	-2.2	2B 3, SS 0	3.2
2021 DC	CHW	MLB	24	540	59	24	2	6	54	31	45	17	7	.301/.352/.399	111	.320	-2.0	2B 3	2.9

Comparables: Breyvic Valera, Jarrett Hoffpauir, Eric Sogard

The Report: How good of a baseball player can you be in the 2020s if you don't hit the ball hard in the air? Madrigal has some of the best contact abilities in the game. He has an elite hit tool, potentially an 80. He's an excellent defensive second baseman, probably skilled enough to play on the other side of the keystone if needed. He runs well. He has more raw power than you'd think given his 20 game power, probably 40 or 45 on balance, and he actually had a 112-mph batted ball in the majors.

In an age where launch angle optimization and exit velocity have become king, Madrigal hits the ball on the ground a whole lot and, on average, not particularly hard. He did not have a single "barrel" as defined by Statcast this year. While there's still the potential for him to at least occasionally start driving the ball in the air, he didn't do it at all in the majors, and that's an upper-bound limitation on his profile unless he actually does hit .340 every year. He's going to single his way into being an awfully good player anyways, but we were already pretty confident of that outcome, and we're less optimistic that gap game power is coming than we were a year ago.

Development Track: Madrigal remains unexpectedly eligible for this list because of a separated shoulder that cost him three-and-a-half weeks around the middle of the season. He had surgery after the season, and he might not be ready for spring training. His slash line was extreme even for his current skill set, owing to a .365 BABIP and a .029 ISO. We'd expect the former to go a bit down and the latter to go a bit up over the longer term even without future adjustments. As ridiculous as this sounds, he might have a little more room for growth in his contact rate, which was "only" 91.2 percent, fourth in the majors for players with 100 or more plate appearances.

Variance: Low, subject to his shoulder not being a long-term concern. If we were still doing our old OFP/likely outcome spread, I'd probably argue for a 60/60 here.

J.P. Breen's Fantasy Take: Some fantasy experts remain skeptical of Madrigal's path to fantasy relevance, but he's a potential #categorycarrier in two troublesome categories: batting average and stolen bases. Madrigal could offer a .300-plus average with 20-plus stolen bases and a boatload of runs. Power is easy to find these days, but average-and-speed guys are not. Madrigal's skill set projects to be incredibly useful—think early-career Jose Altuve, before the power spike.

★ ★ ★ *2021 Top 101 Prospect* **#14** ★ ★ ★

2 Andrew Vaughn 1B

OFP: 60   ETA: Early 2021

Born: 04/03/98   Age: 23   Bats: R   Throws: R   Height: 6'0"   Weight: 215   Origin: Round 1, 2019 Draft (#3 overall)

YEAR	TEAM	LVL	AGE	PA	R	2B	3B	HR	RBI	BB	K	SB	CS	AVG/OBP/SLG	DRC+	BABIP	BRR	FRAA	WARP
2019	WSX	ROK	21	16	3	2	0	1	4	0	3	0	0	.600/.625/.933		.727			
2019	KAN	LO-A	21	103	14	7	0	2	11	14	18	0	0	.253/.388/.410	137	.297	1.2	1B(19) -0.5	0.6
2019	WS	HI-A	21	126	16	8	0	3	21	16	17	0	1	.252/.349/.411	139	.270	-0.3	1B(16) -0.3	0.5
2021 FS	CHW	MLB	23	600	60	26	1	13	58	44	149	0	0	.228/.295/.355	82	.289	-0.4	1B -2	-0.8
2021 DC	CHW	MLB	23	405	40	18	1	8	39	29	100	0	0	.228/.295/.355	82	.289	-0.3	1B -1	-0.3

Comparables: Nick Evans, Max Muncy, Daniel Vogelbach

The Report: Until Spencer Torkelson came around a year later, Vaughn was the highest-drafted college first baseman since the 1990s. (We'll ignore Detroit's suggestion for a moment that Torkelson might really be a third baseman.) Given the industry preference against taking right-handed bat-only players in the top five of the draft, you'd expect Vaughn to be an elite hitting prospect even if you knew absolutely nothing else about him. We're looking at a plus hit tool and plus power, with both of those being light if anything, and one of the best plate approaches of any prospect in the minors. He's a first baseman, occasional fantastical notions about trying third or the outfield aside, so he's going to have to *hit*. And he should.

Development Track: This is one of the reports where we just don't have a lot of fantastically interesting stuff to say about Vaughn's 2020. We got consistently strong reports on his bat from the alternate site at Schaumburg, although he didn't force himself to the majors immediately either. Everything seems perfectly on track, and the White Sox look likely to have plenty of 1B/DH playing time available as soon as he's ready.

Variance: Low. We're pretty confident in this bat.

J.P. Breen's Fantasy Take: Despite posting pedestrian numbers in his professional debut in 2019, Vaughn remains a top-10 dynasty prospect and a top-100 overall dynasty player. He is a potential four-category monster—whether in AVG or OBP leagues—and he should make his big-league debut in 2021. The fact that the White Sox project to be an offensive powerhouse obviously increases his short-term value, but given his glowing scouting reports, Vaughn should be a long-term fantasy stalwart for the foreseeable future. Grab him where you can.

★ ★ ★ *2021 Top 101 Prospect* **#36** ★ ★ ★

3 Garrett Crochet LHP

OFP: 60   ETA: Debuted in 2020

Born: 06/21/99   Age: 22   Bats: L   Throws: L   Height: 6'6"   Weight: 218   Origin: Round 1, 2020 Draft (#11 overall)

YEAR	TEAM	LVL	AGE	W	L	SV	G	GS	IP	H	HR	BB/9	K/9	K	GB%	BABIP	WHIP	ERA	DRA-	WARP
2020	CHW	MLB	21	0	0	0	5	0	6	3	0	0.0	12.0	8	61.5%	.231	0.50	0.00	81	0.1
2021 FS	CHW	MLB	22	9	9	0	26	26	150	145	23	3.7	8.3	137	44.9%	.290	1.38	4.61	106	0.5
2021 DC	CHW	MLB	22	2	3	0	9	9	44	42	6	3.7	8.3	40	44.9%	.290	1.38	4.61	106	0.3

Comparables: Jesús Luzardo, Caleb Ferguson, Luiz Gohara

The Report: In what amounted to a very short amateur track record, Crochet's flashes of dominance could not be overlooked. Starting in only a third of his appearances in college, including just one instance of game action in the spring, the tall, lefty fireballer simply had too much upside to pass up with the 11th-overall pick. Reports last fall indicated his fastball had gained an extra gear up from its already plus velocity, adding some snap to the slider as well. Even the changeup was coming along. With all the arrows trending upward on his projectable frame and present big-league stuff, it was only a minor surprise to see him force his way onto the bullpen late in the season and playoff run. The huge velocity seen in shorter stints is likely to head back into the mid-90s range as he returns to a starter role moving forward and until further notice.

Development Track: With the velo spike came some barking arm troubles, which again flared up in what became the final game of the White Sox season. The amount of power he generates from a short arm action on a lower slot could make starting over a long period of time unmanageable. If that is in fact the case, we all saw just how dominating he was in the late innings. The heater/slider combo is good enough to erase any platoon advantage, however, the increased development of the changeup will help further his case as a future starter beyond any health concerns.

Variance: High. The small sample size is both promising and worrisome.

J.P. Breen's Fantasy Take: With the number of pop-up pitching prospects that annually emerge, as well as the increased value of middle-relief arms in fantasy, Crochet is the type of arm that I value much more highly than most fantasy analysts. If the lefty makes it as a starter or a reliever, he's elite in either role. We're talking an SP2, at least, or an elite closer in the Josh Hader mold. His health remains a gargantuan question mark, but that's always true to some extent with pitching prospects. If I'm going to take up a minor-league roster spot with a pitcher, Crochet is precisely the pitching profile I want to target: the potential fantasy monster. I ain't running a real-life fantasy team after all.

★ ★ ★ *2021 Top 101 Prospect* **#37** ★ ★ ★

---

4 **Michael Kopech** **RHP**   OFP: 60   ETA: Debuted in 2018

Born: 04/30/96   Age: 25   Bats: R   Throws: R   Height: 6'3"   Weight: 225   Origin: Round 1, 2014 Draft (#33 overall)

YEAR	TEAM	LVL	AGE	W	L	SV	G	GS	IP	H	HR	BB/9	K/9	K	GB%	BABIP	WHIP	ERA	DRA-	WARP
2018	CHA	AAA	22	7	7	0	24	24	126¹	101	9	4.3	12.1	170	38.7%	.319	1.27	3.70	105	0.5
2018	CHW	MLB	22	1	1	0	4	4	14¹	20	4	1.3	9.4	15	28.3%	.381	1.53	5.02	152	-0.3
2021 FS	CHW	MLB	25	9	8	0	26	26	150	131	21	5.2	10.3	171	37.2%	.291	1.46	4.66	96	1.4
2021 DC	CHW	MLB	25	5	5	0	102	19	89	78	12	5.2	10.3	101	37.2%	.291	1.46	4.66	96	0.9

Comparables: Trevor Bauer, Henry Owens, Matt Wisler

The Report: It's unusual that we would still be ranking a prospect who debuted in 2018 on our 2021 lists. When it does happen you can usually assume it's a pitcher and Tommy John surgery was involved. Kopech played to the scouting report in his four 2018 outings, mid-90s, high spin heat that touched higher, and a power slider that missed bats. The control gains he showed in the minors continued, at least in those few MLB appearances. He didn't get the chance to convince us he was a starter long term before he tore his UCL, but the stuff will play in any role.

Development Track: Kopech chose not to play in the 2020 season. Besides the completely reasonable concerns about playing in a global pandemic, Kopech was still recovering from Tommy John surgery and would have had a short ramp up. Now he gets a normal offseason and hopefully more normal spring training. For our purposes though, it does limit the information we have about his present stuff. We've chosen to not consider the additional missed year off Tommy John as we really just don't know more than we knew a year ago.

Variance: High. Kopech was major-league-ready pre-surgery, but hasn't thrown a competitive pitch since September 2018.

J.P. Breen's Fantasy Take: Kopech is overrated in re-draft formats and underrated in dynasty circles. The right-hander has too many short-term question marks to be selected in front of guys like Marcus Stroman and James Paxton, which has been true according to early NFBC numbers, but has too much long-term talent to be ranked 100-plus spots behind someone like Nate Pearson on dynasty lists. Kopech has a high-octane fastball-slider combination that misses plenty of bats, and he had shown improvement in his command in the upper minors and the majors before his injury. The problem: The right-hander is coming off Tommy John surgery and hasn't pitched since 2018. Then again, to use someone like Pearson as a comparison, Pearson missed time in 2020 with elbow issues and isn't much less of an injury risk. Kopech is a potential SP2, though he shouldn't be treated as such for those only interested in fantasy production in 2021.

5 **Jared Kelley** **RHP**   OFP: 55   ETA: 2024

Born: 10/03/01   Age: 19   Bats: R   Throws: R   Height: 6'3"   Weight: 215   Origin: Round 2, 2020 Draft (#47 overall)

The Report: As the 2020 draft cycle came into focus, Kelley was in a tight race for the top prep arm in the class and a possible top 10 pick. Unlike many high school players, the early spring season for Texas allowed for further scrutiny that caused many evaluators to soften their opinion. The fastball that was in the mid-to-upper 90s and topping near 100 during the previous summer showcase months dropped a tick and questions about his husky body dropped his stock heading into draft day. One scout referred to him as, "Tyler Kolek with a changeup," which you can interpret however you wish. On the plus side, there were plenty of positive reviews in camp upon signing, signaling the potential steal of a first-round talent in the second.

Development Track: The fastball and changeup, including the command of both pitches, are advanced for his age. What is clearly needed as he transitions to a professional training program is work on his slurvy breaking ball and tightening up the overall physique. That's a pretty solid foundation for a player who was picked apart—perhaps both by sample and recency bias—prior to the draft.

Variance: Extreme. High school pitchers are notoriously risky, especially the strong-armed kind. Enough question marks exist several years down the road to gauge this sort of risk.

J.P. Breen's Fantasy Take: We're now six prospects into this list, and I've officially tapped out. This ain't my bag. Kelley is your prototypical hard-throwing righty about whom we'll know nothing significant for a year or two. If you're in a deep dynasty league, he's worth a dart throw if you love hard-throwing prep arms—the advanced changeup makes him more interesting than most—but I wouldn't advise investing more than a late-round pick in offseason supplemental drafts. You'll be able to find similar arms on the waiver wire or in next year's draft class with little trouble.

6 Jonathan Stiever RHP   OFP: 55   ETA: Debuted in 2020

Born: 05/12/97   Age: 24   Bats: R   Throws: R   Height: 6'2"   Weight: 215   Origin: Round 5, 2018 Draft (#138 overall)

YEAR	TEAM	LVL	AGE	W	L	SV	G	GS	IP	H	HR	BB/9	K/9	K	GB%	BABIP	WHIP	ERA	DRA-	WARP
2018	GTF	ROK	21	0	1	0	13	13	28	23	3	2.9	12.5	39	47.7%	.323	1.14	4.18		
2019	KAN	LO-A	22	4	6	0	14	14	74	88	10	1.7	9.4	77	43.8%	.363	1.38	4.74	123	-0.7
2019	WS	HI-A	22	6	4	0	12	12	71	56	7	1.6	9.8	77	40.4%	.278	0.97	2.15	64	1.7
2020	CHW	MLB	23	0	1	0	2	2	6¹	7	4	5.7	4.3	3	40.9%	.167	1.74	9.95	148	-0.1
2021 FS	CHW	MLB	24	2	2	0	57	0	50	50	8	3.4	7.8	43	40.4%	.287	1.37	4.74	108	-0.1
2021 DC	CHW	MLB	24	2	2	0	25	4	43	43	7	3.4	7.8	37	40.4%	.287	1.37	4.74	108	0.2

Comparables: Beau Burrows, Felix Jorge, Andrew Heaney

The Report: The summer of 2019 saw Stiever go from cold weather fifth-rounder to hot prospect with helium thanks to 71 dominant innings at High-A Winston-Salem. In the Carolina League he showcased a mid-90s fastball and two above-average breaking pitches. Stiever wasn't the perfect starting pitching prospect but he was promising; control over command but with very good control, not racking up all that many strikeouts yet exhibiting swing-and-miss stuff. He's also a good athlete with a repeatable delivery that bodes well for future command gains.

Development Track: There were a couple of concerning trends that cropped up in Stiever's 2020, a season that began with a forearm injury scare and ended with a rocky introduction to the big leagues. The devastating fastball/breaking ball combo that impressed us in 2019 wasn't there when he made his major league debut. The riding fastball that was sitting 94-96 is now running at 92-94, and neither the slider nor the curveball seem to have the bite that they used to. The slider in particular lacks the sharp downward movement that used to distinguish it, and with it most of its swing-and-miss quality. A more encouraging sign is his increasingly viable changeup that would round out a starter's repertoire.

Variance: Medium. The stuff backed up in 2020 but it was an anomalous season in which he was hampered by injury, and it will be interesting to see if it bounces back next spring.

J.P. Breen's Fantasy Take: Stiever's brief cup o' coffee in 2020 was disastrous, but don't hold that against him. The 23-year-old had never thrown a professional inning above High-A before being rocketed to the big leagues, where he had home-run issues, command issues, and bat-missing issues. That performance will ensure that he's available in almost all dynasty formats, either on the waiver wire or via trade, but he's still a potential SP5 who saw his stuff take a step backward in 2020. If your league rosters approximately 250 prospects, he's worth a stash. Dynasty owners in shallower leagues can feel free to move on without a tinge of hesitation.

7 Andrew Dalquist RHP   OFP: 50   ETA: 2024

Born: 11/13/00   Age: 20   Bats: R   Throws: R   Height: 6'1"   Weight: 175   Origin: Round 3, 2019 Draft (#81 overall)

YEAR	TEAM	LVL	AGE	W	L	SV	G	GS	IP	H	HR	BB/9	K/9	K	GB%	BABIP	WHIP	ERA	DRA-	WARP
2019	WSX	ROK	18	0	0	0	3	3	3	2	0	6.0	6.0	2	33.3%	.222	1.33	0.00		
2021 FS	CHW	MLB	20	2	3	0	57	0	50	53	8	5.7	7.3	40	37.5%	.302	1.72	6.24	140	-1.0

Comparables: Juan Minaya, Elvis Luciano, José Torres

The Report: The White Sox took Dalquist as an over-slot prep righty in the third round of the 2019 draft. He was an advanced arm at the time, flashing above-average velocity and working a full four-pitch mix, unusual for even a seven-figure prep.

Development Track: We paired Dalquist with Matthew Thompson on last year's list coming off the 2019 draft, but this year's instructs reports have the California righty showing a more complete arsenal led by a fastball that bumped 96. The curve is the most advanced secondary, but it's a quality overall repertoire, and Dalquist has a better chance to start long term despite lacking Thompson's prototypical size.

Variance: High. There's already four pitches with at least average potential, but Dalquist doesn't have much physical projection or pro experience and is a long ways off from pitching on the South Side.

J.P. Breen's Fantasy Take: A semi-projectable prep righty who is a potential No. 4 starter and had a bit of a velocity bump in instructs? When will one of those ever come around again?! Dalquist is an interesting real-life prospect who has a legit pathway to a useful big-league role in four or five years. For dynasty, the right-hander is just one of a few-dozen projectable teenage arms who could be irrelevant by August. Don't bother for now.

8 Codi Heuer RHP   OFP: 50   ETA: Debuted in 2020

Born: 07/03/96 Age: 25 Bats: R Throws: R Height: 6'5" Weight: 190 Origin: Round 6, 2018 Draft (#168 overall)

YEAR	TEAM	LVL	AGE	W	L	SV	G	GS	IP	H	HR	BB/9	K/9	K	GB%	BABIP	WHIP	ERA	DRA-	WARP
2018	GTF	ROK	21	0	1	0	14	14	38	49	4	3.3	8.3	35	56.3%	.369	1.66	4.74		
2019	WS	HI-A	22	4	1	2	20	0	38¹	34	0	1.9	10.1	43	61.9%	.327	1.10	2.82	73	0.5
2019	BIR	AA	22	2	3	9	22	0	29¹	25	0	2.1	6.8	22	59.8%	.298	1.09	1.84	77	0.3
2020	CHW	MLB	23	3	0	1	21	0	23²	12	1	3.4	9.5	25	50.0%	.193	0.89	1.52	84	0.4
2021 FS	CHW	MLB	24	2	2	4	57	0	50	46	6	4.0	8.3	46	51.4%	.285	1.37	4.22	98	0.2
2021 DC	CHW	MLB	24	2	2	4	52	0	55	50	7	4.0	8.3	51	51.4%	.285	1.37	4.22	98	0.4

Comparables: Alex Claudio, Michael Tonkin, Keynan Middleton

The Report: Heuer went from nondescript starting prospect to high-leverage big league reliever in two seasons thanks to his nasty sinker and deceptive sidearm delivery. His slider flashes plus and is a useful swing-and-miss pitch against both righties and lefties, and he's fared well against both despite initially profiling as more of a right-on-right specialist. His changeup is also viable, if seldom used. Heuer's top-line numbers outpaced his peripherals in his first big league campaign, but even if he regresses a bit he should still be a key cog in the White Sox 'pen for the near term.

Development Track: It's possible he's just about reached his final form, but Heuer could rise on the bullpen depth chart if he refines his command and works to get more consistent results with his secondaries.

Variance: Low. He was a reliable arm out of the 'pen last season and there's nothing indicating that this should be a fluke.

J.P. Breen's Fantasy Take: Our own Mike Gianella has been highlighting the unheralded value of big-league middle relievers in recent weeks. Heuer is worth tracking, as he posted a 14.4 percent swinging-strike rate and gets tons of groundballs. His BABIP should rise going forward, obviously, but we're still talking about a potential late-inning reliever who strikes out more than a batter per inning with decent rates. He needs to refine his command; however, Heuer is closer to fantasy relevance than the previous three prospects. Just remember that Heuer is a potential waiver-wire grab, not someone to target in drafts. There are too many Heuers in Major League Baseball these days to waste draft picks on him.

9 Jimmy Lambert RHP   OFP: 50   ETA: Debuted in 2020

Born: 11/18/94 Age: 26 Bats: R Throws: R Height: 6'2" Weight: 190 Origin: Round 5, 2016 Draft (#146 overall)

YEAR	TEAM	LVL	AGE	W	L	SV	G	GS	IP	H	HR	BB/9	K/9	K	GB%	BABIP	WHIP	ERA	DRA-	WARP
2018	WS	HI-A	23	5	7	0	13	13	70²	57	5	2.7	10.2	80	39.9%	.301	1.10	3.95	67	1.8
2018	BIR	AA	23	3	1	0	5	5	25	20	2	2.2	10.8	30	40.0%	.286	1.04	2.88	56	0.8
2019	BIR	AA	24	3	4	0	11	11	59¹	62	11	4.1	10.6	70	37.0%	.338	1.50	4.55	114	-0.4
2020	CHW	MLB	25	0	0	0	2	0	2	2	0	0.0	9.0	2	33.3%	.333	1.00	0.00	100	0.0
2021 FS	CHW	MLB	26	1	1	0	57	0	50	48	8	3.6	8.8	48	36.7%	.289	1.37	4.63	106	0.0
2021 DC	CHW	MLB	26	1	1	0	13	3	25	24	4	3.6	8.8	24	36.7%	.289	1.37	4.63	106	0.1

Comparables: Sterling Sharp, Patrick Murphy, Brandon Woodruff

The Report / Development Track: Lambert was closing in on the majors when he had Tommy John surgery in summer 2019. We were a bit surprised to see him show back up in the majors to start 2020; in last offseason's list we predicted he'd miss most or all of the season. He threw in two games in July and promptly missed the rest of the season with a flexor strain, which is often related to UCL problems. He's got swing-and-miss stuff, four pitches that can come in at average-to-above from a deceptively high arm slot. The flip side is that he just turned 26 and hasn't even come close to establishing himself as a big-league starter yet. We think he can be an effective MLB pitcher in 2021, we're just not sure in what role he'll hold up in.

Variance: High. On the one hand, he's major-league-ready. On the other hand, he's had Tommy John and a subsequent elbow issue.

J.P. Breen's Fantasy Take: A potential back-end starter who has a history of elbow problems and maybe an elbow problem right now. He'll be on the waiver wire in your dynasty league. If you need pitching, grab him off waivers if he's healthy and in the majors in 2021. Otherwise, don't bother.

10 Matthew Thompson RHP   OFP: 50   ETA: 2024

Born: 08/11/00   Age: 20   Bats: R   Throws: R   Height: 6'3"   Weight: 195   Origin: Round 2, 2019 Draft (#45 overall)

YEAR	TEAM	LVL	AGE	W	L	SV	G	GS	IP	H	HR	BB/9	K/9	K	GB%	BABIP	WHIP	ERA	DRA-	WARP
2019	WSX	ROK	18	0	0	0	2	2	2	2	0	0.0	9.0	2	33.3%	.333	1.00	0.00		
2021 FS	CHW	MLB	20	2	3	0	57	0	50	53	8	5.5	7.5	41	38.2%	.304	1.68	6.10	140	-1.0

Comparables: Nick Adenhart, Will Smith, Elvis Luciano

The Report / Development Track: We paired Thompson and Dalquist on last year's list, and while the latter has moved ahead in 2020, Thompson is a good pitching prospect in his own right, although there were concerns about how much more physicality he will add to his frame, and his fastball velocity was a couple ticks behind Dalquist in the complex. The breaking ball has improved enough that there's a useful reliever role fallback now. As I wrote last year, the story on those two prep arms is far from finished. Check back again next year after both have spent time in full-season ball.

Variance: High. It's a relatively advanced breaking ball, but Thompson hasn't advanced through the minors much

J.P. Breen's Fantasy Take: Thompson can be categorized with the other highly volatile prep pitchers ... except his velocity already fluctuates a ton. More has to go right here than with most high-school hurlers, which means he's not a top-400 dynasty prospect.

The Prospects You Meet Outside The Top Ten:

Safe MLB bats, but less upside than you'd like

Blake Rutherford RF   Born: 05/02/97   Age: 24   Bats: L   Throws: R   Height: 6'3"   Weight: 210   Origin: Round 1, 2016 Draft (#18 overall)

YEAR	TEAM	LVL	AGE	PA	R	2B	3B	HR	RBI	BB	K	SB	CS	AVG/OBP/SLG	DRC+	BABIP	BRR	FRAA	WARP
2018	WS	HI-A	21	487	67	25	9	7	78	34	90	15	8	.293/.345/.436	120	.351	1.1	RF(73) -2.5, LF(15) -2.7, CF(13) -1.4	0.4
2019	BIR	AA	22	480	50	17	3	7	49	37	117	9	2	.265/.319/.365	95	.342	2.4	RF(68) 1.7, LF(29) -1.7, CF(1) -0.1	1.0
2021 FS	CHW	MLB	24	600	58	24	3	11	57	41	172	4	1	.228/.284/.348	74	.309	1.4	LF -16, CF 0	-1.9
2021 DC	CHW	MLB	24	33	3	1	0	0	3	2	9	0	0	.228/.284/.348	74	.309	0.1	LF -1	-0.1

Comparables: Jorge Bonifacio, Daniel Johnson, Bronson Sardinha

Rutherford remains tied in my mind to a different org's center fielder. He and Mickey Moniak were both sure-shot bats among the prep outfield class of 2016. Rutherford didn't have the albatross of "first overall pick" hanging over his development track, but like Moniak he's never really hit as much as the amateur reports prophesied. There were suggestions of some power improvements at the alternate site this year, but like Moniak he might end up "just" a bench outfielder.

Personal Cheeseball, sort of

Jake Burger 3B   Born: 04/10/96   Age: 25   Bats: R   Throws: R   Height: 6'2"   Weight: 210   Origin: Round 1, 2017 Draft (#11 overall)

Comparables: Kelvin Gutierrez, Ty Kelly, Rangel Ravelo

Burger finally made it back on the field after two Achilles tears wiped out his 2018 and 2019 seasons. He spent some time in the CarShield Collegiate Summer League, the alternate site in Schaumberg, and White Sox instructs. Third base isn't really an option anymore, but the plus-plus bat speed and power are still present. It would be a great story if he can make it to the majors, and we aren't gonna bet against the bat even now.

Some upside, but a ways away

Bryan Ramos 3B   Born: 03/12/02   Age: 19   Bats: R   Throws: R   Height: 6'2"   Weight: 190   Origin: International Free Agent, 2018

YEAR	TEAM	LVL	AGE	PA	R	2B	3B	HR	RBI	BB	K	SB	CS	AVG/OBP/SLG	DRC+	BABIP	BRR	FRAA	WARP
2019	WSX	ROK	17	218	36	10	2	4	26	19	44	3	4	.277/.353/.415		.331			
2021 FS	CHW	MLB	19	600	45	26	2	6	48	30	199	5	3	.215/.262/.306	56	.321	-3.1	3B 1, 1B 0	-2.5

Comparables: Lane Thomas, Dilson Herrera, Renato Núñez

The White Sox no longer have a system overflowing with high-upside, high-dollar IFAs, but Ramos—signed for $300k in 2018—can really hit. He'll need to given the corner profile, but the bat stood out in Camelback.

Top Talents 25 and Under (as of 4/1/2021):

1. Yoán Moncada, 3B
2. Eloy Jiménez, OF
3. Luis Robert, OF
4. Nick Madrigal, 2B
5. Andrew Vaughn, 1B
6. Garrett Crochet, LHP
7. Michael Kopech, RHP
8. Dane Dunning, RHP
9. Dylan Cease, RHP
10. Jared Kelley, RHP

The White Sox have three recently-graduated global top 10 prospects, so this is a pretty loaded 25-and-under list. Yoán Moncada topped this list last year, and tops it again this year. At points during and after the season Moncada mentioned battling long-term health issues stemming from a summer bout with COVID-19; given that, talking about his on-field performance seems trite and irrelevant. One only has to go back to 2019 to see a sensational campaign from our 2017 No. 5 prospect, and we hope he'll get back to that moving forward.

Of the recent White Sox list graduates, Eloy Jiménez's development has been the most linear in the majors. Our 2019 No. 4 prospect showed up in 2019 after signing a pre-debut arbitration buyout and was more or less immediately the player we expected him to be: a plus hitter who is getting to nearly all of his 80-grade power in games. He doesn't walk a lot or play defense well, but if you can hit for as much average and power as Jiménez does, it doesn't matter a whole lot.

Luis Robert looked like an emerging superstar early on in the majors. Last year's No. 6 prospect showed enormous power and Gold Glove defense in his debut, and at times flashed enough hit tool and plate approach to hold up as the total package. At other times, contact completely eluded him; he hit .137 with a 34 percent strikeout rate in September. Robert will need to make adjustments, especially against same-side pitching, but all-in-all there were more positives than negatives to take away from his debut.

Dylan Cease was quite a prospect in his own right, topping out at No. 26 on the 2019 Top 101. He has struggled to throw strikes in the majors, and struggled to fool batters as well in 2020, leading to a 7.36 DRA lurking behind his superficially impressive 4.01 ERA. Cease's stuff is too good to be this bad, but we're starting to think about wanting to see what this looks like in relief again.

Nomar Mazara is somehow still eligible for this list as well. Our 2016 No. 5 prospect sure looks like he peaked before he ever hit the majors. He's heading towards a non-tender this winter after the White Sox failed to kickstart his stalled offensive development.

Cincinnati Reds

The State of the System:

The Reds' system feels like a bit of a hodgepodge of player types, a mishmash of developmental preferences, but it's a fairly deep system at least.

The Top Ten:

★ ★ ★ *2021 Top 101 Prospect* **#57** ★ ★ ★

1 **Nick Lodolo** **LHP**   OFP: 60   ETA: 2022, maybe late 2021 if necessary
Born: 02/05/98   Age: 23   Bats: L   Throws: L   Height: 6'6"   Weight: 205   Origin: Round 1, 2019 Draft (#7 overall)

YEAR	TEAM	LVL	AGE	W	L	SV	G	GS	IP	H	HR	BB/9	K/9	K	GB%	BABIP	WHIP	ERA	DRA-	WARP
2019	BIL	ROK+	21	0	1	0	6	6	11¹	12	1	0.0	16.7	21	32.0%	.458	1.06	2.38		
2019	DAY	LO-A	21	0	0	0	2	2	7	6	0	0.0	11.6	9	50.0%	.333	0.86	2.57	69	0.1
2021 FS	CIN	MLB	23	2	3	0	57	0	50	50	8	4.3	7.9	43	38.2%	.296	1.49	5.13	121	-0.5

Comparables: Patrick Sandoval, Cristian Javier, Kris Bubic

The Report: A well-regarded SoCal prep arm out of high school, Lodolo spurned the Pirates in 2016 as the 41st-overall pick and instead attended TCU. The tall, lanky lefty had mixed success his first two years, finally filling out and taking off in his junior season. With a fastball that sits comfortably in the low-to-mid 90s, his repeatable delivery allows for very good command of all his pitches, making each of the individual pitch grades play up. His breaking ball can be manipulated to be a short slider or more slurvy with downer action, while the changeup has good fade and is sold with deceptive arm speed. A workhorse body, clean mechanics, at least three distinct pitches with command of each all equate to a high-end starter worthy of the top 10 selection a year ago.

Development Track: There should be some reluctance to mess too much with a guy who has above-average stuff and can throw quality strikes. If there is one knock against Lodolo, he's never been a "Statcast star" with high spin rates. What he does offer is a wide release point that creates a tough angle to the plate. So while there might be more to unlock with his spin efficiency or tinkering with grips, making sure it's not a significant detriment to what he already does well will be advantageous.

Variance: Medium. There is a fair amount of polish with perhaps a slightly limited ceiling, but you trade that off for an elevated floor.

J.P. Breen's Fantasy Take: Lodolo gets more love in some dynasty circles than his scouting report might warrant, due to his 30-to-zero strikeout-to-walk rate as a professional. He's more of a potential mid-rotation workhorse than a top-end fantasy star, as currently constructed, but that could change with arsenal tweaks or increased spin rates. I love the frame and the high floor, but he's a fringe top-101 dynasty prospect and is on the outside of my personal Top 101.

2 **Austin Hendrick** **CF**   OFP: 60   ETA: 2023
Born: 06/15/01   Age: 20   Bats: L   Throws: L   Height: 6'0"   Weight: 195   Origin: Round 1, 2020 Draft (#12 overall)

The Report: During the big national high school showcases last summer, Hendrick did everything possible to vault himself into the first round as one of the top hitters in the class. Displaying huge raw power from the left side despite standing a listed 6-foot tall, Hendrick is able to generate a ton of bat speed due to his explosive hands. He tends to over-swing, however, causing his mechanics to break down. Pitch recognition might be the issue, as he stays within himself when he's on time. A solid outfielder with enough arm, he profiles best as a future right fielder, but will likely be given a chance to start his pro career in center.

Development Track: Scouts began noticing subtle tweaks to his swing between the high profile all-star events and his travel-ball squad in the fall. Depending on when he was seen, his hand load or stride or foot alignment would be different. Some believed it was a knock against him, others pointed to the fact he was open to coaching and capable of working through new ideas. Either way, his present ability to get natural lift on the ball fits perfectly into the Reds' hitting philosophy, and only needs to find the mechanical tweak that works consistently for him.

Variance: Extreme. Your typical boom-or-bust type who will either slug in the middle of the order or swing-and-miss too much to reach full potential.

J.P. Breen's Fantasy Take: As Gwen Stefani would say, this my s--t, this my s--t. Hendrick possesses some of the best raw power in the minors, but it comes with typical concerns about contact rates and pitch recognition. While I typically advocate shying away from these popular boom-or-bust power hitters, as homers are no longer difficult to obtain on the cheap, I'm a sucker for potential superstars who come from geographic areas that are not baseball powerhouses. When they blossom, it happens in the blink of an eye. Hendrick is one of the few guys outside the top-75 dynasty prospects who has a clear path to becoming a top-25 dynasty prospect with a good few months in 2021.

3 Hunter Greene RHP   OFP: 55   ETA: 2023
Born: 08/06/99   Age: 21   Bats: R   Throws: R   Height: 6'4"   Weight: 215   Origin: Round 1, 2017 Draft (#2 overall)

YEAR	TEAM	LVL	AGE	W	L	SV	G	GS	IP	H	HR	BB/9	K/9	K	GB%	BABIP	WHIP	ERA	DRA-	WARP
2018	DAY	LO-A	18	3	7	0	18	18	68¹	66	6	3.0	11.7	89	42.6%	.355	1.30	4.48	79	1.2

Comparables: Kolby Allard, Roberto Osuna, Jordan Lyles

The Report: Greene was a two-way prospect out of southern California with 1.1 buzz going into the 2017 draft. He ended up going second overall—although received the biggest bonus—and the Reds quickly had him ditch the shortstop's glove to become a full-time moundsman. It wasn't hard to see why. Greene regularly hit triple digits from an athletic, repeatable delivery. He also showed some feel for a slider. Not much has changed since draft day though. Well, one major thing has: He has a new elbow scar from his 2019 Tommy John surgery. The elite arm speed remains, but the fastball runs rather true, and the slider that flashes plus often required him to slow down his arm to really snap it off.

Development Track: Greene was throwing at the alternate site—and getting the fastball back into the high-90s. For a high pick from 2017, he's a ways behind the development curve now due to injury and 2020 being a year where it would be awfully bold of you to fly the Goodyear blimp. None of that really matters if his velocity comes all the way back and the secondaries continue to improve—he's added a cutter, and taken quickly to it—but many of the same questions about the profile remain two years later. The good news is he is healthy and throwing without restrictions.

Variance: High. Given the injury and missed development time, Greene could still go in a number of directions as a prospect. While this is true of all prospects that dealt with a functionally lost season, it's especially true of Greene: We'll know a lot more after 2021.

J.P. Breen's Fantasy Take: The name of the dynasty game with minor-league starters is upside. Given that, I'd rather have Greene than Lodolo in standard dynasty leagues. If the velocity returns and the new cutter is as legit as it sounds, Greene has SP2 projection with room for more. While the injury risk is real and the variance in ultimate outcomes is extreme, there are few pitching prospects with the top-end upside that Greene boasts. That's all I care about.

4 Tyler Stephenson C   OFP: 55   ETA: Debuted in 2020

Born: 08/16/96 Age: 24 Bats: R Throws: R Height: 6'4" Weight: 225 Origin: Round 1, 2015 Draft (#11 overall)

YEAR	TEAM	LVL	AGE	PA	R	2B	3B	HR	RBI	BB	K	SB	CS	AVG/OBP/SLG	DRC+	BABIP	BRR	FRAA	WARP
2018	DAY	HI-A	21	450	60	20	1	11	59	45	98	1	0	.250/.338/.392	116	.301	0.2	C(97) -3.3	1.5
2019	CHA	AA	22	363	47	19	1	6	44	37	60	0	0	.285/.372/.410	128	.331	-2.1	C(87) -11.8	1.3
2020	CIN	MLB	23	20	4	0	0	2	6	2	9	0	0	.294/.400/.647	80	.500	-0.0	C(4) -0.0	0.0
2021 FS	CIN	MLB	24	600	60	23	1	18	62	49	184	0	0	.229/.302/.378	85	.312	-0.4	C 1	1.4
2021 DC	CIN	MLB	24	273	27	10	0	8	28	22	83	0	0	.229/.302/.378	85	.312	-0.2	C 1, 1B 0	0.5

Comparables: Jason Castro, Alex Avila, Christian Vázquez

The Report: We've been writing about Stephenson for more than half a decade now. The good news is we are no longer writing about his injury issues, and the healthy seasons now outnumber the IL-plagued ones. He remains on the larger side for a catcher with commensurate defensive concerns. The arm strength is average but he can be slow to get the ball out. His receiving has improved, but he'll never be super flexible or athletic behind the plate. He projects well enough defensively that you will want to get his bat into the lineup if it plays to the 50 hit, 55 power baked into his OFP below.

Development Track: Stephenson made his major-league debut in 2020 while Tucker Barnhart was on paternity leave. He left quite the impression in his brief appearance. It was a Third Wave Japanese Siphon Machine cup of joe, as he popped two home runs in just 20 plate appearances—including a massive bomb to center in his first major-league at-bat. He also struck out nine times, so you can't exactly say the hit tool concerns have been assuaged, but you can't really say anything about 20 plate appearances. Curt Casali is a trendy trade/non-tender candidate this offseason, so Stephenson could find himself with a relatively clean shot at a time share with Gold Glover Barnhart. He is very unlikely to be as good a defender, but he might be good enough back there to justify getting the bat in the lineup 4-5 days a week.

Variance: Medium. The bat looks major-league ready, but the jury will remain out on the glove until he gets a longer look in Triple-A or our new robot ump overlords arrive.

J.P. Breen's Fantasy Take: The scouting reports have long referenced Stephenson's raw power. However, it has rarely shown up in games. Prior to 2020, the 24-year-old had never clubbed more than 11 homers in a season, and his highest ISO (min. 100 PA) was .142. Although he showed some massive power in his brief big-league debut in 2020, it came with significant swing-and-miss issues. We're left with questions about Stephenson's hit tool and his in-game power. Thus, Stephenson is not a top-500 dynasty guy at this point, especially without a path to short-term playing time, but his proximity to the big leagues probably makes him worth a stash in leagues that roster 200-plus prospects.

5 Jose Garcia SS   OFP: 55   ETA: Debuted in 2020, might be best if you see him again in 2022

Born: 04/05/98 Age: 23 Bats: R Throws: R Height: 6'2" Weight: 175 Origin: International Free Agent, 2017

YEAR	TEAM	LVL	AGE	PA	R	2B	3B	HR	RBI	BB	K	SB	CS	AVG/OBP/SLG	DRC+	BABIP	BRR	FRAA	WARP
2018	DAY	LO-A	20	517	61	22	4	6	53	19	112	13	9	.245/.290/.344	84	.307	1.8	SS(93) -0.7, 2B(29) -1.8	0.3
2019	DAY	HI-A	21	452	58	37	1	8	55	25	83	15	2	.280/.343/.436	143	.329	-0.8	SS(100) 0.7	3.8
2020	CIN	MLB	22	68	4	0	0	0	2	1	26	1	1	.194/.206/.194	45	.317	-0.8	SS(21) 1.3	-0.2
2021 FS	CIN	MLB	23	600	54	22	2	12	56	31	191	7	3	.217/.271/.332	64	.306	-0.8	SS 1, 2B 0	-0.7
2021 DC	CIN	MLB	23	410	37	15	1	8	38	21	130	5	2	.217/.271/.332	64	.306	-0.6	SS 1	-0.5

Comparables: Chris Nelson, Marcus Semien, Gleyber Torres

The Report: Signed out of Cuba as a teenager, Garcia was on a fairly normal development track that featured a breakout 2019 that left him just off last year's Top 101. The bat caught up with the glove in Daytona, although he didn't (and doesn't) project for much power due to an approach that is contact-heavy over loft. The defense isn't spectacular at shortstop, but Garcia does everything well. He's rangy with good hands and has a strong arm that is accurate on the move.

Development Track: Perhaps the Reds called Garcia up this year because they were hoping he would give their rather anemic 2020 lineup a spark beyond what Freddy Galvis and Kyle Farmer had offered. That was a fairly large ask of a glove-over-bat prospect who hadn't seen a single plate appearance in the upper minors. And indeed, Garcia looked like he was just trying to stay above water, prioritizing contact of any sort over driving the ball, and not even making that much contact. He looked overmatched and his swing was mechanical. None of this is a death knell to an above-average projection, and I don't even know that he's a markedly different prospect than he was at this time last year. The bat just wasn't major-league ready. His glove was more or less as advertised, though.

Variance: High. It's unusual that we are putting high variance on a prospect who already debuted in the majors, but most prospects don't jump right from the Florida State League to the bigs. It's not a surprise Garcia was overwhelmed at the plate, but his track record of hitting in the minors isn't particularly long either. It's not a long-term worry, but he will need more consolidation time in Double- and/or Triple-A despite the Reds having an opening for a 2021 shortstop.

J.P. Breen's Fantasy Take: Some dynasty owners adore Garcia, arguing that he possesses more power potential than his numbers have shown to this point. For my money, I am confident in neither his power nor his approach. His walk rates perennially have been low, and his brief big-league appearance did nothing to assuage those concerns. While he's not a top-100 dynasty prospect, his glove-and-speed combo gives him a reasonable dynasty floor. He's comfortably in the Top 150.

6 Jonathan India 3B OFP: 55 ETA: 2021

Born: 12/15/96 Age: 24 Bats: R Throws: R Height: 6'0" Weight: 200 Origin: Round 1, 2018 Draft (#5 overall)

YEAR	TEAM	LVL	AGE	PA	R	2B	3B	HR	RBI	BB	K	SB	CS	AVG/OBP/SLG	DRC+	BABIP	BRR	FRAA	WARP
2018	GRN	ROK	21	62	11	2	1	3	12	15	12	1	0	.261/.452/.543		.290			
2018	BIL	ROK	21	10	1	0	0	0	0	0	4	0	1	.250/.400/.250		.500			
2018	DAY	LO-A	21	112	17	7	0	3	11	13	28	5	0	.229/.339/.396	103	.292	1.5	3B(21) 2.4, SS(4) -0.1	0.6
2019	DAY	HI-A	22	367	50	15	5	8	30	37	84	7	5	.256/.346/.410	129	.319	-1.8	3B(74) -9.2, 2B(5) 0.0	1.0
2019	CHA	AA	22	145	24	3	0	3	14	22	26	4	0	.270/.414/.378	141	.314	0.2	3B(33) -0.4	1.1
2021 FS	CIN	MLB	24	600	67	24	2	17	61	62	182	3	1	.225/.322/.384	96	.309	0.9	3B -7, 2B 0	0.3
2021 DC	CIN	MLB	24	68	7	2	0	2	6	7	20	0	0	.225/.322/.384	96	.309	0.1	3B -1	0.0

Comparables: Kyle Kubitza, Kelvin Gutierrez, Ty France

The Report: India's core skills have been steady throughout college and his time in pro ball. He's a good glove on the dirt and has a nice on-base profile in terms of his willingness to take a walk and a decent feel to hit. Unfortunately, other than his college draft year, he hasn't shown nearly the power you'd like to elevate his profile above that of a steady contributor, and it didn't show up in Double-A or the Arizona Fall League, where he should have easily outclassed his competition.

Development Track: His 2019 Double-A numbers are better in some ways than they look—DRC+ reminds us the Southern League is a tough place to hit, and he certainly got on base plenty. We again heard good things about his approach at the alternate site, and evidently he spent the summer adding second base defense to his portfolio. Given the Reds' depth at second and third, it's not necessarily an indictment that India didn't get time in the bigs in 2020. That said, although the college power is theoretically still in there, the longer it goes without manifesting the more concerned we become.

Variance: Medium. He can probably hold down second or third and get on base at a decent clip without any improvement, but the delta on his power output remains significant.

J.P. Breen's Fantasy Take: Unless injuries have continued to mask his power potential, there's nothing exciting about India's fantasy profile. He won't run much. He will struggle to hit 20 homers. Plus, he's never hit above .270 as a professional. It all seems … fine. It's just difficult for me to get excited about a dude whose best-case fantasy scenario seems to be Eduardo Escobar, circa 2015-2018.

7 Tony Santillan RHP OFP: 55 ETA: 2021

Born: 04/15/97 Age: 24 Bats: R Throws: R Height: 6'3" Weight: 240 Origin: Round 2, 2015 Draft (#49 overall)

YEAR	TEAM	LVL	AGE	W	L	SV	G	GS	IP	H	HR	BB/9	K/9	K	GB%	BABIP	WHIP	ERA	DRA-	WARP
2018	DAY	HI-A	21	6	4	0	15	15	86²	81	5	2.3	7.6	73	42.3%	.302	1.19	2.70	105	0.2
2018	PNS	AA	21	4	3	0	11	11	62¹	65	8	2.3	8.8	61	43.9%	.318	1.30	3.61	88	0.8
2019	CHA	AA	22	2	8	0	21	21	102¹	110	8	4.7	8.1	92	32.8%	.342	1.60	4.84	118	-1.0
2021 FS	CIN	MLB	24	2	3	0	57	0	50	50	9	5.2	7.8	43	37.3%	.286	1.58	5.72	121	-0.5
2021 DC	CIN	MLB	24	2	3	0	40	4	56	56	10	5.2	7.8	48	37.3%	.286	1.58	5.72	121	-0.2

Comparables: Touki Toussaint, Miguel Almonte, Jonathan Hernández

The Report: Have good frame, will travel up the minors. Santillan is the next tier down of mid-rotation types who dot the back of the 101 every year (and he hasn't been that far off the last two list cycles). The fastball backed up a little in 2019 and concern about the secondaries and command projection made the reliever risk loom a little larger.

Development Track: Santillan was at the alternate site and in consideration for major league time—even made the playoff taxi squad. The velocity has ticked back up and the change and breaker both looked potentially average-or-better. There's still some unanswered questions on whether the command and stamina are good enough to start across 162 games, but at least there are fewer questions about the stuff now.

Variance: Medium. There's some profile risk and Santillan might fit best as a bulk inning guy after an opener. He's trending in the right direction though and should see the majors this season.

J.P. Breen's Fantasy Take: We're talking about a potential fourth starter who had injury and performance issues in 2019? That juice ain't worth the squeeze outside of dynasty leagues that roster 200-plus prospects. If Santillan's velocity has returned, as suggested above, he's somewhat more interesting due to his proximity to the big leagues. Still, given that he hasn't struck out more than a batter per inning since 2016 and has a history of command problems, he shouldn't be considered to be anything more than roster backfill.

8 Michael Siani CF   OFP: 50   ETA: 2023/2024

Born: 07/16/99   Age: 21   Bats: L   Throws: L   Height: 6'1"   Weight: 188   Origin: Round 4, 2018 Draft (#109 overall)

YEAR	TEAM	LVL	AGE	PA	R	2B	3B	HR	RBI	BB	K	SB	CS	AVG/OBP/SLG	DRC+	BABIP	BRR	FRAA	WARP
2018	GRN	ROK	18	205	24	6	3	2	13	16	35	6	4	.288/.351/.386		.342			
2019	DAY	LO-A	19	531	75	10	6	6	39	46	108	45	15	.253/.333/.339	95	.317	7.4	CF(112) 24.7, RF(5) -0.7, LF(1) 0.0	4.8
2021 FS	CIN	MLB	21	600	50	25	3	8	53	34	169	29	12	.235/.286/.338	71	.323	-1.9	CF 14, RF 0	1.0

Comparables: Derek Hill, Carlos Gómez, Joe Benson

The Report: Siani continued to get glowing reviews for his center field defense at the alternate site and at instructs, which is consistent with the speed, first step, and throwing arm he had already established as strengths. He won't need to hit too much to be a contributor, but all phases of his offensive game remain raw, and when we last got looks at him, his swing seemed designed for contact over power, which would theoretically take advantage of his plus speed.

Development Track: Given the above, Siani losing a summer of at-bats is particularly painful, both for his development and for our sense of how well he is progressing at the plate. He did get a chance to face older competition at the alternate site, even if it wasn't in formal game action. If his 2019 first-half/second-half narrative was that of a cold weather prep bat adjusting to Low-A, there was theoretically a chance he continued to thrive in High-A and maybe challenge for Double-A this year. With the season gone, there will be that much more pressure to add to his offense next year.

Variance: High. While it sounds like it wasn't a lost year for Siani, he was still deprived of what he needed most: a high volume of at-bats against advanced competition.

J.P. Breen's Fantasy Take: Siani has a profile that can fall through the dynasty cracks. He swiped 45 bases in 2019, which grabs plenty of people's attention, but neither the offensive scouting reports nor the minor-league batting averages have been good. Still, too many dynasty owners discount Siani's defensive abilities. His glove could get him to the big leagues, and at that point, the speed becomes far more attractive. Guys like Leonys Martín, after all, stick around for years. Sure, you say, but Martín is always available on the waiver wire! Yes, which is why Siani is not worth rostering outside of the deepest of fantasy leagues—y'know, the ones that regularly roster guys like Martín in the majors.

9 Rece Hinds SS   OFP: 50   ETA: 2024

Born: 09/05/00   Age: 20   Bats: R   Throws: R   Height: 6'4"   Weight: 215   Origin: Round 2, 2019 Draft (#49 overall)

YEAR	TEAM	LVL	AGE	PA	R	2B	3B	HR	RBI	BB	K	SB	CS	AVG/OBP/SLG	DRC+	BABIP	BRR	FRAA	WARP
2019	GRN	ROK+	18	10	1	0	0	0	1	2	3	0	0	.000/.286/.000		.000			
2021 FS	CIN	MLB	20	600	45	26	2	7	49	35	228			.200/.253/.298	53	.322			-1.9

The Report: Hinds is a big, strong prep draftee, has tons of raw power, swings really, really hard, and just turned 20. As you might imagine, there's plenty of swing-and-miss here and all of the attendant concerns that brings about accessing the power in games and reaching base enough to be a regular.

Development Track: Hinds evidently used the summer to semi-officially transition over to third base and, ironically, the lack of games meant that much more time for him to try to shore up the defensive deficiencies in his game at the alternate site. We heard good things about third base as a fit, as we already knew he had the arm strength for the position, and evidently his hands and feet were promising enough that he may be able to stick there for a while.

Variance: High. He has 10 professional plate appearances and they were in rookie ball.

J.P. Breen's Fantasy Take: Hinds is too far away from the big leagues for the move to third base to matter much for dynasty purposes. As for the bat, he has enough raw power to make him worth monitoring, but he's not worth rostering, even in deep dynasty leagues. The questions about his hit tool and his plate discipline are too loud at the moment.

Lyon Richardson RHP   Born: 01/18/00   Age: 21   Bats: S   Throws: R   Height: 6'2"   Weight: 192   Origin: Round 2, 2018 Draft (#62 overall)

YEAR	TEAM	LVL	AGE	W	L	SV	G	GS	IP	H	HR	BB/9	K/9	K	GB%	BABIP	WHIP	ERA	DRA-	WARP
2018	GRN	ROK	18	0	5	0	11	11	29	37	3	5.0	7.4	24	40.2%	.362	1.83	7.14		
2019	DAY	LO-A	19	3	9	0	26	26	112²	126	10	2.6	8.5	106	39.9%	.341	1.41	4.15	117	-0.7
2021 FS	CIN	MLB	21	2	3	0	57	0	50	51	8	4.7	7.0	38	36.0%	.287	1.55	5.36	124	-0.6

Comparables: Joe Ross, Kyle Ryan, Justus Sheffield

The Report: Richardson is an athletic prep arm with high-effort mechanics who impressed us sufficiently—despite the profile concerns—to make this list last year. Unsurprising for a non-elite prep pitching prospect, Richardson was inconsistent with the quality and command of the non-fastball offerings. So we were not confident he would stay in the rotation. But if he winds up a reliever, there's the material here for a pretty good one.

Development Track: Richardson's velocity was up a tick at the alternate site, sitting 93-94 and touching 96-97, and he was reportedly more consistent with his breaking pitch against the most advanced hitters he has ever faced. On the one hand, that's in a very small sample in non-game action, but on the other hand, pitching prospects with far shinier pedigrees than Richardson's had trouble with their mechanics in the extremely weird "season" and Richardson did not. Every step closer he takes to the majors without being converted to relief is a victory.

Variance: High. If he doesn't improve the consistency of his secondaries considerably he's a reliever and the fallback options from there involve pitching in other countries.

J.P. Breen's Fantasy Take: No, no, don't speak / I know what you're thinkin' / And I don't need your reasons / Don't tell me cuz it hurts

The Prospects You Meet Outside The Top Ten:

Interesting Draft Follows

Christian Roa   Born: 04/02/99   Age: 22   Bats: R   Throws: R   Height: 6'4"   Weight: 220   Origin: Round 2, 2020 Draft (#48 overall)

A solid, albeit modest performer in his first two years at Texas A&M, Roa saw his draft stock bump coinciding with a tick up in his velocity this year. Witnessed by many upper-tier evaluators in town to see Asa Lacy, the performance was enough to vault Roa into the second round despite a loss in command toward the end of his abbreviated season. It's a four-pitch mix that's at least average across the board, and with some room still left on his 6-foot-4 frame. The question becomes what further gains can be made with his velocity and whether he can harness the command.

Bryce Bonnin   Born: 10/11/98   Age: 22   Bats: R   Throws: R   Height: 6'2"   Weight: 190   Origin: Round 3, 2020 Draft (#84 overall)

The Reds' third-round pick has the kind of raw material—a high-spin 95-mph fastball and potential plus slider—that they'd want their current pitching development team working with. He might not be a starter long term, but he will start for now, and it could be a short hop to major league help if and when he moves to the bullpen.

Prospects to dream on a little

Michel Triana   Born: 11/23/99   Age: 21   Bats: L   Throws: R   Height: 6'3"   Weight: 230   Origin: International Free Agent, 2019

Another seven-figure Cuban signee for Cincinnati, the bat here is worth flagging even though he has been playing mostly first base. There's big power potential here, but the hit tool is also more advanced than you might think. He's going to have to hit a lot, obviously, but the early returns are good. Check back after he gets more stateside game time.

Interesting (2019) Draft Follows

Ivan Johnson 2B Born: 10/11/98   Age: 22   Bats: S   Throws: R   Height: 6'0"   Weight: 190   Origin: Round 4, 2019 Draft (#114 overall)

YEAR	TEAM	LVL	AGE	PA	R	2B	3B	HR	RBI	BB	K	SB	CS	AVG/OBP/SLG	DRC+	BABIP	BRR	FRAA	WARP
2019	GRN	ROK+	20	210	27	10	1	6	22	18	46	11	4	.262/.335/.426		.321			
2021 FS	CIN	MLB	22	600	46	26	2	8	51	34	198	19	7	.208/.259/.311	56	.306	0.8		-1.6

Last season's low minors sleeper remains buzzy coming off instructs. He might not be a shortstop long term, but for now you can keep dreaming on a switch-hitting shortstop with pop and some feel for hitting. You can also pencil him in as a 2021 breakout candidate even if he has to slide over to second or third.

Tyler Callihan 2B Born: 06/22/00   Age: 21   Bats: L   Throws: R   Height: 6'1"   Weight: 205   Origin: Round 3, 2019 Draft (#85 overall)

YEAR	TEAM	LVL	AGE	PA	R	2B	3B	HR	RBI	BB	K	SB	CS	AVG/OBP/SLG	DRC+	BABIP	BRR	FRAA	WARP
2019	BIL	ROK+	19	21	3	0	1	1	7	1	4	2	0	.400/.429/.650		.467			
2019	GRN	ROK+	19	217	27	10	5	5	26	9	46	9	3	.260/.297/.439		.313			
2021 FS	CIN	MLB	21	600	45	26	4	8	51	28	195	18	5	.209/.250/.316	54	.303	5.6		-1.2

Callihan is another of the Reds' bat-first infield prospects who they hope to refine enough to manage at second or third while the bat plays up enough to make it worthwhile. A 2019 prep draftee, Callihan also will suffer from the loss of 2020 development. The left-handed swing is pretty, and there's still room for physical development with a professional conditioning program as he ages into his 20s.

Safe MLB bat, but less upside than you'd like

TJ Friedl LF Born: 08/14/95   Age: 25   Bats: L   Throws: L   Height: 5'10"   Weight: 180   Origin: Undrafted Free Agent, 2016

YEAR	TEAM	LVL	AGE	PA	R	2B	3B	HR	RBI	BB	K	SB	CS	AVG/OBP/SLG	DRC+	BABIP	BRR	FRAA	WARP
2018	DAY	HI-A	22	274	40	10	4	3	35	38	44	11	4	.294/.405/.412	135	.350	4.7	LF(39) 2.0, CF(19) -1.0, RF(2) -0.1	1.8
2018	PNS	AA	22	296	47	10	3	2	16	28	56	19	5	.276/.359/.360	111	.345	3.3	LF(53) 5.1, CF(9) -1.0, RF(1) -0.1	1.2
2019	CHA	AA	23	269	38	11	4	5	28	29	50	13	4	.235/.347/.385	112	.277	1.3	RF(42) 2.4, LF(14) -1.4, CF(13) -1.1	1.1
2021 FS	CIN	MLB	25	600	57	26	4	11	58	47	151	13	4	.232/.310/.363	86	.302	3.4	LF 6, CF -6	1.0

Comparables: *John Andreoli, Bryan Petersen, Shane Peterson*

Hey, did you know that Friedl got the highest bonus ever given to a UDFA because most teams didn't even know he was draft eligible? It's been relegated to a fun fact over the years and now he's a good glove at three outfield spots with enough OBP to make him a useful bench player as soon as 2021.

Huge Stuff & Huge Risk

Lyon Richardson RHP Born: 01/18/00   Age: 21   Bats: S   Throws: R   Height: 6'2"   Weight: 192   Origin: Round 2, 2018 Draft (#62 overall)

YEAR	TEAM	LVL	AGE	W	L	SV	G	GS	IP	H	HR	BB/9	K/9	K	GB%	BABIP	WHIP	ERA	DRA-	WARP
2018	GRN	ROK	18	0	5	0	11	11	29	37	3	5.0	7.4	24	40.2%	.362	1.83	7.14		
2019	DAY	LO-A	19	3	9	0	26	26	112²	126	10	2.6	8.5	106	39.9%	.341	1.41	4.15	117	-0.7
2021 FS	CIN	MLB	21	2	3	0	57	0	50	51	8	4.7	7.0	38	36.0%	.287	1.55	5.36	124	-0.6

Comparables: *Joe Ross, Kyle Ryan, Justus Sheffield*

A former 11th-round pick, the Reds added Solomon to their 40-man roster last week, only a few weeks removed from his having Tommy John surgery. The stuff had popped to the high 90s, scraping triple digits, with reports of a hellacious breaking pitch. Sometimes that can be a precursor to injury and, well … there you go. The risk is extreme and we don't know how much stuff he'll retain after his rehab, but the organization clearly believes in the talent and if they're right that's the type of arsenal worth flagging.

Top Talents 25 and Under (as of 4/1/2021):

1. Nick Senzel, OF

2. Nick Lodolo, LHP
3. Austin Hendrick, OF
4. Hunter Greene, RHP
5. Tyler Stephenson, C
6. Jose Garcia, SS
7. Jonathan India, IF
8. Tony Santillan, RHP
9. Mike Siani, OF
10. Rece Hinds, 3B

2016 No. 2-overall pick Nick Senzel is the only young Reds non-prospect to make our list here. The two-time top-10 global prospect still hasn't quite established himself as a good major-league regular yet, mostly through no fault of his own; in 2020, he missed a month with COVID-19 and didn't hit well on his return. We're still in on his long-term potential with the bat, and the longtime infielder seems to have settled in at a surprising position defensively: center field. We'd like to see what he can do over a healthy, full season. Hopefully, that's 2021.

Cleveland

The State of the System:

Like their cross-state National League rivals, this is a very deep system that may lack true impact talent at the top. Well, at least at press time. One suspects it will get deeper and more impactful this offseason.

The Top Ten:

★ ★ ★ *2021 Top 101 Prospect* **#48** ★ ★ ★

1 **George Valera** **CF**   OFP: 60   ETA: 2023
Born: 11/13/00 Age: 20 Bats: L Throws: L Height: 5'11" Weight: 185 Origin: International Free Agent, 2017

YEAR	TEAM	LVL	AGE	PA	R	2B	3B	HR	RBI	BB	K	SB	CS	AVG/OBP/SLG	DRC+	BABIP	BRR	FRAA	WARP
2018	INDB	ROK	17	22	4	1	0	1	6	3	3	1	1	.333/.409/.556		.333			
2019	MV	SS	18	188	22	7	1	8	29	29	52	6	2	.236/.356/.446	132	.296	-0.3	CF(25) 0.7, RF(11) -3.5, LF(5) 4.4	1.1
2019	LC	LO-A	18	26	1	0	1	0	3	2	9	0	2	.087/.192/.174	34	.143	-1.0	RF(3) 1.2, LF(2) 1.6	0.0
2021 FS	CLE	MLB	20	600	50	26	2	13	57	39	217	10	8	.199/.257/.329	60	.299	-9.7	CF -1, RF -2	-2.7

Comparables: Luis Alexander Basabe, Michael Saunders, Harold Ramirez

The Report: Valera's swing is not what you would call traditionally beautiful. And the bar for a pretty lefty swing is high anyway. But it's attractive in the same way a Seijun Suzuki film is—noisy, chaotic, frenetic while just barely under control, and probably best enjoyed in cinemascope. It's also short and to the point once it gets going, and often ends in an explosion of monochromatic violence. There's near-elite bat speed, and the raw power has become the party piece here—he was trending power-over-hit in the Penn League in 2019—although we still expect him to hit for a high enough average as well. He's likely bound for a corner eventually, but the bat should play there.

Development Track: Valera is one of the prospects I'm most personally annoyed didn't get a full 2020 season to crush A-ball. It would make ranking him number one in the Cleveland system far easier. The alternate site and instructional league reports don't give us any reason to move off our aggressive 2019 ranking, but we'd like to see it in games in 2021.

Variance: Extreme. Valera hasn't actually played in full-season ball yet and may end up in an outfield corner. There's significant pressure on the bat to play to projection.

Mark Barry's Fantasy Take: On one hand, all of the reasons to love Valera are still there—excellent bat speed, raw power, budding hit tool. On the other, he didn't play any real games in 2020, and because fantasy managers are nothing if not a fickle, prisoners of the moment, that's likely to cause his value to take a serious hit. Put those hands together and you have a buy-low opportunity on a dude who could be .290ish with 25-30 homers.

★ ★ ★ *2021 Top 101 Prospect* **#52** ★ ★ ★

2 Nolan Jones 3B

OFP: 60   ETA: Late 2021/Early 2022

Born: 05/07/98   Age: 23   Bats: L   Throws: R   Height: 6'2"   Weight: 185   Origin: Round 2, 2016 Draft (#55 overall)

YEAR	TEAM	LVL	AGE	PA	R	2B	3B	HR	RBI	BB	K	SB	CS	AVG/OBP/SLG	DRC+	BABIP	BRR	FRAA	WARP
2018	LC	LO-A	20	389	46	12	0	16	49	63	97	2	1	.279/.393/.464	150	.347	-0.9	3B(76) -4.1	2.3
2018	LYN	HI-A	20	130	23	9	0	3	17	26	34	0	0	.298/.438/.471	154	.418	0.1	3B(28) -0.3	0.9
2019	LYN	HI-A	21	324	48	12	1	7	41	65	84	5	3	.286/.435/.425	172	.396	-1.4	3B(72) -3.4	2.8
2019	AKR	AA	21	211	33	10	2	8	22	31	63	2	0	.253/.370/.466	149	.346	0.8	3B(44) 0.0	1.8
2021 FS	CLE	MLB	23	600	68	27	2	17	62	68	217	1	0	.235/.326/.393	99	.364	0.0	3B -1	1.0
2021 DC	CLE	MLB	23	199	22	9	0	5	20	22	72	0	0	.235/.326/.393	99	.364	0.0	3B 0, RF 0	0.4

Comparables: Austin Riley, Matt Davidson, Tyler O'Neill

The Report: Jones was a cold weather prep shortstop who was going to quickly move off shortstop, but had the bat to carry a corner. So far...mostly so good. The raw power jumped quickly as Jones filled out in his late teens and is now plus-plus, although he's never slugged .500 at any minor league stop. The main culprit there is significant swing-and-miss to his game, with the K-rate peaking over 30 percent in his first taste of Double-A in 2019. He sometimes tries to yank it 450 feet, leading to whiffs when he can't adjust, although his overall approach is solid enough. If this sounds like a TTO slugger, well that's the outcome you are hoping for. Jones is passable at third base for now, but the arm and foot speed outpace the hands and lateral range, so he might be a better fit in right field. That might be more useful given Cleveland's current roster holes anyway.

Development Track: Jones spent the summer at the alternate site in Lake County, but really could have used another crack at the Eastern League to smooth out some of the rough edges of the offensive profile. Now you could argue that for him—and any number of other prospects we'll chronicle on these lists—seeing Triston McKenzie, Sam Hentges, and Nick Sandlin would be at least a comparable level of difficulty, but I'm not sure the instructional league type format is allowing for the kind of hit tool development Jones needs. I'm not sure that it isn't either. We'll see in April ... hopefully.

Variance: High. The power is loud but more raw than game. There is significant swing-and-miss and positional risk in the eventual major-league profile.

Mark Barry's Fantasy Take: The fun part about Cleveland's big-league roster is that Jones could be the "best" outfielder on the team should he get the call. Sure that's damning with faint praise, but whatever. It was probably telling that Jones didn't see any time with the big club in a season where top-75 prospects were being called up on a seemingly daily basis, but like Jeffrey said above, he still could use a little time to sand down the swing-and-miss in his profile. I don't love TTO prospects for fantasy (unless you're in an OBP league), so I'm less than enthused with Jones's upside.

★ ★ ★ *2021 Top 101 Prospect* **#73** ★ ★ ★

3 Triston McKenzie RHP

OFP: 60   ETA: Debuted in 2020

Born: 08/02/97   Age: 23   Bats: R   Throws: R   Height: 6'5"   Weight: 165   Origin: Round 1, 2015 Draft (#42 overall)

YEAR	TEAM	LVL	AGE	W	L	SV	G	GS	IP	H	HR	BB/9	K/9	K	GB%	BABIP	WHIP	ERA	DRA-	WARP
2018	AKR	AA	20	7	4	0	16	16	90²	63	8	2.8	8.6	87	33.3%	.234	1.00	2.68	86	1.4
2020	CLE	MLB	22	2	1	0	8	6	33¹	21	6	2.4	11.3	42	40.0%	.217	0.90	3.24	85	0.6
2021 FS	CLE	MLB	23	9	8	0	26	26	150	133	25	2.9	10.2	170	36.2%	.287	1.21	3.81	90	1.9
2021 DC	CLE	MLB	23	6	7	0	22	22	111	98	18	2.9	10.2	125	36.2%	.287	1.21	3.81	90	1.8

Comparables: Noah Syndergaard, Tyler Skaggs, Jenrry Mejia

The Report: McKenzie was a former Top 101 prospect who dropped off Cleveland's top 10 last year because ... well, he didn't pitch. After missing time in 2018 with a forearm strain, back issues wiped out his 2019. He was reportedly having a normal spring, but given his rather narrow physique, you'd be forgiven for having concerns about whether he'd come back and be able to handle a full starter's workload. The stuff was Top 101 quality two years ago, but we were still relying on a bit of fastball projection to get him to the mid-rotation OFP.

Development Track: I called McKenzie a "mystery box" right before his 2020 debut. But behind Door #1, you got a pitcher pumping 95 with the same above-average 12-6 downer curve. There was also a new slider he had some feel for, and while his change was firm, McKenzie sold it well enough with his arm action to be effective. In a season of impressive pitching prospect debuts, he might have had the most dominant first outing. But the velocity went backward quickly after that first start and he was more 90-92 by his last few abbreviated September outings. He can still be effective in that velocity band given the deception, life, and command on the fastball. McKenzie hadn't thrown in games for almost two years before he was dropped into Cleveland's rotation, so it's not a huge surprise the velocity backslid some, but he also never really sat 95 in the minors either, so it's unclear what to expect here going forward. He does remain remarkably thin, and the physical projection we hoped for out of the draft doesn't seem to be coming.

Variance: High. This all depends on where the fastball/stamina settle after a normal (hopefully healthy) offseason and spring. He can be a useful major league starter in the low 90s, but the role 6 guy probably needs above-average fastball velocity for the rest of the arsenal to play off of. McKenzie also has a bad injury track record, so there will be durability questions until he takes the ball every fifth day while maintaining the stuff and command.

Mark Barry's Fantasy Take: It's hard to call McKenzie's debut anything other than an huge success after spending the better part of two seasons on the sidelines. Where that leaves us, though, uh, your guess is as good as mine. He's probably an SP4 factoring in all of the risk, but I'd be surprised if he's not valued a little better than that on the market. I'm a big fan of the dude and the story, but the variance is high.

★ ★ ★ *2021 Top 101 Prospect* **#87** ★ ★ ★

4 **Gabriel Arias SS**   OFP: 60   ETA: 2022

Born: 02/27/00   Age: 21   Bats: R   Throws: R   Height: 6'1"   Weight: 201   Origin: International Free Agent, 2016

YEAR	TEAM	LVL	AGE	PA	R	2B	3B	HR	RBI	BB	K	SB	CS	AVG/OBP/SLG	DRC+	BABIP	BRR	FRAA	WARP
2018	FW	LO-A	18	504	54	27	3	6	55	41	149	3	3	.240/.302/.352	84	.340	-0.5	SS(111) 6.2, 3B(6) 0.2	1.2
2019	LE	HI-A	19	506	62	21	4	17	75	24	126	8	4	.304/.341/.474	121	.380	1.5	SS(104) -11.4, 3B(10) 1.4, 2B(2) -0.4	2.1
2021 FS	CLE	MLB	21	600	51	26	3	13	59	28	220	1	0	.220/.261/.348	64	.333	0.6	SS -2, 3B 0	-1.0

Comparables: Franklin Barreto, Gleyber Torres, Xander Bogaerts

The Report: Arias's 2019 offensive improvements were hidden some by a rough first half. After July 1st, the 19-year-old slashed .350/.378/.562, smashing 10 of his 17 High-A home runs. It wasn't random small sample size success either, as multiple looks by our staff saw improvements at the plate as the season wore on. While he's unlikely to hit .300 with pop outside of the friendly confines of Lake Elsinore, both his hit and power tools could land at a tick above-average if he continues to further refine an aggressive approach. Even if they don't, the plus shortstop glove should carry the profile at least to a useful fifth infielder.

Development Track: Arias was the main prospect piece sent to Cleveland at the deadline for Mike Clevinger. He may soon enough be putting down his marker as a potential Lindor replacement at the 6. Arias isn't major-league-ready on the whole—although the glove might be—but if you are willing to wait another year, and the bat proves to be above-average, you might end up with merely a Betts-to-Verdugo type downgrade there. I guess here's hopin' if you are a Cleveland fan?

Variance: High. The glove gives Arias a soft landing on a major league bench even if the offensive improvements of 2019 prove to be a Cal League mirage. In that respect, really wish we had another year of improvement with the bat to point to.

Mark Barry's Fantasy Take: First of all, no. How dare you? No "here's hopin' as a Cleveland fan."

Having said that, I do like Arias and don't be fooled by the Josh Naylor-of-it-all, Arias was likely the crown jewel of the Clevinger trade. In the Golden Age of the Fantasy Shortstop, Arias will need to run some to have seasons where he cracks into the Top 10 at the position, but presently gives me 2020 Dansby Swanson-vibes if he continues this trajectory.

★ ★ ★ *2021 Top 101 Prospect* **#100** ★ ★ ★

5 **Daniel Espino RHP**   OFP: 60   ETA: 2023

Born: 01/05/01   Age: 20   Bats: R   Throws: R   Height: 6'2"   Weight: 205   Origin: Round 1, 2019 Draft (#24 overall)

YEAR	TEAM	LVL	AGE	W	L	SV	G	GS	IP	H	HR	BB/9	K/9	K	GB%	BABIP	WHIP	ERA	DRA-	WARP
2019	INDR	ROK	18	0	1	0	6	6	13²	7	1	3.3	10.5	16	48.4%	.207	0.88	1.98		
2019	MV	SS	18	0	2	0	3	3	10	9	1	4.5	16.2	18	31.8%	.381	1.40	6.30	60	0.3
2021 FS	CLE	MLB	20	2	3	0	57	0	50	48	8	6.5	9.8	54	37.3%	.301	1.68	5.86	134	-0.8

The Report: A lightning rod in the 2019 draft, Espino was considered to have the type of arm talent usually associated with a top-10 pick. Enough teams worried about the length in his arm action to question his long-term health projection, causing him to "slip" to the 23rd pick overall. The fastball is lively—routinely in the mid-90s and nearing 100 in shorter outings—and he has surprisingly good command for a young player throwing that kind of fuzz. Additionally, there are the makings of two plus breaking balls, both of which he is unafraid of throwing to righties and lefties alike. The consensus has always been that his premium athleticism on the mound should allow for any necessary adjustments to be integrated seamlessly as he develops into a potential dynamic starter.

Development Track: Despite his age and limited pro experience, Espino was able to get much-needed repetitions this summer and fall at their team's alternate site and training camps. Even after the long spring layoff, his velocity held at previous norms while continuing his path towards throwing high quality strikes. Likened to a "ball of clay," he is being molded by a player development group that has shown a nearly unmatched track record of bettering in-house prospects into eventual major league difference-makers on the mound.

Variance: High. Some of the concerns that plagued his pre-draft report still exist even though they have yet to manifest negatively. As time goes on with the continued reps those worries will dissipate more fully. If everything goes right, he could be a star.

Mark Barry's Fantasy Take: Espino is one of my favorite non-marquee pitching prospects. He's got the velocity, the pitch mix, and the ability to strike tons of dudes out to be a front-line starter. What could possibly go wrong (dammit, oops sorry trying to delete—baseball gods don't read this)?

6 Brayan Rocchio SS   OFP: 55   ETA: 2023/24

Born: 01/13/01   Age: 20   Bats: S   Throws: R   Height: 5'10"   Weight: 150   Origin: International Free Agent, 2017

YEAR	TEAM	LVL	AGE	PA	R	2B	3B	HR	RBI	BB	K	SB	CS	AVG/OBP/SLG	DRC+	BABIP	BRR	FRAA	WARP
2018	INDB	ROK	17	158	21	10	1	1	17	10	17	14	8	.343/.389/.448		.378			
2018	DSL IND1	ROK	17	111	19	2	3	1	12	5	14	8	5	.323/.391/.434		.369			
2019	MV	SS	18	295	33	12	3	5	27	20	40	14	8	.250/.310/.373	106	.276	-1.8	SS(62) 5.5, 2B(7) 0.6	1.8
2021 FS	CLE	MLB	20	600	50	26	3	9	55	26	139	24	13	.237/.277/.347	70	.299	-8.1	SS 5, 2B 0	-0.8

Comparables: Sergio Alcántara, Willi Castro, Amed Rosario

The Report: Bursting out of the gates in his professional debut, despite a modest six-figure signing bonus, the combined offensive and defensive abilities for Rocchio were noticeable from day one. Most notable is his contact rate from both sides of the plate, while appearing more comfortable from the left side, his right-handed swing isn't far behind. His featherweight size won't likely allow for much growth in the power department, but a plus hit tool with plus grades defensively at either shortstop or second base translate to a future starter role.

Development Track: Like many Venezuelans during the pandemic, travel restrictions hampered his ability to make it into the United States for additional training. Cleveland was able to set up online training sessions with many of their international prospects, where Rocchio received glowing reviews for his diligence and information retention while working out on a neighborhood diamond. Strength training is at the top of his list for needed development, followed by the need to face more advanced pitching to test the bat.

Variance: Extreme. Rocchio is the type of player most negatively affected from the lost year. The bat could be special, but it might also be much ado about nothing.

Mark Barry's Fantasy Take: There's a wide range of outcomes for Rocchio right now, as Keanan correctly points out that it is indeed difficult to learn baseball on a Zoom call. His potential is a lot of fun, maybe a little Cesar Hernandez-esque from a fantasy production standpoint, but the mystery of his 2020 development makes it risky to dive in headfirst.

7 Ethan Hankins RHP   OFP: 55   ETA: 2023

Born: 05/23/00   Age: 21   Bats: R   Throws: R   Height: 6'6"   Weight: 200   Origin: Round 1, 2018 Draft (#35 overall)

YEAR	TEAM	LVL	AGE	W	L	SV	G	GS	IP	H	HR	BB/9	K/9	K	GB%	BABIP	WHIP	ERA	DRA-	WARP
2018	INDB	ROK	18	0	0	0	2	2	3	4	0	0.0	18.0	6	28.6%	.571	1.33	6.00		
2019	MV	SS	19	0	0	0	9	8	38²	23	1	4.2	10.0	43	55.1%	.253	1.06	1.40	68	0.8
2019	LC	LO-A	19	0	3	0	5	5	21¹	20	3	5.1	11.8	28	47.2%	.340	1.50	4.64	113	-0.1
2021 FS	CLE	MLB	21	2	3	0	57	0	50	46	8	6.0	8.9	49	46.0%	.283	1.60	5.43	123	-0.5

Comparables: Joe Ross, Pedro Avila, Edgar Olmos

The Report: During the summer showcase season of 2017, Hankins elevated himself to the top spot of the prep arm pecking order due to the sheer movement on his pitches paired with a 6-foot-6 workhorse frame. There was concern that his delivery lacked consistency, at times showing wide variance between starts. When spring 2018 rolled around, Hankins dealt with shoulder soreness, further exacerbating questions about the delivery and the long-term prognosis on his throwing arm. His mechanics have since been simplified, especially in the bottom half, while maintaining the plus movement on his mid-90s fastball. With the revamped delivery he has lost some break to the slider, while the changeup has the potential to be his best secondary pitch when all is said and done.

Development Track: Like his teammate Espino, Hankins got the reps he desperately needed this year. With a focus on strike-throwing and staying within himself, he made positive strides especially in Cleveland's fall camp. Even though there is some risk of an eventual reliever role, he certainly improved his likelihood to stick in the rotation after his 2020 progress. He'll be given every opportunity to start so long as his mechanics continue trending in the right direction and his secondary pitches catch up to his fastball quality.

Variance: High. The building blocks exist to be a full-time starter even though the trajectory so far might not indicate it's likely.

Mark Barry's Fantasy Take: Injury concerns aside (lol), there are worse organizations to bet on when developing young, talented arms. The laws of TINSTAAPP apply, as always, but if you're rostering hurlers who have yet to see High-A, Hankins is the kind of guy I'd like to gamble on, especially in that top-125ish range.

8 Tyler Freeman SS   OFP: 55   ETA: 2022

Born: 05/21/99   Age: 22   Bats: R   Throws: R   Height: 6'0"   Weight: 170   Origin: Round 2, 2017 Draft (#71 overall)

YEAR	TEAM	LVL	AGE	PA	R	2B	3B	HR	RBI	BB	K	SB	CS	AVG/OBP/SLG	DRC+	BABIP	BRR	FRAA	WARP
2018	MV	SS	19	301	49	29	4	2	38	8	22	14	3	.352/.405/.511	180	.372	3.5	SS(52) -0.1, 2B(10) -0.2	2.7
2019	LC	LO-A	20	272	51	16	3	3	24	18	28	11	4	.292/.382/.424	141	.320	2.6	SS(57) 0.5, 2B(3) -0.2	2.6
2019	LYN	HI-A	20	275	38	16	2	0	20	8	25	8	1	.319/.354/.397	129	.350	1.2	SS(57) -1.0, 2B(3) 0.1	1.9
2021 FS	CLE	MLB	22	600	60	28	3	7	57	30	97	10	3	.259/.318/.366	90	.303	1.5	2B -4, SS 2	1.2
2021 DC	CLE	MLB	22	66	6	3	0	0	6	3	10	1	0	.259/.318/.366	90	.303	0.2	2B 0, SS 0	0.1

Comparables: José Rondón, Wilmer Flores, Luis Sardiñas

The Report: I don't mean to step on Mark's toes here, but Freeman is the quintessential "better fantasy prospect than real life one" for me. He's not a bad prospect by any means. Despite a rather mechanical and at times overly-complicated stroke, he makes consistent good contact and you can project a plus hit tool. Freeman is also a plus runner and an efficient base-stealer, so you get batting average and steals from a player who is also likely to have some positional flexibility—that is to say, he's unlikely to have enough glove to be a full-time shortstop. There isn't going to be much in the way of power or OBP to boost the overall offensive profile, so he profiles best as a batting average driven second baseman.

Development Track: The reports from the alternate site don't really move the needle a ton, but he moves up some on attrition elsewhere in the system and the rest on my waning stubbornness about the profile. Still would like to see that swing against better velocity and secondaries in Double-A first, though.

Variance: High. Hit is the carrying tool here and we haven't seen Freeman rake against upper minors pitchers yet.

Mark Barry's Fantasy Take: Yep, I concur. Freeman is a borderline top-50 dynasty prospect for me, and if any semblance of power comes, he could rise a good deal higher than that.

9 Aaron Bracho SS   OFP: 55   ETA: 2023

Born: 04/24/01   Age: 20   Bats: S   Throws: R   Height: 5'11"   Weight: 175   Origin: International Free Agent, 2017

YEAR	TEAM	LVL	AGE	PA	R	2B	3B	HR	RBI	BB	K	SB	CS	AVG/OBP/SLG	DRC+	BABIP	BRR	FRAA	WARP
2019	INDB	ROK	18	137	25	10	2	6	29	23	21	4	1	.296/.416/.593		.306			
2019	MV	SS	18	32	5	1	0	2	4	5	8	0	0	.222/.344/.481	92	.235	0.3	2B(8) -1.4	0.0
2021 FS	CLE	MLB	20	600	49	27	3	10	53	44	181	5	2	.203/.267/.319	62	.283	1.0	2B 1	-0.6

Comparables: J.P. Crawford, Yu Chang, Jesse Winker

The Report: Not unlike his Venezuelan teammate Rocchio, Bracho is a bat-first infielder. The similarities, however, tail off significantly after that. Bracho's body is physically filled out with little projection left even though he won't turn 20 until the presumptive minor league season starts in 2021. It's not that he's round or unathletic, it's more of a ready-made boxy frame that isn't likely to change much. He's only played second base as a professional, yet there are questions as to whether he'd fare better hidden in the outfield. In order for that to happen, the bat needs to carry him into the lineup—which it does in spades. He controls the zone well, squaring fastballs up and fighting off breaking balls consistently to run long counts and get on base. He's adept from both sides of the plate as a switch hitter, and like so many of his organizational teammates, there is a lot to dream on.

Development Track: Injuries delayed his pro debut by over a year, getting only 38 games under his belt in 2019. To make up for lost time, he was given a coveted spot on the 60-man alternate site roster where he competed well against players much more advanced in their careers. Using that experience, he will be one to watch next season as someone who could take several steps forward.

Variance: High. The juxtaposition against the myriad other infielder prospects within the org has Bracho with a higher offensive potential without the backup plan that others might have.

Mark Barry's Fantasy Take: Oh look, another high-contact, middle infielder who gets on base. If I didn't know any better, I'd think these guys grow on trees, but I know we don't have the technology for something like that yet. Anyway, Bracho has a chance to hit a lot, even if his defensive position might ultimately be TBD. He's a fringy top-100 fantasy guy right now, even if he's not a game changer anywhere.

10   Carson Tucker   SS   OFP: 50   ETA: 2025

Born: 01/24/02   Age: 19   Bats: R   Throws: R   Height: 6'2"   Weight: 180   Origin: Round 1, 2020 Draft (#23 overall)

The Report: Carson is Pirates shortstop Cole Tucker's younger brother, and it was a bit of a surprise when he was popped in the first round of the draft. Lacking any flashy tools, he is more of a high-floor type and signed an under-slot deal as Cleveland chose to employ a spread-the-bonus-pool strategy. Tucker is still growing into his body—as evidenced by a two-inch growth spurt his senior year—and working to find a swing he's comfortable with. At present he shows very good foot speed and the defensive chops to stick at short.

Development Track: As his draft year went along, there were some positive signs in the swing that likely helped cement his draft standing with the team. In the time it takes him to gain strength, especially in the lower half, he'll be able to find a better setup that helps begin the swing and engage the top half. His hands are a bit tighter with less movement, limiting all the moving parts that pre-existed throughout. First step: get into that pro strength program.

Variance: Extreme. Tucker is still growing and his swing is protean as a result, so he has a long way to go.

Mark Barry's Fantasy Take: Meh. Tucker could be good, but a lot of things need to happen for that to come to fruition. And even if it does, it's likely not terribly fantasy relevant. Toss Tucker on the watchlist if you'd like, but don't expect returns for a few years.

The Prospects You Meet Outside The Top Ten:

#11

Tanner Burns   RHP   Born: 12/28/98   Age: 22   Bats: R   Throws: R   Height: 6'0"   Weight: 215   Origin: Round 1, 2020 Draft (#36 overall)

An exceptional performer in the SEC over three seasons, Burns improved each year even as he continuously found success. A fastball-first pitcher, he can both cut and sink the pitch while hiding it well during his delivery. He establishes the heater in each quadrant early in the game before turning to his secondary pitches. The curveball is the best of the secondaries, however, the command of the rest of the arsenal lags behind that of his heater. The ceiling may not be as high, but he's likely to find a reliable back-end starter role.

MLB-ready arms, but probably relievers

Emmanuel Clase RHP   Born: 03/18/98   Age: 23   Bats: R   Throws: R   Height: 6'2"   Weight: 206   Origin: International Free Agent, 2015

YEAR	TEAM	LVL	AGE	W	L	SV	G	GS	IP	H	HR	BB/9	K/9	K	GB%	BABIP	WHIP	ERA	DRA-	WARP
2018	SPO	SS	20	1	1	12	22	0	28¹	16	0	1.9	8.6	27	61.1%	.225	0.78	0.64	241	-2.2
2019	DE	HI-A	21	2	0	1	6	0	7	4	0	1.3	14.1	11	76.9%	.308	0.71	0.00	61	0.1
2019	FRI	AA	21	1	2	11	33	1	37²	34	1	1.9	9.3	39	61.3%	.317	1.12	3.35	76	0.4
2019	TEX	MLB	21	2	3	1	21	1	23¹	20	2	2.3	8.1	21	59.1%	.281	1.11	2.31	80	0.4
2021 FS	CLE	MLB	23	2	2	3	57	0	50	47	6	4.0	8.7	48	52.8%	.298	1.40	4.36	98	0.2
2021 DC	CLE	MLB	23	2	2	3	53	0	57	54	6	4.0	8.7	55	52.8%	.298	1.40	4.36	98	0.4

Comparables: Yennsy Diaz, Carlos Sanabria, Germán Márquez

Acquired in the Corey Kluber trade last offseason, Clase had a completely lost season; he suffered a back injury early in spring training and then got popped for a steroid in May and was suspended for the entire shortened season. We'd heard in our canvassing of the system that he was back to full strength, and he looked as much in his first appearance in the Dominican Winter League a few weeks ago. At his best, Clase has one of the best weapons in baseball: a high-90s cutter—and it's a true cutter at that high of a speed, not a fastball with a little bit of natural cut—that regularly hits 100, which you probably saw a bunch of GIFs of in 2019. He also has a plus slider, and generally the whole package is unhittable when he's healthy and throwing strikes. He should be a high-leverage reliever starting right now.

Prospects to dream on a little

Bo Naylor C   Born: 02/21/00   Age: 21   Bats: L   Throws: R   Height: 6'0"   Weight: 195   Origin: Round 1, 2018 Draft (#29 overall)

YEAR	TEAM	LVL	AGE	PA	R	2B	3B	HR	RBI	BB	K	SB	CS	AVG/OBP/SLG	DRC+	BABIP	BRR	FRAA	WARP
2018	INDB	ROK	18	139	17	3	3	2	17	21	28	5	1	.274/.381/.402		.341			
2019	LC	LO-A	19	453	60	18	10	11	65	43	104	7	5	.243/.313/.421	97	.296	0.9	C(85) 3.4	2.2
2021 FS	CLE	MLB	21	600	52	26	5	12	58	41	191	5	2	.221/.277/.355	72	.314	1.8	C 1, 3B 0	0.6

Comparables: Jorge Alfaro, Joe Benson, Greg Golson

Part of the second high-profile set of brothers in the org, the younger of the Naylor brothers is often unfairly compared to his older sibling Josh. While he has a similar squarish frame, his athleticism is much better and gives him a chance to stick behind the plate when paired with his close-to-average catch-and-throw ability. The calling card offensively is a power stroke that is easy-plus on the raw side and shows up plenty in games. Of course there are a lot of strikeouts to go with that, but he fits the mold of what is expected of today's archetypal catcher.

Lenny Torres RHP   Born: 10/15/00   Age: 20   Bats: R   Throws: R   Height: 6'1"   Weight: 190   Origin: Round 1, 2018 Draft (#41 overall)

YEAR	TEAM	LVL	AGE	W	L	SV	G	GS	IP	H	HR	BB/9	K/9	K	GB%	BABIP	WHIP	ERA	DRA-	WARP
2018	INDB	ROK	17	0	0	0	6	5	15¹	14	0	2.3	12.9	22	51.4%	.400	1.17	1.76		

Comparables: Elvis Luciano, Beau Burrows, Abel De Los Santos

One of the youngest players in the 2018 draft class, Torres fit Cleveland's trend of valuing age with its corollary of physical projection. His pro debut in the AZL was very loud, as he showed an athletic delivery with a plus heater, makings of a plus slider, and feel for a change. Unfortunately, the following spring he underwent Tommy John surgery and missed all of 2019. The rehab process during 2020 would have been very cautious regardless, so you can expect Torres to hit the ground running in 2021, especially after adding lean muscle to his frame during the time off from game action.

The New Guys

Joey Cantillo   LHP   Born: 12/18/99   Age: 21   Bats: L   Throws: L   Height: 6'4"   Weight: 220   Origin: Round 16, 2017 Draft (#468 overall)

YEAR	TEAM	LVL	AGE	W	L	SV	G	GS	IP	H	HR	BB/9	K/9	K	GB%	BABIP	WHIP	ERA	DRA	WARP
2018	SD2	ROK	18	2	2	0	11	9	45¹	33	0	2.4	11.5	58	57.3%	.303	0.99	2.18		
2018	FW	LO-A	18	0	1	0	1	1	3²	4	0	7.4	12.3	5	70.0%	.400	1.91	9.82	89	0.0
2019	FW	LO-A	19	9	3	0	19	19	98	58	3	2.5	11.7	127	42.7%	.264	0.87	1.93	44	3.5
2019	LE	HI-A	19	1	1	0	3	3	13²	12	2	4.6	10.5	16	38.5%	.270	1.39	4.61	77	0.2
2021 FS	CLE	MLB	21	2	3	0	57	0	50	43	7	4.7	9.7	54	42.8%	.283	1.39	4.22	103	0.0

Comparables: Tyler Danish, Miguel Castro, José Fernández

Every season there's a few A-ball pitchers who absolutely dominate the level with an advanced changeup and an upper-80s fastball they can move around the zone. Cantillo was far younger than the median of that group—he spent 2019 as still a teenager—and may still add a tick or two, but overall the stats far outpaced the stuff. You could certainly argue Cleveland is the right place for him to add enough velocity and a suddenly viable slide/cutter thing. It wouldn't be the first time. But until we see signs of that, we can't bake it into his projection.

Owen Miller   SS   Born: 11/15/96   Age: 24   Bats: R   Throws: R   Height: 5'11"   Weight: 197   Origin: Round 3, 2018 Draft (#84 overall)

YEAR	TEAM	LVL	AGE	PA	R	2B	3B	HR	RBI	BB	K	SB	CS	AVG/OBP/SLG	DRC+	BABIP	BRR	FRAA	WARP
2018	TRI	SS	21	216	22	8	3	2	20	15	24	4	4	.335/.395/.440	158	.369	-2.5	SS(43) 3.3	1.4
2018	FW	LO-A	21	114	18	11	0	2	13	4	17	0	0	.336/.368/.495	134	.382	0.9	3B(13) -2.8, SS(7) -0.4	0.4
2019	AMA	AA	22	560	76	28	2	13	68	46	86	5	5	.290/.355/.430	112	.328	1.3	SS(71) 5.1, 2B(48) 0.5, 3B(6) -0.3	3.4
2021 FS	CLE	MLB	24	600	63	28	2	13	63	37	129	1	0	.258/.313/.390	93	.315	-0.3	2B 3, 3B 0	1.7
2021 DC	CLE	MLB	24	33	3	1	0	0	3	2	7	0	0	.258/.313/.390	93	.315	0.0	2B 0	0.1

Comparables: Gregorio Petit, Chris Valaika, Eugenio Suárez

Cantillo had the eye-popping numbers in 2019, but we ranked Miller as the better prospect on the 2020 Padres list. He's broadly similar to Tyler Freeman, with a bit more pop, but more likely to end up as a utility type than an everyday middle infielder. But this ranking—or lack thereof—overstates the gap between them as prospects.

Safe MLB bats, but less upside than you'd like

Daniel Johnson   RF   Born: 07/11/95   Age: 25   Bats: L   Throws: L   Height: 5'10"   Weight: 200   Origin: Round 5, 2016 Draft (#154 overall)

YEAR	TEAM	LVL	AGE	PA	R	2B	3B	HR	RBI	BB	K	SB	CS	AVG/OBP/SLG	DRC+	BABIP	BRR	FRAA	WARP
2018	HBG	AA	22	391	48	19	7	6	31	23	90	21	4	.267/.321/.410	95	.338	-2.3	RF(54) 6.3, CF(33) -2.9, LF(4) -0.7	0.2
2019	AKR	AA	23	167	25	7	2	10	33	16	39	6	3	.253/.337/.534	121	.276	-2.3	CF(24) -2.3, RF(10) -0.3, LF(4) -0.6	0.2
2019	COL	AAA	23	380	51	27	5	9	44	34	79	6	7	.306/.371/.496	122	.370	-1.5	RF(48) 6.4, CF(21) 1.2, LF(9) 0.0	2.4
2020	CLE	MLB	24	13	0	0	0	0	0	1	5	0	0	.083/.154/.083	77	.143		RF(4) -0.6, LF(1) -0.1	-0.1
2021 FS	CLE	MLB	25	600	59	24	3	18	65	39	168	11	4	.231/.293/.389	86	.298	0.7	RF 4, LF 0	1.1
2021 DC	CLE	MLB	25	266	26	10	1	8	28	17	74	5	2	.231/.293/.389	86	.298	0.3	RF 2	0.4

Comparables: Wladimir Balentien, Ben Francisco, Corey Hart

Johnson got a brief look in the bigs in 2020, where he continued to try and swing very, very hard at major league stuff. He has a plus power/speed combo, and the arm is even better than that, but until he reins in his aggressive, leveraged stroke, he'll struggle to establish himself as more than an optionable 26th man.

Top Talents 25 and Under (as of 4/1/2021):

1. Shane Bieber, RHP
2. George Valera, OF
3. Nolan Jones, 3B
4. James Karinchak, RHP
5. Triston McKenzie, RHP

6. Franmil Reyes, DH/OF
7. Gabriel Arias, SS
8. Daniel Espino, RHP
9. Brayan Rocchio, SS
10. Ethan Hankins, RHP

Shane Bieber, the reigning American League Cy Young Award winner, has developed into one of the very best pitchers in baseball. I've written previously on how even merely solid prospects have a 99th-percentile outcome of a superstar; that's Bieber's present trajectory.

James Karinchak, our 2020 No. 101 prospect, lived up to his billing and finished sixth in Rookie of the Year balloting. He trotted in from the bullpen with Wild Thing blaring over the speakers, stomped around the mound like a maniac, threw a bunch of 70-to-80-grade fastballs and curveballs, walked just a few too many for comfort, and struck out 53 of the 109 batters he faced. It was everything we'd hoped for, and just about the only real negative was that his velocity was a little down at times, not that it made his fastball less effective. Karinchak seems poised to take over the closer's role as soon as this year, and should continue to be one of the more entertaining and dominant relievers for the foreseeable future.

Franmil Reyes is generously listed with a secondary position in the outfield, which is sort of true in that he can stand there if you really want him to for some reason. He started 58 games in 2020 and 57 of them were at DH, matching his poor defensive reputation. Reyes has light-tower power and crushes the ball when he hits it, posting exit velocities near the top of the league. His overall offensive performance has been more above-average than star-level so far, and DH carries a high enough offensive burden that he could stand to inch that production up.

With a deep farm system—the top eight prospects in the system are all viable Top 101 candidates—only those three non-prospect eligible players made the 25 and under list. But that obscures the strength of Cleveland's young major-league talent a bit. In a weaker system, Aaron Civale, Josh Naylor, Jake Bauers, Logan Allen, and Yu Chang all might've made this list.

Colorado Rockies

The State of the System:

I've rewritten this four or five times now because I thought it was too mean. It's not a good system.

The Top Ten:

★ ★ ★ *2021 Top 101 Prospect* **#49** ★ ★ ★

1 **Zac Veen** **OF** OFP: 60 ETA: Late 2024
Born: 12/12/01 Age: 19 Bats: L Throws: R Height: 6'4" Weight: 190 Origin: Round 1, 2020 Draft (#9 overall)

The Report: After solid showings in last summer's high school all-star games, Veen's momentum continued into the fall and brief spring season, and he garnered mentions as a possible top-5 pick. It was a minor coup for the Rockies that he was still available at the ninth slot, where he was clearly the best player on the board. The smooth-swinging lefty has an advanced approach for his age, knowing when to be aggressive and when to be patient, and can do significant damage when ahead in the count. He's also more athletic than he's given credit for; his long limbs and long strides are surprisingly quick, allowing for plus speed on the basepaths and gap-to-gap coverage in the outfield. The so-so arm and likelihood he eventually loses a step probably paints him into a corner outfield spot in the future.

Development Track: Living on Florida's Atlantic coast, Veen was able to get more game action than almost any other high profile prospect prior to the shutdown thanks to the area's early start and preseason tournaments. There is room for growth on his frame, although keeping him light on his feet to maintain his athleticism would be ideal over bulky muscle. The bat looked as advertised at instructs, but his defense will need some work. With patience, one day he could terrorize opposing pitchers at Coors Field.

Variance: Medium. All the pieces are there to accommodate a modest floor while also including an All-Star potential ceiling.

J.P. Breen's Fantasy Take: Top-end bats in Colorado's system will always be overvalued, due to the #CoorsEffect. Veen, however, might be worth the lofty price tag. His advanced approach at the plate and his feel for hitting give him an attractive dynasty floor, whether with the Rockies or elsewhere, and the power-speed potential could make him fantasy stud. His pure upside is the highest of anyone selected in the 2020 MLB Draft.

2 **Ryan Rolison** **LHP** OFP: 55 ETA: Late 2021/Early 2022
Born: 07/11/97 Age: 23 Bats: R Throws: L Height: 6'2" Weight: 213 Origin: Round 1, 2018 Draft (#22 overall)

YEAR	TEAM	LVL	AGE	W	L	SV	G	GS	IP	H	HR	BB/9	K/9	K	GB%	BABIP	WHIP	ERA	DRA-	WARP
2018	GJ	ROK	20	0	1	0	9	9	29	15	2	2.5	10.6	34	65.7%	.200	0.79	1.86		
2019	ASH	LO-A	21	2	1	0	3	3	14²	8	0	1.2	8.6	14	37.8%	.216	0.68	0.61	49	0.5
2019	LAN	HI-A	21	6	7	0	22	22	116¹	129	22	2.9	9.1	118	43.6%	.327	1.44	4.87	94	0.6
2021 FS	COL	MLB	23	1	1	0	57	0	50	50	8	4.0	7.9	44	43.1%	.296	1.46	5.06	115	-0.3
2021 DC	COL	MLB	23	1	1	0	4	4	21	21	3	4.0	7.9	18	43.1%	.296	1.46	5.06	115	0.0

Comparables: Braxton Garrett, Kris Bubic, Patrick Sandoval

The Report: Given the Rockies' early competitiveness in the truncated season, there were whispers of bringing up Rolison for the stretch run. They were operating without a left-handed reliever in the bullpen for the majority of the year, not that James Pazos or Phillip Diehl inspired much confidence in the first place. Colorado ultimately didn't make the call, but it wasn't for a lack of success and stuff as Rolison showed an improved fastball and a sharper slider than before. The two-pitch mix ran through his teammates at the alternate site while Rolison showed improved strike-throwing ability.

Development Track: The Rockies are committed to developing Rolison as a starter, hence why they did not want him to work out of a bullpen without a clear spot for a starting pitcher. He will start 2021 on Double-A team "TBD" and most likely spend the whole season there. The Rockies hardly put guys on the fast track, even the advanced college picks who are supposed to move quickly.

Variance: Medium. Coors Field hasn't exactly been kind to pitchers without premium velocity, or to players who rely on their curveball as an out pitch (see Hoffman, Jeff).

J.P. Breen's Fantasy Take: While too many dynasty owners overestimate the #CoorsEffect for batters, I don't believe that's true on the pitching side. Dynasty owners tend to shy away from Rockies pitching prospects, and they should. Rolison is no different. At the absolute best, he's a mid-rotation arm who can strike out a batter per inning, thanks to his curveball, but even that is an undesirable profile at Coors. Even worse, Rolison is a fly-ball pitcher who had home-run issues in High-A. He's not a Top-300 dynasty prospect for me, though he'd be more interesting with a different organization.

3 Ryan Vilade SS   OFP: 50   ETA: 2022
Born: 02/18/99   Age: 22   Bats: R   Throws: R   Height: 6'2"   Weight: 226   Origin: Round 2, 2017 Draft (#48 overall)

YEAR	TEAM	LVL	AGE	PA	R	2B	3B	HR	RBI	BB	K	SB	CS	AVG/OBP/SLG	DRC+	BABIP	BRR	FRAA	WARP
2018	ASH	LO-A	19	533	77	20	4	5	44	49	96	17	13	.274/.353/.368	112	.333	-1.9	SS(116) -6.3	1.1
2019	LAN	HI-A	20	587	92	27	10	12	71	56	94	24	7	.303/.367/.466	118	.341	2.5	SS(83) -4.0, 3B(46) -4.3	2.6
2021 FS	COL	MLB	22	600	55	26	4	10	57	49	157	10	6	.242/.310/.362	87	.322	-2.7	SS -5, 3B -1	-0.1

Comparables: Tyler Wade, Amed Rosario, Yolmer Sánchez

The Report: Going into 2020, Vilade was prepared to play the outfield for the first time. It wasn't going to work as a shortstop, although we felt the Rockies may have given him more leash as a third baseman given his relative inexperience there before the 2019 season. There is much less uncertainty about Vilade at the plate, as he uses the whole field, doesn't strikeout often, and can put a charge into baseballs. Given the large dimensions of Coors Field, expect to see a lot of extra-base hits. But he keeps moving down the defensive spectrum, putting more pressure on the bat to perform.

Development Track: Vilade hasn't faced Double-A pitching yet. He will have to do that next year while playing a new position. Coors Field isn't exactly small, and being a below-average runner might be an issue even in the corners.

Variance: High. Vilade is learning a new position, hasn't faced advanced pitching yet, and had a notable split between Lancaster and everywhere else.

J.P. Breen's Fantasy Take: I am cooler on Vilade than most dynasty experts. He stole 17 bases in 2018 and 24 bases in 2019, but the 21-year-old doesn't profile to be a league-average runner. He'll be hard-pressed to reach double-digit steals, especially since his minor-league success rates have been very poor. Vilade reportedly has significant power potential; however, he has yet to post an ISO over .200 as a professional. He's a fringe top-200 prospect who will need to hit for major power to be fantasy relevant whatsoever in shallow leagues.

4 Michael Toglia 1B   OFP: 50   ETA: 2023
Born: 08/16/98   Age: 22   Bats: S   Throws: L   Height: 6'5"   Weight: 226   Origin: Round 1, 2019 Draft (#23 overall)

YEAR	TEAM	LVL	AGE	PA	R	2B	3B	HR	RBI	BB	K	SB	CS	AVG/OBP/SLG	DRC+	BABIP	BRR	FRAA	WARP
2019	BOI	SS	20	176	25	7	0	9	26	28	45	1	1	.248/.369/.483	131	.290	0.3	1B(38) -0.2	0.6
2021 FS	COL	MLB	22	600	50	26	2	12	56	40	209	1	0	.198/.256/.321	58	.292	-0.2	1B 0	-2.4

Comparables: Shane Peterson, Joe Mahoney, Ali Solis

The Report: Toglia is a switch-hitter with plus power. He can drive the ball all over, but the swing-and-miss became more of an issue as he transitioned from college to the pros. Three true outcome hitters don't typically rank high on a team prospect list, especially when they are playing mostly first base. The defense there is plus, at least, and he is athletic enough that they will give him opportunities in the outfield to add some versatility.

Development Track: The lack of a 2020 season—where you would have hoped for his advanced college bat to power its way to Double-A—leaves us without answers to just how much the big pop will play in games against better competition. Toglia will have to wait for 2021 to make his full-season debut, which will likely be in a less hitter-friendly park than Lancaster's. He will move through first base and the two outfield corners, but wherever he stands he will have to tighten up the plate discipline to project for long term impact with the bat.

Variance: Medium. While Toglia's pro resume is short, he does show quality game power already and good defense at first base, which gives him a higher floor than other three true outcome types.

J.P. Breen's Fantasy Take: Toglia is a good example of why defense matters in dynasty formats. Without a good glove, Toglia is a low-average power hitter who needs to absolutely mash to reach the majors in any capacity. With his good first-base defense, there are multiple paths available to fantasy relevance. The 2021 season will give us a better idea as to whether he's truly a drag in terms of batting average. Toglia is a top-150 dynasty prospect, better than Vilade thanks to role certainty and better current power.

5 Chris McMahon   OFP: 50   ETA: 2023
Born: 02/04/99   Age: 22   Bats: R   Throws: R   Height: 6'2"   Weight: 217   Origin: Round 2, 2020 Draft (#46 overall)

The Report: Among the top performers for last year's Collegiate National Team, McMahon was finally healthy and showing stuff area scouts believed was first-round caliber. After leading the team in strikeouts, he came out in fall workouts up to 98 mph and dominated in his few spring starts. Had the NCAA season continued, it's possible he could have worked his way further up draft boards in what was an incredibly deep college pitching class. The delivery is consistent, staying a hair upright and tall on his front leg without pushing off much with his back hip. So his mid-90s fastball is rooted in arm strength with the potential to add a tick or two with more lower half engagement. The breaking ball is a slurvy, downer-type that flashes good movement as a chase pitch even though it can be inconsistent.

Development Track: Staying healthy has been the issue during McMahon's amateur career. He has solid tools as a starting pitcher, needing sustained reps to work on his secondaries, including a changeup that has improved over time. Between the stout body, mechanics, and lack of mileage on his arm, there is some hope that there is a lot of projection left to be tapped into.

Variance: High. You just want to see more of what was on display in his four starts at The U this spring, but there's also the chance he could be a mid-rotation piece if all goes well.

J.P. Breen's Fantasy Take: Projectable collegiate pitchers are always intriguing, but the combination of health issues and inconsistent secondary stuff takes away most of that shine. Of course, there's also the Coors thing. The upside isn't high enough to warrant drafting in your offseason supplemental drafts, and he didn't even make the Honorable Mentions in Bret and Jesse's recap of the top-40 dynasty prospects from the 2020 MLB Draft.

6 Aaron Schunk 3B   OFP: 50   ETA: Late 2022
Born: 07/24/97   Age: 23   Bats: R   Throws: R   Height: 6'2"   Weight: 205   Origin: Round 2, 2019 Draft (#62 overall)

YEAR	TEAM	LVL	AGE	PA	R	2B	3B	HR	RBI	BB	K	SB	CS	AVG/OBP/SLG	DRC+	BABIP	BRR	FRAA	WARP
2019	BOI	SS	21	192	31	12	2	6	23	14	25	4	1	.306/.370/.503	138	.329	1.8	3B(37) 7.4	2.2
2021 FS	COL	MLB	23	600	55	27	3	13	61	36	144	6	2	.232/.287/.367	80	.290	1.3	3B 7	0.6

Comparables: Matt Skole, Gaby Sanchez, J.D. Davis

The Report: Schunk had a power spike his junior year at Georgia which jumped him into the second round of the draft. The ball continued to fly off his bat in the friendly confines of Boise, and the power is the most likely tool to reach above-average. The rest of the scouting report is a 45 or 50. Schunk has all the physical tools to be average at the hot corner, and might be athletic enough to play some second as well, which is the kind of infield positional flexibility the Rockies like to develop. There's not a long track record of the kind of power you'd want from an everyday third baseman, though.

Development Track: Schunk got some 2020 reps in at instructs and the profile looked more or less the same. He was on the older side for a college draftee and will turn 24 in the middle of the 2021 season, so you'd like to see him hit the ground running.

Variance: Medium. There's a broad base of potentially average tools, so between that and potential flexibility to move around the infield, Schunk should get major league reps. For example, Colorado gave Pat Valaika 400+ PAs across four seasons. But like Toglia, the missing year of mashing full-season ball injects some uncertainty.

J.P. Breen's Fantasy Take: Oof, it's never a great sign, at least in terms of dynasty value, when Pat Valaika appears in your write-up. Schunk hit .306/.370/.503 in 2019, but that came in the NWL and he was an experienced college bat. That stat line doesn't tell us much. Maybe he's a utility bat who hits 15-20 homers with a decent average, but that ain't worth more than a wait-and-see approach.

7   Brenton Doyle   RF   OFP: 50   ETA: 2023

Born: 05/14/98   Age: 23   Bats: R   Throws: R   Height: 6'3"   Weight: 200   Origin: Round 4, 2019 Draft (#129 overall)

YEAR	TEAM	LVL	AGE	PA	R	2B	3B	HR	RBI	BB	K	SB	CS	AVG/OBP/SLG	DRC+	BABIP	BRR	FRAA	WARP
2019	GJ	ROK+	21	210	42	10	3	8	31	30	46	17	3	.381/.474/.608		.480			
2021 FS	COL	MLB	23	600	48	26	3	7	50	43	197	20	4	.218/.279/.320	65	.326	8.1		-0.1

The Report: Doyle was a potential breakout prospect for 2020. He has tools, athleticism, physicality, and a relatively inexperienced background to make it all dangerous enough to cause trouble. He still has all that, and we are moving him up based on the upside he offers relative to other players who lack those tools. Everything you want he has: power, arm strength, above-average speed, outfield instincts; he just has not been consistently tested against better players yet.

Development Track: Doyle may start off in Low-A "TBD" in 2021, but could move quickly onward to stiffer competition if he sets it ablaze. He needs the repetitions.

Variance: High. D2 background, only one short season of pro experience (albeit very good), missing a year of games and experience.

J.P. Breen's Fantasy Take: >Doyle is the unheralded gem of this system. He's a potential everyday outfielder with five-category production, and those are difficult to find outside the top-250 dynasty prospects. Doyle may not make keeper cuts this winter in deep leagues—and is likely unrostered in shallower leagues—and is a sneaky target for supplemental drafts. He's a strong half-season away from being a dynasty darling.

8   Colton Welker   3B   OFP: 50   ETA: Late 2021/Early 2022

Born: 10/09/97   Age: 23   Bats: R   Throws: R   Height: 6'1"   Weight: 235   Origin: Round 4, 2016 Draft (#110 overall)

YEAR	TEAM	LVL	AGE	PA	R	2B	3B	HR	RBI	BB	K	SB	CS	AVG/OBP/SLG	DRC+	BABIP	BRR	FRAA	WARP
2018	LAN	HI-A	20	509	74	32	0	13	82	42	103	5	1	.333/.383/.489	139	.395	1.1	3B(92) -9.3, 1B(6) -0.7	1.2
2019	HFD	AA	21	394	37	23	1	10	53	32	68	2	1	.252/.313/.408	112	.281	-2.8	3B(63) -1.5, 1B(27) 2.2	1.3
2021 FS	COL	MLB	23	600	64	26	2	17	67	38	146	3	1	.252/.306/.403	89	.314	-0.2	1B 5, 3B -5	0.3
2021 DC	COL	MLB	23	100	10	4	0	2	11	6	24	0	0	.252/.306/.403	89	.314	0.0	1B 1, 3B -1	0.0

Comparables: Matt Dominguez, Lonnie Chisenhall, Andy LaRoche

The Report: Welker hit his first professional speed bump in 2019. He got off to a hot start in Hartford, but his aggressive, pull-and-lift approach got exposed as the season went on, and he struggled to adjust to Double-A arms who could move their fastball around the zone and break off quality secondaries in hitter's counts. Welker doesn't get cheated up there, and anything he squares is a threat to go for extra base hits, but he will need to tone down the aggressiveness and find a balance to his approach for the plus raw to get into games enough to carry a corner infield profile. He's a better fit at first than third, as the range and arm are a little light for the hot corner at times. He moves well laterally despite a sturdy frame, so maybe they will try him at second too.

Development Track: Welker spent the summer at the Rockies' alternate site and likely never had much of a chance to break into a crowded major league corner infield situation. That might open up some with a potential Nolan Arenado trade, but he could use some consolidation time in Triple-A Albuquerque or whatever their affiliate is in 2021. I'm sure Major League Baseball will let us all know at some point.

Variance: Medium. Welker's approach and defensive limitations could make him more of a short-side platoon bench piece.

J.P. Breen's Fantasy Take: Welker lacks a carrying fantasy tool. Scouting reports have long talked about his power potential, but he hasn't posted an ISO over .162 in his professional career. Plus, his average took a step backward against more advanced pitching. If we're talking about a potential platoon bat, as mentioned above, we're talking about dynasty irrelevance. He's not a top-300 dynasty prospect for me.

9   Drew Romo   C   OFP: 50   ETA: 2025
Born: 08/29/01   Age: 19   Bats: S   Throws: R   Height: 6'1"   Weight: 205   Origin: Round 1, 2020 Draft (#35 overall)

The Report: One Texas area scout said of Romo that he was the best defensive backstop to come out of high school in the last 20 years. High praise, considering the position has been notoriously difficult to draft and develop without players first going to college. As expected, he receives excellent grades with the glove and the arm while the offensive marks are decidedly behind. There is some thump in the bat, more from the right side as a switch-hitter, as both strokes tend to get slightly disconnected and need greater consistency.

Development Track: Romo's deficiencies are correctable, that is the good news. The two hardest skill-sets to master in baseball are switch-hitting and everything that encompasses the catcher position. In trying to do both, he has a very tall task ahead of him.

Variance: Very High. The list of successful catchers drafted out of high school in recent memory is miniscule. If he only maintains what he can do behind the plate, the bar is set so low as a hitter nowadays it won't take much to clear it.

J.P. Breen's Fantasy Take: Glove-first prep catchers are not worth rostering, even in deep dynasty leagues. And that's coming from someone who notoriously overvalues catching prospects.

10   Sam Weatherly   OFP: 50   ETA: 2023
Born: 05/28/99   Age: 22   Bats: L   Throws: L   Height: 6'4"   Weight: 205   Origin: Round 3, 2020 Draft (#81 overall)

The Report: A former two-way player out of cold-weather Michigan, it hasn't been long since Weatherly committed to pitching. Since that transition he has become demonstrably better, as his fastball/slider combo needed a ton of work on the control side. After previously walking more than a batter per inning, he took charge as the Friday night starter for Clemson this past spring and put up insane strikeout rates, to the tune of almost two per inning while cutting the walk rate by half. The 6-foot-4 frame offers a lot of arms and legs in the delivery, when he gets out of sync the command issues begin. When repeated, the fastball is TrackMan-friendly with carry up in the zone while sitting in the mid-90s. The real story is the slider, featuring a wipeout quality, oftentimes located better than his heater.

Development Track: He's shown just how good he can be when fully focusing on pitching. Ensuring he doesn't take a step back with the bases-on-balls will be necessary if he's to remain a starter long-term. Additionally, the changeup–which has mostly been a show-me pitch–will also need to come along at some point. Like any other college strikeout artist, you run him out there as a starter as long as possible knowing if things don't work out he can always rely on a dynamic 1-2 punch as a reliever.

Variance: High. In order for him to make it into the rotation he's going to need to clear two distinct hurdles (command and third pitch) that are far from gimmes. However, he does offer something as a valued relief pitcher in the event he stumbles.

J.P. Breen's Fantasy Take: Friends don't let friends draft potential relievers when they have yet to appear on a professional mound (outside of instructs).

The Prospects You Meet Outside The Top Ten

Solid pitching prospects, but limited upside

Karl Kauffmann   RHP   Born: 08/15/97   Age: 23   Bats: R   Throws: R   Height: 6'2"   Weight: 200   Origin: Round 2, 2019 Draft (#77 overall)

The staff ace of the 2019 College World Series runner-up rode his amateur success into being a Competitive Balance B pick that July. After throwing 114 innings that spring and summer, the Rockies shut him down in preparation for what was hoped to be a fast-moving pro trajectory in 2020. Since 2020 didn't happen, the Rockies added him to alternate site to get reps. The profile lacks upside as it doesn't feature a true out pitch, but instead relies on preventing hard contact and throwing strikes with an above-average fastball and slider.

Prospects to dream on a little

Warming Bernabel SS   Born: 06/06/02   Age: 19   Bats: R   Throws: R   Height: 6'0"   Weight: 180   Origin: International Free Agent, 2018

YEAR	TEAM	LVL	AGE	PA	R	2B	3B	HR	RBI	BB	K	SB	CS	AVG/OBP/SLG	DRC+	BABIP	BRR	FRAA	WARP
2019	DSL ROC	ROK	17	79	11	6	1	0	14	3	9	0	1	.300/.342/.414		.328			
2019	DSL COL	ROK	17	162	26	7	1	4	17	13	20	3	6	.225/.309/.373		.233			

Signed for $900,000 out of the Dominican in 2018, Bernabel isn't selling jeans but also isn't selling out for the kind of bat speed and barrel control that can handle plus major league velocity. I don't know if he will be ready for a full-season ball assignment in 2021, but I'll be asking around the AZ complex about him.

MLB-ready arms, but probably relievers

Lucas Gilbreath LHP   Born: 03/05/96   Age: 25   Bats: L   Throws: L   Height: 6'1"   Weight: 185   Origin: Round 7, 2017 Draft (#206 overall)

YEAR	TEAM	LVL	AGE	W	L	SV	G	GS	IP	H	HR	BB/9	K/9	K	GB%	BABIP	WHIP	ERA	DRA-	WARP
2018	ASH	LO-A	22	7	8	2	26	21	116	133	9	1.9	9.2	119	42.9%	.359	1.35	5.04	90	1.2
2019	LAN	HI-A	23	5	10	0	28	28	144	168	22	4.6	8.9	143	41.9%	.350	1.68	5.81	129	-2.2
2021 FS	COL	MLB	25	1	2	0	57	0	50	51	8	5.0	7.5	41	39.1%	.296	1.59	5.66	122	-0.5
2021 DC	COL	MLB	25	1	2	0	15	4	31	31	5	5.0	7.5	25	39.1%	.296	1.59	5.66	122	-0.1

Comparables: Sterling Sharp, Jimmy Lambert, Roberto Gómez

Perhaps it's a little odd to see a 40-man add who was last seen posting a near-6 ERA in Advanced-A as a 23-year-old here, but when said 40-man add is a lefty popping 100 in short bursts, it becomes quite explicable. Gilbreath more likely settles in as a 95-and-a-slider guy, but he's a *lefty* 95-and-a-slider guy, and could be a useful bullpen arm in 2021. And if he can be a 100-and-a-slider guy, there's an argument for him in the 10 spot over Weatherly.

You were going to ask about him in the comments

Riley Pint RHP   Born: 11/06/97   Age: 23   Bats: R   Throws: R   Height: 6'5"   Weight: 225   Origin: Round 1, 2016 Draft (#4 overall)

YEAR	TEAM	LVL	AGE	W	L	SV	G	GS	IP	H	HR	BB/9	K/9	K	GB%	BABIP	WHIP	ERA	DRA-	WARP
2018	BOI	SS	20	0	2	0	3	3	8	4	0	10.1	9.0	8	41.2%	.250	1.62	1.12	286	-0.8
2019	ASH	LO-A	21	0	1	0	21	3	17²	12	0	15.8	11.7	23	44.7%	.324	2.43	8.66	154	-0.6
2021 FS	COL	MLB	23	2	3	0	57	0	50	48	7	9.2	8.1	44	49.2%	.286	1.99	6.99	144	-1.1

Comparables: Yennsy Diaz, Jefry Rodriguez, Jordan Holloway

Pint was not added to the 40-man, although he was hitting triple digits in instructs himself. In what is becoming an unfortunately familiar refrain for the former fourth-overall pick, reports varied, from upper-90s heat and a plus-plus flashing slider around the zone enough to make it work to 20 command/control of a low-90s fastball. And these reports came a week apart.

Top Talents 25 and Under (as of 4/1/2021):

1. Zac Veen, OF
2. Brendan Rodgers, SS/2B
3. Ryan Rolison, LHP
4. Ryan Vilade, SS/3B
5. Michael Toglia, OF
6. Chris McMahon, RHP
7. Aaron Schunk, 3B
8. Brenton Doyle, OF
9. Colton Welker, 3B
10. Drew Romo, C

We were already preliminarily dreading ranking Brendan Rodgers as a prospect again this offseason when he was removed from our immediate purview by the changes to the service time rules. But that just left him to my purview on the 25-and-under beat. Alas.

For a few years now, we've been concerned about Rodgers' approach against advanced pitching negatively impacting his hit tool. In very limited MLB time, that's borne out in a 4/33 BB/K ratio and poor all-around offensive performance. We're now also worried about what seem to be chronic shoulder injuries; after a season-ending surgery in 2019 for a torn labrum, he missed all of September 2020 with a capsule strain in the same shoulder. There's still a lot of underlying talent and skill here, but there's a lot of ifs now, too.

For the rest of the eligible non-prospects ... well, it's kind of bleak. Peter Lambert made this list last year, just barely, and then blew out his elbow in summer camp and had Tommy John surgery in July. He missed all of 2020 and rates to miss much or all of 2021, too. Ryan Castellani took a regular turn in Colorado's rotation for much of the season. He put up a 7.92 DRA and walked more hitters than he struck out. The date cutoffs probably hurt more here than in most systems, with Germán Márquez and Antonio Senzatela both missing by fewer than three months.

Detroit Tigers

The State of the System:

The high-end pitching talent has scuffled recently and the system is now led by two potential impact bats. You still wonder if it's enough to fill out a competitive AL Central roster heading into Year Four of the rebuild.

The Top Ten:

─────────────── ★ ★ ★ *2021 Top 101 Prospect* **#13** ★ ★ ★ ───────────────

1 **Spencer Torkelson 3B**   OFP: 70   ETA: 2022, after a few weeks in the minors to "work on his defense."
Born: 08/26/99 Age: 21 Bats: R Throws: R Height: 6'1" Weight: 220 Origin: Round 1, 2020 Draft (#1 overall)

The Report: Rare is the player who is selected as a virtually ready-made product straight out of college. There may not be much left to the imagination, except for maybe where he ends up defensively. The draft card read by Rob Manfred listed Torkelson as a third baseman despite his never having appeared at the position in college. His defensive home is inconsequential—whether it's at third or first or a corner outfield spot—because the bat is what made him the first overall pick and it will carry him to the big leagues. It's an above-average hit tool thanks to a selective approach and plus-plus power to all fields. If there is a weakness offensively, it has yet to be exposed.

Development Track: All Torkelson did while at Arizona State is obliterate most of Barry Bonds' school records. He pummeled the Pac-12 every year, crushed in the Cape Cod League, and cruised on the U.S. Collegiate National Team. He can now turn the page to be tested against pro pitching (finally), after performing very well at fall instructs. How long he spends in the minors will depend on how quickly the bat forces the Tigers' hand.

Variance: Low. Defense is almost irrelevant when 30 homers annually might be the floor.

Mark Barry's Fantasy Take:

"All Torkelson did while at Arizona State is obliterate most of Barry Bonds' school records."

Lol.

I think Torkelson is very good at hitting and that will translate to the MLB. He's a no-doubt, top-10 dynasty guy for me and could be closer to five than 10.

─────────────── ★ ★ ★ *2021 Top 101 Prospect* **#19** ★ ★ ★ ───────────────

2 **Riley Greene RF**   OFP: 70   ETA: Late 2022/Early 2023
Born: 09/28/00 Age: 20 Bats: L Throws: L Height: 6'3" Weight: 200 Origin: Round 1, 2019 Draft (#5 overall)

YEAR	TEAM	LVL	AGE	PA	R	2B	3B	HR	RBI	BB	K	SB	CS	AVG/OBP/SLG	DRC+	BABIP	BRR	FRAA	WARP
2019	TIW	ROK	18	43	9	3	0	2	8	5	12	0	0	.351/.442/.595		.478			
2019	NOR	SS	18	100	12	3	1	1	7	11	25	1	0	.295/.380/.386	127	.403	-1.5	CF(21) 3.5	0.7
2019	WM	LO-A	18	108	13	2	2	2	13	6	26	4	0	.219/.278/.344	62	.268	0.8	CF(20) 1.9, RF(4) -0.0	0.2
2021 FS	DET	MLB	20	600	48	26	3	9	53	33	209	6	2	.214/.265/.323	61	.323	1.5	CF 8, RF 0	-0.1

Comparables: Luis Alexander Basabe, Harold Ramirez, Manuel Margot

The Report: Greene's profile is one of balance. He has the five-tool potential you'd expect from a prep outfielder drafted fifth overall, but he arrived in the pro ranks in 2019 with a fairly advanced offensive game for his age and experience level. He had room to fill out and add strength, but the present frame looked the part of a future major leaguer. The hit and power tools both projected as plus despite a late hand load due to his bat speed and solid approach. The physical tools showed a potential above-average outfield glove, but Greene did struggle with his routes and reads in the big Norwich outfield and his arm might be the one place on the scouting sheet you struggle to give him at least a 5. The performance might not have been immediately loud, but you didn't have to squint hard to see a future plus regular, with breakout potential past that.

Development Track: About that breakout potential: We are about as confident as we can be for a prospect with uh ... zero 2020 games played that a breakout of some sort happened. Greene added the good weight and the game power seems to be catching up to the raw. More reps in the outfield at the alternate site and instructs have smoothed out the defensive game and he's maintained most of his straight line speed for now, although I'd expect continued physical maturation in his 20s to make him a better fit in left than center. The bat will play there.

Variance: High. He did have zero real 2020 games. So we're hedging some until he's showing the same tools/skills gains in the upper minors. There was at least some discussion about whether he should rank over Torkelson though, if you want to talk about positive variance.

Mark Barry's Fantasy Take: There's no doubt that Torkelson is the No. 1 dude in this system, but Green might be my personal favorite. He has a chance to contribute in all five categories, with a plus batting average (a stat that has been exceedingly hard to find as of late). Because I'm typically one to value dynasty bats more than arms (really going out on a limb there), I'd have Green hovering around my personal top-20 list.

★ ★ ★ *2021 Top 101 Prospect* **#27** ★ ★ ★

3 Casey Mize RHP   OFP: 60   ETA: Debuted in 2020

Born: 05/01/97   Age: 24   Bats: R   Throws: R   Height: 6'3"   Weight: 220   Origin: Round 1, 2018 Draft (#1 overall)

YEAR	TEAM	LVL	AGE	W	L	SV	G	GS	IP	H	HR	BB/9	K/9	K	GB%	BABIP	WHIP	ERA	DRA-	WARP
2018	TIW	ROK	21	0	0	0	1	1	2	0	0	4.5	18.0	4	100.0%	.000	0.50	0.00		
2018	LAK	HI-A	21	0	1	0	4	4	11²	13	2	1.5	7.7	10	44.1%	.344	1.29	4.63	91	0.1
2019	LAK	HI-A	22	2	0	0	6	6	30²	11	0	1.5	8.8	30	45.1%	.157	0.52	0.88	37	1.2
2019	ERI	AA	22	6	3	0	15	15	78²	69	5	2.1	8.7	76	41.7%	.295	1.11	3.20	85	0.8
2020	DET	MLB	23	0	3	0	7	7	28¹	29	7	4.1	8.3	26	38.2%	.268	1.48	6.99	129	-0.2
2021 FS	DET	MLB	24	8	9	0	26	26	150	151	24	3.0	8.1	134	39.2%	.297	1.35	4.78	111	0.1
2021 DC	DET	MLB	24	6	10	0	24	24	126	127	20	3.0	8.1	113	39.2%	.297	1.35	4.78	111	0.6

Comparables: Shawn Chacon, Tyler Mahle, Archie Bradley

The Report: We really had no idea what to do with Mize last offseason. For the first half of 2019, he was the best pitching prospect in baseball, an absolute monster with a mid-90s fastball that he manipulated well and three plus off-speeds that all flashed plus-plus. The command was there and he looked like a potential future ace pitching in High-A and Double-A. Then he had a shoulder injury. While he came back briefly as a diminished version of himself and pitched poorly, he was quickly shut down after that, and we really didn't know what version of Mize to expect when the Tigers called him up in August.

Development Track: In Mize's first start in the majors, he flashed some of the ace potential, albeit with a little less command and a little less in-game endurance than you would have liked to see with all the question marks coming out of 2019. Those command and endurance issues lingered for his remaining six starts, and he also didn't always sit mid-90s as the season progressed. On balance, he was kind of terrible, and we're leaning a lot on our priors here to even have him this high.

Variance: High. Mize has shown us more than this in the past, and even flashed it for three and four inning spurts in the majors. He could put it back together very quickly—or never do so at all. I'd like to be optimistic here, but he really needs an uninterrupted season where nothing major goes wrong.

Mark Barry's Fantasy Take: Things were weird this year and everything should be taken with a grain of salt. Still, Mize was really bad in his debut, taking a huge step back with his command, failing to get many whiffs, and serving up dingers like they were macarons during Biscuit Week. Fold in his prior arm ailments and I am, as they say, worried. I'm in wait-and-see mode with Mize, so it's likely I won't have him on any fantasy teams in the near future.

www.baseballprospectus.com

★ ★ ★ *2021 Top 101 Prospect* **#46** ★ ★ ★

4 Matt Manning RHP OFP: 60 ETA: 2021

Born: 01/28/98 Age: 23 Bats: R Throws: R Height: 6'6" Weight: 195 Origin: Round 1, 2016 Draft (#9 overall)

YEAR	TEAM	LVL	AGE	W	L	SV	G	GS	IP	H	HR	BB/9	K/9	K	GB%	BABIP	WHIP	ERA	DRA-	WARP
2018	WM	LO-A	20	3	3	0	11	11	55²	47	3	4.5	12.3	76	40.5%	.346	1.35	3.40	69	1.3
2018	LAK	HI-A	20	4	4	0	9	9	51¹	32	4	3.3	11.4	65	45.8%	.243	0.99	2.98	76	1.0
2018	ERI	AA	20	0	1	0	2	2	10²	11	0	3.4	11.0	13	39.3%	.423	1.41	4.22	65	0.3
2019	ERI	AA	21	11	5	0	24	24	133²	93	7	2.6	10.0	148	47.2%	.259	0.98	2.56	56	3.6
2021 FS	DET	MLB	23	9	8	0	26	26	150	125	18	4.4	9.4	156	43.5%	.274	1.33	3.87	97	1.3
2021 DC	DET	MLB	23	3	4	0	12	12	63	52	7	4.4	9.4	65	43.5%	.274	1.33	3.87	97	0.8

Comparables: Luis Severino, Ian Anderson, Stephen Gonsalves

The Report: Manning profiles as a mid-rotation starting pitcher with some tantalizing hints that he might be even better. His fastball sits in the low-to-mid-90s, touching 96, and he gets great extension and angle on it. His power curveball profiles as a true plus pitch and flashes plus-plus potential, although it's a little humpier than you'd like. The changeup is going to make or break the profile as a starter; we projected that it would settle in as an average offering on balance last year, when it sometimes flashed higher and sometimes was too firm and looked like it needed to pick up a grade for him to stay in the rotation. Manning seems to have largely overcome past repeatability and delivery issues, and all-in-all he's a very fine pitching prospect.

Development Track: Manning probably would have debuted in the majors in 2020 were it not for a forearm strain. The Tigers shut him down in August, although we've been assured that he's healthy and ready to go for 2021. He was added to the 40-man roster after the season.

Variance: Medium, still. We still have concerns that he'll end up in the bullpen if the changeup consistency doesn't improve, and the forearm issues aren't exactly great. But there's positive variance here too, with his fastball/breaking ball combination hinting at higher-end outcomes if the rest sorts out.

Mark Barry's Fantasy Take: Potential mid-rotation starter, you say? With forearm issues? How could I possibly resist? As far as guys with that profile, however, I like Manning a little more than the rest. I think he'll strike enough guys out that he'll still be useful, even if the rate stats aren't great. He's an SP3 for me with the upside of a little more, but also a downside of a reliever.

★ ★ ★ *2021 Top 101 Prospect* **#99** ★ ★ ★

5 Tarik Skubal LHP OFP: 55 ETA: Debuted in 2020

Born: 11/20/96 Age: 24 Bats: L Throws: L Height: 6'3" Weight: 215 Origin: Round 9, 2018 Draft (#255 overall)

YEAR	TEAM	LVL	AGE	W	L	SV	G	GS	IP	H	HR	BB/9	K/9	K	GB%	BABIP	WHIP	ERA	DRA-	WARP
2018	TIW	ROK	21	1	0	0	2	1	3	2	0	3.0	15.0	5	85.7%	.286	1.00	0.00		
2018	NOR	SS	21	0	0	1	4	0	12	8	0	1.5	12.8	17	45.8%	.333	0.83	0.75	61	0.3
2018	WM	LO-A	21	2	0	1	3	0	7¹	5	0	1.2	13.5	11	21.4%	.357	0.82	0.00	40	0.3
2019	LAK	HI-A	22	4	5	0	15	15	80¹	62	5	2.1	10.9	97	39.0%	.294	1.01	2.58	68	1.7
2019	ERI	AA	22	2	3	0	9	9	42¹	25	2	3.8	17.4	82	39.1%	.343	1.02	2.13	49	1.3
2020	DET	MLB	23	1	4	0	8	7	32	28	9	3.1	10.4	37	27.4%	.253	1.22	5.62	137	-0.3
2021 FS	DET	MLB	24	9	8	0	26	26	150	129	24	3.3	10.7	177	32.4%	.287	1.23	3.84	94	1.5
2021 DC	DET	MLB	24	4	6	0	21	21	86	74	13	3.3	10.7	101	32.4%	.287	1.23	3.84	94	1.2

Comparables: Brendan McKay, Eric Lauer, Nick Margevicius

The Report: The Tigers made a bet on Skubal after he missed most of two college seasons following Tommy John surgery, and struggled with his control and command when he returned to the mound in 2018. It paid off in 2019, as a healthy Skubal dominated two levels with a plus fastball/slider combo. His Double-A K-rate was absurd, as he struck out nearly half of the Eastern League batters he faced. The raw pitch grades wouldn't suggest that level of dominance. His velocity is plus, but not spectacular when stretched out, and the fastball is high-spin but runs pretty true. The slider flashes plus-plus, but he can't always command it in a way that elicits chases against better hitters. But both pitches can play up to the deception and angle created in Skubal's delivery. There were still reliever markers even in his breakout campaign, but at worst we'd expect him to be a very good, potential multi-inning fireman.

Detroit Tigers - 97

Development Track: Skubal was promoted to Detroit the same week as Mize and Paredes. All three had their struggles adjusting to major league competition. Skubal leaned heavily on his fastball and hitters were able to hit it hard in the zone, although he got his fair share of swings-and-misses with it as well. They were able to lay off the slider and other secondaries enough to force Skubal into fastball counts, and it may not be enough fastball to turn over a lineup multiple times without further command and secondary improvement. He threw his change a lot, but it doesn't have a ton of action or deception, and his curveball is potentially average, but more a change-of-breaking-ball look for now. Despite the MLB struggles, we don't think the profile has changed all that much, although that multi-inning fireman role looks more likely.

Variance: Medium. The breaker is good enough you will find a role for him on a major-league staff, but the command, change, and durability issues mean it might be in a late-inning shutdown role.

Mark Barry's Fantasy Take: During his debut, Skubal's ERA more than doubled the second time through the order. It's a small sample, sure, but it's also the stuff multi-inning relievers are made of. It's too early to relegate him to that role (and the Tigers aren't good enough to have that pressing need), but his current profile is awfully Carlos Rodón-y and not in a good way.

6   Dillon Dingler   C   OFP: 55   ETA: 2023
Born: 09/17/98   Age: 22   Bats: R   Throws: R   Height: 6'3"   Weight: 210   Origin: Round 2, 2020 Draft (#38 overall)

The Report: You will be hard-pressed to find a player in the 2020 draft who improved his stock more given the very short season. After arriving at Ohio State as primarily a center fielder, the Buckeyes started to try him at catcher due to his overall athleticism. The transition to a full-time catcher role hit its peak this spring. Dingler showed an impressive ability to block pitches, flashed a plus arm, and demonstrated improved receiving. Not only did the defense now look above-average, so did his right-handed swing, as he consistently barreled balls while showing an advanced approach. Dingler is the rare projectable college catcher where both the offensive and defensive tools could end up above-average.

Development Track: Catching is still a relatively new position for Dingler. Even with the rapid improvements, he will need to continue to refine those skills and build upon them. He's a plus athlete for a backstop, which should help him handle the defensive rigors. The track record is limited yet promising, with reports out of post-draft workouts noting continued high performance.

Variance: Very High. All signs are trending upward, even if it is just a snapshot in time. There exists a scenario where the bat develops faster than the glove and you try to get him defensive reps a bunch of places. This could go in a bunch of different directions.

Mark Barry's Fantasy Take: Dingler could be very good, but as he's new to the position, it could take awhile. And that position is catcher. I don't think you have to take the plunge right away, and if he develops into the next, say, Daulton Varsho, then we'll cross that bridge when we come to it.

7   Isaac Paredes   3B   OFP: 50   ETA: Debuted in 2020
Born: 02/18/99   Age: 22   Bats: R   Throws: R   Height: 5'11"   Weight: 213   Origin: International Free Agent, 2015

YEAR	TEAM	LVL	AGE	PA	R	2B	3B	HR	RBI	BB	K	SB	CS	AVG/OBP/SLG	DRC+	BABIP	BRR	FRAA	WARP
2018	LAK	HI-A	19	347	50	19	2	12	48	32	54	1	0	.259/.338/.455	126	.274	0.3	SS(59) 3.2, 2B(22) 0.5, 3B(3) -0.1	2.0
2018	ERI	AA	19	155	20	9	0	3	22	19	22	1	0	.321/.406/.458	141	.358	0.3	3B(18) 0.6, SS(15) 0.9, 2B(2) 0.1	1.2
2019	ERI	AA	20	552	63	23	1	13	66	57	61	5	3	.282/.368/.416	137	.298	-2.3	3B(81) -3.4, SS(32) 0.1	3.4
2020	DET	MLB	21	108	7	4	0	1	6	8	24	0	0	.220/.278/.290	81	.280	-0.4	3B(33) -2.4	-0.3
2021 FS	DET	MLB	22	600	67	27	2	15	66	48	125	1	0	.244/.315/.390	97	.291	0.5	3B 0, 2B 0	1.5
2021 DC	DET	MLB	22	463	51	21	2	11	51	37	97	0	0	.244/.315/.390	97	.291	0.4	3B 0	0.8

Comparables: Wilmer Flores, Francisco Lindor, J.P. Crawford

The Report: Since being acquired from the Cubs in 2017 Paredes has been a mainstay on the Tigers' list, ranking as high as third two years ago. The bat has always been the carrying tool and he's displayed the ability to hit at every level in his minor league tenure. There is plus raw power, but with the swing geared more for contact it plays average in game. Defensively, he's outgrown any possibility of sticking up the middle and has settled in at third base.

Development Track: Paredes started hot but never got back on track after a rough 1-for-29 late August slump. The final slash line (.220/.278/.290) was disappointing, but his youth and track record of hitting should give hope for a rebound. Detroit is in full rebuild mode and Paredes will get plenty of major league at bats next year.

Variance: Medium. This profile is tough when it's limited to a corner infield position. It's unlikely Parades ever becomes a star, but his offensive game gives a pathway to a major league starting role.

Mark Barry's Fantasy Take: Lazy Teammate Comp Alert: the future fantasy line for Parades reminds me a lot of Jeimer Candelario, which is also fun because they came over together from the Cubs. I'm still in for .280ish and 20 homers at peak, which is pretty useful, if not transcendent.

8 Alex Faedo RHP   OFP: 50   ETA: 2021, if healthy
Born: 11/12/95   Age: 25   Bats: R   Throws: R   Height: 6'5"   Weight: 225   Origin: Round 1, 2017 Draft (#18 overall)

YEAR	TEAM	LVL	AGE	W	L	SV	G	GS	IP	H	HR	BB/9	K/9	K	GB%	BABIP	WHIP	ERA	DRA-	WARP
2018	LAK	HI-A	22	2	4	0	12	12	61	49	3	1.9	7.5	51	32.0%	.263	1.02	3.10	66	1.5
2018	ERI	AA	22	3	6	0	12	12	60	54	15	3.3	8.8	59	26.3%	.250	1.27	4.95	94	0.6
2019	ERI	AA	23	6	7	0	22	22	115¹	104	17	2.0	10.5	134	32.5%	.299	1.12	3.90	77	1.7
2021 FS	DET	MLB	25	2	3	0	57	0	50	49	8	3.3	8.8	48	31.5%	.295	1.35	4.54	114	-0.3

Comparables: Jordan Yamamoto, Ryan Helsley, Robert Dugger

The Report: Faedo was one of the best pitchers in University of Florida history—he was the Most Outstanding Player of the 2017 College World Series—and was an early candidate to go first-overall in the 2017 MLB Draft. He fell to the middle of the round and has settled in as a good-not-great pitching prospect, but that's still fun. Faedo lives off a low-90s fastball and a plus slider that has been his go-to out pitch since college, and he commands and manipulates both pitches well. His changeup has lagged a bit behind, and that's the pitch he's going to need to improve to establish himself as a long-term starting option in the bigs. Given his fastball has touched higher velocities in the past and the quality of the slider, he should have a decent bullpen fallback, too.

Development Track: Faedo had a lost 2020, even by prospect standards; he tested positive for COVID-19 in July and was shut down for the season with a forearm strain not that long after he got ramped up at the alternate site. He was working out at instructs, and was added to the 40-man roster after the season.

Variance: Medium. We had "low" last year, and he hasn't actually pitched in games since then so there's no known additional talent variance or anything. But you really can't give a prospect low variance when he hasn't pitched since being shut down with a forearm strain.

Mark Barry's Fantasy Take: In this space last season, I had Faedo pegged as having fantasy SP5 upside. Since he pretty much hasn't pitched since then, I'm sticking to it.

9 Joey Wentz LHP   OFP: 50   ETA: 2022
Born: 10/06/97   Age: 23   Bats: L   Throws: L   Height: 6'5"   Weight: 220   Origin: Round 1, 2016 Draft (#40 overall)

YEAR	TEAM	LVL	AGE	W	L	SV	G	GS	IP	H	HR	BB/9	K/9	K	GB%	BABIP	WHIP	ERA	DRA-	WARP
2018	FLO	HI-A	20	3	4	0	16	16	67	49	3	3.2	7.1	53	44.4%	.251	1.09	2.28	86	0.9
2018	DAY	HI-A	20	0	0	0	1	1	4	1	0	2.2	4.5	2		.091	0.50	0.00		
2019	ERI	AA	21	2	0	0	5	5	25²	20	3	1.4	13.0	37	19.3%	.315	0.94	2.10	67	0.5
2019	MIS	AA	21	5	8	0	20	20	103	90	13	3.9	8.7	100	32.6%	.283	1.31	4.72	113	-0.7
2021 FS	DET	MLB	23	2	3	0	57	0	50	47	8	5.0	8.6	47	32.4%	.288	1.50	4.93	117	-0.3

Comparables: Trevor Rogers, Génesis Cabrera, Lucas Giolito

The Report: Wentz never consistently found the top-end, mid-90s velocity he showed as a prep his draft year, but after varying velocity reports and curveball effectiveness across his pro career, he had settled back in as a solid pitching prospect after being dealt to the Tigers at the 2019 deadline. A mechanical tweak upped the effectiveness of his low-90s fastball, and both the curve and change projected to above-average...

Development Track: ... and then Wentz was one of the handful of pitchers who blow out every spring, going under the knife for Tommy John surgery in March. His recovery is as expected so far and he should be back throwing in games by mid-season 2021. Perhaps this will allow him a reset from the past couple seasons of injury and inconsistency, but you never want to have major elbow surgery as a pitcher. Coming back 100 percent is not a guarantee as the surgery is common but not routine.

Variance: High. I suppose there are worse seasons to lose to a torn UCL and Tommy John, but even if Wentz has had a normal recovery so far, we won't know what he looks like until he's back on a mound next season.

Mark Barry's Fantasy Take: I'd keep a heralded southpaw on my watchlist as he treks back from Tommy John surgery, but I wouldn't go out and trade for such an arm.

10 Parker Meadows CF

OFP: 50   ETA: 2023

Born: 11/02/99   Age: 21   Bats: L   Throws: R   Height: 6'5"   Weight: 205   Origin: Round 2, 2018 Draft (#44 overall)

YEAR	TEAM	LVL	AGE	PA	R	2B	3B	HR	RBI	BB	K	SB	CS	AVG/OBP/SLG	DRC+	BABIP	BRR	FRAA	WARP
2018	TIW	ROK	18	85	16	2	1	4	8	8	25	3	1	.284/.376/.500		.378			
2018	NOR	SS	18	21	4	1	0	0	2	2	6	0	0	.316/.381/.368	97	.462	0.1	CF(6) 0.0	0.0
2019	WM	LO-A	19	504	52	15	2	7	40	47	113	14	8	.221/.296/.312	78	.277	-1.1	CF(101) -2.3, RF(16) 0.8	0.0
2021 FS	DET	MLB	21	600	49	25	2	10	53	35	205	8	4	.213/.265/.323	60	.317	-3.0	CF 1, RF 0	-1.4

Comparables: Derrick Robinson, Mickey Moniak, Carlos Tocci

The Report: Tall, lean, and athletic, Meadows has all the physical tools to be a top-flight center fielder. It takes a few steps for his 6-foot-5 frame to reach top gear, but when it does he has exceptional speed. Not the type of speed that will produce a ton of steals, but it will allow him to take extra bases and cover large swaths of ground in the outfield. He will grow into some power eventually as the swing develops.

Development Track: The lost season was particularly rough for Meadows. A solid year at Lakeland could have allowed us to chalk up his rough 2019 to the growing pains of a prep player in his first full season. We did get some good reports about his development during his brief stint at Toledo, but we will have to wait and see if real strides have been made offensively.

Variance: High. The athleticism and glove give him a path to the majors as a reserve type, but we're going to need to see him hit consistently if he's going to be anything more.

Mark Barry's Fantasy Take: I love the high ceiling for Meadows, but he's the type of prospect that suffers the most by missing out on competitive games. He still has a big ceiling, but without reps (and without steals), it's a fantasy risk I won't be taking.

The Prospects You Meet Outside The Top Ten

Prospects to dream on a little

Roberto Campos   Born: 06/14/03   Age: 18   Bats: R   Throws: R   Height: 6'3"   Weight: 200   Origin: International Free Agent, 2019

Campos is the Tigers' version of Jasson Dominguez without the Instagram highlights. Both signed their respective teams' largest international free agent contract and have yet to play stateside. Campos might not be as powerful as his Yankees counterpart, but reports tell of a similarly offensive-minded outfielder with a knack for barreling up the baseball. He's still just a teenager and until we get some live looks against real pitching, it's going to be a challenge to slot Campos into the prospect ranks.

Interesting Draft Follow

Gage Workman   Born: 10/24/99   Age: 21   Bats: S   Throws: R   Height: 6'4"   Weight: 195   Origin: Round 4, 2020 Draft (#102 overall)

Workman was the third baseman "blocking" Torkelson from playing there at Arizona State. He's a plus defender there with enough on-base skills due to a patient approach to be a useful left-side infield bench piece. He'll have to show a bit more pop to project as an everyday third baseman though.

Safe MLB bats, but less upside than you'd like

Daz Cameron **CF** Born: 01/15/97 Age: 24 Bats: R Throws: R Height: 6'2" Weight: 185 Origin: Round 1, 2015 Draft (#37 overall)

YEAR	TEAM	LVL	AGE	PA	R	2B	3B	HR	RBI	BB	K	SB	CS	AVG/OBP/SLG	DRC+	BABIP	BRR	FRAA	WARP
2018	LAK	HI-A	21	246	35	9	3	3	20	25	69	10	4	.259/.346/.370	117	.366	2.5	CF(38) 1.9, RF(18) 0.9	1.2
2018	ERI	AA	21	226	32	12	5	5	35	25	53	12	5	.285/.367/.470	123	.366	3.4	CF(34) -7.0, RF(16) 1.5	0.7
2018	TOL	AAA	21	62	8	4	1	0	6	2	15	2	2	.211/.246/.316	55	.279	0.7	CF(14) 0.3, RF(1) 0.0	-0.1
2019	TOL	AAA	22	528	68	22	6	13	43	62	152	17	8	.214/.330/.377	86	.291	2.4	CF(93) -1.0, RF(19) 5.4	1.3
2020	DET	MLB	23	59	4	2	1	0	3	2	19	1	0	.193/.220/.263	68	.289	0.1	RF(16) 0.5	-0.1
2021 FS	DET	MLB	24	600	59	23	7	12	58	50	204	16	7	.216/.293/.355	77	.322	2.8	RF 19, LF 0	2.3
2021 DC	DET	MLB	24	198	19	7	2	4	19	16	67	5	2	.216/.293/.355	77	.322	0.9	RF 6	0.6

Comparables: Anthony Gose, Michael Saunders, Dalton Pompey

When the Tigers called Cameron up in September, I wrote much of our Call-Up article about his contact and plate approach issues. His swing and contact rates weren't *catastrophically* bad in his 59 PA late season run, but they weren't good either, and from an outcome perspective he walked only twice and struck out 19 times. The hit tool is the big question here; if he can hit .250 consistently the rest of the profile will carry him into being a good regular, but there's a lot of evidence he might not be able to hit .250 consistently without significant hit tool development.

Top Talents 25 and Under (as of 4/1/2021):

1. Spencer Torkelson, 3B/1B
2. Riley Greene, OF
3. Casey Mize, RHP
4. Matt Manning, RHP
5. Tarik Skubal, LHP
6. Dillon Dingler, C
7. Isaac Paredes, 3B
8. Alex Faedo, RHP
9. Joey Wentz, LHP
10. Willi Castro, SS

Willi Castro is the lone major-leaguer to make the list. The switch-hitting former Cleveland farmhand grabbed hold of the starting shortstop job in September and thrived, hitting .349 on the season with power over 140 plate appearances and ending up fourth in Rookie of the Year voting. While the performance was superficially impressive, his DRC+ was a mere 103, and his WARP was actually negative due to poor defensive performance. There's not a whole lot to suggest .349 with pop is attainable again and he's probably not really a shortstop, but there's a reasonable enough chance he levels out at useful or better to run it back in 2021.

Most of the rest of Detroit's top young talent is still prospect eligible. Other than Castro, the main player of note is Rony García, the top pick in the 2019 Rule 5 Draft who stuck on the roster all season. While I liked him some in the Yankees' system, he pitched very poorly in the majors and is not a better bet for long-term future success than Faedo or Wentz.

Houston Astros

The State of the System:

The Astros have had a long run of success hitting on their OFP 50/55 arms. That will need to continue, because that's most of the system now.

The Top Ten:

★ ★ ★ *2021 Top 101 Prospect* **#69** ★ ★ ★

1 Forrest Whitley RHP   OFP: 60   ETA: 2021, pending health

Born: 09/15/97   Age: 23   Bats: R   Throws: R   Height: 6'7"   Weight: 238   Origin: Round 1, 2016 Draft (#17 overall)

YEAR	TEAM	LVL	AGE	W	L	SV	G	GS	IP	H	HR	BB/9	K/9	K	GB%	BABIP	WHIP	ERA	DRA-	WARP
2018	CC	AA	20	0	2	0	8	8	26¹	15	2	3.8	11.6	34	37.7%	.220	0.99	3.76	70	0.6
2019	AST	ROK	21	0	2	0	2	2	4¹	2	0	18.7	20.8	10	50.0%	.333	2.54	8.31		
2019	FAY	HI-A	21	1	0	0	2	2	8¹	4	0	1.1	11.9	11	44.4%	.222	0.60	2.16	46	0.3
2019	CC	AA	21	2	2	0	6	6	22²	18	2	7.5	14.3	36	46.7%	.372	1.63	5.56	112	-0.1
2019	RR	AAA	21	0	3	0	8	5	24¹	35	9	5.5	10.7	29	30.7%	.400	2.05	12.21	157	-0.2
2021 FS	HOU	MLB	23	8	9	0	26	26	150	132	28	5.3	10.7	177	37.3%	.288	1.48	5.09	110	0.2
2021 DC	HOU	MLB	23	4	4	0	12	12	64	56	12	5.3	10.7	75	37.3%	.288	1.48	5.09	110	0.3

Comparables: Julio Urías, Lucas Sims, Jonathan Hernández

The Report: As recently as the 2019 Arizona Fall League, Whitley was showing off four plus-or-better offerings: a mid-90s fastball, a diving changeup that tunnels well with the fastball, and two distinct swing-and-miss breakers, a power slider with late tilt and a curveball with strong depth. That AFL stint got us to hold the line on a 70 OFP grade last year despite a woeful regular season. Whitley has struggled with his command and hasn't always had his best stuff coming off injuries; particularly concerning, he's had a string of lat and shoulder issues dating back to 2018. But when he's on, he looks like a top-of-the-rotation starter.

Development Track: Whitley came down with arm soreness during summer camp and wasn't on the mound much in 2020. Ultimately, it was another lost year for the big righty, which particularly stings given all the opportunities that opened up with the big-league club. Although he's yet to suffer any singular particularly serious injury, he just hasn't pitched a whole lot in the last three years, and it's hard to peg him to a particular role until we get a full healthy season.

Variance: High. The No. 2 starter projection is clearly still there somewhere.

J.P. Breen's Fantasy Take: Dynasty owners should always prioritize starters with top-of-the-rotation stuff, and Whitley fits the bill. However, it's hard to justify the righty's current standing as a top-30 dynasty prospect, given his history of injuries, control problems, and bloated ERAs. His dominant appearance in front of scouts in the 2019 AFL has overly inflated his stock, in my mind, as we haven't seen sustained, elite performance since 2017. Given the price tags, I'd rather roll the dice on someone like Michael Kopech. The upside is real, though.

★ ★ ★ *2021 Top 101 Prospect* **#82** ★ ★ ★

2 Jeremy Peña SS OFP: 55 ETA: Late-2021

Born: 09/22/97 Age: 23 Bats: R Throws: R Height: 6'0" Weight: 202 Origin: Round 3, 2018 Draft (#102 overall)

YEAR	TEAM	LVL	AGE	PA	R	2B	3B	HR	RBI	BB	K	SB	CS	AVG/OBP/SLG	DRC+	BABIP	BRR	FRAA	WARP
2018	TRI	SS	20	156	22	5	0	1	10	18	19	3	0	.250/.340/.309	133	.282	-1.0	SS(32) -0.5, 2B(4) 0.0	0.5
2019	QC	LO-A	21	289	44	8	4	5	41	35	57	17	6	.293/.389/.421	153	.357	3.3	SS(60) -2.1, 2B(2) -0.3	2.9
2019	FAY	HI-A	21	185	28	13	3	2	13	12	33	4	3	.317/.378/.467	144	.383	1.8	SS(29) -0.2, 2B(11) 0.1, 3B(1) -0.0	1.7
2021 FS	HOU	MLB	23	600	60	26	3	12	58	42	150	8	4	.239/.301/.370	83	.306	-1.2	SS -9, 2B 0	-0.4
2021 DC	HOU	MLB	23	68	6	2	0	1	6	4	17	0	0	.239/.301/.370	83	.306	-0.1	SS -1	0.0

Comparables: Darnell Sweeney, Zach Walters, Andy Burns

The Report: The 2018 third-rounder was one of 2019's biggest breakout prospects, showing off not just the expected strong defense but surprising offensive skills across both full-season A-ball levels. Peña has strong bat-to-ball abilities and controls the strike zone well. He's never going to be a huge power threat, but he hits the ball in the gaps already and projects to get to at least fringe-average game pop. Defensively, he's a sure-shot shortstop, with better-than-required range, instincts, and arm for the position.

Development Track: Peña was a late addition to the alternate site roster, as Houston took one of the most veteran-heavy groups and only brought in more of their top prospects in September. He got strong reviews for his development there and in instructs, and he's looked very good in the Dominican Winter League so far.

Variance: Medium. We were hoping to see a consolidation season from Peña building on his 2020 breakout, but, well, you know. The circumstantial evidence indicates that he's still on course or perhaps even higher.

J.P. Breen's Fantasy Take: This system gets dynasty-ugly real quick. Peña hit a combined .303/.385/.440 in 2019 with seven homers and 20 stolen bases, and while that's a nice little breakout campaign, it's not exciting in fantasy contexts. The 23-year-old is unlikely to hit for significant power. That puts a lot of pressure on his batting average and stolen bases, and we're not talking about elite skills in either area. We'll need to see another .300-plus season with 20-plus steals before I consider moving him into the top-300 dynasty prospects.

3 Luis Garcia RHP OFP: 55 ETA: Debuted in 2020

Born: 12/13/96 Age: 24 Bats: R Throws: R Height: 6'1" Weight: 244 Origin: International Free Agent, 2017

YEAR	TEAM	LVL	AGE	W	L	SV	G	GS	IP	H	HR	BB/9	K/9	K	GB%	BABIP	WHIP	ERA	DRA-	WARP
2018	TRI	SS	21	0	0	0	5	3	16¹	7	0	4.4	15.4	28	43.3%	.233	0.92	0.00	237	-1.1
2018	QC	LO-A	21	7	2	0	19	10	69	58	4	4.3	9.1	70	37.3%	.300	1.32	2.48	74	1.3
2019	QC	LO-A	22	4	0	1	9	6	43	23	4	3.3	12.6	60	41.1%	.221	0.91	2.93	55	1.2
2019	FAY	HI-A	22	6	4	0	15	12	65²	43	5	4.7	14.8	108	45.3%	.311	1.17	3.02	66	1.4
2020	HOU	MLB	23	0	1	0	5	1	12¹	7	1	3.6	6.6	9	41.2%	.182	0.97	2.92	110	0.0
2021 FS	HOU	MLB	24	2	3	0	57	0	50	43	8	5.3	10.1	56	40.6%	.283	1.46	4.74	101	0.1
2021 DC	HOU	MLB	24	0	0	0	3	3	13	11	2	5.3	10.1	14	40.6%	.283	1.46	4.74	101	0.1

Comparables: Vince Velasquez, Jorge Alcala, Cristian Javier

The Report: My biggest miss across our 2020 list product was Luis Garcia. He was in discussion for the Next Ten, but we had a fairly muted report from early in the season on a particularly cold night in the Midwest League. Shortly after the Astros' list went live, I got a text from a scout: "Where was Luis Garcia on your 101?" After figuring out they weren't talking about the Phillies' or Nats' Luis Garcia, I gave a deep sigh and asked for the report. I got back above-average fastball, and the change might be a 70. Yeah, that would explain the 14 K/9 in A-ball. Yes, he was an older signee, but the stuff was advanced, with a full five-pitch mix, featuring three distinct breaking ball looks. The mechanics are a little funky with some deception, which led to some wildness and command scuffles, but Garcia was already built like a major leaguer with the arsenal to match.

Development Track: And he quickly became a major leaguer. The Astros had to lean heavily on their organizational pitching depth in 2020, and Garcia ended up playing a utility arm role for them in September. He pitched well enough to make a playoff roster—and take a playoff start—and the performance didn't look all that out of place for a pitcher with no experience in the upper minors. The fastball can be a bit straight and a bit hittable since Garcia has more control than command at present, but he mixes in the off-speed enough to think he can keep MLB hitters off the fastball. The change has a 10+ mph spread of the fastball and shows big fade and some sink. The slider was more a glove-side chase pitch that didn't always get chases, but the shape of the offering is good and you could see it being above-average with further refinement. I don't know if Garcia fits perfectly as a 180-inning mid-rotation starter, but he's in the right organization to slot in with Framber Valdez andCristian Javier as 130-inning type utility arms who post the rate stats of a good mid-rotation starter That's not quite a Top 101 prospect, but he's certainly on the long list.

Variance: Medium. Garcia pitched well enough in his major-league cameo that he may just slot back into the Astros' 2021 pitching staff in a similar role. A little more minor league time could see him develop into a "real" No. 3 starter, but there is some reliever risk if the fastball remains too hittable across longer outings.

J.P. Breen's Fantasy Take: The 2021 version of Cristian Javier or Jose Urquidy or whoever. The Astros have a ton of these guys. They're useful, but unexciting. Garcia's big-league cameo should make him slightly less available in most dynasty leagues than Javier was 12 months ago. However, he could offer solid rates and volume without costing much on draft day.

4 Alex Santos II   RHP   OFP: 55   ETA: 2025
Born: 02/10/02   Age: 19   Bats: R   Throws: R   Height: 6'3"   Weight: 185   Origin: Round 2, 2020 Draft (#72 overall)

The Report: It's hard enough to draft in a normal year. Add in further complications like a reduction to five rounds—plus losing your first two picks because of the sign-stealing punishment—and the Astros were left with very little opportunity to add to their system. But even with their first pick being 72nd overall, they got a heck of a player in Santos, a right-hander out of the Bronx who was closer to a top-50 talent. With a projectable 6-foot-3 frame paired with an athletic delivery, he fits the mold of the Astros' preferred pitching prospect type, especially when you consider an arsenal that features a high-spin fastball paired with an equally high-spin curveball.

Development Track: Hailing from one of the New York boroughs means baseball season kicks off a little later in the spring, too late for games to begin before the COVID-19 shutdown. Santos was drafted largely off the pedigree from his summer performance the year prior, especially since there had been anticipation to see where a potential velocity spike might have leveled off after winter workouts. The heater still sits in the low 90s while topping out at 96, with many believing he could end up cruising in the mid-to-upper 90s sooner than later. Reports from instructs mentioned his competitive edge despite being the youngest pitcher in camp.

Variance: Very High. Any cold-weather prep pitcher has risk built into their profile. Houston's player development department knows how and whom to identify with a certain set of skills on the mound, and Santos looks like another Jose Urquidy, Cristian Javier, Josh James et al.

J.P. Breen's Fantasy Take: Every organization has one or two high-upside prep pitchers who could pop at any moment. Put him on a 2021 watch list, but don't bother rostering Santos this winter. The lead time is too long, the risk is too high, and there are too many similar arms on the waiver wire every year.

5 Korey Lee   C   OFP: 50   ETA: 2023
Born: 07/25/98   Age: 22   Bats: R   Throws: R   Height: 6'2"   Weight: 205   Origin: Round 1, 2019 Draft (#32 overall)

YEAR	TEAM	LVL	AGE	PA	R	2B	3B	HR	RBI	BB	K	SB	CS	AVG/OBP/SLG	DRC+	BABIP	BRR	FRAA	WARP
2019	TRI	SS	20	259	31	6	4	3	28	28	49	8	5	.268/.359/.371	139	.328	2.5	C(30) 0.7, LF(5) -0.9, 1B(2) -0.2	1.8
2021 FS	HOU	MLB	22	600	49	25	3	8	52	37	177	9	5	.219/.276/.327	67	.305	-2.3	C 1, LF -1	-0.5

Comparables: Luis Torrens, Richie Martin, Boog Powell

The Report: With the final pick in the first round of the 2019 draft, the Astros surprised many by drafting and then signing Lee to an under-slot deal. Considered by some in the industry as more of a potential third-rounder, Lee's splashy junior year at Cal was undeniably impressive. His slash line improved by nearly 100 points across the board, with his slugging percentage jumping nearly 200 points alone while hitting behind Andrew Vaughn. The raw power flashed plus, but he's unlikely to get to all of it in games while he tries to rework his swing to be less pull-happy. He especially tended to pull off on pitches away. The arm flashes plus as well, even though he wasn't the full-time catcher in college until his junior year, and his raw receiving skills need significant refinement.

Development Track: During his collegiate career, Lee had shown an ability to play multiple positions before settling in solely at catcher. However, upon being drafted, he again was asked to show his versatility by getting time in both left field and first base during his stint in the New York-Penn League. Seldom do you see a first-round catcher—already with limited innings behind the dish—do anything but continue their needed work at the position. This suggests the Astros may value his bat above any defensive value he brings, where he could become a super utility player who can also catch a couple times a week.

Variance: Very High. You had hoped 2020 and a full-season campaign would show evidence of growth both offensively and defensively, instead, we are left with a lot of uncertainty.

J.P. Breen's Fantasy Take: Lee is a more-athletic-than-you-might-think maybe-catcher who would become interesting in fantasy circles if he can develop his skills behind the plate. Think of him like Daulton Varsho, with less speed and an inferior hit tool. In other words, he's a dynasty afterthought for now.

6 Bryan Abreu RHP   OFP: 50   ETA: Debuted in 2019
Born: 04/22/97   Age: 24   Bats: R   Throws: R   Height: 6'1"   Weight: 225   Origin: International Free Agent, 2013

YEAR	TEAM	LVL	AGE	W	L	SV	G	GS	IP	H	HR	BB/9	K/9	K	GB%	BABIP	WHIP	ERA	DRA-	WARP
2018	TRI	SS	21	2	0	0	4	2	16	11	2	3.4	12.4	22	29.4%	.281	1.06	1.12	273	-1.4
2018	QC	LO-A	21	4	1	3	10	5	38¹	22	2	4.0	16.0	68	47.0%	.317	1.02	1.64	55	1.1
2019	FAY	HI-A	22	1	0	0	3	3	14²	9	2	3.7	15.3	25	38.5%	.292	1.02	3.68	63	0.3
2019	CC	AA	22	6	2	2	20	13	76²	60	6	5.6	11.9	101	42.5%	.310	1.41	5.05	87	0.6
2019	HOU	MLB	22	0	0	0	7	0	8²	4	0	3.1	13.5	13	50.0%	.250	0.81	1.04	95	0.1
2020	HOU	MLB	23	0	0	0	4	0	3¹	1	0	18.9	8.1	3	37.5%	.125	2.40	2.70	121	0.0
2021 FS	HOU	MLB	24	2	3	0	57	0	50	43	8	5.9	10.8	59	40.7%	.290	1.52	5.08	106	0.0
2021 DC	HOU	MLB	24	0	0	0	10	0	11	9	1	5.9	10.8	13	40.7%	.290	1.52	5.08	106	0.0

Comparables: Jorge Alcala, Cristian Javier, Demarcus Evans

The Report: This is an unusually high ranking for a pitcher who broadly falls into the "95-and-a-slider" class of arms. Working in Abreu's favor are two things: (1) It's a really good slider, a potential plus-plus weapon that sits in the mid-80s and touches higher with big two-plane break. (2) He's already pitched in the majors and shown an ability there to miss bats with his stuff. He's also shown issues with command and control, which does limit the upside in the late innings here.

Development Track: Abreu should have been a strong candidate to step into the closer role after the incumbent, Roberto Osuna, tore his UCL shortly into the 2020 season. Abreu showed up to summer camp out of shape though, per *The Athletic*'s Jake Kaplan, and looked more like a "93-and-a-slider" arm who struggled to find the plate. We can't handwave that entirely, but there were going to be some pitchers who struggled to adjust to the unusual start-stop nature of the season, and there's no reason to think Abreu will come into 2021 with the same issues. Well, the control stuff is a little troubling, as even in the minors Abreu's has never been a dart-thrower.

Variance: Medium. Abreu's stuff plays in the bullpen, but how many high-quality strikes he can throw with his stuff will determine the outcome here, which ranges from viable closer to frustrating middle reliever.

J.P. Breen's Fantasy Take: As Mike Gianella has reminded us all offseason, quality middle relievers have underappreciated fantasy value. Abreu has the swing-and-miss stuff to be useful, as shown by his 19.2 percent swinging-strike rate in his big-league debut in 2019, but he'll have to show that he can throw strikes consistently before fantasy owners can trust Abreu to not torpedo their rate stats. The righty is worth a dart throw, though. He might be 2021's Jonathan Hernandez.

7 Freudis Nova SS   OFP: 50   ETA: 2024
Born: 01/12/00   Age: 21   Bats: R   Throws: R   Height: 6'1"   Weight: 180   Origin: International Free Agent, 2016

YEAR	TEAM	LVL	AGE	PA	R	2B	3B	HR	RBI	BB	K	SB	CS	AVG/OBP/SLG	DRC+	BABIP	BRR	FRAA	WARP
2018	AST	ROK	18	157	21	3	1	6	28	6	21	9	5	.308/.331/.466		.317			
2019	QC	LO-A	19	299	35	20	1	3	29	15	67	10	7	.259/.301/.369	104	.330	-0.4	SS(32) -3.0, 2B(23) -0.0, 3B(18) -0.6	0.8
2021 FS	HOU	MLB	21	600	47	27	2	9	53	28	172	14	7	.219/.260/.326	59	.298	-4.1	SS -6, 2B 0	-2.5

Comparables: Tim Beckham, Ryan Mountcastle, Javy Guerra

The Report: Despite the seven-figure bonus number, Nova's profile has developed into more of a steady hand as an infield prospect, rather than "seven-figure IFA shortstop prospect." He's played all around the infield the last couple seasons, although he has the physical tools to be an above-average shortstop once he gets more reps at the 6 in higher game speed situations. Nova has struggled against velocity at times despite above-average, whippy bat speed and doesn't project for significant game power. He does enough things well enough that you can squint and see it all come together as a starter in a few years, but given the collection of tools the pro performance so far, you do have to squint a bit.

Development Track: Squint as hard as you want, but you wouldn't have seen much of Nova in 2020. He didn't play at the alternate site; the Astros' camp tilted more toward the major-league-ready. He did spend some time at domestic instructs, but will be 21 next year and yet to play above Low-A, while still needing refinement at shortstop and physical maturation at the plate.

Variance: High. The loss of a potential season of offensive development stings here more than it might other places, given the needed improvements at the plate.

J.P. Breen's Fantasy Take: Some dynasty experts still consider Nova to be a top-300 prospect. In those cases, however, he's still riding the 2018 hype wave, when many (including myself) were enamored with the young infielder. A couple of years later, it's hard to see the impact. Either his approach needs to improve or the power needs to pop. Otherwise, we're looking at a potential utility infielder who is freely available on most big-league waiver wires.

8 Hunter Brown RHP   OFP: 55   ETA: 2022

Born: 08/29/98   Age: 22   Bats: R   Throws: R   Height: 6'2"   Weight: 203   Origin: Round 5, 2019 Draft (#166 overall)

YEAR	TEAM	LVL	AGE	W	L	SV	G	GS	IP	H	HR	BB/9	K/9	K	GB%	BABIP	WHIP	ERA	DRA-	WARP
2019	TRI	SS	20	2	2	0	12	6	23²	13	0	6.8	12.5	33	52.9%	.255	1.31	4.56	79	0.3
2021 FS	HOU	MLB	22	2	3	0	57	0	50	47	8	7.6	9.1	50	42.4%	.289	1.79	6.09	132	-0.8

Comparables: Cristian Javier, Akeel Morris, James Norwood

The Report: Brown was a small college find in the 2019 draft; the Astros popped him out of D2 Wayne State, where he'd only become a regular starting pitcher in his draft year. He was sitting mid-to-upper-90s in the short-season Low-A New York-Penn League after the draft and flashing some interesting secondaries, including a curveball that he added as a pro. But Brown was pitching shorter outings, never even completing three innings, and the command was fringe-at-best, so we had a relief projection on him last year.

Development Track: Our reports highlighted Brown as one of the big risers from instructs, and Jake Kaplan of *The Athletic* reported that he hit 100 mph on a Rapsodo while throwing at home over the summer. It's hard to fully separate the signal from the noise here, because we don't have 2020 live looks and our 2019 post-draft live look wasn't great, but we've got enough overall for the arrow to be pointing up.

Variance: High. It may sound like a broken record here, but we need to see him jump up in a game to fully buy in.

J.P. Breen's Fantasy Take: Brown is one of many pop-up candidates in the lower levels. If he were an offensive player, I'd be interested. Since he's a pitcher, I'll wait and separate the wheat from the chaff in the summer.

9 Colin Barber OF   OFP: 55   ETA: 2024

Born: 12/04/00   Age: 20   Bats: L   Throws: L   Height: 6'0"   Weight: 185   Origin: Round 4, 2019 Draft (#136 overall)

YEAR	TEAM	LVL	AGE	PA	R	2B	3B	HR	RBI	BB	K	SB	CS	AVG/OBP/SLG	DRC+	BABIP	BRR	FRAA	WARP
2019	AST	ROK	18	119	19	5	1	2	6	19	29	2	1	.263/.387/.394		.353			
2021 FS	HOU	MLB	20	600	47	26	2	8	51	40	220	4	1	.209/.266/.313	60	.328	0.4	CF -4, LF -3	-2.1

Comparables: Ronald Acuña Jr., Byron Buxton, Monte Harrison

The Report: The Astros went way, way over-slot to snag Barber as a California prep in the fourth round last year. Early returns are promising; he's a sweet-swinging lefty with a very quick bat and plus power potential. With no minor-league season, he found his way to the City of Champions Cup this summer, a four-team league formed by the independent Joliet Slammers. Barber hit .203/.353/.348 as the youngest player in the league, playing against pitchers who were all far older, many with significant pro track records and a few with big-league time.

Development Track: Barber was invited to the alternate site in September after he played in Joliet, and hit a homer on his first swing in Corpus. Like Brown, Barber was highlighted to us as a player who made a big jump this fall, and the Astros were conservative with alternate site invites and still brought him in, which is a great sign. We're honestly not sure how facing much more advanced pitching than planned is going to influence young hitting prospects; players like Barber got thrown in on the deep end in ways they usually wouldn't have in the pandemic season.

Variance: High. Things are looking quite promising here, but he just turned 20 and hasn't even made his full-season debut yet.

J.P. Breen's Fantasy Take: Folks are always clamoring for the next breakout prospect in the lower levels. That could be Barber in 2021. He's a coveted power-speed type of prospect who few outside of the dynasty diehards have heard about. Don't expect him to ever hit for average, but Barber should be on your supplemental draft board this winter.

10 Jairo Solis RHP   OFP: 50   ETA: Late-2022 or early-2023

Born: 12/22/99 Age: 21 Bats: R Throws: R Height: 6'2" Weight: 160 Origin: International Free Agent, 2016

YEAR	TEAM	LVL	AGE	W	L	SV	G	GS	IP	H	HR	BB/9	K/9	K	GB%	BABIP	WHIP	ERA	DRA-	WARP
2018	QC	LO-A	18	2	5	0	13	11	50²	49	1	5.7	9.1	51	44.3%	.345	1.60	3.55	119	-0.2

Comparables: Julio Teheran, Noah Syndergaard, Kolby Allard

The Report: Going back a few years, Solis was on a meteoric rise. He blew through both complex levels and the Appy League in his age-17 season in 2017, and popped up in full-season Low-A the next year at 18 years old. He was extremely, extremely impressive given his age in the Midwest League, with a low-to-mid-90s fastball, a curve flashing plus, and a change flashing above-average. The Astros handled him extremely carefully, reasonably so given his age, with a shortened season and relatively light outings, but he tore his UCL and had Tommy John surgery in the fall anyway. He missed the entire 2019 season, and was still working his way back in 2020.

Development Track: Solis is now fully recovered and ready to go, and he was at fall instructs. He was added to the 40-man roster this offseason, so the option clock is ticking now; we're hoping he picks right back up where he left off.

Variance: Very High. He hasn't pitched competitively in two years and only has 112 pro innings.

J.P. Breen's Fantasy Take: Against my better judgment, I kinda dig Solis. I'd rather take a punt on Solis than Santos or any other non-elite prep hurler. Few non-top-400 have a legit pathway to being a big-league starter. Solis is one of them—though it's far more likely that the Astros develop him into one of their 120-inning swingman types.

The Prospects You Meet Outside The Top Ten

MLB-Ready Arms, But Less Upside Than You'd Like

Shawn Dubin RHP Born: 09/06/95 Age: 25 Bats: R Throws: R Height: 6'1" Weight: 154 Origin: Round 13, 2018 Draft (#402 overall)

YEAR	TEAM	LVL	AGE	W	L	SV	G	GS	IP	H	HR	BB/9	K/9	K	GB%	BABIP	WHIP	ERA	DRA-	WARP
2018	TRI	SS	22	2	1	0	14	5	29¹	23	4	3.4	9.5	31	37.2%	.257	1.16	4.60	220	-1.7
2019	QC	LO-A	23	1	0	2	3	1	12	7	0	3.0	14.2	19	69.6%	.304	0.92	0.75	58	0.3
2019	FAY	HI-A	23	6	5	1	22	18	98²	71	3	3.8	12.0	132	49.4%	.294	1.15	3.92	69	1.9
2021 FS	HOU	MLB	25	2	3	0	57	0	50	45	7	5.2	9.7	53	44.6%	.289	1.48	4.82	114	-0.3

Comparables: Adonis Rosa, Matt Strahm, Alex Reyes

Dubin stood out as one of the few prospects to be invited to summer camp initially who didn't have upper-level minors experience; he pitched most of 2019 in High-A. He didn't make it to the majors even as the Astros rotated through a lot of arms (an early unexplained IL stint set him back), but he was on the postseason taxi squad. The lanky righty has bat-missing stuff, led by a mid-90s fastball and tough slider, but might not have the frame to start long term.

Austin Hansen RHP Born: 08/25/96 Age: 24 Bats: R Throws: R Height: 6'0" Weight: 195 Origin: Round 8, 2018 Draft (#252 overall)

YEAR	TEAM	LVL	AGE	W	L	SV	G	GS	IP	H	HR	BB/9	K/9	K	GB%	BABIP	WHIP	ERA	DRA-	WARP
2018	TRI	SS	21	2	3	2	14	2	30²	14	2	3.8	13.2	45	46.0%	.197	0.88	1.76	208	-1.6
2019	QC	LO-A	22	4	1	1	9	7	41²	20	1	4.1	11.2	52	39.6%	.211	0.94	0.86	51	1.3
2019	FAY	HI-A	22	3	2	1	14	7	52¹	32	4	5.3	13.1	76	41.1%	.269	1.20	3.10	76	0.7
2021 FS	HOU	MLB	24	2	3	0	57	0	50	44	8	6.6	10.4	57	40.2%	.292	1.63	5.35	122	-0.5

Comparables: Luis Garcia, Enoli Paredes, Brandon Bailey

Hansen is maybe the most obvious reliever of this group, although he was still used within the Astros' tandem starting model in 2019. The 2018 eighth rounder was a dominant reliever for Oklahoma in college, and while the Astros stretched him back out, the whirling dervish, high effort delivery will work best in short bursts, where his fastball might play into the upper-90s and complement two power breakers he can use to miss bats.

Peter Solomon RHP Born: 08/16/96 Age: 24 Bats: R Throws: R Height: 6'4" Weight: 201 Origin: Round 4, 2017 Draft (#121 overall)

YEAR	TEAM	LVL	AGE	W	L	SV	G	GS	IP	H	HR	BB/9	K/9	K	GB%	BABIP	WHIP	ERA	DRA-	WARP
2018	QC	LO-A	21	8	1	0	19	10	77²	62	2	3.2	10.2	88	47.8%	.302	1.16	2.43	62	2.0
2018	FAY	HI-A	21	1	0	0	5	3	23	16	0	1.6	10.2	26	58.9%	.286	0.87	1.96	56	0.7
2019	FAY	HI-A	22	0	0	0	2	2	7²	7	1	4.7	16.4	14	33.3%	.429	1.43	2.35	82	0.1
2021 FS	HOU	MLB	24	2	3	0	57	0	50	45	8	4.7	9.4	52	44.1%	.285	1.43	4.65	104	0.0
2021 DC	HOU	MLB	24	0	0	0	10	0	11	9	1	4.7	9.4	11	44.1%	.285	1.43	4.65	104	0.0

Comparables: Cristian Javier, Vince Velasquez, Hunter Wood

Solomon's elbow blew out very early in the 2019 season and he ended up undergoing Tommy John surgery. Like Solis, he's now recovered and should be a full go for the 2021 season, and was added to the 40-man roster in the offseason. Back in 2018, the 2017 fourth-rounder out of Notre Dame profiled with a mid-90s fastball and advanced secondaries led by a quality breaker; he could move quickly once back in games, but the elbow surgery increases the reliever risk here.

Tyler Ivey RHP Born: 05/12/96 Age: 25 Bats: R Throws: R Height: 6'4" Weight: 195 Origin: Round 3, 2017 Draft (#91 overall)

YEAR	TEAM	LVL	AGE	W	L	SV	G	GS	IP	H	HR	BB/9	K/9	K	GB%	BABIP	WHIP	ERA	DRA-	WARP
2018	QC	LO-A	22	1	3	2	9	6	41²	36	2	1.7	11.4	53	47.3%	.315	1.06	3.46	48	1.4
2018	FAY	HI-A	22	3	3	1	15	12	70¹	50	3	2.7	10.5	82	53.6%	.269	1.01	2.69	61	2.0
2019	CC	AA	23	4	0	0	11	8	46	28	5	3.1	11.9	61	37.7%	.230	0.96	1.57	58	1.1
2021 FS	HOU	MLB	25	1	1	0	57	0	50	45	8	4.2	9.7	54	37.8%	.288	1.37	4.48	102	0.1
2021 DC	HOU	MLB	25	1	1	0	31	0	33	29	5	4.2	9.7	35	37.8%	.288	1.37	4.48	102	0.2

Comparables: Brandon Bailey, Ryan Helsley, Dane Dunning

Hmm, the Astros sure seem to like righties with unorthodox, often effortful mechanics and multiple breaking ball looks (to be fair, they also like lefties like that). Ivey is another in this group with mid-90s heat and two useable breaking balls. Like Hansen, the mechanics portend a move to the pen, where Ivey could fill a setup or multi-inning role.

MLB-Ready Bat, But Less Upside Than You'd Like

Chas McCormick RF Born: 04/19/95 Age: 26 Bats: R Throws: L Height: 6'0" Weight: 208 Origin: Round 21, 2017 Draft (#631 overall)

YEAR	TEAM	LVL	AGE	PA	R	2B	3B	HR	RBI	BB	K	SB	CS	AVG/OBP/SLG	DRC+	BABIP	BRR	FRAA	WARP
2018	FAY	HI-A	23	209	26	13	3	2	27	19	34	7	0	.264/.332/.401	109	.305	0.9	RF(44) 1.9, LF(7) 0.0	0.5
2018	CC	AA	23	282	33	10	1	2	28	24	32	12	4	.280/.344/.352	108	.308	-0.2	RF(24) 1.9, LF(23) -1.8, CF(22) 1.0	0.4
2019	CC	AA	24	223	26	3	3	4	22	39	28	9	3	.277/.426/.395	151	.310	0.7	LF(40) 5.2, CF(6) -0.3, RF(3) -0.9	2.1
2019	RR	AAA	24	225	39	3	3	10	44	28	34	7	1	.262/.347/.466	101	.261	0.0	RF(22) 0.2, CF(16) 0.6, LF(12) 1.2	0.8
2021 FS	HOU	MLB	26	600	65	24	3	15	62	54	119	7	2	.248/.324/.392	96	.293	3.1	RF 3, LF 4	2.4
2021 DC	HOU	MLB	26	378	41	15	2	9	39	34	75	4	1	.248/.324/.392	96	.293	1.9	RF 2, LF 3	1.5

Comparables: Jerry Owens, Mike Tauchman, JB Shuck

McCormick was a Day 3, Division II senior sign outfielder, who paved a fairly non-descript path to the upper minors. He was always old for his levels, but also always hit enough that he'd have to find a new apartment in a new town around mid-season. Then McCormick hit enough at the alternate site in 2020 to find himself a surprise playoff roster addition, although that was more likely due to his speed. He's never hit for much power outside of the 2019 PCL, but there's maybe a bit more game power than Myles Straw, and the plus speed and approach might make him a useful bench outfielder in that type of mold.

Top Talents 25 and Under (as of 4/1/2021):

1. Kyle Tucker, OF
2. Yordan Alvarez, DH/OF
3. Forrest Whitley, RHP
4. Jose Urquidy, RHP
5. Cristian Javier, RHP

6. Jeremy Peña, SS
7. Luis Garcia, RHP
8. Alex Santos, RHP
9. Abraham Toro, 3B
10. Korey Lee, C

After several years of coming just short of fully breaking through, Kyle Tucker settled in as a very good major-league regular in 2020. As Houston's regular left fielder (occasionally flipping over to right), he put up a 116 DRC+ in his age-23 season, and he hit fifth or sixth in every playoff game. We think there's even better to come from his talented lefty bat.

It's very difficult to place Yordan Alvarez in context right now. Just six months ago, it would've been unthinkable to put him behind Tucker, but there he is. Alvarez only played in two games in 2020 amid injuries to both knees that started in spring training, and he had surgery on both in August after tearing his right patella tendon. He's an offensive force when healthy, but there's a lot of uncertainty now.

2019 breakout star Urquidy missed much of the 2020 season with COVID-19. When he came back, he looked like the Urquidy of 2019 again, 92-94 with a plus changeup and the occasional deadly slider. He looked solid in the postseason, and is probably just a present mid-rotation type, albeit with a bit more risk since he still only has 12 regular-season MLB starts.

Coming into the season, we had Cristian Javier projected with some serious bullpen risk, but he took a regular turn in Houston's rotation and ended up netting a third place in AL Rookie of the Year voting. The righty mostly works off a low-90s fastball and a slurvy breaker, with the occasional changeup mixed in. He was effective in the playoffs shifted to a multi-inning role, and that was closer to the projection we had on him last year. But right now he looks like a present third or fourth starter with a bit of upside past that.

Abraham Torostuck on the Astros roster in 2020, albeit in a backup role. He saw semi-regular time when Alex Bregman was injured and filled in a bit as a reserve corner infielder when Bregman was healthy. He hit poorly in a small sample— a .149 batting average and 80 DRC+—but we still see him as a well-rounded future regular overall.

Kansas City Royals

The State of the System:

This looked like a system on the rise last year. Some of that was interrupted by a lost minor league season, but a strong draft helped out.

The Top Ten:

★ ★ ★ *2021 Top 101 Prospect* **#9** ★ ★ ★

1 Bobby Witt Jr. SS   OFP: 70   ETA: 2022
Born: 06/14/00   Age: 21   Bats: R   Throws: R   Height: 6'1"   Weight: 190   Origin: Round 1, 2019 Draft (#2 overall)

YEAR	TEAM	LVL	AGE	PA	R	2B	3B	HR	RBI	BB	K	SB	CS	AVG/OBP/SLG	DRC+	BABIP	BRR	FRAA	WARP
2019	ROY	ROK	19	180	30	2	5	1	27	13	35	9	1	.262/.317/.354		.323			
2021 FS	KC	MLB	21	600	43	25	4	6	48	29	193	13	3	.211/.253/.305	52	.308	7.4	SS 3	-0.7

Comparables: Erick Mejia, Erik González, Michael A. Taylor

The Report: Witt was in contention to go 1.1 in the 2019 draft, and the tools at the time were loud enough to carry the mantle of "first-overall prep shortstop." The athletic tools both grade out at 6 or better, and he had the infield actions to project at shortstop long term. The raw power was plus, with potential projection beyond that if he filled out more physically. The one place you could quibble with the profile was exactly how much he would hit. Projecting the hit tool for any prep bat is going to be an exercise in high variance, but even a fringe hit tool with swing-and-miss issues—a below median, but not unreasonable projection on draft day—would be enough given the rest of the skill set. A couple steps past that though, and Witt might be a superstar.

Development Track: Witt jumped from the AZL to the alternate site where he faced a fair amount of major-league-quality arms. He showed improving contact ability and a real two-strike approach, which portend the kind of hit tool improvements that would really make the offensive profile pop. The raw power has started to translate into (simulated) games as well, and he could be a 25-plus home run bat at his peak. He has seen some time at third base as well. That might be a better fit for him if he fills out more and has a clearer path to the majors in Kansas City at the moment. Witt is clearly trending up despite not having a real minor league season, and he was already quite a good prospect this time last year.

Variance: High. My initial instinct here was to put medium, but despite the positive alternate site reports and the strong tools across the board, Witt hasn't seen real game time outside of the complex, where he slugged .354. So we will remain somewhat cautious.

Mark Barry's Fantasy Take: In this Golden Age of Fantasy Shortstops, Witt's potential pilgrimage to the hot corner doesn't affect his fantasy value all that much. He's a top-20ish dynasty name with or without shortstop eligibility. The steals will be the deciding factor for his fantasy ceiling. If he runs consistently, we're looking at a potential top-five prospect, and a guy who could see plenty of time in the first three rounds of standard roto drafts.

★ ★ ★ *2021 Top 101 Prospect* **#21** ★ ★ ★

2 Asa Lacy LHP   OFP: 60   ETA: Late 2022/Early 2023
Born: 06/02/99   Age: 22   Bats: L   Throws: L   Height: 6'4"   Weight: 215   Origin: Round 1, 2020 Draft (#4 overall)

The Report: There was little question of who was the best pitching prospect entering the draft, with Lacy setting himself above the rest of a strong group of college arms. Surprisingly, he wasn't the first pitcher taken and fell into the Royals' laps at the fourth pick. Lacy's combination of physical build and an advanced four-pitch mix allow us to project him as a frontline starter, with far less reliever risk than most pitching prospects. While the mechanics could be classified by some as "funky," he repeats the delivery well and does a very good job of hiding the ball before release. It helps an already plus fastball in the mid-to-upper 90s jump on hitters and shorten the reaction time available on anything breaking or off-speed.

Development Track: The shortened college season may have helped Lacy where it hurt others. Many players needed the season to showcase and improve their skills, whereas in limited innings, Lacy not only was able to demonstrate his abilities, but also kept close to 100 innings off his arm without any risk of overuse. Being prepped and ready to go for a full season in 2021 is all that is required at present.

Variance: Medium. Pitchers are always a fickle bunch to forecast. There seems to be a low risk he won't pan out as a starter, and it's not out of the realm of outcomes he turns into an ace.

Mark Barry's Fantasy Take: Lacy was my favorite pitcher in the 2020 draft by far, and was probably closer to my favorite player in the draft than was appropriate. I'm not sure what more you could ask for than a lefty with four pitches who can flirt with high-90s heat. It's hard to bet on pitching prospects in dynasty leagues, so when you do, make sure there's ace upside. Lacy has ace upside, and is probably one of my five favorite pitching prospects in baseball.

★ ★ ★ *2021 Top 101 Prospect* **#70** ★ ★ ★

3   Daniel Lynch   LHP   OFP: 60   ETA: Late 2021/Early 2022

Born: 11/17/96   Age: 24   Bats: L   Throws: L   Height: 6'6"   Weight: 190   Origin: Round 1, 2018 Draft (#34 overall)

YEAR	TEAM	LVL	AGE	W	L	SV	G	GS	IP	H	HR	BB/9	K/9	K	GB%	BABIP	WHIP	ERA	DRA-	WARP
2018	BUR	ROK	21	0	0	0	3	3	11^1	9	0	1.6	11.1	14	55.2%	.310	0.97	1.59		
2018	LEX	LO-A	21	5	1	0	9	9	40	35	1	1.4	10.6	47	48.0%	.351	1.02	1.57	83	0.6
2019	ROY	ROK	22	0	0	0	3	3	9	6	0	3.0	12.0	12	55.6%	.333	1.00	1.00		
2019	BUR	ROK+	22	1	0	0	2	2	9	13	1	3.0	7.0	7	55.2%	.429	1.78	4.00		
2019	WIL	HI-A	22	5	2	0	15	15	78^1	76	4	2.6	8.8	77	46.9%	.324	1.26	3.10	91	0.5
2021 FS	KC	MLB	24	2	2	0	57	0	50	46	6	3.5	8.3	45	45.8%	.285	1.32	3.96	99	0.1

Comparables: Julio Urías, Albert Abreu, Tarik Skubal

The Report: Lynch's fastball jumped shortly after being drafted and it's been all systems go for his prospect track since. It's mid-90s heat from the left side with two potential above-average secondaries in his slider and change. The slider was ahead when he was last pitching in minor league games, although both secondaries needed more refinement and consistency. Even with the potential for a robust three-pitch mix, Lynch's mechanics have always suggested reliever, and he missed some time in 2019 with an arm injury.

Development Track: Lynch continued pumping his 70 fastball down the road at the alternate site at T-Bones Stadium. The changeup was his main developmental focus and he's made strides with the pitch. There have been general command improvements as well. The last hurdle for him is to throw 100+ innings in the upper minors, but if those go as well as his low minors outings, his last few 2021 appearances could be in the majors.

Variance: Medium. A lefty who can run it up into the upper 90s will get major league chances if he can stay healthy. There are also good second and third options in the arsenal. The profile and injury risks are not insignificant, though.

Mark Barry's Fantasy Take: No shade at Lynch—he's a backend, top-100 guy—but my excitement in this system really drops off after the top two dudes. I think there's a very strong chance Lynch is a reliever, so he's less interesting in a fantasy sense. There's upside to dream on, but I'm not terribly confident he gets there.

★ ★ ★ *2021 Top 101 Prospect* **#95** ★ ★ ★

4 Jackson Kowar RHP   OFP: 60   ETA: 2021

Born: 10/04/96   Age: 24   Bats: R   Throws: R   Height: 6'5"   Weight: 180   Origin: Round 1, 2018 Draft (#33 overall)

YEAR	TEAM	LVL	AGE	W	L	SV	G	GS	IP	H	HR	BB/9	K/9	K	GB%	BABIP	WHIP	ERA	DRA-	WARP
2018	LEX	LO-A	21	0	1	0	9	9	26¹	19	2	4.1	7.5	22	53.4%	.239	1.18	3.42	80	0.4
2019	WIL	HI-A	22	5	3	0	13	13	74	68	4	2.7	8.0	66	44.9%	.305	1.22	3.53	97	0.3
2019	NWA	AA	22	2	7	0	13	13	74¹	73	8	2.5	9.4	78	45.5%	.323	1.26	3.51	96	0.3
2021 FS	KC	MLB	24	2	3	0	57	0	50	48	6	4.2	7.8	43	42.5%	.289	1.44	4.76	113	-0.2
2021 DC	KC	MLB	24	0	0	0	3	3	14	13	1	4.2	7.8	12	42.5%	.289	1.44	4.76	113	0.0

Comparables: Robert Dugger, Jorge Alcala, Anthony Misiewicz

The Report: Another in the long line of high-pick pitchers to come out of Kevin O'Sullivan's Florida program, Kowar featured an unusually good changeup for a college pitcher and it's been his out pitch as a pro as well. It plays well off his mid-90s fastball although the command, although his mechanics have never screamed sure-shot starter, and the curve has been fringy. He's pitched well in the minors, but hasn't dominated quite as much as you'd expect from a major college arm with a plus fastball/change combo. That's left him in the kind of mid-rotation starter or late-inning reliever prospect who is on the outside of our Top 101 zone rather than in the 80-100 range somewhere. That's not a large distinction in projection, to be fair.

Development Track: Kowar continued to get his velocity back at the alternate site, getting up to 99 while sitting comfortably in the mid-90s. The curve has reportedly improved enough to be an average offering, and that's all he will really need given the fastball and change. You'd like to see the command get to the happy side of average to feel a bit more confident about his having immediate success, but he's basically major-league ready, and will likely make the cut for the 101 this time around.

Variance: Medium. The breaking ball is good enough now that he's less likely to end up as a fastball/change reliever, and the changeup might be good enough that he ends up the Chris Paddack who was promised. He's probably just a third starter though. And that's fine.

Mark Barry's Fantasy Take: Kowar strikes guys out, but doesn't post gaudy numbers. He has solid rates, but they're not spectacular. He's got a Backend Starter, uh, starter's kit, which is certainly useful irl but less so in fantasy circles.

★ ★ ★ *2021 Top 101 Prospect* **#97** ★ ★ ★

5 Erick Pena CF   OFP: 60   ETA: 2024/2025

Born: 02/20/03   Age: 18   Bats: L   Throws: R   Height: 6'3"   Weight: 180   Origin: International Free Agent, 2019

The Report: Shortly after signing, we started hearing that Peña was clearly the second best prospect of his IFA class, behind only Jasson Dominguez. While Dominguez looks likes a middle linebacker who hits dingers, Peña is your typical toolsy, projectable center field prospect with a present swing to make scouts blush. There's always going to be a fairly high level of uncertainty with a 17-year-old outfielder, and that was certainly true of Peña at this time last year. He was high potential, but needed to add strength and professional experience.

Development Track: Despite not having games in which to to play, Peña was invited to postseason camp at Kauffman and instructs. Sending him up to face the likes of Lynch and Kowar was a big ask, and he was overmatched early on, but adjusted to the level of competition and then shined at instructs against more age-appropriate pitching. Peña has added some good weight already and should continue to fill out and turn his present doubles power into plus over-the-fence game power in his 20s. He remains a potential five-tool center fielder, and we're more bullish on that this year than last.

Variance: Extreme. This cuts both ways. He has very little professional experience and won't turn 18 until spring training. But I've suspected for a bit that he's eventually going to grow into an elite outfield prospect, and nothing I've heard this year has dissuaded me of that possibility.

Mark Barry's Fantasy Take: Last year in this space, I wrote that Peña could be a decent fallback in FYPDs if you missed out on Jasson Dominguez. Since, Peña has surged up prospect boards despite literally not playing in a real game. The lesson, as always, is these J2 guys come with helium. You need to get in early if you're getting in at all. I'd have Peña in the top-75 or so, but even that is all on speculation at this point.

6 Kyle Isbel OF   OFP: 55   ETA: Mid-to-late-2021

Born: 03/03/97 Age: 24 Bats: L Throws: R Height: 5'11" Weight: 183 Origin: Round 3, 2018 Draft (#94 overall)

YEAR	TEAM	LVL	AGE	PA	R	2B	3B	HR	RBI	BB	K	SB	CS	AVG/OBP/SLG	DRC+	BABIP	BRR	FRAA	WARP
2018	IDF	ROK	21	119	27	10	1	4	18	14	17	12	3	.381/.454/.610		.429			
2018	LEX	LO-A	21	174	30	12	1	3	14	12	43	12	3	.289/.345/.434	110	.377	2.8	CF(27) 0.8, LF(11) -0.5	0.7
2019	ROY	ROK	22	27	9	2	0	2	7	2	5	3	1	.360/.407/.680		.389			
2019	WIL	HI-A	22	214	26	7	3	5	23	15	44	8	3	.216/.282/.361	85	.253	1.8	CF(32) -2.3, RF(12) 0.5	0.2
2021 FS	KC	MLB	24	600	55	26	3	13	60	39	173	17	7	.228/.285/.361	78	.307	-0.6	CF 1, RF 1	0.2

Comparables: Paulo Orlando, Abraham Almonte, Rosell Herrera

The Report: Isbel was aggressively assigned to High-A Wilmington to start his first full campaign in 2019, and shined there until he broke his hamate and missed several months. When he came back, he struggled badly in one of MiLB's worst hitting environments, tanking his offensive numbers for the season. Despite the low average, he projects as an above-average hitter with strong feel for contact. He has a good plate approach and pitch recognition and sneaky power, especially to the pull side. He's also a plus runner and fielder. Basically, if the average is what we think it could be, and not what it was in 2019, he's going to be a solid regular with a broad base of offensive and defensive abilities.

Development Track: Along with Witt, Isbel was one of Kansas City's top performers at the alternate site, continuing his strong run from the 2019 Arizona Fall League. We said last year that we wanted to see him pull everything together for a full season, and that holds true. He has not even moved up in the rankings here given the strong nature of the system overall. But make no mistake, his stock is decently up year-over-year.

Variance: Medium. We're still missing the single big season, but he's done everything other than that now.

Mark Barry's Fantasy Take: I think Isbel is a little under-the-radar on the dynasty scene. As Jarrett mentioned, his hit tool projects as above average and the 23-year-old has displayed some efficiency on the bases. There's 20/20 potential for Isbel, and I don't think you'd have to pay that price on the current market.

7 Nick Loftin   OFP: 55   ETA: Late 2022 or early 2023

Born: 09/25/98 Age: 22 Bats: R Throws: R Height: 6'1" Weight: 185 Origin: Round CBA, 2020 Draft (#32 overall)

The Report: Loftin was one of the names that was floated around a bunch of different landing spots on draft night. There isn't one particularly loud tool that stands out, which perhaps limits his overall ceiling. However, his at least average grades across the board and positional versatility creates a relatively high floor. Loftin has a balanced swing that creates a ton of contact to all fields and some pull-side pop.

Development Track: Even with the possibility of playing multiple spots on the diamond, he's more than capable of handling short. The swing and the approach are tied together so any adjustments made will affect the other side of the equation. It would be wise to get him situated his first full year, with any alterations offensively or defensively coming later. He could be a quick mover who ascends alongside the others on this list as the next wave makes their way to Kansas City.

Variance: Low. The difference between his likely outcome and worst case scenario as a valued bench player isn't all that much. He's a big league asset one way or another.

Mark Barry's Fantasy Take: The deeper the league, the more interest I'd have in a guy like Loftin. Adding a guy who can play a few different spots and won't kill you anywhere offensively is a nice luxury, but the lack of impact anywhere keeps me from endorsing him in any format shallower than 15 teams.

8 Khalil Lee CF   OFP: 55   ETA: 2021
Born: 06/26/98   Age: 23   Bats: L   Throws: L   Height: 5'10"   Weight: 170   Origin: Round 3, 2016 Draft (#103 overall)

YEAR	TEAM	LVL	AGE	PA	R	2B	3B	HR	RBI	BB	K	SB	CS	AVG/OBP/SLG	DRC+	BABIP	BRR	FRAA	WARP
2018	WIL	HI-A	20	301	42	13	4	4	41	48	75	14	3	.270/.402/.406	140	.371	2.2	CF(57) 3.8, RF(9) 0.3	2.2
2018	NWA	AA	20	118	15	5	0	2	10	11	28	2	2	.245/.330/.353	82	.319	0.6	CF(17) 0.3, LF(9) 0.7	0.0
2019	NWA	AA	21	546	74	21	3	8	51	65	154	53	12	.264/.363/.372	117	.374	3.7	RF(55) -6.0, CF(45) -5.7, LF(8) -0.1	1.2
2021 FS	KC	MLB	23	600	61	28	4	11	56	56	218	18	7	.217/.303/.350	81	.345	1.0	RF -9, LF 0	-0.5
2021 DC	KC	MLB	23	66	6	3	0	1	6	6	24	2	0	.217/.303/.350	81	.345	0.1	RF -1	-0.1

Comparables: Clint Frazier, Austin Jackson, Luis Alexander Basabe

The Report: Lee has long been a bit of a prospect enigma. He has big bat speed and plus raw power, but hasn't really gotten to it since he was in Low-A in 2017. His groundball rates spiked absolutely huge once he was promoted to Double-A; 59 percent over the late stage of 2018 and 2019 combined. Throw in some serious swing-and-miss—his swing gets long and out of sync, which contributes to both issues—and we've been concerned about Lee's long-term offensive trajectory for a while. He does run like the wind and can play anywhere in the outfield, and even moderate swing adjustments could get him on the fast track.

Development Track: Lee was a part of the summer camp and alternate site group all season. The Royals believe he made some of the adjustments to make better and more contact there, and added him to the 40-man roster after the season.

Variance: High. We're going to need to see his adjustments in games—and make sure that they don't cause his hit tool to cave in—before we truly believe in it.

Mark Barry's Fantasy Take: Lee stole 53 bases in 2019. That's it. That's the reason we're clinging to hope in a fantasy sense. It's also the reason we'll keep clinging to that hope, probably against our collective better judgment.

9 MJ Melendez C   OFP: 55   ETA: 2022/2023
Born: 11/29/98   Age: 22   Bats: L   Throws: R   Height: 6'1"   Weight: 185   Origin: Round 2, 2017 Draft (#52 overall)

YEAR	TEAM	LVL	AGE	PA	R	2B	3B	HR	RBI	BB	K	SB	CS	AVG/OBP/SLG	DRC+	BABIP	BRR	FRAA	WARP
2018	LEX	LO-A	19	472	52	26	9	19	73	43	143	4	6	.251/.322/.492	103	.327	-1.7	C(73) 1.4	0.8
2019	WIL	HI-A	20	419	34	23	2	9	54	44	165	7	5	.163/.260/.311	50	.259	-0.9	C(71) 2.4	-0.4
2021 FS	KC	MLB	22	600	49	27	4	13	57	44	256	3	2	.180/.246/.319	53	.303	-0.5	C -1	-1.3

Comparables: Javy Guerra, Estevan Florial, Trevor Story

The Report: As you can see in his statistics box, Melendez absolutely *cratered* in 2019 in Wilmington. It was a complete collapse of his hit tool; his timing fell apart and he didn't make enough contact or hit it in good spots when he did. Yet you only need to run it back another year to see a potential star catcher. Melendez was our No. 67 overall prospect entering the 2019 season, with huge raw power and big defensive talents. If his hit tool can even get to below-average, he'll be a pretty good regular, and if it can get past that he'll be a star. But it's pretty hard to stay afloat hitting .163.

Development Track: Melendez was at the alternate site all season, gaining valuable experience and reps. He impressed early on, though he wore down over the course of training. He's still a year away from being added to the 40-man, and we'd like to see a consolidation season here.

Variance: Extreme. There's severe hit tool variance here, both to push him above the OFP and to implode his entire offensive skill set a la 2019.

Mark Barry's Fantasy Take: I'm working on a theory that catching prospects are a little like Highlanders in that there can be only one. Right now it's Adley Rutschman, and pretty much everyone else is off my radar. Also Melendez struck out almost 40 percent of the time during his last bout with competitive pitching, so he'll need to iron out those issues before getting back into the mix.

10 Carlos Hernández RHP   OFP: 50   ETA: Debuted in 2020
Born: 03/11/97   Age: 24   Bats: R   Throws: R   Height: 6'4"   Weight: 250   Origin: International Free Agent, 2016

YEAR	TEAM	LVL	AGE	W	L	SV	G	GS	IP	H	HR	BB/9	K/9	K	GB%	BABIP	WHIP	ERA	DRA-	WARP
2018	LEX	LO-A	21	6	5	0	15	15	79¹	71	7	2.6	9.3	82	41.4%	.299	1.18	3.29	130	-0.9
2019	ROY	ROK	22	0	2	0	5	5	11	14	1	2.5	9.8	12	41.2%	.394	1.55	7.36		
2019	BUR	ROK+	22	0	0	0	3	3	10²	11	1	10.1	11.0	13	33.3%	.345	2.16	9.28		
2019	LEX	LO-A	22	3	3	0	7	7	36	34	5	2.2	10.8	43	37.2%	.326	1.19	3.50	86	0.4
2020	KC	MLB	23	0	1	0	5	3	14²	19	4	3.7	8.0	13	42.6%	.349	1.70	4.91	111	0.0
2021 FS	KC	MLB	24	8	10	0	26	26	150	146	21	5.0	8.2	137	41.2%	.293	1.53	5.14	116	-0.3
2021 DC	KC	MLB	24	3	6	0	16	16	71	69	10	5.0	8.2	65	41.2%	.293	1.53	5.14	116	0.1

Comparables: Luis Perdomo, Nick Neidert, Seranthony Domínguez

The Report: An over-aged signee out of Venezuela in 2016, Hernández found mid-90s heat as a late-bloomer. He's pitched well in the minors, but his large frame hasn't proved as durable as you'd like, and there's some effort in the delivery. The profile might play better in relief, but he does have feel for both a change and curve, although the change can be a bit firm and flat, and the 12-6 curve lacking tight, late depth.

Development Track: Despite not pitching above the South Atlantic League, Hernández was called up as an available arm on the 40-man roster, and briefly slotted into the Royals' rotation in place of Matt Harvey. The results were mixed at best. He touched the upper-90s with regularity and both the curve and change flashed above-average, but when they weren't flashing, they got hit hard, and the fastball command was well-below-average. Hernández has the potential to have big, bat-missing stuff, but he looked like a pitcher who needed another year-plus in the minors to harness it all.

Variance: Medium. I'm fairly confident Hernández would be a useful reliever, if the arsenal doesn't end up deep enough, or the durability issues continue. But he's not a major-league ready reliever, and there's limited upside as a rotation piece.

Mark Barry's Fantasy Take: Hernández wasn't great in his first stint with the big club, being used as an opener in three of his five appearances. I'm not sure you need to spend a ton of time contemplating his fantasy future, but if you want to do so as an attempt to take your mind off of the world's insanity, I won't begrudge you.

The Prospects You Meet Outside The Top Ten

#11

Nick Pratto 1B   Born: 10/06/98   Age: 22   Bats: L   Throws: L   Height: 6'1"   Weight: 195   Origin: Round 1, 2017 Draft (#14 overall)

YEAR	TEAM	LVL	AGE	PA	R	2B	3B	HR	RBI	BB	K	SB	CS	AVG/OBP/SLG	DRC+	BABIP	BRR	FRAA	WARP
2018	LEX	LO-A	19	537	79	33	2	14	62	45	150	22	5	.280/.343/.443	110	.375	1.4	1B(125) -0.6	0.3
2019	WIL	HI-A	20	472	48	21	1	9	46	49	164	17	7	.191/.278/.310	64	.286	0.5	1B(123) 5.2	-0.5
2021 FS	KC	MLB	22	600	52	26	2	14	58	40	233	11	4	.201/.260/.334	61	.317	-0.7	1B 6	-1.6

Comparables: Anthony Rizzo, Javy Guerra, Matt Davidson

Pratto has been disappointing as a prospect, given he was a first-round prep bat, and his 2019 at Wilmington was an out-and-out disaster, even factoring in how hard it is to hit there. But he also got one of the strongest positive reports among prospects at the alternate site. The swing has improved, and if he can get more aggressive with his approach in the zone, a potential average regular is back in play.

Prospects to dream on a little

Wilmin Candelario SS   Born: 09/11/01   Age: 19   Bats: S   Throws: R   Height: 5'11"   Weight: 165   Origin: International Free Agent, 2018

YEAR	TEAM	LVL	AGE	PA	R	2B	3B	HR	RBI	BB	K	SB	CS	AVG/OBP/SLG	DRC+	BABIP	BRR	FRAA	WARP
2019	DSL ROY2	ROK	17	213	33	7	8	4	27	23	62	11	11	.315/.396/.505		.450			

Signed for $850,000 out of the Dominican as part of Kansas City's 2018 J2 class, Candelario needs to add some physical strength to up the oomph in his natural hitting ability, but could be year or two away from being a very intriguing two-way shortstop prospect.

Darryl Collins OF Born: 09/16/01 Age: 19 Bats: L Throws: R Height: 6'2" Weight: 185 Origin: International Free Agent, 2018

YEAR	TEAM	LVL	AGE	PA	R	2B	3B	HR	RBI	BB	K	SB	CS	AVG/OBP/SLG	DRC+	BABIP	BRR	FRAA	WARP
2019	ROY	ROK	17	208	24	7	7	0	25	22	30	1	2	.320/.401/.436		.382			
2021 FS	KC	MLB	19	600	46	26	5	6	50	32	166	1	1	.221/.269/.322	62	.303	2.2	LF -7	-1.7

Comparables: Ramón Flores, Tim Lopes, Trent Grisham

Signed out of the Dutch League, Collins found himself back with the Curaçao Neptunus in 2020 before heading back for instructs. His is a frame that portends power although the approach at the plate is still raw and he can't consistently lift and pull the ball at present. There's some feel for contact already, so he may be able to unlock some poolside power at some point, but he'll have to hit a bunch as the arm will limit him to left field.

Rothaikeg Seijas RF Born: 07/22/02 Age: 18 Bats: R Throws: R Height: 5'11" Weight: 170 Origin: International Free Agent, 2018

YEAR	TEAM	LVL	AGE	PA	R	2B	3B	HR	RBI	BB	K	SB	CS	AVG/OBP/SLG	DRC+	BABIP	BRR	FRAA	WARP
2019	DSL ROY1	ROK	16	162	19	6	1	1	17	27	37	4	1	.220/.354/.303		.295			

Seijas was reputed to be the best pure hitter of the recent Kansas City IFA classes, but he is on the shorter and already-filled-out side. There's some power potential here, but he may end up as more of a tweener, which does feel like an unnecessarily specific thing to write about an 18-year-old who hasn't even come stateside yet.

You always need catching

Sebastian Rivero C Born: 11/16/98 Age: 22 Bats: R Throws: R Height: 6'1" Weight: 195 Origin: International Free Agent, 2015

YEAR	TEAM	LVL	AGE	PA	R	2B	3B	HR	RBI	BB	K	SB	CS	AVG/OBP/SLG	DRC+	BABIP	BRR	FRAA	WARP
2018	LEX	LO-A	19	306	41	16	0	7	34	17	59	0	1	.258/.301/.391	91	.300	-0.4	C(60) 1.0	0.4
2019	WIL	HI-A	20	326	23	14	1	1	24	19	75	2	2	.212/.270/.278	58	.276	-1.3	C(68) 0.9	-0.2
2021 FS	KC	MLB	22	600	48	26	1	11	55	26	168	0	0	.215/.255/.329	59	.285	-0.5	C 0	-0.8

Comparables: Francisco Peña, Pedro Severino, Carson Kelly

Rivero is a career .250/.291/.345 hitter in the minors. Even considering he's a catcher, he would have to be a really good glove to be much more than a fringe backup. But the defensive improvements this year do give him a really good glove. And as the sign says, you always need catching.

Good upside but a ways away

Zach Haake RHP Born: 10/08/96 Age: 24 Bats: R Throws: R Height: 6'4" Weight: 186 Origin: Round 6, 2018 Draft (#182 overall)

YEAR	TEAM	LVL	AGE	W	L	SV	G	GS	IP	H	HR	BB/9	K/9	K	GB%	BABIP	WHIP	ERA	DRA-	WARP
2018	ROY	ROK	21	0	0	0	5	4	9²	7	1	1.9	9.3	10	40.0%	.250	0.93	1.86		
2019	LEX	LO-A	22	4	6	0	18	18	75²	60	2	4.3	10.7	90	36.9%	.317	1.27	2.85	88	0.8
2021 FS	KC	MLB	24	2	3	0	57	0	50	46	7	5.5	8.5	47	35.5%	.286	1.55	4.96	114	-0.3

Comparables: Steven Matz, Pierce Johnson, Matt Purke

We had very strong 2019 reports on Haake, who flashed three above-average or plus pitches as a breakout arm who thrived in the pros after struggling at Kentucky. If the season had happened, he might've broken out even further; instead, he ended up a bit behind due to shoulder soreness (which also cost him some time in 2019) and never made it to the alternate site. He's healthy now, but he's entering his age-24 season having never pitched above Low-A and there's durability and secondary consistency issues present. It sure feels like there's a lot of bullpen risk, in other words.

You were going to ask about him in the comments

Seuly Matias	**RF**	Born: 09/04/98	Age: 22	Bats: R	Throws: R	Height: 6'3"	Weight: 198	Origin: International Free Agent, 2015											
YEAR	TEAM	LVL	AGE	PA	R	2B	3B	HR	RBI	BB	K	SB	CS	AVG/OBP/SLG	DRC+	BABIP	BRR	FRAA	WARP
2018	LEX	LO-A	19	376	62	13	1	31	63	24	131	6	0	.231/.303/.550	95	.264	0.7	RF(75) -2.1	-0.4
2019	WIL	HI-A	20	221	23	10	4	4	22	25	98	2	4	.148/.259/.307	47	.270	-0.6	RF(51) 5.6	-0.2
2021 FS	KC	MLB	22	600	45	26	3	11	52	39	279	3	1	.167/.233/.290	42	.309	0.4	RF 2	-2.8

Comparables: Estevan Florial, Jorge Bonifacio, Willy García

Matias is now over three years removed from his breakout in the Appy, and two years removed from hitting 31 home runs in just over 90 games in the South Atlantic League. The hit tool completely collapsed in 2019. The swing-and-miss that was always a concern has borne out, so while the line-to-line power is elite, it seems unlikely Matias will get it into games against advanced arms. There were some marginal approach gains at the alternate site, but the profile is trending more towards "wins a lot of Double-A Home Run Derbies" than "major league masher." It's a shame, because it's a really fun batting practice.

Top Talents 25 and Under (as of 4/1/2021):

1. Bobby Witt Jr., SS
2. Brady Singer, RHP
3. Adalberto Mondesi, SS
4. Asa Lacy, LHP
5. Kris Bubic, LHP
6. Daniel Lynch, LHP
7. Jackson Kowar, RHP
8. Erick Pena, OF
9. Brad Keller, RHP
10. Kyle Isbel, OF

Brady Singer stepped into the major-league rotation a bit ahead of schedule. He was immediately a good No. 3 starter, which was exactly our projection for him on last year's prospect list. He's mostly a sinker/slider guy, with the occasional changeup mixed in. Both of his primary offerings are effective, and although he's never going to miss a ton of bats and doesn't have elite upside, the whole is greater than the sum of the individual parts due to pitchability and command. We expect him to continue on at this level for quite some time.

Adalberto Mondesi makes his last 25U list this year. He remains a frustrating offensive player, unable to get on base enough to take advantage of his blazing speed or to leverage his power. He's put up two terrible offensive seasons in a row, 75 DRC+ in 2019 and 61 in 2020, and Witt is starting to loom as a long-term threat to his job. There's still a chance this all comes together, but he might just stay a speed-and-defense type, too.

Kris Bubic made it even more ahead of schedule than Singer, having jumped straight from High-A to The Show. He was slightly-above replacement level by DRA, though with a shinier 4.32 ERA and striking out nearly a batter an inning. He gave up a few too many walks and dingers, but for that big of a jump it didn't go that badly. He works mostly off his fastball and changeup, with a curve that's a better third offering than most of the type. Like Singer, he projects to be a mid-rotation starter, but unlike Singer he's not actually there quite yet.

Brad Keller is one of the better recent Rule 5 finds. That's not saying that much, since he's only a fourth starter-type, but getting a fourth starter for free is always a plus. Edward Olivares, our No. 14 prospect in a loaded Padres system last year, landed here in the Trevor Rosenthal trade, and warrants a brief mention as well; he graduated on service time without establishing himself as a regular, but we think he's got a shot to get there.

Los Angeles Angels

The State of the System:

We aren't too sad that we don't have to figure out where exactly to rank Jo Adell now, but his graduation does take a bite out of the impact prospect group at the top.

The Top Ten:

★ ★ ★ *2021 Top 101 Prospect* **#44** ★ ★ ★

1 **Brandon Marsh** **CF**   OFP: 60   ETA: 2021
Born: 12/18/97   Age: 23   Bats: L   Throws: R   Height: 6'4"   Weight: 215   Origin: Round 2, 2016 Draft (#60 overall)

YEAR	TEAM	LVL	AGE	PA	R	2B	3B	HR	RBI	BB	K	SB	CS	AVG/OBP/SLG	DRC+	BABIP	BRR	FRAA	WARP
2018	BUR	LO-A	20	154	26	12	1	3	24	21	40	4	0	.295/.390/.470	136	.400	2.9	CF(14) 1.2, RF(13) -1.3, LF(6) 0.7	1.2
2018	IE	HI-A	20	426	59	15	6	7	46	52	118	10	4	.256/.348/.385	107	.356	4.3	CF(50) -0.8, RF(33) 3.0, LF(7) 0.5	1.1
2019	MOB	AA	21	412	48	21	2	7	43	47	92	18	5	.300/.383/.428	141	.384	2.6	CF(55) -0.7, RF(19) 1.8, LF(13) -3.0	2.9
2021 FS	LAA	MLB	23	600	62	26	4	13	60	46	194	7	2	.240/.303/.377	85	.345	3.1	CF 0, LF 0	0.9
2021 DC	LAA	MLB	23	68	7	3	0	1	6	5	22	0	0	.240/.303/.377	85	.345	0.4	CF 0	0.1

Comparables: Michael Saunders, Jordan Schafer, Chris Young

The Report: Marsh is a well-rounded outfielder who can contribute in a variety of ways. At 6-foot-4 and 215-pounds, the left-handed hitter has yet to tap into his reservoir of power, but his display of hard contact to all fields while hitting .300 at Double-A in 2019 is a great sign of his future offensive potential. His speed translates to plus range in the outfield and he has the arm strength to play all three positions. Marsh is an excellent baserunner and a capable thief, stealing 18-of-23 bases while in the Southern League. Marsh could entrench himself in the middle of a big-league lineup very soon.

Development Track: Marsh's versatility and undeniable talent could allow him to force his way into the lineup as soon as next season.

Variance: Low. Additional leverage in the swing would equate to more power, as long as it doesn't compromise the already impressive hard contact ability.

Mark Barry's Fantasy Take: OK, so the dream is for Marsh to add a little more pop to an already pretty well-rounded base of skills. And while that would certainly be very cool (as the kids say), Marsh could still be awfully valuable in a fantasy sense even without prodigious power. There are faint whiffs of an Adam Eaton-esque floor, even if Marsh only slugs 12-15 homers. An Eaton floor with plenty of upside to be better puts Marsh firmly amongst the top-30 dynasty prospects on my personal list.

─────── ★ ★ ★ *2021 Top 101 Prospect* **#76** ★ ★ ★ ───────

2 **Jordyn Adams   CF**   OFP: 60   ETA: 2022
Born: 10/18/99   Age: 21   Bats: R   Throws: R   Height: 6'2"   Weight: 180   Origin: Round 1, 2018 Draft (#17 overall)

YEAR	TEAM	LVL	AGE	PA	R	2B	3B	HR	RBI	BB	K	SB	CS	AVG/OBP/SLG	DRC+	BABIP	BRR	FRAA	WARP
2018	ANG	ROK	18	82	8	2	2	0	5	10	23	5	2	.243/.354/.329		.362			
2018	ORM	ROK	18	40	5	4	1	0	8	4	7	0	1	.314/.375/.486		.379			
2019	ANG	ROK	19	14	4	1	0	0	4	1	3	4	0	.538/.571/.615		.700			
2019	BUR	LO-A	19	428	52	15	2	7	31	50	94	12	5	.250/.346/.358	122	.316	2.4	CF(73) -1.2, LF(9) 2.5, RF(8) -0.4	2.6
2019	IE	HI-A	19	40	7	1	1	1	1	5	14	0	1	.229/.325/.400	94	.350	0.2	CF(4) 0.4, LF(2) -0.3, RF(2) -0.3	0.1
2021 FS	LAA	MLB	21	600	50	26	3	9	54	41	200	5	2	.218/.278/.332	68	.323	-0.5	CF 0, LF 1	-0.5

Comparables: Aaron Hicks, Kyle Tucker, Slade Heathcott

The Report: Adams is an elite defender in center field and continues to develop his dynamic offensive game. The speed, agility, and soft hands that made him a highly recruited prep wide receiver are apparent as he ranges gap-to-gap on defense. He's demonstrated advanced strike zone awareness in his two seasons thus far (.353 career OBP), and reportedly held his own while facing older pitching at the Angels' alternate site in 2020.

Development Track: While advanced pitching has been able to knock the bat out of his hands on occasion, those days are dwindling as the young outfielder develops into an offensive presence. While he may never hit more than 20-25 home runs in a season, his middle-of-the field approach and high rate of contact should equate to a perennial .270-.290 hitter.

Variance: Medium. The bat-to-ball ability requires improvement before he can solidify his spot in a lineup.

Mark Barry's Fantasy Take: Admittedly, I might be a sucker for Angels outfield prospects with the initials J.A., but I quite like Adams. Adams is never going to reach Jo Adell's power potential, but he can get on base and run, and he'll also get plenty of shots thanks to superb defense. Production-wise, might I interest you in a ceiling of Deluxe Ender Inciarte

─────── ★ ★ ★ *2021 Top 101 Prospect* **#86** ★ ★ ★ ───────

3 **Reid Detmers   LHP**   OFP: 55   ETA: 2022
Born: 07/08/99   Age: 21   Bats: L   Throws: L   Height: 6'2"   Weight: 210   Origin: Round 1, 2020 Draft (#10 overall)

The Report: It would be difficult to find a better performing starting pitcher at the collegiate level the past two years than Detmers. He racked up strikeouts at an eye-popping rate and displayed good control with low walk totals, so you'd expect it to be coming from an electric flame-thrower. Not the case with Detmers, whose fastball is average on pure velocity, but plays up due to his plus command of the pitch inside the strike zone. The separator in the arsenal is a big breaking curveball that locks up hitters with regularity. Hitters often attempt to protect against the curve, leaving them susceptible to swinging late on the heater. His build is solid with a strong lower half and he has mechanics that stay consistent, lending evaluators to feel confident about a starter's role, albeit with a limited ceiling.

Development Track: There is some belief the fastball has potential left if Detmers can develop more efficient back-spin and work up in the zone with the pitch to further complement the curve. Without much room left to add on his frame, the velocity is likely to remain in the low 90s, necessitating improvement in other areas to help on the overall quality of his pitches. His changeup has some feel to it with late sinking action; having been able to get through lineups in college mostly as a two-pitch pitcher, further work wouldn't hurt to make it a weak-contact option against righties.

Variance: Low. The flags and question marks are limited. With the state of the big league club's pitching staff, they could really use some consistency in the rotation.

Mark Barry's Fantasy Take: Typically I'm out on low-velocity, two-pitch hurlers like Detmers, but I'm definitely more interested when plus command is involved. The changeup will likely determine the southpaw's upside, and while we won't know about its development before most FYPDs, I'm taking a flyer on Detmers as a top-150 prospect and a potential top-10 FYPD selection.

4 Kyren Paris SS   OFP: 55   ETA: 2024

Born: 11/11/01   Age: 19   Bats: R   Throws: R   Height: 6'0"   Weight: 165   Origin: Round 2, 2019 Draft (#55 overall)

YEAR	TEAM	LVL	AGE	PA	R	2B	3B	HR	RBI	BB	K	SB	CS	AVG/OBP/SLG	DRC+	BABIP	BRR	FRAA	WARP
2019	ANG	ROK	17	13	4	1	0	0	2	3	4	0	0	.300/.462/.400		.500			
2021 FS	LAA	MLB	19	600	44	26	2	6	47	35	238	4	1	.204/.255/.296	52	.341	0.7	SS -1	-1.9

Comparables: Michael Chavis, Travis Demeritte, Jay Bruce

The Report: A big "arrow up" pop-up player out of southern California the spring before the 2019 draft, Paris is a promising infielder in a number of ways, perhaps most notably via the analytics. As one of the youngest players in the draft, data-driven models weigh age relative to potential since there is a presumption of more room for all-encompassing growth. Paris clearly fit that bill and is said to have been working his tail off in the weight room. Whether he stays at shortstop or moves to another position is contingent on how fully he fills out the uniform. He could also be at second or third, or even the outfield thanks to his rangy foot-speed and quick reactions. The swing is simple and includes ideal actions with the hands, balanced throughout and a bat-path that stays level through the zone.

Development Track: Paris missed most of his pro debut after the draft thanks a broken hamate bone, and then we had the lost year of 2020, meaning he's sorely needing the game reps to get his feet wet. The good news, experience notwithstanding, reports have been favorable with regards to his training makeup. With no games to play, all indicators point to making the most of the time off, now requiring a healthy 2021 to make up for lost time.

Variance: Extreme. He's young, very young when you consider how long it's been since he's played in meaningful games. Until he gets on the field for a sustained season it's impossible to know where he's at as a position player with a two-year layoff.

Mark Barry's Fantasy Take: Paris has 13 professional plate appearances, thanks to a broken hamate bone and, well, 2020. There's a chance he could be a "solid-across-the-board" contributor, but he's still very far away in terms of development, so everything is a complete guess right now for our purposes. I think I speak for us all when I say that I hope Paris is very good, if not great, for a handful of years before bowing out of the fantasy spotlight, so we can all knowingly glance at one another and earnestly say, "We'll always have Paris."

5 Chris Rodriguez RHP   OFP: 55   ETA: 2022

Born: 07/20/98   Age: 22   Bats: R   Throws: R   Height: 6'2"   Weight: 185   Origin: Round 4, 2016 Draft (#126 overall)

YEAR	TEAM	LVL	AGE	W	L	SV	G	GS	IP	H	HR	BB/9	K/9	K	GB%	BABIP	WHIP	ERA	DRA-	WARP
2019	IE	HI-A	20	0	0	0	3	3	9¹	6	0	3.9	12.5	13	68.4%	.316	1.07	0.00	64	0.2
2021 FS	LAA	MLB	22	2	3	0	57	0	50	45	7	4.0	8.7	48	43.1%	.283	1.35	4.26	105	0.0

Comparables: Ian Anderson, Danny Duffy, Beau Burrows

The Report: Rodriguez has been severely limited by injuries, throwing just 9 ⅓ innings across the 2018-19 seasons. When healthy, the 22-year-old right-hander showcases an electric four-pitch repertoire featuring a heavy, mid-90s fastball. Accompanying the heat are two different breaking balls, a hard lateral slider and a downward-tumbling curveball, along with an effective, dawdling changeup.

Development Track: Strictly utilized as a starter up to this point in his career, Rodriguez's injury history and power repertoire make the bullpen an option. Reportedly healthy and impressive at the Angels' alternate site and instructs in 2020, Rodriguez is more than ready to resume his promising career.

Variance: High. Has to stay on the field to progress.

Mark Barry's Fantasy Take: Four-pitch mixes are wonderful. However, they're less useful if one can't stay on the field. I'll keep Rodriguez on the watchlist for now and act accordingly if/when he stays healthy for an extended period of time.

6 Jeremiah Jackson SS   OFP: 55   ETA: 2023

Born: 03/26/00   Age: 21   Bats: R   Throws: R   Height: 6'0"   Weight: 165   Origin: Round 2, 2018 Draft (#57 overall)

YEAR	TEAM	LVL	AGE	PA	R	2B	3B	HR	RBI	BB	K	SB	CS	AVG/OBP/SLG	DRC+	BABIP	BRR	FRAA	WARP
2018	ANG	ROK	18	91	13	4	2	5	14	7	25	6	1	.317/.374/.598		.396			
2018	ORM	ROK	18	100	13	6	3	2	9	8	34	4	1	.198/.260/.396		.286			
2019	ORM	ROK+	19	287	47	14	2	23	60	23	96	5	1	.265/.331/.609		.314			
2021 FS	LAA	MLB	21	600	42	26	3	9	49	32	256	5	1	.176/.226/.286	36	.302	2.7	SS -3, 2B 0	-3.0

The Report: We were impressed with Jackson's pop out of a presently thin but projectable frame during his 2019 Pioneer League jaunt and saw him as a potential plus power/speed shortstop. He was a long way from that projection due to an aggressive approach coupled with an unorthodox hand load that created length and left him vulnerable to better spin. The defense in the infield was shaky at times as well, although the underlying tools were enough to man the position given year-over-year development.

Development Track: Jackson got alternate site and instructional league reps, but we didn't get the kind of reports that would markedly move him one way or the other. Which, given where he was entering the season, is a bit of a net negative for the projection.

Variance: Very High. It was high last year for the hit tool and lack of full-season experience/performance. Another year older, and deeper in debt (to variance).

Mark Barry's Fantasy Take: We're currently smack dab in the middle of the Golden Age of Fantasy Shortstops, but at his peak, Jackson could sneak into the back end of the top 15 at the position, thanks to some solid pop. He's a top-150 prospect, but it's hard to imagine him scraping into the top 50.

7 D'Shawn Knowles OF   OFP: 55   ETA: 2023/2024

Born: 01/16/01   Age: 20   Bats: S   Throws: R   Height: 6'0"   Weight: 165   Origin: International Free Agent, 2017

YEAR	TEAM	LVL	AGE	PA	R	2B	3B	HR	RBI	BB	K	SB	CS	AVG/OBP/SLG	DRC+	BABIP	BRR	FRAA	WARP
2018	ANG	ROK	17	130	19	4	1	1	14	15	27	7	4	.301/.385/.381		.384			
2018	ORM	ROK	17	123	27	9	2	4	15	13	38	2	3	.321/.398/.550		.463			
2019	ORM	ROK+	18	286	38	11	4	6	28	25	76	5	4	.244/.311/.392		.312			
2021 FS	LAA	MLB	20	600	45	26	3	7	49	37	221	7	3	.199/.254/.300	50	.315	-1.3	CF 0, RF 0	-2.5

The Report: Knowles is a fleet-of-foot, up-the-middle type with some feel to hit and above-average bat speed from both sides of the plate. The swing isn't built for much game power, but he could add some doubles and maybe even 40 over-the-fence pop if he gets stronger in his 20s—and he did show off some ability to lift the ball in last winter's Bahamian Home Run Derby (look, there hasn't been much baseball this year, so I will use what little I have). Realistically though, you are hoping for a slash-and-burn center fielder who hits it in the gaps enough to get to 40 doubles. And he still hasn't seen full-season pitching and just lost an important year of development time.

Development Track: I wrote in our Rule 5 Draft recap that one of the reasons that perhaps a better class of prospect was available this year was that teams didn't have the extra season of reps in which to evaluate if a player should be protected (or put another way, would be likely to get taken). That also applies to the BP Prospect Team as we try to evaluate a certain class of prospect. On our first list I suggested it would be primarily prospects with upside, but little or no full-season experience. Knowles is a prime example of this problem. One could argue that ranking him on the 101 last year was a year too early. We make this kind of bet on occasion, especially towards the very back of the list. The difference in evaluation and projection between the 100th-best prospect and 150th best is marginal, but one gets a line on the prospect's b-ref page and one doesn't. Knowles was very high variance coming into 2020. I believed in the hit tool. I thought he might add some power. But there was certainly a non-zero chance he would go to the Midwest League and flop. There was also a non-zero chance he would end the year in the Cal League as a borderline Top 50 prospect in baseball. Neither of those happened. He didn't stand out at instructs in particular, but in a year like this, how much do you hold that against him? We don't know anything more than we did last year. I'm not moving the line much here. But Knowles won't make the 101, and where I do have information about improvements in the system, he's been passed for now.

Variance: Extreme. Using the same basic principle as Jackson, Knowles was very high last year and only got some instructs reps in 2020.

Mark Barry's Fantasy Take: First and foremost, I'm currently petitioning BP to send me to next year's Bahamanian Home Run Derby, you know, for research.

After that, well, not much has happened in the last year for Knowles to have improved his profile. Unfortunately, Knowles needs reps to develop and the last 365 days haven't been helpful in that regard. I would have pushed for Knowles to be added to the dynasty farm system last season around this time, but currently, I think he's a watchlist guy.

8 Jack Kochanowicz   OFP: 55   ETA: 2024
Born: 12/22/00   Age: 20   Bats: L   Throws: R   Height: 6'6"   Weight: 220   Origin: Round 3, 2019 Draft (#92 overall)

The Report: A tall, sturdy, cold weather prep arm, Kochanowicz still technically hasn't thrown a professional pitch. When he was drafted he was sitting low 90s, touching higher, along with having a projectable curve and firm change. Your standard cold weather pitching starter kit. Despite his size, the mechanics are repeatable, and he shows good body control keeping all his moving parts in line. A quick arm action and long stride makes the fastball play up and get on hitters quickly, and he stays tall to create plane on the pitch as well. It's a starter's frame and delivery. Kochanowicz just needs the three-pitch arsenal to develop.

Development Track: Despite not being a particular projectable 6-foot-6, Kochanowicz showed up to instructs sitting mid-90s rather than bumping there. That's a strong base for development, and it also creates a little more separation off his changeup. He might have headed to (checks crib sheet) Inland Empire in 2021 regardless, but the lack of short-season landing spots means he will have to try and develop his secondaries in the less-than-friendly confines of the Cal League.

Variance: Extreme. Very limited pro experience, more than the usual secondary development needed for a prep arm.

Mark Barry's Fantasy Take: The bones are there, to be sure. But the reps against anything nearing professional hitters have not been, so Kochanowicz should be on the radar in leagues with 350ish prospects, but probably not otherwise—you know, until we see him be a professional pitcher or whatever.

9 Orlando Martinez   RF   OFP: 50   ETA: 2022
Born: 02/17/98   Age: 23   Bats: L   Throws: L   Height: 6'0"   Weight: 185   Origin: International Free Agent, 2017

YEAR	TEAM	LVL	AGE	PA	R	2B	3B	HR	RBI	BB	K	SB	CS	AVG/OBP/SLG	DRC+	BABIP	BRR	FRAA	WARP
2018	ORM	ROK	20	53	11	5	0	2	10	4	9	3	2	.375/.415/.604		.421			
2018	BUR	LO-A	20	238	27	12	1	3	25	17	56	6	5	.289/.340/.394	106	.373	-1.2	RF(20) 1.9, LF(18) -1.0, CF(13) 0.3	0.4
2019	IE	HI-A	21	422	55	21	4	12	49	36	79	5	4	.263/.325/.434	110	.299	1.4	CF(41) 3.4, RF(21) -2.2, LF(20) 1.6	1.9
2021 FS	LAA	MLB	23	600	57	27	2	15	64	36	172	3	2	.236/.285/.379	80	.313	-1.5	CF 6, LF 1	0.8

Comparables: César Puello, Kirk Nieuwenhuis, Jake Cave

The Report: An ideal fourth outfielder, Martinez hits for average, draws walks, runs well, plays all three outfield positions, and has enough power to pinch hit off the bench in any scenario. In 88 games in the 2019 season, Martinez totaled 12 homers and 21 doubles, alluding to the sneaky pop and offensive capabilities of the 6-foot, 180-pound lefty. He's a well-rounded ballplayer who can hit throughout the lineup, bunts, runs, provides above-average defense, and takes one for the team.

Development Track: The 22-year-old has yet to play above High-A, but is equipped with an advanced baseball IQ and the savvy skills to advance quickly to the big leagues. While his consistent but unspectacular game may not suit every lineup, his value may be greatest on a good team, where he can be utilized in favorable matchups and off of the bench.

Variance: High. While his skill set is broad, he might like a carrying tool, and he wasn't major league-ready enough to be picked in the Rule 5.

Mark Barry's Fantasy Take: I'm not sure you have to take too much action on Martinez until he a) hits for more power or 2) becomes more efficient on the bases. I don't have a ton of faith in either option, so he's probably a deep, deep or only-league play.

10 Adrian Placencia   OFP: 50   ETA: 2025
Born: 06/02/03   Age: 18   Bats: S   Throws: R   Height: 5'11"   Weight: 155   Origin: International Free Agent, 2019

The Report: One of two seven-figure shortstops in the Angels' 2019 July 2nd class, Placencia doesn't have Arol Vera's physical projection, but his present offensive tools are advanced and he's a good enough athlete to handle short although he clearly needs more experience on the dirt because his reads off the bat reflect how few reps he's had in the grand scheme of things.

Development Track: Placencia didn't look overmatched against older and more advanced competition at domestic instructs. He has plus bat speed and a plan at the plate. The defensive tools are behind the offensive ones at present, but he's a good athlete with the hands to stay up the middle. There's some tools projection and Placencia stings the ball enough to hope he adds some power with maturity, but the overall profile is both lower ceiling and less of a lottery ticket than your median million-dollar IFA shortstop.

Variance: Extreme. The profile could go in several different directions, both generally and positionally. Placencia has been a professional baseball player for just over a year now and it's been a weird year. If you wanted to call him a 55 / Extreme right now based on holding his own against better than usual instructs competition, I wouldn't disagree strongly.

Mark Barry's Fantasy Take: Low-ceiling, not necessarily lottery ticket potential = meh on the fantasy side. The offensive skills are ahead of the defensive prowess at present, so that's something, but at present, Placencia is an assistant-to-the-watchlist as opposed to assistant watchlist.

The Prospects You Meet Outside The Top Ten

Interesting Draft Follow

Werner Blakely SS Born: 02/21/02   Age: 19   Bats: L   Throws: R   Height: 6'3"   Weight: 185   Origin: Round 4, 2020 Draft (#111 overall)

One draft heuristic the Angels employ is prioritizing premium physical attributes, trusting that they can convert them into baseball skills. They went over slot in the fourth round to pry Blakely away from Auburn because of the explosive traits to his swing, which are apparent even as he's trying to find a comfortable setup. He also displays loose actions with the glove and arm, despite the question of where he will end up on the field as his 6-foot-3 body matures.

Interesting Rule 5 Draft Follow

Jose Rivera 2B   Born: 05/26/99   Age: 22   Bats: R   Throws: R   Height: 5'10"   Weight: 165   Origin: International Free Agent, 2016

José Soriano was at the back of this Top 10 list right up until the 2020 Rule 5 draft started. I'm loathe to write up Rule 5 eligible players for these lists for just that reason, but both he and Martinez were too good to leave off entirely. You could make a case to slot Rivera right in Soriano's old spot at 9 or 10. It's a broadly similar profile as I noted in our draft recap. Unlike Soriano, Rivera isn't recovering from Tommy John surgery, which isn't necessarily a positive when you have to roster him all season. His command is behind Soriano's, which is the main reason he's also outside the Top Ten and also less likely to stick on the Angels 26-(or however many) man for all of 2021. If they do manage to keep him around, they will be getting a potential fourth starter out of the deal with three 50 to 55 offerings. But either way he will still be in the Angels chapter when the Futures Guide publishes.

MLB arms, but probably relievers

Hector Yan LHP   Born: 04/26/99   Age: 22   Bats: L   Throws: L   Height: 5'11"   Weight: 180   Origin: International Free Agent, 2015

YEAR	TEAM	LVL	AGE	W	L	SV	G	GS	IP	H	HR	BB/9	K/9	K	GB%	BABIP	WHIP	ERA	DRA-	WARP
2018	ORM	ROK	19	0	4	0	10	10	29²	29	3	6.1	8.8	29	45.6%	.342	1.65	4.55		
2019	BUR	LO-A	20	4	5	1	26	20	109	74	5	4.3	12.2	148	39.9%	.291	1.16	3.39	77	1.7
2021 FS	LAA	MLB	22	2	3	0	57	0	50	46	8	6.8	9.8	54	35.9%	.295	1.69	5.96	127	-0.6

Comparables: Huascar Ynoa, Keury Mella, Rony García

Yan's fastball can touch the upper 90s and his slider can flash plus. The split is good enough he won't need to drop it in relief, but relief is where he's going to end up given the control issues emanating from his unorthodox delivery. He'll need to smooth that all out even in one-inning stints, though, to be more than a Jekyll-or-Hyde extra 'pen arm.

MLB bats, but less upside than you'd like

Jahmai Jones 2B Born: 08/04/97 Age: 23 Bats: R Throws: R Height: 6'0" Weight: 204 Origin: Round 2, 2015 Draft (#70 overall)

YEAR	TEAM	LVL	AGE	PA	R	2B	3B	HR	RBI	BB	K	SB	CS	AVG/OBP/SLG	DRC+	BABIP	BRR	FRAA	WARP
2018	IE	HI-A	20	347	47	10	5	8	35	43	63	13	3	.235/.338/.383	111	.272	1.5	2B(70) -6.9	-0.1
2018	MOB	AA	20	212	33	10	4	2	20	24	51	11	1	.245/.335/.375	103	.323	-1.5	2B(45) -1.7	-0.1
2019	MOB	AA	21	544	66	22	3	5	50	50	109	9	11	.234/.308/.324	79	.288	2.3	2B(110) 14.4, CF(7) 0.3, LF(4) -0.6	2.3
2020	LAA	MLB	22	7	2	0	0	0	1	0	2	0	0	.429/.429/.429	89	.600	-0.1	2B(2) -0.0	0.0
2021 FS	LAA	MLB	23	600	61	25	3	12	59	46	160	11	4	.227/.295/.357	81	.297	0.6	2B 6, LF 0	1.3
2021 DC	LAA	MLB	23	34	3	1	0	0	3	2	9	0	0	.227/.295/.357	81	.297	0.0	2B 0	0.1

Comparables: *Luis Valbuena, Eddie Rosario, Abraham Toro*

The former Top 101 prospect—two years and one position switch ago—finally made the majors in 2020. The game power never consistently showed up outside of the Cal League, and Jones struggled more generally in Double-A. He's significantly changed his swing in recent seasons, and now is very quiet with just a toe tap and an exaggerated hand position that simplifies his route to the pitch. The profile is still a little short for a starting second baseman, but if you add an outfield glove back to his locker, Jones could be a useful bench piece.

Top Talents 25 and Under (as of 4/1/2021):

1. Jo Adell, OF
2. Brandon Marsh, OF
3. Griffin Canning, RHP
4. Jordyn Adams, OF
5. Reid Detmers, LHP
6. Kyren Paris, SS
7. Chris Rodriguez, RHP
8. Jeremiah Jackson, SS
9. D'Shawn Knowles, OF
10. Patrick Sandoval, LHP

Jo Adell, our No. 2 prospect in baseball the past two seasons, (barely) graduated from rookie-eligibility with the modified service time rules. He still ranks first here quite comfortably, but that saved us from some difficult discussions about how much to shade down his hit tool projection based on how bad he looked in the majors in 2020. Adell missed in the zone so much that I had a semi-serious conversation with Craig Goldstein right towards the end of the season about whether he might be having trouble seeing the ball, a la Wilson Ramos. It was only 132 plate appearances at 21-years-old in a pandemic season, so we're not exactly alarmed, but making contact on less than 65 percent of pitches in the strike zone is cause for at least moderate concern.

Griffin Canning is the rare third starter prospect who seems to be settling in as exactly a third starter. He's had somewhat chronic elbow injuries dating back to college, and probably wouldn't have been ready if the 2020 season had started on time with UCL injuries. But he avoided surgery, and was fine by summer camp. Ultimately, he made 11 league-average starts. We're shading Canning behind Marsh this year given the lack of superior upside and the shaky medical history, but he's likely to keep trucking as a mid-rotation pitcher as long as he's healthy.

Patrick Sandoval is a lefty with a feel for spin and velocity who has been ridiculously homer-prone in the majors but could yet round out into a decent major-league starter. Jaime Barria had his first above-replacement season in 2020 by DRA, with 32 ⅓ semi-effective innings; he's got a usable fastball/slider combination but could use to miss more bats if he's going to be more than a bulk innings type. Luis Rengifo was a long-time favorite of our late colleague and friend Rob McQuown; he's failed to hit for average much in part-time play in two MLB seasons even though he was a hit-tool oriented prospect. Matt Thaiss is a walks-first first baseman who has started picking up other positions; he'd be even more interesting if he picked back up the catching mitt he left at the University of Virginia. José Suarez barely made the back of this list last year, before he made two starts that lasted 2 ⅓ innings combined.

Los Angeles Dodgers

The State of the System:

The depth and overall quality of the system has taken a dip from recent years. A lot of that has been because of graduated prospects who contributed to a World Series title, so you know, they're probably feeling okay on Vin Scully Ave.

The Top Ten:

★ ★ ★ *2021 Top 101 Prospect* **#55** ★ ★ ★

1 **Josiah Gray** **RHP** OFP: 60 ETA: 2021
Born: 12/21/97 Age: 23 Bats: R Throws: R Height: 6'1" Weight: 190 Origin: Round 2, 2018 Draft (#72 overall)

YEAR	TEAM	LVL	AGE	W	L	SV	G	GS	IP	H	HR	BB/9	K/9	K	GB%	BABIP	WHIP	ERA	DRA-	WARP
2018	GRN	ROK	20	2	2	0	12	12	52¹	29	1	2.9	10.1	59	36.4%	.219	0.88	2.58		
2019	GL	LO-A	21	1	0	0	5	5	23¹	13	0	2.7	10.0	26	37.0%	.241	0.86	1.93	46	0.8
2019	RC	HI-A	21	7	0	0	12	12	67¹	52	3	1.7	10.7	80	36.3%	.293	0.97	2.14	47	2.2
2019	TUL	AA	21	3	2	0	9	8	39¹	33	0	2.5	9.4	41	34.3%	.317	1.12	2.75	67	0.8
2021 FS	LAD	MLB	23	1	1	0	57	0	50	44	6	3.7	8.8	48	35.8%	.279	1.30	4.03	97	0.2
2021 DC	LAD	MLB	23	1	1	0	27	0	29	25	4	3.7	8.8	28	35.8%	.279	1.30	4.03	97	0.2

Comparables: Yohander Méndez, Brett Cecil, Carl Edwards Jr.

The Report: Gray was recruited to be primarily a shortstop at D-II LeMoyne College, albeit one that could throw a few innings here and there as well. By his junior year he was starting full time and dominating with a fastball that sat mid-90s. He's not a mere arm strength prospect at this point. Nor does he looks like a position player converted to the mound. Gray has a fluid, repeatable, uptempo delivery. He still sits mid-90s and both his slider and change have a chance to be above-average. There was some reliever risk coming out of college, but that was more due to demographics (cold weather arm, late pitching convert) than the idea that his stuff would especially play up in shorter bursts, and Gray might lack a true late-inning wipeout secondary, even though both have progressed well to this point. Now he just looks like a solid mid-rotation pitching prospect.

Development Track: Gray didn't look out of place in Dodgers instraquad games facing parts of ... well, literally a World Series-winning lineup. He spent the balance of the summer at the alternate site to try and refine his secondaries, but he's about ready to be deployed in whatever role the Dodgers like, which I'd guess won't be a traditional 32 start /180 inning workhorse, but he'd likely be capable of that in time.

Variance: Medium. If Gray played for Kansas City or Miami, he probably would have seen time in the bigs and been able to acquit himself well enough. The Dodgers had pitching depth to spare in 2020, which does give Gray time to further tighten up his short, power slider and overall command.

Mark Barry's Fantasy Take: Typically "mid-rotation starter" is a term that is met with derision in fantasy circles. With Gray, however, I think his mid-rotation-ness (mid-rotation-osity?) stems more from organization and role than skill level. I like Gray quite a bit as a set-and-forget fantasy SP3-4, one capable of piling up strikeouts and wins, even if his spot in the rotation doesn't come with lofty innings totals.

★ ★ ★ *2021 Top 101 Prospect* **#74** ★ ★ ★

2 Keibert Ruiz C OFP: 60 ETA: Debuted in 2020

Born: 07/20/98 Age: 22 Bats: S Throws: R Height: 6'0" Weight: 225 Origin: International Free Agent, 2015

YEAR	TEAM	LVL	AGE	PA	R	2B	3B	HR	RBI	BB	K	SB	CS	AVG/OBP/SLG	DRC+	BABIP	BRR	FRAA	WARP
2018	TUL	AA	19	415	44	14	0	12	47	26	33	0	1	.268/.328/.401	92	.266	-3.8	C(86) 3.5	0.5
2019	TUL	AA	20	310	33	9	0	4	25	28	21	0	0	.254/.329/.330	104	.261	-3.5	C(61) 0.5	1.1
2019	OKC	AAA	20	40	6	0	0	2	9	2	1	0	0	.316/.350/.474	87	.286	0.9	C(9) -0.5	0.2
2020	LAD	MLB	21	8	1	0	0	1	1	0	3	0	0	.250/.250/.625	91	.250		C(2) -0.0	0.0
2021 FS	LAD	MLB	22	600	67	25	2	18	69	35	106	0	0	.262/.311/.416	97	.293	-0.2	C -4	1.8
2021 DC	LAD	MLB	22	69	7	2	0	2	7	4	12	0	0	.262/.311/.416	97	.293	0.0	C -1	0.2

Comparables: Ryan Sweeney, Jake Bauers, Michael Brantley

The Report: Ruiz burst onto the prospect scene during the 2017 season, hitting .300 at two A-ball levels as an 18-year-old. The hit tool looked above-average, there was some raw power in the swing, and he was a precocious defender for his age. Wilson Karaman called him "a quality catching prospect with the ingredients to develop into a big-league starter, with room for a bit more if the right-handed swing maxes out." 2018 was more of the same, although an aggressive approach in Double-A cut into our confidence in the offensive tools. Kevin Carter liked the glove still: "His upside is tied to his approach and how much of his average raw power he taps into and with large improvements he could produce fringe-all-star value." Ruiz didn't really tame the aggressive approach in 2019—despite walking more than he struck out—and both the pop and quality of contact regressed. He added weight as well and Kevin now thought that: "All in all, his profile is starting to blur the line a bit between a major league regular projection and a quality tandem or backup."

There's a point to having as many citations here as Sam Fuld's Wikipedia page. Ruiz is six months younger than Adley Rutschman, but is a prime example of prospect fatigue, or perhaps John Sickels' Young Catcher Stagnation Syndrome. The development hasn't been along that nice y=x slope you'd want, and maybe some of his prospect helium was tied up in age-relative-to-league, but he still has potentially average offensive tools and above-average defensive ones. That's a good catching prospect, but one who still needs to take that next step, three years later.

Development Track: Ruiz got a couple games behind the plate while Will Smith was dealing with a neck issue and promptly hit a home run in his first major-league at-bat. That's pretty nice. However, his playing time may continue to be contingent on Will Smith's health, as the Dodgers' primary backstop looks like he might already be a top-five catcher in baseball, and his backup, Austin Barnes, is functionally Clayton Kershaw's personal catcher. Ruiz is only 22, and hasn't dominated the high minors yet, so he has a little more time to burn. He'll spend some of that time in 2021 hanging out in Oklahoma City, where we hope to see the bat take a step or two back forward.

Variance: High. Ruiz's prospect track has seen more fits and starts than you'd expect from a player about to make his fourth consecutive Top 101. The staff reports were downright mediocre in 2019, and while he appears to have righted the ship, there's still uncertainty around both the offensive and defensive parts of his game.

Mark Barry's Fantasy Take: As far as catching prospects are concerned, Ruiz is a pretty good one. The backstop hasn't seen a strikeout rate over 10 percent in any meaningful sample since 2017, which is certainly notable as batting averages dwindle league wide. Still, he's a catcher, and one who doesn't project to hit for much power. He's a top-200 guy, perhaps a little higher if you're in a two-catcher format.

★ ★ ★ *2021 Top 101 Prospect* **#77** ★ ★ ★

3 **Miguel Vargas** **3B**   OFP: 60   ETA: 2022
Born: 11/17/99 Age: 21 Bats: R Throws: R Height: 6'3" Weight: 205 Origin: International Free Agent, 2017

YEAR	TEAM	LVL	AGE	PA	R	2B	3B	HR	RBI	BB	K	SB	CS	AVG/OBP/SLG	DRC+	BABIP	BRR	FRAA	WARP
2018	OGD	ROK	18	103	25	11	1	2	22	8	13	6	1	.394/.447/.596		.443			
2018	DOD2	ROK	18	37	6	3	1	0	2	5	3	1	0	.419/.514/.581		.464			
2018	GL	LO-A	18	89	4	1	1	0	6	10	20	0	0	.213/.307/.253	68	.281	-0.5	3B(19) 3.1	0.1
2019	GL	LO-A	19	323	53	20	2	5	45	35	43	9	1	.325/.399/.464	162	.363	-2.5	3B(59) 2.2, 1B(2) 0.4, 2B(2) 0.4	3.1
2019	RC	HI-A	19	236	23	18	1	2	32	20	40	4	3	.284/.353/.408	127	.341	-2.3	3B(43) -1.9, 1B(6) 0.4	0.8
2021 FS	LAD	MLB	21	600	55	28	3	10	58	42	142	3	1	.245/.304/.365	84	.312	0.4	3B 0, 1B 1	0.1

Comparables: Matt Dominguez, Mike Moustakas, Rafael Devers

The Report: Vargas is a naturally gifted hitter with plus bat-to-ball ability and is able to drive the ball gap-to-gap, which has led to 53 doubles in just 177 minor league games. Advanced strike-zone awareness limits his strikeouts, prevents him from chasing bad pitches, and helped him establish a .387 career OBP. While his power has yet to fully develop, his sturdy base and strong physique are sure to produce more home runs as he matures. His mobility and range are somewhat limited, but Vargas has the soft hands and the arm strength to play a competent third base, while he also has seen time at first base or even second.

Development Track: Vargas didn't get an invite to the alternate site, but his offensive performance at instructs played to the pre-season scouting report. The body is on the high maintenance side now, but he still looked fine at the hot corner, although the Dodgers are already moving him around the infield some. Vargas would have been ticketed to start 2020 in Double-A and given the limited 2020 game time, I'd expect that to be his starting point in 2021. The bat is capable of forcing the issue if his power continues to develop, even given a crowded major-league roster.

Variance: Medium. Despite the limited action, the bat gives Vargas a high floor, although we'd feel better about everything if he spent 2020 conquering the upper minors.

Mark Barry's Fantasy Take: Plenty of patience and lots of contact, you say? Vargas' loud arrival on the dynasty scene was quieted only by, uh, not playing real games in 2020, an issue we'll hopefully get to rectify in 2021. This profile is one I really like, especially with budding power reaching maturity as he gets closer to a debut. Vargas still has something to prove, as he hasn't faced pitching above High-A, but he's probably flirting with the top-100 dynasty prospects right now, and could even tick higher in the future.

★ ★ ★ *2021 Top 101 Prospect* **#91** ★ ★ ★

4 **Michael Busch** **2B**   OFP: 55   ETA: Late 2021/Early 2022
Born: 11/09/97 Age: 23 Bats: L Throws: R Height: 6'0" Weight: 207 Origin: Round 1, 2019 Draft (#31 overall)

YEAR	TEAM	LVL	AGE	PA	R	2B	3B	HR	RBI	BB	K	SB	CS	AVG/OBP/SLG	DRC+	BABIP	BRR	FRAA	WARP
2019	DOD1	ROK	21	16	1	0	0	0	0	1	2	0	0	.077/.250/.077		.091			
2019	GL	LO-A	21	19	4	0	0	0	2	6	3	0	0	.182/.474/.182	132	.222	0.6	2B(4) 0.2	0.2
2021 FS	LAD	MLB	23	600	53	26	2	12	56	46	173	3	1	.211/.284/.335	74	.286	0.5	2B 1	0.4

Comparables: Santiago Espinal, Rafael Ynoa, Mark Canha

The Report: The Dodgers popped Busch at the end of the first round in 2019 based on the strength of his bat. He raked his junior year at UNC, and while he doesn't have the loudest offensive tools you'll see, he does everything well. Hit, approach, pop, everything is above-average. While the bat might have been worthy of going in the top half of the first round, Busch was primarily a 1B/LF in college. That's going to put a bit of a damper on the overall profile, but the Dodgers being the Dodgers, they made him a second baseman. So we will list him at the keystone, although I suspect he will play there in the same way Max Muncy does—on occasion and not particularly well.

Development Track: "Busch is awesome." The praise for his performance in instructs was effusive. He showed good feel for contact and control of the zone, with burgeoning power. The hit and power tools could both end up above-average or better. He has settled into second base and while he's unlikely to grade out as average there, it's playable. The bat might be good enough now that it doesn't matter where he stands.

Variance: Medium. Busch is going to hit, and should be good enough defensively that you're happy enough to have him in the lineup wherever. Still need to see him do it in the upper minors though, and the glove might eat into his value some.

Mark Barry's Fantasy Take: Speaking of the Dodgers player development, it seems like Busch's profile (read: patience, power, no defensive position) is one that typically thrives in the organization. He got next to zero run after being drafted in 2019, so there's a good chance he's still a little unheralded in the dynasty world. I think he's a top-125ish guy that could even sneak into that top-100 on my personal list.

5 Diego Cartaya C   OFP: 55   ETA: 2024
Born: 09/07/01   Age: 19   Bats: R   Throws: R   Height: 6'2"   Weight: 199   Origin: International Free Agent, 2018

YEAR	TEAM	LVL	AGE	PA	R	2B	3B	HR	RBI	BB	K	SB	CS	AVG/OBP/SLG	DRC+	BABIP	BRR	FRAA	WARP
2019	DSL BAU	ROK	17	57	11	2	2	1	9	5	11	0	0	.240/.316/.420		.282			
2019	DOD2	ROK	17	150	25	10	0	3	13	11	31	1	0	.296/.353/.437		.359			
2021 FS	LAD	MLB	19	600	45	27	2	7	50	28	202	1	0	.214/.257/.312	55	.319	0.2	C 0	-1.0

Comparables: Bryan Anderson, Luis Campusano, Miguel Gonzalez

The Report: The Dodgers put Cartaya on the Keibert Ruiz track of catching development. They aggressively brought him stateside at 17 as soon as the AZL started and he was living with their Triple-A manager and former roving catcher instructor, Travis Barbary, during the shutdown. The similarities end there though. Cartaya has more raw power projection and a potential plus hit tool, but the defensive game is not as advanced as it was for teenaged Ruiz. Cartaya lacks some of the quick-twitch actions a modern catcher is expected to have and his receiving is more brute strength than finesse at present. Some of that will smooth out with more professional instruction and reps, but the profile is hit-over-glove, and that doesn't always fly behind the plate. There's potential on both sides of the ball though.

Development Track: Cartaya got about the fullest 2020 a prospect could get, spending time at both the alternate site and instructs. Reports on the bat in Camelback were a bit muted, but it was an unusual season, and he was facing a better caliber arm than your usual instructional league crop. Cartaya just turned 19, but I'd expect given how aggressively the Dodgers have handled him that he will be ticketed for a full-season affiliate in 2021.

Variance: Extreme. The bat is ahead of the glove here, and the bat hasn't really been tested by better pitching yet.

Mark Barry's Fantasy Take: If you wanted to push Cartaya ahead of Ruiz on your personal list, I wouldn't begrudge you too much. Cartaya projects to have more power than his colleague behind the dish, and while his hit tool might not be as renowned as Ruiz's, it's still pretty solid. His defense will need to improve to stay at catcher, though, and if he doesn't stay at catcher, he's less interesting for fantasy purposes.

6 Bobby Miller RHP   OFP: 55   ETA: 2023 as a starter, 2022 as a reliever
Born: 04/05/99   Age: 22   Bats: L   Throws: R   Height: 6'5"   Weight: 220   Origin: Round 1, 2020 Draft (#29 overall)

The Report: The other half of the best tandem of collegiate pitchers, Miller actually has the edge over his former Louisville teammate Reid Detmers in terms of dynamic stuff despite being picked 19 spots later in the first round. As our own Ben Spanier witnessed, Miller features a live fastball in the mid-90s that holds it's heat late into games and can ramp the pitch up to 99 at times. His ability to command it to either side of the plate gilds the lily further. He backs it up with a curling slider in the low 80s that is his second-best offering. A cutter and firm changeup round-out the mix, both needing to improve in order to reach average grades.

Development Track: Given Miller's athletic frame, there is a chance the fastball velocity can still find another gear, even though that's the least of concerns with the profile. The arm stroke is rather elongated, forcing his glove hand to reach out front to maintain balance. This makes his secondaries a little difficult to repeat. Already lacking finish on both the cutter and change, without improvement in the other two secondaries, there will be relief concerns. Having never spent an entire year as a starter while in school, he will need to prove his stuff can be sustained across an entire season.

Variance: High. There is a lot of potential in the arm that could blossom or stagnate. The requisite off-speed improvements may be difficult to make without adversely affecting the electric heater.

Mark Barry's Fantasy Take: A couple things worry me about Miller. First, he hasn't spent a full year as a starter. And second, he has two very good pitches, but the rest of the arsenal is underdeveloped. Usually that screams reliever. Too negative? Fine. First, he hasn't spent a full year as a starter, so he doesn't have the same wear and tear on his arm. And second, he's in a great organization for developing secondary offerings. Better? Good.

Keep Miller on the watchlist for now, or scoop him up in leagues with 200+ prospects.

7   Andre Jackson   RHP   OFP: 50   ETA: Late 2021/Early 2022

Born: 05/01/96   Age: 25   Bats: R   Throws: R   Height: 6'3"   Weight: 210   Origin: Round 12, 2017 Draft (#370 overall)

YEAR	TEAM	LVL	AGE	W	L	SV	G	GS	IP	H	HR	BB/9	K/9	K	GB%	BABIP	WHIP	ERA	DRA-	WARP
2018	DOD2	ROK	22	2	0	0	4	3	18^1	18	0	2.0	15.2	31	40.0%	.450	1.20	3.44		
2018	GL	LO-A	22	1	5	0	14	14	49^2	48	3	7.4	8.2	45	46.2%	.319	1.79	4.35	153	-1.1
2019	GL	LO-A	23	4	1	0	10	10	48^1	29	1	3.5	9.3	50	46.7%	.237	0.99	2.23	66	1.1
2019	RC	HI-A	23	3	1	0	15	15	66^1	61	5	5.2	12.3	91	45.9%	.368	1.49	3.66	96	0.3
2021 FS	LAD	MLB	25	2	3	0	57	0	50	45	7	6.6	9.2	51	41.9%	.287	1.65	5.36	119	-0.4

Comparables: Mike Montgomery, T.J. Zeuch, Alex Reyes

The Report: A former college outfielder, the 6-foot-3 Jackson utilizes a high release point and a mid-90s fastball to consistently challenge hitters up in the zone. Pairing perfectly with the high heat is a plunging upper-70s curveball. His mid-80s changeup is a work in progress, but there has been progression. While Jackson's command will need to improve, his competitiveness will serve him well in either a starter or reliever role in the big leagues.

Development Track: The 24-year-old has learned and developed quickly while playing across four levels in two minor league seasons. While he may only start next season in Double-A, Jackson could appear in a Dodgers uniform as soon as 2021.

Variance: Medium. Improved command and fewer walks issued would expedite his big-league arrival.

Mark Barry's Fantasy Take: Jackson is probably a reliever, but his path to the doorstep of the big leagues has been anything but conventional, so there's still space to dream on his role. For now, he's a fringe-watchlist guy, but be sure to have that quick claim finger ready, should he pop as a starter in early 2021.

8   Kody Hoese   3B   OFP: 50   ETA: 2022

Born: 07/13/97   Age: 23   Bats: R   Throws: R   Height: 6'4"   Weight: 200   Origin: Round 1, 2019 Draft (#25 overall)

YEAR	TEAM	LVL	AGE	PA	R	2B	3B	HR	RBI	BB	K	SB	CS	AVG/OBP/SLG	DRC+	BABIP	BRR	FRAA	WARP
2019	DOD2	ROK	21	68	14	5	1	3	13	10	11	1	0	.357/.456/.643		.395			
2019	GL	LO-A	21	103	15	3	1	2	16	8	14	0	0	.264/.330/.385	102	.286	-0.2	3B(12) 0.7	0.3
2021 FS	LAD	MLB	23	600	53	26	3	9	56	40	156	1	0	.240/.298/.353	80	.317	1.0	3B 0	-0.2

Comparables: Ty Kelly, Rangel Ravelo, Kelvin Gutierrez

The Report: Hoese followed up a strong 2018 Cape Cod campaign with an outrageous junior year at Tulane. Nearly scraping .400 with 23 homers and more walks than strikeouts, he played his way into the first round of the draft. The power is plus, but it takes some length and leverage from his large, sturdy frame to tap into it, which can lead to swing-and-miss issues. The approach is solid enough in terms of knowing what to zone to get the most out of his pop, so the offensive profile may lean towards the Three True Outcomes. That's fine in an everyday third baseman, although Hoese is not a lock to stick there given his size and stiffness in the field.

Development Track: It's easy to pair Hoese and Busch as advanced college bats taken in the first round of the same draft, and a mere six spots apart at that. Hoese is more power-over-hit though, and despite having a more clear cut position, looked downright rusty at third in instructs. The reports on his defense have been decidedly mixed for a while, and Keanan had a 40 on the third base glove pre-2019 draft. Hoese looked more comfortable at shortstop this fall, but that's a stretch even for the Dodgers, so you hope the recent issues at the hot corner were just a product of the weirdness of player development in 2020. None of this matters if he continues to hit and hit for power mind you.

Variance: High. Hoese is 23 and has 22 games outside of college or the complex. There's hit tool and positional questions as well.

Mark Barry's Fantasy Take: For fantasy, I might have Hoese challenging Gray for the top spot on this list. Hoese made a bunch of contact in the small sample of his 2019 debut, and while that ultimately might not carry over against advanced pitching, his plate discipline and power should more than make up for any swing-and-miss in his profile. Lazy organizational comp coming: he's basically right-handed Max Muncy.

9   Jacob Amaya   SS   OFP: 50   ETA: 2022

Born: 09/03/98   Age: 22   Bats: R   Throws: R   Height: 6'0"   Weight: 180   Origin: Round 11, 2017 Draft (#340 overall)

YEAR	TEAM	LVL	AGE	PA	R	2B	3B	HR	RBI	BB	K	SB	CS	AVG/OBP/SLG	DRC+	BABIP	BRR	FRAA	WARP
2018	OGD	ROK	19	155	41	9	3	3	24	27	29	11	4	.346/.465/.535		.432			
2018	GL	LO-A	19	119	13	1	0	1	5	20	18	3	3	.265/.390/.306	130	.316	-1.8	SS(21) 2.2, 2B(5) -0.2	0.7
2019	GL	LO-A	20	470	68	25	4	6	58	74	83	4	4	.262/.381/.394	145	.314	-0.5	SS(51) -3.8, 2B(49) 1.9, 3B(4) 0.1	3.6
2019	RC	HI-A	20	89	14	3	2	1	13	7	15	1	3	.250/.307/.375	98	.292	0.3	SS(14) -2.1, 2B(4) 1.0, 3B(1) -0.0	0.2
2021 FS	LAD	MLB	22	600	55	27	3	9	55	57	161	3	2	.237/.314/.351	86	.321	-1.8	SS -1, 2B 3	1.0

Comparables: Eugenio Suárez, Pete Kozma, Sean Rodríguez

The Report: Although Amaya might struggle to crack double-digit home runs, he's far from an offensive zero. He's a tough out due to his strong strike zone awareness and plus contact ability that he can work gap-to-gap. This has led him to run high OBPs, which should continue in the majors. Amaya can potentially pair that with a .280 batting average and plenty of doubles. A natural shortstop, his soft hands and strong arm will enable him to play all three infield positions at the highest level. His speed and baserunning savvy make him dangerous every time he makes his way to first.

Development Track: While he last played at the High-A level, Amaya's strong fundamentals and well-rounded game will allow him to progress quickly. Further development of his offensive skills would hasten his ascension to the show.

Variance: Medium. His broad base of offensive and defensive skills give him a bunch of ways to help your major league club, although the overall ceiling is somewhat limited.

Mark Barry's Fantasy Take: Amaya does a bunch of things pretty well, without doing anything *very* well. He should have a major-league role, but his fantasy usefulness might be limited to NL-only leagues.

10   Gerardo Carrillo   RHP   OFP: 50   ETA: 2022

Born: 09/13/98   Age: 22   Bats: R   Throws: R   Height: 5'10"   Weight: 154   Origin: International Free Agent, 2016

YEAR	TEAM	LVL	AGE	W	L	SV	G	GS	IP	H	HR	BB/9	K/9	K	GB%	BABIP	WHIP	ERA	DRA-	WARP
2018	DOD2	ROK	19	2	0	1	4	1	11	6	0	1.6	10.6	13	57.7%	.231	0.73	0.82		
2018	GL	LO-A	19	2	1	0	9	9	49	35	3	2.8	6.8	37	49.6%	.235	1.02	1.65	80	0.9
2019	RC	HI-A	20	5	9	0	23	21	86	87	3	5.3	9.0	86	54.2%	.339	1.60	5.44	107	-0.2
2021 FS	LAD	MLB	22	2	3	0	57	0	50	49	7	4.9	7.5	41	46.9%	.289	1.54	5.37	123	-0.5

Comparables: Rony García, Rob Kaminsky, Junior Fernández

The Report: The 22-year-old right-hander has as electric an arm as any pitcher in the Dodgers organization. Emanating from a seemingly effortless motion, Carrillo's fastball sits comfortably in the high-90s and can reach triple-digits. His secondary offerings remain a work in progress, consisting of a slurvy breaking ball with varying velocity and shape, a high-80s changeup, and a hard cutter that he can work inside against lefties. He's sometimes struggled with command as a pro, but has also demonstrated the ability to make adjustments and improvements required to develop into a quality major-league hurler.

Development Track: Carrillo has yet to throw more than 86 innings in a professional season. While he's worked primarily as a starter in the minors, a transition to the bullpen is always an option for the hard-throwing righty.

Variance: High. The natural velocity is impressive, but Carrillo must refine his command and further develop his craft to become a successful big-leaguer.

Mark Barry's Fantasy Take: It would be nice to see Carillo consistently put together some heavy-inning workloads to assuage fears of a role spent in relief, but as it stands, he's probably just a reliever, and not terribly exciting for fantasy purposes.

The Prospects You Meet Outside The Top Ten

Almost an entire draft class

Landon Knack   Born: 07/15/97   Age: 23   Bats: L   Throws: R   Height: 6'2"   Weight: 220   Origin: Round 2, 2020 Draft (#60 overall)

Not your typical fifth-year senior sign, Knack had one of the most unique profiles in this year's draft. Due to injuries that cost him most of three different seasons while he was a two-way player, Knack has been a full-time pitcher for only a year, and the stuff dramatically improved over that period. With the lack of miles on the arm, the velocity already peaking in the mid-90s, potentially average secondary pitches, and very good control, there is a ton to build on here.

Clayton Beeter   RHP   Born: 10/09/98   Age: 22   Bats: R   Throws: R   Height: 6'2"   Weight: 220   Origin: Round 2, 2020 Draft (#66 overall)

Injuries plagued Beeter throughout his senior year of high school and freshman year at Texas Tech, resulting in two elbow surgeries including Tommy John. Beeter returned as a reliever for his sophomore campaign in 2019 and struck out nearly two batters an inning. It was an effectively wild approach, though as he walked nearly a batter per as well. The dynamic arsenal was too good sequestered in the bullpen, so last spring he was given the chance to start, and made the most of his four starts. Even with the 2020 success, however abbreviated, the injury history is difficult to ignore, likely relegating him to a late-inning role to maximize his value. It's lights-out stuff that could play well in high leverage situations, featuring upper 90s heat and plus-plus slider.

Jake Vogel   OF   Born: 10/12/01   Age: 19   Bats: R   Throws: R   Height: 5'11"   Weight: 165   Origin: Round 3, 2020 Draft (#100 overall)

In the running—no pun intended—for fastest player in this year's prep class, the SoCal product had to be enticed by a well over-slot deal to sign with the Dodgers. Vogel garnered mixed reviews on his offensive potential, mostly because of his light frame and compact swing. That featherweight body allows for the elite foot-speed to play on the bases and especially in the outfield. The quick-twitch athleticism is what highlights the profile, with significant improvements to the swing necessary to reach his full potential.

Prospects to dream on a little

Andy Pages   RF   Born: 12/08/00   Age: 20   Bats: R   Throws: R   Height: 6'1"   Weight: 180   Origin: International Free Agent, 2018

YEAR	TEAM	LVL	AGE	PA	R	2B	3B	HR	RBI	BB	K	SB	CS	AVG/OBP/SLG	DRC+	BABIP	BRR	FRAA	WARP
2018	DSL SHO	ROK	17	178	34	8	0	9	33	23	31	9	6	.236/.393/.486		.238			
2018	DOD2	ROK	17	34	5	1	0	1	3	6	4	1	1	.192/.382/.346		.190			
2019	OGD	ROK+	18	279	57	22	2	19	55	26	79	7	6	.298/.398/.651		.364			
2021 FS	LAD	MLB	20	600	49	27	2	10	52	38	212	13	7	.192/.263/.307	58	.291	-6.4	RF 6, LF 2	-1.5

Pages moves from Low Minors Sleeper to uh ... Low Minors Prospect, I guess. He looked good at instructs, still every bit the potential plus hit/power combo he'll need to carry a corner outfield profile, but the lost year hurts here more than most.

Pitchers that are either good or unavailable, too often unavailable

Mitch White RHP Born: 12/28/94 Age: 26 Bats: R Throws: R Height: 6'3" Weight: 210 Origin: Round 2, 2016 Draft (#65 overall)

YEAR	TEAM	LVL	AGE	W	L	SV	G	GS	IP	H	HR	BB/9	K/9	K	GB%	BABIP	WHIP	ERA	DRA-	WARP
2018	TUL	AA	23	6	7	0	22	22	105¹	114	12	2.9	7.5	88	47.6%	.319	1.41	4.53	108	0.0
2019	TUL	AA	24	1	0	0	7	7	30	18	3	2.1	11.1	37	43.1%	.217	0.83	2.10	61	0.7
2019	OKC	AAA	24	3	6	0	16	13	63²	73	13	3.4	9.6	68	41.6%	.351	1.52	6.50	101	1.0
2020	LAD	MLB	25	1	0	0	2	3	3	1	0	3.0	6.0	2	12.5%	.125	0.67	0.00	110	0.0
2021 FS	LAD	MLB	26	9	9	0	26	26	150	142	25	4.1	9.0	150	40.8%	.290	1.40	4.71	105	0.7
2021 DC	LAD	MLB	26	3	3	0	24	8	49	46	8	4.1	9.0	49	40.8%	.290	1.40	4.71	105	0.3

Comparables: Chase De Jong, Andrew Moore, Nabil Crismatt

White has long been a favorite of the west coast branch of our prospect team. Granted, that's mostly because they have been the only ones able to catch the about-to-be 26-year-old. And that's never been as frequently as they'd like. The various maladies have depleted the stuff at times, but the fastball is back to mid-90s in short bursts and he pairs it with an above-average slider/cutter thing and low-80s curve. He might just be a 95-and-a-breaking-ball guy, but at least he is healthy now as far as we know.

Michael Grove RHP Born: 12/18/96 Age: 24 Bats: R Throws: R Height: 6'3" Weight: 200 Origin: Round 2, 2018 Draft (#68 overall)

YEAR	TEAM	LVL	AGE	W	L	SV	G	GS	IP	H	HR	BB/9	K/9	K	GB%	BABIP	WHIP	ERA	DRA-	WARP
2019	RC	HI-A	22	0	5	0	21	21	51²	61	7	3.3	12.7	73	29.7%	.412	1.55	6.10	110	-0.2
2021 FS	LAD	MLB	24	2	3	0	57	0	50	47	8	4.5	9.2	50	30.6%	.292	1.45	4.78	114	-0.3

Comparables: Eric Jokisch, Robert Dugger, T.J. Zeuch

Grove was coming off Tommy John surgery last year, so that at least explains his limited reps. He's worked on ironing out some of the mechanical issues we saw last year, and the fastball has ticked up to plus, and an improving change-up could get there as well. There's still a ways to go here, but signs are pointing in the right direction for Grove to be inside the Top 10 this time next year.

The Dodgers' next out of nowhere player development success story

Zach McKinstry 2B Born: 04/29/95 Age: 26 Bats: L Throws: R Height: 6'0" Weight: 180 Origin: Round 33, 2016 Draft (#1001 overall)

YEAR	TEAM	LVL	AGE	PA	R	2B	3B	HR	RBI	BB	K	SB	CS	AVG/OBP/SLG	DRC+	BABIP	BRR	FRAA	WARP
2018	GL	LO-A	23	72	12	2	2	3	8	16	16	2	1	.377/.542/.660	191	.500	-0.7	SS(11) -1.2, 2B(5) 0.1, LF(1) -0.1	0.7
2018	RC	HI-A	23	114	20	7	1	2	8	17	22	0	0	.308/.447/.473	124	.388	0.3	2B(17) -0.5, 3B(5) 1.7, SS(5) -0.1	0.5
2018	TUL	AA	23	87	7	2	1	2	8	4	21	0	0	.193/.230/.313	54	.233	-0.2	3B(14) 0.8, 2B(9) 0.5, SS(2) -0.2	-0.2
2019	TUL	AA	24	384	53	16	4	12	52	37	74	8	8	.279/.352/.455	146	.323	-0.5	2B(49) -2.7, SS(29) 1.8, 3B(10) -0.1	2.7
2019	OKC	AAA	24	95	17	8	2	7	26	6	18	0	1	.382/.421/.753	152	.422	-0.4	SS(17) -0.1, 2B(3) 0.4, 3B(2) 0.2	1.0
2020	LAD	MLB	25	7	1	1	0	0	0	0	3	0	0	.286/.286/.429	69	.500		2B(1) -0.0, RF(1) 0.1	0.0
2021 FS	LAD	MLB	26	600	66	23	3	20	67	55	173	3	1	.242/.321/.412	98	.319	1.0	2B 1, SS 3	2.3
2021 DC	LAD	MLB	26	276	30	10	1	9	30	25	79	1	0	.242/.321/.412	98	.319	0.5	2B 1, SS 2	1.1

Comparables: Rougned Odor, German Duran, Cesar Hernandez

McKinstry was a 33rd rounder out of Central Michigan. A solid college performer whose best tool was his approach, he seemed destined to be the kind of player who bounced around a minor league bench for a few seasons before becoming a coach or an insurance adjuster. He slugged .295 in the Cal League in 2017. Come on now, you know how this ends. Well two years and one swing change later, McKinstry socked 19 home runs in the upper minors. He can play all over the diamond, and while the power might not reach the heights he found with the Triple-A ball in PCL parks, the Dodgers might not miss Enrique Hernandez as much as you'd think in 2021.

Top Talents 25 and Under (as of 4/1/2021):

1. Cody Bellinger, OF/1B
2. Dustin May, RHP

3. Gavin Lux, 2B
4. Julio Urías, LHP
5. Josiah Gray, RHP
6. Keibert Ruiz, C
7. Brusdar Graterol, RHP
8. Miguel Vargas, 3B
9. Michael Busch, 2B
10. Diego Cartaya, C

This is one of the most loaded crops of young major-league talent in the league, just in case you were worried that the Dodgers were going anywhere anytime soon. Kicking us off is Cody Bellinger, the 2019 National League MVP. Bellinger was not quite able to match his 8 WARP 2019 pace in 2020, with his batting average dropping from .305 to .239 in the shortened season. He was still really good, and he continued his move up the defensive spectrum by taking about two-thirds of his playing time in center. He's one of the best players in baseball and may not have hit his true peak yet.

The next three names could be in virtually any order. Dustin May was the No. 8 prospect in baseball entering last season, and the surprising Opening Night starter after Clayton Kershaw was a late scratch. He pitched most of the season in the rotation, working mostly off stupendous high-90s sinkers and low-90s cutters. He didn't miss as many bats as you'd expect given the velocity and movement, but he was extremely impressive.

Gavin Lux was the highest-rated prospect of this trio, topping out at No. 2 last offseason. The Dodgers seemed surprisingly uninterested in playing him in 2020, dispatching him to the alternate site long enough to not only claw back a year of service time but likely a year of Super 2 eligibility as well. He saw only partial playing time at second base down the stretch, and didn't even make the NLCS or World Series rosters. This was enough of a lost year to swap him with May, who wasn't much worse of a prospect and established himself as a good major-league pitcher, but we're still looking for Lux to be an offensive force starting very soon.

Julio Urías was the No. 6 prospect on the 101 five years ago. In the intervening years, he's still never actually thrown a full-length season between shoulder capsule surgery and workload concerns. He might never, but he's an extremely effective pitcher no matter the role, as you saw in the closing innings of Game 7 of the World Series.

The Dodgers picked up big righty Brusdar Graterol in the second version of the Mookie Betts deal. He was used in a wide variety of short roles in the regular season, from opener to the eighth inning and everywhere in between, before settling in as a primary setup man in the postseason. Graterol throws 100-plus regularly with a nasty slider, and if he continues along his present path he's going to be quite a fine reliever. We'd still like to see him get a shot at starting long-term, but it's hard to see him getting the opportunity given all of Los Angeles's pitching depth.

Two more non-prospect pitchers lurk just off the list and warrant a mention. Like Graterol, lefties Caleb Ferguson and Victor González are both starters by trade who have thrived airing it out in relief roles for the Dodgers. It is a huge competitive advantage to have enough pitching depth to let them do it.

Miami Marlins

The State of the System:

The Marlins might not be able to repeat their surprise playoff run in 2021, but they are well-positioned for next year and beyond with a deep pipeline of talent.

The Top Ten:

★ ★ ★ *2021 Top 101 Prospect* **#4** ★ ★ ★

1 **Sixto Sánchez** **RHP**   OFP: 70   ETA: Debuted in 2020
Born: 07/29/98   Age: 22   Bats: R   Throws: R   Height: 6'0"   Weight: 234   Origin: International Free Agent, 2015

YEAR	TEAM	LVL	AGE	W	L	SV	G	GS	IP	H	HR	BB/9	K/9	K	GB%	BABIP	WHIP	ERA	DRA-	WARP
2018	CLR	HI-A	19	4	3	0	8	8	46^2	39	1	2.1	8.7	45	51.5%	.295	1.07	2.51	76	0.9
2019	JUP	HI-A	20	0	2	0	2	2	11	14	1	1.6	4.9	6	60.5%	.351	1.45	4.91	117	-0.1
2019	JAX	AA	20	8	4	0	18	18	103	87	5	1.7	8.5	97	47.3%	.288	1.03	2.53	83	1.1
2020	MIA	MLB	21	3	2	0	7	7	39	36	3	2.5	7.6	33	58.0%	.303	1.21	3.46	79	0.8
2021 FS	MIA	MLB	22	9	8	0	26	26	150	150	17	2.8	8.2	136	50.7%	.306	1.31	4.09	95	1.5
2021 DC	MIA	MLB	22	7	9	0	25	25	134	134	16	2.8	8.2	121	50.7%	.306	1.31	4.09	95	1.7

Comparables: Brett Anderson, David Holmberg, Jack Flaherty

The Report: Sánchez has long been one of the hardest throwing prospects in baseball, and has long had a wide variety of other stuff with plus-or-better potential. He consistently sits in the upper-90s and touches higher with both his four-seam and two-seam fastballs, generating different looks and manipulating the pitches well, but with relatively below-average spin and more horizontal funk than vertical. For some years, we've been waiting for one or more of Sánchez's offspeed pitches to break out of a kitchen sink of above-average offerings that flashed plus. Frankly, he'd pitched to contact a lot in the minors, breezing through easily in terms of results by generating weak swings but never really burying hitters to the level you'd think given the fastball and multiple plus-flashing offspeeds.

Development Track: Well, the changeup got there. What was as recently as 2019 one of three "potential plus, flash plus-plus" offerings looked more like a steady plus-plus offering in the majors. The slider didn't look far off, either. Sánchez was one of the better pitchers in the majors after being called up in late-August—though once again without posting whiff rates commensurate with his stuff and overall performance—and he's pretty close to his OFP already. He's one of the best prospects in baseball.

Variance: Medium. As early as spring 2017 and as recently as yesterday, I have made arguments that Sánchez could be an 80 OFP because his 75th-percentile outcome is awful close to a true ace given the breadth and quality of stuff. There's enough against that to hold the line at a role 7 for now—health and durability concerns, occasionally wavering command, lack of elite swing-and-miss generation—but there's certainly more positive variance here than for your typical 70 OFP pitching prospect.

J.P. Breen's Fantasy Take: Sánchez has taken gargantuan steps forward. Folks had questioned whether his fastball could miss enough bats, and it had a 12.7 percent whiff rate in 2020. The fastball-changeup combination is good enough for a top-of-the-rotation profile, as noted above. However, without an improved slider, Sánchez has an eerily similar profile to Chris Paddack, who had a disappointing 2020 campaign, or even Kevin Gausman. The health concerns should also keep dynasty owners from pushing in all their chips. Make no mistake, though, Sánchez is one of the most exciting young pitchers in Major League Baseball, and few minor leaguers have his upside.

★ ★ ★ *2021 Top 101 Prospect* **#33** ★ ★ ★

2 JJ Bleday RF   OFP: 60   ETA: 2021

Born: 11/10/97   Age: 23   Bats: L   Throws: L   Height: 6'3"   Weight: 205   Origin: Round 1, 2019 Draft (#4 overall)

YEAR	TEAM	LVL	AGE	PA	R	2B	3B	HR	RBI	BB	K	SB	CS	AVG/OBP/SLG	DRC+	BABIP	BRR	FRAA	WARP
2019	JUP	HI-A	21	151	13	8	0	3	19	11	29	0	0	.257/.311/.379	105	.306	-1.1	RF(32) -0.9	0.1
2021 FS	MIA	MLB	23	600	55	26	2	13	60	39	168	1	0	.232/.286/.361	78	.308	0.2	RF -14	-1.7

Comparables: Lorenzo Cain, Socrates Brito, Rymer Liriano

The Report: Bleday features one of the most well-rounded offensive profiles of any prospect, and could make contributions to the big league club very early in the 2021 season. He will offer the Marlins' lineup a combination of advanced bat-to-ball abilities for a slugger of his ilk, as he is able to get the barrel to the ball quickly with a quick left-handed stroke. The hands can get a bit bouncy with a whippy bat pre-release, still at a great firing position with a high elbow that creates plenty of loft in the swing, too, leading to plus power. As for another plus tool, he's a good fit for right field thanks to a plus arm that has both carry and accuracy to his throws. The hulking outfielder isn't exactly the speediest, which is perhaps the only knock against his game.

Development Track: Bleday was believed to have been penciled-in for a 2020 campaign in Double-A, and as such, hasn't played above A-ball. He got plenty of time this year at the Marlins' complex; still, he'll likely get some extra seasoning in the minors before leveling-up to the majors.

Variance: Low. He's done it at every level so far, showing a good eye at the plate and minimal swing-and-miss, all which add to the confidence with the outcome.

J.P. Breen's Fantasy Take: Bleday doesn't generate as much dynasty excitement as he should. He won't run much, and he hit just .257/.311/.379 in his professional debut. It's important to remember, though, that Bleday plied his trade in Jupiter, which is one of the least power-friendly ballparks in one of the least hitter-friendly leagues. Trust the scouting reports. Bleday still boasts one of the best power-average combinations in the minors. He's a top-200 dynasty player and a top-40 dynasty prospect.

★ ★ ★ *2021 Top 101 Prospect* **#45** ★ ★ ★

3 Edward Cabrera RHP   OFP: 60   ETA: 2021

Born: 04/13/98   Age: 23   Bats: R   Throws: R   Height: 6'5"   Weight: 217   Origin: International Free Agent, 2015

YEAR	TEAM	LVL	AGE	W	L	SV	G	GS	IP	H	HR	BB/9	K/9	K	GB%	BABIP	WHIP	ERA	DRA-	WARP
2018	GBO	LO-A	20	4	8	0	22	22	100¹	105	11	3.8	8.3	93	43.4%	.329	1.47	4.22	139	-1.7
2019	JUP	HI-A	21	5	3	0	11	11	58	37	1	2.8	11.3	73	47.3%	.281	0.95	2.02	62	1.4
2019	JAX	AA	21	4	1	0	8	8	38²	28	6	3.0	10.0	43	48.5%	.242	1.06	2.56	70	0.7
2021 FS	MIA	MLB	23	1	2	0	57	0	50	47	7	4.0	8.7	48	44.3%	.292	1.40	4.74	112	-0.2
2021 DC	MIA	MLB	23	1	2	0	6	6	27	25	4	4.0	8.7	26	44.3%	.292	1.40	4.74	112	0.1

Comparables: Jonathan Hernández, Gerrit Cole, Frankie Montas

The Report: Despite an early season outbreak of COVID-19 that decimated the Marlins' pitching staff, Cabrera was not among those called to fill the void. Not because of talent or readiness, but due to a bad case of timing with a minor injury. Those minor injuries—also experienced in 2019—have prevented him from skyrocketing up prospect lists, as evaluators resoundingly agree on the legit stuff exploding out of his right arm. When healthy, it's a lively fastball that cruises 95-97 and can even sit in the 97-99 range for extended periods. Both the breaking ball and changeup feature above average qualities; depending on the day one can seem superior over the other. The ease of the delivery and the finish on his pitches point toward an impact starter needing to shed pesky ailments to realize top-of-the-rotation potential.

Development Track: The Marlins have been consistent with their top-end pitching prospects, handling them with kid gloves to try and avoid any major complications as they matriculate out of the system. Cabrera has been on a familiar parallel path to Sánchez, only once eclipsing the 100-inning mark in a season. He could have easily been called up in 2020, and barring any further annoyances will get the call in 2021.

Variance: Medium. Everything is there to be a complete pitcher. What is missing is a track record over the course of a full season of major league sized workload.

J.P. Breen's Fantasy Take: Explosive fastball. Secondary pitches that can all flash plus, depending on the day. Some durability/health concerns. You'd be forgiven for thinking that this sounds a lot like Sixto Sánchez's write-up from 12 months ago. The right-hander is perhaps the best pitching prospect about whom no one is talking. He's an easy top-100 dynasty prospect for me, and I like the combination of scouting profile and organization enough to put him ahead of more heralded pitching prospects.

──────── ★　★　★ *2021 Top 101 Prospect* **#51** ★　★　★ ────────

4   **Max Meyer**   **RHP**   OFP: 60   ETA: 2022 as a reliever, 2023 as a starter
Born: 03/12/99   Age: 22   Bats: L   Throws: R   Height: 6'0"   Weight: 196   Origin: Round 1, 2020 Draft (#3 overall)

The Report: A strong showing for the Collegiate National Team put Meyer into first-round consideration for the 2020 draft. He had previously been the closer at the University of Minnesota before shifting to the weekend rotation his sophomore year, showing he could handle a starter's workload and then outright dominating his abbreviated draft year. Many of the questions regarding whether he's a future starter or reliever stem from his 6-foot stature. The Marlins took this into account, but inevitably sided with the pure arm talent over any height concerns. Using a fastball that rides comfortably in the mid-to-upper 90s and an upper 80s slider that one scout called, "the best I've seen in 20 years," it looks like a typical late-inning reliever profile. However, between his athletic, repeatable delivery, and two present plus pitches, Meyer has a good shot to break the obvious reliever mold and become a dynamic starter.

Development Track: Two questions will determine whether or not Meyer sticks in the rotation. Can his build hold up over the course of a season, and can the changeup develop into a usable third pitch? If both are answered in the affirmative, there is a little doubt he will end up as a starter. Failing those, he could be an elite closer with velocity readings reaching 100 and a slider that could be near-unhittable. Prior to the draft, the industry considered him a high variance player for valid reasons—some teams had him towards the back-half of the first round, and at least one had him at the top of their board. The Marlins believed his make-up, combined with the fastball/slider pairing, made him the easy choice at third overall.

Variance: High. It's not the ideal frame for a 30-start pitcher. There are plenty of examples of guys with similar builds who overcome the maxim that you need to be a certain height and weight to survive the rigors of a season. It's not uncommon, but Meyer will need to prove he's capable.

J.P. Breen's Fantasy Take: Meyer is a top-100 dynasty prospect, thanks to a dynamic slider that should lead to gaudy strikeout totals. If he can stick in the rotation, he's a 200-plus strikeout starter. If he transitions to the bullpen, the above scouting report suggests that he could be a top-10 fantasy closer with enough strikeouts to remain fantasy relevant as a non-closer. The latter currently seems more likely, and that's still a good enough fantasy arm that the SP3 upside makes him worth a first-round pick in offseason supplemental drafts.

──────── ★　★　★ *2021 Top 101 Prospect* **#58** ★　★　★ ────────

5   **Jazz Chisholm**   **SS**   OFP: 60   ETA: Debuted in 2020
Born: 02/01/98   Age: 23   Bats: L   Throws: R   Height: 5'11"   Weight: 184   Origin: International Free Agent, 2015

YEAR	TEAM	LVL	AGE	PA	R	2B	3B	HR	RBI	BB	K	SB	CS	AVG/OBP/SLG	DRC+	BABIP	BRR	FRAA	WARP
2018	KC	LO-A	20	341	52	17	4	15	43	30	97	8	2	.244/.311/.472	101	.303	-1.4	SS(75) -0.3	0.9
2018	VIS	HI-A	20	160	27	6	2	10	27	9	52	9	2	.329/.369/.597	138	.443	0.5	SS(36) -0.7	0.9
2019	JXN	AA	21	364	51	6	5	18	44	41	123	13	4	.204/.305/.427	108	.261	2.9	SS(88) -5.8	1.7
2019	JAX	AA	21	94	6	4	2	3	10	11	24	3	0	.284/.383/.494	103	.370	-0.5	SS(22) -1.8	0.4
2020	MIA	MLB	22	62	8	1	1	2	6	5	19	2	2	.161/.242/.321	74	.200	-0.4	2B(13) -1.7, SS(9) -0.1	-0.2
2021 FS	MIA	MLB	23	600	59	24	5	17	63	47	218	10	3	.208/.277/.366	75	.310	5.8	SS -2	0.4
2021 DC	MIA	MLB	23	267	26	10	2	7	28	21	97	4	1	.208/.277/.366	75	.310	2.6	2B 0, SS -1	0.2

Comparables: Yu Chang, Cameron Maybin, Trevor Story

The Report: The Marlins seemed to target loud tools and extreme variance profiles in trade as the Jeter-era began. Chisholm certainly fits the bill, although like the rest of this group, it hasn't all quite clicked at the plate for him yet. He has plus raw and plus bat speed that unfurls itself from a violent uppercut out of a noisy setup. There's better bat control than you'd think, but Chisholm can really sell out for pullside power, which exacerbates what will be at best above-average swing-and-miss. He may hit the ball hard enough, and grab enough infield hits, to make the hit tool play to average, but there's not much of a floor to his contact rate at present. In the field, he's a sure-handed, rangy shortstop with enough arm for the left side. Ultimately, how much Chisholm reins in his aggressive, free-swinging tendencies will determine the outcome, but plus regular remains a distinct possibility.

Development Track: Chisholm didn't exactly dominate Double-A in 2019, so it's not a surprise he struggled at times after he was promoted to the Fish from the alternate site. His playing time was also erratic, as he didn't really unseat Miguel Rojas or Jon Berti from the middle infield spots despite the pair's defensive flexibility. Chisholm never really got into a rhythm against major league arms, although the upside certainly. He could use some consolidation time in Triple-A in 2021, but he's not that far off a more permanent role with the Marlins, although the range of outcomes remains broad.

Variance: High. I wouldn't call his debut a disaster, but a 30 percent K-rate and 74 DRC+ doesn't exactly assuage concerns about how the bat will play against top-level pitching. Given the present speed, pop, and glove though, Chisholm should be able to carve out a decently long career even if it's only as a bench infielder.

J.P. Breen's Fantasy Take: Given the long-term questions regarding his hit tool, Chisholm appears poised to be a poor man's Javier Báez—exciting power, speed, and defense without the .280 batting average. Dynasty owners will need Chisholm to be a 20-20 guy to justify the poor average. Even then, he's not far from a Rougned Odor-type fantasy profile. Chisholm, for me, is a better real-life prospect than a dynasty one. His high strikeout rate and low batting average put too much pressure on his power and speed.

★ ★ ★ *2021 Top 101 Prospect* **#94** ★ ★ ★

6 **Trevor Rogers** **LHP**   OFP: 60   ETA: Debuted in 2020
Born: 11/13/97   Age: 23   Bats: L   Throws: L   Height: 6'5"   Weight: 217   Origin: Round 1, 2017 Draft (#13 overall)

YEAR	TEAM	LVL	AGE	W	L	SV	G	GS	IP	H	HR	BB/9	K/9	K	GB%	BABIP	WHIP	ERA	DRA-	WARP
2018	GBO	LO-A	20	2	7	0	17	17	72²	86	4	3.3	10.5	85	46.7%	.398	1.56	5.82	94	0.6
2019	JUP	HI-A	21	5	8	0	18	18	110¹	97	7	2.0	10.0	122	40.8%	.307	1.10	2.53	80	1.5
2019	JAX	AA	21	1	2	0	5	5	26	25	3	3.1	9.7	28	28.8%	.319	1.31	4.50	102	0.0
2020	MIA	MLB	22	1	2	0	7	7	28	32	5	4.2	12.5	39	46.1%	.380	1.61	6.11	80	0.6
2021 FS	MIA	MLB	23	9	8	0	26	26	150	140	21	3.5	9.4	156	42.5%	.299	1.33	4.20	97	1.3
2021 DC	MIA	MLB	23	4	6	0	21	21	84	78	11	3.5	9.4	87	42.5%	.299	1.33	4.20	97	1.0

Comparables: Kris Bubic, Brock Burke, Patrick Sandoval

The Report: I must admit that when we started our offseason list project, I was surprised to see Rogers pop up in strong 101 consideration. He's been a pretty high profile prospect for awhile, and what I saw as the season went along in the majors seemed pretty true to form to his pre-2020 profile, which was a level below that—a nice three-pitch starting prospect. Then I dug deeper.

Development Track: It turns out Rogers was a hell of a lot more impressive than I thought in the majors, making a bunch of incremental improvements off his previous profile that added up to significant development. His fastball averaged 94 mph, continuing a fairly consistent upward trend since his 2018 pro debut, and with quite a lot of spin attached too. His changeup looked plus and the slider wasn't far behind, both progressing along ahead of schedule. Rogers had an ugly ERA owing to a nightmare outing in Philadelphia, but overall he pitched well, with a shiny DRA and decent peripherals. He could use another half-grade of command and slider development, but given that he barely had 200 minor-league innings, this has already come together really fast. He's a 101 guy now.

Variance: Medium. Rogers has already shown up in the majors, and things are pointing in the right direction.

J.P. Breen's Fantasy Take: For as much as we've lauded Sixto Sánchez's changeup, Rogers had a better whiff rate than Sánchez on his changeup in 2020 (23.77 percent to 17.7 percent, respectively). He'll need to throw strikes more consistently to avoid an unattractive WHIP, but the lefty is one of the higher-upside arms among those who currently sit outside our Top-500 Dynasty Rankings.

7 Jesús Sánchez RF   OFP: 55   ETA: Debuted in 2020

Born: 10/07/97   Age: 23   Bats: L   Throws: R   Height: 6'3"   Weight: 222   Origin: International Free Agent, 2014

YEAR	TEAM	LVL	AGE	PA	R	2B	3B	HR	RBI	BB	K	SB	CS	AVG/OBP/SLG	DRC+	BABIP	BRR	FRAA	WARP
2018	CHA	HI-A	20	378	56	24	2	10	64	15	71	6	3	.301/.331/.462	133	.350	-1.5	RF(78) 1.8, CF(7) -1.4	1.2
2018	MTG	AA	20	110	14	8	0	1	11	11	21	1	1	.214/.300/.327	93	.263	0.7	RF(26) -0.8, CF(1) -0.0	-0.1
2019	MTG	AA	21	316	32	11	1	8	49	24	65	5	4	.275/.332/.404	121	.327	0.1	RF(72) 0.0	1.4
2019	NO	AAA	21	78	11	1	0	4	9	9	15	0	0	.246/.338/.446	73	.250	0.3	CF(8) -1.6, RF(8) 3.6	0.2
2019	DUR	AAA	21	71	6	2	1	1	5	6	20	0	0	.206/.282/.317	52	.279	-0.3	RF(15) 0.7	-0.2
2020	MIA	MLB	22	29	1	1	0	0	2	4	11	0	0	.040/.172/.080	81	.071	0.0	RF(10) 0.4	0.0
2021 FS	MIA	MLB	23	600	60	26	4	16	65	40	172	2	0	.234/.289/.387	82	.309	1.7	RF -1, CF -4	0.0
2021 DC	MIA	MLB	23	200	20	8	1	5	21	13	57	0	0	.234/.289/.387	82	.309	0.6	RF 0, CF -1	0.0

Comparables: Brandon Moss, Tyler Austin, Jeff Francoeur

The Report: The overriding theme of our reports and list blurbs on Sánchez over the last few seasons has been: "Well he will have to hit, but we think he will hit." Carrying a corner outfield profile even as a teenager, Sánchez tore up the low minors while being young for his assignments. His combination of compact stroke, plus bat speed, and projectable strength made us confident he would hit—and hit the ball hard enough—to carry a corner outfield profile. The approach has always been on the aggressive side, but Sánchez generally had the bat control to make it work and do damage. He's fast enough to be fine in either corner, but not a major defensive asset.

Development Track: In August, Sánchez joined the litany of Marlins prospects pressed into MLB service in 2020. His 10 days in the majors did not go well, as he looked overmatched, his swing out of sorts and out of sync. Unlike several of his still prospect-eligible teammates, Sánchez has a fair amount of upper minors experience, including six weeks at Triple-A in 2019. And zooming out further, he hasn't really hit in the upper minors at all. There's still a chance Sánchez puts it all together, and the underlying ability is still there for a plus hit/power right fielder, but at a certain point the projection has to make its way into the real world. You don't want to ding him too much for 10 bad games in a weird season, but we often talk on the prospect team about whether it "looked right" in the majors. Sánchez didn't in 2020.

Variance: High. The question with Sánchez has always been when it would click at the plate and how loud it would be when it did. The longer it doesn't happen, the more you wonder if it ever will, and the swing-and-miss issues in the majors were stark enough to make you worry about the realistic floor.

J.P. Breen's Fantasy Take: The physical tools are loud, but the statistics are ugly. He has power projection but has not posted an ISO over .200 since 2016. And the ground-ball rate has been 50-plus percent. He has the tools to hit for average, if it all comes together, but he has only hit .275 at one stop since reaching Double-A in 2018. And now the strikeout rate has spiked. If Sánchez weren't a top-100 dynasty prospect, he might be worth a low-stakes gamble. As it stands, though, he looks to be Lewis Brinson with prospect eligibility. And that's not a compliment.

8 Nasim Nunez SS   OFP: 55   ETA: 2023

Born: 08/18/00   Age: 20   Bats: S   Throws: R   Height: 5'9"   Weight: 160   Origin: Round 2, 2019 Draft (#46 overall)

YEAR	TEAM	LVL	AGE	PA	R	2B	3B	HR	RBI	BB	K	SB	CS	AVG/OBP/SLG	DRC+	BABIP	BRR	FRAA	WARP
2019	MRL	ROK	18	214	37	5	1	0	12	34	43	28	2	.211/.340/.251		.276			
2021 FS	MIA	MLB	20	600	42	25	2	5	45	40	202	28	10	.190/.249/.276	45	.288	0.9	SS 2, 2B 0	-2.0

Comparables: Gavin Cecchini, Ramón Torres, José Rondón

The Report: For a light-hitting shortstop to claw his way into the top 10 of a very deep and talented system, there must be some special talents to justify the ranking. In the case of Nunez, there's a series of skills that grade out towards the top of the scale. To start, he has elite plate discipline that allows him to get on base with an uncanny ability for his age. So even though his switch-hitting stroke lacks any sort of thump—and may never even get to below-average power—he should make enough contact and draw plenty of walks to buoy his on-base percentage. Which is where his second near-elite skill comes into play: his plus-plus speed and baserunning instincts makes him a terror on the base-paths for pitchers and catchers alike. And finally, and perhaps the most important of his positive traits, is a glove and arm that could contend for hardware in the future.

Development Track: The challenge for Nunez will be to add strength without putting too much of a damper on his straight-line speed. He has remained lean since his drafting, but has added some good weight to help with his durability and add some oomph at the plate. As he continues to advance and face better pitching, the foundation of hitting is there to improve the hit tool to a potentially average grade, which would lock him in as an everyday player.

Variance: High. It's all contingent on the bat and whether it's a liability, good enough, or better than hoped. If it's either of the last two options, he could be a special player.

J.P. Breen's Fantasy Take: Nunez is a great late-round target for supplemental drafts. He has a legitimate pathway to the big leagues and has category-carrying speed potential. If the batting average takes a positive step in 2021, we might be looking at the infield version of Cristian Pache. Oh, and after reading the above scouting report, I wanted to add this for my buddy Craig: Hardware.

9 Dax Fulton LHP   OFP: 55   ETA: 2024
Born: 10/16/01   Age: 19   Bats: L   Throws: L   Height: 6'6"   Weight: 230   Origin: Round 2, 2020 Draft (#40 overall)

The Report: Despite being injured during the tail-end of the summer showcase portion of his draft year, the book was already out on Fulton as one of the top lefty arms in the 2020 class. He's a monster for his age, standing 6-foot-6 with a solid build, a bit narrow-chested, but with overall a good frame. His height really allows for him to attack with his heater down in the zone, which he then follows up with a big breaking curveball that locks up hitters on their front foot. Like most high schoolers, he toyed around with a changeup which will eventually come into play. What's important is the projectable body and the potential for at least two plus pitches.

Development Track: It's never a good thing to have Tommy John surgery, especially during your draft year. The Marlins saw past Fulton's injury that occurred in late 2019, and in a way, couldn't have been hurt at a better time. Focusing on the rehab process during the pandemic will allow him to toe the rubber come 2021 without missing any games of consequence.

Variance: Extreme. Recently drafted 19-year-olds coming off TJ are about as far away from the majors as possible. Every pitcher recovers differently, and we need to see how things look in 2021 as he gets back into form. The eventual grade here could be off one or two standard deviations depending on the rehab and how he develops.

J.P. Breen's Fantasy Take: Prep arms are risky enough in dynasty. Add in the Tommy John surgery, and y'all don't need to bother until next winter. Even then, he's years away.

10 Peyton Burdick OF   OFP: 55   ETA: 2022
Born: 02/26/97   Age: 24   Bats: R   Throws: R   Height: 6'0"   Weight: 210   Origin: Round 3, 2019 Draft (#82 overall)

YEAR	TEAM	LVL	AGE	PA	R	2B	3B	HR	RBI	BB	K	SB	CS	AVG/OBP/SLG	DRC+	BABIP	BRR	FRAA	WARP
2019	BAT	SS	22	25	3	0	1	1	5	2	5	1	1	.318/.400/.545	114	.375	0.2	RF(4) 0.4	0.1
2019	CLI	LO-A	22	288	57	20	3	10	59	32	67	6	6	.307/.408/.542	164	.380	-0.2	LF(59) 10.1, RF(2) 0.5	3.7
2021 FS	MIA	MLB	24	600	58	27	3	16	65	38	187	5	4	.225/.290/.379	87	.310	-3.7	LF 12, RF 0	1.5

Comparables: Khris Davis, Jaycob Brugman, Eric Fryer

The Report: Some of the words that have been used to describe Burdick: "animal," "beast," "bulldog," among other monstrous varieties. The former third-round pick out of Wright State parlayed a productive summer at the Cape into an eye-popping stat line the following spring, walking nearly twice as much as he struck out, clobbering 15 homers, and stealing 24 bases. Seamlessly transitioning to pro ball, he continued his mashing ways as one of the most productive hitters in Low-A. At 6-foot, he's not the towering individual you'd expect to be launching majestic home runs, but he's good at using his stout lower half and jacked arms to generate power from a balanced swing.

Development Track: Continuing the nickname barrage, "gym rat" and "workout warrior" can also be added to the list. He's received high praise for his work ethic and makeup, forcing his way into the discussion to be part of a crowded future outfield. As long as he continues to adjust to each new level of pitching, there is little tangible development left to make beyond those adjustments.

Variance: Medium. As hot as Burdick was for all of 2019, you hate to have anything prevent you from continuing that streak. After the layoff, if he comes out on fire yet again, we'll know just how for real he is, with a 55 potentially being on the low end of outcomes.

J.P. Breen's Fantasy Take: Burdick has been a trendy name in the dynasty community for the past 12-14 months. He's a top-200 dynasty prospect and could skyrocket up lists with a strong 2021 campaign. Word to the wise: Pay attention to how successful he is stealing bases next season. He stole seven bags in 2019 but was caught seven times. If that ratio doesn't improve, he won't be a double-digit steal threat at the big-league level, as no manager will give him the green light enough to matter.

The Prospects You Meet Outside The Top Ten

Top Ten Prospects in a shallower system

Braxton Garrett LHP Born: 08/05/97   Age: 23   Bats: L   Throws: L   Height: 6'2"   Weight: 202   Origin: Round 1, 2016 Draft (#7 overall)

YEAR	TEAM	LVL	AGE	W	L	SV	G	GS	IP	H	HR	BB/9	K/9	K	GB%	BABIP	WHIP	ERA	DRA-	WARP
2019	JUP	HI-A	21	6	6	0	20	20	105	92	13	3.2	10.1	118	53.9%	.294	1.23	3.34	99	0.2
2019	JAX	AA	21	0	1	0	1	1	1²	4	0	16.2	5.4	1	55.6%	.444	4.20	16.20	209	-0.1
2020	MIA	MLB	22	1	1	0	2	2	7²	8	3	5.9	9.4	8	61.9%	.278	1.70	5.87	103	0.1
2021 FS	MIA	MLB	23	1	1	0	57	0	50	47	6	5.7	8.7	48	50.4%	.295	1.57	4.98	109	-0.1
2021 DC	MIA	MLB	23	1	1	0	4	4	19	17	2	5.7	8.7	18	50.4%	.295	1.57	4.98	109	0.1

Comparables: Pedro Avila, Trevor Rogers, Jonathan Hernández

It's been a long year, but that's only part of the reason it feels like it's been ages since Garrett was the seventh overall draft pick. The elevator pitch for him as a top 10 talent was "second-best lefty curve in the draft." Which means plus-plus potential when you are only beat out by Jay Groome Garrett missed 2018 with Tommy John surgery, but the curve remains a pristine plus hook. The pitch got some foolish swings from major league hitters, but it's a below-average fastball in terms of both velocity and movement, so Garrett will have to walk a fine line as a starter. An improving change-up gives him a chance to be at least an average one though.

Kameron Misner OF Born: 01/08/98   Age: 23   Bats: L   Throws: L   Height: 6'4"   Weight: 218   Origin: Round 1, 2019 Draft (#35 overall)

YEAR	TEAM	LVL	AGE	PA	R	2B	3B	HR	RBI	BB	K	SB	CS	AVG/OBP/SLG	DRC+	BABIP	BRR	FRAA	WARP
2019	MRL	ROK	21	38	2	2	0	0	4	9	7	3	0	.241/.421/.310		.318			
2019	CLI	LO-A	21	158	25	7	0	2	20	21	35	8	0	.276/.380/.373	136	.357	2.2	CF(32) 7.1	2.0
2021 FS	MIA	MLB	23	600	55	26	2	11	57	52	186	11	1	.225/.298/.345	79	.320	5.1	CF 19, RF 0	2.8

Comparables: Ryan LaMarre, Mitch Haniger, Gary Brown

A conundrum of a prospect before he was drafted, Misner has obvious physical tools but lacked the college production to back it up. With his size, speed, and lofty swing you'd expect him to put up big power and stolen base numbers, but they've been modest relative to what you see on video. Misner routinely puts together professional at-bats, but it's a borderline passive approach, attempting to get into counts where he can sit on a pitch and location to jump on. He maintained that strategy at instructs while playing all three outfield positions and is referred to often as a potentially dynamic player.

Major League-ready bats, but less upside than you'd like

Lewin Díaz **1B** Born: 11/19/96 Age: 24 Bats: L Throws: L Height: 6'4" Weight: 217 Origin: International Free Agent, 2013

YEAR	TEAM	LVL	AGE	PA	R	2B	3B	HR	RBI	BB	K	SB	CS	AVG/OBP/SLG	DRC+	BABIP	BRR	FRAA	WARP
2018	FTM	HI-A	21	310	21	11	3	6	35	10	56	1	0	.224/.255/.344	67	.255	-1.8	1B(74) 2.7	-1.3
2019	FTM	HI-A	22	234	34	11	1	13	36	14	40	0	0	.290/.333/.533	157	.297	-1.3	1B(52) 4.9	2.0
2019	JAX	AA	22	129	16	6	0	8	14	11	28	0	1	.200/.279/.461	122	.188	-0.2	1B(30) -2.2	0.5
2019	PNS	AA	22	138	12	16	1	6	26	8	23	0	0	.302/.341/.587	130	.320	-0.6	1B(31) -0.2	0.9
2020	MIA	MLB	23	41	2	2	0	0	3	2	12	0	0	.154/.195/.205	73	.222	-0.1	1B(11) 0.9	0.0
2021 FS	MIA	MLB	24	600	63	24	2	23	78	36	166	0	0	.227/.280/.409	85	.279	1.0	1B 4	0.2
2021 DC	MIA	MLB	24	133	14	5	0	5	17	8	36	0	0	.227/.280/.409	85	.279	0.2	1B 1	0.0

Comparables: Kendrys Morales, Russ Canzler, Ben Paulsen

Díaz made the top 10 last year, and also was awfully close this year. The system improved around him, but he also badly flopped in a short major-league trial. He's a power-hitting first baseman who had a breakout 2019; he's hurt by not having the consolidation year in 2020. We expect him to get another shot at MLB time in 2021, but even though he adds some value as a good defender and has some hit tool potential, the margins to be an everyday first baseman remain tight.

Prospects to dream on a little

José Devers **SS** Born: 12/07/99 Age: 21 Bats: L Throws: R Height: 6'0" Weight: 174 Origin: International Free Agent, 2016

YEAR	TEAM	LVL	AGE	PA	R	2B	3B	HR	RBI	BB	K	SB	CS	AVG/OBP/SLG	DRC+	BABIP	BRR	FRAA	WARP
2018	GBO	LO-A	18	362	46	12	4	0	24	15	49	13	6	.273/.313/.332	92	.318	-2.6	SS(58) 2.2, 2B(15) 0.0	0.2
2019	MRL	ROK	19	46	7	3	1	0	2	4	4	3	1	.275/.370/.400		.306			
2019	JUP	HI-A	19	138	13	3	1	0	3	8	20	5	0	.325/.384/.365	128	.387	-1.8	SS(32) -1.9	0.6
2021 FS	MIA	MLB	21	600	49	26	3	6	51	32	143	12	4	.237/.288/.334	71	.307	2.5	SS -4, 2B 1	-0.3

Comparables: Ketel Marte, Cole Tucker, Sergio Alcántara

Devers was just 20 for the entire 2020 season. He didn't make his MLB debut, but he wasn't overmatched at all at the alternate site, enough that he was on the MLB taxi squad down the stretch. He's an above-average defender with promising bat-to-ball and pitch selection, and he runs well too. The profile is limited by a lack of power, but he'd have made most Top 10s, and he's deceptively close to the majors for a 21-year-old who has never played in the high-minors.

Osiris Johnson **SS** Born: 10/18/00 Age: 20 Bats: R Throws: R Height: 6'0" Weight: 181 Origin: Round 2, 2018 Draft (#53 overall)

YEAR	TEAM	LVL	AGE	PA	R	2B	3B	HR	RBI	BB	K	SB	CS	AVG/OBP/SLG	DRC+	BABIP	BRR	FRAA	WARP
2018	MRL	ROK	17	111	12	8	2	1	13	4	19	7	2	.301/.333/.447		.353			
2018	GBO	LO-A	17	88	4	3	0	2	6	1	34	0	2	.188/.205/.294	28	.280	-1.3	SS(23) -6.3	-1.2

Comparables: Javy Guerra, Brendan Rodgers, Marco Hernández

As has been often referenced, those who missed a lot of time prior to 2020 really needed to take advantage of the opportunities afforded to them at either the alternate site or instructs. Having lost his 2019 season due to injury, Johnson turned heads this fall with a clean bill of health allowing his elite bat-speed to finally recover to pre-injury form. Still maturing into his 20-year-old body, Johnson is likely to be shifted over to third base next season where his offensive profile and arm strength should work just fine.

Connor Scott **OF** Born: 10/08/99 Age: 21 Bats: L Throws: L Height: 6'3" Weight: 187 Origin: Round 1, 2018 Draft (#13 overall)

YEAR	TEAM	LVL	AGE	PA	R	2B	3B	HR	RBI	BB	K	SB	CS	AVG/OBP/SLG	DRC+	BABIP	BRR	FRAA	WARP
2018	MRL	ROK	18	119	15	1	4	0	8	14	29	8	5	.223/.319/.311		.307			
2018	GBO	LO-A	18	89	4	2	0	1	5	10	27	1	3	.211/.295/.276	58	.300	-1.9	CF(22) -3.0	-0.8
2019	CLI	LO-A	19	413	56	24	4	4	36	31	91	21	9	.251/.311/.368	98	.322	1.6	CF(85) -2.6, LF(1) -0.1	1.1
2019	JUP	HI-A	19	111	12	4	1	1	5	11	26	2	1	.235/.306/.327	85	.301	0.9	CF(24) -1.5	0.1
2021 FS	MIA	MLB	21	600	48	27	4	8	52	42	199	12	8	.213/.272/.322	63	.317	-6.1	CF -4, LF 0	-1.9

Comparables: Mickey Moniak, Rey Fuentes, Derrick Robinson

The former first-round pick hasn't been mentioned in the same breath as the other members of his 2018 prep class (Jarred Kelenic, Nolan Gorman, Jordyn Adams, Triston Casas, etc.) yet Scott has been steadily improving outside of the spotlight. With average future hit and power tools—and more potentially more to come with minor swing tweaks—he also offers plus speed and a plus glove patrolling center field.

Top Talents 25 and Under (as of 4/1/2021):

1. Sixto Sánchez, RHP
2. Sandy Alcantara, RHP
3. Pablo Lopez, RHP
4. JJ Bleday, OF
5. Edward Cabrera, RHP
6. Max Meyer, RHP
7. Jazz Chisholm SS
8. Trevor Rogers, LHP
9. Isan Díaz, 2B
10. Elieser Hernandez, RHP

Folks, the Marlins might be good for awhile. Sandy Alcantara would be the most promising young pitcher for the majority of MLB organizations. He's a present mid-rotation innings eater with an All-Star nod under his belt already. The upper-90s heat and three average-or-better offspeeds hint at even more, if he can take the final steps.

Pablo López would be the most promising young pitcher in many organizations. He's always had plus command, but he's picked up velocity in the majors, and he's found a real out pitch in a changeup that he spammed almost 30 percent of the time. The entire 2020 MLB season was a short sample, granted, but López was seventh in pitching WARP, with most of the names in front of him being established aces.

Isan Díaz opted out of the season during the Marlins' COVID-19 outbreak. He opted back in right before the trade deadline, only to suffer a season-ending groin injury right after his return. Díaz still has big power potential, but he hasn't had much of a MLB opportunity yet and hasn't hit for average when he has. His stock will likely be way up or way down depending on how his 2021 goes.

Elieser Hernandez slides onto the back of this list in place of Jordan Yamamoto, whose 2020 never much got going at all. Hernandez, a former Rule 5 pick, is a homer-prone fastball/slider type who seems to be settling in well as a fourth or fifth starter.

Milwaukee Brewers

The State of the System:

The Brewers system fired a lot of bullets in trades and graduations to build a roster that made the playoffs three years running. Have they fired them all? Well, let's just say for 2021, the rest of the NL Central might be feeling lucky.

The Top Ten:

1 Brice Turang SS   OFP: 55   ETA: Late 2021 / Early 2022

Born: 11/21/99   Age: 21   Bats: L   Throws: R   Height: 6'0"   Weight: 173   Origin: Round 1, 2018 Draft (#21 overall)

YEAR	TEAM	LVL	AGE	PA	R	2B	3B	HR	RBI	BB	K	SB	CS	AVG/OBP/SLG	DRC+	BABIP	BRR	FRAA	WARP
2018	BRG	ROK	18	57	11	2	0	0	7	9	6	8	1	.319/.421/.362		.357			
2019	WIS	LO-A	19	357	57	13	4	2	31	49	54	21	4	.287/.384/.376	141	.339	3.2	SS(43) 0.6, 2B(28) 0.9	3.2
2019	CAR	HI-A	19	207	25	6	2	1	6	34	47	9	1	.200/.338/.276	99	.268	1.6	SS(35) -2.6, 2B(5) -0.8	0.6
2021 FS	MIL	MLB	21	600	52	26	3	7	52	52	161	15	4	.234/.304/.336	78	.319	5.2	SS -2, 2B -2	0.4

Comparables: José Peraza, Asdrúbal Cabrera, Jorge Polanco

The Report: Turang does everything well, but nothing so well that he's cracked national lists yet. In some ways it's a tough profile. He doesn't project for much power, and while he has a good approach and good contact skills, without putting consistent sting on the baseball, pitchers may challenge him further up the ladder, eroding those low minors walk rates. So the offensive profile may come down to the hit tool, which is solid, maybe even plus. You combine that with solid, but probably not plus shortstop defense, and you have a solid regular. But it all has to break right, and he hasn't seen the upper minors and struggled after a promotion to Advanced-A in 2019. He's a plus runner and good on the basepaths, so if Turang is able to get on base at a .350 or so clip, he'll add some extra value there.

Development Track: Turang was at the Brewers alternate site where reports were ... solidly positive. There's more hard contact and he's driving the ball into the gaps, but those doubles aren't turning into home runs yet, and given his frame, I doubt they ever will to any significant extent. Turang remains a perfectly fine shortstop prospect if still a half-step below the Jeremy Peñas and Gerardo Perdomos you find towards the back of the 101.

Variance: High. There may not be a true carrying tool in the profile, so we have just kicked the can down the road another year waiting to see him continue to produce against pitchers outside of the Midwest League.

J.P. Breen's Fantasy Take: It's never a great sign for an organization, at least in terms of dynasty, when the org's No. 1 prospect isn't a top-101 guy. We're talking Nico Hoerner< with a little less on the hit tool. We're talking Andres Gimenez with a little less speed. Ultimately, we're talking about a dude whose absolute upside is a MI slot ... which, in the parlance of my people, uff da.

2 Garrett Mitchell OF   OFP: 55   ETA: 2023

Born: 09/04/98   Age: 22   Bats: L   Throws: R   Height: 6'3"   Weight: 215   Origin: Round 1, 2020 Draft (#20 overall)

The Report: Depending on which scout you asked prior to the 2020 draft, Mitchell was either one of the most physically-gifted, tooled-up college players they had ever seen, or someone largely overhyped due to mechanical shortcomings. It really is a test of whether the glass is half full or half empty, with both arguments based on equally-considered evidence. Built like a strong safety with a big chest and broad shoulders, Mitchell runs well even given his size, grading out as a plus-plus runner. It helps defensively as there should be no issues staying in center field chasing down balls in the gap. The debate comes down to the swing and if a guy who has every bit of strength you'd expect from a 30-home run slugger will ever show any semblance of moderate game power. Right now Mitchell makes enough contact and uses his speed to take extra bases, but the difference between that player and one who produces what his physical attributes say he can are entirely different things at present.

Development Track: It's not to say the necessary swing changes can't be made. Mitchell's back elbow never gets to a good position for power, and the front shoulder bars his arm out. Both of these swing elements sap a ton of potential out of the bat. In short: His front-side is weak and back-side collapses. The slap and dash approach may work for him, but it just seems odd coming from someone who looks like a middle-of-the-order masher. From a training standpoint there is little left to accomplish with the body. It is now just a matter of what the Brewers player dev and hitting instruction can do to maximize the swing output.

Variance: High. It's all about the bat. If nothing changes to his game the value is derived solely from his glove and legs, and maybe a hit tool that is average.

Major league ETA: 2023

J.P. Breen's Fantasy Take: Mitchell is the dynasty prospect you want from this org. He'll be a guy who is undervalued in prospect circles because he hasn't been as good—or even been the kind of player—that people want him to be. Even if the bat is disappointing, however, we're looking at a glove-and-speed dude who has fantasy relevance from his speed alone. Remember, even Leonys Martin was worth rostering for a handful of years. And if the Brewers are able to develop him at the dish, we're looking at a potential five-category producer.

3   Aaron Ashby   LHP   OFP: 55   ETA: Mid to Late 2021

Born: 05/24/98   Age: 23   Bats: R   Throws: L   Height: 6'2"   Weight: 181   Origin: Round 4, 2018 Draft (#125 overall)

YEAR	TEAM	LVL	AGE	W	L	SV	G	GS	IP	H	HR	BB/9	K/9	K	GB%	BABIP	WHIP	ERA	DRA-	WARP
2018	HEL	ROK	20	1	2	1	6	3	20¹	18	3	3.5	8.4	19	48.3%	.273	1.28	6.20		
2018	WIS	LO-A	20	1	1	0	7	7	37¹	40	1	2.2	11.3	47	50.5%	.398	1.31	2.17	59	1.1
2019	WIS	LO-A	21	3	4	0	11	10	61	47	4	4.1	11.8	80	48.9%	.319	1.23	3.54	91	0.5
2019	CAR	HI-A	21	2	6	0	13	13	65	54	1	4.4	7.6	55	47.3%	.286	1.32	3.46	98	0.2
2021 FS	MIL	MLB	23	2	3	0	57	0	50	47	7	5.3	8.5	47	44.9%	.287	1.54	5.06	118	-0.4

Comparables: Patrick Sandoval, Cristian Javier, Brock Burke

The Report: Ashby was one of the later additions to the alternate site, but he didn't waste any time making himself known and went on to impress at instructs, too. The lanky lefty improved the velocity on his already above-average fastball, holding mid-90s late into games and touching 98. Paired with a slow curve with nasty, late breaking action, he boasts a one-two punch of plus pitches to keep batters on their toes. He rounds out his four pitch mix with an equally devastating slider and a developing changeup. He's racked up strikeouts, with the ability to tunnel pitches and elicit swings and misses. Unfortunately, sometimes he's racked up walks too.

Development Track: What good is multiple plus pitches if you can't hit your target? Ashby has the stuff, but command issues still linger. He did a better job at keeping the ball in the strike zone and hitting the glove during instructional league. There's signs he's about to turn a corner, but as he rises through the system he'll have to truly refine his command to find success at higher levels. Ashby feels close to making it to the big club, despite the lack of professional experience under his belt; he's got major league caliber pitches and improved upon his biggest weakness. It wouldn't be much of a surprise if the Brewers were aggressive with his promotions and put him on a fast track.

Variance: Low. There's still some talk of Ashby ending up in the bullpen, but the org is high on him, and it's likely he contributes soon, one way or another.

J.P. Breen's Fantasy Take: Plenty of minor-league pitchers can post gaudy strikeout numbers. When the strikeouts are paired with a high walk rate—his 2019 walk rate was north of 11 percent at both Class-A and High-A—it's a tough needle to thread. Ashby might be better in a multi-inning relief role, too, though the WHIP might not be good enough to make him valuable in standard roto leagues. The next pitcher on this list profiles as the better dynasty gamble.

4   Ethan Small   LHP   OFP: 55   ETA: Mid to Late 2021

Born: 02/14/97   Age: 24   Bats: L   Throws: L   Height: 6'4"   Weight: 215   Origin: Round 1, 2019 Draft (#28 overall)

YEAR	TEAM	LVL	AGE	W	L	SV	G	GS	IP	H	HR	BB/9	K/9	K	GB%	BABIP	WHIP	ERA	DRA-	WARP
2019	BRG	ROK	22	0	0	0	2	2	3	0	0	0.0	15.0	5	50.0%	.000	0.00	0.00		
2019	WIS	LO-A	22	0	2	0	5	5	18	11	0	2.0	15.5	31	30.3%	.333	0.83	1.00	51	0.6
2021 FS	MIL	MLB	24	2	3	0	57	0	50	45	7	4.4	10.2	56	36.7%	.295	1.40	4.47	110	-0.2

Comparables: Brendan McKay, Brock Burke, Victor González

The Report: Alongside Ashby, Small was one of the standouts at the Brewers alternate site. He boasts a four pitch mix; a lively fastball that sits either side of 90, a mid 70s changeup with late fade, a solid curve, and a newly developed slider. The fastball velocity plays up a bit due to a deceptive delivery, and he has average command of all four pitches, occasionally better. He's not afraid to use every weapon he has to disrupt a hitter's timing, often varying the rhythm of his wind up or slightly changing his leg kick.

Development Track: Small added a slider to his arsenal earlier this year and he's already developed it into an out pitch rather than a get me over one, improving it a full grade since spring training. He spent his season enhancing his secondaries and turning the trio into average offerings with flashes of something more. The fastball is still the star of the show, but now that it's accompanied by multiple other options, Small's on track to break into a major league rotation. The true test comes once he starts facing higher levels, as he's not yet pitched above Low-A ball.

Variance: Medium. Now that his offspeed pitches are legit offerings he looks a lot like an actual major leaguer. He'll still have to prove he's just as effective in-game next season as he was at the alternate site.

J.P. Breen's Fantasy Take: While not an exciting dynasty piece in the long term, Small could generate some significant buzz by Summer 2021. His improved secondary offerings, plus the quality command, should allow him to carve up minor-league hitting. A bloated strikeout rate and a shiny ERA might make him one of the summer's hottest trading chips. Long term, though, we're not looking at someone with the upside of a top-50 fantasy starter, unless the command is impeccable or the fastball adds a few ticks. Still, he's worth adding in deep dynasty leagues.

5   Mario Feliciano   C   OFP: 50   ETA: 2022

Born: 11/20/98   Age: 22   Bats: R   Throws: R   Height: 6'1"   Weight: 200   Origin: Round 2, 2016 Draft (#75 overall)

YEAR	TEAM	LVL	AGE	PA	R	2B	3B	HR	RBI	BB	K	SB	CS	AVG/OBP/SLG	DRC+	BABIP	BRR	FRAA	WARP
2018	CAR	HI-A	19	165	20	7	1	3	12	13	59	2	0	.205/.282/.329	53	.318	0.5	C(25) -0.6	-0.5
2019	CAR	HI-A	20	482	62	25	4	19	81	29	139	2	1	.273/.324/.477	118	.351	-5.1	C(61) -0.4	1.7
2021 FS	MIL	MLB	22	600	58	25	3	14	59	35	188	2	0	.214/.268/.351	70	.295	1.5	C -1	0.2
2021 DC	MIL	MLB	22	67	6	2	0	1	6	3	21	0	0	.214/.268/.351	70	.295	0.2	C 0	0.0

Comparables: Wilin Rosario, Wilson Ramos, Nick Williams

The Report: Feliciano exploded offensively at the alternate site. The potential with the bat has always been there, and he fully tapped into it this year. The contact rate is up, as his overall bat to ball skills have really come along and he's refined his approach at the plate. He sends hard line drives deep to all fields and has arguably the most power on the top ten.

Development Track: His ability to catch isn't quite the question mark it once was, but there's definitely still room for improvement. Currently the catching skills are just passable, good enough to get the job done with flashes of something more every so often. The strength of his arm is his best asset behind the dish and there's enough pure athleticism to ensure he remains at least average defensively. Feliciano's a bat-first backstop with the possibility of providing impact on both sides of the ball as long as he keeps making steady progress with the glove.

Variance: Medium. His offensive production is here to stay, but he's a catcher who still needs to improve defensively. The bat carries the profile.

J.P. Breen's Fantasy Take: Although I'm not allowed to advocate for dynasty catchers, other than one or two elite prospects, Feliciano has been one of my personal favorites for several years. Still, I'm not allowed to tell you to roster him. Mark Barry will yell at me.

6 Tristen Lutz OF   OFP: 50   ETA: 2022
Born: 08/22/98 Age: 22 Bats: R Throws: R Height: 6'2" Weight: 210 Origin: Round 1, 2017 Draft (#34 overall)

YEAR	TEAM	LVL	AGE	PA	R	2B	3B	HR	RBI	BB	K	SB	CS	AVG/OBP/SLG	DRC+	BABIP	BRR	FRAA	WARP
2018	WIS	LO-A	19	503	63	33	3	13	63	46	139	9	3	.245/.321/.421	114	.322	-0.9	RF(68) -11.4, LF(29) 1.9, CF(14) -2.9	-0.2
2019	CAR	HI-A	20	477	62	24	3	13	54	46	137	3	2	.255/.335/.419	108	.343	-1.5	CF(71) -3.0, RF(39) -2.4	0.9
2021 FS	MIL	MLB	22	600	55	27	3	16	63	36	214	2	1	.211/.268/.361	71	.309	0.3	CF -2, RF -6	-1.5

Comparables: Michael Saunders, Yorman Rodriguez, Jordan Schafer

The Report: Completely filled out, Lutz is strong and athletic despite his large frame.
Likewise, he runs better than one might think, both on the base paths and in the field. He is destined to make the move to right field at some point. Lutz has the speed and the range to handle center, but he's a big guy with a strong accurate arm who's overall better suited for a corner spot. Defensively he's above average across the board, with power at the plate to match.

Development Track: Lutz's biggest hurdle is difficulty making consistent solid contact. When he gets the barrel on the ball he can hit it hard to every part of the park, plus game pop, even more raw power, but the hit tool just isn't where you want it to be. He's made some steps in the right direction this year, taking better swings and making mechanical adjustments, and also benefiting from daily at-bats against skilled arms at the alternate site. Whether or not he reaches his true ceiling relies heavily on him continuing to make contact and really showing off his plus power. He's slipped down the ranks, but he still has the potential to be a real difference maker.

Variance: Medium. Contact issues still plague Lutz, but he's made decent progress and his other tools are impressive enough to relieve some previous risk.

J.P. Breen's Fantasy Take: The raw power makes Lutz worth monitoring; however, he hasn't posted a .200 ISO in full-season ball and projects to be a drag in terms of batting average. To me, Lutz feels like Brandon Marsh with more questions about his hit tool. That's a hard pass from me for the moment, at least until we see tangible evidence of positive development at the plate.

7 Antoine Kelly LHP   OFP: 50   ETA: Late-2022
Born: 12/05/99 Age: 21 Bats: L Throws: L Height: 6'6" Weight: 205 Origin: Round 2, 2019 Draft (#65 overall)

YEAR	TEAM	LVL	AGE	W	L	SV	G	GS	IP	H	HR	BB/9	K/9	K	GB%	BABIP	WHIP	ERA	DRA-	WARP
2019	BRB	ROK	19	0	0	0	9	9	28²	21	0	1.6	12.9	41	43.5%	.339	0.91	1.26		
2019	WIS	LO-A	19	0	1	0	1	1	3	5	2	12.0	12.0	4	44.4%	.500	3.00	18.00	153	-0.1
2021 FS	MIL	MLB	21	2	3	0	57	0	50	46	8	4.9	9.3	51	40.0%	.292	1.48	4.89	116	-0.3

Comparables: Luis Severino, Edwin Escobar, Adrian Morejon

The Report: A big JuCo popup arm from the 2019 Draft as a lefty who could touch triple digits, Kelly has developed well since getting into pro ball. He sits in the mid-90s with the fastball and it's free and easy heat. His slider projects as above-average to plus, and his changeup is coming along too. Kelly has had issues with his command—he's just a year off walking over 5 batters per 9 in the Great Rivers Athletic Conference, after all—but he seems to be putting things together ahead of schedule.

Development Track: Kelly gained valuable experience at the alternate site against more experienced hitters, working on his command and changeup. It's not clear to us that the alternate site and instructional league format was actually worse for starting pitchers than a normal season, given that it was much more controlled and it's not like pitching prospects throw 180 innings anyway.

Variance: High. He's got three innings of official game action above the complex level. The envelope of outcomes is quite high here, including ones where he's a lot better than a No. 4 starter. Full-season ball will be quite telling.

J.P. Breen's Fantasy Take: Kelly may not be a prep draftee, but it's not incorrect to treat him like one in terms of dynasty. He's one of several dozen interesting young arms in the complex leagues, but he has far too many questions about his command and his changeup to be worth rostering at the moment.

8   Freddy Zamora   SS   OFP: 50   ETA: 2023/2024

Born: 11/01/98   Age: 22   Bats: R   Throws: R   Height: 6'1"   Weight: 190   Origin: Round 2, 2020 Draft (#53 overall)

The Report: A collegiate shortstop who was among those with a big "arrow up" heading into this past Spring, Zamora didn't see the field at all after tearing his ACL in the pre-season. His reputation as a glove-first infielder with quick reactions, solid arm, and good body control were never in question. They were fully on display during his first two years at The U. Scouts wanted to see if he could begin driving the ball with more authority, having maintained decent batting averages and never striking out more than he walked. Signs of more power appeared to be in the cards following his sophomore season; even so, a plus defender with a solid eye at the plate and above-average contact rates would be worth a second round selection even with the injury.

Development Track: Torn knee ligaments aren't necessarily a career-altering injury thanks to modern medicine. But for a player whose skills are reliant upon fluid movements, it is a little more of a concern. Even if Zamora had a full, healthy junior year, there were going to be concerns to quell about the profile. You'd have liked to see more offensive development with more hard-hit contact, more muscle on his frame. Now we just need to see him fully rehabbed and on the field at all.

Variance: High. The good news is the variance is high because there is a far better chance he becomes a 55 rather than a 45. Playing a premium position and being more than capable defensively gets you pretty far on its own. His offensive value will determine his overall potential.

J.P. Breen's Fantasy Take: If you're getting Brice Turang vibes and aren't too excited about it, you're not alone. That might say more about Turang's fantasy upside than Zamora's, though. The injury adds more uncertainty. Don't worry about the former Cane until we see some professional reps.

9   Carlos Rodriguez   OF   OFP: 50   ETA: 2023/2024

Born: 12/07/00   Age: 20   Bats: L   Throws: L   Height: 5'10"   Weight: 150   Origin: International Free Agent, 2017

YEAR	TEAM	LVL	AGE	PA	R	2B	3B	HR	RBI	BB	K	SB	CS	AVG/OBP/SLG	DRC+	BABIP	BRR	FRAA	WARP
2018	DSL BRW	ROK	17	230	38	13	1	2	32	7	19	12	8	.323/.358/.419		.347			
2019	RMV	ROK+	18	157	20	3	1	3	12	4	20	4	6	.331/.350/.424		.364			
2021 FS	MIL	MLB	20	600	49	25	2	8	54	21	130	16	10	.248/.280/.347	70	.308	-10.1	CF 1, LF 3	-1.0

Comparables: Eddie Rosario, Billy McKinney, Jahmai Jones

The Report: Rodriguez doesn't have the physicality or projection of your typical seven-figure IFA outfielder. What he has done is hit every place he's played in an admittedly brief pro career. Even here his profile confounds further, his .300+ batting averages don't originate from a typical "pretty" lefty swing. Rodriguez's mechanics are unorthodox, with an awkward, poking leg kick for timing. Obviously it hasn't been an issue so far; he stays back well and the upper body works just fine. But it's definitely something you'd want to see work against better competition, which wasn't going to happen for him in 2020. And he'll need to hit: The lack of physicality and projection mean below-average power at best, and while he has the range for center field, we need to see more reps there as well.

Development Track: As you see throughout this list, the Brewers were extremely aggressive with assigning prospects—even low-level ones—to their alternate site. Rodriguez at least had a year of stateside reps before heading to Grand Chute this Summer, and it will be interesting to see if the Brewers considered his work there equivalent to significant A-ball reps. He'll spend all of next season as a 20-year-old, so "holding him back" in the Carolina League (gonna have to get used to this) wouldn't be all that conservative an assignment.

Variance: Extreme. This report may read as somewhat muted for a Top Ten outfield prospect, and sure, Milwaukee isn't the best or deepest system. But I do actually really like Rodriguez quite a bit. I think he'll hit, and I think there's positive variance here once we see that bat at higher levels. Sure, the swing isn't gonna end up hanging in the Louvre, but I find it pleasingly similar to the alien beauty of like, Charline von Heyl.

J.P. Breen's Fantasy Take: Think Gilberto Jimenez (Red Sox) with a little better hit tool and slightly worse speed. He'll have to hit .300-plus for him to be an everyday guy. He has a legit chance to do that, though, and it's a good sign that the Brewers have continuously been aggressive with his assignments. Just remember that the best-case scenario is, like, Ender Inciarte—who is a nice little player but is easily replaceable in fantasy.

10 Hedbert Perez OF   OFP: 50   ETA: 2025ish
Born: 04/04/03   Age: 18   Bats: L   Throws: L   Height: 5'10"   Weight: 160   Origin: International Free Agent, 2019

The Report: Two years after signing Rodriguez out of Venezuela for a little over a million dollars, the Brewers inked Perez for $700,000. Perez has much more present strength and enough pop to generate good bat speed and loft from a fairly simple swing path, but both are advanced hitters for their age and experience level with a broad base of tools, even if they won't be sharing a wardrobe anytime soon. Or a position, as the barrel-chested Perez is likely destined for a corner outfield spot. He might well have the above-average hit and power tools to fit the profile.

Development Track: Perez was one of several high-profile 2019 J2s to get alternate site invites. We'd describe his performance as "buzzy." Buzzy enough to get him sent to a full-season affiliate for his 18th birthday? It's not impossible. I'm guessing he won't be the 10th best prospect in the Brewers system for 2022. And I'm guessing he won't be lower. But until he gets game reps, I am guessing more than I generally prefer.

Variance: Extreme. In a prospect list soaked with high variance profiles, Perez hasn't played an official game yet and doesn't turn 18 until Opening Day 2021.

J.P. Breen's Fantasy Take: Given Perez's post-J2 buzz, it's unlikely that he's available in deeper dynasty leagues. And very little has changed over the past 12 months. He's an intriguing young hitter who could potentially produce in terms of average and power. We just have very little on which to go, outside of a few buzzy reports. With that said, I won't blame you for rolling the dice in a deep dynasty, if he's available in your league.

The Prospects You Meet Outside The Top Ten

Zavier Warren   Born: 01/08/99   Age: 22   Bats: S   Throws: R   Height: 6'0"   Weight: 190   Origin: Round 3, 2020 Draft (#92 overall)

The ultimate baseball swiss-army knife—a player who can play any position-- Warren bounced all over the diamond during his college career, getting the bulk of his starts at shortstop. He has the arm strength to throw out runners from behind the plate, or from the 6-hole, or across the diamond at third base; it's possible his value is derived from not having a clear defensive home. He's also a capable switch-hitter with the ability to spray line-drives from foul line to foul line thanks to short, compact swing that is a little better from the left side, where the bat speed and swing plane are more evident, not that his right-handed stroke is that far off.

Eduardo Garcia SS Born: 07/10/02   Age: 18   Bats: R   Throws: R   Height: 6'2"   Weight: 160   Origin: International Free Agent, 2019

YEAR	TEAM	LVL	AGE	PA	R	2B	3B	HR	RBI	BB	K	SB	CS	AVG/OBP/SLG	DRC+	BABIP	BRR	FRAA	WARP
2019	DSL BRW	ROK	16	40	6	2	0	1	3	6	9	1	1	.312/.450/.469		.409			

Milwaukee's big IFA signing of 2018 checks in just outside the top ten after a fractured ankle cut short his time in the Dominican complex last Summer. It's a broadly similar profile to Zamora, right down to the recent bad leg injury. Garcia is a potential plus shortstop whose offensive tools lag behind the glove, but there's enough of a chance that the bat gets to average that the ordinal gap between them on this list overstates the projection gap. Honestly you could put 5-12 in this system in almost any permutation depending on your risk tolerance and profile preference.

Top Talents 25 and Under (as of 4/1/2021):

1. Keston Hiura, 2B
2. Brice Turang, SS
3. Garrett Mitchell, OF
4. Freddy Peralta, RHP
5. Luis Urías, IF
6. Aaron Ashby, LHP
7. Ethan Small, LHP
8. Mario Feliciano, C
9. Tristen Lutz, OF

10. Eric Lauer, LHP

Well, it gets a little better down here, I suppose. Keston Hiura never really got going in 2020, striking out nearly 35 percent of the time and hitting the ball an average of 4 MPH softer when he did hit it. Despite that, he was still close to a league-average hitter (98 DRC+), and we're extremely confident in the underlying hitting ability that made him the No. 6 prospect in baseball two years ago and drove his big 2019 rookie campaign.

Freddy Peralta has been a whiff machine for the Brewers, mostly out of the bullpen. He's virtually eliminated his changeup in favor of a new slider; there's only a handful of true fastball/slider/curveball starters around the league, so he might need to drop the occasional change in just for an armside look if he's going to slide back to the rotation. But there's nothing else really saying he can't at least be a twice through the order guy, and a lot of his relief appearances have already come in long relief. We'd like the Brewers to give it a shot.

Luis Urías was a top 25 prospect not that long ago based on a high-end hit tool projection, and now he's hit .226 over parts of three MLB seasons. He's not making as much contact as we thought he would and he's not hitting it all that hard when he does, which is a bad combo. The latent bat-to-ball is probably still there and he's a versatile defender, so we're not totally out, but his stock is slipping.

Eric Lauer was pretty awful this year coming off a trade from the Padres. In literally any other system, he wouldn't have made this list. But it's the Brewers and he looked like a No. 4 starter in 2019, so…

Minnesota Twins

The State of the System:

The Twins' system remains deep enough that I am once again annoyed by some of the names I couldn't make room for in the top ten.

The Top Ten:

1 Royce Lewis   SS   OFP: 70   ETA: Late-2021 or early-2022

Born: 06/05/99   Age: 22   Bats: R   Throws: R   Height: 6'2"   Weight: 200   Origin: Round 1, 2017 Draft (#1 overall)

YEAR	TEAM	LVL	AGE	PA	R	2B	3B	HR	RBI	BB	K	SB	CS	AVG/OBP/SLG	DRC+	BABIP	BRR	FRAA	WARP
2018	CR	LO-A	19	327	50	23	0	9	53	24	49	22	4	.315/.368/.485	151	.349	3.7	SS(67) 0.8	3.2
2018	FTM	HI-A	19	208	33	6	3	5	21	19	35	6	4	.255/.327/.399	106	.291	1.7	SS(45) -4.8	0.3
2019	FTM	HI-A	20	418	55	17	3	10	35	27	90	16	8	.238/.289/.376	96	.281	-1.5	SS(84) 4.0	1.8
2019	PNS	AA	20	148	18	9	1	2	14	11	33	6	2	.231/.291/.358	66	.287	2.0	SS(29) -2.6, 2B(1) 0.0, 3B(1) -0.0	0.3
2021 FS	MIN	MLB	22	600	62	27	3	14	63	40	151	14	5	.230/.288/.369	82	.290	0.1	SS 0, CF 1	0.6
2021 DC	MIN	MLB	22	101	10	4	0	2	10	6	25	2	0	.230/.288/.369	82	.290	0.0	SS 0, CF 0	0.1

Comparables: José Rondón, Amed Rosario, Tony Wolters

The Report: We've written as extensively on Lewis as any other prospect over the past few years. We'll start with the good stuff: Lewis has lightning-quick hands and generates a whole lot of bat speed with them. At times, with his best swings, we've projected him as a plus hitter. He projects for above-average-to-plus power. He has the defensive chops to play nearly anywhere on the diamond—short, second, third, center, you name it. And he runs very well too. There's true five-tool potential here.

There's also a level of hit tool variance which is nearly unprecedented for a former No. 1 overall pick who has already reached Double-A and is still a great prospect. Lewis gets seriously out of sync between his upper and lower halves, with a ton of moving parts, and his swing is inconsistent at best and kind of a disaster at worst.

Development Track: There's obviously an outcome where everything comes together in a flash for Lewis and he's a star with an average-or-better hit tool—we have people on staff who believe in that outcome—but our confidence in that solution is no higher than last year, and time is not an ally here. Lewis wasn't called up from the alternate site, which you can read a few ways. He didn't have to be added to the 40-man this offseason, so there were reasons within the context of roster construction not to call him up. But at the same time, if he

had

gotten everything together, he probably would've pushed his way to the MLB roster, right? Jeffers did, and Kirilloff did, even if just for the playoffs. In the 2020 video we saw, the swing issues Lewis has been battling for the past couple years didn't exactly look like they'd gone away.

Variance: Extreme. Somehow it got higher here?

J.P. Breen's Fantasy Take: Lewis is a tough dynasty prospect to value. On one hand, he has five-category upside, if it all comes together. He's easily a top-two-round talent in that case. On the other hand, if the swing issues don't improve, we're talking about a low-average super utility player who would derive most of his fantasy value from stolen bases and volume—though volume would be tough to come by if he's hitting .230 with a sub-.300 OBP. Here's the main dynasty problem: Lewis's value (currently our 15th-ranked dynasty prospect) reflects his upside, not the likelihood that he ever reaches that upside. He's basically impossible to acquire, and it'd be foolish to pay the going rate, given his extreme volatility. If you're already rostering him, you'll probably have to hold him. If you don't have him, you won't like the asking price.

★ ★ ★ *2021 Top 101 Prospect* **#71** ★ ★ ★

2 **Alex Kirilloff** **RF**   OFP: 60   ETA: Debuted in 2020

Born: 11/09/97 Age: 23 Bats: L Throws: L Height: 6'2" Weight: 195 Origin: Round 1, 2016 Draft (#15 overall)

YEAR	TEAM	LVL	AGE	PA	R	2B	3B	HR	RBI	BB	K	SB	CS	AVG/OBP/SLG	DRC+	BABIP	BRR	FRAA	WARP
2018	CR	LO-A	20	281	36	20	5	13	56	24	47	1	1	.333/.391/.607	162	.364	-0.8	RF(53) -4.0, CF(0) -0.0	1.5
2018	FTM	HI-A	20	280	39	24	2	7	45	14	39	3	2	.362/.393/.550	162	.399	-0.8	RF(51) 0.4, CF(3) 0.3	1.7
2019	PNS	AA	21	411	47	18	2	9	43	29	76	7	6	.283/.343/.413	120	.333	-3.3	RF(41) -4.0, 1B(35) 0.3, LF(8) -1.0	0.6
2021 FS	*MIN*	*MLB*	*23*	*600*	*65*	*26*	*3*	*16*	*69*	*35*	*143*	*1*	*0*	*.252/.301/.401*	*92*	*.311*	*0.4*	*1B 1, LF -1*	*0.8*
2021 DC	*MIN*	*MLB*	*23*	*505*	*55*	*22*	*2*	*14*	*58*	*29*	*120*	*1*	*0*	*.252/.301/.401*	*92*	*.311*	*0.3*	*1B 1, LF -1*	*0.6*

Comparables: Brandon Moss, Carlos González, Tyler Austin

The Report: For a system that we are quite bullish on overall, we've been skeptical about the top two names here in recent years. The Q+D on Kirilloff: A post-draft breakout in short-season coming off a cold weather prep career made us all think perhaps there was more in the tank. Tommy John surgery cost him the next season, so we had to wait to see it at full-season ball. His performance on the field in 2018 was quite good, but the underlying swing had us skeptical about just how loud the hit and power tools would be given the corner profile. In 2019 Kirilloff dealt with a wrist injury and played almost as much first base as outfield. There's the potential for a plus-or-better hit tool with plus power, but he can get pull-power-happy and out of sync, leading to suboptimal contact. And he doesn't consistently lift the ball either, struggling to hit for corner bat game power above Low-A. Yes, there's that pesky wrist injury mention again, but it's all a bit muddled still.

Development Track: Kirilloff was a surprise add to the playoff roster for an injured Josh Donaldson after spending the summer at the alternate site. Conversely to the Royce Lewis discussion above, you could read into it that the Twins thought Kirilloff was the best option for that spot even though it wasn't a straight like-for-like swap. We're not going to fill the evaluation vacuum by reading too much into his four Wild Card Series plate appearances, but it did appear like he was still stuck between his 2018 and 2019 swings. Kirilloff could use some consolidation time in Triple-A, but once you are willing to start a player in the playoffs—and opened a theoretical spot for him by non-tendering Eddie Rosario—well, one could look at these as signals.

Variance: High. We don't think Kirilloff will have the weird orphan "Postseason Batting" baseball-reference page for long, the range of outcomes can go to fringe regular if the bat merely plays a little above average, to frequent All-Star if he unlocks (re-unlocks) something in the swing.

J.P. Breen's Fantasy Take: Assuming he winds up at first base, Kirilloff has an Eric Hosmer feel about him. That is, the average is good and the raw power is present, but there's a significant risk that none of those skills transition over to in-game power—making him a 20-homer, solid-average first baseman who has the occasional hot stretch. Kirilloff is more interesting as a corner outfielder, just not as much as you might think. Perhaps he puts everything together in 2021. I just don't plan on being the one who's betting on that outcome.

★ ★ ★ *2021 Top 101 Prospect* **#83** ★ ★ ★

3 **Trevor Larnach** **RF**   OFP: 60   ETA: 2021, as needed

Born: 02/26/97 Age: 24 Bats: L Throws: R Height: 6'4" Weight: 223 Origin: Round 1, 2018 Draft (#20 overall)

YEAR	TEAM	LVL	AGE	PA	R	2B	3B	HR	RBI	BB	K	SB	CS	AVG/OBP/SLG	DRC+	BABIP	BRR	FRAA	WARP
2018	ELZ	ROK	21	75	10	5	0	2	16	10	11	2	0	.311/.413/.492		.340			
2018	CR	LO-A	21	102	17	8	1	3	10	11	17	1	0	.297/.373/.505	149	.338	0.7	RF(17) -1.5	0.5
2019	FTM	HI-A	22	361	33	26	1	6	44	35	74	4	1	.316/.382/.459	165	.389	-1.4	RF(59) -8.1, LF(9) -0.4	1.9
2019	PNS	AA	22	181	26	4	0	7	22	22	50	0	0	.295/.387/.455	146	.390	-0.3	RF(29) -2.2, LF(5) -0.1	0.8
2021 FS	*MIN*	*MLB*	*24*	*600*	*65*	*27*	*2*	*15*	*64*	*51*	*170*	*0*	*0*	*.237/.307/.378*	*91*	*.318*	*-0.2*	*LF 0, RF -2*	*0.5*
2021 DC	*MIN*	*MLB*	*24*	*337*	*36*	*15*	*1*	*8*	*35*	*28*	*96*	*0*	*0*	*.237/.307/.378*	*91*	*.318*	*-0.1*	*LF 0, RF -1*	*0.3*

Comparables: Mac Williamson, Preston Tucker, Marcell Ozuna

The Report: Larnach and Kirilloff were merely one spot apart on the Top 101 coming into 2020. They remain close to a pick 'em of corner bats with plus hit and power potential who haven't dominated the minor leagues to the point where we are supremely confident they'd be plus regulars in the majors. Larnach's swing is more geared for power than Kirilloff, but his slugging percentages have mostly started with a four. The soon-to-be 24-year-old had a sturdy, mature frame, so any further power gains will have to come from lifting some of those doubles in the gap over the fence. Larnach is a perfectly adequate corner outfielder, but that still leaves a world of value in the gap between being a .270, 20 home-run hitter in the majors, versus .290 and 30.

Development Track: Flipping Kirilloff and Larnach this year isn't merely because the Twins chose to add one to the playoff roster over the other—Kirilloff was going to need to be added to the 40 anyway, Larnach wasn't—but it does point us in a direction. That said, the gap between the two remains fairly insignificant with Kirilloff having more upside. That's what wins out this year. The alternate site was roughly an appropriate level of competition for where Larnach was as a prospect, and he should be ready for the majors sometime in 2021.

Variance: High. While the top-line Double-A numbers were a tad better than Kirilloff's—however much you want to read into a month of performance—The K-rate did spike some, and Larnach's swing is geared for more swing-and-miss along with the additional game pop.

J.P. Breen's Fantasy Take: The Twins' minor-league system reminds me of

Game of Thrones

. Many of your intelligent friends hype it up, but when you sit down and finally dig into the beginning of it, you realize that you're looking at something solid enough that has the potential to be incredible. Larnach is the third consecutive Twins dynasty prospect who is profile-over-production, whose value treats him like a safe 30-homer corner masher, when he only hit 13 bombs in 542 PA between High-A and Double-A as a 22-year-old. Let's hope Larnach reaches his potential more fully than George R. R. Martin's series did.

4 Ryan Jeffers C   OFP: 60   ETA: Debuted in 2020
Born: 06/03/97   Age: 24   Bats: R   Throws: R   Height: 6'4"   Weight: 235   Origin: Round 2, 2018 Draft (#59 overall)

YEAR	TEAM	LVL	AGE	PA	R	2B	3B	HR	RBI	BB	K	SB	CS	AVG/OBP/SLG	DRC+	BABIP	BRR	FRAA	WARP
2018	ELZ	ROK	21	129	29	7	0	3	16	20	16	0	1	.422/.543/.578		.482			
2018	CR	LO-A	21	155	19	10	0	4	17	14	30	0	0	.288/.361/.446	144	.343	0.4	C(22) 0.2	1.2
2019	FTM	HI-A	22	315	35	11	0	10	40	28	64	0	0	.256/.330/.402	121	.297	-2.7	C(57) 0.7	1.6
2019	PNS	AA	22	99	13	5	0	4	9	9	19	0	0	.287/.374/.483	142	.328	1.4	C(17) -0.9	0.8
2020	MIN	MLB	23	62	5	0	0	3	7	5	19	0	0	.273/.355/.436	92	.364	-0.5	C(25) -0.1	0.1
2021 FS	MIN	MLB	24	600	71	25	1	19	71	48	168	1	0	.256/.327/.417	108	.336	-0.5	C 0	3.1
2021 DC	MIN	MLB	24	269	32	11	0	8	32	21	75	0	0	.256/.327/.417	108	.336	-0.2	C 0	1.3

Comparables: Devin Mesoraco, Danny Jansen, Jake Fox

The Report: We noted Jeffers was moving fast last year when he made it to Double-A in his first full pro season. He's not the world's most exhilarating prospect in written form—average hit tool projection, above-average power—but he's turned out to be much more advanced than we thought. More importantly, he's turned out to be a pretty nifty framer and overall defender despite his size. A bunch of 5s and 55s plays better behind the plate than anywhere else, at least in the age where there's like all of five good two-way catchers in all of MLB at any given time.

Development Track: Jeffers was unexpectedly called up in 2020 just two years after being drafted. That's very fast for a catcher, and he was an above-average framer in the small sample. His hitting stats weren't facially hugely impressive, but he hit the ball

hard

: 91.6 mph average exit velocity, with six batted balls out of 38 over 105 mph and a max of 112.9 mph. His stock is rising.

Variance: Medium, although that's low as catchers go. There's only a couple catching prospects more likely to be a decent regular or semi-regular.

J.P. Breen's Fantasy Take: Jeffers has hit .270-plus at every professional stop, save his 2019 stint in High-A, but the Florida State League is rarely friendly to hitters. Jeffers could be a top-10 fantasy catcher. Only seven catchers hit .270-plus with at least 15 homers in 2019. Jeffers has the skills and track record to join that club as quickly as 2021. The presence of Mitch Garver on the roster, however, makes forecasting when he'll get the chance to log 350 PA very difficult.

5   Jhoan Duran   RHP   OFP: 60   ETA: 2021, as needed

Born: 01/08/98   Age: 23   Bats: R   Throws: R   Height: 6'5"   Weight: 230   Origin: International Free Agent, 2014

YEAR	TEAM	LVL	AGE	W	L	SV	G	GS	IP	H	HR	BB/9	K/9	K	GB%	BABIP	WHIP	ERA	DRA-	WARP
2018	CR	LO-A	20	2	1	0	6	6	36	19	2	2.5	11.0	44	66.2%	.218	0.81	2.00	55	1.1
2018	KC	LO-A	20	5	4	0	15	15	64²	69	6	3.9	9.9	71	51.1%	.348	1.50	4.73	75	1.3
2019	FTM	HI-A	21	2	9	0	16	15	78	63	5	3.6	11.0	95	51.6%	.317	1.21	3.23	90	0.6
2019	PNS	AA	21	3	3	0	7	7	37	34	2	2.2	10.0	41	63.0%	.330	1.16	4.86	128	-0.6
2021 FS	MIN	MLB	23	8	9	0	26	26	150	137	23	4.2	8.7	145	51.6%	.280	1.39	4.55	109	0.3
2021 DC	MIN	MLB	23	2	2	0	8	8	34	31	5	4.2	8.7	32	51.6%	.280	1.39	4.55	109	0.2

Comparables: Adonis Medina, Johan Oviedo, Huascar Ynoa

The Report: If you were building a starting pitching prospect on paper you could do far worse than Duran. He's a 6-foot-5, well-built righty. He's tossed more than 100 innings in each of his last two actual seasons. Oh yeah, he has three potential plus pitches, including a fastball that routinely hits triple digits, a high-80s power curve, and a sinker/split hybrid. The minor league performance has matched the stuff, as he has posted 25%+ K-rates in 2018 and 2019. He generally finds the zone with his plus stuff. This sounds like one of the better pitching prospects in baseball, no? But if I may put on my bucket hat and Kohl's clearance rack color block polo for a moment, the games aren't played on paper, sport-o. Duran's delivery is high effort and the command profile has lagged behind the control. The splittish thing is a neat pitch, but it's not a true armside option against lefties, who had some success against him in 2019. So there remains some reliever risk. We're mostly nitpicking, but nitpickability is the difference between a Top 50 prospect in baseball and merely in consideration for the back of the 101.

Development Track: It's entirely possible Duran could have helped the 2020 Twins pitching staff on merit. And I'm a little surprised they didn't try to use him as a 'pen weapon late in the season and into the postseason, but honestly their pitching staff ran deep enough if it would have been a bit of a luxury. And you'd want to keep him stretched out as a starter for 2021 where he could make the most near-term impact. I'd expect Duran to start in Triple-A, but he could easily be the first arm up, and it's not impossible he beats out Randy Dobnak and Devin Smeltzer with a strong camp if the Twins don't bolster their rotation elsewhere.

Variance: Medium. If Duran does end up in the 'pen long term, the fastball/curve combo will play in high leverage. There's the usual pitcher health risks too of course.

J.P. Breen's Fantasy Take: Duran has a lot going for him. He has the stuff and the track record to make one comfortable that he'll miss bats in the majors; he has the size you'd ideally want in a starter; and he's poised to make his big-league debut in 2021. However, the questions about his command and his potential platoon split make Duran a potential roto risk in terms of rates. Overall, you're looking at a borderline top-100 dynasty prospect.

6   Jordan Balazovic   RHP   OFP: 55   ETA: 2021 or 2022

Born: 09/17/98   Age: 22   Bats: R   Throws: R   Height: 6'5"   Weight: 215   Origin: Round 5, 2016 Draft (#153 overall)

YEAR	TEAM	LVL	AGE	W	L	SV	G	GS	IP	H	HR	BB/9	K/9	K	GB%	BABIP	WHIP	ERA	DRA-	WARP
2018	CR	LO-A	19	7	3	0	12	11	61²	54	5	2.6	11.4	78	46.5%	.327	1.17	3.94	65	1.6
2019	CR	LO-A	20	2	1	0	4	4	20²	15	1	1.7	14.4	33	42.2%	.318	0.92	2.18	40	0.8
2019	FTM	HI-A	20	6	4	0	15	14	73	52	3	2.6	11.8	96	44.3%	.283	1.00	2.84	66	1.6
2021 FS	MIN	MLB	22	1	2	0	57	0	50	47	7	3.8	9.6	53	38.2%	.299	1.38	4.69	115	-0.3
2021 DC	MIN	MLB	22	1	2	0	6	6	29	27	4	3.8	9.6	30	38.2%	.299	1.38	4.69	115	0.1

Comparables: Stephen Gonsalves, Lucas Giolito, Dustin May

The Report: When drafting projectable—albeit ultra skinny—cold-weather pitchers, you hope to see them blossom into what Balazovic is turning into. A slow mover to date, the 6-foot-5 righty has continued to add strength and could be in line for a big league promotion in the coming year. His extremely long levers act as a slight-of-hand during his delivery, with his mid-90s heater getting on hitters quickly. The release point is lower than you'd think for such a tall pitcher, which gives the fastball a sideways sink in its action. Despite the late movement, it doesn't play like a typical sinker because of all the deception. Atypical describes a lot of his game, being able to repeat his mechanics and throw a lot of strikes for his age while also mixing in at least two average-to-better breaking balls is a credit to his body control.

Development Track: The knock until now was the concern over whether his frame could add the necessary weight to survive a full season of starting. There have been no hiccups yet, succeeding at every challenge thrown his way thus far. Now as he begins to round out his game in preparation for The Show, what's left is continued work on a changeup that should be able to play off his fastball shape against lefty batters.

Variance: Medium. Nothing about what he does on the mound is conventional by almost any measure. He shouldn't have such control of his pitches, his arm should have had something barking by now, and yet he's proving what works for him is still getting better.

J.P. Breen's Fantasy Take: Balazovic profiles as a safe (at least, safe for a pitching prospect) bet to make it as a starter. When we normally hear about deceptive fastballs, they're struggling to stay above 90 mph, but the right-hander runs it into the mid-90s and misses bats with it. Balazovic also throws strikes and has a pair of breaking balls. I love high-floor profiles when they're paired with moderate upside, and it's not a stretch to think that, if the changeup develops a bit, Balazovic can flirt with an SP2 season or two. I'd take Balazovic over Duran in both redraft and dynasty formats in 2021.

7 Matt Canterino RHP   OFP: 55   ETA: 2022

Born: 12/14/97 Age: 23 Bats: R Throws: R Height: 6'2" Weight: 222 Origin: Round 2, 2019 Draft (#54 overall)

YEAR	TEAM	LVL	AGE	W	L	SV	G	GS	IP	H	HR	BB/9	K/9	K	GB%	BABIP	WHIP	ERA	DRA-	WARP
2019	CR	LO-A	21	1	1	0	5	5	20	6	0	3.1	11.2	25	48.8%	.146	0.65	1.35	41	0.7
2021 FS	MIN	MLB	23	2	3	0	57	0	50	47	8	5.2	8.9	49	40.0%	.291	1.53	5.14	122	-0.5

Comparables: Cal Quantrill, James Russell, Ben Lively

The Report: The Twins used their second-round pick in 2019 on a very second-roundish college arm. Canterino was a three-year starter at Rice who missed bats with a potential plus fastball/slider combo. The minimal physical projection, along with a hitchy delivery made it easy to cast him as a 95-and-a-slider type reliever. Which we did last year. He had upside past that, but was an OFP 50 type with relief risk in a very good and deep system, so it would be easy for him to get lost in the shuffle and end up, say, 18th on last year's Twins list.

Development Track: One of the themes of the prospect team's Fungo essay in this year's Baseball Prospectus *Annual* is the difficulty in identifying breakout prospects given the dearth of data for players who didn't accrue major league time. With Canterino though there were two notable skill changes: He added a tick or two on the fastball, but more importantly, his changeup—previously a below-average afterthought in his arsenal, now has plus projection. That rounds out a starter's arsenal with three potential above-average MLB offerings. We need to see how it all works in real games, and the delivery and command concerns remain, but the arrow is clearly pointing up.

Variance: High. The gains in the profile haven't been seen in games yet, and he might give the velocity back on a more regular pitching schedule. Also worth noting that while Rice isn't as Ricey as they once were, Canterino was used heavily there by modern college pitching standards. There's positive variance here as well though. If we see the improvements translate on-field in 2021 he's not all that far off from a Top-101 arm.

J.P. Breen's Fantasy Take: File Canterino's name away and take him as a late-round pick in your dynasty supplemental draft. I'm reluctant to get too high on the righty until we see him throwing (and producing) every fifth day in Double-A this season. However, he's worth a speculative add in deeper dynasties, as he'll miss enough bats to be rosterable in all formats, if the latest reports prove accurate. And dynasty owners rarely have time to wait and see whether a prospect breakout is legit. Pounce early and cross your fingers.

8 Aaron Sabato 1B   OFP: 50   ETA: 2023

Born: 06/04/99 Age: 22 Bats: R Throws: R Height: 6'2" Weight: 230 Origin: Round 1, 2020 Draft (#27 overall)

The Report: Picture in your mind the prototypical slugging first baseman. What does he look like? A largely built, sometimes wide-bodied, plodding strongman who hits the ball really far and needs a position on the field to hide his lack of foot-speed and lateral movement. That appropriately describes Sabato, the first-round pick whose value will likely be exclusive to how much he hits. It's more power than contact—he's still able to work a count and take his fair share of walks—and the swing is catered to generate loft thanks to his back posture bent slightly at the waist. The above-average bat-speed also helps with the exit velo, staying mostly in control without selling out too much for hard contact.

Development Track: While technically "old" for a draft-eligible sophomore, he's around the same age as most juniors in this class. The calling card being the power bat, he will need to see as much quality pitching as possible to be tested. His body is ready-made as is, the defense and running will likely plateau soon if not already. Get the man in the lineup and see where it takes him.

Variance: High. If it turns out his swing can be exposed and he can't adjust, there is little left he can contribute.

J.P. Breen's Fantasy Take: A top-20 dynasty player in the 2020 draft class, Sabato must hit for both average and power to be both fantasy and real-life relevant. Currently, as the above report indicates, it's power-over-hit, which is readily obtainable from a first baseman. He'll get popped earlier than he probably should be in offseason supplemental drafts, as first-round first basemen often are, but he has a legit pathway to being an impact big-league bat.

9 Keoni Cavaco SS   OFP: 50   ETA: 2025
Born: 06/02/01   Age: 20   Bats: R   Throws: R   Height: 6'2"   Weight: 195   Origin: Round 1, 2019 Draft (#13 overall)

YEAR	TEAM	LVL	AGE	PA	R	2B	3B	HR	RBI	BB	K	SB	CS	AVG/OBP/SLG	DRC+	BABIP	BRR	FRAA	WARP
2019	TWI	ROK	18	92	9	4	0	1	6	4	35	1	1	.172/.217/.253		.275			
2021 FS	MIN	MLB	20	600	41	26	2	7	47	25	276	6	2	.196/.236/.289	42	.365	-0.8	SS 1	-2.5

Comparables: Niko Goodrum, Kaleb Cowart, Steven Baron

The Report: No player in the 2019 draft had as much helium attached to their name as Cavaco, whose growth spurt and sterling spring high school season helped him fly up draft boards, ultimately landing with the Twins 13

th

pick in the first round. The 6-foot-2 19-year-old is strong, and has smooth transitions with his hands that could play at multiple positions, and with measurables off the charts. Despite the present strength, he still projects for more, and the raw power is present even when the swing gets a little disconnected. He's the kind of player you dream on after a lot of little things go right, and he needs more experience to get there.

Development Track: Add him to the group of players who were likely most impacted by not having a year's worth of games to help them developmentally. He was hampered by a minor injury after being drafted and was expected to get his feet underneath him with a full 2020 campaign. Slotted in at shortstop during his brief pro debut, it will be interesting to see how much rust is attached to the glove in 2021. He has the ability to cover any number of positions, including second, third, or perhaps even center field.

Variance: Extreme. There's nothing to suggest he couldn't become a stud, but the delta remains huge given that it remains mostly projection at this stage. Such a high variance on a young player, we look forward to getting a better look soon.

J.P. Breen's Fantasy Take: Cavaco is a high-variance, high-reward prospect. Unlike Royce Lewis, however, Cavaco isn't a consensus top-100 dynasty prospect, thanks to injuries and the COVID-19 shutdown of Minor League Baseball. That should make the gamble much more attractive to dynasty owners. Cavaco is a hyped prospect who could fly into the top-30 prospects with a big 2021 campaign. In that sense, now is the time to acquire him. Conversely, he could spin his wheels in 2021 and quickly be forgotten like Estevan Florial.

10 Brent Rooker OF   OFP: 50   ETA: Debuted in 2020
Born: 11/01/94   Age: 26   Bats: R   Throws: R   Height: 6'3"   Weight: 225   Origin: Round 1, 2017 Draft (#35 overall)

YEAR	TEAM	LVL	AGE	PA	R	2B	3B	HR	RBI	BB	K	SB	CS	AVG/OBP/SLG	DRC+	BABIP	BRR	FRAA	WARP
2018	CHA	AA	23	568	72	32	4	22	79	56	150	6	1	.254/.333/.465	115	.316	-4.7	1B(47) -5.7, LF(44) -8.2	-1.2
2019	TWI	ROK	24	7	2	0	0	0	0	1	0	0	0	.333/.429/.333		.333			
2019	ROC	AAA	24	274	41	16	0	14	47	35	95	2	0	.281/.398/.535	122	.417	2.6	LF(56) -0.6	1.5
2020	MIN	MLB	25	21	4	2	0	1	5	0	5	0	0	.316/.381/.579	102	.385		RF(4) -0.1, LF(1) -0.1	0.0
2021 FS	MIN	MLB	26	600	61	25	2	17	67	50	207	1	0	.209/.288/.364	83	.301	0.1	LF -9, 1B 0	-0.8
2021 DC	MIN	MLB	26	269	27	11	0	8	30	22	92	0	0	.209/.288/.364	83	.301	0.0	LF -4	-0.3

Comparables: Travis Demeritte, Matt Clark, Will Craig

The Report: The Twins drafted Rooker twice, finally getting their man as a redshirt junior, following a season where he laid waste to the SEC to the tune of a .387/.495/.810 slash line. He's hit everywhere since. Rooker is not quite the hulking corner slugger you might envision, he's stooping but on the lean side, shorter with the bat path than you might expect, but with the requisite strength, stiffness, and leverage to bring plenty of pop but commensurate swing-and-miss as well. If he hits .250, the walks and power make him a useful regular, and he turns on enough inside fastballs you might project him to get there. Rooker also swings through enough breakers in the zone where you worry he might be a Quad-A slugger. But so far no level of pitching has been able to keep him from his appointed mashing.

Development Track: Rooker got a spot of major league time when Max Kepler hit the IL in early September and cracked his first major league home run and a couple extra base hits to go with it. He's 26 now and there's some surety in the profile. Given enough playing time he can hit you 30 home runs, get on base enough to prop up fringy batting averages, and stand in a few different spots. You're buying the bat here, and it's a good bat.

Variance: Low. Rooker has never not hit, up to and including his brief 2020 Twins cameo, but the underlying offensive tools might not be loud enough to carry the overall profile past useful. But hey, that's useful.

J.P. Breen's Fantasy Take: Rooker has strong Hunter Renfroe vibes, and not the Hunter Renfroe from the first half of 2019. The breaking-ball issues will always make Rooker a platoon risk, and the power needs to be special to overcome his projected AVG and SB shortcomings in fantasy. Treat him like a fringe top-250 dynasty prospect.

The Prospects You Meet Outside The Top Ten

Prospects to dream on a little bit

Josh Winder RHP Born: 10/11/96 Age: 24 Bats: R Throws: R Height: 6'5" Weight: 210 Origin: Round 7, 2018 Draft (#214 overall)

YEAR	TEAM	LVL	AGE	W	L	SV	G	GS	IP	H	HR	BB/9	K/9	K	GB%	BABIP	WHIP	ERA	DRA-	WARP
2018	ELZ	ROK	21	3	1	0	9	9	38²	37	1	1.4	9.8	42	33.9%	.333	1.11	3.72		
2019	CR	LO-A	22	7	2	0	21	21	125²	93	10	2.1	8.5	118	35.8%	.252	0.98	2.65	66	2.9
2021 FS	MIN	MLB	24	2	3	0	57	0	50	50	7	3.5	7.5	41	32.0%	.292	1.39	4.59	111	-0.2

Comparables: Bryan Price, Wes Parsons, Austin Voth

The Twins' seventh round pick in 2018 out of VMI, Winder showed up at instructs this year sitting mid-90s with his fastball, a big bump over his college velocity. He has a full mix of secondaries backing the fastball, all of which have above-average potential. Like with Canterino—and really even more so given their respective track records—we'll need to see the stuff in a more normal year before we jot down these improvements in ink, but you could certainly argue on upside and perhaps even OFP that he deserves to pip Rooker for the 10th spot in the system.

Misael Urbina CF Born: 04/26/02 Age: 19 Bats: R Throws: R Height: 6'0" Weight: 175 Origin: International Free Agent, 2018

YEAR	TEAM	LVL	AGE	PA	R	2B	3B	HR	RBI	BB	K	SB	CS	AVG/OBP/SLG	DRC+	BABIP	BRR	FRAA	WARP
2019	DSL TWI	ROK	17	217	34	14	5	2	26	23	14	19	8	.279/.382/.443		.290			

We got strong reports on Urbina in 2019, but tend to play it safe with IFAs with minimal stateside experience. It was going to be tough for Urbina to "break out" in 2020 given he was thrown to the lions, or at least a bunch of the pitchers residing in the top half of the list. Urbina held his own at the alternate site despite the degree of difficulty, which is all you can really ask of your teenaged hitting prospects in 2020.

MLB bats, but less upside than you'd like

Gilberto Celestino CF Born: 02/13/99 Age: 22 Bats: R Throws: L Height: 6'0" Weight: 170 Origin: International Free Agent, 2015

YEAR	TEAM	LVL	AGE	PA	R	2B	3B	HR	RBI	BB	K	SB	CS	AVG/OBP/SLG	DRC+	BABIP	BRR	FRAA	WARP
2018	ELZ	ROK	19	117	13	4	1	1	13	6	16	8	2	.266/.308/.349		.301			
2018	TRI	SS	19	142	18	8	0	4	21	10	25	14	0	.323/.387/.480	167	.374	1.6	CF(16) 0.9, RF(12) 2.6, LF(3) -0.8	1.2
2019	CR	LO-A	20	503	52	24	3	10	51	48	81	14	8	.276/.350/.409	137	.317	-3.6	CF(83) 3.7, RF(25) -3.6	3.0
2019	FTM	HI-A	20	33	6	4	0	0	3	2	4	0	0	.300/.333/.433	124	.333	0.2	CF(4) -0.8, RF(3) -0.3	0.0
2021 FS	MIN	MLB	22	600	58	27	2	11	59	36	170	13	3	.228/.280/.348	74	.307	2.9	CF 2, RF 0	0.3

Comparables: Jake Cave, Domonic Brown, Dalton Pompey

Celestino also had a case for No. 10 in the system, a ranking he held this time last year. He's a near mirror image of Rooker, a center fielder who can go get it in the gaps, but has limited upside with the bat. He's not an empty wizard, to quote one of my predecessors, and even average production with the stick would make him a solid or better regular. He shows good bat speed, but not much loft so he will need to sting a fair amount of doubles into the gap to make it as an everyday center fielder. For now we will bet on the player we are more confident will hit (to be the 10th best prospect in a good system).

Interesting Draft Follows

Alerick Soularie OF Born: 07/05/99 Age: 22 Bats: R Throws: R Height: 6'0" Weight: 175 Origin: Round 2, 2020 Draft (#59 overall)

A big time producer, first in JuCo and then at the University of Tennessee, Soularie's game can best be summarized by the characteristics of his swing: It's in-between. He's not really an infielder, lacking the arm to play anywhere but second base. He's not really a center fielder, with decent speed it's not the plus wheels or instincts you'd prefer there. Not really a power hitter, despite showing an ability to carry his raw power into games thanks to an innate ability to lift the ball. The hands get really loose as the pitch approaches, finishing belt-high with an elongated stride. It's funky, but it works. Fact is: he gets the job done, it isn't always pretty, and maybe with some refinement there's more there.

Marco Raya Born: 08/07/02 Age: 18 Bats: R Throws: R Height: 6'0" Weight: 165 Origin: Round 4, 2020 Draft (#128 overall)

The Twins' fourth-round pick in 2020, Raya is a non-traditional Texas prep arm. Listed at 6-foot-0 (so probably 5-foot-10) and with minimal physical projection, he's a relatively advanced high school arm who will show four potentially average-or-better pitches. The fastball is low-90s with good spin, but you may not wring much more out there. His loose, uptempo delivery only has mild effort given his size, and he's worth … well, a follow to see how the secondaries progress under pro instruction.

Top Talents 25 and Under (as of 4/1/2021):

1. Royce Lewis, IF/OF
2. Luis Arraez, 2B
3. Alex Kirilloff, OF/1B
4. Trevor Larnach, OF
5. Ryan Jeffers, C
6. Jhoan Duran, RHP
7. Jordan Balazovic, RHP
8. Matt Canterino, RHP
9. Aaron Sabato, 1B
10. Jorge Alcala, RHP

Luis Arraez is now a .331 hitter over 487 plate appearances in the majors, which is a lot more than you can reasonably fluke your way into. He's probably not
that

good because hardly anybody is a true talent .330-plus hitter, but Arraez clearly has elite bat-to-ball skills. There's little power here and really the hit tool is carrying the entire profile, but all that's okay if you're a batting champion-in-waiting, and he might be.

Just tagging along on the bottom of the list is reliever Jorge Alcala. Alcala was the last player omitted from our top 20 prospects last year, when he was still mid-relief conversion. He made the full-time switch for 2020, and his velocity jumped more consistently into the upper-90s; he also threw nearly as many hard sliders as he threw fastballs, along with the occasional hard change. He was very effective, and seems headed down a late-game reliever path.

New York Mets

The State of the System:

The Mets' new ownership and front office will have to do a fair bit of work to build out a very shallow system, but aggressive moves at the top of the last two drafts mean the cupboard isn't completely bare.

The Top Ten:

★ ★ ★ *2021 Top 101 Prospect* **#42** ★ ★ ★

1 Ronny Mauricio SS   OFP: 60   ETA: Late-2022

Born: 04/04/01   Age: 20   Bats: S   Throws: R   Height: 6'3"   Weight: 166   Origin: International Free Agent, 2017

YEAR	TEAM	LVL	AGE	PA	R	2B	3B	HR	RBI	BB	K	SB	CS	AVG/OBP/SLG	DRC+	BABIP	BRR	FRAA	WARP
2018	MTS	ROK	17	212	26	13	3	3	31	10	31	1	6	.279/.307/.421		.310			
2018	KNG	ROK	17	35	6	3	0	0	4	3	9	1	0	.233/.286/.333		.304			
2019	COL	LO-A	18	504	62	20	5	4	37	23	99	6	10	.268/.307/.357	100	.330	2.9	SS(106) -0.1	2.3
2021 FS	NYM	MLB	20	600	45	26	3	7	50	30	168	3	4	.220/.263/.318	57	.301	-5.0	SS 2	-1.6

Comparables: Cole Tucker, Alcides Escobar, Andrew Velazquez

The Report: Mauricio was aggressively sent to the South Atlantic League in 2019, making his full-season debut on his 18th birthday. He didn't exactly shine there statistically, but he held his own given his age. His hit tool plays as a potential plus, with good feel for hitting and plus bat speed. His game power is theoretical at present, but he has above-average-to-plus raw and could get there in games with further physical development and additional loft in his swing. Both his hit tool and power are currently limited in games by his aggressiveness at the plate; he walked less than five percent of the time in 2019. Defensively, Mauricio currently has the range for shortstop, with an obvious third base fallback if he grows off the position. There is still a lot of projection here, so there are several different forms his ultimate MLB profile could take.

Development Track: Mauricio was brought to the alternate site in mid-August. He struggled there against more advanced pitching than he was ready for, although his abilities still flashed well. Mets fall instructs were cut short, so he didn't have a major opportunity to rebound there. We're holding his report largely steady since we don't have a ton to go on, honestly; what information we have suggests that he was about where he would've been had he played 2020 as a teenager in High-A as expected.

Variance: High. A year of lost reps at 19 probably isn't great here, and we're optimistic he gets on track in 2021.

Mark Barry's Fantasy Take: The promise of a little extra pop in Mauricio's stick is nice, but honestly, you had me at the potentially plus hit tool. There's very little chance you're getting steals from Mauricio, as he's been thrown out twice as often as he has been successful, but at peak he's a four-category contributor. As it stands now, I'd have him in the top-40ish range for dynasty prospects.

★ ★ ★ *2021 Top 101 Prospect* **#79** ★ ★ ★

2 Matthew Allan   RHP   OFP: 60   ETA: Late 2022 / Early 2023

Born: 04/17/01   Age: 20   Bats: R   Throws: R   Height: 6'3"   Weight: 225   Origin: Round 3, 2019 Draft (#89 overall)

YEAR	TEAM	LVL	AGE	W	L	SV	G	GS	IP	H	HR	BB/9	K/9	K	GB%	BABIP	WHIP	ERA	DRA-	WARP
2019	MTS	ROK	18	1	0	0	5	4	8¹	5	0	4.3	11.9	11	31.6%	.263	1.08	1.08		
2019	BRK	SS	18	0	0	0	1	1	2	5	0	4.5	13.5	3	42.9%	.714	3.00	9.00	136	0.0
2021 FS	NYM	MLB	20	2	3	0	57	0	50	51	8	6.2	8.7	48	35.6%	.308	1.72	6.20	141	-1.0

Comparables: Tyler Glasnow, Eduardo Rodriguez, Noah Syndergaard

The Report: Allan was a first-round talent in the 2019 draft who slipped to the third reportedly because of bonus demands. The Mets scraped together $2.5 million, picking almost entirely under-slot senior signs after him to make the money work. It sure looks like it's paying early dividends. Allan showed mid-90s heat and a potential plus curveball in the complex and at Coney Island, and the pitchability and command were advanced for a teenaged arm. His 6-foot-3, 225-lb. frame is functionally the ideal size for a pitching prospect and there's no concerning markers in his delivery. The only real quibbles you could have with Allan coming into 2020 is the changeup needed work—although, again less so compared to most of his cohort—he hadn't pitched a full pro season, and the track record of non-elite righty prep arms is a lot more noise than signal.

Development Track: Allan spent about a month at the Mets' alternate site in Brooklyn, then a little less than that at instructs. When on the mound, he showed a little more top-end velocity and big spin rates on both his fastball and curveball. Without a 2020 season, the same quibbles remain, but the stuff is getting harder to ignore. Arms of this quality dictate their own time table, and while I'd expect Allan to start the season in Low-A St. Lucie, he might be back on the beaches of Kings County before the water is warm enough to take a dip.

Variance: High. All the usual young pitching prospect concerns here. Limited pro track record, command and change need grade jumps, generic injury risk. Conversely he's one good, healthy year with moderate improvements in the profile from potential being a Top 50 prospect in baseball. That happens to 20-year-old arms with this kind of stuff, too.

Mark Barry's Fantasy Take: We were all robbed of something in 2020, but dynasty-wise, it's not hard to envision Allan putting up a dominant performance in A-ball and shooting up prospect lists across the industry. The fact that it didn't happen, while bad for his publicist, is good for dynasty managers, as there's still some time to get in on a high-upside prep arm before he takes off (or, you know, before he falls apart because pitchers). The risks are evergreen, but his ceiling makes Allan an interesting gamble.

★ ★ ★ *2021 Top 101 Prospect* **#84** ★ ★ ★

3 Francisco Alvarez   C   OFP: 60   ETA: 2024

Born: 11/19/01   Age: 19   Bats: R   Throws: R   Height: 5'11"   Weight: 220   Origin: International Free Agent, 2018

YEAR	TEAM	LVL	AGE	PA	R	2B	3B	HR	RBI	BB	K	SB	CS	AVG/OBP/SLG	DRC+	BABIP	BRR	FRAA	WARP
2019	MTS	ROK	17	31	8	4	0	2	10	4	4	0	1	.462/.548/.846		.500			
2019	KNG	ROK+	17	151	24	6	0	5	16	17	33	1	1	.289/.385/.453		.356			
2021 FS	NYM	MLB	19	600	49	26	2	9	53	36	194	2	1	.219/.273/.324	64	.318	-1.1	C 0	-0.4

Comparables: Wil Myers, Joey Gallo, Oscar Hernández

The Report: If you've got two recent big ticket IFAs with 60 OFPs in your top three, you've done pretty well in your international scouting department. Alvarez is a power-over-hit prospect offensively, driven by great bat speed and strength. Unlike Mauricio, his power has already shown up in games. The hit tool isn't bad either, and it's buoyed by an advanced plate approach for his age. We're not 100 percent sure he's going to stick at catcher, but all of the signs are positive; he's looked like a good receiver with an above-average arm so far. If the rigors of catching don't cause him to stagnate, he has a chance to be a very good player in a few years time.

Development Track: Alvarez is down a spot on this list, but don't mistake that for us being down on him. His stock is actually slightly up, it's just that Allan's stock is up more. Alvarez performed well at the alternate site after being added around the same time as the prior two players. He tweaked his swing to try and tap into even more power, and got some catching time in. Given that short-season would've been a reasonable 2020 assignment anyway, we don't think much developmental time was lost for him, either.

Variance: Extreme. He's a teenage catcher who hasn't played above rookie ball yet.

Mark Barry's Fantasy Take: I remember 2019. It was a simpler time. I hung out with people. My favorite team wasn't on the verge of trading its best player *(Ed. Note: Cleveland)*. And I still believed in catching prospects. I'm not here to question your beliefs. If you're still a compiler of dynasty catchers, that's fine, and Alvarez is definitely one of your better options. He's just really far away and probably won't see returns for another 3-4 seasons, so be patient.

4 Pete Crow-Armstrong OF OFP: 55 ETA: 2024
Born: 03/25/02 Age: 19 Bats: L Throws: L Height: 6'1" Weight: 180 Origin: Round 1, 2020 Draft (#19 overall)

The Report: Playing at one of the premiere baseball factory high schools in the country, PCA was an early add to the "follow list" for area scouts in southern California. He uses his feet to his benefit in every facet of the game, whether it's ranging in center field where his advanced glove is evident, or putting the ball in play and letting the wheels take over. It's a contact-oriented approach with the main question about his future being his eventual game power: Will it be too much of a line-drive swing resulting in below-average pop? Or can added muscle help with lift in the bat path?

Development Track: His draft stock was back on the upswing following an up-and-down three years that unfairly hyped him as a top-5 pick and then just as unfairly saw the pendulum swing the opposite way. There were flashes in the spring that the regular doubles and triples were turning into the four-bagger variety of extra base hits, something that will continue to hang over him as he gets into pro ball. His lean body keeps him fleet of foot, so adding too much weight might sacrifice his greatest asset.

Variance: High. There is a lot of belief that the bat will come along eventually. Relying so much on his glove and speed, finding a way to impact the game in other ways will not only improve the variance but also vault his OFP upwards. If not, then he's a bench player reserved for specific roles.

Mark Barry's Fantasy Take: The fantasy perception of PCA will rest with his power. If he can provide some pop, he'll be a top-50 guy in short order. That's not to say he'll get there, however. If the bat doesn't really develop he'd be relegated to a role as a speedy defensive replacement or fourth outfielder, good for a handful of steals for your fantasy fortune, but not much else.

5 Brett Baty 3B OFP: 55 ETA: 2023
Born: 11/13/99 Age: 21 Bats: L Throws: R Height: 6'3" Weight: 210 Origin: Round 1, 2019 Draft (#12 overall)

YEAR	TEAM	LVL	AGE	PA	R	2B	3B	HR	RBI	BB	K	SB	CS	AVG/OBP/SLG	DRC+	BABIP	BRR	FRAA	WARP
2019	MTS	ROK	19	25	5	3	0	1	8	5	6	0	0	.350/.480/.650		.462			
2019	KNG	ROK+	19	186	30	12	2	6	22	24	56	0	0	.226/.344/.445		.312			
2019	BRK	SS	19	17	2	1	0	0	3	6	3	0	0	.200/.529/.300	173	.286	-0.3	3B(2) -0.2	0.1
2021 FS	NYM	MLB	21	600	47	27	2	8	48	50	231	1	0	.186/.262/.291	53	.306	0.7	3B 0	-2.3

Comparables: Joey Gallo, Jamie Romak, Joc Pederson

The Report: Baty was picked in the top half of the first round on the strength of his bat, and the Texan projects as a middle-of-the-order slugger if the offense continues to develop. Baty's approach and plate discipline are advanced, and he already shows plus power to all fields in-game. While the body is already leaning a bit first base-ish and maybe he's not as smooth as you'd like at the hot corner, he's fine at third for now and the arm's strong enough for the left side. Baty can put a real sting into a baseball, but so far he's struggled to make consistent contact against high-level pitching. He drives the ball well the other way, but doesn't always turn around some of the better fastballs he sees.

Development Track: Baty's *raison d'etre* as he enters full season ball will be refining the hit tool so that the patience and power really play, and making sure he remains at third so that the value of these things plays up. So he's still got most of the ladder to climb.

Variance: High. He hasn't yet played full-season ball and the hit tool that should be his calling card hasn't yet solidified.

Mark Barry's Fantasy Take: For dynasty, Baty is probably the second-best prospect in the system. He still has work to do, sure, but the bat is projectable and for our purposes, it really doesn't matter whether he plays first base or third base (or, what the hell, left field—shout out Dom Smith).

6 J.T. Ginn RHP   OFP: 55   ETA: 2024
Born: 05/20/99   Age: 22   Bats: R   Throws: R   Height: 6'2"   Weight: 200   Origin: Round 2, 2020 Draft (#52 overall)

The Report: Originally drafted in the first round by the Dodgers in 2018, Ginn opted to go to Mississippi State and bet on himself for a bigger payday. Following a very strong freshman season for the Bulldogs, he was primed and ready for a breakout season as a draft-eligible sophomore. That season was even shorter than most this past spring, as Ginn needed Tommy John surgery after only one start. When healthy, he possesses one of the best fastballs around because of its elite movement. Still pumping in the low-to-mid 90s, he can locate to either side with arm-side run reminiscent of a Wiffle ball. The secondaries could use some work, with both a slider and changeup lagging behind the quality of the heater.

Development Track: Ginn will enter spring training nearly a year removed from reconstructive elbow surgery, so there will be no rush to get him into games until the Mets believe he's fully capable. There is some reliever risk to the profile, so maybe it wouldn't be the worst thing to build him up through a bullpen role in 2021 before lengthening him back out.

Variance: High. As good as modern elbow surgeries have become, recovery is still different for everyone. Second, there was bullpen-role risk even before the injury It's wait-and-see until he steps on the field.

Mark Barry's Fantasy Take: If there's room on your roster to stash Ginn, I'd take a flier on the talent and pre-TJ stuff. If not, he's a watchlist candidate, for sure, keeping a special eye on how his secondaries come back post-surgery.

7 Mark Vientos 3B   OFP: 55   ETA: 2022
Born: 12/11/99   Age: 21   Bats: R   Throws: R   Height: 6'4"   Weight: 185   Origin: Round 2, 2017 Draft (#59 overall)

YEAR	TEAM	LVL	AGE	PA	R	2B	3B	HR	RBI	BB	K	SB	CS	AVG/OBP/SLG	DRC+	BABIP	BRR	FRAA	WARP
2018	KNG	ROK	18	262	32	12	0	11	52	37	43	1	0	.287/.389/.489		.312			
2019	COL	LO-A	19	454	48	27	1	12	62	22	110	1	4	.255/.300/.411	122	.311	-5.2	3B(100) -3.0	1.5
2021 FS	NYM	MLB	21	600	51	27	1	13	58	38	186	0	0	.210/.266/.336	64	.291	-1.4	3B 0, SS 0	-1.7

Comparables: Nick Castellanos, Neftali Soto, Rio Ruiz

The Report: The profile on Vientos is actually pretty similar to Baty's, just with less pedigree and an approach at the plate that's not quite as advanced. Though he's lean with some physical projection remaining, Vientos shows plus power to all fields; if there's a tool that will pave his path forward it's the pop. The third base defense is average but he should be able to stay there. The swing is a bit long and the hit tool will be, as it often is, the determining factor here.

Development Track: Wherever 2021 finds him, Vientos will be looking to improve his contact rate, and a bump in plate discipline wouldn't hurt either. How far he goes next year and beyond will be contingent on this. Whatever happens, he's still got a ways to go.

Variance: High. There's uncertainty in the hit tool and he hasn't played above Low-A.

Mark Barry's Fantasy Take: I wish Vientos would strike out less. Sitting down to strikes a quarter of the time in A-ball is not something that particularly bodes well for the future. Still, there's some power in the bat, and I'd be willing to roll the dice in deeper leagues. As it stands not, Vientos is probably a fringe-top-150 dude.

8 Josh Wolf RHP   OFP: 55   ETA: 2023
Born: 09/01/00   Age: 20   Bats: R   Throws: R   Height: 6'3"   Weight: 170   Origin: Round 2, 2019 Draft (#53 overall)

YEAR	TEAM	LVL	AGE	W	L	SV	G	GS	IP	H	HR	BB/9	K/9	K	GB%	BABIP	WHIP	ERA	DRA-	WARP
2019	MTS	ROK	18	0	1	0	5	5	8	9	0	1.1	13.5	12	40.0%	.450	1.25	3.38		
2021 FS	NYM	MLB	20	2	3	0	57	0	50	50	8	4.9	8.4	46	37.5%	.299	1.55	5.37	127	-0.6

Comparables: Hunter Harvey, Elvis Luciano, Liam Hendriks

The Report: Wolf comes right out of central casting for a projectable second-round Texas prep arm. A lean 6-foot-3 with a velocity spike his draft year, Wolf projects to sit mid-90s as he fills out and adds strength in his 20s. The second pitch is a big downer curve. He was drafted as a two-pitch power arm who was a ways off from that projection—which is the difference between first-round Texas prep arms and second-round Texas prep arms, generally speaking—but Wolf injected some upside into an organization that badly needed it on the pitching side.

Development Track: As already mentioned, the Mets were very conservative with regards to bringing non-40-man prospects to the alternate site. Wolf threw at instructs where the reports were uneven, but given the nature of the 2020 "season" we're generally giving a pass to guys where that's the case. 2021 will be an important year for his development, which is boilerplate language for our lists at this point, but still holds true for a lot of 2019 draftees.

Variance: High. Functionally everything that applies to Allan also applies to Wolf. There's also more reliever/durability risk.

Mark Barry's Fantasy Take: There was this FIFA World Cup video game (in, I wanna say, 2006) where the pre-programmed commentary would get awfully excited about an American named Wolf, breaking through the defense to goal. There wasn't much to it, just a supremely English gentleman screaming "WOLF" at the top of his lungs. At the time, my roommate and I found it extremely funny and would yell "Wolf" at each other a lot. Anyway, Mets Wolf is a high-upside dude with only two pitches at present. Right now it's watchlist stuff for me, but I hope he hits so I can scream "WOLF" at the top of my lungs and be the only one that thinks it's funny.

9 Isaiah Greene   OFP: 50   ETA: 2025
Born: 08/29/01   Age: 19   Bats: L   Throws: L   Height: 6'1"   Weight: 180   Origin: Round 2, 2020 Draft (#69 overall)

The Report: With a shortened draft and equally short evaluation period, there were bound to be numerous surprises, and you can mark Greene's selection prior to the third round as one such revelation. He performed very well in stints, flashing some pop as a natural low-ball hitter thanks to his trebuchet of a swing. It's a bit whippy with his hands and wrists twisting at load with a long follow-through. The swing is inefficient at present but despite the length Greene has some feel for the barrel. There is plenty of fluidity in his movements as a plus runner and he should be able to compete for reps with PCA in center field.

Development Track: It certainly is a high variance profile due to the questions about what becomes of the swing. Given that they were both high-pick prep center fielders by the Mets, there will naturally be comparisons between Greene and Crow-Armstrong. Whereas PCA has a longer track record of hitting, Greene may have the better power potential. In the latter's case, finding a consistent launch point and carrying that into games will be pivotal as he receives pro hitting instruction.

Variance: Extreme. The thing about selecting high variance high schoolers in a pandemic-rattled year is that they lose out on all the time that could have been spent tightening up areas of needed focus. It may be a slow start professionally while he works to adjust to everything new being thrown at him.

Mark Barry's Fantasy Take: Plus runner, you say? As the villainous Leonardo Dicaprio said in *Django Unchained*, you had my curiosity, now you have my attention. There's still a long time before that speed will translate to steals for your fantasy roster, but Greene is a sneaky-good name to keep an eye on after the usual suspects in your first-year player drafts.

10 Jaylen Palmer   3B   OFP: 50   ETA: 2024
Born: 07/31/00   Age: 20   Bats: R   Throws: R   Height: 6'3"   Weight: 195   Origin: Round 22, 2018 Draft (#650 overall)

YEAR	TEAM	LVL	AGE	PA	R	2B	3B	HR	RBI	BB	K	SB	CS	AVG/OBP/SLG	DRC+	BABIP	BRR	FRAA	WARP
2018	MTS	ROK	17	100	13	4	1	1	11	8	27	5	2	.310/.394/.414		.441			
2019	KNG	ROK+	18	276	41	12	2	7	28	31	108	1	3	.272/.357/.431		.471			
2021 FS	NYM	MLB	20	600	42	26	2	6	46	34	272	4	2	.188/.241/.283	43	.350	-1.6	3B 1, SS -1	-3.1

The Report: The Wilpon-era Mets loved a local kid, and Flushing's own Jaylen Palmer went to high school less than five miles from Citi Field. A high school growth spurt has left him a very projectable 6-foot-3 with already present plus raw pop. As he fills out you'd expect him to move off shortstop—he was already splitting time at third in the Appy—but he has the ranginess and arm to fit well at a number of spots in both the infield and outfield. The swing has some length to it, and he struggled with better spin even in rookie ball, so there's not much of a floor to the hit tool. But conversely you could argue he's got the most upside in the system as he could end up with plus game power with the ability to be average-or-better at multiple defensive spots. Palmer is a long way off from those heady heights, though.

Development Track: And of course he didn't get much closer to it in 2020. Palmer could have really used day-in and day-out reps in A-ball to get more comfortable seeing better velocity and secondaries. He spent some time at instructs, working on multiple defensive spots—I posited last year he'd be an intriguing center field prospect, and still think that holds true—but we won't have a good feel for how he's developing until 2021 game action. He functionally moves up on system attrition.

Variance: Extreme. Palmer has made real gains as a pro, but this is still mostly a projection bet. Two years from now he could be a Top 101 prospect, or have stalled out in A-ball.

Mark Barry's Fantasy Take: Oh lovely, two years away from a top-101 spot, which means he's two years away from being two years away from a spot in your fantasy lineup (it was clunky, but I sure do love the "two years away from being two years away" reasoning from Fran Fraschilla). Let's make a pact to meet back here in two years to figure out what we should do with Palmer.

The Prospects You Meet Outside The Top Ten

MLB-arms, but probably relievers

Franklyn Kilome   RHP   Born: 06/25/95   Age: 26   Bats: R   Throws: R   Height: 6'6"   Weight: 175   Origin: International Free Agent, 2013

YEAR	TEAM	LVL	AGE	W	L	SV	G	GS	IP	H	HR	BB/9	K/9	K	GB%	BABIP	WHIP	ERA	DRA-	WARP
2018	REA	AA	23	4	6	0	19	19	102	96	7	4.5	7.3	83	44.8%	.309	1.44	4.24	99	0.8
2018	BNG	AA	23	0	3	0	7	7	38	31	3	2.4	9.9	42	41.0%	.289	1.08	4.03	94	0.4
2020	NYM	MLB	25	0	1	1	4	0	11^1	14	5	7.1	10.3	13	34.3%	.310	2.03	11.12	138	-0.1
2021 FS	NYM	MLB	26	1	1	0	57	0	50	49	8	5.3	8.4	46	40.0%	.291	1.57	5.62	118	-0.4
2021 DC	NYM	MLB	26	1	1	0	34	0	36	35	6	5.3	8.4	33	40.0%	.291	1.57	5.62	118	-0.1

Comparables: Bryan Mitchell, Adrian Houser, Myles Jaye

Kilomé missed all of 2019 with Tommy John surgery. The Mets used him as an up-and-down depth arm in 2020, and he flashed the former Top 101 form from when he was in the Phillies system in glimpses while also getting shelled in general. Kilomé's been inconsistent with his command and velocity going back a long time now—one of the first things I wrote at BP was about his inconsistency from start-to-start and even inning-to-inning, and I've been here five years now. As a starter, he's probably no more than a back-end arm, and we'd really like to see him air it out with the fastball, which is sometimes mid-90s and touching higher, and the breaking ball, which we've had a plus projection on forever.

Sam McWilliams   RHP   Born: 09/04/95   Age: 25   Bats: R   Throws: R   Height: 6'7"   Weight: 230   Origin: Round 8, 2014 Draft (#232 overall)

YEAR	TEAM	LVL	AGE	W	L	SV	G	GS	IP	H	HR	BB/9	K/9	K	GB%	BABIP	WHIP	ERA	DRA-	WARP
2018	CHA	HI-A	22	0	1	0	3	3	11^2	13	0	2.3	5.4	7	47.5%	.325	1.37	3.86	88	0.1
2018	VIS	HI-A	22	1	1	0	5	5	25^2	20	1	2.1	11.2	32	50.8%	.317	1.01	2.10	67	0.6
2018	MTG	AA	22	6	7	0	19	15	100^1	111	13	3.6	8.4	94	37.0%	.338	1.50	5.02	118	-0.4
2019	MTG	AA	23	6	3	0	15	11	87^2	80	3	3.1	6.8	66	42.0%	.303	1.25	2.05	107	-0.4
2019	DUR	AAA	23	1	6	0	11	8	44	72	7	3.5	8.8	43	44.8%	.442	2.02	8.18	167	-0.6
2021 FS	NYM	MLB	25	1	1	0	57	0	50	50	7	3.5	7.3	40	40.8%	.292	1.41	4.91	111	-0.2
2021 DC	NYM	MLB	25	1	1	0	21	4	18	18	5	3.5	7.3	14	40.8%	.292	1.41	4.91	111	0.0

Comparables: Rookie Davis, Jakob Junis, Blake Wood

It's highly unusual to find a minor league free agent on a prospect list. The shallowness of this system has a lot to do with that, but McWilliams also wasn't your average MiLB FA. The Mets gave him a major league deal worth $750,000 to win a bidding war for the tall righty. He's been used as a starter for almost his entire minor league career, but a velocity bump into the upper-90s at the Rays alternate site makes him a logical candidate for the Mets 2021 pen. He could have substantial impact in that role, but the real impact might be the signal that the organization is getting more creative in acquiring talent. That will hopefully lead to the next McWilliams not being roughly the 13th-best prospect in the system.

Prospects to dream on a little

Freddy Valdez **RF** Born: 12/06/01 Age: 19 Bats: R Throws: R Height: 6'3" Weight: 212 Origin: International Free Agent, 2018

YEAR	TEAM	LVL	AGE	PA	R	2B	3B	HR	RBI	BB	K	SB	CS	AVG/OBP/SLG	DRC+	BABIP	BRR	FRAA	WARP
2019	DSL MET1	ROK	17	257	36	15	3	5	36	28	46	6	1	.268/.358/.432		.312			
2021 FS	NYM	MLB	19	600	45	26	2	7	49	35	225	28	9	.206/.257/.303	53	.329	2.1	RF -6	-2.7

Comparables: Joey Gallo, Bobby Bradley, Wil Myers

Valdez made last season's Mets list thanks in large part to the seven-figure bonus he got in 2018 and a scarcity of system depth. He's made this year's list as well, and I would be engaging in deceit if I were to tell you these factors weren't still at play. He did show promise in the Instructional League, and the fog surrounding his skill set is beginning to lift just a bit. 6-foot-3 and north of 200 lbs, the (just turned) 19-year-old really drives the ball and power-hitting right-fielder is the projection, but a realization of this potential is still beyond the horizon and contingent on what his hit tool looks like in full-season ball.

Alexander Ramírez Born: 01/13/03 Age: 18 Bats: R Throws: R Height: 6'3" Weight: 170 Origin: International Free Agent, 2019

Ramírez also signed for seven figures, inking a bonus above $2 million in 2019. The 17-year-old outfielder is strong defensively, plays a well-rounded game, and is already showing a bit of pop. As with Valdez, we'll have to see how the hit tool shows as he climbs the ladder and how well the power plays in-game.

Robert Dominguez **RHP** Born: 11/30/01 Age: 19 Bats: R Throws: R Height: 6'5" Weight: 195 Origin: International Free Agent, 2019

At 6-foot-5, 200 lbs, the 19-year-old Domínguez has what you might call a prototypical pitcher's frame. He also has a big right arm, popping the upper-90s consistently and touching triple digits with his fastball while showing secondary stuff and pitching sensibilities that are advanced for his age. There is naturally quite a bit of buzz around the 2019 signee, certainly more than is typical for an over-aged IFA who signed for five figures. There is stuff to dream on here, but also much that is yet to be revealed. We should have a better grasp of his command and control profile, for instance, once we get to see him face live competition.

Top Talents 25 and Under (as of 4/1/2021):

1. Dominic Smith, 1B/OF
2. Andres Gimenez, SS
3. Amed Rosario, SS
4. Ronny Mauricio, SS
5. Matthew Allan, RHP
6. Francisco Alvarez, C
7. Pete Crow-Armstrong, OF
8. Brett Baty, 3B
9. David Peterson, LHP
10. J.T. Ginn, RHP

This was one of the weirder 25U lists to place the MLB talent on—and I watch nearly every game of this team. Dominic Smith is on the verge of stardom, having already turned into a very good MLB hitter with surprising defensive versatility. He's hit .299/.366/.571 with 21 homers over 396 plate appearances stretching over 2019 and 2020, and he got well-deserved down-ballot MVP consideration in 2020. While he will never be a good defender in the outfield, he's worked like hell to become playable in left in a part-time role, and that's let the Mets get his bat in the lineup more.

Andrés Giménez and Amed Rosario feel like two ships passing in the night. Rosario was 2017's No. 7 overall prospect, and might've ranked even higher in 2018 if he hadn't graduated by a few weeks. But he's never consistently hit in the majors—he's just not able to put together good enough at-bats—and his glove at short has been disappointing as well, leading to talk of a move to third or center.

That opened the door for Giménez, who had fallen from No. 38 on our 2019 101 to No. 90 in 2020 amidst a backslide with his own hit tool projection as he tried to maximize his power. The Mets surprisingly broke camp with him, and even more surprisingly he stuck the entire season, playing his way up from fifth infielder to quasi-regular shortstop by the end of the season. Giménez's hit tool projection looked better, although not quite all the way back to the plus he was flashing in 2018, and his defense was extremely slick all over the infield even though he'd barely played second and third before.

I decided to put Giménez ahead of Rosario for now. Giménez is a plus defensive shortstop and younger, and offensively they're probably pretty close on true talent. Because of Rosario's bat speed and latent hit tool projection, he almost certainly still has higher upside, but he's over 1500 plate appearances deep and his plate approach has, if anything, regressed.

We've projected David Peterson as a no. 4 starter basically since he was drafted. He came up in 2020 and posted a 4.62 DRA, which is pretty much in line with that. Because he has a true out pitch—a gnarly slider—and the changeup flashed, he could theoretically start missing more bats at some point. If that happens, or his command improves, he could slide in as more of a no. 3 starter. Since he's proven the profile can work in the majors as-is, he slots in between the tier of 101 candidate prospects and the next group down, which is a tick up from his prospect days last year, where he was behind Wolf.

New York Yankees

The State of the System:
A deep, talent-rich org with immediate help for 2021 and beyond, finally things are looking up for the New York Yankees.

The Top Ten:

★ ★ ★ *2021 Top 101 Prospect* **#17** ★ ★ ★

1 **Deivi García** **RHP**   OFP: 70   ETA: Debuted in 2020
Born: 05/19/99   Age: 22   Bats: R   Throws: R   Height: 5'9"   Weight: 163   Origin: International Free Agent, 2015

YEAR	TEAM	LVL	AGE	W	L	SV	G	GS	IP	H	HR	BB/9	K/9	K	GB%	BABIP	WHIP	ERA	DRA-	WARP
2018	CSC	LO-A	19	2	4	0	8	8	40²	31	5	2.2	13.9	63	27.5%	.310	1.01	3.76	50	1.4
2018	TAM	HI-A	19	2	0	0	5	5	28¹	19	0	2.5	11.1	35	35.4%	.297	0.95	1.27	65	0.7
2018	TRN	AA	19	1	0	0	1	1	5	0	0	3.6	12.6	7	37.5%	.000	0.40	0.00	71	0.1
2019	TAM	HI-A	20	0	2	0	4	4	17²	14	0	4.1	16.8	33	50.0%	.438	1.25	3.06	72	0.3
2019	TRN	AA	20	4	4	0	11	11	53²	43	2	4.4	14.6	87	40.5%	.363	1.29	3.86	88	0.4
2019	SWB	AAA	20	1	3	0	11	6	40	39	8	4.5	10.1	45	36.7%	.313	1.48	5.40	105	0.6
2020	NYY	MLB	21	3	2	0	6	6	34¹	35	6	1.6	8.7	33	34.0%	.293	1.19	4.98	105	0.2
2021 FS	NYY	MLB	22	9	8	0	26	26	150	134	26	3.4	10.2	169	37.3%	.288	1.27	4.28	97	1.3
2021 DC	NYY	MLB	22	8	7	0	22	22	124	111	21	3.4	10.2	139	37.3%	.288	1.27	4.28	97	1.5

Comparables: Bryse Wilson, Sixto Sánchez, Luis Severino

The Report: Yes, García is deceptive, but don't let that term fool you—he has four average-or-better pitches and misses a ton of bats. His fastball is anywhere from 90-96 mph, and while it doesn't have particularly notable spin rates, it fools hitters; we think this is a combination of good shape and a difficult to pick up release point that comes from deception in his delivery and his height. His curveball is just a straight plus-plus breaking ball, a classic high-spin, two-plane bender that will serve as his out pitch and plays very well off his fastball. García also has a changeup that functions as an average arm-side offering and a slider which he developed over the course of 2019 that has flashed higher. Despite the deception, his delivery is low-effort, and he's run huge strikeout rates all over the minors even though he's always been one of the youngest players at his level.

Development Track: The Yankees called García up at the end of August. He flashed glimpses of frontline brilliance while making six league-average starts down the stretch just a few months after his 21st birthday. His command was significantly sharper than he'd shown in the minors; he was able to spot all of his pitches effectively around the zone.

Variance: Medium. We know the stuff can get past major-league hitters already, and the command profile looked a lot more consistent than it did previously. He's still a pitcher with an oddball profile, but that's about all that's working against him here.

Mark Barry's Fantasy Take: García was only okay in his first stint against big-league hitters, but let's not overthink this. Unless the Yankees go on a major spending spree between now and Opening Day, García should begin the season as the number-two starter in the Bronx. We don't know what kind of workload he'll be able to withstand early, but I'd expect plenty of strikeouts and wins in the meantime.

2 Jasson Dominguez CF   OFP: 70   ETA: 2024 or 2025
Born: 02/07/03   Age: 18   Bats: S   Throws: R   Height: 5'10"   Weight: 190   Origin: International Free Agent, 2019

The Report / Development Track: In last year's blurb we noted that we had very limited information with which to pin down a ranking for Dominguez. Almost nothing has changed in that regard. The demographics which suggest he's a top prospect (signing bonus, teenage showcase and tricky league reports) also would have applied to Kevin Maitan a few years ago. The reports were good mind you, a potential five-tool outfielder with light tower power. Dominguez was briefly stateside for spring training pre-shutdown, but was not invited to the alternate site, and the Yankees did not run domestic instructs in the Fall. Occasional Instagram video emerged of the 17-year-old—now built like a short-yardage running back that Gene Stallings would have recruited for his early 90s Alabama teams—taking massive home run cuts in some sort of live batting practice. We can safely conclude the raw power is still present, but beyond that we really have no idea what kind of prospect Dominguez is at this point.

Variance: Extreme. If I could go higher than extreme I would.

Mark Barry's Fantasy Take: Dominguez is a prime mystery box guy. He could be anything. He could be two tickets to a comedy club, or he could be a boat. Unfortunately he's being priced as a boat. He could absolutely be worth it, and judging on his Instagram feed, he could be quite exciting. It's just that his stock is already sky-high, so if you didn't already get in, you're likely to be priced out. I think Dominguez is a top-20ish dynasty prospect, and he's absolutely the type of player I'd be likely to flip for a veteran.

3 Clarke Schmidt RHP   OFP: 60   ETA: Debuted in 2020
Born: 02/20/96   Age: 25   Bats: R   Throws: R   Height: 6'1"   Weight: 200   Origin: Round 1, 2017 Draft (#16 overall)

YEAR	TEAM	LVL	AGE	W	L	SV	G	GS	IP	H	HR	BB/9	K/9	K	GB%	BABIP	WHIP	ERA	DRA-	WARP
2018	YAE	ROK	22	0	2	0	3	2	7²	8	1	2.3	14.1	12	50.0%	.412	1.30	7.04		
2018	YAW	ROK	22	0	0	0	3	3	7¹	4	0	2.5	9.8	8	68.8%	.250	0.82	1.23		
2018	SI	SS	22	0	1	0	2	2	8¹	4	0	2.2	10.8	10	36.8%	.211	0.72	1.08	245	-0.6
2019	YAE	ROK	23	0	0	0	3	3	8¹	6	1	3.2	15.1	14	56.2%	.333	1.08	3.24		
2019	TAM	HI-A	23	4	5	0	13	12	63¹	59	2	3.4	9.8	69	54.6%	.333	1.31	3.84	84	0.7
2019	TRN	AA	23	2	0	0	3	3	19	14	1	0.5	9.0	19	45.1%	.260	0.79	2.37	79	0.3
2020	NYY	MLB	24	0	1	0	3	1	6¹	7	0	7.1	9.9	7	42.1%	.368	1.89	7.11	90	0.1
2021 FS	NYY	MLB	25	8	9	0	26	26	150	147	26	4.1	8.8	146	39.9%	.295	1.44	5.05	111	0.1
2021 DC	NYY	MLB	25	5	6	0	19	19	93	91	16	4.1	8.8	91	39.9%	.295	1.44	5.05	111	0.4

Comparables: Dillon Peters, Jonathan Loaisiga, Elieser Hernandez

The Report: Schmidt's calling card is an elite two-plane breaking ball. It has slider velocity, sitting in the mid-80s, with curveball shape. Schmidt calls it a curveball. Whatever the nomenclature, the spin rates on it are top-of-the-league (3085 average rpm in 2020) and it's a visually stunning pitch. If he can command it, it has a chance to be one of the best breaking balls in the majors. Schmidt also has both four-seam and two-seam fastball varieties in the mid-90s, with the two-seamers generally looking the best to us and the four-seamers often showing significant cut.

Changeup development, command, and durability are all significant drags on Schmidt's profile. His change was a show-me pitch in the minors in 2019, and that continued in his brief 2020 MLB stint; he threw it less than 9 percent of the time. His command has come and gone. And Schmidt just hasn't pitched a whole lot as a pro, as the Yankees brought him back very slowly and very carefully from pre-draft Tommy John surgery, limiting his workload into the 2019 season.

Development Track: A few days after they called on García, the Yankees brought up Schmidt. He didn't pitch much, and he was wild and relatively ineffective, but his curveball spin rates remained obscene. Before things got shut down, Schmidt was one of the most impressive pitchers in the Grapefruit League, and we suspect he'd have gotten much more of an opportunity in a normal season.

Variance: High. Schmidt has a scant professional track record through his first four seasons, and the command and changeup would carry significant bullpen risk on their own.

Mark Barry's Fantasy Take: We've seen fewer than 120 professional innings from Schmidt, and he has been relatively steady, if not dominant. I'm a little worried about volume for Schmidt, but he has displayed a knack for missing bats at every stop, and should continue to do so in the Bronx if he can stay on the bump. His situation and upside keeps him above streamer status for me.

4 Luis Gil RHP   OFP: 60   ETA: Late 2022/2023

Born: 06/03/98 Age: 23 Bats: R Throws: R Height: 6'2" Weight: 185 Origin: International Free Agent, 2015

YEAR	TEAM	LVL	AGE	W	L	SV	G	GS	IP	H	HR	BB/9	K/9	K	GB%	BABIP	WHIP	ERA	DRA-	WARP
2018	PUL	ROK	20	2	1	0	10	10	39¹	21	1	5.7	13.3	58	34.2%	.256	1.17	1.37		
2018	SI	SS	20	0	2	0	2	2	6²	11	1	8.1	13.5	10	39.1%	.455	2.55	5.40	300	-0.9
2019	CSC	LO-A	21	4	5	0	17	17	83	60	1	4.2	12.1	112	47.2%	.311	1.19	2.39	80	1.3
2019	TAM	HI-A	21	1	0	0	3	3	13	11	0	5.5	7.6	11	40.5%	.297	1.46	4.85	115	-0.1
2021 FS	NYY	MLB	23	2	3	0	57	0	50	44	8	7.2	9.8	54	38.7%	.282	1.69	5.54	121	-0.5

Comparables: Domingo Germán, Albert Abreu, Gregory Infante

The Report: Out of the pitchers in the Yankees org who haven't debuted in the majors, Gil possibly has the highest ceiling. Owning the best fastball in the system, Gil creates downhill plane along with electrifying, late life on a pitch that can comfortably sit in the upper-90s. The heater is a true swing-and-miss offering already. During 2020, Gil worked on honing his strike-throwing ability, which was a concern after 2019. He also worked on getting his slurvy breaking ball to resemble more of a slider, adding a few ticks to it as well. Gil's low-90s changeup, similar to a power sinker, is also a potential plus offering.

Development Track: Gil has yet to eclipse 100 innings in his minor league career, and with no games during 2020, he may not be able to pass that mark in 2021 either. But right now, developing his breaking ball is more important. How this pitch develops will determine how fast he moves.

Variance: High. Although the fastball is currently plus, tinkering with the arsenal means there is still much that is unknown. Until we can see the secondary improvements play out in live games, and Gil has more successful innings above Low-A, reliever risk is still present—albeit with high-leverage potential.

Mark Barry's Fantasy Take: The lack of true secondary offerings keeps me off Gil Island for the time being, as I'm having a hard time shaking the reliever risk. He could be a very good reliever, mind you, but that's not something you should go out looking for. I'm passing for now, but I'll monitor the progress.

5 Luis Medina RHP   OFP: 60   ETA: Late 2022/2023

Born: 05/03/99 Age: 22 Bats: R Throws: R Height: 6'1" Weight: 175 Origin: International Free Agent, 2015

YEAR	TEAM	LVL	AGE	W	L	SV	G	GS	IP	H	HR	BB/9	K/9	K	GB%	BABIP	WHIP	ERA	DRA-	WARP
2018	PUL	ROK	19	1	3	0	12	12	36	32	3	11.5	11.8	47	42.7%	.337	2.17	6.25		
2019	CSC	LO-A	20	1	8	0	20	20	93	86	9	6.5	11.1	115	43.6%	.344	1.65	6.00	145	-2.1
2019	TAM	HI-A	20	0	0	0	2	2	10²	7	0	2.5	10.1	12	67.9%	.250	0.94	0.84	72	0.2
2021 FS	NYY	MLB	22	2	3	0	57	0	50	47	9	8.9	9.3	51	43.0%	.286	1.93	6.98	142	-1.1
2021 DC	NYY	MLB	22	0	0	0	3	3	14	13	2	8.9	9.3	14	43.0%	.286	1.93	6.98	142	-0.2

Comparables: Huascar Ynoa, Beau Burrows, Jefry Rodriguez

The Report: Medina's big turnaround happened late in the 2019 season. The key change for the right-hander's surge began when he started using his curveball more than half the time, helping his plus-plus fastball, which has touched as high as 102, play up even more. But it wasn't just the pitch mix that helped Medina. Gradually, he began throwing more strikes, cutting his walk rate down. In winter ball, that trend has continued. Over 11 2/3 innings in Liga de Baseball Professional Roberto Clemente, Medina has fanned 25 against just four walks. There are no obvious mechanical culprits for his previous wildness, so improving his strike rate even more with the curveball has been a point of emphasis throughout the year. With the curveball and fastball getting most of the attention, it is easy to forget about the 90 mph changeup. Even though it will mostly be used against lefties, it is a solid offering to round out a menacing arsenal.

Development Track: The 2020 season was lined up for Medina to make a significant jump in innings, after throwing around 100 the previous two years. He did get innings at the alternate site and in Puerto Rico, but the lost frames surely will push his timeline back. How much will depend on how normal the minors are in 2021 and if his dominant performances from High-A continues. Medina will only be entering his age-22 season so don't expect the Yankees to push him too fast.

Variance: High. Although the variance has shrunk over the last year-plus, the track record isn't quite there yet to alleviate all concerns. Medina has certainly raised the floor, but there's still a ways to go for the young hurler.

Mark Barry's Fantasy Take: Of the Bronx Luises, I actually prefer Medina to Gil for dynasty purposes. I have more confidence in Medina's ability to start long-term, and his arsenal is already fairly well developed. He'll need some polishing this season, but if he continues on this development path, it isn't difficult to imagine some SP2-SP3 seasons from Medina. I'm not sure that's enough to crack the top-100, but he'd be in that next group of 50 names for me.

6 Estevan Florial CF   OFP: 55   ETA: Debuted in 2020

Born: 11/25/97 Age: 23 Bats: L Throws: R Height: 6'1" Weight: 195 Origin: International Free Agent, 2015

YEAR	TEAM	LVL	AGE	PA	R	2B	3B	HR	RBI	BB	K	SB	CS	AVG/OBP/SLG	DRC+	BABIP	BRR	FRAA	WARP
2018	TAM	HI-A	20	339	45	16	3	3	27	44	87	11	10	.255/.354/.361	102	.353	-0.9	CF(59) 1.8, RF(6) -0.2, LF(3) -0.1	0.4
2019	TAM	HI-A	21	301	38	10	3	8	38	24	98	9	5	.237/.297/.383	92	.335	1.0	CF(64) 2.9	1.1
2020	NYY	MLB	22	3	0	0	0	0	0	0	2	0	0	.333/.333/.333	90	1.000		CF(1) -0.1	0.0
2021 FS	NYY	MLB	23	600	54	21	3	15	59	45	235	10	5	.208/.272/.344	66	.330	-1.9	CF 4, LF 0	-0.5
2021 DC	NYY	MLB	23	33	2	1	0	0	3	2	12	0	0	.208/.272/.344	66	.330	-0.1	CF 0	0.0

Comparables: Keon Broxton, Tommy Pham, Daniel Fields

The Report: Three years ago, we ranked Florial as the No. 26 prospect in baseball. He'd shown thunderous bat speed from the left side with big power potential, and we were pretty optimistic about him finding a good plate approach and ending up with an above-average hit tool. He'd shown up in the Double-A Eastern League playoffs as a teenager after seemingly mastering both full-season A-ball levels, and there was about as much scout buzz as any player in baseball.

Just about nothing has gone right for Florial since. He battled recurring hamate and wrist problems during 2018 and 2019, hitting poorly at return engagements in High-A when on the field. The pitch recognition and plate approach went backwards, and we haven't seen the potentially above-average hit tool in a few years either. The bat speed and raw power are still there, but he hasn't been able to get to it in games.

Development Track: The Yankees called Florial up as a spare outfielder when needed; you can probably tell throughout this chapter that they weren't shy about calling prospects up. He started a game in center and looked overmatched twice against Michael Wacha before roping a single off Walker Lockett. He did go to the Dominican this winter and got some at-bats in during the LIDOM season, playing well there, but a mostly-lost season for a player who needed to get things back on track is never good.

Variance: High. Florial really needed a healthy consolidation season, and it's hard to tell where he's at lacking much new information.

Mark Barry's Fantasy Take: Florial's prospect status joins the long list of New York falls from grace that includes former mayors, former shortstops (before a return to grace?), and the Knicks. Admittedly that's a bit harsh, but since peaking at number 26 on the 2018 101, Florial has done little else to instill confidence that he can restore the buzz. I hope he has a moment, but I think the consistency(or lack thereof) those moments will keep the ceiling low.

7 Anthony Volpe 2B   OFP: 55   ETA: 2023

Born: 04/28/01 Age: 20 Bats: R Throws: R Height: 5'11" Weight: 180 Origin: Round 1, 2019 Draft (#30 overall)

YEAR	TEAM	LVL	AGE	PA	R	2B	3B	HR	RBI	BB	K	SB	CS	AVG/OBP/SLG	DRC+	BABIP	BRR	FRAA	WARP
2019	PUL	ROK+	18	150	19	7	2	2	11	23	38	6	1	.215/.349/.355		.289			
2021 FS	NYY	MLB	20	600	48	26	3	8	51	40	220	11	3	.213/.273/.319	63	.337	4.0		-0.7

The Report: The less-heralded prep teammate of likely top 2021 selection Jack Leiter, Volpe was the one who actually went in the first round in 2019. He's a well-rounded infield prospect, and I liked him a good deal in high school. Volpe has above-average bat speed, and his quick hands lend well to a positive future hit tool outcome, although he's had so few reps against professional hitting that it's hard to be aggressive until we see him more as a pro. His swing plane has not shown optimization for power yet, and whether or not he can develop significant game power is an open question. Defensively, he has a shot to remain at shortstop, with second and third as potential fallback spots. With his lack of experience, there's a bit of a mystery box flair here, but as of before he was shut down in 2019, there was not an obvious carrying tool present, even if there were several that could get there.

Development Track: The Yankees were conservative with alternate site invites, bypassing most of their far-away prospect crop, and then they didn't hold domestic fall instructs at all. So there's not much official action for us to update going on here, although we've heard that Volpe is training well in the tri-state area.

Variance: High. His entire pro experience is 34 games in the Appy League.

Mark Barry's Fantasy Take: Volpe is fine. Maybe he's even a little better than that. But the ability to "stick at short" isn't as much of a selling point as it once was, with the current batch of MLBers at the six providing real, top-of-draft output. If you want to tab Volpe as a future second baseman, and roll the dice in leagues with at least 200 prospects, that sounds about right.

8 Kevin Alcantara OF   OFP: 55   ETA: Late 2023/2024

Born: 07/12/02   Age: 18   Bats: R   Throws: R   Height: 6'6"   Weight: 188   Origin: International Free Agent, 2018

YEAR	TEAM	LVL	AGE	PA	R	2B	3B	HR	RBI	BB	K	SB	CS	AVG/OBP/SLG	DRC+	BABIP	BRR	FRAA	WARP
2019	YAE	ROK	16	128	19	5	2	1	13	3	27	3	3	.260/.289/.358		.326			
2019	DSL NYY	ROK	16	46	7	3	1	0	6	5	9	2	0	.237/.348/.368		.300			
2021 FS	NYY	MLB	18	600	42	26	3	6	47	23	207	13	6	.206/.243/.297	45	.311	-1.8	CF -5	-3.0

Comparables: Isaac Galloway, Rey Fuentes, Xavier Avery

The Report: Alcantara showed his upside in flashes after coming stateside as a 16-year-old in 2019. In the GCL, he chased out of the zone regularly and overall showed an inconsistent swing. However across 2020, Alcantara began controlling the zone better while cutting down on the big movements in his swing. Mechanically, he's now more repeatable and plays much better against all pitch types. There is a chance Alcantara will hit for both power and average, as his plus bat speed will help both tools grow. The long and slender 6-foot-6 outfielder also added much needed strength to his frame, lifting his power tool floor without taking away speed yet, but that will remain a concern down the road. Defensively, the arm is plus and Alcantara has the potential to be a center fielder in the long term. As he physically develops, however, he may get pushed to right field.

Development Track: With Alcantara purportedly making big strides this year, some expect him to move quickly over the next season or two as he gets his feet under him stateside. But regardless, he still has lots of work to do in front of him, with playing close to a full season near the top of the to-do list.

Variance: Very high. The possible mix of five above-average to plus tools make Alcantara an enticing prospect. But with little to no track record and still only 18 years old, he makes for a better dream than a sure-fire bet at this point.

Mark Barry's Fantasy Take: As dynasty managers, we're always on the lookout for the next, shiny thing. Estevan Florial isn't cool anymore. You know what's cool? Kevin Alcantara. The latter offers five above-average tools and hasn't yet trailed off in production, or had the bloom fall off his rose. As such, he's a top 100-125 guy in dynasty circles, almost exclusively based on speculative value.

9 Ezequiel Duran 2B   OFP: 55   ETA: 2023

Born: 05/22/99   Age: 22   Bats: R   Throws: R   Height: 5'11"   Weight: 185   Origin: International Free Agent, 2017

YEAR	TEAM	LVL	AGE	PA	R	2B	3B	HR	RBI	BB	K	SB	CS	AVG/OBP/SLG	DRC+	BABIP	BRR	FRAA	WARP
2018	PUL	ROK	19	235	34	8	2	4	20	9	65	7	0	.201/.251/.311		.265			
2019	SI	SS	20	277	49	12	4	13	37	25	77	11	4	.256/.329/.496	160	.314	0.6	2B(57) 7.6	3.0
2021 FS	NYY	MLB	22	600	48	26	4	13	58	26	229	13	5	.206/.247/.338	57	.318	2.1	2B 6, SS 0	-0.4

Comparables: Patrick Wisdom, Darrell Ceciliani, Shane Peterson

The Report: Duran profiles as a power-hitting second baseman who had already figured out how to get much of his plus raw power into games as a teenager. He led the Penn League in home runs in 2019, rarely having to sell out to yank the ball over the fence, while just as comfortably driving the ball into the gaps. The power will eventually play line-to-line if his approach improves. The approach was lacking in short-season, as he didn't always see spin well, and would hunt fastballs out of the zone. Nothing that looked unfixable, however.

On the dirt, Duran projects as a plus defender at second. While the straight-line speed and range are merely average, he's an instinctual defender who shows excellent actions and a strong, accurate arm for the right side of the infield.

Development Track: Duran showed approach gains especially against breaking balls, while continuing to post major-league quality exit velocities. It was a lost year of game reps, though, and it's difficult to gauge exactly where he is now until we see him in Tampa or Hudson Valley in 2021.

Variance: High. This was a tough lost year for the variance profile, given the hit tool concerns and lack of games above short-season.

Mark Barry's Fantasy Take: I read reports like this on Duran and get irrationally excited before seeing Ben's Jonathan Schoop comp from last year and oh right, that's where I've seen this before. I'm considerably less interested in a guy who strikes out almost 30 percent of the time in Low-A, even if said guy has the tools to be a high-power, good defender at the keystone.

10   Austin Wells   C   OFP: 50   ETA: 2023

Born: 07/12/99   Age: 21   Bats: L   Throws: R   Height: 6'2"   Weight: 220   Origin: Round 1, 2020 Draft (#28 overall)

The Report: Sometimes you're meant to be a Yankee. Originally drafted by the pinstripes in the 35th round out of high school and then again in the first round this past draft, Wells' reputation as an offensive-minded player carried over to college at the University of Arizona—a notoriously hitter-friendly home park. An impressive summer at the Cape dispelled the notion he was a park-created slugger, but a major question remains: where does he end up defensively? He's spent a majority of his college time at catcher, with starts mixed-in at first base and in the outfield. His receiving skills are so-so at best and his arm is below-average. With such an advanced stick, it may push his inevitable transition from out behind home plate even more quickly.

Development Track: The Yankees have been known to push defensively-challenged catchers before (see: Sánchez, Gary). Wells projects as a complete hitter with contact and power to all fields, so of course that type of player would be of supreme value if he could stick at the position. We'll know within the first week of the (assumed) minor league season what Yankees player development has in store.

Variance: Medium. There is little worry he'll be able to hit his way up the system. He's more athletic than a traditional plodding DH, so you'd like to find a home for him somewhere on the field to keep him in the lineup every day.

Mark Barry's Fantasy Take: Personally I think the Yankees should just have an entire roster of catchers that can't really catch. That should be their thing. Honestly, I might have wells as the third-best dynasty prospect in this system. I think he can hit, and the only question is where he'll play defensively, which pretty much only matters if he sticks behind the plate.

The Prospects You Meet Outside The Top Ten

Top Ten prospects in a shallower system

Josh Breaux   C   Born: 10/07/97   Age: 23   Bats: R   Throws: R   Height: 6'1"   Weight: 220   Origin: Round 2, 2018 Draft (#61 overall)

YEAR	TEAM	LVL	AGE	PA	R	2B	3B	HR	RBI	BB	K	SB	CS	AVG/OBP/SLG	DRC+	BABIP	BRR	FRAA	WARP
2018	SI	SS	20	105	6	9	0	0	13	3	20	0	0	.280/.295/.370	96	.341	-2.1	C(21) -0.3	-0.2
2019	CSC	LO-A	21	216	28	10	0	13	49	15	59	0	0	.271/.324/.518	137	.320	0.4	C(22) -0.2	1.4
2021 FS	NYY	MLB	23	600	48	26	2	12	55	35	196	1	0	.198/.250/.319	56	.280	-0.2	C 0	-1.0

Comparables: Ryan O'Hearn, Jesús Aguilar, Matt Adams

After playing in only 51 games in 2019, one might think losing the 2020 season would be a huge detriment for Breaux. From all indications, however, it had the opposite effect, as he has reportedly made some of the biggest strides in the org this year anyway. The big-framed catcher's throwing elbow has fully recovered from his 2019 injury, and did not affect his development this year. But his plus-plus arm strength was never the main concern behind the plate. Going forward the glove may not be a problem either with Breaux showing improvements across the board defensively. At the dish in 2019, he swatted an impressive 13 homers in his abbreviated Sally League campaign—albeit with swing-and-miss issues as well. He spent 2020 fine-tuning his swing mechanics to try and cut down on inconsistencies and whiffs, which has so far been positive. A big 2021 campaign from Breaux—assuming a somewhat normal season—would not be surprising.

Roansy Contreras   RHP   Born: 11/07/99   Age: 21   Bats: R   Throws: R   Height: 6'0"   Weight: 175   Origin: International Free Agent, 2016

YEAR	TEAM	LVL	AGE	W	L	SV	G	GS	IP	H	HR	BB/9	K/9	K	GB%	BABIP	WHIP	ERA	DRA-	WARP
2018	SI	SS	18	0	0	0	5	5	28²	15	1	2.8	10.0	32	46.2%	.226	0.84	1.26	96	0.3
2018	CSC	LO-A	18	0	2	0	7	7	34²	29	4	3.1	7.3	28	34.3%	.255	1.18	3.38	93	0.3
2019	CSC	LO-A	19	12	5	0	24	24	132¹	105	10	2.4	7.7	113	39.9%	.256	1.07	3.33	81	1.9
2021 FS	NYY	MLB	21	2	3	0	57	0	50	51	8	4.2	7.1	39	37.1%	.286	1.49	5.14	122	-0.5

Comparables: Brad Keller, Eduardo Rodriguez, Brad Hand

Compared to the other young Dominican starting pitching prospects in the Yankees org—Gil, Medina, and Alexander Vizcaino—Contreras is far from the flashiest, but he has shown plenty of upside in his own right. In 2019, he excelled in the Sally while throwing plenty of strikes with a three-pitch arsenal: fastball, curveball and changeup. Contreras worked on his curveball this past year to improve consistency and shape, a pitch he needs to stick as a starter. Adding strength and gaining more body control will be top priorities as well.

Prospects to dream on a little

Alexander Vizcaino   RHP   Born: 05/22/97   Age: 24   Bats: R   Throws: R   Height: 6'2"   Weight: 160   Origin: International Free Agent, 2016

YEAR	TEAM	LVL	AGE	W	L	SV	G	GS	IP	H	HR	BB/9	K/9	K	GB%	BABIP	WHIP	ERA	DRA-	WARP
2018	PUL	ROK	21	3	3	0	11	11	54	49	7	3.5	9.2	55	52.0%	.290	1.30	4.50		
2019	CSC	LO-A	22	5	5	0	16	16	87²	80	6	2.8	10.4	101	46.4%	.326	1.22	4.41	113	-0.3
2019	TAM	HI-A	22	1	1	0	5	5	27¹	33	2	3.6	8.9	27	51.9%	.408	1.61	4.28	141	-0.6
2021 FS	NYY	MLB	24	1	1	0	57	0	50	51	10	4.8	8.0	44	44.0%	.287	1.56	5.88	129	-0.7
2021 DC	NYY	MLB	24	1	1	0	22	0	24	24	5	4.8	8.0	21	44.0%	.287	1.56	5.88	129	-0.2

Comparables: Luis Perdomo, Amir Garrett, Randy Rosario

Sporting one of the best changeups in the org, Vizcaino made significant improvements during the 2019 season, especially throwing strikes. But one area still in need of development is his fastball, as his mid-to-upper-90s offering got hit harder than you'd think it would in A-ball given the velocity. Avoiding the hard contact on the four-seamer became the main area of focus for the 23-year-old during the pandemic-ridden year. Like Contreras, adding strength to the frame to help with his body control has been a point of emphasis. For what it's worth, the slider will be fine.

Alexander Vargas   SS   Born: 10/29/01   Age: 19   Bats: S   Throws: R   Height: 5'11"   Weight: 148   Origin: International Free Agent, 2018

YEAR	TEAM	LVL	AGE	PA	R	2B	3B	HR	RBI	BB	K	SB	CS	AVG/OBP/SLG	DRC+	BABIP	BRR	FRAA	WARP
2019	DSL NYY	ROK	17	44	6	5	2	0	2	4	6	2	3	.289/.364/.526		.333			
2019	YAE	ROK	17	173	23	5	5	1	16	14	22	13	0	.219/.301/.335		.250			
2021 FS	NYY	MLB	19	600	43	26	4	6	48	29	154	29	7	.203/.249/.301	50	.267	10.8	SS -2	-0.9

Comparables: Engelb Vielma, Erick Mejia, Dixon Machado

With a plus speed/glove combo at shortstop, Vargas' ceiling hinges on his hit tool development, due to the lack of projectable power. In 2019 he showed a good swing and approach from both sides while taking his walks. The main concern for Vargas was lack of strength, which he worked on adding in 2020. He fits the mold of the other shortstops in the org: high defensive floor with limited offensive upside.

Maikol Escotto   SS   Born: 06/04/02   Age: 19   Bats: R   Throws: R   Height: 5'11"   Weight: 180   Origin: International Free Agent, 2018

YEAR	TEAM	LVL	AGE	PA	R	2B	3B	HR	RBI	BB	K	SB	CS	AVG/OBP/SLG	DRC+	BABIP	BRR	FRAA	WARP
2019	DSL NYY	ROK	17	218	47	11	4	8	26	32	57	13	3	.315/.429/.552		.422			

Although he hasn't made his stateside debut yet, Escotto is someone worth keeping an eye on. During the 2019 Dominican Summer League, the now 18-year-old slashed .315/.429/.552 with 13 stolen bases, 11 doubles and eight homers over 45 games. Escotto can reach triple-digit exit velos using a smooth right-handed swing with plus bat speed and plays both middle infield positions as well as third base.

Oswald Peraza SS   Born: 06/15/00   Age: 21   Bats: R   Throws: R   Height: 6'0"   Weight: 176   Origin: International Free Agent, 2016

YEAR	TEAM	LVL	AGE	PA	R	2B	3B	HR	RBI	BB	K	SB	CS	AVG/OBP/SLG	DRC+	BABIP	BRR	FRAA	WARP
2018	PUL	ROK	18	159	25	3	2	1	11	14	41	8	1	.250/.333/.321		.343			
2019	SI	SS	19	85	7	1	1	2	7	5	9	5	2	.241/.294/.354	116	.250	0.0	SS(18) 1.9	0.7
2019	CSC	LO-A	19	208	31	5	0	2	13	16	28	18	5	.273/.348/.333	112	.310	-0.4	SS(44) 0.8	1.2
2021 FS	NYY	MLB	21	600	51	25	3	9	54	36	159	20	6	.227/.285/.335	72	.302	4.3	SS 4, 2B 0	0.7

Comparables: Luis Sardiñas, Abiatal Avelino, J.P. Crawford

A bit of a surprise 40-man add given his total lack of experience above A-ball, Peraza's potential plus shortstop glove and speed might have made him a target in the Rule 5. He was overmatched at the plate at times in the South Atlantic League, but there's some whippy bat speed and above-average raw that could come out with more game experience.

MLB arms, but probably relievers

Albert Abreu RHP   Born: 09/26/95   Age: 25   Bats: R   Throws: R   Height: 6'2"   Weight: 190   Origin: International Free Agent, 2013

YEAR	TEAM	LVL	AGE	W	L	SV	G	GS	IP	H	HR	BB/9	K/9	K	GB%	BABIP	WHIP	ERA	DRA-	WARP
2018	TAM	HI-A	22	4	3	0	13	13	62²	54	9	4.2	9.3	65	43.4%	.278	1.32	4.16	81	1.0
2019	TRN	AA	23	5	8	0	23	20	96²	103	9	4.9	8.5	91	41.2%	.339	1.61	4.28	139	-2.2
2020	NYY	MLB	24	0	1	0	2	0	1¹	4	1	13.5	13.5	2	33.3%	.600	4.50	20.25	112	0.0
2021 FS	NYY	MLB	25	2	2	0	57	0	50	50	9	6.0	8.4	46	39.7%	.296	1.69	6.24	128	-0.7
2021 DC	NYY	MLB	25	2	2	0	45	0	48	48	8	6.0	8.4	44	39.7%	.296	1.69	6.24	128	-0.4

Comparables: Hector Perez, Jordan Yamamoto, Keury Mella

We ranked Abreu third on this list last year, because both Jeffrey and I saw starts where he was still projecting as a mid-rotation starter with electric stuff. He was pretty similar to Medina and Gil as prospects. Where they still have time, Abreu is now 25, and instead of making a quick major-league impact the command was abysmal and his stuff was down in his limited major-league time; he didn't exactly get sterling reviews from the alternate site either, although he's pitched okay in LIDOM this winter (albeit with too many walks, a running theme). Abreu can still hit the upper-90s and there's been a plus breaker projection down there for a half-decade, but he's quickly running out of time to develop the command and sequencing to start, and there were no brilliant outings to ensorcel us for another year in 2020.

T.J. Sikkema LHP   Born: 07/25/98   Age: 22   Bats: L   Throws: L   Height: 6'0"   Weight: 221   Origin: Round 1, 2019 Draft (#38 overall)

YEAR	TEAM	LVL	AGE	W	L	SV	G	GS	IP	H	HR	BB/9	K/9	K	GB%	BABIP	WHIP	ERA	DRA-	WARP
2019	SI	SS	20	0	0	0	4	4	10²	6	0	0.8	11.0	13	52.0%	.240	0.66	0.84	41	0.4
2021 FS	NYY	MLB	22	2	3	0	57	0	50	51	8	4.5	8.1	45	41.4%	.299	1.52	5.23	125	-0.6

Comparables: Humberto Castellanos, Vance Worley, Clay Buchholz

Sikkema is a polished lefty crossfire guy that can hit 95 and show you two different breaking ball looks. 95-and-a-slider-and-a-curve isn't as pithy, but the end result is likely the same—a good major leaguer reliever. Of course this is also the exact type of arm the Yankees are good at coaching up into an OFP 55 in the Florida State League, but that didn't happen this year for obvious reasons.

Miguel Yajure RHP Born: 05/01/98 Age: 23 Bats: R Throws: R Height: 6'1" Weight: 175 Origin: International Free Agent, 2015

YEAR	TEAM	LVL	AGE	W	L	SV	G	GS	IP	H	HR	BB/9	K/9	K	GB%	BABIP	WHIP	ERA	DRA-	WARP
2018	CSC	LO-A	20	4	3	0	14	14	64²	64	3	2.1	7.8	56	50.3%	.316	1.22	3.90	104	0.2
2019	TAM	HI-A	21	8	6	0	22	18	127²	110	5	2.0	8.6	122	54.8%	.301	1.08	2.26	78	1.8
2019	TRN	AA	21	1	0	0	2	2	11	9	0	1.6	9.0	11	35.5%	.290	1.00	0.82	104	0.0
2020	NYY	MLB	22	0	0	0	3	0	7	3	1	6.4	10.3	8	40.0%	.143	1.14	1.29	93	0.1
2021 FS	NYY	MLB	23	1	1	0	57	0	50	51	9	3.4	7.9	43	38.2%	.291	1.41	5.07	112	-0.2
2021 DC	NYY	MLB	23	1	1	0	34	0	36	36	7	3.4	7.9	31	38.2%	.291	1.41	5.07	112	0.0

Comparables: Jonathan Hernández, Rony García, Zack Littell

Unlike Abreu, Yajure looked pretty good in his limited major-league time. He's also not strictly or even necessarily probably a reliever—he's a four-pitch righty with an advanced changeup and good feel for pitching—but he fits in this oeuvre even if it isn't strictly speaking the right category. Yajure has been a scout favorite for years and projects as a fourth starter, but that's the result from after he got his developmental boosts.

You always need catching

Anthony Seigler C Born: 06/20/99 Age: 22 Bats: S Throws: S Height: 6'0" Weight: 200 Origin: Round 1, 2018 Draft (#23 overall)

YEAR	TEAM	LVL	AGE	PA	R	2B	3B	HR	RBI	BB	K	SB	CS	AVG/OBP/SLG	DRC+	BABIP	BRR	FRAA	WARP
2018	PUL	ROK	19	53	4	1	0	0	5	8	5	0	0	.209/.340/.233		.231			
2018	YAW	ROK	19	41	7	2	0	1	4	6	7	0	0	.314/.415/.457		.370			
2019	CSC	LO-A	20	120	10	3	0	0	6	20	28	1	0	.175/.328/.206	73	.246	-0.2	C(23) 0.4	0.2
2021 FS	NYY	MLB	22	600	53	26	2	8	53	54	172	2	0	.225/.301/.331	77	.313	0.1	C 0	0.8

Comparables: Adrian Nieto, Danny Jansen, Roberto Pérez

For the third year in-a-row, the 2018 first rounder lost out on crucial game development. In 2019, Seigler only managed to play in 30 games because of two injuries. Defensively, there isn't much worry. He's seen as a plus defender behind the dish, throwing arm especially, with his dexterity helping him make pitch framing improvements. At the plate, however, question marks remain. There really is no projectable power, so the upside offensively will be his ability to get on base and draw walks, which Seigler has shown to be an average strength thus far.

Top Talents 25 and Under (as of 4/1/2021):

1. Gleyber Torres, SS/2B
2. Deivi García, RHP
3. Jasson Dominguez, OF
4. Clarke Schmidt, RHP
5. Luis Gil, RHP
6. Luis Medina, RHP
7. Estevan Florial, OF
8. Anthony Volpe, SS
9. Kevin Alcantara, OF
10. Ezequiel Duran, 2B

Gleyber Torres went from hitting 38 homers in 2019 to 3 in 2020. Sure, the pandemic skews that number, but he still went from slugging .535 to .368, and he also struggled badly at shortstop after previously playing a fine second base. The outcome moving forward is probably going to lie in the middle of all this; he's projected for plus game power since he was a prospect, but 2019 suggested he might contend for home run titles. If only he could play all his games against 2019 Orioles pitching…

I thought about putting Michael King, long a personal favorite, on this list. But he's pretty similar to Yajure, except without the plus change; neither has had much MLB success yet and neither has much more than a fourth starter upside.

Oakland Athletics

The State of the System:
Why doesn't Billy Beane's shit work in the org rankings?

The Top Ten:

1 **A.J. Puk** **LHP**   OFP: 60   ETA: Debuted in 2019
Born: 04/25/95   Age: 26   Bats: L   Throws: L   Height: 6'7"   Weight: 248   Origin: Round 1, 2016 Draft (#6 overall)

YEAR	TEAM	LVL	AGE	W	L	SV	G	GS	IP	H	HR	BB/9	K/9	K	GB%	BABIP	WHIP	ERA	DRA-	WARP
2019	STK	HI-A	24	0	0	0	3	3	6	5	2	6.0	13.5	9	33.3%	.300	1.50	6.00	109	0.0
2019	MID	AA	24	0	0	0	6	1	8^1	9	2	3.2	14.0	13	57.9%	.412	1.44	4.32	121	-0.1
2019	LV	AAA	24	4	1	0	9	0	11	7	3	2.5	13.1	16	41.7%	.190	0.91	4.91	46	0.4
2019	OAK	MLB	24	2	0	0	10	0	11^1	10	1	4.0	10.3	13	44.8%	.321	1.32	3.18	70	0.2
2021 FS	OAK	MLB	26	9	7	0	26	26	150	124	18	3.5	10.6	176	43.8%	.286	1.21	3.39	82	2.6
2021 DC	OAK	MLB	26	6	5	0	39	16	97	80	11	3.5	10.6	114	43.8%	.286	1.21	3.39	82	1.8

Comparables: Thomas Pannone, Bryan Garcia, Gregory Soto

The Report: When healthy, Puk has some serious high-end stuff. His fastball velocity is regularly in the high-90s, and because of his height and release point, if anything it plays up from the radar gun readings. His slider is another potential plus-plus weapon, a hard-boring pitch around 90 with significant tilt. His changeup has flashed plus too, and he mixes in a show-me curveball as well. Puk has had significant command issues, and carries some bullpen risk even without accounting for health.

Development Track: Puk hasn't been healthy a whole lot lately. He missed all of 2018 and some of 2019 following Tommy John surgery, although he pitched very well in a late-season MLB bullpen stint. He was expected to be a big factor for the A's last year, but was placed on the injured list again shortly before the 2020 season began, and underwent labrum and rotator cuff debridement surgery in September. The history of pitchers with significant shoulder injuries is … not great.

Variance: Extreme. Shoulder surgery is about as big of a red flag as you can get.

J.P. Breen's Fantasy Take: Shoulder surgery and relief risk isn't a great combination, even for someone who has the kind of stuff that Puk does. The lefty is technically still a top-100 dynasty prospect because he's one of the few MLB-ready hurlers with legit SP2 upside. Plus, the fact that the A's are already penciling him into the 2021 starting rotation only bolsters his value. But, man, I don't feel great about ranking a pitcher in the Top 100 who hasn't thrown more than 40 innings since 2017 due to Tommy John and shoulder surgery.

2 **Tyler Soderstrom** **C**   OFP: 55   ETA: 2023/2024
Born: 11/24/01   Age: 19   Bats: L   Throws: R   Height: 6'2"   Weight: 200   Origin: Round 1, 2020 Draft (#26 overall)

The Report: It was nearly a dead-heat finish to see which high school position player would take the mantle as the best pure hitter of the 2020 class. Depending on the team, many liked either Robert Hassell or Soderstrom as the standouts, with both displaying aesthetically pleasing strokes from the left side. It's easy to compare the two, both having mechanically ideal swings—under control with a solid approach and already showing the prospect of big power to go along with a sustainable hit tool. Where Soderstrom is different is his defensive home, or rather, we are left with the question of his defensive home. A prep catcher by trade, he projects to handle the defensive duties fine enough, but with an offensive profile that has such a promising outlook, you'd be sorely tempted to take the development behind the plate off of his to focus on getting his bat to the majors.

Development Track: Soderstrom has seen time in the field at third base, both corner outfield spots, and assuredly could get looks at first base down the road. The unknown position debate is in the glass half empty camp, because he's not the premium athlete you can stick anywhere and expect him to flourish. It reflects more where you can hide him and let the bat play.

Variance: High. Prep catchers have a bad track record, but if the bat is good enough that they don't need to stay behind the plate (Wil Myers, Neil Walker), the outlook gets sunnier. But that just keeps Soderstrom from an extreme variance profile as he's still a prep bat who hasn't been tested in the pros yet.

J.P. Breen's Fantasy Take: <whispers> I'm not allowed to like catching prospects, but I like Soderstrom. </whispers> In all seriousness, Soderstrom has been undervalued in the dynasty lists that I've seen, as they're overwhelmingly treating him as a long-term catcher. This seems like a Daulton Varsho situation. Rank the bat. Worry about the rest later. For what it's worth, I'd rather have Soderstrom than fellow first-rounder Austin Wells.

3 Robert Puason SS   OFP: 60   ETA: 2025
Born: 09/11/02   Age: 18   Bats: S   Throws: R   Height: 6'3"   Weight: 165   Origin: International Free Agent, 2019

The Report / Development Track: Jarrett covered Puason's signing background in appropriately thorough detail on last year's edition of the A's list. On some level his prospect narrative will always be tied up in being at the center of one of the biggest amateur bonus scandals in baseball history, but he deserves to be evaluated as a prospect on the merits. Unfortunately given that his first real pro season was 2020, that evaluation remains muddled. The A's were among the more aggressive teams in baseball in terms of bringing prospects—even low level ones—to their alternate site, so Puason spent his age-17 season facing older and significantly more experienced arms. The tools flashed, the frame remains uber-projectable, he's quick-twitch enough to stay up the middle. Past that, hope for a more normal year, and a more tangible evaluation in 2021.

Variance: Extreme. Like with his fellow $5 million 2019 bonus baby, Jasson Dominguez, if I could go higher than extreme I would.

J.P. Breen's Fantasy Take: Echoing what's been written above, Puason's value is mostly treading water due to the lost season. He was a top-150 guy last winter. He's still a top-150 guy. All of the same caveats remain the same, too.

4 Nick Allen SS   OFP: 55   ETA: 2021/2022
Born: 10/08/98   Age: 22   Bats: R   Throws: R   Height: 5'8"   Weight: 166   Origin: Round 3, 2017 Draft (#81 overall)

YEAR	TEAM	LVL	AGE	PA	R	2B	3B	HR	RBI	BB	K	SB	CS	AVG/OBP/SLG	DRC+	BABIP	BRR	FRAA	WARP
2018	BEL	LO-A	19	512	51	17	6	0	34	34	85	24	8	.239/.301/.302	75	.289	3.7	SS(121) 5.2	1.1
2019	STK	HI-A	20	328	45	22	5	3	25	28	52	13	5	.292/.362/.434	134	.348	-4.4	SS(45) 4.7, 2B(24) -1.6	2.1
2021 FS	OAK	MLB	22	600	55	26	4	7	52	36	152	13	5	.226/.279/.327	68	.297	-0.2	SS 10, 2B 0	0.5
2021 DC	OAK	MLB	22	67	6	3	0	0	5	4	17	1	0	.226/.279/.327	68	.297	0.0	SS 1	0.1

Comparables: José Rondón, Amed Rosario, Sergio Alcántara

The Report / Development Track: Allen was a standout Cal League shortstop with High-A Stockton in 2019 despite only playing 72 games because he missed a significant part of the second half with a high-ankle sprain. He made up for some lost time at the Fall League, playing in 18 games there, and spending 2020 at the alternate site. He's someone whose plus quickness and ability to hit for average sets him up to be a top-of-the-order hitter. He really doesn't have much power, but he can probably hit a fair amount of doubles and triples. He's also a plus defender in the middle of the infield, spending a third of the time playing second base in Stockton. He's extremely athletic on the field, especially as a defender and it shows with his glovework, footwork, and transfers.

Variance: Medium. He's already shown himself to be capable in the middle infield role, but needs some more reps coming back from all the missed time to solidify if he can make it to the A's bench.

J.P. Breen's Fantasy Take: In terms of fantasy, Allen gives me David Fletcher vibes. Perhaps he runs a bit more, but I mention Fletcher to emphasize how important it will be for Allen to hit for a high average to have any relevance in fantasy circles. Without it, he's José Iglesias, circa 2016-2018. He's not a top-300 dynasty prospect.

5 Jeff Criswell RHP   OFP: 55   ETA: Late 2022/Early 2023

Born: 03/10/99 Age: 22 Bats: R Throws: R Height: 6'4" Weight: 225 Origin: Round 2, 2020 Draft (#58 overall)

The Report: What looks like an up-and-down career at the University of Michigan actually has all the signs of a development arc trending in the right direction at the right time. Criswell had been used in multiple roles on the Wolverine's pitching staff—one of the best in the country during his time on campus. He wasn't able to nail down a bona fide starter's role until this past season due to a lack of control and less-than-ideal walk rate. This stems from a delivery that requires a lot of effort to generate the mid-90s velocity and movement on his fastball. However, he was throwing more strikes in the spring with both his hits and walks allowed down from previous years while still maintaining his strikeout numbers. Reports from after the draft suggest more consistency in his delivery and his full three-pitch mix ticking up.

Development Track: There will still be concerns about the starter/reliever prognosis moving forward, but at this juncture it appears many of those questions are being answered in the affirmative towards a starting role. Criswell has the body to endure the typical workload stresses. What needs to happen to maintain this projection? The slider and changeup flash as potential plus pitches, but need more consistency to go along with improved location of his sinking fastball. With the continued cleanup of the delivery being an ongoing process, giving him an opportunity to start every fifth day and work through the routine issues will be integral to becoming the more valued starter over bullpen piece.

Variance: Medium. There's still significant relief risk but the stuff is pointing in the right direction for some impact major league role assuming Criswell keeps throwing strikes.

J.P. Breen's Fantasy Take: Mark always tells me that I'm too negative, but it seems like every decent pitching prospect saw their stuff "tick up" in 2020. I'm skeptical. Criswell has role uncertainty and a history of control issues, without the upside of a frontline starter. That's comfortably outside the top-300 dynasty prospects for me.

6 Austin Beck OF   OFP: 55   ETA: 2022

Born: 11/21/98 Age: 22 Bats: R Throws: R Height: 6'1" Weight: 200 Origin: Round 1, 2017 Draft (#6 overall)

YEAR	TEAM	LVL	AGE	PA	R	2B	3B	HR	RBI	BB	K	SB	CS	AVG/OBP/SLG	DRC+	BABIP	BRR	FRAA	WARP
2018	BEL	LO-A	19	534	58	29	4	2	60	30	117	8	6	.296/.335/.383	105	.377	-4.8	CF(113) 2.0	0.9
2019	STK	HI-A	20	367	40	22	4	8	49	24	126	2	2	.251/.302/.411	92	.372	-0.1	CF(69) -0.3, RF(10) 2.7	1.1
2021 FS	OAK	MLB	22	600	48	27	3	8	52	37	224	3	1	.214/.267/.324	61	.339	0.2	CF -7, RF 0	-1.7

Comparables: Yorman Rodríguez, Mickey Moniak, Willy García

The Report: Though Beck's 2019 season was interrupted by injury multiple times, he has been very solid defensively with a good arm for the outfield and natural athleticism. His offense was more of a question mark due to his inconsistent production at the plate. He's got good bat speed and bat control. At times, he showed some hints of a solid offensive package. Taken together, Beck has all of the tools to be a solid outfielder, but the question remains if he can just put his hitting together.

Development Track: Beck was only at instructs in 2020, but the team was happy with his play there and he worked on balancing his contact and power.

Variance: High. No one can ever go wrong with good defense, but he still needs to polish his hitting a bit.

J.P. Breen's Fantasy Take: In terms of context, Beck has a similar dynasty value to Tristen Lutz, and their offensive profiles are relatively similar. As I'm not high on Lutz, I'm not high on Beck. The modest potential is present—and he lacked exposure to high-end competition prior to being drafted—but Beck has struggled to tap into his raw power due to swing and approach issues. On the plus side, though, the defensive skills give Beck a better chance of being an everyday big leaguer than Lutz.

7 Daulton Jefferies RHP   OFP: 55   ETA: Debuted in 2020

Born: 08/02/95   Age: 25   Bats: L   Throws: R   Height: 6'0"   Weight: 182   Origin: Round 1, 2016 Draft (#37 overall)

YEAR	TEAM	LVL	AGE	W	L	SV	G	GS	IP	H	HR	BB/9	K/9	K	GB%	BABIP	WHIP	ERA	DRA-	WARP
2018	ASGR	ROK	22	0	0	0	1	1	2	1	0	0.0	22.5	5	0.0%	.500	0.50	0.00		
2019	STK	HI-A	23	1	0	0	5	3	15	10	1	1.2	12.6	21	44.1%	.273	0.80	2.40	52	0.4
2019	MID	AA	23	1	2	0	21	12	64	63	7	1.0	10.1	72	41.0%	.329	1.09	3.66	69	1.1
2020	OAK	MLB	24	0	1	0	1	1	2	5	2	9.0	4.5	1	30.0%	.375	3.50	22.50	116	0.0
2021 FS	OAK	MLB	25	9	8	0	26	26	150	139	23	2.4	8.9	148	39.6%	.286	1.20	3.79	94	1.6
2021 DC	OAK	MLB	25	4	5	0	16	16	77	71	11	2.4	8.9	76	39.6%	.286	1.20	3.79	94	1.1

Comparables: Dean Kremer, Jharel Cotton, Jose Urquidy

The Report / Development Track: Jefferies spent 2020 at the alternate site, save for one start in the first game of a doubleheader. Two innings of work showed that he mostly used an above-average fastball that showed some arm-side run but was very hittable and induced a lot of fly balls. His velocity seems to be there—his fastball averaged 95 while his cutter, which is his best secondary, averaged 91. That's over a very small major league sample size, of course.

He hasn't had a full, healthy season since 2015, his sophomore year at Cal. Since then, Tommy John surgery in 2017, and some rehab issues in 2018, he needed more healthy innings in 2020. And as you may have heard, that was hard to come by in 2020. 2019 saw him throw 79 innings, but he averaged only three innings an appearance, while only throwing 3 1/3 and 3 2/3 innings once each.

Jefferies still has stuff. There's enough velocity, but he needs to work on improving his command. More healthy innings is key, and getting stretched out after that, depending on if he stays as a starter or not.

Variance: High. Having a full, injury-free season would be paramount for the young righty, but if Jefferies can stay healthy and improve how he commands the ball, he could be highly valuable on the A's pitching staff.

J.P. Breen's Fantasy Take: Jefferies is the fourth-best dynasty prospect in this system. I've got questions about the ultimate effectiveness of his fastball; however, sitting outside the top-200 dynasty prospects and on the cusp of the big leagues, Jefferies is worth adding in most formats. He should throw strikes, and the cutter could be very good. If he can post a double-digit swinging-strike rate, he could be a nice source of rates without killing you in strikeouts.

8 Brayan Buelvas CF   OFP: 55   ETA: 2024

Born: 06/08/02   Age: 19   Bats: R   Throws: R   Height: 5'11"   Weight: 155   Origin: International Free Agent, 2018

YEAR	TEAM	LVL	AGE	PA	R	2B	3B	HR	RBI	BB	K	SB	CS	AVG/OBP/SLG	DRC+	BABIP	BRR	FRAA	WARP
2019	DSL ATH	ROK	17	88	4	5	1	0	14	8	14	4	4	.244/.330/.333		.297			
2019	ASGR	ROK	17	186	26	10	7	3	27	22	46	12	5	.300/.392/.506		.402			
2021 FS	OAK	MLB	19	600	44	26	5	6	48	33	223	27	14	.205/.254/.307	52	.326	-5.3	CF -5, LF -1	-2.9

Comparables: Clint Frazier, Colby Rasmus, Byron Buxton

The Report: A low six-figure signing out of Columbia, Buelvas isn't the toolsiest or most projectable teenaged outfielder you will find, but he's a fleet-footed, advanced defender with some hit and pop potential. He is a plus runner who already has good reads and routes out on the grass, projecting as an above-average center fielder. At the plate Buelvas wrings a fair bit of loud contact out of a smaller frame and relatively short swing, but tends to work all fields at present over trying to tap into his raw power. Overall the approach is on the aggressive side, although he's worked on taming that some and developing more plate discipline.

Development Track: Buelvas was another of Oakland's young prospects that got a fair bit of run in 2020. Spending time at both the alternate site and instructs, the present skills popped more than Puason's, but he lacks the same projection in the body and the bat. After what seemed to be a strong developmental year for the outfielder, he should be ready for a full-season assignment as a 19-year-old in 2021.

Variance: High. The present glovesmanship makes me slightly more confident in a reasonable floor that earns some MLB per diems, but he's still a teenaged outfielder without a ton of physicality that hasn't seen full-season fastballs yet. So there's still significant risk in the profile.

J.P. Breen's Fantasy Take: Mark and I talked about Buelvas on TINO over the summer, arguing that he was an attractive under-the-radar dynasty add. Why? Oakland prioritized his professional development by sending him to the Alternate Site. Buelvas could be a solid contributor across the board, with a solid hit tool and a bit of speed. The questions revolve around his power production. If he can hit 15-plus homers with a .275 batting average and double-digit steals, we're looking at a potential top-250 dynasty guy. I simply remain cautious because he hasn't even reached full-season ball yet.

9 Sheldon Neuse 3B OFP: 50 ETA: Debuted in 2019

Born: 12/10/94 Age: 26 Bats: R Throws: R Height: 6'0" Weight: 232 Origin: Round 2, 2016 Draft (#58 overall)

YEAR	TEAM	LVL	AGE	PA	R	2B	3B	HR	RBI	BB	K	SB	CS	AVG/OBP/SLG	DRC+	BABIP	BRR	FRAA	WARP
2018	NAS	AAA	23	537	48	26	3	5	55	32	172	4	1	.263/.304/.357	74	.385	-0.4	3B(130) -3.1, 2B(1) 0.0, SS(1) 0.7	-0.6
2019	LV	AAA	24	560	99	31	2	27	102	56	132	3	3	.317/.389/.550	117	.384	0.3	3B(96) 12.3, 2B(15) 0.6, SS(9) 1.2	4.4
2019	OAK	MLB	24	61	3	3	0	0	7	4	19	0	0	.250/.295/.304	69	.368	0.3	2B(20) -1.4, 3B(5) -0.3	-0.2
2021 FS	OAK	MLB	26	600	64	24	2	16	65	42	196	2	1	.237/.294/.382	87	.334	0.6	2B -4, 3B 5	0.5
2021 DC	OAK	MLB	26	67	7	2	0	1	7	4	21	0	0	.237/.294/.382	87	.334	0.1	2B 0, 3B 1	0.1

Comparables: Mike Costanzo, Alex Liddi, Todd Frazier

The Report: Neuse turned 26 this year and has been bouncing around the fringes of Nats and Athletics prospect lists ever since he was drafted. Even as a second-round college pick, there were questions around how the offensive tools would fare, and his minor league career has been uneven in that regard. He looked like a fast-moving, hit-over-power college bat, then the bat stagnated, then the power popped in Triple-A. All along he's shown passable third base defense due to his strong arm, and he has spent time at all four infield positions in the minors—he was a college shortstop at Oklahoma. At the point where we click the shutter on this snapshot in time, Neuse has the potential for an average hit/power combo you'll want to leverage against lefties whenever possible, and some defensive flexibility.

Development Track: Neuse was at Oakland's alternate site, but got passed over for third base reps after Matt Chapman went down in favor of a waiver-claimed Jake Lamb. I suppose that's a data point of some sort. He does have a fairly open path to a 2021 bench role on the A's, at least at press time.

Variance: Medium. Neuse has some platoon issues, and may end up a short-side corner bat if he can't solve major-league righties, but if the pop isn't just a desert mirage, you can always use a lefty masher with some defensive flex.

J.P. Breen's Fantasy Take: Neuse desperately needs consistent big-league reps to determine whether he can handle righties. I'm not confident. Maybe he can become the next Jesús Aguilar, but that kind of upside is not worth rostering in dynasty without the assured playing time. Neuse might just be a low-average corner masher on the short side of the platoon—useful in real baseball, not so much in fantasy.

10 Colin Peluse RHP OFP: 50 ETA: 2022/2023

Born: 06/11/98 Age: 23 Bats: R Throws: R Height: 6'3" Weight: 230 Origin: Round 9, 2019 Draft (#284 overall)

YEAR	TEAM	LVL	AGE	W	L	SV	G	GS	IP	H	HR	BB/9	K/9	K	GB%	BABIP	WHIP	ERA	DRA-	WARP
2019	VER	SS	21	2	1	0	8	5	24	21	1	2.2	9.8	26	50.7%	.303	1.12	2.25	102	0.0
2021 FS	OAK	MLB	23	2	3	0	57	0	50	49	8	4.6	7.4	41	41.2%	.286	1.51	5.22	125	-0.6

Comparables: Humberto Mejía, Jordan Montgomery, Justin Berg

The Report: Peluse was a known but not significant college pitching prospect whose poor junior year probably knocked him from early on Day Two to the end of Day Two once the 2019 draft rolled around. He pitched well in the Penn League post-draft, and flashed improved stuff in Instructs this past fall. The sturdy righty was sitting mid-90s with his fastball and touched as high as 98, and his slider is solid enough at present, although it will need further improvements to be a true out pitch. The delivery is uptempo and high effort and he's struggled to consistently throw strikes because of it. It also makes a long-term starter projection difficult.

Development Track: As a college arm with an above-average two-pitch combo at the top of his arsenal, Peluse should move fast if the instructs performance carries over. It's probably worth keeping him stretched out in a minor league rotation for now, just to make up for some lost game reps, but his likely role is a fastball/slider reliever.

Variance: Medium. Health and control/command permitting, Peluse has all the tools to be a useful major league arm. But that's two things that cloud the projection, and he's yet to see full-season bats.

J.P. Breen's Fantasy Take: Yes, middle relievers who can miss bats are increasingly valued in fantasy circles. No, you shouldn't bother rostering them in dynasty until they're already producing in the bigs.

The Prospects You Meet Outside The Top Ten

#11

Logan Davidson SS Born: 12/26/97   Age: 23   Bats: S   Throws: R   Height: 6'3"   Weight: 185   Origin: Round 1, 2019 Draft (#29 overall)

YEAR	TEAM	LVL	AGE	PA	R	2B	3B	HR	RBI	BB	K	SB	CS	AVG/OBP/SLG	DRC+	BABIP	BRR	FRAA	WARP
2019	VER	SS	21	238	42	7	0	4	12	31	55	5	0	.239/.345/.332	132	.308	1.5	SS(50) 11.8	3.0
2021 FS	OAK	MLB	23	600	51	26	2	11	56	38	198	4	0	.214/.270/.332	67	.310	1.5	SS 11	0.7

Comparables: Yamaico Navarro, Andy Parrino, David Adams

The A's first-round pick from just a year ago, file Davidson among those with an "incomplete" report card. He's a balanced switch-hitter with pop from both sides and may move off shortstop eventually to third base, but still, he's very much one to watch. His pro debut in the short season New York-Penn League was undeniably sluggish, but he finished the second half of his games very well, looking to carry that into his 2020 campaign. If a normal season had been played, something resembling his August 2019 slash line of .301/.400/.408 would have undoubtedly run him up the list with the expanded stat lines and everything next to his name rather than as an extra guy footnote.

MLB arms, but probably relievers

Wandisson Charles RHP Born: 09/07/96   Age: 24   Bats: R   Throws: R   Height: 6'4"   Weight: 263   Origin: International Free Agent, 2015

YEAR	TEAM	LVL	AGE	W	L	SV	G	GS	IP	H	HR	BB/9	K/9	K	GB%	BABIP	WHIP	ERA	DRA-	WARP
2018	BEL	LO-A	21	0	0	0	11	0	11	6	1	13.9	15.5	19	52.6%	.278	2.09	4.09	80	0.1
2019	BEL	LO-A	22	1	0	0	13	0	22¹	12	1	8.1	14.9	37	48.8%	.275	1.43	3.22	76	0.3
2019	STK	HI-A	22	2	0	2	18	0	25²	14	1	6.3	13.7	39	32.7%	.277	1.25	3.16	68	0.4
2019	MID	AA	22	1	0	0	9	0	14¹	9	1	3.1	10.7	17	31.4%	.235	0.98	1.88	68	0.2
2021 FS	OAK	MLB	24	2	3	0	57	0	50	40	7	10.6	13.1	72	36.4%	.305	1.99	6.56	135	-0.9

Comparables: Cristian Javier, Steven Okert, Seth Elledge

Charles was a bit of a surprise add to the A's 40-man, although relievers with mid-90s and higher heat are often in demand in the Rule 5. Despite his dominant 2019 across three levels, the profile outside of the fastball velocity is a bit rough. Grip it and rip it mechanics mean the fastball command is below average, and his slider and split only flash. This merely starts the option clock, and Charles has had some Double-A success already, so he has time to work out the kinks to become a setup arm.

James Kaprielian RHP Born: 03/02/94   Age: 27   Bats: R   Throws: R   Height: 6'3"   Weight: 225   Origin: Round 1, 2015 Draft (#16 overall)

YEAR	TEAM	LVL	AGE	W	L	SV	G	GS	IP	H	HR	BB/9	K/9	K	GB%	BABIP	WHIP	ERA	DRA-	WARP
2019	STK	HI-A	25	2	2	0	11	10	36¹	35	6	2.0	10.7	43	32.0%	.319	1.18	4.46	92	0.2
2019	MID	AA	25	2	1	0	7	5	27²	18	2	2.6	8.5	26	40.8%	.232	0.94	1.63	61	0.6
2019	LV	AAA	25	0	0	0	1	1	4	6	0	0.0	13.5	6	16.7%	.500	1.50	2.25	70	0.1
2020	OAK	MLB	26	0	0	0	2	0	3²	4	2	4.9	9.8	4	36.4%	.222	1.64	7.36	112	0.0
2021 FS	OAK	MLB	27	2	3	0	57	0	50	46	8	3.3	9.1	50	38.2%	.287	1.30	4.25	101	0.1
2021 DC	OAK	MLB	27	2	3	0	58	0	62	57	9	3.3	9.1	62	38.2%	.287	1.30	4.25	101	0.3

Comparables: Joe Musgrove, Walker Lockett, Dillon Tate

Somehow, Kaprielian still remains on prospect lists entering his age-27 season. After seasons upon seasons of arm injuries, he popped up in the majors a couple times in relief, sitting mid-90s and leaning on his hard slider as his primary off-speed, which was also his best off-speed in 2019. Given that he's only thrown 101 innings in a five-and-a-half year pro career, I'd probably bet on a relief outcome here, but there's still mid-rotation stuff present when he can take the ball.

MLB bats, but less upside than you'd like

Luis Barrera CF Born: 11/15/95 Age: 25 Bats: L Throws: L Height: 6'0" Weight: 195 Origin: International Free Agent, 2012

YEAR	TEAM	LVL	AGE	PA	R	2B	3B	HR	RBI	BB	K	SB	CS	AVG/OBP/SLG	DRC+	BABIP	BRR	FRAA	WARP
2018	STK	HI-A	22	351	51	18	7	3	46	32	63	10	4	.284/.354/.415	118	.345	1.3	CF(39) 5.1, RF(37) 3.7, LF(12) 0.7	1.7
2018	MID	AA	22	144	24	8	4	0	18	9	18	13	3	.328/.378/.450	110	.377	3.5	CF(22) 3.1, RF(6) -0.5, LF(3) -0.1	0.9
2019	MID	AA	23	240	35	9	11	4	24	12	48	9	7	.321/.357/.513	136	.393	-1.0	CF(36) -5.5, RF(14) 3.0, LF(1) -0.0	1.1
2021 FS	OAK	MLB	25	600	59	26	7	10	60	33	164	13	5	.242/.289/.372	80	.323	4.0	CF -1, RF 2	0.7

Comparables: Roman Quinn, Blake Tekotte, Lorenzo Cain

Barrera was well on his way to a useful slap-and-dash bench outfielder outcome when a shoulder injury cut short his 2019 season. He was at the alternate site in 2020, and should be in play for major league reps in 2021.

Prospects to dream on a little

Lazaro Armenteros LF Born: 05/22/99 Age: 22 Bats: R Throws: R Height: 6'0" Weight: 182 Origin: International Free Agent, 2016

YEAR	TEAM	LVL	AGE	PA	R	2B	3B	HR	RBI	BB	K	SB	CS	AVG/OBP/SLG	DRC+	BABIP	BRR	FRAA	WARP
2018	BEL	LO-A	19	340	43	8	2	8	39	36	115	8	6	.277/.374/.401	118	.427	2.1	LF(69) -0.7	1.1
2019	STK	HI-A	20	538	65	22	5	17	61	73	226	22	6	.222/.336/.403	101	.394	2.4	LF(112) -1.3, CF(7) -0.1	1.4
2021 FS	OAK	MLB	22	600	47	26	3	9	51	40	266	9	4	.193/.260/.305	55	.354	-0.1	LF 5, CF 1	-1.1

Comparables: Nick Williams, Tyler O'Neill, Estevan Florial

It's not ideal that almost five years on from signing out of Cuba has a relatively advanced teenaged hitter, Lazarito finds himself in the "prospects to dream on a little" subhead. The underlying traits of a plus hit/power combination are present in the swing, but the approach even in A-ball has been so poor it's undercut the offensive projection. The defensive profile is corner outfield, so we may wake up with a start in 2022 if he doesn't hit once games resume.

Top Talents 25 and Under (as of 4/1/2021):

1. Jesús Luzardo, LHP
2. A.J. Puk, LHP
3. Tyler Soderstrom, C
4. Robert Puason, SS
5. Nick Allen, SS
6. Jeff Criswell, RHP
7. Austin Beck, OF
8. Daulton Jefferies, RHP
9. Brayan Buelvas, OF
10. Colin Peluse, RHP

If you're only going to have one non-prospect in the 25U, a potential top-of-the-rotation arm is a good pull. Jesús Luzardo was our No. 9 prospect last year. He pitched in the majors in 2019 and flashed dominance with his mid-to-upper-90s fastball, changeup, and slider, all of which look like plus-or-better pitches. He's poised for a huge breakout in 2021.

Philadelphia Phillies

The State of the System:

There's not nothing for Dave Dombrowski to "work with" here, but the Phillies' system continues its slow slide since the peak of the rebuild years.

The Top Ten:

───────────── ★ ★ ★ *2021 Top 101 Prospect* **#54** ★ ★ ★ ─────────────

1 **Mick Abel** **RHP**   OFP: 60   ETA: Late 2023, more likely 2024
Born: 08/18/01   Age: 19   Bats: R   Throws: R   Height: 6'5"   Weight: 190   Origin: Round 1, 2020 Draft (#15 overall)

The Report: Abel emerged as the best prep pitcher in the 2020 class. Heading into the spring evaluation period prior to the draft, you could have argued for one of maybe three different arms, but two of those—including Abel—never pitched in games. What we knew from the previous summer: he had a projectable 6-foot-4 frame, showed good movement on a mid-90s fastball, a snappy breaking ball with swing-and-miss potential, and feel for a changeup. During pre-draft workouts and especially after the Phillies selected him, it became increasingly clear not only that he was clearly the best high school arm, but also may have been a steal at the 15th pick. He's already getting stronger, as expected, with velocity readings ticking up into the upper-90s.

Development Track: For pitchers coming from cold weather parts of the country, there's usually a certain level of caution when first integrating them into a professional routine. First priority is building up strength, something Abel has already shown an ability to do. His natural proclivity to spin a ball with fluid mechanics gives him the complete starter kit to quickly pick up whatever he needs to on his path to a potential top-of-the-rotation monster.

Variance: Medium. It's rare to see a high school pitcher with only a "medium" variance, but Abel has everything you want in a future frontline stud.

J.P. Breen's Fantasy Take: We haven't seen such dynasty excitement surrounding a high school pitcher since Hunter Greene. The more apt example, however, might be Lucas Giolito, as Greene didn't have the advanced repertoire that Abel does. But dynasty owners would be wise to keep Greene and Giolito in their minds as cautionary tales, of sorts. Both righties had (or continue to have) uneven journeys to Major League Baseball. Giolito saw his stock drop dramatically before becoming a high-end major-league starter. Thus, while Abel is a top-10 dynasty option from the 2020 draft, it's unlikely that he arrives in the majors quickly or without hiccups. Still, Abel is my favorite dynasty arm among this year's draftees, including Asa Lacy.

★ ★ ★ *2021 Top 101 Prospect* **#65** ★ ★ ★

2 Spencer Howard   RHP   OFP: 60   ETA: Debuted in 2020

Born: 07/28/96   Age: 24   Bats: R   Throws: R   Height: 6'3"   Weight: 210   Origin: Round 2, 2017 Draft (#45 overall)

YEAR	TEAM	LVL	AGE	W	L	SV	G	GS	IP	H	HR	BB/9	K/9	K	GB%	BABIP	WHIP	ERA	DRA-	WARP
2018	JS	LO-A	21	9	8	0	23	23	112	101	6	3.2	11.8	147	37.8%	.351	1.26	3.78	73	2.3
2019	PHE	ROK	22	0	0	0	1	1	2¹	3	1	3.9	11.6	3	71.4%	.333	1.71	11.57		
2019	PHW	ROK	22	0	0	0	1	1	3	1	0	3.0	15.0	5	60.0%	.200	0.67	0.00		
2019	CLR	HI-A	22	2	1	0	7	7	35	19	1	1.3	12.3	48	44.3%	.261	0.69	1.29	46	1.2
2019	REA	AA	22	1	0	0	6	6	30²	20	2	2.6	11.2	38	42.5%	.254	0.95	2.35	60	0.8
2020	PHI	MLB	23	1	2	0	6	6	24¹	30	6	3.7	8.5	23	38.0%	.329	1.64	5.92	108	0.1
2021 FS	PHI	MLB	24	9	8	0	26	26	150	138	23	3.0	9.3	155	37.2%	.289	1.26	4.00	93	1.7
2021 DC	PHI	MLB	24	6	6	0	22	22	102²	94	16	3.0	9.3	105	37.2%	.289	1.26	4.00	93	1.5

Comparables: Dylan Cease, Archie Bradley, Cristian Javier

The Report: Howard entered 2020 with high-end stuff, but no track record of holding it over an extended period of time. The Phillies held him down to open the year to steal a year of free agency before he made his major league debut in early August. A blister issue and ultimately shoulder soreness caused a shortened start and ultimately led to him missing two weeks late in the season. When he was on the mound, Howard flashed everything but the absolute top-end velocity. His fastball sat mid-90s early in games before losing 2-3 mph after a few innings. He is able to locate the pitch well, elevating for swings and misses or painting the low corners to play off the changeup. His changeup is a plus pitch with good deception and fade. His slider will show plus, but can get a bit long and loopy. It functions as primarily a chase pitch. Howard rarely used his curveball in 2020, and while it showed improvement, it functions more as a change-of-pace pitch. He has tightened it up some and when he gets on top of it, it can be a weapon for him.

Howard has plus control, and solid command, especially of the fastball and changeup, but he has had spurts of wildness where he will fail to locate any of his pitches before locking back in. The pieces are there, especially if the high-end velocity returns, for Howard to be a front-end starting pitcher, but there are a lot more questions now about his ability to actually put it all together for a sustained period of time. It looks more likely that he will be a solid starter, but never consistently sustains the ceiling he flashes.

Development Track: Given his age, development, and the Phillies' needs, Howard should open the season in the big league rotation. Given the lack of consistency in his 2020 season, the hope is getting on a regular turn in the rotation will bring some improvements to his results. Given that he has not really been a regular turn through a rotation since 2018, there could still be bumps ahead.

Variance: Medium. Howard is major-league ready and has impactful stuff, but has logged surprisingly little time pitching against upper minors competition given his age. He does have some minor injury concerns as well, all of which leads to a higher level of risk than you'd expect a pitcher of this profile to have.

J.P. Breen's Fantasy Take: While I have no interest in bumping down Howard on my dynasty rankings because of his 5.92 ERA and 2.22 HR/9 in 2020, I am more concerned about his long-term ability to miss a ton of bats. He only had a 9.8 percent swinging strike rate in 2020, and the above report about his inconsistent breaking stuff is worrisome. Still, Howard remains a top-200 overall dynasty player and a top-50 dynasty prospect. He profiles as a mid-rotation starter with the potential to be more.

3 Francisco Morales   RHP   OFP: 60   ETA: 2022

Born: 10/27/99   Age: 21   Bats: R   Throws: R   Height: 6'4"   Weight: 185   Origin: International Free Agent, 2016

YEAR	TEAM	LVL	AGE	W	L	SV	G	GS	IP	H	HR	BB/9	K/9	K	GB%	BABIP	WHIP	ERA	DRA-	WARP
2018	WIL	SS	18	4	5	0	13	13	56¹	54	6	5.3	10.9	68	40.9%	.324	1.54	5.27	283	-5.1
2019	JS	LO-A	19	1	8	1	27	15	96²	82	8	4.3	12.0	129	44.5%	.325	1.32	3.82	90	0.7
2021 FS	PHI	MLB	21	2	3	0	57	0	50	47	9	6.3	9.5	52	37.8%	.290	1.64	5.72	129	-0.7

Comparables: Lucas Sims, Aaron Sanchez, Lance McCullers Jr.

The Report: A projectable power arm, Morales already sits in the mid-90s and touches higher, and if he moved to relief we'd expect him to threaten triple digits. The slider is plus to plus-plus depending on the day. The changeup is developing, but has only gotten to fringe-average projection as of 2019 looks, which might not be good enough for starting. His delivery is deceptive but he doesn't always repeat great, and he's had command issues. Basically, he's a very typical big stuff/high variance pitching prospect who very easily could end up in the bullpen, but has major rotational upside if the changeup, command, and repeatability come around.

Development Track: Morales wasn't at the alternate site, which was a little surprising but not particularly concerning. Instructs reports on him were pretty solid, especially on his fastball/slider combo, so we expect him to come out in 2021 without missing a beat.

Variance: High. The command and changeup are still going to need to develop, or he's going to end up in the bullpen, albeit with a very high ceiling there too.

J.P. Breen's Fantasy Take: Morales "has major rotational upside if the changeup, command, and repeatability come around." Oh, is that all that needs to come around? I'm 100 percent buying Morales as a potential impact reliever in a couple of years—maybe like Seranthony Dominguez was a couple of seasons ago. But that currently leaves him outside my top-200 dynasty prospects. If your dynasty league has larger pitching staffs or carries specific roster spots for relievers, he's a touch more valuable than that.

4 Bryson Stott SS   OFP: 55   ETA: 2022
Born: 10/06/97 Age: 23 Bats: L Throws: R Height: 6'3" Weight: 200 Origin: Round 1, 2019 Draft (#14 overall)

YEAR	TEAM	LVL	AGE	PA	R	2B	3B	HR	RBI	BB	K	SB	CS	AVG/OBP/SLG	DRC+	BABIP	BRR	FRAA	WARP
2019	PHE	ROK	21	11	3	1	1	1	3	2	0	0	0	.667/.727/1.333		.625			
2019	WIL	SS	21	182	27	8	2	5	24	22	39	5	3	.274/.370/.446	149	.336	1.1	SS(34) -1.0, 2B(2) -0.1, 3B(2) -0.1	1.4
2021 FS	PHI	MLB	23	600	56	26	3	14	62	40	180	9	3	.228/.286/.368	81	.311	1.6	SS 1, 2B 0	0.7

Comparables: Garrett Hampson, Ryan Flaherty, Jake Cronenworth

The Report: Stott's college performance at UNLV far outpaced his tools, but he's a well-rounded two-way infielder whose hit and power tools should play at least to average with a strong approach making the total package at the plate play up. The swing can be a little timing-heavy with a double toe tap that gets him out of sync and cuts off some of the above-average raw, but he will then put a charge into plus velocity when you don't expect it. So there's some additional upside in the bat despite the polished college profile. Stott's unlikely to stick at shortstop long term, but could play there once a week or so, and the arm is strong enough to handle third, and he's rangy enough to handle second. Nothing sticks out as a clear plus or carrying tool, which will mean performance up the minor league ladder will be important to narrow our confidence interval on Stott landing in Philly as a good regular.

Development Track: Stott impressed at the alternate site, showing the same good approach and control of the zone against more advanced arms. He added some good weight and bat speed as well, although the hit tool still remains ahead of the game power. The added weight might kibosh even occasional shortstop duty though, which will put more pressure on the potential 20-home run power to manifest. Everything is advanced enough that I'd expect Stott to move quickly if and when minor league games resume.

Variance: Medium. The converse of there being no real carrying tool is there isn't a particular hole in his profile either. Sometimes that means you only get a fifth infielder, but the reasonable floor here is some kind of major league bench piece. We'd feel more confident about that once he hits in the upper minors of course.

J.P. Breen's Fantasy Take: Stott would be more exciting if he either hit for more average or stole more bases, but he projects as more of a steady contributor who you'd rather have as your MI guy than your everyday guy at second or short. He might hit 20 homers with a .265 average and 10 stolen bases, which is basically what Asdrubal Cabrera has done over the past decade and a half. Stott is a "safe" prospect on the fringes of the Top 100.

5   Johan Rojas   CF   OFP: 60   ETA: 2023

Born: 08/14/00   Age: 20   Bats: R   Throws: R   Height: 6'1"   Weight: 165   Origin: International Free Agent, 2018

YEAR	TEAM	LVL	AGE	PA	R	2B	3B	HR	RBI	BB	K	SB	CS	AVG/OBP/SLG	DRC+	BABIP	BRR	FRAA	WARP
2018	DSL PHR	ROK	17	292	42	12	4	2	31	18	37	19	8	.320/.376/.421		.360			
2019	PHW	ROK	18	84	13	6	5	0	4	9	12	3	2	.311/.393/.527		.371			
2019	WIL	SS	18	172	17	5	6	2	11	5	29	11	4	.244/.273/.384	81	.284	-0.6	CF(17) -3.1, RF(13) 0.9, LF(12) 0.3	-0.1
2021 FS	PHI	MLB	20	600	47	26	6	7	52	29	160	21	9	.232/.275/.341	68	.311	1.8	CF 2, RF -1	-0.3

Comparables: Billy McKinney, Eddie Rosario, Jahmai Jones

The Report: An overaged signee in 2018, Rojas was a 2019 breakout showing big bat speed and raw power from a small frame, with more than enough foot speed and present outfield instincts to project an above-average big league center fielder. His limited professional reps at the plate did show at times in the Penn League, as he struggled with offspeed and only flashed that sweet 5 o'clock swing in games, but you can't teach this kind of bat speed.

Development Track: Rojas added some good weight in 2020 and could still carry significantly more on his frame without losing his straight line speed and plus defensive projection in center. He's continued to struggle with offspeed stuff at times, but that can be written off for now at least as an age/lack of reps issue. The offensive upside here outpaces Stott's by a fair bit, but he ranks behind him due to the high variance in the hit tool and distance from the majors. However, if you can be a breakout prospect twice, I wouldn't bet against Rojas doing it again in 2021.

Variance: Extreme. Rojas has a Top 101 OFP, but the questions about the hit tool and approach need to be answered before we pull the trigger. This ranking/report could look very different in a year for good or for ill.

J.P. Breen's Fantasy Take: The dynasty community has cooled dramatically on Rojas, who is outside most Top 250 lists at this point. Rojas, however, has immense power-speed potential and has more upside than many J2 guys over whom dynasty owners went nuts just 12 months ago. He's somehow a post-hype prospect at just 20 years old. I'll be targeting Rojas in many supplemental drafts.

6   Rafael Marchan   C   OFP: 55   ETA: Debuted in 2020

Born: 02/25/99   Age: 22   Bats: S   Throws: R   Height: 5'9"   Weight: 170   Origin: International Free Agent, 2015

YEAR	TEAM	LVL	AGE	PA	R	2B	3B	HR	RBI	BB	K	SB	CS	AVG/OBP/SLG	DRC+	BABIP	BRR	FRAA	WARP
2018	WIL	SS	19	210	28	8	2	0	12	11	18	9	6	.301/.343/.362	134	.330	0.3	C(47) 2.7	1.2
2019	JS	LO-A	20	265	21	16	0	0	20	24	31	1	3	.271/.347/.339	130	.311	0.7	C(48) 1.8	2.1
2019	CLR	HI-A	20	86	6	4	0	0	3	6	8	1	2	.231/.291/.282	84	.254	-0.4	C(22) -0.3	0.2
2020	PHI	MLB	21	9	3	0	0	1	3	1	2	0	0	.500/.556/.875	90	.600	-0.3	C(3) 0.1	0.0
2021 FS	PHI	MLB	22	600	56	24	2	8	54	31	108	6	3	.245/.289/.343	73	.289	-2.5	C -1	0.0
2021 DC	PHI	MLB	22	271	25	11	0	3	24	14	49	2	1	.245/.289/.343	73	.289	-1.1	C -1	0.0

Comparables: Travis d'Arnaud, Rob Brantly, Tucker Barnhart

The Report: IFA catchers can have a slow burn development process, especially when their defensive tools lag behind the bat, as they have for most of Marchan's pro career. His fourth professional season was his first in A-ball, and while he continued to develop behind the plate, he didn't seem like he was particularly close to major league utility there. At the plate he showed good feel for contact from both sides, but the power was limited to the outfield gaps—Marchan didn't hit a single home run in those first four pro campaigns. The likely outcome here felt like more of a backup than a starter, although he showed enough improvements in all aspects of his game to keep that OFP on the starter's side of the ledger.

Development Track: After not protecting Marchan from exposure in the 2019 Rule 5 draft, he made his major league debut in 2020 and hit his first professional home run in the bigs—wonder if that has been done since the Bonus Baby Rule days? His arrival was much quicker than expected—a minor hip injury for J.T. Realmuto led to the Phillies needing some extra catching depth. But the fact that Marchan was the name called speaks to the improvements he's made both at the plate and behind it. He's likely to head back to the minors in 2021, but given that Philadelphia might now have a Realmuto-sized hole at catcher, Marchan could be back in the team's major league plans sooner rather than later.

Variance: High. Marchan arrived in the majors far quicker than we could have anticipated, and the strides he's made with the glove suggest he will definitely be back in the majors behind the plate soon enough, but it's still unclear if he will hit enough to be a starter.

J.P. Breen's Fantasy Take: Marchan doesn't have a clear path to playing time in 2021 and has just one professional homer in five seasons. It's basically like if Jeff Mathis could hit for average. Dynasty owners can just keep on walking.

7   Simon Muzziotti   CF   OFP: 55   ETA: 2022

Born: 12/27/98   Age: 22   Bats: L   Throws: L   Height: 6'1"   Weight: 175   Origin: International Free Agent, 2015

YEAR	TEAM	LVL	AGE	PA	R	2B	3B	HR	RBI	BB	K	SB	CS	AVG/OBP/SLG	DRC+	BABIP	BRR	FRAA	WARP
2018	JS	LO-A	19	299	33	12	2	1	20	14	40	18	4	.263/.299/.331	84	.303	1.7	CF(66) 4.6, RF(1) 0.0	0.5
2019	CLR	HI-A	20	465	52	21	3	3	28	32	60	21	12	.287/.337/.372	107	.327	2.1	CF(80) 0.0, RF(16) 0.8, LF(6) 1.6	2.2
2021 FS	PHI	MLB	22	600	49	26	3	7	53	30	113	16	7	.241/.282/.343	70	.289	-2.4	CF 2, RF 0	-0.4

Comparables: Carlos Tocci, Gorkys Hernández, Derrick Robinson

The Report: With some prospects it's difficult to find their future roles, while others are relatively easy. Muzziotti has four potential plus tools and one tool that is well below average. His carrying tool is plus defense in center field, showing off a combination of good instincts, plus speed, and a plus arm. It is not a Gold Glove ceiling, but he could play there in the majors now. At the plate he has an innate feel for contact, but has a tendency to swing at pitches he shouldn't, which leads to poor quality of that contact. Muzziotti will put one out of the ballpark occasionally, but the Phillies are more working with him on adding enough lift to his swing to put line drives in the gap rather than trying to make him a home run hitter. Muzziotti was added to the 40-man roster this offseason, and despite not playing above High-A yet, he is very nearly major league ready.

Development Track: The biggest knock on Muzziotti has been his lack of strength, and he got stronger during the lost year, but will still need to add more muscle to hold up to the rigors of a full season in the majors. Since he is on the 40-man roster he could see time in Philadelphia in 2021, but presently he slots in behind three other flawed center fielders in the pecking order.

Variance: Medium. While his tools and profile have a high floor, Muzziotti has not faced Double-A or Triple-A pitching, and his aggressive approach could be exposed against high level pitchers.

J.P. Breen's Fantasy Take: Muzziotti must hit for average and run to be relevant in fantasy circles. His aggressive approach and his lack of premium batting-average production in the minors makes me skeptical that he can flirt with .300 in the majors. In the end, you're looking at a speed-and-glove guy, and the speed isn't otherworldly. He's not currently a top-400 dynasty prospect for me.

8   Casey Martin   OFP: 55   ETA: 2023

Born: 04/07/99   Age: 22   Bats: R   Throws: R   Height: 5'11"   Weight: 175   Origin: Round 3, 2020 Draft (#87 overall)

The Report: With Martin, the Phillies may have gotten a first round talent in the third round, although there are questions about how his profile projects going forward. Everything in his game is predicated on aggressiveness, whether at the plate or on the basepaths or in the field. That can be a good thing when harnessed; other times, it can seem out of control. Martin has plenty of juice in his bat, but it's a leveraged swing that does have swing-and-miss tendencies that put a drag on the hit tool projection. If he can be more patient with his pitch selection, it may split the difference enough for him to be an impact player at the plate. On the field, there were more than a few errors made at shortstop over the last few years, so it's unclear where he settles in defensively.

Development Track: The physical tools are loud, but it's unknown yet how the swing and approach will play against professional arms. While many draft prospects enter organizations needing their body to mature to catch up with their baseball skills, Martin is all about refining what he already has. From near top-of-the-scale speed with a dynamic offensive profile, the Phillies have a potential impact prospect on their hands with Martin, but the risk is also significantly higher than you'd expect from a college bat.

Variance: Very High. Bordering on extreme variance, because Martin could be an everyday starter on a first division team and make some all-star games. Or, he could be a quad-A player who sits at the end of the bench more often than not. That's unusual in a recent major college pick.

J.P. Breen's Fantasy Take: Martin is unlikely to slip in dynasty drafts this winter because he boasts premium speed, but if he's available outside the top-20 picks in your offseason supplemental draft, grab him. It's a volatile prospect profile with a low likelihood of coming good, but potential All-Star talents with impact speed are rarely available in dynasty.

9 Luis Garcia SS   OFP: 55   ETA: 2024
Born: 10/01/00 Age: 20 Bats: S Throws: R Height: 5'11" Weight: 170 Origin: International Free Agent, 2017

YEAR	TEAM	LVL	AGE	PA	R	2B	3B	HR	RBI	BB	K	SB	CS	AVG/OBP/SLG	DRC+	BABIP	BRR	FRAA	WARP
2018	PHW	ROK	17	187	33	11	3	1	32	15	21	12	8	.369/.433/.488		.418			
2019	JS	LO-A	18	524	36	14	3	4	36	44	132	9	8	.186/.261/.255	57	.247	-5.0	SS(72) -0.2, 2B(55) -5.3	-1.4
2021 FS	PHI	MLB	20	600	46	25	3	7	50	33	174	10	6	.216/.265/.315	57	.299	-6.2	SS -2, 2B -4	-2.5

Comparables: Leury García, Juan Lagares, Andrew Velazquez

The Report: The last time we saw Garcia in game action, in Low-A in 2019, he was completely overmatched, especially from the left side. He had some barrel control and bat-to-ball ability, but he just couldn't hit the ball hard in the air, so he made an awful lot of weak groundball contact. He almost certainly wasn't ready for a full-season assignment, but the Phillies didn't have an Appy League team to send him to. Defensively, he showed very well at shortstop, and should be able to stay there up the chain. We do think that he might grow into his swing and gain enough power to profile as a regular with the defense.

Development Track: Garcia was likely headed to a Low-A repeat engagement, and coming off a dreadful season is the worst time for him to lose developmental reps. We heard he looked stronger at instructs, and given that he's going to play the entire 2021 season at 20, there's still time.

Variance: Extreme. We still have no idea if he can hit or not.

J.P. Breen's Fantasy Take: Dynasty owners shouldn't get too excited about glove-first prospects who have hit-tool questions without the premium power potential. Even if Garcia hits his top-end projects, it remains a non-impact fantasy profile. If the gap-to-gap profile somehow becomes a 20-homer profile, we'll adjust accordingly.

10 Adonis Medina RHP   OFP: 50   ETA: Debuted in 2020
Born: 12/18/96 Age: 24 Bats: R Throws: R Height: 6'1" Weight: 187 Origin: International Free Agent, 2014

YEAR	TEAM	LVL	AGE	W	L	SV	G	GS	IP	H	HR	BB/9	K/9	K	GB%	BABIP	WHIP	ERA	DRA-	WARP
2018	CLR	HI-A	21	10	4	0	22	21	111¹	103	11	2.9	9.9	123	49.7%	.318	1.25	4.12	95	0.9
2019	REA	AA	22	7	7	0	22	21	105²	103	11	3.5	7.0	82	45.3%	.291	1.36	4.94	123	-1.3
2020	PHI	MLB	23	0	1	0	1	1	4	3	0	6.8	9.0	4	81.8%	.273	1.50	4.50	80	0.1
2021 FS	PHI	MLB	24	8	10	0	26	26	150	152	23	4.5	7.7	128	45.7%	.294	1.51	5.45	118	-0.4
2021 DC	PHI	MLB	24	1	2	0	8	8	32	32	5	4.5	7.7	27	45.7%	.294	1.51	5.45	118	0.0

Comparables: Paul Blackburn, Alex Cobb, Jonathan Hernández

The Report: It has been five years since Medina first broke onto the scene, and the scouting report has barely changed in that time period. While Medina has flashed the ability to hit 96-97, his fastball sits mostly 91-94, occasionally showing a tick or two above that. The pitch has solid run and sink, which leads to a decent amount of ground balls, but disappointing swing-and-miss rates. Medina's changeup has become his best secondary pitch, and it's a plus pitch sitting the mid-to-high 80s with very good sink and fade. His pair of breaking balls have never really developed over the years. The slider flashes plus, but will sometimes get slow and slurvy. The curveball will do the same, getting a bit firm and lacking bite. Medina's control can get a bit loose, but he generally is around the strike zone. However his command continues to lag behind his control, as he still struggles to locate in the zone. Medina sports a very slight frame and tends to lose velocity over the course of his starts. Given his upper minors struggles, he may end up in the bullpen, where he could potentially sit in the higher range of his velocity with sharper secondary pitches.

Development Track: After a disappointing year in Double-A in 2019, Medina was slated for a return to Reading, but instead spent most of the season at the Phillies' alternate site before coming up in late September for his major league debut in a spot start against the Blue Jays. Medina is only 24 and should theoretically get all of 2021 in Triple-A to work through his issues in the rotation, however this is his last option year, so the Phillies are going to need to make a decision on whether he starts or relieves very shortly.

Variance: Medium. Medina has a year in Double-A and a year at the alternate site and is essentially a finished product stuff-wise. The high-end ceiling is likely out of range for Medina, and his ability to start is slipping as well. It is likely his stuff plays up in the bullpen so a move there might not be a huge value hit if he clicks there.

J.P. Breen's Fantasy Take: Medina's long-term prospect pedigree has him still sitting in the Top 400 on some dynasty prospect lists, but that's prioritizing big-league proximity over potential impact. Medina won't miss many bats and is unlikely to offer above-average ratios. You can feel comfortable passing on the righty.

The Prospects You Meet Outside The Top Ten

MLB-ready arms, but probably relievers

Connor Brogdon **RHP** Born: 01/29/95 Age: 26 Bats: R Throws: R Height: 6'6" Weight: 205 Origin: Round 10, 2017 Draft (#293 overall)

YEAR	TEAM	LVL	AGE	W	L	SV	G	GS	IP	H	HR	BB/9	K/9	K	GB%	BABIP	WHIP	ERA	DRA-	WARP
2018	JS	LO-A	23	5	3	5	31	7	69¹	59	3	2.1	10.3	79	33.3%	.316	1.08	2.47	77	1.1
2019	CLR	HI-A	24	2	0	0	10	0	20	11	1	2.2	10.3	23	32.6%	.222	0.80	1.80	51	0.5
2019	REA	AA	24	1	1	2	15	0	23²	12	4	2.7	14.8	39	28.6%	.216	0.80	2.66	50	0.6
2019	LHV	AAA	24	3	1	2	26	0	32¹	23	4	3.3	12.2	44	38.2%	.268	1.08	3.06	59	1.0
2020	PHI	MLB	25	1	0	0	9	0	11¹	5	3	4.0	13.5	17	36.4%	.105	0.88	3.97	85	0.2
2021 FS	PHI	MLB	26	2	2	0	57	0	50	41	7	4.6	11.3	62	36.5%	.289	1.35	4.17	94	0.3
2021 DC	PHI	MLB	26	2	2	0	46	0	49	41	7	4.6	11.3	61	36.5%	.289	1.35	4.17	94	0.4

Comparables: Kodi Whitley, Phil Maton, Bryan Garcia

Brogdon added some stability to a gas can Phillies bullpen down the stretch. On some level that's damning with faint praise since he did give up three home runs in 11 innings of work. He's a 95-and-a-cutter reliever, but flashes a good change as well. The 95 part is important though. While the fastball has decent spin, Brogdon's command is fringy and when he doesn't have the top-end velocity, he gets hit hard, which he didn't in his first major league spin in August. He came back from the alternate site in September with 95+ though, and much better outings followed. If he carries the borderline plus-plus heat into 2021 he could slot right into the seventh or eighth inning for the Phillies.

JoJo Romero **LHP** Born: 09/09/96 Age: 24 Bats: L Throws: L Height: 5'11" Weight: 200 Origin: Round 4, 2016 Draft (#107 overall)

YEAR	TEAM	LVL	AGE	W	L	SV	G	GS	IP	H	HR	BB/9	K/9	K	GB%	BABIP	WHIP	ERA	DRA-	WARP
2018	REA	AA	21	7	6	0	18	18	106²	97	13	3.5	8.4	100	51.8%	.289	1.29	3.80	95	1.1
2019	REA	AA	22	4	4	0	11	11	57²	58	4	1.9	8.1	52	47.7%	.325	1.21	4.84	102	0.0
2019	LHV	AAA	22	3	5	0	13	13	53²	68	8	5.9	6.7	40	49.5%	.347	1.92	6.88	163	-0.6
2020	PHI	MLB	23	0	0	0	12	0	10²	13	1	1.7	8.4	10	48.5%	.387	1.41	7.59	78	0.2
2021 FS	PHI	MLB	24	2	2	5	57	0	50	50	7	4.3	7.5	41	46.6%	.293	1.48	5.04	110	-0.2
2021 DC	PHI	MLB	24	2	2	5	52	0	55	55	8	4.3	7.5	46	46.6%	.293	1.48	5.04	110	0.0

Comparables: Logan Allen, Génesis Cabrera, Drew Anderson

Once a mid-rotation starting pitching prospect, Romero continued his 'pen conversion that began in the 2019 AFL. He's consolidated down to one breaking ball, the slider, which was always the better of the two, and he's continued to throw his plus-flashing changeup. His fastball velocity jumped up a few ticks in relief, and he's now sitting mid-90s. He's still got mid-rotation starting stuff, basically, but it seems to work best in the pen, and even though he's a lefty he's more suited for multi-inning work than LOOGYness.

Damon Jones **LHP** Born: 09/30/94 Age: 26 Bats: L Throws: L Height: 6'5" Weight: 233 Origin: Round 18, 2017 Draft (#533 overall)

YEAR	TEAM	LVL	AGE	W	L	SV	G	GS	IP	H	HR	BB/9	K/9	K	GB%	BABIP	WHIP	ERA	DRA-	WARP
2018	JS	LO-A	23	10	7	0	23	22	113¹	105	7	4.0	9.8	123	55.8%	.329	1.37	3.41	83	1.6
2019	CLR	HI-A	24	4	3	0	11	11	58¹	38	3	3.7	13.6	88	56.9%	.315	1.06	1.54	64	1.4
2019	REA	AA	24	1	0	0	4	4	22	9	0	3.7	12.7	31	52.5%	.225	0.82	0.82	54	0.6
2019	LHV	AAA	24	0	1	0	8	8	34	27	4	6.9	8.7	33	51.6%	.258	1.56	6.62	103	0.6
2021 FS	PHI	MLB	26	8	10	0	26	26	150	134	24	6.5	10.4	174	46.4%	.293	1.61	5.44	119	-0.5
2021 DC	PHI	MLB	26	1	2	0	8	8	35	31	5	6.5	10.4	40	46.4%	.293	1.61	5.44	119	0.0

Comparables: Anthony Kay, Alex Reyes, Gregory Soto

Jones really should've popped up in the majors in 2020 given the needs of the major-league team; it was his age-25 season and he'd already made Triple-A. That he didn't is a red flag, and sure enough he had issues with pitch location and consistency at the alternate site. There was always some reliever risk given his age and command woes, and it's trending more so that way now, although as a lefty who throws gas he'll probably do fine there in the end.

Ramón Rosso RHP Born: 06/09/96 Age: 25 Bats: R Throws: R Height: 6'4" Weight: 240 Origin: International Free Agent, 2015

YEAR	TEAM	LVL	AGE	W	L	SV	G	GS	IP	H	HR	BB/9	K/9	K	GB%	BABIP	WHIP	ERA	DRA-	WARP
2018	JS	LO-A	22	5	1	0	12	12	67²	45	3	2.7	10.8	81	48.1%	.278	0.96	1.33	67	1.6
2018	CLR	HI-A	22	6	2	0	11	10	55²	49	1	3.2	9.4	58	48.3%	.322	1.24	2.91	78	1.0
2019	REA	AA	23	3	2	0	10	10	54¹	46	8	2.5	8.6	52	32.4%	.273	1.12	3.15	90	0.4
2019	LHV	AAA	23	2	4	0	14	14	68²	67	13	4.1	8.4	64	39.7%	.283	1.43	5.50	93	1.4
2020	PHI	MLB	24	0	1	0	7	1	9²	9	1	7.4	10.2	11	15.4%	.320	1.76	6.52	126	0.0
2021 FS	PHI	MLB	25	2	3	0	57	0	50	48	9	5.1	9.0	50	33.6%	.290	1.54	5.60	120	-0.4
2021 DC	PHI	MLB	25	2	3	0	39	4	57	55	11	5.1	9.0	57	33.6%	.290	1.54	5.60	120	-0.2

Comparables: Hunter Harvey, Mike Shawaryn, Ryan Helsley

Rosso's velocity jumped during spring training, and he was on the verge of making the team when things shut down. He was used as an up-and-down reliever in the pandemic season, and was sitting low-to-mid-90s and touching 97 pretty regularly; given that he was previously sitting around 90 or even less and had a hard time cracking 92, that's a pretty big jump. He's probably just a 95-and-a-slider setup guy, but I would've never projected that having seen him a half-dozen times in Low-A.

MLB-ready bats, but less upside than you'd like

Mickey Moniak CF Born: 05/13/98 Age: 23 Bats: L Throws: R Height: 6'2" Weight: 195 Origin: Round 1, 2016 Draft (#1 overall)

YEAR	TEAM	LVL	AGE	PA	R	2B	3B	HR	RBI	BB	K	SB	CS	AVG/OBP/SLG	DRC+	BABIP	BRR	FRAA	WARP
2018	CLR	HI-A	20	465	50	28	3	5	55	22	100	6	5	.270/.304/.383	85	.334	-0.1	CF(99) -7.3, LF(9) -0.3, RF(2) -0.5	-1.1
2019	REA	AA	21	504	63	28	13	11	67	33	111	15	3	.252/.303/.439	96	.307	1.4	CF(94) -2.2, RF(24) 0.5	1.3
2020	PHI	MLB	22	18	3	0	0	0	0	4	6	0	0	.214/.389/.214	83	.375	0.2	LF(5) 0.5, RF(1) 0.1	0.1
2021 FS	PHI	MLB	23	600	56	23	5	13	56	37	178	7	3	.215/.270/.347	65	.292	2.6	LF -4, RF 1	-0.9
2021 DC	PHI	MLB	23	237	22	9	2	5	22	14	70	2	1	.215/.270/.347	65	.292	1.0	LF -2, RF 0	-0.5

Comparables: Brett Phillips, Dustin Fowler, Carlos Tocci

Nearly five years after he was selected first overall, and with plenty of digital ink spilled at Baseball Prospectus and elsewhere about his professional struggles, Moniak debuted in the majors looking like a perfectly fine fourth outfielder. His approach and swing have never really developed, leaving the plus-plus hit tool projected as an amateur as mere vaporware. Moniak remains a solid enough center fielder with sneaky pop and should have a 5-10 year career as a good bench outfielder and occasional starter.

Nick Maton SS Born: 02/18/97 Age: 24 Bats: L Throws: R Height: 6'2" Weight: 178 Origin: Round 7, 2017 Draft (#203 overall)

YEAR	TEAM	LVL	AGE	PA	R	2B	3B	HR	RBI	BB	K	SB	CS	AVG/OBP/SLG	DRC+	BABIP	BRR	FRAA	WARP
2018	JS	LO-A	21	466	52	26	5	8	51	43	103	5	3	.256/.330/.404	102	.318	1.6	SS(110) 7.4, 2B(3) -0.3	2.2
2019	CLR	HI-A	22	384	35	14	3	5	45	41	71	11	8	.276/.358/.380	126	.335	-5.9	SS(65) -2.0, 2B(15) -0.1, 3B(8) -0.1	1.6
2019	REA	AA	22	72	6	3	0	2	6	9	14	1	1	.210/.306/.355	94	.234	0.1	2B(11) -0.1, SS(8) -0.2	0.2
2021 FS	PHI	MLB	24	600	61	26	3	14	59	48	170	5	3	.228/.296/.365	81	.305	-1.9	2B -2, SS 2	0.3
2021 DC	PHI	MLB	24	203	20	8	1	4	20	16	57	1	1	.228/.296/.365	81	.305	-0.7	2B -1, SS 1	0.1

Comparables: Nick Ahmed, Tyler Smith, Todd Frazier

Maton might be the infield version of Moniak—although he got some outfield reps at the alternate site as well. There's enough glove up the middle to carve out a decent bench role, and he's added strength and started hitting the ball harder. The hard contact will likely result in more doubles than home runs, but it's a positive sign. Seeing and adjusting to upper minors secondary stuff in 2021 will give us a better idea if Maton is just a useful bench piece or a potential major league starter.

Prospects to dream on a little

Kendall Simmons SS Born: 04/11/00 Age: 21 Bats: R Throws: R Height: 6'2" Weight: 180 Origin: Round 6, 2018 Draft (#167 overall)

YEAR	TEAM	LVL	AGE	PA	R	2B	3B	HR	RBI	BB	K	SB	CS	AVG/OBP/SLG	DRC+	BABIP	BRR	FRAA	WARP
2018	PHE	ROK	18	113	21	7	0	3	11	9	30	2	4	.232/.345/.400		.302			
2019	WIL	SS	19	205	31	7	3	12	34	20	54	5	6	.234/.333/.520	126	.255	0.1	2B(23) -2.0, 3B(16) -0.9, SS(8) -1.1	0.7
2021 FS	PHI	MLB	21	600	51	26	3	13	57	32	222	10	7	.198/.258/.328	59	.303	-8.2	SS -2, 2B -1	-2.5

Comparables: Zach Green, Christopher Bostick, Dylan Cozens

By going under slot for Alec Bohm in 2018 the Phillies were able to give Simmons an overslot bonus. He has one of the better collections of physical tools in the Phillies' system, and posts some of the highest exit velocities of any hitter in the organization. During the lost season, Simmons added even more muscle, and impressed in his short time at the instructional league before an injury limited his reps. There are still a lot of swing-and-miss issues that he will need to work through, but he also has the ability to impact the baseball in a special way. On defense, Simmons has made strides, but probably isn't a shortstop full time, rather more likely to end up at second or third. A first pass at full-season ball in 2021 could see Simmons exposed against better arms, or rocketing up lists.

Erik Miller LHP Born: 02/13/98 Age: 23 Bats: L Throws: L Height: 6'5" Weight: 240 Origin: Round 4, 2019 Draft (#120 overall)

YEAR	TEAM	LVL	AGE	W	L	SV	G	GS	IP	H	HR	BB/9	K/9	K	GB%	BABIP	WHIP	ERA	DRA-	WARP
2019	WIL	SS	21	0	0	0	6	4	20	13	0	3.1	13.1	29	52.2%	.289	1.00	0.90	48	0.6
2019	JS	LO-A	21	1	0	0	3	2	13	10	0	4.2	11.8	17	29.0%	.323	1.23	2.08	88	0.1
2021 FS	PHI	MLB	23	2	3	0	57	0	50	47	7	5.5	9.4	52	39.5%	.297	1.56	5.31	122	-0.5

Comparables: Tarik Skubal, Austin Voth, Murphy Smith

The Phillies took Miller in the fourth round of the 2019 draft with the hope that they could get him to command the high-end stuff he flashed in college. In his first season, he was able to make command improvements, but his velocity was down, sitting mostly in the low 90s. The Phillies did not invite him to their alternate site, but he did pitch in the instructional league where he reportedly dominated. His fastball velocity was back up near its college peak, routinely up to 95, touching 96-97. Miller will also show a plus slider and an average changeup. If the command and velocity improvements are real, there is a path to a mid-rotation starter ceiling with some changeup growth. However, given past inconsistency there is still a significant chance that Miller ends up in the bullpen long term. He likely opens 2021 in Double-A where hopefully the OFP will start to become clearer.

Logan O'Hoppe C Born: 02/09/00 Age: 21 Bats: R Throws: R Height: 6'2" Weight: 185 Origin: Round 23, 2018 Draft (#677 overall)

YEAR	TEAM	LVL	AGE	PA	R	2B	3B	HR	RBI	BB	K	SB	CS	AVG/OBP/SLG	DRC+	BABIP	BRR	FRAA	WARP
2018	PHW	ROK	18	124	19	10	1	2	21	10	28	2	1	.367/.411/.532		.458			
2019	WIL	SS	19	177	20	12	2	5	26	12	49	3	0	.216/.266/.407	77	.270	-0.1	C(34) 0.3	0.4
2021 FS	PHI	MLB	21	600	49	27	3	12	57	32	219	4	1	.205/.251/.331	57	.309	1.3	C 0	-0.7

Comparables: Lou Marson, Will Middlebrooks, Oscar Hernández

Due to a whole series of circumstances and his physical proximity to Philadelphia, O'Hoppe found himself jumping directly from the New York-Penn League to summer camp and then the Phillies' alternate site. In both places, O'Hoppe impressed both on and off the field. He reportedly made progress on his bat-to-ball skills, and with a .216 average and 27.7 percent K-rate in 2019, there was certainly improvement to be made. He showed solid power and good defensive tools and got rave reviews for his makeup and leadership skills from the Phillies. O'Hoppe has a chance to be an everyday catcher, and he may be in the middle of a breakout of sorts, but jumping from short season to facing the same Triple-A pitchers everyday is not the same as putting up improvement day in and day out in full-season ball.

Top Talents 25 and Under (as of 4/1/2021):

1. Alec Bohm, 3B
2. Mick Abel, RHP
3. Spencer Howard, RHP

4. Francisco Morales, RHP
5. Bryson Stott, IF
6. Johan Rojas, OF
7. Adam Haseley, OF
8. Rafael Marchan, C
9. Simon Muzziotti, OF
10. Casey Martin, IF

Alec Bohm just keeps hitting. He posted a .338 average as a rookie, although it was on the emptyish side and his DRC+ was a more down-to-earth 100. We expect his power to show up—a 90.2 mph average exit velocity bodes well there—but as has been true since he was drafted, he really could use to start lifting the ball more to get to all of his game power.

Back when Adam Haseley was a prospect, we were concerned he was a bit tweenerish—not enough power to carry a corner, not enough range to want to play him in center. Through 334 major league plate appearances, he's slugged .382 and spent about 37 percent of his outfield in a corner, so, yeah. He gets on base enough to be useful, at least.

Pittsburgh Pirates

The State of the System:

There's plenty of high upside talent in the Pirates' system now, but this rebuild is probably going to last a while longer given the lack of overall depth.

The Top Ten:

───────────────── ★ ★ ★ *2021 Top 101 Prospect* **#7** ★ ★ ★ ─────────────────

1   **Ke'Bryan Hayes   3B**   OFP: 70   ETA: Debuted in 2020

Born: 01/28/97   Age: 24   Bats: R   Throws: R   Height: 5'10"   Weight: 205   Origin: Round 1, 2015 Draft (#32 overall)

YEAR	TEAM	LVL	AGE	PA	R	2B	3B	HR	RBI	BB	K	SB	CS	AVG/OBP/SLG	DRC+	BABIP	BRR	FRAA	WARP
2018	ALT	AA	21	508	64	31	7	7	47	57	84	12	5	.293/.375/.444	128	.344	-0.8	3B(116) 9.0	3.5
2019	IND	AAA	22	480	64	30	2	10	53	43	90	12	1	.265/.336/.415	96	.311	2.3	3B(104) 8.2	2.3
2020	PIT	MLB	23	95	17	7	2	5	11	9	20	1	0	.376/.442/.682	115	.450	0.6	3B(24) 3.0	0.7
2021 FS	PIT	MLB	24	600	68	28	4	14	64	51	139	7	2	.254/.327/.403	99	.319	4.0	3B 14	3.0
2021 DC	PIT	MLB	24	564	64	26	4	13	60	48	131	7	2	.254/.327/.403	99	.319	3.8	3B 13	2.8

Comparables: Andy Marte, Ian Stewart, Willy Aybar

The Report: If you got to the park by 4 p.m., Hayes looked like a perennial All-Star in waiting. He'd flash plus-plus raw power at the end of batting practice, and early on when he was taking it easy and getting loose, would still crack laser beam line drives from gap to gap. The plus-or-better glove at third base was obvious as well. At 7 p.m.? Well, he still looked like a very good third base prospect. The glove was more obviously plus-plus as he'd slow the game down, or fire an accurate strike from a step or two into foul territory. There was a strong approach at the plate, and he'd hit the ball incredibly hard—it's at least 70-grade bat speed. But Hayes didn't lift pitches consistently, instead ripping doubles down the left field line when he really got into one. He never managed double-digit home run totals until 2019 with the Triple-A rabbit ball, in what was overall a bit of a disappointing campaign. The lack of game power seemed to limit the upside to merely a good regular as Hayes stood on the precipice of the majors.

Development Track: After implying that Hayes could have the everyday third base job if he just signed a cheap extension, the Pirates finally gave him some run at the hot corner at the end of a lost season. If you want a bright spot for the 2020 season—in addition to securing the first overall pick, I guess—he immediately found that missing over-the-fence game power. And these home runs weren't cheapies. It's not a large enough sample size to be sure it will play as plus going forward—he's still list eligible, after all—but it looked very, very right. As did the rest of the offensive profile and the glove at third. But we've long been pretty sure about those.

Variance: Medium. Hayes was always likely to be a good regular given the approach, plus hit tool, and plus-plus glove. How real the 2020 power breakout is will dictate exactly how good a regular.

Mark Barry's Fantasy Take: I long loved Hayes, believing his minor-league numbers masked his true upside. Then around this time last year, I hedged like a coward and tempered expectations as to whether Hayes could be an impact bat. Yes, it's fewer than 100 plate appearances, but Hayes looks every bit like That Dude, making a ton of loud contact and finding a way to consistently leave the yard. Hayes is a top-10 dynasty name, for me, pushing top five, and I'm sorry for doubting him.

2 Nick Gonzales SS   OFP: 60   ETA: 2023

Born: 05/27/99   Age: 22   Bats: R   Throws: R   Height: 5'10"   Weight: 190   Origin: Round 1, 2020 Draft (#7 overall)

The Report: This is not your typical top-of-the-draft, top-of-the-system prospect. Undersized, from a smaller school, playing a non-premium position, Gonzales somehow managed to win over the detractors to the point where his selection didn't even merit the bat of an eye. Look past the video game numbers racked up at the friendly confines of New Mexico State's extreme hitter's park and toward the campaign he put up at the Cape Cod League. As the 2019 MVP he slashed .351/.451/.630 against consistently better competition and in a pitcher's league. The swing is lightning quick with excellent hand-speed, angling his torso at the waist to create tons of natural lift. He may get a few looks at other positions, second base seems like the most likely fit where his offense would play up comparatively against his peers.

Development Track: Consider this next part as an extension of his report, but one attribute that might be his best tool is his makeup. One scout at the Cape likened him to Bryce Harper as the quintessential gym rat, constantly working out and trying to improve his game. While at school, he even reportedly was giving switch-hitting a try in the batting cages. All this to impress upon the point that even though his defense may be lacking, it's not because of any lack of effort. He's known to flash a stellar play a time or two, what he needs is more consistency and concentration in the field with his physical ability taking over.

Variance: Medium. Borderline low variance, but still needs to adjust to quality pitching day-in, day-out. Knowing how much he'll likely work his tail off, it helps quell most fear associated with his future.

Mark Barry's Fantasy Take: There are a couple of questions re: Gonzales from a fantasy standpoint: 1) How real was the power in such a power-friendly environment like New Mexico? and 2) Will he run at all? I think he'll make a ton of contact, but it might not be fantasy impact unless the answers to those questions are 1) Real/spectacular and 2) Yes, some. He's a top-five pick in FYPD depending on how you view pitching, though, and will probably be a top-40 prospect.

3 Liover Peguero SS   OFP: 60   ETA: Late 2022/Early 2023

Born: 12/31/00   Age: 20   Bats: R   Throws: R   Height: 6'1"   Weight: 160   Origin: International Free Agent, 2017

YEAR	TEAM	LVL	AGE	PA	R	2B	3B	HR	RBI	BB	K	SB	CS	AVG/OBP/SLG	DRC+	BABIP	BRR	FRAA	WARP
2018	DSL DB1	ROK	17	90	14	3	3	1	16	6	12	4	1	.309/.356/.457		.343			
2018	DIA	ROK	17	71	8	0	0	0	5	5	17	3	2	.197/.254/.197		.265			
2019	MIS	ROK+	18	156	34	7	3	5	27	12	34	8	1	.364/.410/.559		.448			
2019	HIL	SS	18	93	13	4	2	0	11	8	17	3	1	.262/.333/.357	103	.328	0.1	SS(18) -0.1	0.4
2021 FS	PIT	MLB	20	600	46	26	4	7	51	29	188	13	4	.227/.268/.329	62	.327	4.1	SS 4	-0.2

Comparables: Eduardo Núñez, Amed Rosario, Sergio Alcántara

The Report: Peguero stands out right away for the verve he brings onto the diamond. Then his batting practice starts, and he stands out for loud, hard contact. The swing is incredibly short, but he has elite hand/wrist strength that allows him to punish baseballs. Peguero is still prone to chase, but the barrel control is strong enough that he can get to most pitches thrown his way. He does not cut the most physical figure on the field, but as a player who just turned 20, he already has most of his man strength. Oh, he is also a plus runner with above-average arm strength in the field. Most of the mistakes I have seen from him at shortstop can be ironed out over time and with more defensive reps—not getting enough on a throw, being too casual, going too fast when not needed.

Development Track: Peguero may partner up with Gonzales as the everyday double play combination for Low-A Bradenton in 2021. He could also be pushed more aggressively since he is Rule 5 eligible after next season and is an obvious protection candidate. A full-season worth of games can have Peguero shoot up next year's Pirates list and into the Top 101.

Variance: Medium. There are enough tools here that even if he moves off SS, he will find an above-average defensive position somewhere. The home run power may be less than you would hope given his frame but this is still nearly a five-tool player, and tools play.

Mark Barry's Fantasy Take: Reason 2,304,283 that I'm mad about 2020 is that it deprived us of seeing Peguero's progression in Pittsburgh. The dude makes a ton of contact and could even see some of those high-contact batted balls wind up over the fence. He reminds me a little of Jean Segura or Whit Merrifield (minus some steals), and while those aren't overly sexy names, they still keep Peguero in the top-75 dynasty prospects or so.

4 Quinn Priester RHP   OFP: 60   ETA: 2023
Born: 09/15/00   Age: 20   Bats: R   Throws: R   Height: 6'3"   Weight: 195   Origin: Round 1, 2019 Draft (#18 overall)

YEAR	TEAM	LVL	AGE	W	L	SV	G	GS	IP	H	HR	BB/9	K/9	K	GB%	BABIP	WHIP	ERA	DRA-	WARP
2019	PIR	ROK	18	1	1	0	8	7	32²	29	1	2.8	10.2	37	57.3%	.322	1.19	3.03		
2019	WV	SS	18	0	0	0	1	1	4	3	0	9.0	9.0	4	90.0%	.300	1.75	4.50	100	0.0
2021 FS	PIT	MLB	20	2	3	0	57	0	50	50	8	5.4	8.1	44	47.9%	.297	1.61	5.68	131	-0.7

Comparables: Junior Fernández, Brad Keller, Ronald Herrera

The Report: As one evaluator during instructs put it, "He looks like a young Gerritt Cole with blonde hair". This is rather high praise, but fits in some regards. Priester has obvious physical similarities, looking much more imposing than his listed 6-foot-3, 195 lbs. The fastball velocity has climbed as a pro, now comfortably sitting 95 and touching as high as 97. He throws strikes with the heater and repeats his delivery well, The breaking ball isn't a slider, instead a firm 12-6 curve in the low-80s with quality depth. He located the breaker with ease in my viewing. Plus grades on the fastball and curve are well within reach and could end up as high as plus-plus for both. The gains Priester has made since his name was first written in these pages last year have come ahead of schedule.

Development Track: Not that he would've likely thrown 130+ innings in Low-A ball in 2020, but yeah, full-season innings would've been nice. The physical gains that Priester has made has translated to stuff on the mound, leading to an overall diminished projection. The velocity gains need to be put to the test over a long season and full workload, as does the strike-throwing.

Variance: High. Priester is a recent first-round selection with obviously projectable stuff he has already started to realize. There will be a future for him, as well as quite a long development leash as a starting pitcher.

Mark Barry's Fantasy Take: I wrote last season that Priester was pretty far away and amounted to a dart throw for dynasty managers. While he's reportedly made some improvements since, not a lot has changed with his timeline. Still, I'd add him in super-deep leagues, or keep him on the watchlist for anything shallower.

5 Brennan Malone RHP   OFP: 60   ETA: 2024
Born: 09/08/00   Age: 20   Bats: R   Throws: R   Height: 6'4"   Weight: 205   Origin: Round 1, 2019 Draft (#33 overall)

YEAR	TEAM	LVL	AGE	W	L	SV	G	GS	IP	H	HR	BB/9	K/9	K	GB%	BABIP	WHIP	ERA	DRA-	WARP
2019	DIA	ROK	18	1	2	0	6	3	7	4	0	6.4	9.0	7	33.3%	.222	1.29	5.14		
2019	HIL	SS	18	0	0	0	1	0	1	0	0	0.0	9.0	1	50.0%	.000	0.00	0.00	68	0.0
2021 FS	PIT	MLB	20	2	3	0	57	0	50	52	8	6.6	7.9	44	35.9%	.300	1.77	6.37	143	-1.1

Comparables: Elvis Luciano, Devin Williams, Randy Rosario

The Report/Developmental Track: One of the most physically mature prep pitchers you'll ever see, Malone was settling nicely into the D'backs' organization after being selected 33rd overall, even getting into a playoff race game with short-season Hillsboro. He was then part of the package shipped to the Pirates in the Starling Marte deal, and by all accounts was set to take off in 2020. The filled-out 6-foot-5 frame delivers plenty of velocity into the mid-90s and three distinct secondary pitches that could each be weapons in the future. Everything about his profile screams workhorse starter.

Variance: Very High. You hate to see young pitchers miss out on the first full season of development. (insert guy shrugging emoji)

Mark Barry's Fantasy Take: There's a chance that Malone could eventually outpace Priester, but ultimately I have more faith in Priester's secondaries. Malone still has big strikeout upside, I'm just not interested beyond leagues with 200+ prospects.

6 Tahnaj Thomas RHP   OFP: 55   ETA: 2023/2024

Born: 06/16/99   Age: 22   Bats: R   Throws: R   Height: 6'4"   Weight: 190   Origin: International Free Agent, 2016

YEAR	TEAM	LVL	AGE	W	L	SV	G	GS	IP	H	HR	BB/9	K/9	K	GB%	BABIP	WHIP	ERA	DRA-	WARP
2018	INDR	ROK	19	0	0	0	8	6	19²	13	2	4.6	12.4	27	54.8%	.275	1.17	4.58		
2019	BRS	ROK+	20	2	3	0	12	12	48¹	40	5	2.6	11.0	59	41.6%	.292	1.12	3.17		
2021 FS	PIT	MLB	22	2	3	0	57	0	50	49	9	7.8	8.9	49	38.0%	.294	1.86	6.72	144	-1.1

The Report: After being traded to the Pirates from Cleveland during the 2018 offseason, Thomas quickly found success the following year in the Appalachian League, posting career-best numbers across the board. The former infielder hurled 48 1/3 innings across 12 starts and pitched to a 3.17 ERA with 59 strikeouts against 14 walks. The stuff matched the stats in this case. Thomas' fastball sits in the mid-to-high-90s and can touch triple digits with plus ride. In 2020, he became more comfortable throwing the pitch at the top of the zone and focused on command to all four quadrants. The slider also took a step forward as he gained better feel for the offering and began using it in a wider variety of counts. Once Thomas deploys those two pitches with more consistent efficiency, the changeup will need to be addressed. The development of the change will determine the ultimate role for him, but the stuff projects to have late-inning impact if he does end up in the bullpen.

Development Track: Thomas has only been a full-time pitcher since 2017, so he is still a ways away from mapping out a definitive time table—his 48 1/3 innings in 2019 were a career high after all. Depending on where the Pirates assign Thomas at the beginning of the 2021 season—seemingly either the complex league or Low-A Bradenton—will be a good clue to where he is developmentally.

Variance: Extreme. Although Thomas has made solid progress over the last two years, players who go from the field to the mound have tons of risk. Plus, there is still a nice chunk of development left. Check back in a year, or two.

Mark Barry's Fantasy Take: My pal J.P. Breen loves Thomas. I like Thomas fine, but wish we had more to go on. Pitchers are notoriously risky, but I'd much rather take a shot on a guy like Thomas, who definitely has impact upside.

7 Travis Swaggerty OF   OFP: 55   ETA: Late 2021 / Early 2022

Born: 08/19/97   Age: 23   Bats: L   Throws: L   Height: 5'11"   Weight: 180   Origin: Round 1, 2018 Draft (#10 overall)

YEAR	TEAM	LVL	AGE	PA	R	2B	3B	HR	RBI	BB	K	SB	CS	AVG/OBP/SLG	DRC+	BABIP	BRR	FRAA	WARP
2018	WV	SS	20	158	22	9	1	4	15	15	40	9	3	.288/.365/.453	146	.379	0.9	CF(36) -0.6	0.7
2018	WV	LO-A	20	71	6	1	1	1	5	7	18	0	0	.129/.225/.226	43	.159	-0.6	CF(16) 0.7	-0.3
2019	BRD	HI-A	21	524	79	20	3	9	40	57	116	23	8	.265/.347/.381	123	.334	-0.2	CF(121) 7.4	3.7
2021 FS	PIT	MLB	23	600	54	26	2	13	60	42	191	9	4	.221/.281/.353	75	.311	-0.9	CF 6	0.5

Comparables: Aaron Hicks, Jake Cave, Anthony Alford

The Report: At times in 2019 Swaggerty struggled, but he finished the second half on a strong note, as he slashed .306/.375/.430 over his final 63 games in the rough offensive environment of Bradenton. He made adjustments controlling his forward movement, getting to his hitting position on time more and honing in his launch position. With these positive progressions, paired with his approach and bat control, a continued, if delayed, surge could happen in 2021. In the outfield, Swaggerty's instincts and speed make him a plus center fielder. Additionally, in 2019 he swiped 23 bags in the Florida State League, tied for fifth in the circuit, which, along with his defense, will be his two most notable calling cards in the majors.

Development Track: So far, the Pirates have been fairly aggressive with the former first rounder. After scuffling at the end of 2018 in the South Atlantic League, Swaggerty was sent to High-A Bradenton to begin 2019. So an assignment to start 2021 in Double-A Altoona, or even Triple-A Indianapolis after competing at the alternate site, to test Swaggerty's revamped swing wouldn't be a shock, especially given the way he finished 2019.

Variance: Medium. The glove and speed tools should carry Swaggerty to an outfield bench role in the bigs. How much impact he has with the bat is the question here.

Mark Barry's Fantasy Take: It will be very interesting to see how Swaggerty's adjustments will carry over to competitive action. He already has a solid fantasy skillset with contact/speed, and if he can add anything to it, that's a super playable profile. I'd be making some inquiries on Swaggerty before we kick off the 2021 campaign, because if he starts out the season hitting, he won't be cheap.

8 Cal Mitchell RF   OFP: 55   ETA: 2022

Born: 03/08/99   Age: 22   Bats: L   Throws: L   Height: 6'0"   Weight: 209   Origin: Round 2, 2017 Draft (#50 overall)

YEAR	TEAM	LVL	AGE	PA	R	2B	3B	HR	RBI	BB	K	SB	CS	AVG/OBP/SLG	DRC+	BABIP	BRR	FRAA	WARP
2018	WV	LO-A	19	494	55	29	3	10	65	41	108	4	5	.281/.345/.428	126	.347	-4.4	RF(99) 0.5, LF(10) -1.6	0.8
2019	BRD	HI-A	20	493	54	21	2	15	64	32	142	1	1	.251/.304/.406	104	.328	0.0	RF(111) -0.4	1.0
2021 FS	PIT	MLB	22	600	58	26	2	17	65	41	196	1	0	.227/.287/.376	80	.320	-0.7	RF 1, LF 0	0.1

Comparables: Oswaldo Arcia, Gabriel Guerrero, Yorman Rodriguez

The Report: If we were doing our old The Good/The Bad format, we'd list "The Good" here as the hit and power tools and "The Bad" as basically everything else. Mitchell has an effortless and compact swing from the left side, enough to project to a plus hit tool if the plate approach holds up. He has plus power and the ball jumps off his bat. Of course, the "if" is carrying a lot of weight there; he ran a 142/32 K/BB ratio in High-A in 2019, and he was much too aggressive against offspeed pitches there. Mitchell's not going to produce much defensive value, so the bat is going to have to carry him, and while we still like the swing a lot, he's coming off a mediocre year and then a nearly lost one.

Development Track: We don't have much new to say on Mitchell. He was bypassed for the alternate site, which is telling us a little something; he was at instructs in the fall, but we didn't get any particularly notable feedback on his performance there. He should get a crack at Double-A in 2021.

Variance: High. We didn't get a better handle on the hit tool risk in 2020.

Mark Barry's Fantasy Take: I'm super into Good Hit and Power Tools for fantasy, because defense, shmeefense. However, I am extremely not into striking out nearly 30 percent of the time at High-A. I wouldn't write anyone off at 21 years old, but Mitchell is off my radar for now.

9 Cody Bolton RHP   OFP: 55   ETA: Late 2021/Early 2022

Born: 06/19/98   Age: 23   Bats: R   Throws: R   Height: 6'3"   Weight: 185   Origin: Round 6, 2017 Draft (#178 overall)

YEAR	TEAM	LVL	AGE	W	L	SV	G	GS	IP	H	HR	BB/9	K/9	K	GB%	BABIP	WHIP	ERA	DRA-	WARP
2018	WV	LO-A	20	3	3	0	9	9	44¹	43	6	1.4	9.1	45	41.3%	.308	1.13	3.65	81	0.7
2019	BRD	HI-A	21	6	3	0	12	12	61²	39	1	2.0	10.1	69	48.1%	.245	0.86	1.61	56	1.7
2019	ALT	AA	21	2	3	0	9	9	40	37	6	3.6	7.4	33	33.9%	.279	1.32	5.85	88	0.3
2021 FS	PIT	MLB	23	2	3	0	57	0	50	49	8	3.5	8.0	44	35.3%	.290	1.38	4.46	110	-0.2

Comparables: Edwin Díaz, Rony García, Tyler Mahle

The Report: Bolton began 2019 with High-A Bradenton and absolutely shoved, where he compiled a 1.61 ERA with 69 strikeouts over 61 2/3 innings, which led to a midseason promotion to Double-A Altoona. While there, however, Bolton struggled mightily in his nine starts, getting victimized by the long ball. To bounce back from the rough stretch, Bolton needs to improve pitch execution for all three offerings, especially working on his changeup development, as that pitch lagged behind the fastball and slider in 2019. Bolton's fastball sits in the low-to-mid-90s showing some cut and life to it, while the slider is a power breaker in the high-80s with average command that he pairs with the fastball well. He made some strides with his changeup at the alternate site, but needs to continue to work on starting it in the zone and getting it to consistently turn over to make it the needed third pitch in the arsenal.

Development Track: Given Bolton's struggles in his first Altoona stint there's a chance he returns to the Eastern League in 2021. He will only turn 23 next season, so there isn't a need to rush him to the bullpen yet, but to stay a starter long term, he will need to keep developing the changeup and add more innings to his ledger.

Variance: Medium. As mentioned above, the fastball and slider will play at the highest level and should earn Bolton a late-inning role in the bigs. Although, a mid-rotation starter projection is still in play for now.

Mark Barry's Fantasy Take: I think Bolton is probably a reliever, so he doesn't need to be on your radar until he lands a ninth-inning job.

10 Max Kranick RHP   OFP: 50   ETA: Late 2022/Early 2023

Born: 07/21/97 Age: 23 Bats: R Throws: R Height: 6'3" Weight: 175 Origin: Round 11, 2016 Draft (#345 overall)

YEAR	TEAM	LVL	AGE	W	L	SV	G	GS	IP	H	HR	BB/9	K/9	K	GB%	BABIP	WHIP	ERA	DRA-	WARP
2018	WV	LO-A	20	4	5	1	17	16	78	72	7	2.1	8.9	77	35.6%	.302	1.15	3.81	127	-0.8
2019	BRD	HI-A	21	6	7	0	20	20	109^1	100	11	2.5	6.4	78	41.9%	.276	1.19	3.79	99	0.3
2021 FS	PIT	MLB	23	2	3	0	57	0	50	52	8	3.3	6.6	36	36.7%	.291	1.43	4.95	119	-0.4

Comparables: Jorge López, Blake Snell, Rony García

The Report: Although Kranick has battled injury problems the last couple of years, the righty has pitched well and thrown strikes when he's been on the mound. During the quarantine year, he made a mechanical change while keeping his velocity in the mid-90s. Besides injury concerns, inducing whiffs has been another knock on Kranick. This past year, however, he began missing bats at a higher rate, as his secondaries showed more effectiveness than they had before. The changeup, sitting in the mid-80s, is deceptive out of the hand, and he shows a slider look in the low-80s and a cutter look in the upper-80s. It's not a flashy profile but Kranick does enough things well.

Development Track: Even with the injury problems, Kranick has steadily increased his innings over the years, peaking at 109 1/3 in 2019 with High-A Bradenton. From all indications, he held his own at the alternate site in Altoona this year against advanced hitters. So Kranick should be set to return there in 2021 as a Double-A starter. If the ability to miss bats continues in games next year, Kranick could push for a quick promotion. Although he will need to stay healthy long enough.

Variance: High. He throws strikes at a high rate but the injury bug is still worrisome. Until he can show signs of better durability the variance will stay. However, the report from this year is intriguing.

Mark Barry's Fantasy Take: Intriguing, yes. Kranick should be widely available if/when he gets called up, so you can make a decision then. I'm not sure he's more than a streamer.

The Prospects You Meet Outside The Top Ten

MLB arms, but less upside than you'd like

Carmen Mlodzinski RHP Born: 02/19/99 Age: 22 Bats: R Throws: R Height: 6'2" Weight: 232 Origin: Round 1, 2020 Draft (#31 overall)

Scouts had been witnessing the pure stuff for years, yet the performances and injuries kept the true potential from doing more than flashing. Finally healthy, Mlodzinski had a very strong performance at the Cape and backed that up again with another solid spring before the shutdown. His fastball is a power sinker with good movement that gets up to 95 and is located much better to his glove-side—which hitters began picking up on. He'll need to get more comfortable moving his spots around and working on his changeup to play off the sinker movement. If not, there is some reliever risk with his slider/cutter being just average as his preferred offspeed pitch.

Blake Cederlind RHP Born: 01/04/96 Age: 25 Bats: R Throws: R Height: 6'4" Weight: 205 Origin: Round 5, 2016 Draft (#165 overall)

YEAR	TEAM	LVL	AGE	W	L	SV	G	GS	IP	H	HR	BB/9	K/9	K	GB%	BABIP	WHIP	ERA	DRA-	WARP
2018	WV	LO-A	22	3	2	1	19	1	28^1	21	1	2.9	11.4	36	50.0%	.312	1.06	2.86	62	0.6
2018	BRD	HI-A	22	1	2	3	17	0	21^1	26	2	8.0	7.6	18	58.0%	.358	2.11	7.59	135	-0.4
2019	BRD	HI-A	23	0	0	2	7	0	7^2	4	0	7.0	9.4	8	50.0%	.200	1.30	1.17	77	0.1
2019	ALT	AA	23	5	1	2	31	0	45^2	31	1	3.2	8.3	42	48.8%	.252	1.03	1.77	81	0.4
2019	IND	AAA	23	0	0	2	3	0	6	11	1	3.0	7.5	5	52.0%	.435	2.17	7.50	166	-0.1
2020	PIT	MLB	24	0	0	0	5	0	4	3	0	2.2	9.0	4	54.5%	.273	1.00	4.50	87	0.1
2021 FS	PIT	MLB	25	1	1	0	57	0	50	49	7	5.6	8.2	45	45.9%	.297	1.61	5.65	118	-0.4
2021 DC	PIT	MLB	25	1	1	0	25	0	27	26	3	5.6	8.2	24	45.9%	.297	1.61	5.65	118	-0.1

Comparables: Stephen Nogosek, José Ruiz, James Norwood

If it seems like we've been writing a lot of 95-and-a-slider relievers this year, well, Cederlind's a 100-and-a-cutter guy, so that's at least a little different. He sits high-90s and touches triple-digits with a two-seam fastball that has some nasty sink on it. His "offspeed" pitch is a cutter that gets up into the low-90s. He put it together very quickly in 2019 and kept it going at the end of the 2020 season at the majors; he's got a chance to get into high-leverage work very quickly

Wil Crowe RHP Born: 09/09/94 Age: 26 Bats: R Throws: R Height: 6'2" Weight: 228 Origin: Round 2, 2017 Draft (#65 overall)

YEAR	TEAM	LVL	AGE	W	L	SV	G	GS	IP	H	HR	BB/9	K/9	K	GB%	BABIP	WHIP	ERA	DRA-	WARP
2018	AUB	SS	23	0	0	0	1	1	3	2	0	6.0	3.0	1	62.5%	.250	1.33	0.00	106	0.0
2018	FBG	HI-A	23	11	0	0	16	15	87	71	6	3.1	8.1	78	45.8%	.270	1.16	2.69	71	2.0
2018	HBG	AA	23	0	5	0	5	5	26¹	31	4	5.5	5.1	15	42.5%	.325	1.78	6.15	100	0.2
2019	HBG	AA	24	7	6	0	16	16	95¹	85	8	2.1	8.4	89	48.1%	.297	1.12	3.87	92	0.5
2019	FRE	AAA	24	0	4	0	10	10	54	66	7	4.3	6.8	41	41.2%	.337	1.70	6.17	126	0.3
2020	WAS	MLB	25	0	2	0	3	3	8¹	14	5	8.6	8.6	8	27.6%	.375	2.64	11.88	180	-0.3
2021 FS	*PIT*	*MLB*	*26*	*8*	*10*	*0*	*26*	*26*	*150*	*154*	*27*	*4.7*	*7.3*	*122*	*38.6%*	*.291*	*1.55*	*5.53*	*121*	*-0.7*
2021 DC	*PIT*	*MLB*	*26*	*3*	*4*	*0*	*12*	*12*	*59*	*60*	*10*	*4.7*	*7.3*	*48*	*38.6%*	*.291*	*1.55*	*5.53*	*121*	*0.0*

Comparables: Mitch White, Brady Lail, Joel Payamps

Dealt to the Pirates as part of the Josh Bell trade, Crowe is a major-league-ready utility arm, who has never really shown enough stuff or durability to project as an average starter. His low-90s fastball is a little too hittable due to fringy command and only occasional sink. He leaned heavily on his slider in his 2020 MLB cameo, and it might end up a tick above average. There's a curve and change as well. Crowe was unlikely to get much major-league run in Washington, but he could fulfill a variety of roles for the Pirates.

Prospects to dream on a little

Jared Jones RHP Born: 08/06/01 Age: 19 Bats: L Throws: R Height: 6'1" Weight: 180 Origin: Round 2, 2020 Draft (#44 overall)

One of the most electric arms in the draft regardless of age, Jones has one of the largest ranges of possible career outcomes. Working a heater in the upper-90s—with a lot of effort, mind you—and a snapping power curveball, it looks like the kind of stuff you see at the back-end of a bullpen right now in the majors, none in a recently drafted 19-year-old. Despite all that effort, he actually shows quite good body control, varying his delivery motion to mess with hitters trying to cheat early on the velocity. The two questions he'll face developmentally are whether he can throw enough strikes and if a third pitch can be brought along.

Mason Martin 1B Born: 06/02/99 Age: 22 Bats: L Throws: R Height: 6'0" Weight: 201 Origin: Round 17, 2017 Draft (#508 overall)

YEAR	TEAM	LVL	AGE	PA	R	2B	3B	HR	RBI	BB	K	SB	CS	AVG/OBP/SLG	DRC+	BABIP	BRR	FRAA	WARP
2018	BRS	ROK	19	269	42	10	1	10	40	42	87	2	2	.233/.357/.422		.328			
2018	WV	LO-A	19	173	16	8	0	4	18	18	62	1	1	.200/.302/.333	82	.310	0.0	1B(43) -3.0	-0.8
2019	GBO	LO-A	20	355	58	19	3	23	83	46	103	8	2	.262/.361/.575	163	.311	-1.5	1B(77) 4.1	2.9
2019	BRD	HI-A	20	201	32	13	1	12	46	22	65	0	1	.239/.333/.528	129	.303	-0.8	1B(47) 3.4	1.1
2021 FS	*PIT*	*MLB*	*22*	*600*	*55*	*27*	*2*	*15*	*60*	*55*	*241*	*2*	*1*	*.188/.270/.333*	*65*	*.304*	*-0.6*	*1B 6, RF 0*	*-1.2*

Comparables: Bobby Bradley, Chris Carter, Tyler O'Neill

Sporting prodigious power from the left side, Martin smacked 35 homers across both A-ball levels in 2019, but struck out 168 times in 556 plate appearances. He also drew 68 walks so this feels like a boom-or-bust, three true outcomes profile. Reducing those strikeout numbers, by having him hone in and be more aggressive in his hitting zone, will be crucial going forward.

Matthew Fraizer OF Born: 01/12/98 Age: 23 Bats: L Throws: R Height: 6'3" Weight: 205 Origin: Round 3, 2019 Draft (#95 overall)

YEAR	TEAM	LVL	AGE	PA	R	2B	3B	HR	RBI	BB	K	SB	CS	AVG/OBP/SLG	DRC+	BABIP	BRR	FRAA	WARP
2019	WV	SS	21	171	20	5	1	0	15	14	38	5	3	.221/.287/.266	74	.288	0.1	RF(22) 3.4, CF(11) -0.9, LF(3) 0.4	0.3
2021 FS	*PIT*	*MLB*	*23*	*600*	*46*	*26*	*2*	*7*	*50*	*35*	*193*	*10*	*5*	*.212/.263/.309*	*57*	*.308*	*-2.5*	*RF 4, CF -1*	*-1.7*

Comparables: Bryce Brentz, Bryan Petersen, DJ Stewart

After suffering a hamate injury prior the 2019 draft, Fraizer struggled in the New York Penn League, slashing .221/.287/.266 in 43 games. One issue was his contact point, which led into another, his launch angle. The return on the work in instructs has so far improved the chances of Fraizer finding some power in the stroke. How much of that will be gap-to-gap and how much over-the-fence power will need to be demonstrated in 2021.

Eddy Yean RHP Born: 06/25/01 Age: 20 Bats: R Throws: R Height: 6'1" Weight: 180 Origin: International Free Agent, 2017

YEAR	TEAM	LVL	AGE	W	L	SV	G	GS	IP	H	HR	BB/9	K/9	K	GB%	BABIP	WHIP	ERA	DRA-	WARP
2018	DSL NAT	ROK	17	1	2	0	11	10	43²	57	1	4.7	6.6	32	50.0%	.384	1.83	5.98		
2019	NAT	ROK	18	1	2	0	8	8	35¹	30	3	3.1	9.2	36	49.5%	.293	1.19	3.82		
2019	AUB	SS	18	1	1	0	2	2	11	7	0	4.1	5.7	7	40.6%	.219	1.09	2.45	89	0.1
2021 FS	PIT	MLB	20	2	3	0	57	0	50	55	8	5.6	7.4	41	41.7%	.308	1.72	6.32	141	-1.0

Comparables: José Torres, Miguel Yajure, Ronald Herrera

The other half of the Josh Bell trade return, Yean is an undersized righty with some feel for a changeup. His velocity ticked up in 2020, but he hasn't pitched above the complex level, and we haven't seen the velocity stick in a real season yet. Check back in this space in a year.

José Soriano RHP Born: 10/20/98 Age: 22 Bats: R Throws: R Height: 6'3" Weight: 220 Origin: International Free Agent, 2016

YEAR	TEAM	LVL	AGE	W	L	SV	G	GS	IP	H	HR	BB/9	K/9	K	GB%	BABIP	WHIP	ERA	DRA-	WARP
2018	BUR	LO-A	19	1	6	0	14	14	46¹	34	1	6.8	8.2	42	45.3%	.284	1.49	4.47	89	0.6
2019	ANG	ROK	20	0	1	0	3	3	4²	5	0	5.8	15.4	8	25.0%	.417	1.71	1.93		
2019	BUR	LO-A	20	5	6	0	17	15	77²	53	5	5.6	9.7	84	54.0%	.262	1.30	2.55	90	0.7
2021 FS	PIT	MLB	22	1	2	0	57	0	50	49	8	6.5	8.3	46	44.2%	.295	1.71	6.05	130	-0.7
2021 DC	PIT	MLB	22	1	2	0	22	3	33	32	5	6.5	8.3	30	44.2%	.295	1.71	6.05	130	-0.3

Comparables: Chris Flexen, Alex Reyes, Huascar Ynoa

The Pirates used the first overall pick in the 2020 Rule 5 draft to pluck arguably the best overall prospect left unprotected. Soriano hasn't pitched above A-ball and will spend at least the first few months of 2021 recovering and rehabbing from Tommy John surgery, but if healthy he could soak up some 'pen innings for the Pirates, and they might come out the other side with a potential average MLB starter or setup guy down the line given the potentially above-average fastball/curve combo.

Rodolfo Castro 2B Born: 05/21/99 Age: 22 Bats: S Throws: R Height: 6'0" Weight: 200 Origin: International Free Agent, 2015

YEAR	TEAM	LVL	AGE	PA	R	2B	3B	HR	RBI	BB	K	SB	CS	AVG/OBP/SLG	DRC+	BABIP	BRR	FRAA	WARP
2018	WV	LO-A	19	426	47	19	4	12	50	26	100	6	3	.231/.278/.395	83	.276	2.9	2B(88) 4.3, SS(11) 1.6	0.6
2019	GBO	LO-A	20	246	33	13	2	14	46	18	68	6	5	.242/.306/.516	127	.271	2.1	2B(34) -0.2, SS(17) -0.9, 3B(7) 0.5	1.6
2019	BRD	HI-A	20	215	26	13	1	5	27	13	54	1	0	.243/.288/.391	105	.308	0.3	2B(37) 1.9, SS(16) -1.2, 3B(4) -0.1	0.9
2021 FS	PIT	MLB	22	600	53	27	3	16	62	36	204	4	2	.207/.260/.356	64	.294	0.0	2B 3, SS 0	-0.5

Comparables: Luke Hughes, Cory Spangenberg, Christopher Bostick

Castro has some interesting pieces in his game; pro scouts have pegged him as a favorite to us going back to 2018. He's a switch-hitter who takes loose swings that are well-suited for power both in the gaps and over the fences. Primarily a second baseman, he can play all around the dirt. The downside is his pitch recognition, and that limits the hit tool presently. Castro was at the alternate site and added to the 40-man this offseason even though he's never played above A-ball, and the team liked his development this season.

Top Talents 25 and Under (as of 4/1/2021):

1. Ke'Bryan Hayes, 3B
2. Nick Gonzales, IF
3. Mitch Keller, RHP
4. Liover Peguero, SS
5. Quinn Priester, RHP
6. Brennan Malone, RHP
7. Bryan Reynolds, OF
8. Tahnaj Thomas, RHP
9. Travis Swaggerty, OF

10. Cole Tucker, SS

Mitch Keller's 2020 performance was the opposite of his 2019: shiny ERA (2.91), awful underlying rates (7.06 DRA and more walks than strikeouts). It feels like we've been writing about Keller's inconsistency and wavering command since the earth started spinning, but somehow he only has 69 2/3 MLB innings; he missed a bunch of time in 2020 with oblique problems. He continued down the 2019 path as a fastball/slider/curve pitcher when he was on the mound, only throwing his changeup 3.4 percent of the time. My cheeky past prediction that he'll be a future Rays ace after a change of scenery trade and better pitch design is a year closer to reality, if nothing else.

If you had told me that Bryan Reynolds would hit .280/.349/.463 over his first two seasons in the majors, I'd have thought he'd be higher than this. But after a fourth place in the 2019 Rookie of the Year race, Reynolds fell flat on his face in 2020, hitting .189 with an 87 DRC+. That's not going to cut it in a corner, though the Pirates will certainly run it back and hope that 2020 is the small sample fluke instead of 2019.

Cole Tucker needs to hit a little more to fill his destiny as a second-division shortstop. Luckily, he's on a second-division franchise.

San Diego Padres

The State of the System:

A strong farm system can help your big club in two ways. One, your prospects can turn into good major leaguers. Two, you can trade your prospects for good major leaguers. The Padres seem to have turned toward the second path.

The Top Ten:

★ ★ ★ *2021 Top 101 Prospect* **#10** ★ ★ ★

1 **CJ Abrams** **SS** OFP: 70 ETA: Late 2022/Early 2023
Born: 10/03/00 Age: 20 Bats: L Throws: R Height: 6'2" Weight: 185 Origin: Round 1, 2019 Draft (#6 overall)

YEAR	TEAM	LVL	AGE	PA	R	2B	3B	HR	RBI	BB	K	SB	CS	AVG/OBP/SLG	DRC+	BABIP	BRR	FRAA	WARP
2019	SD1	ROK	18	156	40	12	8	3	22	10	14	14	6	.401/.442/.662		.425			
2019	FW	LO-A	18	9	1	1	0	0	0	1	0	1	0	.250/.333/.375	121	.250	0.1	SS(1) -0.1	0.0
2021 FS	SD	MLB	20	600	47	27	5	8	53	31	132	30	10	.225/.270/.337	66	.280	6.1	SS 5	0.5

Comparables: Yu Chang, Christian Arroyo, Tyrone Taylor

The Report: Adley Rutschman was always going first overall in the 2019 draft, but Abrams was one of a handful of bats who were in the mix for the second pick. He "slid" to the Padres at six, and if you wanted to quibble with him last June, the bat perhaps didn't have the same upside as Bobby Witt Jr. or Riley Greene, and certainly lacked the safety of JJ Bleday or Andrew Vaughn. Abrams did offer plus-plus speed and the range and actions for shortstop, along with projectable hit and power combination. As soon as he landed in the complex though—and even accounting for the launching pads in Arizona—the bat looked much less like a laggard in the profile. While Abrams might never smash 20 home runs, fringe game power with plenty of doubles and triples looked more likely. The arm strength might be a bit light for shortstop—although his actions and quick release help it play up—but he'd be plus at second and has seen some time in center field as well, where his speed would be a significant asset.

Development Track: Abrams spent time at both the alternate site and instructs, where he looked about as much of a steal as a sixth overall pick can be. He's continued stinging the ball, driving plus major league velocity to the gaps consistently. It's still not entirely clear what his defensive landing home will be, but he could theoretically be average-or-better at all three up-the-middle spots. I'd expect him to start at Advanced-A next year and reach Double-A—and near the top of our 2022 prospect list—by the end of the year.

Variance: High. So it isn't a huge surprise that a top prep draft pick took a step forward in his first full pro season—or whatever this was—and moved from good prospect with some questions about the bat to top-ten-in-baseball type. However when your "first full pro season" was 2020, we are gonna keep the risk/variance factor on the high side.

Mark Barry's Fantasy Take: I'm not saying Abrams should be the No. 1 dynasty prospect, but I am saying that if he can keep doing what he's doing against more advanced pitching—that's the stuff No. 1 dynasty prospects are made of.

★ ★ ★ *2021 Top 101 Prospect* **#11** ★ ★ ★

2 MacKenzie Gore LHP OFP: 70 ETA: 2021

Born: 02/24/99 Age: 22 Bats: L Throws: L Height: 6'2" Weight: 197 Origin: Round 1, 2017 Draft (#3 overall)

YEAR	TEAM	LVL	AGE	W	L	SV	G	GS	IP	H	HR	BB/9	K/9	K	GB%	BABIP	WHIP	ERA	DRA-	WARP
2018	FW	LO-A	19	2	5	0	16	16	60²	61	5	2.7	11.0	74	40.5%	.354	1.30	4.45	59	1.8
2019	LE	HI-A	20	7	1	0	15	15	79¹	36	4	2.3	12.5	110	36.5%	.212	0.71	1.02	34	3.2
2019	AMA	AA	20	2	1	0	5	5	21²	20	3	3.3	10.4	25	44.6%	.321	1.29	4.15	86	0.2
2021 FS	SD	MLB	22	9	8	0	26	26	150	126	22	4.0	10.3	171	39.8%	.278	1.29	3.95	98	1.3
2021 DC	SD	MLB	22	4	4	0	12	12	64	53	9	4.0	10.3	73	39.8%	.278	1.29	3.95	98	0.8

Comparables: Brailyn Marquez, Deivi García, José Suarez

The Report: Gore entered the season as the best pitching prospect in baseball, and in our estimation he's still the best pitching prospect who hasn't made the majors yet. He has ace potential if he throws strikes and keeps developing. His fastball gets up into the mid-90s with late life. His curveball rates as plus-to-plus-plus, a majestic two-plane bender that he commands and tunnels extremely well. His slider is advanced, a tight above-average offering, and his changeup consistently also shows above-average. That's four above-average pitches or better. Except for blister issues and occasional wandering command, he's been the absolute total package in our live looks.

Development Track: Gore clearly should've made the majors this year given San Diego's pitching needs and his developmental timetable. He was repeatedly passed up for call-ups, although that could be the club being more comfortable using Luis Patiño and Ryan Weathers in relief. Because San Diego wasn't in the alternate site share and Gore didn't throw at instructs, there's basically no third-party scouting information available on him from the summer or fall. Dennis Lin of The Athletic talked to Gore in December and reported that he struggled during summer camp and fought his mechanics at the alternate site, which is broadly in line with industry scuttlebutt.

Variance: High. There's a lot of unanswered questions here. Gore could come firing bullets and make us look foolish for doubting him. Or he could not.

Mark Barry's Fantasy Take: Two things can be true: 1) Gore still has no-doubt, ace upside and 2) There are more questions about Gore today than there were last year at this time. It's a little concerning that he kept getting passed over for opportunities, but like Jarrett mentioned, that could just be the team not wanting to use him out of the 'pen. I might float some offers for Gore heading into 2021, to take the temperature of any managers skittish from his 2020 struggles. Even if he's not the best pitching prospect in baseball right now, he still could be a rotational anchor, and should be treated as such.

★ ★ ★ *2021 Top 101 Prospect* **#61** ★ ★ ★

3 Luis Campusano C OFP: 60 ETA: Debuted in 2020

Born: 09/29/98 Age: 22 Bats: R Throws: R Height: 5'11" Weight: 232 Origin: Round 2, 2017 Draft (#39 overall)

YEAR	TEAM	LVL	AGE	PA	R	2B	3B	HR	RBI	BB	K	SB	CS	AVG/OBP/SLG	DRC+	BABIP	BRR	FRAA	WARP
2018	FW	LO-A	19	284	26	11	0	3	40	19	43	0	1	.288/.345/.365	116	.335	-1.1	C(38) -0.8, 1B(4) 0.2	0.8
2019	LE	HI-A	20	482	63	31	1	15	80	52	57	0	0	.321/.394/.508	167	.336	-4.4	C(76) -2.6, 1B(2) 0.0	3.9
2020	SD	MLB	21	4	2	0	0	1	1	0	2	0	0	.333/.500/1.333	81				0.0
2021 FS	SD	MLB	22	600	61	26	1	17	72	40	138	0	0	.248/.304/.398	94	.299	-0.6	C -1, 1B 0	1.8
2021 DC	SD	MLB	22	130	13	5	0	3	15	8	29	0	0	.248/.304/.398	94	.299	-0.1	C 0	0.4

Comparables: Alejandro Kirk, Jarrod Saltalamacchia, Chance Sisco

The Report: Campusano's offensive game is loud. The 2019 California League batting champion and co-MVP has the potential to hit for a significant average like you'd expect, and he has a very refined eye and plate approach. He barrels up and drives pitches, and while his power has been more gap-oriented so far, we think he's got the chance to get to above-average-to-plus game power as he further develops. Defensively, he has a strong arm, but needs to refine his overall throwing and receiving. He's a decent bet to stay at catcher, but doesn't currently project for defensive stardom; if he did, he'd be one of the top small handful of catching prospects in the game. He's not far off as-is.

Development Track: Campusano was called up in September and promptly smacked a homer in his first major-league game. He was scratched from his first start at catcher the next day and missed the rest of the regular season with a wrist injury, although he did pop back up as the third catcher on the postseason roster. In October, he was charged with felony marijuana possession after a traffic stop in Georgia. It is patently absurd that possession of slightly less than three ounces of weed constitutes a felony, to say nothing of broader systemic racial bias in the criminal justice system.

Variance: Medium, on skill.

Mark Barry's Fantasy Take: Going along with my "There Can Only Be One Dynasty Catcher" theory, I'm not stoked to pay a premium to acquire Campusano, as he's not Adley Rutschman. Still, if dynasty catchers are your thing, Campusano is neck-and-neck with Joey Bart for me as the next guy in line for the throne. There's a good offensive skill set here.

★ ★ ★ *2021 Top 101 Prospect* **#64** ★ ★ ★

4   Robert Hassell III   CF   OFP: 60   ETA: 2023
Born: 08/15/01   Age: 19   Bats: L   Throws: L   Height: 6'2"   Weight: 195   Origin: Round 1, 2020 Draft (#8 overall)

The Report: The first high school player off the board in last year's draft, the Padres had their target in the crosshairs regardless of the presumptive best prep—Zac Veen—still being available. Hassell was as steady as they come throughout the evaluation process thanks to a swing and projected hit tool well beyond any others in his class. The sweet lefty stroke is balanced throughout and contains both contact and power potential to all fields. While that is certainly what grabbed the most attention, he is a better defender than given credit for, and was even considered a two-way prospect at one point. The arm off the mound worked in the low-90s and easily translates to either center or right field.

Development Track: If there's one thing you could copy-and-paste into virtually any of the players spotlighted it's that, "boy it sucked having them lose 2020 developmentally." If there were two things you could copy-and-paste to specifically the high schoolers from this (and any) draft, it's that Hassell will need to get into the weight room and fill out the rest of his frame. He's lean and strong as-is, but could stand to put on 10-15 pounds without losing a step.

Variance: Medium. The hitting ability and approach seems so good so early you just hope it's not messed with too much. It's fine to take some knocks, learn what works and what doesn't before making any big changes.

Mark Barry's Fantasy Take: It's always nice to be referred to as a pure hitter or having an advanced hit tool. It's better than the alternative at least. How that translates to fantasy typically depends on the other stuff in the profile. Can Hassell be discount Michael Brantley? Maybe. Is discount Michael Brantley just Melky Cabrera? Also maybe. I like Hassell as a top-75 name, but will need to see more (read: something) before going all in.

5   Ryan Weathers   LHP   OFP: 55   ETA: Debuted in 2020, sort of
Born: 12/17/99   Age: 21   Bats: R   Throws: L   Height: 6'1"   Weight: 230   Origin: Round 1, 2018 Draft (#7 overall)

YEAR	TEAM	LVL	AGE	W	L	SV	G	GS	IP	H	HR	BB/9	K/9	K	GB%	BABIP	WHIP	ERA	DRA-	WARP
2018	SD2	ROK	18	0	2	0	4	4	9¹	8	2	2.9	8.7	9	69.0%	.222	1.18	3.86		
2018	FW	LO-A	18	0	1	0	3	3	9	11	0	1.0	9.0	9	54.8%	.367	1.33	3.00	82	0.1
2019	FW	LO-A	19	3	7	0	22	22	96	101	6	1.7	8.4	90	44.6%	.348	1.24	3.84	112	-0.3
2021 FS	*SD*	*MLB*	*21*	*1*	*1*	*0*	*57*	*0*	*50*	*50*	*7*	*3.3*	*7.1*	*39*	*43.1%*	*.285*	*1.37*	*4.70*	*114*	*-0.3*
2021 DC	*SD*	*MLB*	*21*	*1*	*1*	*0*	*4*	*4*	*20*	*20*	*3*	*3.3*	*7.1*	*15*	*43.1%*	*.285*	*1.37*	*4.70*	*114*	*0.1*

Comparables: Brailyn Marquez, Noah Syndergaard, Luis Severino

The Report: The son of righty bullpen stalwart David, Ryan Weathers is a lefty with a better chance to start than pops. The frame is a bit shorter and stouter, but Weathers repeats his slingy, uptempo, compact delivery well and can run his fastball up into the mid-90s. He also offers a potentially above-average curve and an average change. He mixes his stuff well and stays off barrels, so while he may lack a true bonafide out pitch, he does get a lot out of the current arsenal. Which is good, because given that stout frame, there isn't a ton of projection left.

Development Track: Like Alex Kirilloff and Shane McLanahan, Weathers found himself in the unusual circumstance of making his major-league debut in the playoffs. He was a bit of a surprise addition to the Padres' NLDS roster and immediately got some middle innings work in Game 1, showing a tick more on his fastball in the short burst outing. Granted, that's more info than we have on any Padres prospect who didn't show up in the majors or instructs. Weathers hasn't pitched above A-ball otherwise, and while he's not all that far off from the majors—he was an advanced arm for a prep pick—he'll likely start 2021 in Double-A, and the Friars' rotation is a bit more crowded now than it was last October.

Variance: High. Weathers is a 20-year-old pitching prospect with more present than projection, so we will have to see how that present plays in the near future in Double-A and higher.

Mark Barry's Fantasy Take: Oh hey, another Padres pitching prospect who got called up instead of Gore. I don't think Weathers has the stuff to be an impact starter in fantasy. If Weathers is going to have impact, it's going to be in the bullpen, and if Weathers pitches out of the bullpen, he's not really going to impact your fantasy lineup. Clear as mud? Good.

6 Hudson Head CF   OFP: 55   ETA: 2023

Born: 04/08/01   Age: 20   Bats: L   Throws: L   Height: 6'1"   Weight: 180   Origin: Round 3, 2019 Draft (#84 overall)

YEAR	TEAM	LVL	AGE	PA	R	2B	3B	HR	RBI	BB	K	SB	CS	AVG/OBP/SLG	DRC+	BABIP	BRR	FRAA	WARP
2019	SD1	ROK	18	141	19	7	3	1	12	15	29	3	3	.283/.383/.417		.363			
2021 FS	SD	MLB	20	600	45	26	3	7	49	32	203	7	4	.205/.257/.304	53	.307	-1.6	CF-11	-2.9

Comparables: Byron Buxton, Ronald Acuña Jr., Aaron Hicks

The Report: Head was a 2019 pop-up draft prospect who got overslot, late-first-round money from the Padres. He's a potential five-tool center fielder, but a lot of that is physical projection that might also move him to a corner. He has good bat speed and extension, and should be able to launch some baseballs as he fills out more. He's an above-average runner and an advanced defensive outfielder for his age. There's some tweenerish potential in the profile, but he's also a little bit safer than your median prep outfielder due to the present broad base of skills.

Development Track: Last year when we pegged Head as a potential big riser in the Padres' system for 2020, we expected it would be more due to further skill development then, uh, 10 or so guys ahead of him on the list being traded. His time at instructs was limited due to injury, but there were some positive reports on his bat.

Variance: High. Complex-league resume combined with some tweenerish signs and some stiffness in his load make for profile risk, but there's also the potential for five above-average tools in center field. That kind of profile plays up.

Mark Barry's Fantasy Take: This guy is pretty far away, but he has that nice blend of skills that could easily translate to a well-rounded fantasy profile. None of them really stand out as category carriers, however, so he's a watch list guy for me right now while we see how he fairs in full-season ball.

7 Justin Lange RHP   OFP: 55   ETA: 2024 as a reliever, 2025 as a starter

Born: 09/11/01   Age: 19   Bats: R   Throws: R   Height: 6'4"   Weight: 220   Origin: Round 1, 2020 Draft (#34 overall)

The Report: Lange is basically the inverse of fellow Texan Jared Kelley, who was long thought to be at-worst the second-best high school pitcher in the 2020 draft, but ended up falling to the 47th pick. Blessed with an ideal pitcher's frame, Lange shot up draft boards after adding close to 20 pounds of muscle during a six-month offseason period. What once was velocity in the low 90s was now up several ticks and hitting 100 on occasion during the spring. There is also some feel for a changeup that has a mimicking run similar to his fastball. In the inverse of the traditional prep arm, it's the breaking ball that is inconsistent. Like any rapidly maturing teenager, there isn't a ton of body control just yet and it shows in his command.

Development Track: Lange is a project pitcher. There's never-ending promise, but a lot of work to be done. The delivery in particular is worrisome, with a low slot that creates a lot of side spin to his pitches, it also puts a ton of stress on his elbow at the bottom of the arm swing and again with a recoiling follow-through at deceleration. He'll need to clean that up for his own long-term benefit while also finding something that he can comfortably repeat.

Variance: Extreme. There doesn't seem to be a ton of middle-ground/gray area in the profile. It will either all fall into place, or it won't. ---Keanan Lamb

Mark Barry's Fantasy Take: Lange has a bunch of stuff you look for in pitching prospects, but he's still a prep righty that hasn't thrown a professional pitch. That's not his fault, mind you, but I don't think you need to rush in for another couple years, at least.

8 Jorge Oña OF   OFP: 50   ETA: Debuted in 2020
Born: 12/31/96   Age: 24   Bats: R   Throws: R   Height: 6'0"   Weight: 235   Origin: International Free Agent, 2016

YEAR	TEAM	LVL	AGE	PA	R	2B	3B	HR	RBI	BB	K	SB	CS	AVG/OBP/SLG	DRC+	BABIP	BRR	FRAA	WARP
2018	LE	HI-A	21	410	44	24	2	8	44	33	110	0	2	.239/.312/.380	88	.317	-2.1	RF(59) -1.3	-1.3
2019	AMA	AA	22	103	11	2	0	5	18	11	26	2	1	.348/.417/.539	170	.433	0.7	LF(15) -2.3	0.6
2020	SD	MLB	23	15	3	1	0	1	2	2	7	0	0	.250/.400/.583	78	.500	0.1	RF(1) -0.0	0.0
2021 FS	SD	MLB	24	600	60	20	2	18	65	47	211	1	0	.218/.290/.364	82	.319	0.4	RF -6, LF -4	-0.9
2021 DC	SD	MLB	24	293	29	9	0	8	32	23	103	0	0	.218/.290/.364	82	.319	0.2	RF -3, LF -2	-0.4

Comparables: Rymer Liriano, Zoilo Almonte, Marcell Ozuna

The Report: Oña is a big man who wants to hit big bombs. Every time he is up at the plate the plan is swing hard, hit it 450. He gets to his power with a fairly short swing, but it's max effort and leveraged at the expense of barrel control or the ability to adjust to offspeed. That said, even his mishits can go for extra bases given how strong he is, and he has enough of an eye that he could get enough of all three outcomes to carry a corner outfield profile. Oña has the arm strength for right field, but his range and footspeed will be below-average in any outfield spot. He might be better suited for DH, assuming Rob Manfred works out whether or not there will be one in the National League in 2021 at some point.

Development Track: Oña got called up as an extra bat for a couple weeks in September. He struck out in almost half his plate appearances, but also hit one laser beam into the second deck at PetCo. He will need to balance the bombs and Ks a bit better going forward to be more than some fun pop off the bench, but given that he only has a month's worth of at-bats in Double-A—he missed most of 2019 after shoulder surgery—there's still time to work that out.

Variance: Medium. The K-rate may eat into enough of the hit tool—and with it some of the game power—that Oña is limited to pinch hitter with pop. But even marginal improvements on the swing-and-miss can lead to an exponential production boost based on how hard he can hit the ball when he does make contact.

Mark Barry's Fantasy Take: Oña back? An abbreviated 2019 Double-A breakout put Oña back onto the dynasty radar, culminating in a 2020 debut with the big club. There is a lot to like with this profile, but there are probably going to be too many strikeouts to feel comfortable rolling him out everyday.

9 Reiss Knehr RHP   OFP: 50   ETA: Late 2021/Early 2022
Born: 11/03/96   Age: 24   Bats: L   Throws: R   Height: 6'2"   Weight: 205   Origin: Round 20, 2018 Draft (#591 overall)

YEAR	TEAM	LVL	AGE	W	L	SV	G	GS	IP	H	HR	BB/9	K/9	K	GB%	BABIP	WHIP	ERA	DRA-	WARP
2018	SD1	ROK	21	3	0	2	12	0	19	12	2	3.8	11.8	25	51.1%	.222	1.05	2.84		
2018	FW	LO-A	21	0	1	0	8	1	15²	14	1	4.0	11.5	20	48.7%	.351	1.34	4.02	59	0.4
2019	LE	HI-A	22	3	5	1	17	12	66¹	71	11	3.8	11.3	83	43.5%	.347	1.49	5.43	113	-0.4
2021 FS	SD	MLB	24	2	3	0	57	0	50	47	9	5.3	9.1	50	41.6%	.289	1.55	5.29	121	-0.5

Comparables: Jeremy Beasley, Albert Abreu, T.J. Zeuch

The Report: A Day 3 small college arm who didn't even get full pool, Knehr has had an uneven pro career despite pretty good stuff. He's a stocky righty with a delivery that starts a little drop and drive, but ends pretty upright, and there's effort throughout. So the command and control have been an issue even going back to college. He can run his fastball up in the mid-90s though, and has a pretty good cutter and changeup backing it up. Ultimately between the mechanics and shaky production as a pro starter, Knehr probably ends up in the 'pen, where the fastball/cutter combo might play up.

Development Track: Knehr pitched at instructs, where reports were better on the fastball velocity and secondaries, but until we see that translate into better outputs on his player page, the major league OFP here is going to be a little muted.

Variance: Medium. There's pretty significant reliever markers here, and it's not necessarily going to be late inning stuff in the pen unless it pops in short bursts. Yes, that usually happens, but it's not a guarantee.

Mark Barry's Fantasy Take: Knehr has the mix of a starter, but is probably destined for relief. Pass.

10 Tucupita Marcano 2B   OFP: 50   ETA: 2023
Born: 09/16/99   Age: 21   Bats: L   Throws: R   Height: 6'0"   Weight: 170   Origin: International Free Agent, 2016

YEAR	TEAM	LVL	AGE	PA	R	2B	3B	HR	RBI	BB	K	SB	CS	AVG/OBP/SLG	DRC+	BABIP	BRR	FRAA	WARP
2018	SD2	ROK	18	160	33	4	1	0	17	26	10	10	7	.395/.497/.444		.419			
2018	TRI	SS	18	77	12	1	2	1	9	4	6	5	0	.314/.355/.429	162	.328	2.1	2B(11) -0.4, SS(6) 1.0	0.7
2019	FW	LO-A	19	504	55	19	3	2	45	35	45	15	16	.270/.323/.337	92	.293	-2.9	3B(42) -1.1, SS(40) -5.6, 2B(32) 0.1	0.3
2021 FS	SD	MLB	21	600	52	26	3	6	52	44	98	15	9	.252/.311/.345	83	.297	-7.3	2B 1, SS -2	-0.3

Comparables: Donovan Solano, Wilfredo Tovar, Luis Sardiñas

The Report: Marcano is a smooth infielder with an advanced approach and good feel for contact. The hit too projection is plus, contingent on him adding some more physical strength, but the game power will likely stall out at well-below-average. Marcano is a plus runner with the range for either middle infield spot—and he's played some third as a pro as well, but his arm strength would really only play at the keystone in an every day role.

Development Track: The Padres were reasonably aggressive with their prospects in 2020 and Marcano saw time at the alternate site and instructs. It's a slow burn profile given the slighter frame, and he will have to show harder contact against minor league pitching to project as more than a utility infielder.

Variance: High. Marcano has some skills that should give him some sort of major league career. He can hit, run, and play multiple infield spots. But he lacks physicality and we haven't really seen the bat tested by better arms yet.

Mark Barry's Fantasy Take: Normally, guys like Marcano are my jam. I love the heavy-contact, low-strikeout dudes that can run a little. Unfortunately, Marcano isn't all that efficient on the bases, snagging 15 bases in 31 tries in High-A. Love the bat-- need to see more success in the base thievery.

The Prospects You Meet Outside The Top Ten

Prospects to dream on a little

Joshua Mears RF   Born: 02/21/01   Age: 20   Bats: R   Throws: R   Height: 6'3"   Weight: 230   Origin: Round 2, 2019 Draft (#48 overall)

YEAR	TEAM	LVL	AGE	PA	R	2B	3B	HR	RBI	BB	K	SB	CS	AVG/OBP/SLG	DRC+	BABIP	BRR	FRAA	WARP
2019	SD1	ROK	18	195	30	4	3	7	24	23	59	9	1	.253/.354/.440		.343			
2021 FS	SD	MLB	20	600	44	25	3	6	47	34	249	13	2	.202/.254/.296	50	.350	6.1	RF 1, LF -2	-1.9

Comparables: Alex Jackson, Jorge Bonifacio, Estevan Florial

You would think a second-round prep outfielder in this subhead would be somewhat of a projection bet, and Mears will have to improve some things for sure. That said, he's already built like a major league right fielder in the midst of his physical prime. He has that kind of power too, although the swing is going to need a fair bit of fine tuning to get to it. He should be fine in right field and is a good runner for his size. It's going to need to click, and I don't know how likely that is, but you can dream on it.

Tirso Ornelas OF   Born: 03/11/00   Age: 21   Bats: L   Throws: R   Height: 6'3"   Weight: 200   Origin: International Free Agent, 2017

YEAR	TEAM	LVL	AGE	PA	R	2B	3B	HR	RBI	BB	K	SB	CS	AVG/OBP/SLG	DRC+	BABIP	BRR	FRAA	WARP
2018	FW	LO-A	18	355	45	13	3	8	40	40	68	5	1	.252/.341/.392	106	.297	1.2	RF(63) -1.8, CF(5) 1.8, LF(3) -0.7	0.5
2019	SD1	ROK	19	97	6	2	0	0	11	9	22	4	0	.205/.278/.227		.273			
2019	LE	HI-A	19	374	41	10	5	1	30	43	89	3	1	.220/.307/.290	66	.295	-1.8	RF(74) -2.9, CF(3) 0.2	-0.9
2021 FS	SD	MLB	21	600	49	25	3	8	52	44	191	0	0	.218/.279/.324	66	.317	1.6	RF 0, CF -2	-1.2

Comparables: Dylan Carlson, Leody Taveras, Anthony Gose

Ornelas slides out of the Top Ten because he badly needed a consolidation year in the minors in 2020. The physical tools are among the best for position players in the system, but he's struggled with his swing and approach the last time we saw him in game action.

MLB bats, but less upside than you'd like

Eguy Rosario 2B Born: 08/25/99 Age: 21 Bats: R Throws: R Height: 5'9" Weight: 150 Origin: International Free Agent, 2015

YEAR	TEAM	LVL	AGE	PA	R	2B	3B	HR	RBI	BB	K	SB	CS	AVG/OBP/SLG	DRC+	BABIP	BRR	FRAA	WARP
2018	LE	HI-A	18	505	60	28	1	9	45	38	119	9	8	.239/.307/.363	83	.302	-0.7	2B(101) -8.0, 3B(14) 0.2, SS(1) -0.1	-1.7
2019	LE	HI-A	19	507	58	25	8	6	71	37	101	21	9	.277/.330/.405	97	.337	1.0	3B(69) -0.3, SS(19) -0.5, 2B(15) -0.6	1.3
2021 FS	SD	MLB	21	600	51	27	3	11	56	39	181	16	8	.217/.275/.340	67	.300	-4.7	2B -3, 3B -2	-1.7

Comparables: Rougned Odor, Andrés Giménez, Amed Rosario

Rosario is a future utility infielder that can handle all three spots and shows some feel for contact. The game power is limited, he probably won't get on base a ton, and he's swung and missed a little too much in two shots at the Cal League. He had a nice little instructs campaign, but the upside remains limited.

MLB arms, but probably relievers

Reggie Lawson RHP Born: 08/02/97 Age: 23 Bats: R Throws: R Height: 6'4" Weight: 205 Origin: Round 2, 2016 Draft (#71 overall)

YEAR	TEAM	LVL	AGE	W	L	SV	G	GS	IP	H	HR	BB/9	K/9	K	GB%	BABIP	WHIP	ERA	DRA-	WARP
2018	LE	HI-A	20	8	5	0	24	22	117	130	11	3.9	9.0	117	42.2%	.350	1.55	4.69	108	-0.1
2019	AMA	AA	21	3	1	0	6	6	27²	28	4	4.2	11.7	36	37.5%	.358	1.48	5.20	102	0.0
2021 FS	SD	MLB	23	2	3	0	57	0	50	46	8	5.5	9.0	50	38.2%	.284	1.55	5.27	122	-0.5
2021 DC	SD	MLB	23	0	0	0	3	3	12	11	2	5.5	9.0	12	38.2%	.284	1.55	5.27	122	0.0

Comparables: Robbie Ray, Jeremy Jeffress, Jason Adam

Lawson offers mid-90s heat and a potential plus hook, but our missing 2020 means that he hasn't been able to follow up on his rather electric 2019 AFL performance that itself followed an injury-marred regular season. We noted in last year's blurb that he was just 22, but next year he will be 24, so it might be time to move him to the pen and let him move quickly. He could be a boon to the Padres' 2021 relief corps.

You always need catching

Jonny Homza C Born: 06/13/99 Age: 22 Bats: R Throws: R Height: 6'0" Weight: 185 Origin: Round 5, 2017 Draft (#138 overall)

YEAR	TEAM	LVL	AGE	PA	R	2B	3B	HR	RBI	BB	K	SB	CS	AVG/OBP/SLG	DRC+	BABIP	BRR	FRAA	WARP
2018	SD2	ROK	19	185	25	7	1	3	21	26	37	0	0	.226/.351/.342		.278			
2019	TRI	SS	20	211	18	14	1	0	13	21	62	2	0	.216/.313/.303	78	.325	0.7	C(35) 0.5, 3B(20) 1.6, 2B(1) -0.1	0.8
2021 FS	SD	MLB	22	600	44	27	2	6	46	38	220	2	1	.192/.254/.285	48	.306	-0.8	C 0, 3B -1	-2.3

Comparables: Xavier Scruggs, Tomás Nido, Raudy Read

Prep catchers are a risky proposition. Cold weather prep catchers? Even riskier. Well, it doesn't get much colder than Anchorage, Alaska. Homza, the first player ever drafted out of South Anchorage High School has taken a very conservative path through the minors and still hasn't seen full-season ball yet. He's a good defender though, and there's some projection in the bat that might be starting to bubble up after a good instructs.

Top Talents 25 and Under (as of 4/1/2021):

1. Fernando Tatis Jr., SS
2. C.J. Abrams, SS
3. MacKenzie Gore, LHP
4. Chris Paddack, RHP
5. Luis Campusano, C
6. Robert Hassell III, OF
7. Trent Grisham, OF
8. Adrian Morejon, LHP

9. Ryan Weathers, LHP
10. Hudson Head, OF

Fernando Tatis Jr. is one of the best young players in baseball. He's an emerging two-way superstar who hits for average, hits for power, and makes some fantastic plays at shortstop. There isn't even much more to say.

Chris Paddack could really, really use a workable third pitch. As a fastball/changeup starter, the league has seemed to catch up to him multiple times through, and he's had a harder time inducing whiffs and weak contacts. His curveball isn't getting there, and he introduced a cutter late in 2020. If he can figure out something that breaks gloveside, he still could be a top-of-the-rotation starter.

Trent Grisham's DRC+ numbers (90 in Milwaukee in 2019, 95 in San Diego in 2020) have not lived up to his slash line (.243/.342/.437 career) so far, but they're still usable. The speedster has settled in in center field and looked great out there in 2020, and even at a slightly below-average DRC+ he's a nifty regular as long as that's true.

Adrian Morejon graduated on service time in 2020 after spending the second half of August and all of September bouncing between being an opener and a long reliever. He gave up an absolute boat load of homers (7 in 19 1/3 innings), though the stuff was still pretty good and his DRA was slightly above-average. Our concerns about whether he has enough command and durability to start remain, but even in a shorter role he's on the way to being a nifty weapon.

San Francisco Giants

The State of the System:

The Giants' system is good, folks. There's no other way to say it. I know, it's weird to me too.

The Top Ten:

★   ★   ★   *2021 Top 101 Prospect* **#8** ★   ★   ★

1 Marco Luciano   SS   OFP: 70   ETA: Late 2022/2023
Born: 09/10/01   Age: 19   Bats: R   Throws: R   Height: 6'2"   Weight: 178   Origin: International Free Agent, 2018

YEAR	TEAM	LVL	AGE	PA	R	2B	3B	HR	RBI	BB	K	SB	CS	AVG/OBP/SLG	DRC+	BABIP	BRR	FRAA	WARP
2019	GIO	ROK	17	178	46	9	2	10	38	27	39	8	6	.322/.438/.616		.378			
2019	SK	SS	17	38	6	4	0	0	4	5	6	1	0	.212/.316/.333	96	.259	-0.2	SS(9) -0.8	0.0
2021 FS	SF	MLB	19	600	46	27	2	7	50	39	198	13	7	.205/.263/.306	58	.303	-4.0	SS 2	-1.5

Comparables: Sergio Alcántara, Jonathan Araúz, Hanser Alberto

The Report: Luciano has a hell of a swing. He takes lightning-fast cuts with a great bat path, producing loft and excellent bat speed. His bat-to-ball skills are solid given his age and how hard his move is to the ball. He's a strong young man, with plus power already and the potential for more. He has one of the highest offensive ceilings in baseball. There are some warts here, albeit the ones you would expect from a teenage hitting sensation. His plate approach is a bit aggressive; it's manifested more in weak contact than swing-and-miss so far, which bodes well for future adjustments, but he will have to make them. Defensively, he currently has the range and arm to play shortstop, though we wouldn't be surprised if he slides over to third if he loses a step as he gets older.

Development Track: Luciano hit an instructional league homer with a 119-mph exit velocity, per the @SFGProspects Twitter. He was at the alternate site and then fall instructs, and he held his own and then some against players who were way older. Luciano should make his full-season debut whenever full-season baseball returns, and we expect him to move pretty fast once he gets going.

Variance: High. Despite our optimism, he did just lose a bunch of game reps and has barely played outside the complex.

J.P. Breen's Fantasy Take: We're talking about a potential five-category contributor, and he could be a monster in four of those categories. Luciano is a top-15 dynasty prospect and a top-100 overall guy. Perhaps he slows down a bit and struggles to reach double-digit stolen bases; however, that's a minor quibble. All the normal caveats apply to the 19-year-old who has not yet played full-season ball, but he's one of the special ones.

★ ★ ★ *2021 Top 101 Prospect* **#29** ★ ★ ★

2 Joey Bart C   OFP: 60   ETA: Debuted in 2020

Born: 12/15/96 Age: 24 Bats: R Throws: R Height: 6'2" Weight: 238 Origin: Round 1, 2018 Draft (#2 overall)

YEAR	TEAM	LVL	AGE	PA	R	2B	3B	HR	RBI	BB	K	SB	CS	AVG/OBP/SLG	DRC+	BABIP	BRR	FRAA	WARP
2018	GIO	ROK	21	25	3	1	1	0	1	1	7	0	0	.261/.320/.391		.375			
2018	SK	SS	21	203	35	14	2	13	39	12	40	2	1	.298/.369/.613	146	.318	1.2	C(32) -1.0	1.0
2019	SJ	HI-A	22	251	37	10	2	12	37	14	50	5	2	.265/.315/.479	112	.291	1.0	C(50) -1.9	1.2
2019	RIC	AA	22	87	9	4	1	4	11	7	21	0	2	.316/.368/.544	163	.382	-1.2	C(15) 0.2	0.8
2020	SF	MLB	23	111	15	5	2	0	7	3	41	0	0	.233/.288/.320	48	.387	-0.5	C(32) 0.1	-0.4
2021 FS	*SF*	*MLB*	*24*	*600*	*66*	*24*	*5*	*19*	*73*	*30*	*200*	*2*	*1*	*.236/.289/.406*	*93*	*.330*	*2.3*	*C 0*	*2.2*
2021 DC	*SF*	*MLB*	*24*	*302*	*33*	*12*	*2*	*10*	*37*	*15*	*101*	*1*	*0*	*.236/.289/.406*	*93*	*.330*	*1.2*	*C 0*	*1.0*

Comparables: Luis Exposito, John Hicks, Jose Lobaton

The Report: At the plate, Bart is at least above average. He's got decent pitch recognition and some power, which may fare very well with the fences moved in now at Oracle Park, but he still needs to work on polishing his hitting some more. He has a swing that can almost resemble a golf swing at times and really tries to attack low and middle of the zone pitches because of it. When he can get under a ball, he can really lift the ball up deep into the outfield. Behind the plate, though, he is a plus defender with a plus arm, often posting sub-2.0 pop times. When he's not trying to rush the throw, he can throw down to second with pinpoint accuracy. His framing has improved a fair amount and he seems more confident in that aspect of his defense.

Development Track: Bart started 2020 at the alternate site, but because of the Giants' catching situation after Buster Posey opted out of the season, Bart's missed time in 2019 because of freak hand injuries (a fractured left hand with High-A San Jose, a right thumb fracture in Arizona Fall League), and the everything about 2020, it seemed to be worth a shot to give Bart some regular playing time at the major league level. Making the jump from Double-A to MLB was not without the obvious struggles, but started to adjust as he got more reps in. Of course, with how short the season was, there wasn't necessarily enough time to really fully settle in if one is called up with only a little over a month left to play. It's clear that with more reps, his talent will truly show.

Variance: Medium. The hand injuries don't seem to be much of an issue but a lot depends on if he can harness his power as a hitter. Otherwise, do the bartman.

J.P. Breen's Fantasy Take: It's important to realize that 20-homer catchers don't grow on trees. The majors only had eight of them in 2019. Bart has the potential to reach the 25-homer plateau with 400-plus plate appearances, which would easily make him a top-10 catcher, even in disappointing years. I don't think he'll ever walk enough to be a Yasmani Grandal-type fantasy catcher; however, he should hit for more average.

★ ★ ★ *2021 Top 101 Prospect* **#32** ★ ★ ★

3 Heliot Ramos CF   OFP: 60   ETA: Late 2021/Early 2022

Born: 09/07/99 Age: 21 Bats: R Throws: R Height: 6'0" Weight: 188 Origin: Round 1, 2017 Draft (#19 overall)

YEAR	TEAM	LVL	AGE	PA	R	2B	3B	HR	RBI	BB	K	SB	CS	AVG/OBP/SLG	DRC+	BABIP	BRR	FRAA	WARP
2018	AUG	LO-A	18	535	61	24	8	11	52	35	136	8	7	.245/.313/.396	106	.319	1.8	CF(113) -4.5	0.7
2019	SJ	HI-A	19	338	51	18	0	13	40	32	85	6	6	.306/.385/.500	142	.385	0.1	CF(71) -5.1	1.7
2019	RIC	AA	19	106	13	6	1	3	15	10	33	2	3	.242/.321/.421	120	.339	-1.6	CF(19) -1.5	0.2
2021 FS	*SF*	*MLB*	*21*	*600*	*63*	*25*	*5*	*15*	*65*	*37*	*217*	*6*	*4*	*.226/.284/.377*	*84*	*.339*	*-1.2*	*CF 0*	*0.6*
2021 DC	*SF*	*MLB*	*21*	*33*	*3*	*1*	*0*	*0*	*3*	*2*	*11*	*0*	*0*	*.226/.284/.377*	*84*	*.339*	*-0.1*	*RF 0*	*0.0*

Comparables: Jo Adell, Anthony Gose, Cristian Pache

The Report: Ramos is a potential plus hit/plus power corner outfielder. The plus hit tool doesn't necessarily derive from above-average feel for contact—Ramos's power comes from some length, and swing-and-miss comes with it—but from the damage he can do when he does make contact. Ramos hits the ball hard, and he can hit it over the fence. He's a pretty good runner despite his somewhat square frame, and in an other than San Francisco's cavernous park, could play a bit of center field. He should be a good right fielder though, and the arm strength isn't an issue there.

Development Track: Ramos's season—such as it was—ended up bookended by oblique issues: one in Spring that would have delayed his start to the season, and one in the fall which cut short his time in instructs. This just continues his up and down prospect trajectory. 2020 was perhaps down a little due to the injuries and global pandemic limiting his ability to build off his strong 2019. A strong start to 2021 could find him in the Giants outfield mix quickly though. Some odd-year bullshit in the Bay Area would be refreshing at least.

Variance: Medium. Because of the oscillating arc of his development, Ramos has never really put together the kind of sustained, year-over-year performance that makes you completely confident that it's a plus corner outfield profile. That's a high offensive bar, but the tools are certainly there to vault it.

J.P. Breen's Fantasy Take: Ramos's long-term potential is something like Eloy Jimenez with less power. Ramos has better speed, of course, but he's already slowing down and only stole eight bases in 444 plate appearances in 2019. If everything comes good, Ramos is a 30-homer guy who hits .280 with 10 stolen bases. That's really damn good—Austin Meadows, circa 2019, good—but he carries significant volatility. His proximity to the big leagues puts him in the top-30 dynasty prospects.

───────────── ★ ★ ★ *2021 Top 101 Prospect* **#75** ★ ★ ★ ─────────────

4 Hunter Bishop OF   OFP: 60   ETA: 2022
Born: 06/25/98   Age: 23   Bats: L   Throws: R   Height: 6'5"   Weight: 210   Origin: Round 1, 2019 Draft (#10 overall)

YEAR	TEAM	LVL	AGE	PA	R	2B	3B	HR	RBI	BB	K	SB	CS	AVG/OBP/SLG	DRC+	BABIP	BRR	FRAA	WARP
2019	GIO	ROK	21	29	4	3	0	1	3	9	11	2	0	.250/.483/.550		.500			
2019	SK	SS	21	117	21	1	1	4	9	29	28	4	2	.224/.427/.400	176	.278	-0.3	CF(22) -2.2	0.7
2021 FS	SF	MLB	23	600	54	26	2	12	57	56	217	10	4	.204/.286/.335	74	.315	0.1	CF -8	-0.9

Comparables: Rico Noel, Matt Angle, Garrett Hampson

The Report: Like most of the class of 2019, attempting to rank Bishop based on such a small pro sample size is a difficult task. Reports out of Giants camp were all positive, especially with an emphasis on his defensive ability improving to the point he might stay in center field. His long strides and plus straight line speed play up in the gaps, it's a matter of getting the right reads of the bat. The athletic parts of his game are distinct even as he was labeled a "late bloomer" in college. The hit tool remains questionable until we see it against live pitching, but will note he fits the mold of the traditional high OBP/power corner outfielder.

Development Track: Playing center in San Francisco is no easy feat, with some of the biggest territory to cover this side of the Polo Grounds. If Bishop can make it work using his range, it only helps his overall outlook. The biggest area of development is simply proving he can handle high-quality offspeed in the upper levels of the minors.

Variance: Medium. There are a few finite qualities, like taking walks and hitting bombs, that seem to be inherent in nature that translate up and down whatever level being played at. Even if he's an average hitter, that likely gets you into all-star caliber territory.

J.P. Breen's Fantasy Take: Although defensive improvements are rarely celebrated in dynasty, they matter for Bishop. A defensive step forward puts less pressure on the development of his hit tool. We've all seen no-glove, low-average sluggers flame out after a year or two in the big leagues. Good-glove, low-average sluggers, however, can hold down everyday roles for years. The fact that Bishop can steal double-digit bases only enhances his dynasty value. I've really come around on Bishop over the past 12 months and now am fully on board with his being a fringe top-50 dynasty prospect. He's even more valuable in OBP leagues.

5 Patrick Bailey C   OFP: 55   ETA: 2023, 2022 if needed
Born: 05/29/99   Age: 22   Bats: S   Throws: R   Height: 6'2"   Weight: 207   Origin: Round 1, 2020 Draft (#13 overall)

The Report: Apparently the new market inefficiency is hoarding catchers. Bailey landed in the range of where many predicted he would be selected, although it came somewhat of a surprise hearing the Giants call his name. Unlike the NFL or NBA, you never draft for need in baseball with the amount of developmental and team fluctuations from year to year. Behind Buster Posey and Joey Bart, Bailey is a very solid catcher with the added value of being a switch-hitter with no real platoon weakness. There is nothing to his game that illuminates as a star quality, however, the sum of his tools project him as a starting backstop with some offensive upside.

Development Track: Maintaining a balanced work ethic between servicing your swing from both sides of the plate, while managing a pitching staff and game planning against an opponent, is perhaps the most difficult time management conundrum a professional player can endure. With the possibility he could be splitting time one day with Bart in the same lineup, alternating days between catching and first base, it might be worth doubly-focusing on the offensive output.

Variance: High. Catching is hard.

J.P. Breen's Fantasy Take: Bailey will either need to display impact in-game power potential or have a clear pathway to the big leagues before he's worth rostering in most dynasty formats. There are more interesting and higher-upside catchers in the minors if you insist on dipping your toes into the forbidden catching waters.

6 Will Wilson SS   OFP: 55   ETA: 2022
Born: 07/21/98   Age: 22   Bats: R   Throws: R   Height: 6'0"   Weight: 184   Origin: Round 1, 2019 Draft (#15 overall)

YEAR	TEAM	LVL	AGE	PA	R	2B	3B	HR	RBI	BB	K	SB	CS	AVG/OBP/SLG	DRC+	BABIP	BRR	FRAA	WARP
2019	ORM	ROK+	20	200	23	10	3	5	18	14	47	0	0	.281/.335/.449		.353			
2021 FS	SF	MLB	22	600	44	26	3	7	48	32	204	1	0	.202/.250/.300	51	.303	1.3		-1.9

6. Will Wilson, SS

The Report: Wilson does a little bit of everything well. At the plate, his swing is smooth and balanced, with enough hand and wrist strength to get the barrel anywhere in the zone and drive the ball. He's got a well-built, mature frame that should generate average game power. He's an average runner that might slow down as he moves through his twenties, and that does make the defensive profile fit better at second base than shortstop. But he should be a sure-handed, solid enough defender there. This is a pretty dry recitation, but it's a pretty dry profile. It's also a major league one.

Development Track: As Keanan noted with Bishop, the 2019 draft class is difficult to deal with this year. Wilson is particularly tricky in that he doesn't have the loud tools of his organization mate. You want to see him hit at every level to stay confident he'll hit at the highest one. The lack of a carrying tool here means each individual one will have to scrape the projection for the OFP to become a reality.

Variance: Medium. Minimal pro track record, may lack a carrying tool, and could slide down the defensive spectrum.

J.P. Breen's Fantasy Take: Wilson is the ideal late-round pick in a supplemental draft, or the perfect last keeper. He's unexciting, but he's probably a big leaguer. He's the type of player that competitive dynasty teams have waiting in the wings or sitting in their MI slot. He's the type of boring 1.5-win player who's a fringe starter five years from now, who I'll be shamelessly defending on TINO as the perfect dynasty depth piece. Now that I'm writing this blurb, I'm surprised that I don't have Wilson on a single dynasty roster—I guess we'll have to change that soon.

7 Luis Matos OF   OFP: 55   ETA: 2024
Born: 01/28/02   Age: 19   Bats: R   Throws: R   Height: 5'11"   Weight: 160   Origin: International Free Agent, 2018

YEAR	TEAM	LVL	AGE	PA	R	2B	3B	HR	RBI	BB	K	SB	CS	AVG/OBP/SLG	DRC+	BABIP	BRR	FRAA	WARP
2019	DSL GIA	ROK	17	270	60	24	2	7	47	19	30	20	2	.362/.430/.570		.386			
2019	GIO	ROK	17	20	5	1	0	0	1	1	1	1	1	.438/.550/.500		.467			
2021 FS	SF	MLB	19	600	45	26	2	7	49	28	188	41	8	.211/.259/.306	55	.304	17.4	CF -7	-0.4

Comparables: Alex Verdugo, Victor Robles, Luis Arraez

The Report: Signed as part of the Giants' rather loaded 2018 IFA class, Matos is a projectable, potential five-tool center fielder. The swing is advanced for his experience level, staying in the zone for a while, with good bat speed, and hinting at enough loft to tap into power as he fills out. His speed should keep him in center for the near future at least, and he's got a good shot to stick there as an above-average glove over the long term.

Development Track: Last year we told you to check back on Matos in four years. As it turns out though, we have to do prospect lists every year, so here we are. Matos looked good at instructs and while it would be an aggressive assignment, he could see full-season ball in 2021.

Variance: Extreme. He hasn't played significant games stateside. You can check back in three years now, but there's the potential the profile pops well before then. And anyway, there will be another list in 2022.

J.P. Breen's Fantasy Take: It's uncommon to find a teenager who is both a potential five-tool hitter and someone who isn't whiffing 25-plus percent of the time as a professional. Matos's plate discipline numbers suggest that he has a decent idea at the plate, and the tools are loud enough that he could be an impact guy in five years. The fact that he hasn't even seen full-season ball to this point is why Matos currently isn't a top-50 dynasty prospect. But he already ain't far off it.

8 Luis Toribio 3B   OFP: 55   ETA: 2024
Born: 09/28/00   Age: 20   Bats: L   Throws: R   Height: 6'1"   Weight: 165   Origin: International Free Agent, 2017

YEAR	TEAM	LVL	AGE	PA	R	2B	3B	HR	RBI	BB	K	SB	CS	AVG/OBP/SLG	DRC+	BABIP	BRR	FRAA	WARP
2018	DSL GIA	ROK	17	274	44	13	1	10	39	51	62	4	1	.270/.423/.479		.333			
2019	GIO	ROK	18	234	45	15	3	3	33	45	54	4	5	.297/.436/.459		.400			
2019	SK	SS	18	13	2	1	0	0	0	2	5	0	0	.273/.385/.364	105	.500	-1.4	3B(3) -0.6	-0.2
2021 FS	SF	MLB	20	600	48	27	2	7	49	48	224	4	1	.199/.270/.303	58	.322	0.7	3B -10	-3.1

Comparables: Austin Riley, Ryan McMahon, Sherten Apostel

The Report: Signed for $300,000 while the Giants were in the penalty after inking Lucius Fox the previous summer, Toribio's bat has developed quickly as a pro. The stick was always going to be driving the profile, although the stout Toribio should be fine at third base. The hit and power tools are both potentially above-average and he's shown good plate discipline early in his pro career, albeit at levels where it's not all that hard to draw a walk.

Development Track: Toribio had alternate site and instructs time and should be well-situated for a full-season ball assignment in 2021 when we will get a better test of the offensive carrying tools.

Variance: Extreme. He hasn't played significant games stateside. You can check back in three years now, but there's the potential the profile pops well before then. And anyway, there will be another list in 2022.

J.P. Breen's Fantasy Take: Toribio doesn't have much physical projection remaining and won't be a threat on the basepaths, which puts all the pressure on his bat to carry his fantasy profile. He could be a power-average slugger. However, there's platoon risk and risk that he's simply been more physically developed than his peers in rookie ball. Toribio is a fringe top-200 dynasty prospect, though I have him a touch lower on my personal rankings list due to his age and how infrequently this type of fantasy profile translates to an impact big leaguer.

9 Alexander Canario CF   OFP: 55   ETA: 2024
Born: 05/07/00   Age: 21   Bats: R   Throws: R   Height: 6'1"   Weight: 165   Origin: International Free Agent, 2016

YEAR	TEAM	LVL	AGE	PA	R	2B	3B	HR	RBI	BB	K	SB	CS	AVG/OBP/SLG	DRC+	BABIP	BRR	FRAA	WARP
2018	GIB	ROK	18	208	36	5	2	6	19	27	51	8	5	.250/.357/.403		.317			
2019	GIO	ROK	19	46	13	3	1	7	14	2	9	1	0	.395/.435/1.000		.370			
2019	SK	SS	19	219	38	17	1	9	40	18	71	3	1	.301/.365/.539	158	.419	-1.0	CF(26) -8.1, RF(16) -1.1	0.5
2021 FS	SF	MLB	21	600	46	27	3	9	51	36	211	13	6	.199/.253/.310	53	.302	-1.5	CF -7, RF 2	-2.6

Comparables: Greg Halman, Victor Robles, Austin Meadows

The Report: Canario's swing should go in the BP Prospect Team handbook as our dictionary definition of controlled violence. And it's just barely restrained, but it creates incredible bat speed and whippy loft that could generate big home run totals in the majors some day. It could also generate 200 strikeouts in Double-A. So you can probably guess the variance you will see below. Canario is an average runner better suited to right field than center, but he has the potential power to fit the corner outfield prospect mold.

Development Track: Canario's offensive profile was going to be more boom or bust than Toribio or even Matos, but man it would be a heckuva boom. There's an alternate history where he has a normal A-ball season this year and goes 110+ mph exit velo for 110+ mph exit velo with Luciano. Instead, his season ended with a dislocated shoulder and torn labrum during instructs. He's had shoulder surgery since and given the recovery time for that, the start of his 2021 might be in doubt.

Variance: Extreme. Take the copypasta from the two teenagers ahead of him on the list and add a significant shoulder injury. And given the effort in the swing, any erosion of the shoulder strength could be a big problem

J.P. Breen's Fantasy Take: I fully acknowledge the upside, but we're talking about a 20-year-old who hasn't yet played full-season ball and had a 32.4 percent strikeout rate at his most recent minor-league stop. Add in the shoulder surgery, and I've got nightmares of Gregory Polanco dancing through my head. Most lists have Canario as a top-100 dynasty prospect. He's much lower than that for me.

10 Seth Corry LHP   OFP: 50   ETA: 2022
Born: 11/03/98   Age: 22   Bats: L   Throws: L   Height: 6'2"   Weight: 195   Origin: Round 3, 2017 Draft (#96 overall)

YEAR	TEAM	LVL	AGE	W	L	SV	G	GS	IP	H	HR	BB/9	K/9	K	GB%	BABIP	WHIP	ERA	DRA-	WARP
2018	GIO	ROK	19	3	1	0	9	9	38	38	1	4.0	9.9	42	42.6%	.352	1.45	2.61		
2018	SK	SS	19	1	2	0	5	5	19²	14	1	6.9	7.8	17	51.9%	.245	1.47	5.49	300	-2.2
2019	AUG	LO-A	20	9	3	0	27	26	122²	73	4	4.3	12.6	172	43.2%	.272	1.07	1.76	68	2.7
2021 FS	SF	MLB	22	2	3	0	57	0	50	46	7	7.1	9.6	53	40.7%	.297	1.72	5.88	128	-0.7

Comparables: Brailyn Marquez, Huascar Ynoa, Johan Oviedo

The Report: Corry spent 2019 dominating the South Atlantic League with a K/9 of 12.6. The lefty has a fastball he can dial up to 95 with good extension and deception. He also has a potentially above-average curve and change. The stuff is not in question, but control has been an issue for him throughout his pro career.

Development Track: Corry impressed at instructs with his above-average three pitch mix. He still struggles with walks, and improving his control will be the biggest developmental step for him moving forward as a potential starting pitcher.

Variance: High. Could be a back of the rotation guy if the stuff sticks/command is good, could be a reliever.

J.P. Breen's Fantasy Take: Until the control/command takes a massive step forward, you can feel free to remove Corry from your dynasty lists. Don't be enticed by the shiny A-ball ERA.

The Prospects You Meet Outside The Top Ten

MLB arms, but less upside than you'd like

Sean Hjelle   RHP   Born: 05/07/97   Age: 24   Bats: R   Throws: R   Height: 6'11"   Weight: 228   Origin: Round 2, 2018 Draft (#45 overall)

YEAR	TEAM	LVL	AGE	W	L	SV	G	GS	IP	H	HR	BB/9	K/9	K	GB%	BABIP	WHIP	ERA	DRA-	WARP
2018	SK	SS	21	0	0	0	12	12	21¹	24	4	1.7	9.3	22	49.3%	.317	1.31	5.06	212	-1.2
2019	AUG	LO-A	22	1	2	0	9	9	40²	41	3	2.0	9.7	44	62.4%	.336	1.23	2.66	109	-0.1
2019	SJ	HI-A	22	5	5	0	14	14	77²	73	2	2.2	8.5	73	65.5%	.329	1.18	2.78	84	0.9
2019	RIC	AA	22	1	2	0	5	5	25¹	38	1	3.2	7.5	21	47.1%	.430	1.86	6.04	153	-0.8
2021 FS	SF	MLB	24	2	3	0	57	0	50	49	7	3.4	7.4	40	43.0%	.288	1.38	4.60	113	-0.2

Comparables: Beau Burrows, Jeremy Bleich, Braden Shipley

Potentially one of the tallest major leaguers in history, the 6-foot-11 Hjelle drops his low-90s fastball off a metaphorical skyscraper on hitters and pairs it with a viable curve and change. The arsenal all grades out as average, but Hjelle bucks the usual tall pitcher issues—maybe he's too tall for them—with a repeatable delivery and above-average command. He did get knocked around a bit in his brief 2019 Double-A appearances, but once he conquers the upper minors in 2021, he should be ready to be a number four starter in San Francisco by 2022.

Interesting 2020 draft follows

Casey Schmitt   3B   Born: 03/01/99   Age: 22   Bats: R   Throws: R   Height: 6'2"   Weight: 200   Origin: Round 2, 2020 Draft (#49 overall)

Schmitt does a little bit of everything. He was San Diego State's closer his first two years there, running his fastball into the mid-90s and pairing it with a potential above-average splitter. He was announced as a third baseman only though, and while he has the raw power for the hot corner, the pop never consistently showed up in games in the pitcher-friendly confines of his home park. That power comes with some wrap and length though, so although his track record with wood bats is all right, there might be some adjusting to do against pro arms.

Kyle Harrison   Born: 08/12/01   Age: 19   Bats: R   Throws: L   Height: 6'2"   Weight: 200   Origin: Round 3, 2020 Draft (#85 overall)

Taken in the third round by the Giants and given a first round bonus, and he's absolutely confounding as an overslot prep arm. We all have a picture of our head of what this profile looks like on the mound. The frame is about right, 6-foot-2 and 200 lbs, although perhaps that's less projection than you'd like. The fastball is more low-90s than mid-90s, the profile more pitchability than power stuff. There's even an advanced change for a prep. He's difficult to pigeonhole among the 2020 prep arm class, but he's a solid pitching prospect nonetheless.

MLB arms, but probably relievers

Conner Menez   **LHP**   Born: 05/29/95   Age: 26   Bats: L   Throws: L   Height: 6'2"   Weight: 206   Origin: Round 14, 2016 Draft (#425 overall)

YEAR	TEAM	LVL	AGE	W	L	SV	G	GS	IP	H	HR	BB/9	K/9	K	GB%	BABIP	WHIP	ERA	DRA-	WARP
2018	SJ	HI-A	23	2	5	0	11	11	50¹	48	2	3.8	12.5	70	44.1%	.374	1.37	4.83	67	1.1
2018	RIC	AA	23	6	4	0	15	15	74	73	1	4.1	11.2	92	37.3%	.381	1.45	4.38	84	1.2
2018	SAC	AAA	23	1	1	0	2	2	11	6	0	4.1	7.4	9	50.0%	.214	1.00	3.27	82	0.2
2019	RIC	AA	24	3	3	0	11	11	59²	37	5	3.0	10.6	70	35.7%	.237	0.96	2.72	71	1.1
2019	SAC	AAA	24	3	1	0	12	11	61¹	60	12	4.4	12.3	84	32.0%	.345	1.47	4.84	78	1.7
2019	SF	MLB	24	0	1	0	8	3	17	13	4	6.4	11.6	22	28.2%	.265	1.47	5.29	83	0.3
2020	SF	MLB	25	1	0	0	7	0	11¹	6	2	4.0	6.4	8	29.0%	.143	0.97	2.38	128	-0.1
2021 FS	SF	MLB	26	9	8	0	26	26	150	124	20	4.5	9.6	160	35.0%	.270	1.33	4.11	98	1.2
2021 DC	SF	MLB	26	5	6	0	21	21	84	69	11	4.5	9.6	89	35.0%	.270	1.33	4.11	98	0.9

Comparables: Matt Hall, Gregory Soto, Anthony Misiewicz

Menez's 2020 stint with the Giants went better than his 2019 one on paper, but he continued to have some struggles with the long ball. His recently developed slider looks promising though, and gives him a second breaking ball look from the left side. He'd be assured of more major league time pre-three-batter-rule, but he could still be a useful reliever to deploy as is.

Dedniel Nunez   **RHP**   Born: 06/05/96   Age: 25   Bats: R   Throws: R   Height: 6'2"   Weight: 180   Origin: International Free Agent, 2016

YEAR	TEAM	LVL	AGE	W	L	SV	G	GS	IP	H	HR	BB/9	K/9	K	GB%	BABIP	WHIP	ERA	DRA-	WARP
2018	KNG	ROK	22	4	1	1	11	7	40¹	38	2	3.6	8.0	36	45.7%	.319	1.34	3.79		
2019	COL	LO-A	23	3	1	0	4	3	22¹	14	2	1.2	13.3	33	48.9%	.267	0.76	4.03	59	0.6
2019	STL	HI-A	23	2	3	0	12	12	57²	59	3	3.1	9.5	61	36.3%	.339	1.37	4.53	110	-0.2
2021 FS	SF	MLB	25	1	2	0	57	0	50	49	7	4.4	8.4	46	35.3%	.297	1.47	4.98	119	-0.4
2021 DC	SF	MLB	25	1	2	0	28	3	40	39	5	4.4	8.4	37	35.3%	.297	1.47	4.98	119	-0.1

Comparables: Elieser Hernandez, Brandon Brennan, Jeff Brigham

Plucked out of the Mets org in December's Rule 5 draft, Nunez has a high-spin fastball he can run up to 95—although it sits a few ticks lower—and a fringy slider and change. He's best suited to relief, but given that he's been a starter for most of his pro career and has three pitches, he could help out in a multi-innings stints or as the occasional bulk guy. Or he could get returned to Mets in March.

Top Talents 25 and Under (as of 4/1/2021):

1. Marco Luciano, SS
2. Joey Bart, C
3. Heliot Ramos, OF
4. Hunter Bishop, OF
5. Patrick Bailey, C
6. Will Wilson, SS
7. Luis Matos, OF
8. Luis Toribio, 3B
9. Alexander Canario, OF
10. Logan Webb, RHP

When I agreed to write all 30 of these 25U lists back in the fall, the first thing I did was put together a spreadsheet of all of the 40-man players who were eligible here who aren't rookie-eligible. The Giants had exactly one entry on my list—Logan Webb—and I wasn't even sure if he was going to make the list. He's a back-of-the-rotation starter or bulk guy type and I decided that was probably better than Seth Corry. So, basically, there's not a lot going on here.

Seattle Mariners

The State of the System:

The system is too good now to indulge in our usual trope of a sad Death Cab for Cutie lyric here. Maybe there's a happy Death Cab song, we don't know. Frankly, we don't want to know.

The Top Ten:

───────────── ★ ★ ★ *2021 Top 101 Prospect* **#3** ★ ★ ★ ─────────────

1 **Julio Y. Rodríguez** **OF**   OFP: 70   ETA: Late 2021/Early 2022
Born: 12/29/00   Age: 20   Bats: R   Throws: R   Height: 6'3"   Weight: 180   Origin: International Free Agent, 2017

YEAR	TEAM	LVL	AGE	PA	R	2B	3B	HR	RBI	BB	K	SB	CS	AVG/OBP/SLG	DRC+	BABIP	BRR	FRAA	WARP
2018	DSL SEA	ROK	17	255	50	13	9	5	36	30	40	10	0	.315/.404/.525		.364			
2019	WV	LO-A	18	295	50	20	1	10	50	20	65	1	3	.293/.359/.490	159	.351	0.0	RF(40) 4.7, CF(22) -0.2	2.8
2019	MOD	HI-A	18	72	13	6	3	2	19	5	10	0	0	.462/.514/.738	254	.528	0.5	CF(13) -3.4, RF(3) -0.5	0.9
2021 FS	SEA	MLB	20	600	55	27	5	13	62	35	177	4	1	.231/.285/.375	81	.314	3.7	RF 4, CF -4	0.5

Comparables: Bryce Harper, Jason Heyward, Chris Marrero

The Report: Here's the one sentence version of this report: Rodríguez hits the ball harder than any other prospect in any system.

The longer version adds some more feats of strength. Rodríguez played the entire 2019 season at age 18. He was one of the best hitters in the Low-A South Atlantic League for the bulk of the season, then went up and torched High-A for a few weeks at the end, then shined in the Arizona Fall League. His swing is compact and quick, and he's starting to lift the ball more in a way that belies future high-end power. He manages the strike zone very well, with an extremely advanced approach for his age. He's an above-average runner, and though we think his defensive profile will play best in right given his excellent arm, he has some chance to play center too.

Development Track: The only downside we can find is that he's missed a good deal of time with injuries. Rodríguez was out for a couple months in 2019 with a hand injury from a hit-by-pitch, and he missed some time this summer from a wrist injury from baserunning practice. What we heard and saw of his 2020 developmental time was loud enough that we're still bumping him up.

Variance: Medium. The injuries and lack of pro experience are, I guess, slight concerns. But you can make a cogent argument that Rodríguez is the best prospect in baseball right now.

Mark Barry's Fantasy Take: Do you like really good baseball players that are really good at hitting baseballs? I don't know that he'll run for very much longer (or with a ton of volume), but it wouldn't shock me to see future seasons of .300/35 homers, perhaps even near futures. Do whatever you can to get Julio Rodríguez on your fantasy team.

★ ★ ★ *2021 Top 101 Prospect* **#6** ★ ★ ★

2 Jarred Kelenic OF   OFP: 70   ETA: 2021

Born: 07/16/99   Age: 21   Bats: L   Throws: L   Height: 6'1"   Weight: 190   Origin: Round 1, 2018 Draft (#6 overall)

YEAR	TEAM	LVL	AGE	PA	R	2B	3B	HR	RBI	BB	K	SB	CS	AVG/OBP/SLG	DRC+	BABIP	BRR	FRAA	WARP
2018	KNG	ROK	18	200	33	8	4	5	33	22	39	11	1	.253/.350/.431		.300			
2018	MTS	ROK	18	51	9	2	2	1	9	4	11	4	0	.413/.451/.609		.514			
2019	WV	LO-A	19	218	33	14	3	11	29	25	45	7	4	.309/.394/.586	180	.356	-0.5	CF(33) -1.8, RF(8) -0.1, LF(3) 2.3	2.3
2019	MOD	HI-A	19	190	36	13	1	6	22	17	49	10	3	.290/.353/.485	137	.368	1.4	CF(32) 1.1, RF(8) -1.2, LF(2) -0.1	1.3
2019	ARK	AA	19	92	11	4	1	6	17	8	17	3	0	.253/.315/.542	134	.246	0.6	CF(12) 0.6, RF(5) 0.6, LF(3) -0.2	0.7
2021 FS	SEA	MLB	21	600	67	27	4	22	73	39	181	11	4	.237/.292/.423	93	.310	1.7	CF -5, LF 0	1.1
2021 DC	SEA	MLB	21	99	11	4	0	3	12	6	29	1	0	.237/.292/.423	93	.310	0.3	CF -1	0.2

Comparables: Oscar Taveras, Byron Buxton, Travis Snider

The Report: Kelenic has a classic lefty swing. He's got a very good chance to be at least a plus hit, plus power player based on his improved bat path and move to the ball. He has an advanced plate approach, and because of that and how quickly he advanced in 2019, we're confident he'll hit in the majors, about as much as we can be for a prospect who hasn't played in the majors yet and has fewer than 100 plate appearances in the upper minors.

Kelenic is a plus runner at present, and combined with his plus arm he has a shot to remain in center field long term. He's going to have to improve routes and closing instincts to stick there long-term, and with all the competition in the Seattle outfield picture it's quite possible he ends up in a corner anyway. He'd project extremely well in either right or left.

Development Track: We are not at all down on Kelenic even though he's no longer the top prospect in the system. He's moving up, not down, on the Top 101 list. Seattle had one of the more open alternate site and instructs setups, posting quite a bit of video and TrackMan data on their team social media accounts, and nothing we saw has us down on Kelenic at all. He's still on track to be a great player and be up next year. We just have an even better (if only slightly so) projection on Rodríguez right now.

Variance: Medium. Low on that bat in and of itself, higher on the chance that he has to slide to a corner, where hitting a 70 OFP is a really high offensive bar.

Mark Barry's Fantasy Take: Though I also like Rodríguez slightly more, I wouldn't really put up too much of a fight if you prefer Kelenic for your fantasy roster. Kelenic is a great hitter, he's polished, and he might even steal 15 bases for you, at least in the short term. Both of these two are top-five options in dynasty, which is pretty exciting if you're a Mariners fan.

★ ★ ★ *2021 Top 101 Prospect* **#38** ★ ★ ★

3 Logan Gilbert RHP   OFP: 60   ETA: 2021

Born: 05/05/97   Age: 24   Bats: R   Throws: R   Height: 6'6"   Weight: 225   Origin: Round 1, 2018 Draft (#14 overall)

YEAR	TEAM	LVL	AGE	W	L	SV	G	GS	IP	H	HR	BB/9	K/9	K	GB%	BABIP	WHIP	ERA	DRA-	WARP
2019	WV	LO-A	22	1	0	0	5	5	22²	9	2	2.4	14.3	36	22.5%	.184	0.66	1.59	31	1.0
2019	MOD	HI-A	22	5	3	0	12	12	62¹	52	3	1.7	10.5	73	45.5%	.322	1.03	1.73	65	1.4
2019	ARK	AA	22	4	2	0	9	9	50	34	2	2.7	10.1	56	32.5%	.274	0.98	2.88	73	0.8
2021 FS	SEA	MLB	24	1	2	0	57	0	50	44	7	3.7	9.6	53	34.5%	.285	1.30	4.10	100	0.1
2021 DC	SEA	MLB	24	1	2	0	6	6	30	26	4	3.7	9.6	32	34.5%	.285	1.30	4.10	100	0.3

Comparables: Jordan Yamamoto, David Price, Sean Nolin

The Report: Gilbert is a polished, four-pitch college righty who got a little more velocity in his first full pro season and saw his profile bump into the top half of the 101. There's no 70-grade bullet in the arsenal, but he commands four above-average or better pitches, with the curve having plus swing-and-miss projection. His arsenal plays up given the advanced pitchability and despite his height, Gilbert repeats everything well and gets good extension. Is he the most exciting pitching prospect in baseball? No. Is he likely to be a good mid-rotation starter as soon as 2021? Yep.

Development Track: I suspect in a more normal season, Gilbert could have very well pitched himself into a late season call-up, given the Double-A success he already had in 2019. Instead, he pitched at the alternate site and waits to see how the Mariners rotation mix shakes out in 2021. If he's not ready on Opening Day, I'd expect him up as soon as there is a spot.

Variance: Low. Look, there's a reason I shy away from calling any pitching prospect "safe" or even "high-floor." But Gilbert checks every box to be an above-average major league starter in the near term.

Mark Barry's Fantasy Take: Under normal circumstances, we probably would have seen Gilbert on the bump at Safeco at some point in 2020. I might be a touch lower on Gilbert than most, but there's no-doubt he's one of the 10-best pitching prospects in baseball, I'm just not sold on the ceiling.

───────────────── ★ ★ ★ *2021 Top 101 Prospect* **#50** ★ ★ ★ ─────────────────

4   Emerson Hancock   RHP   OFP: 60   ETA: 2022
Born: 05/31/99   Age: 22   Bats: R   Throws: R   Height: 6'4"   Weight: 213   Origin: Round 1, 2020 Draft (#6 overall)

The Report: It's hard to build a more ideal pitching prospect at the top of the draft. Hancock, who one scout said would have been a top-10 pick if he were draft eligible after his sophomore year, fulfilled that destiny a year later, becoming the third straight college pitcher chosen in the first round by Seattle. While the previous two are known for their plus command/control and good stuff, Hancock not only satisfies the plus command, but the stuff is arguably the best of the bunch. Featuring a fastball that sits comfortably mid-90s and can touch higher, he also brings a slider and changeup that flash plus and a curveball that isn't far behind. His ability to control his body through the delivery and play off each of his pitches with advanced control is seldom found in college. Last but not least, he has the ready-made build of a future front-line starter. Literally every box is checked.

Development Track: Sure, there is plenty to ogle at on Hancock's scouting sheet, but it hasn't always been smooth sailing during his collegiate days. He took his lumps his freshman year, dealt with a minor injury the following season, and didn't get off to a fast beginning of his abbreviated draft year. All signs point toward what you want to see out of a top draft pick, yet there still is that prickly pickiness of wanting to see more. Assuming we see around 20-plus starts and over 100 innings in 2021, he will quickly shoot up preference lists.

Variance: Medium. Barring something catastrophic happening (go ahead and find some wood to knock on as you read this), Hancock has everything needed to remain a starter. Maybe the stuff backs up, but even then he's probably a number four in a rotation.

Mark Barry's Fantasy Take: I'm typically more likely to roll the dice on a guy like Hancock than Gilbert. Hancock isn't as polished, and he's not as close, but I think there's more strikeout upside, and with it, a better likelihood that he can be a front-of-the-rotation ace.

───────────────── ★ ★ ★ *2021 Top 101 Prospect* **#72** ★ ★ ★ ─────────────────

5   Taylor Trammell   CF   OFP: 60   ETA: 2021
Born: 09/13/97   Age: 23   Bats: L   Throws: L   Height: 6'2"   Weight: 213   Origin: Round 1, 2016 Draft (#35 overall)

YEAR	TEAM	LVL	AGE	PA	R	2B	3B	HR	RBI	BB	K	SB	CS	AVG/OBP/SLG	DRC+	BABIP	BRR	FRAA	WARP
2018	DAY	HI-A	20	461	71	19	4	8	41	58	105	25	10	.277/.375/.406	125	.358	-0.8	CF(60) -1.7, LF(29) 4.5, RF(14) -0.7	1.7
2019	AMA	AA	21	133	14	4	1	4	10	13	36	3	4	.229/.316/.381	89	.295	-0.6	CF(31) -1.4	0.1
2019	CHA	AA	21	381	47	8	3	6	33	54	86	17	4	.236/.349/.336	110	.299	2.1	LF(91) -0.7, CF(1) 0.1	1.5
2021 FS	SEA	MLB	23	600	63	25	4	14	59	57	185	19	7	.229/.307/.372	89	.321	2.4	LF 3, CF 0	1.5

Comparables: Ryan Kalish, Michael Saunders, Brandon Nimmo

The Report: Trammell has long been a divisive prospect. At his best, he projects as a center fielder with plus hit and power tools. At other times he looks like a bench outfielder who might be limited to left. The culprit here is a swing that has undergone several tweaks and even overhauls, both in Cincy and then in San Diego. Trammell didn't hit for average or power in Double-A in 2019 and played mostly left field, as his arm is well-below average. He's a plus-plus runner though and the outfield instincts are good enough to stick in center otherwise.

Development Track: It's unusual for a top prospect to get traded twice before debuting in the majors. It's more unusual for that second trade to be for a 30-year-old catcher who had fewer than 400 plate appearances. You can look at this a couple ways. Two teams have looked to offload Trammell. But two teams have also tried to acquire him. The Mariners have already started fiddling with his swing some more, and he did flash that plus raw power again at the alternate site and instructs, but his inconsistency at the plate continues.

Variance: High. It's unclear exactly when the tradition of the Captain going down with the ship began. It's often traced back to the sinking of the HMS Birkenhead, immortalized in the Rudyard Kipling poem "Soldier an' Sailor Too."

Mark Barry's Fantasy Take: It's a little worrying that Trammell is already on his third team at the ripe old age of 23, but since I'm the sunniest of sunny optimists, I'll take that to mean there are just multiple teams that value his skill set. The fantasy upside for Trammell is still there as a high-OBP guy that can steal bases and at least contribute in four categories. The likelihood of him reaching that upside might have diminished slightly, however.

★ ★ ★ *2021 Top 101 Prospect* **#68** ★ ★ ★

6   George Kirby   RHP   OFP: 60   ETA: 2022

Born: 02/04/98   Age: 23   Bats: R   Throws: R   Height: 6'4"   Weight: 215   Origin: Round 1, 2019 Draft (#20 overall)

YEAR	TEAM	LVL	AGE	W	L	SV	G	GS	IP	H	HR	BB/9	K/9	K	GB%	BABIP	WHIP	ERA	DRA-	WARP
2019	EVE	SS	21	0	0	0	9	8	23	24	1	0.0	9.8	25	45.3%	.365	1.04	2.35	72	0.5
2021 FS	SEA	MLB	23	2	3	0	57	0	50	50	7	3.4	7.3	40	40.2%	.290	1.38	4.58	112	-0.2

Comparables: Sam Gaviglio, Luis Perdomo, Humberto Mejía

The Report: With a broadly similar profile to Gilbert coming out of the draft, Kirby featured plus-plus command of an otherwise average-to-solid-average four pitch mix. An elite strikethrower in a calendar year across the Cape, his draft season at Elon, and his first pro summer in the Northwest League, he posted a 156:7 K:BB ratio in 124 ⅓ innings. It would be fair to ask what the ultimate upside was at this point. Command is not an out pitch, and while Kirby's arsenal was fine, there wasn't an obvious plus pitch projection. Then Kirby showed up this spring sitting more mid-90s than low-90s without losing any of the command. OK, now we're cooking with some gas.

Development Track: Kirby technically hasn't seen full-season ball yet, but I don't see a particularly good reason to start him lower than Advanced-A in 2021, and I wouldn't be shocked if he kicks off in the Texas League. He could be a major league factor as soon as this season, but a full year getting him accustomed to a pro workload and schedule isn't the worst idea in the world.

Variance: Medium. Kirby has a lot of the same positive markers as a starter as Gilbert. He even has a few more ticks on the fastball now. He also has far less pro experience.

Mark Barry's Fantasy Take: Gilbert and Hancock are definitely the marquee arms in this org, but Kirby might be my personal favorite. Admittedly, I'm a sucker for high control/command guys, and Kirby definitely fits that bill. It also seems like there's a chance his 2020 development could have raised his ceiling, and his dynasty cost will certainly be lower than the team's other big arms.

7   Noelvi Marte   SS   OFP: 60   ETA: 2024

Born: 10/16/01   Age: 19   Bats: R   Throws: R   Height: 6'1"   Weight: 181   Origin: International Free Agent, 2018

YEAR	TEAM	LVL	AGE	PA	R	2B	3B	HR	RBI	BB	K	SB	CS	AVG/OBP/SLG	DRC+	BABIP	BRR	FRAA	WARP
2019	DSL SEA	ROK	17	299	56	18	4	9	54	29	55	17	7	.309/.371/.511		.351			

The Report / Development Track: One of the pain points for our 2021 lists is if I already wrote a navel-gazing, process-oriented blurb about a recent big bonus IFA with no stateside experience in 2020, I don't really have anything to fall back on this time around. And we do have slightly more information about Marte, who was both at the Mariners' alternate site and instructs. He ended up literally being the last cut off our 101—we have an orphan blurb and everything—because we think the bat will play to at least above-average on both hit and power, and he's likely to stick at shortstop. That's the type of profile that makes our national list. But while we have more information about Marte, it's hard to say we have enough information about Marte.

Variance: Extreme. Our old generic risk profile would look something like this—complex-league resume, uncertainty about the long term hit tool projection, needs to prove it against better competition.

Mark Barry's Fantasy Take: Your mileage may vary on Marte, or guys like Marte. Part of the dynasty-league fun is identifying "The Next Guy", and after a breakout 2019, Marte shot up a ton of fantasy lists for just that reason. The only problem is that his experience stateside has been limited to Mariners camp in non-competitive situations. That's fine, but there's still a lot we don't know, and with guys like Marte, you can't wait around to find out. Marte could be very, very good, but I'd be more likely to take advantage of his shiny "Next" status and cash in for someone that could help sooner.

8 Juan Then RHP   OFP: 60   ETA: 2023

Born: 02/07/00   Age: 21   Bats: R   Throws: R   Height: 6'1"   Weight: 175   Origin: International Free Agent, 2016

YEAR	TEAM	LVL	AGE	W	L	SV	G	GS	IP	H	HR	BB/9	K/9	K	GB%	BABIP	WHIP	ERA	DRA-	WARP
2018	YAE	ROK	18	0	3	0	11	11	50	38	2	2.0	7.6	42	45.4%	.259	0.98	2.70		
2019	MAR	ROK	19	0	0	0	1	0	2	2	0	0.0	9.0	2	20.0%	.400	1.00	0.00		
2019	EVE	SS	19	0	3	0	7	6	30¹	24	1	2.7	9.5	32	34.6%	.299	1.09	3.56	65	0.7
2019	WV	LO-A	19	1	2	0	3	3	16	7	1	2.2	7.9	14	29.3%	.150	0.69	2.25	59	0.4
2021 FS	SEA	MLB	21	2	3	0	57	0	50	49	7	3.6	7.8	43	38.0%	.293	1.40	4.60	112	-0.2

Comparables: Rony García, Luis Severino, Antonio Santos

The Report: Then is on his second spell as a Mariners prospect—the Dipoto special—but the version that came back from the Yankees was better than the one traded away. The undersized righty comfortably sits mid-90s with a potential above-average curve and change as well. It's not the easiest velocity given his size, but the mechanics aren't prohibitive for a starter.

Development Track: We predicted a bump in velocity in this space last year and Then is running his fastball into the upper-90s more now. We don't know how the velocity holds up over a full season, and he's on the shorter and slighter side. There's the makings of a deep enough arsenal to start, but there will always be the temptation to fast track him as a power relief arm. Then will only be 21, so keeping him stretched out for the starter's reps in the near term makes the most sense. And hey, sometimes the starter stays a starter longer than you'd think.

Variance: Very High. Then's career high in innings pitched is 61, which came in 2017 in the Dominican Summer League. He has yet to pitch above A-ball and the frame is … uh, not a traditional starter's build.

Mark Barry's Fantasy Take: Last year, I took a "wait and see" approach with Then, and then, well, 2020 happened. I still don't know if Then needs to be on your dynasty radar quite yet, but if you wanted to toss him on a watch list, I wouldn't argue.

9 Cal Raleigh C   OFP: 55   ETA: Late 2021 / 2022

Born: 11/26/96   Age: 24   Bats: S   Throws: R   Height: 6'3"   Weight: 215   Origin: Round 3, 2018 Draft (#90 overall)

YEAR	TEAM	LVL	AGE	PA	R	2B	3B	HR	RBI	BB	K	SB	CS	AVG/OBP/SLG	DRC+	BABIP	BRR	FRAA	WARP
2018	EVE	SS	21	167	25	10	1	8	29	18	29	1	1	.288/.367/.534	140	.309	0.3	C(25) -0.2	0.7
2019	MOD	HI-A	22	348	48	19	0	22	66	33	69	4	0	.261/.336/.535	150	.267	0.8	C(55) 0.9	3.1
2019	ARK	AA	22	159	16	6	0	7	16	14	47	0	0	.228/.296/.414	108	.286	-0.6	C(26) -0.0	0.6
2021 FS	SEA	MLB	24	600	72	26	1	30	86	43	174	1	0	.238/.298/.459	103	.290	-0.4	C 2	2.9

Comparables: Jason Castro, Yasmani Grandal, Max Ramirez

The Report: Raleigh was drafted as a bat-first, switch-hitting catcher with potential plus pop, but quickly made strides behind the plate as well to get his defense past passable and in the average range. The power plays from both sides, and while there's swing-and-miss concerns that might limit the batting averages to .240 or .250, the bat speed and loft should get Raleigh 20 or so bombs a year. He's unspectacular defensively but he moves and receives well, although the throwing arm is a bit light.

Development Track: Raleigh went to the alternate site for 2020, and currently sits third on the catching depth chart for Seattle behind the likely MLB tandem of Tom Murphy and Luis Torrens. Murphy provides a good model for what a good major league outcome might look like for Raleigh, a bigger framed catcher with raw power, who gets just enough of it into games, and who worked himself into a good enough defender to be a solid 1A or 1B catcher. That might have to wait a season though as you'd like to see a consolidation period against upper minors pitching first.

Variance: Medium. The stiffness in the swing might get exposed against better pitching—and that K-rate in the first pass of Double-A was a little worrisome—limiting Raleigh to more of a backup with a bit of pop. But the bar for catcher offense is low enough that even an OBP that flirts with the wrong side of .300 doesn't mean he's not a viable regular if the pop and glove plays.

Mark Barry's Fantasy Take: I could see tossing a buck on Raleigh at the end of an auction in a two-catcher draft. Whether that buck is well spent, however, is questionable.

10   Zach DeLoach   OFP: 50   ETA: 2023

Born: 08/18/98   Age: 22   Bats: L   Throws: R   Height: 6'1"   Weight: 205   Origin: Round 2, 2020 Draft (#43 overall)

The Report: What exactly are the Mariners getting with their second round pick out of Texas A&M? Are they getting the mediocre offensive player with good physical tools from his first two years in the SEC? Or the juggernaut who lit up summer wood-bat leagues and torched subpar pitching during his brief spring? DeLoach is two sides of the same coin and it's tough to tell which direction the production levels will go next. The fact he has a proven record excelling with wood bats is helpful, showing excellent power potential to the pull side. He's also been a good runner at times, although some added bulk may start weighing that down, and he's already been playing more corner outfield than center.

Development Track: DeLoach is going to have to prove the newfound hitting ability is real. Every draft pick has some element of, "prove it, rook" to back up why they were taken. He will need to do that and then some. Assuming the changes to the swing—he's more closed off than he was before, which seems to help quiet his movements and track the ball better—remain from when he was at his best, it won't seem like such a buy-high pick after all.

Variance: Medium. He's unlikely to rock the boat too much one way or the other. He's not as bad as he was early in his college days, and he's not playing on God Mode, either. Something in-between that seems far more realistic.

Mark Barry's Fantasy Take: It doesn't take much for good-not-great upside to slide into the realm of fourth outfielders.

The Prospects You Meet Outside The Top Ten

Interesting 2019 draft follows

Brandon Williamson   **LHP**   Born: 04/02/98   Age: 23   Bats: L   Throws: L   Height: 6'6"   Weight: 210   Origin: Round 2, 2019 Draft (#59 overall)

YEAR	TEAM	LVL	AGE	W	L	SV	G	GS	IP	H	HR	BB/9	K/9	K	GB%	BABIP	WHIP	ERA	DRA-	WARP
2019	EVE	SS	21	0	0	0	10	9	15¹	9	0	2.9	14.7	25	55.2%	.310	0.91	2.35	46	0.5
2021 FS	SEA	MLB	23	2	3	0	57	0	50	47	7	5.1	9.4	52	42.5%	.296	1.52	5.05	119	-0.4

Comparables: Humberto Mejía, Radhames Liz, Nick Hagadone

Williamson certainly has a case to slot onto the back of the top ten somewhere. A four-pitch lefty whose 6-foot-6 frame creates a touch angle on his low-90s fastball, he also has two viable breaking ball looks already. The change needs some work, and Williamson has a very limited pro track record, but there's the makings of a backend starter with some projection past that.

Isaiah Campbell   **RHP**   Born: 08/15/97   Age: 23   Bats: R   Throws: R   Height: 6'4"   Weight: 225   Origin: Round 2, 2019 Draft (#76 overall)

Campbell could also claim that he was passed over for a top ten spot. There's more reliever risk here, as he already has the 95 mph, the slider, and a college elbow injury on his resume. After a heavy workload his draft year at Arkansas, the Mariners elected not to have him pitch in 2019, so he still hasn't officially made his pro debut—although he did pitch at the alternate site. There's just a bit more mystery here than players like DeLoach or Raleigh.

Interesting 2020 draft follows

Connor Phillips   Born: 05/04/01   Age: 20   Bats: R   Throws: R   Height: 6'2"   Weight: 190   Origin: Round CBB, 2020 Draft (#64 overall)

Phillips decided to forgo his LSU commitment to go to junior college, and ended up getting picked by Seattle in the Comp B round. He has a very live arm, showing at times upper-90s velocity, but the radar gun readings can be inconsistent. The delivery is very upper-body heavy—which may explain the wide fastball range—and he's a bit of a project. I suppose you can't spell projectable without "project" though, and Phillips is projectable too. Still, I get reliever vibes here.

MLB-ready relievers

Sam Delaplane **RHP**   Born: 03/27/95   Age: 26   Bats: R   Throws: R   Height: 5'11"   Weight: 175   Origin: Round 23, 2017 Draft (#693 overall)

YEAR	TEAM	LVL	AGE	W	L	SV	G	GS	IP	H	HR	BB/9	K/9	K	GB%	BABIP	WHIP	ERA	DRA-	WARP
2018	CLI	LO-A	23	4	2	10	39	0	59²	54	5	3.3	15.1	100	49.3%	.386	1.27	1.96	39	2.1
2019	MOD	HI-A	24	3	2	2	21	0	31²	22	2	4.0	17.6	62	36.0%	.417	1.14	4.26	62	0.6
2019	ARK	AA	24	3	1	5	25	0	37	13	2	2.2	14.1	58	35.9%	.180	0.59	0.49	32	1.4
2021 FS	SEA	MLB	26	1	1	0	57	0	50	39	7	4.0	12.5	69	39.3%	.289	1.23	3.66	90	0.4
2021 DC	SEA	MLB	26	1	1	0	29	0	30	23	4	4.0	12.5	41	39.3%	.289	1.23	3.66	90	0.3

Comparables: Bryan Garcia, Kodi Whitley, Tyler Rogers

I'm a little disappointed we didn't get to see Delaplane in the majors if only to see how ludicrous the pitch data was. The fastball/breaking ball combo on paper is plus/plus, but there's late life/bite that has led to some video game-like strikeout numbers in the minors. We'll have to wait until 2021 to see him unleashed in the majors, but he's likely a ready-made seventh/eighth inning type.

MLB arms, but less upside than you'd like

Ljay Newsome **RHP**   Born: 11/08/96   Age: 24   Bats: R   Throws: R   Height: 5'11"   Weight: 210   Origin: Round 26, 2015 Draft (#785 overall)

YEAR	TEAM	LVL	AGE	W	L	SV	G	GS	IP	H	HR	BB/9	K/9	K	GB%	BABIP	WHIP	ERA	DRA-	WARP
2018	MOD	HI-A	21	6	10	0	26	26	138²	169	24	0.8	8.0	123	31.3%	.339	1.31	4.87	90	1.4
2019	MOD	HI-A	22	6	6	0	18	18	100²	105	11	0.8	11.1	124	25.5%	.357	1.13	3.75	87	0.9
2019	ARK	AA	22	3	4	0	9	9	48²	41	4	1.3	6.5	35	34.9%	.262	0.99	2.77	83	0.5
2020	SEA	MLB	23	0	1	0	5	4	15²	20	4	0.6	5.2	9	42.1%	.302	1.34	5.17	118	0.0
2021 FS	SEA	MLB	24	9	9	0	26	26	150	156	28	1.7	7.2	120	37.6%	.289	1.24	4.39	104	0.8
2021 DC	SEA	MLB	24	3	4	0	14	14	61	63	11	1.7	7.2	49	37.6%	.289	1.24	4.39	104	0.5

Comparables: Tyler Mahle, Chih-Wei Hu, José Ureña

A personal cheeseball made good. Newsome was an extreme control artist in the minors who bumped his fastball from the upper-80s to the low-90s, which paired with an average enough breaking ball and change, racked up strikeouts in the minors in 2019. That last step is the steepest though, and his major league fate—albeit in a very small sample—was not uncommon for prospect arms whose control far outpaces their stuff. When in the zone, Newsome got hit hard, which led to a bit more nibbling, a few more walks, and far less whiffs. He might be crowded out of the Mariners' rotation plans, if he was ever really in them to begin with, but he might still be a useful utility arm. I'll be rooting for him anyway.

Prospects to dream on a little

Austin Shenton **3B**   Born: 01/22/98   Age: 23   Bats: L   Throws: R   Height: 6'0"   Weight: 195   Origin: Round 5, 2019 Draft (#156 overall)

YEAR	TEAM	LVL	AGE	PA	R	2B	3B	HR	RBI	BB	K	SB	CS	AVG/OBP/SLG	DRC+	BABIP	BRR	FRAA	WARP
2019	EVE	SS	21	92	16	10	1	2	16	8	15	0	0	.367/.446/.595	192	.429	0.1	3B(14) -0.7, 2B(1) 0.0, RF(1) 0.2	1.0
2019	WV	LO-A	21	134	13	7	1	5	20	11	29	0	0	.252/.328/.454	107	.291	-1.0	2B(8) -1.2, 3B(7) 0.1, LF(6) -0.1	0.2
2021 FS	SEA	MLB	23	600	57	27	3	14	63	36	176	1	0	.234/.292/.375	83	.316	0.8	3B -2, 2B -1	0.0

Comparables: James Darnell, Brandon Allen, Mark Trumbo

The rare projectable college bat, Shenton can really hit. There were two main questions with the profile. Would he be able to tap into his raw power given the shortness of the swing. Well he did hit a bomb over the ridiculous center field fence in Tacoma last summer. The other question is his ultimate defensive home, which remains undetermined. He was our low minors sleeper last year. So let's run that back.

Alberto Rodriguez RF   Born: 10/06/00   Age: 20   Bats: L   Throws: L   Height: 5'11"   Weight: 180   Origin: International Free Agent, 2017

YEAR	TEAM	LVL	AGE	PA	R	2B	3B	HR	RBI	BB	K	SB	CS	AVG/OBP/SLG	DRC+	BABIP	BRR	FRAA	WARP
2018	DSL BLJ	ROK	17	263	44	9	1	5	34	32	55	21	6	.254/.350/.368		.314			
2019	BLU	ROK	18	195	19	13	1	2	29	19	32	13	2	.301/.364/.422		.352			
2021 FS	SEA	MLB	20	600	45	27	2	7	50	33	197	22	6	.212/.258/.309	53	.311	5.0	RF 13, CF 0	-0.4

Comparables: José Martínez, César Puello, Gabriel Guerrero

The player to be named later in the Taijuan Walker deal, Rodriguez can also really hit. His ultimate defensive home is probably left field though, as his arm is below-average and he doesn't have the foot speed for center. He hits the ball incredibly hard, but that might not translate into plus game power. Still, he can really hit, so keep an eye on him.

Top Talents 25 and Under (as of 4/1/2021):

1. Julio Rodríguez, OF
2. Jarred Kelenic, OF
3. Kyle Lewis, OF
4. Logan Gilbert, RHP
5. Emerson Hancock, RHP
6. Justus Sheffield, LHP
7. Taylor Trammell, OF
8. George Kirby, RHP
9. Noelvi Marte, SS
10. Evan White, 1B

Kyle Lewis deservedly won the AL Rookie of the Year award, marking off another step on a phenomenal ascension. He cut his strikeout rate and raised his walk rate, and his performance was driven by all-around offense instead of an all-or-nothing power spike. This level of production is probably sustainable for him moving forward, and though it's not totally clear how the outfield spots in Seattle will shake out positionally quite yet, Lewis has made himself a major part of the mix.

Just a year after being demoted to Double-A, Justus Sheffield took a regular turn in the Seattle rotation. He's remade himself as something of a sinkerballer, and he doesn't quite throw as hard as he did as a prospect, but the plus slider is still there and the changeup has shown some late development. He's probably settling in as a mid-rotation starter, although given his previous bouts of wildness and ineffectiveness we'd like to see everything hold together for longer than a couple months.

Evan White and Justin Dunn occupy a similar space as players who had horrid 2020s. White, who looked for all the world like he was ready to be a quality major-league hitter, instead hit .176 in the first year of his long-term contract. Dunn also took a regular rotation turn, but walked more than six batters per 9 and posted a 7.46 DRA. White was a better prospect and Dunn might be headed for relief, so I ranked White here; Dunn would've been about 12th or 13th.

St. Louis Cardinals

The State of the System:

A combination of power bats, intriguing close-to-ready arms, and marginal depth all adds up to an averagish system.

The Top Ten:

★ ★ ★ *2021 Top 101 Prospect* **#16** ★ ★ ★

1 **Dylan Carlson** **RF**   OFP: 70   ETA: Debuted in 2020

Born: 10/23/98   Age: 22   Bats: S   Throws: L   Height: 6'2"   Weight: 205   Origin: Round 1, 2016 Draft (#33 overall)

YEAR	TEAM	LVL	AGE	PA	R	2B	3B	HR	RBI	BB	K	SB	CS	AVG/OBP/SLG	DRC+	BABIP	BRR	FRAA	WARP
2018	PEO	LO-A	19	57	5	3	0	2	9	10	10	2	0	.234/.368/.426	134	.257	-0.7	RF(10) 2.3, CF(4) -0.3	0.4
2018	PMB	HI-A	19	441	63	19	3	9	53	52	78	6	3	.247/.345/.386	113	.286	1.7	RF(50) 4.7, LF(37) -0.1, CF(1) -0.1	1.2
2019	SPR	AA	20	483	81	24	6	21	59	52	98	18	7	.281/.364/.518	150	.315	3.1	CF(87) -10.2, RF(9) -0.3, LF(5) -0.5	2.7
2019	MEM	AAA	20	79	14	4	2	5	9	6	18	2	1	.361/.418/.681	141	.429	0.1	CF(8) -0.5, LF(7) 0.0, RF(3) -0.2	0.6
2020	STL	MLB	21	119	11	7	1	3	16	8	35	1	1	.200/.252/.364	80	.260	-0.4	RF(18) 1.8, CF(17) -0.8, LF(10) -0.3	0.2
2021 FS	STL	MLB	22	600	65	23	3	19	68	49	180	4	2	.216/.287/.381	87	.282	1.0	CF -8, LF 1	-0.1
2021 DC	STL	MLB	22	534	58	20	3	17	60	44	160	4	1	.216/.287/.381	87	.282	0.9	CF -7, LF 1	0.0

Comparables: Colby Rasmus, Nomar Mazara, Lastings Milledge

The Report: A 2016 draftee who was young for his class, Carlson showed flashes of the five-tool outfield prospect he would become during aggressive A-ball assignments in 2017 and 2018, but a combination of seeing a lot of older, more experienced arms, and some brutal hitting environments meant the overall line somewhat underwhelmed. It all clicked for Carlson in 2019, as he torched the upper minors, making notable improvements to his power stroke and his quick-twitch speed—leading to an above-average center field glove projection after barely playing there the previous two years—and he established himself as a top 20 prospect in baseball. Carlson does everything well, a potential plus hit/power center fielder with a solid approach, who has the foot speed and arm to play any of the three outfield spots.

Development Track: Carlson got a shot at regular playing time early in 2020 as the Cardinals dealt with a COVID-19 outbreak. The early returns were better than the top line stats, as he took good at-bats and hit the ball hard, but lined some balls right at defenders and ended up with a few too many Ks running those deep counts. Carlson hit the reset button back at the alternate site, and blistered the ball after coming back up for the last few weeks of the season. He started for the Cardinals in the playoffs and looks to be a starting outfielder for them going forward. The overall line doesn't look amazing for a major league debut, but going forward we'd expect him to be closer to the .800 OPS he posted in September.

Variance: Medium. If we were still doing OFP/Likely, I think the likely 60 outcome here is pretty stable, given the broad base of skills and adjustments Carlson has made already in the majors. He will have to fine tune the hit tool and approach to get to the All-Star level, though, and those last little skill jumps in the majors can be the hardest.

Mark Barry's Fantasy Take: It was a disappointing 2020 for Carlson, but it was a disappointing 2020 for me too, so who am I to judge? I'm not sure much has changed since this time last year. Maybe the ceiling is slightly lower, but the floor is still pretty high, as is the potential for five-category impact.

───────── ★ ★ ★ *2021 Top 101 Prospect* **#23** ★ ★ ★ ─────────

2 **Nolan Gorman** **3B**   OFP: 60   ETA: Late 2021/Early 2022
Born: 05/10/00   Age: 21   Bats: L   Throws: R   Height: 6'1"   Weight: 210   Origin: Round 1, 2018 Draft (#19 overall)

YEAR	TEAM	LVL	AGE	PA	R	2B	3B	HR	RBI	BB	K	SB	CS	AVG/OBP/SLG	DRC+	BABIP	BRR	FRAA	WARP
2018	JC	ROK	18	167	41	10	1	11	28	24	37	1	3	.350/.443/.664		.411			
2018	PEO	LO-A	18	107	8	3	0	6	16	10	39	0	2	.202/.280/.426	77	.255	-0.5	3B(25) 3.9	0.3
2019	PEO	LO-A	19	282	41	14	3	10	41	32	79	2	0	.241/.344/.448	128	.312	0.4	3B(51) 8.4	2.6
2019	PMB	HI-A	19	230	24	16	3	5	21	13	73	0	1	.256/.304/.428	107	.365	-2.1	3B(49) -5.9	0.0
2021 FS	STL	MLB	21	600	55	27	3	15	62	43	224	1	0	.209/.272/.354	70	.320	0.9	3B 3	-0.7

Comparables: Ryan McMahon, Austin Riley, Tyler Goeddel

The Report: Gorman's pre-draft buzz had him among the top prep bats in 2018, but concerns about hit hit tool and ultimate defensive home caused him to slide to the 19th pick. He responded by destroying the Appalachian League in June and July, earning a full-season assignment a scant few months after his 18th birthday. The power continued to show up in A-ball in 2019, and it's true elite raw with potential 30+ home run seasons to come once Gorman hones his approach against better pitching. The strikeouts also piled up against A-ball pitching, and he does take Paul Bunyan-esque cuts at the ball, so he may never show better than an average hit tool. The defense has consistently looked average at the hot corner as a pro, and given how filled out Gorman already is, there's less concern he will grow off the position. It's not a lock though, and he's unlikely to be much better than a tick above-average there. That's fine as long as the thunder in the bat is as loud as we expect.

Development Track: Gorman was a monster at the plate in March, and looked to be taking another step forward this spring before the shutdown. After cooling his heels for a few months, the alternate site reports were a little more muted. In this case I will defer to the mountain of knowledge we have about the bat that didn't come in the midst of a global pandemic, while granting that the concerns about the hit tool and third base defense will only be dispelled for certain with upper level game action.

Variance: High. There's absolutely All-Star upside here if Gorman can make enough high-quality contact to run some .280+ batting averages. There's also still risk the swing-and-miss eats into the overall line and the third base glove ends up fringy or worse.

Mark Barry's Fantasy Take: It would have been nice to see Gorman finally test himself against advanced-level pitching, but realistically the only question left for the former-first rounder is whether he'll hit for enough contact to be a fantasy stud. The power is legit and could lead to plenty of 30+ homer campaigns, but the average will be the deciding factor as to whether those dingers will be empty or not.

───────── ★ ★ ★ *2021 Top 101 Prospect* **#43** ★ ★ ★ ─────────

3 **Matthew Liberatore** **LHP**   OFP: 60   ETA: 2022
Born: 11/06/99   Age: 21   Bats: L   Throws: L   Height: 6'4"   Weight: 200   Origin: Round 1, 2018 Draft (#16 overall)

YEAR	TEAM	LVL	AGE	W	L	SV	G	GS	IP	H	HR	BB/9	K/9	K	GB%	BABIP	WHIP	ERA	DRA-	WARP
2018	RAY	ROK	18	1	2	0	8	8	27²	16	0	3.6	10.4	32	45.2%	.258	0.98	0.98		
2018	PRN	ROK	18	1	0	0	1	1	5	5	0	3.6	9.0	5	41.7%	.417	1.40	3.60		
2019	BG	LO-A	19	6	2	0	16	15	78¹	70	2	3.6	8.7	76	55.7%	.312	1.29	3.10	98	0.4
2021 FS	STL	MLB	21	2	3	0	57	0	50	48	7	5.4	7.9	44	47.4%	.287	1.56	5.16	120	-0.4

Comparables: Brailyn Marquez, Randall Delgado, Tyler Chatwood

The Report: Liberatore had top-10 pick buzz going into the 2018 draft as a tall, projectable prep lefty with feel for spin. His height gives him good extension and plane on a fastball with above-average velocity for a southpaw, although the command is more on the fringy side. His best secondary is an 11-6 curve that comes from a tough angle and might have enough late action to miss bats at the highest level. Like most prep pitching prospects, the change was a developmental need, but he has solid, if inconsistent feel for it already.

Development Track: Well, Liberatore looks more or less like the same good lefty pitching prospect with advanced feel for spin. The trade that brought him to St. Louis looks a little bit different though. Obviously we won't hold that against him, but the lost year of game reps hurts a bit. Liberatore was at the alternate site and could start 2021 in Double-A, so he might not be that far off the majors himself, but we'll be looking for a more obvious out pitch against upper minors bats in 2021.

Variance: Medium. Liberatore has never really "felt" like a prep prospect, as he's been more polish than stuff—and I suppose is now roughly college junior age. There's the outline of four pitches, some feel for the change. The command outcome here will dictate if there's upside past mid-rotation, or if he's more of a backend guy. There's been some arm worries in the past too, but I mean, he's a pitcher.

Mark Barry's Fantasy Take: Without tweaks to his pitch mix or refinement of secondary offerings, Liberatore might be looking at a Marco Gonzales-esque ceiling. And that's not a knock, Gonzales is pretty good—it's just not the most enticing best case scenario. The most likely outcome is that Liberatore turns out to be a back-end starter that hangs around forever because he's a lefty.

★ ★ ★ *2021 Top 101 Prospect* **#92** ★ ★ ★

---

4 Jordan Walker 3B   OFP: 60   ETA: 2023
Born: 05/22/02   Age: 19   Bats: R   Throws: R   Height: 6'5"   Weight: 220   Origin: Round 1, 2020 Draft (#21 overall)

The Report: Walker offered big power and big upside with a frame that might not allow him to stick at third base long term. Sound familiar? The 6-foot-5 Walker gets to his prodigious raw pop with longer levers than Gorman's, and the swing-and-miss concerns are just as … well, concerning. There's very few third basemen in the majors who look like him either, just on build, so a move to a corner outfield spot or first base might be in the cards. The arm will play just fine at third base—or in right field for that matter—as Walker was up to 93 off the mound as a prep.

Development Track: We started getting big reports on Walker almost as soon as he landed at the alternate site. He can match Gorman for raw pop and posted elite exit velocities as an 18-year-old seeing far older and more advanced pitching. Gorman had a similar jump post-draft himself, but we'd feel a lot better pushing Walker as hard if those big bombs had come in Appalachian League games in Johnson City rather than the alternate site in Springfield. In the converse of the Gorman situation, we don't want to strap too big of a rocket to Walker until we see it in games—and given how aggressive the Cardinals have been recently with their top prospect bats, that could be in Advanced-A in 2021—but maybe we can attach a little V2 to the 21st overall pick, as a treat.

Variance: Extreme. It's easy to get ahead of yourself a bit with this kind of player doing these kinds of things against far more advanced pitching. We do still want to see how the swing plays against more age-appropriate pitching in real games. This could be a bit of a slow burn with a prospect track that requires some patience.

Mark Barry's Fantasy Take: "CTRL C" the Gorman analysis, but add a longer timeline and probably a final destination in the outfield. There's a lot to dream on with Walker, but we've literally seen nothing yet.

5 Zack Thompson LHP   OFP: 55   ETA: 2021 as a reliever / 2022 or later as a starter
Born: 10/28/97   Age: 23   Bats: L   Throws: L   Height: 6'2"   Weight: 215   Origin: Round 1, 2019 Draft (#19 overall)

YEAR	TEAM	LVL	AGE	W	L	SV	G	GS	IP	H	HR	BB/9	K/9	K	GB%	BABIP	WHIP	ERA	DRA-	WARP
2019	CAR	ROK	21	0	0	0	2	2	2	3	0	0.0	18.0	4	66.7%	.500	1.50	0.00		
2019	PMB	HI-A	21	0	0	0	11	0	13¹	16	0	2.7	12.8	19	48.6%	.471	1.50	4.05	137	-0.3
2021 FS	STL	MLB	23	2	3	0	57	0	50	48	8	4.3	8.6	47	42.4%	.293	1.46	4.97	120	-0.4

Comparables: Julio Urías, Jesús Luzardo, Ryan Perry

The Report: When you've been as competitive as the Cardinals have been for the better part of a generation—just one losing season in the last 20 years—and Major League Baseball operates the amateur draft with a reverse record order, it's tough to get really good players. Yet, somehow and some way they snag guys like Thompson, who for one reason or another fall into their laps. In this particular case, despite having probably the best stuff of any college pitcher in the 2019 draft, Thompson slid because of durability concerns as a starter. Using a mid-90s heater that has good wiggle to it, he has a very deceptive arm action that hides his intended pitch selection, which also includes a hard-biting breaking ball and steady changeup.

Development Track: Past arm injuries will always put into question the possibility of a reliever profile, especially as Thompson has done when deployed as a reliever. The stuff and frame are plenty good to start, no denying that's where you keep running him out every fifth day for as long as possible. If the decision is made he'll hold up better in the bullpen, he could be fast-tracked very quickly to the majors.

Variance: High. Until he can show a full season of starting the confidence level associated with the reliever risk is too much to ignore.

Mark Barry's Fantasy Take: It wouldn't surprise me if Thompson was up in 2021 and was pretty good. It also wouldn't surprise me if he comes up and gets rocked. It also wouldn't surprise me if sometimes he was good and sometimes he was bad. And it also wouldn't surprise me if he got hurt again, as he has been wont to do. The mean outcome for all these possibilities is that Thompson is decent, and worth rostering in 200+ prospect leagues, but I'm not sure if the ceiling is super high.

6 Ivan Herrera C   OFP: 55   ETA: Late 2021/Early 2022

Born: 06/01/00   Age: 21   Bats: R   Throws: R   Height: 5'11"   Weight: 220   Origin: International Free Agent, 2016

YEAR	TEAM	LVL	AGE	PA	R	2B	3B	HR	RBI	BB	K	SB	CS	AVG/OBP/SLG	DRC+	BABIP	BRR	FRAA	WARP
2018	CAR	ROK	18	130	23	6	4	1	25	11	20	1	1	.348/.423/.500		.409			
2019	PEO	LO-A	19	291	41	10	0	8	42	35	56	1	1	.286/.381/.423	138	.337	-0.1	C(64) -1.0	2.4
2019	PMB	HI-A	19	65	7	0	0	1	5	5	16	0	0	.276/.338/.328	116	.357	-1.1	C(18) -0.1	0.3
2021 FS	STL	MLB	21	600	60	24	2	10	58	34	178	1	0	.241/.294/.352	82	.333	0.5	C -2	1.0
2021 DC	STL	MLB	21	66	6	2	0	1	6	3	19	0	0	.241/.294/.352	82	.333	0.1	C 0	0.1

Comparables: Chance Sisco, Wil Myers, Hank Conger

The Report: The latest in a long line of catching prospects stuck behind Yadier Molina, Herrera doesn't have Andrew Knizner's upside with the bat nor Carson Kelly's with the glove, but there's no real weakness in his game either. The hit tool is ahead of the power, although he will show some pullside pop, but his short stroke and feel for contact should play against better velocity. He's still developing behind the plate, but Herrera is a sure shot catcher who is average or above-average at all aspects of backstop defense.

Development Track: With Molina set to hit free agency post-2020, you would have liked to see Herrera establish himself in the upper minors and put himself in position to win the job at some point in 2021. Instead, he was one of the Cardinals' six catchers at their alternate site where he didn't do anything to dissuade us from his above-average projection or stake his claim to the long term catching job. There's always 2021.

Variance: High. Catchers are weird.

Mark Barry's Fantasy Take: I want to pitch a Succession-like show, but the objective is not to take over a multimedia conglomerate, but to be the next starting catcher for the St. Louis Cardinals. Molina is in a coma and Knizner and Herrera vie to take the throne. And for some reason, Kelly is there too. Herrera could be an above-average fantasy catcher, but in one-catcher leagues, I'm not sure that means much.

7 Johan Oviedo RHP   OFP: 55   ETA: Debuted in 2020

Born: 03/02/98   Age: 23   Bats: R   Throws: R   Height: 6'5"   Weight: 245   Origin: International Free Agent, 2016

YEAR	TEAM	LVL	AGE	W	L	SV	G	GS	IP	H	HR	BB/9	K/9	K	GB%	BABIP	WHIP	ERA	DRA-	WARP
2018	PEO	LO-A	20	10	10	1	25	23	121²	108	6	5.8	8.7	118	36.5%	.304	1.54	4.22	92	1.3
2019	PMB	HI-A	21	5	0	0	6	5	33²	29	1	3.2	9.4	35	46.7%	.308	1.22	1.60	87	0.3
2019	SPR	AA	21	7	8	0	23	23	113	120	9	5.1	10.2	128	42.0%	.368	1.63	5.65	130	-1.9
2020	STL	MLB	22	0	3	0	5	5	24²	24	3	3.6	5.8	16	40.7%	.269	1.38	5.47	134	-0.2
2021 FS	STL	MLB	23	8	10	0	26	26	150	153	27	4.8	7.7	127	38.7%	.289	1.56	5.74	127	-1.2
2021 DC	STL	MLB	23	4	8	0	22	22	99	101	17	4.8	7.7	84	38.7%	.289	1.56	5.74	127	-0.4

Comparables: Rony García, Touki Toussaint, Huascar Ynoa

The Report: Oviedo is a big dude who throws mostly power stuff and comes at you from a difficult angle due to his extension and arm slot. His best offering is his heavy mid-90s fastball, which touched 99 mph in the majors this season. His primary offspeed is a hard slider that sits in the mid-80s and has improved greatly. The slider looks like a second above-average-to-plus pitch now. The issues here are command and whether he can find a usable third pitch. Oviedo doesn't always throw enough strikes, and sometimes when he is hitting the zone he's missing within the zone, dead red when he needs to hit a corner. He throws both a changeup and curveball, but the change is too firm and the curve is too soft at present. There's significant relief risk present unless something jumps.

Development Track: Oviedo was impressive enough during summer camp and at the alternate site that he got called up to make five starts down the stretch. He was pretty bad, and frankly he probably wasn't ready to be in the majors. But the fastball and slider were there, and he threw more strikes than he had in the minors.

Variance: Medium. He could really use a jump in a secondary offering or command, but he's already made the majors and there's an obvious bullpen fallback with the fastball and slider.

Mark Barry's Fantasy Take: This profile feels very reliever-y, so Oviedo doesn't need to be on your radar until the day he takes over ninth-inning duties (which also might not happen).

8 Masyn Winn   SS
Born: 03/21/02   Age: 19   Bats: R   Throws: R   Height: 5'11"   Weight: 180   Origin: Round 2, 2020 Draft (#54 overall)

The Report: The old football adage, "if you have two quarterbacks, you really have none," is similar in baseball when speaking of two-way players. Contemporary players have become so specialized to harness their best attributes that most often those who actually try to both hit and pitch usually struggle to advance quickly in either. With all that said, Winn actually might have a shot at succeeding at both. At one of the biggest amateur scouting events in Jupiter, Fla., he cruised at 93-95, topping out at 97 with feel to spin some nasty breaking balls. In that same game, he crushed a monster home run into the wind. Every indication from the Cardinals suggest he will be developed simultaneously on the mound and at shortstop.

Development Track: He lacks the ideal size you want to see out of a typical starting pitcher, appearing more like a prototypical shortstop. Maintaining his body to contribute every day he will have to work on building the best base possible in his legs. Watch him being brought along slowly to give every aspect of his game time to grow.

Variance: Extreme. Will it work? Who knows. Maybe he'll have to give up one or the other at some point. The success stories are so rare it's hard to project in the most optimistic terms where it will end up.

Mark Barry's Fantasy Take: Clearly as a middle infielder/pitcher prospect, Winn's pedigree is reminiscent of, uh, well, it's a bit of a current anomaly. The idea that the Cardinals are going to develop him as a two-way player further muddies the dynasty waters. And that's totally fine, it's just hard to gauge how good/valuable he'll be until we see the development in practice. Winn is a fine dart throw, and maybe even a good one, but that's all he is right now.

9 Kodi Whitley   RHP   OFP: 50   ETA: Debuted in 2020
Born: 02/21/95   Age: 26   Bats: R   Throws: R   Height: 6'3"   Weight: 220   Origin: Round 27, 2017 Draft (#814 overall)

YEAR	TEAM	LVL	AGE	W	L	SV	G	GS	IP	H	HR	BB/9	K/9	K	GB%	BABIP	WHIP	ERA	DRA-	WARP
2018	PEO	LO-A	23	4	2	9	41	2	71²	67	2	3.3	8.5	68	45.4%	.322	1.30	2.51	72	1.3
2019	PMB	HI-A	24	0	0	0	3	0	4¹	1	0	4.2	10.4	5	37.5%	.125	0.69	0.00	63	0.1
2019	SPR	AA	24	1	4	7	31	0	39¹	31	3	3.0	10.5	46	40.0%	.277	1.12	1.83	57	0.9
2019	MEM	AAA	24	2	0	2	16	0	23²	21	0	1.5	10.3	27	27.7%	.323	1.06	1.52	45	0.9
2020	STL	MLB	25	0	0	0	4	0	4²	2	1	1.9	9.6	5	36.4%	.100	0.64	1.93	95	0.1
2021 FS	STL	MLB	26	1	2	0	57	0	50	46	8	2.5	8.8	49	35.6%	.285	1.22	3.88	95	0.3
2021 DC	STL	MLB	26	1	2	0	39	0	41	38	6	2.5	8.8	40	35.6%	.285	1.22	3.88	95	0.3

Comparables: Cody Ege, Wei-Chieh Huang, Colton Murray

The Report: Whitely always dominated in the minors, but as a 27th round redshirt junior with a Tommy John in college, the Cardinals didn't exactly push him as aggressively as some of the more notable names higher up the list. He forced the issue in 2019 though as a velocity bump into the upper-90s, paired with his plus slider, caused him to blitz three levels and left him on the doorstep of a major league bullpen role. Whitley is not just a two-pitch reliever either, as the changeup has some utility due to the deception from his arm speed.

Development Track: Whitely's pop-up velocity didn't entirely stick, as he was more of a 95-and-a-slider guy in his brief major league stint than an upper-90s-and-a-slider guy. He did deal with a minor elbow injury which might explain some of that, but also is a little concerning on its own. The slider was as advertised though, mid-80s with late, tight break. The straight change looked pretty good as well. Whitely could use those couple extra ticks back on the fastball to have true end of game utility, but he should slot in as a useful setup level reliever regardless.

Variance: Low. Whitley is ready for a major league bullpen role right now. How good the fastball is going forward will determine which inning he's utilized in however.

Mark Barry's Fantasy Take: Whitley got a bunch of whiffs in an abbreviated stint with the big club in 2020, but didn't see many high-leverage innings. His ideal role might be as a bulk reliever, which is only useful in the deepest of leagues.

10   Tink Hence   RHP   OFP: 50   ETA: 2025
Born: 08/06/02   Age: 18   Bats: R   Throws: R   Height: 6'1"   Weight: 175   Origin: Round 2, 2020 Draft (#63 overall)

The Report: Go down the list of things you want when drafting a prep pitching prospect and Hence would satisfy nearly every quality required. Except for one, but we'll get to that later. From an athletic, repeatable, and balanced delivery, the ball explodes out of his hand. Sitting in the low 90s at present, he's touched 95 on occasion with late life that also explains the late finish to his breaking ball. The arm swing and athletic control of his body through release make him a perfectly suitable Comp B round pick to dream on.

Development Track: Why not higher? Everything sounded great above, there must be a catch. Truth is: he's very skinny, with a frame that won't likely allow for much gains in the strength department. Stamina and durability might also creep into concerns without the usual mass needed to sustain a long season.

Variance: Very High. There's a lot to like to go along with the hard-to-forget barriers.

Mark Barry's Fantasy Take: I'm not writing off an 18-year-old kid, but until he can find a reliable third pitch, he's probably a reliever.

The Prospects You Meet Outside The Top Ten

Interesting 2020 Draft Follows

Alec Burleson   Born: 11/25/98   Age: 22   Bats: L   Throws: L   Height: 6'2"   Weight: 212   Origin: Round 2, 2020 Draft (#70 overall)

Another two-way player? Unlikely, even though Burleson starred at East Carolina University as one of the better ones in the country. His path to the big leagues is as a position player with a bat-first profile. With an arm that is serviceable off the mound (future blowout position player pitching?) you'd think he'd be a surefire right fielder to let the arm play up, however his lack of mobility probably relegates him to left field or first base. There is some decent barrel control and a line-drive swing that provides enough carry to get some of his raw power.

Ian Bedell   Born: 09/05/99   Age: 21   Bats: R   Throws: R   Height: 6'2"   Weight: 198   Origin: Round 4, 2020 Draft (#122 overall)

A trendy name in the 2020 draft thanks to a lights-out Cape performance, there is still a great deal unknown to his game thanks to his very short track record as a starter. In fact, he started more in the Cape than he had in his previous two years at Mizzou. A very repeatable and consistent delivery that allows for maximum strike-throwing lifts an overall average repertoire into something a bit more interesting than Bedell's typically would suggest. Along with a low-90s fastball he shows a curve that has some plus qualities to it and a cutter and changeup. Throw in the Cardinals player dev(il) magic, and the fuzzy picture of a back-end starter begins to take focus.

Prospects to dream on a little

Edwin Nunez   RHP   Born: 11/05/01   Age: 19   Bats: R   Throws: R   Height: 6'3"   Weight: 185   Origin: International Free Agent, 2019

Signed last summer at 18 for $525,000 after having to sit out due to a misrepresented age, Nuñez has regularly been hitting triple digits—and not stopping at 100. He's mostly just an arm strength prospect at this point, but it's a lot of arm strength and he still has some room to fill out further.

MLB bats, but less upside than you'd like

Evan Mendoza 3B Born: 06/28/96 Age: 25 Bats: R Throws: R Height: 6'2" Weight: 200 Origin: Round 11, 2017 Draft (#334 overall)

YEAR	TEAM	LVL	AGE	PA	R	2B	3B	HR	RBI	BB	K	SB	CS	AVG/OBP/SLG	DRC+	BABIP	BRR	FRAA	WARP
2018	PMB	HI-A	22	162	22	7	0	3	16	9	27	1	0	.349/.394/.456	156	.412	-2.4	3B(37) -0.4	0.9
2018	SPR	AA	22	402	36	12	2	5	26	30	77	1	1	.254/.315/.339	83	.309	-2.3	3B(88) 3.5, SS(9) -1.3	-0.2
2019	SPR	AA	23	223	20	8	1	1	20	14	44	5	1	.248/.293/.311	71	.307	1.2	3B(31) 5.8, 1B(21) 1.7	1.0
2021 FS	STL	MLB	25	600	53	26	2	10	57	35	157	1	0	.242/.292/.358	80	.318	0.7	3B 8, 1B 0	0.6

Comparables: Carlos Rivero, Josh VanMeter, Andy Burns

Mendoza has never really recaptured his Top Ten system shine whether it was injury or the bat stagnating some in the upper minors, or both. But even though the average raw power might never really play in games, there's still enough of a hit tool and defensive flexibility to make him a useful utility type.

Top Talents 25 and Under (as of 4/1/2021):

1. Jack Flaherty, RHP
2. Dylan Carlson, OF
3. Nolan Gorman, 3B
4. Matthew Liberatore, LHP
5. Jordan Walker, 3B
6. Zack Thompson, LHP
7. Tommy Edman, IF/OF
8. Ivan Herrera, C
9. Johan Oviedo, RHP
10. Masyn Winn, RHP/SS

Sometimes mid-rotation starting prospects become top-of-the-rotation starters. Jack Flaherty wasn't at his best for a lot of 2020, but he still turned in a decent campaign, and in the two seasons before that he was one of the better pitchers in the National League. He's got a big fastball/slider combination he can ride, and he could contend for a Cy Young in any given year.

Tommy Edman was a sensational find for the Cards. He can play nearly anywhere on the field—in just 170 MLB games he's already started more than 10 times at third, second, right field, and short—and he's useful at the plate, even if the power backed up. Cardinals Devil Magic never ends.

Tampa Bay Rays

The State of the System:

Comparing farm systems across eras is incredibly tricky, but if you told me this was the deepest collection of prospect talent ever, I'd be inclined to believe you.

The Top Ten:

───────────── ★ ★ ★ *2021 Top 101 Prospect* **#1** ★ ★ ★ ─────────────

1   **Wander Franco**   **SS**   OFP: 70   ETA: 2021, as needed

Born: 03/01/01   Age: 20   Bats: S   Throws: R   Height: 5'10"   Weight: 189   Origin: International Free Agent, 2017

YEAR	TEAM	LVL	AGE	PA	R	2B	3B	HR	RBI	BB	K	SB	CS	AVG/OBP/SLG	DRC+	BABIP	BRR	FRAA	WARP
2018	PRN	ROK	17	273	46	10	7	11	57	27	19	4	3	.351/.418/.587		.346			
2019	BG	LO-A	18	272	42	16	5	6	29	30	20	14	9	.318/.390/.506	158	.318	0.1	SS(53) -1.0	2.6
2019	CHA	HI-A	18	223	40	11	2	3	24	26	15	4	5	.339/.408/.464	175	.346	4.3	SS(45) 8.1	3.9
2021 FS	TB	MLB	20	600	63	28	5	11	64	38	88	9	7	.265/.315/.394	95	.298	-6.7	SS 6	1.5
2021 DC	TB	MLB	20	67	7	3	0	1	7	4	9	1	0	.265/.315/.394	95	.298	-0.7	SS 1	0.2

Comparables: Jurickson Profar, Carlos Correa, Ronald Torreyes

The Report: What more is there really to say about the best prospect in baseball? Franco is a potentially elite hitter, who should regularly hit .300 and post high OBPs due to one of the most advanced approaches you'll see in a teenaged hitter—yes he's still a teenager until March. The raw power is plus, but may play higher in games due to the sheer volume of quality contact. The left-handed swing is ahead of the right-handed one in terms of both hit and power, but that's not uncommon for a switch-hitter of his age, and that should smooth out with more reps against quality southpaws. Franco is an above-average runner for now, but has a blocky physique, and I'd expect the speed to play more in the average range by the time he's in his mid-20s. He's a solid infielder, rangey with smooth actions, but everything might fit a little better at second base than shortstop, and he's prone to the occasional young infielder hiccup.

Development Track: Franco played at the alternate site and even made the playoff taxi squad—you might have caught him on the field in a cutoff T-shirt showing off some bigger arms while celebrating the Rays' ALCS win. He then went to the Dominican Winter League for a bit, before a sore bicep caused him to be shut down. It sounds fairly minor, so expect Franco to be in the major league mix as soon as the Rays want to start his service time clock in 2021.

Variance: Low. You could argue because of the positional value and merely plus power that there are a small handful of prospects with a better 90th percentile outcome than Franco. He's the most likely to be at least a good regular for a decade though.

Mark Barry's Fantasy Take: So many things are different in the world since the last time we put out a Rays list. One thing not different: Wander Franco. He's the best prospect in the system, the best prospect in baseball, and probably a top-30 overall dynasty option.

★ ★ ★ *2021 Top 101 Prospect* **#20** ★ ★ ★

2 **Randy Arozarena** **LF**   OFP: 60   ETA: Debuted in 2019

Born: 02/28/95   Age: 26   Bats: R   Throws: R   Height: 5'11"   Weight: 185   Origin: International Free Agent, 2016

YEAR	TEAM	LVL	AGE	PA	R	2B	3B	HR	RBI	BB	K	SB	CS	AVG/OBP/SLG	DRC+	BABIP	BRR	FRAA	WARP
2018	SPR	AA	23	102	22	5	0	7	21	6	25	9	3	.396/.455/.681	193	.492	1.0	RF(12) 1.6, CF(6) -0.4, LF(5) 0.9	1.3
2018	MEM	AAA	23	311	42	16	0	5	28	28	59	17	5	.232/.328/.348	81	.278	0.8	LF(49) -2.7, RF(18) 0.2, CF(10) -0.9	-0.5
2019	SPR	AA	24	116	14	7	2	3	15	13	23	8	5	.309/.422/.515	160	.380	-0.5	CF(13) 0.9, LF(5) 0.0, RF(5) -0.7	0.9
2019	MEM	AAA	24	283	51	18	2	12	38	24	48	9	7	.358/.435/.593	154	.404	-1.2	CF(25) -3.4, RF(20) 4.6, LF(14) 0.5	2.7
2019	STL	MLB	24	23	4	1	0	1	2	2	4	2	1	.300/.391/.500	84	.333	-1.7	RF(6) -0.1, CF(5) 0.5, LF(1) -0.1	-0.1
2020	TB	MLB	25	76	15	2	0	7	11	6	22	4	0	.281/.382/.641	115	.306	0.5	LF(14) -0.4, RF(3) -0.3, CF(2) 0.1	0.4
2021 FS	TB	MLB	26	600	79	25	2	24	73	49	159	14	5	.251/.341/.446	116	.315	0.2	LF -3, CF 0	2.7
2021 DC	TB	MLB	26	574	76	24	2	23	69	47	152	13	5	.251/.341/.446	116	.315	0.2	LF -3	2.5

Comparables: Brandon Jones, Dwight Smith, Chris Pettit

The Report: It's entirely possible Arozarena started his breakout at the end of 2019. Long more of a hit-over-power, speedy, maybe tweener type as a prospect, he popped 12 home runs in 64 games with the Triple-A Memphis Redbirds. But that's the Pacific Coast League with the MLB rabbit ball. Whenever it happened, the power breakout is real. It might be 30+ home run power, as Arozarena sure looks like he has the loft and strength now to have plus-plus game power. Even if the aggressive approach—especially against same-side breaking stuff—limits him to an average hit tool, and 20 or so home runs, his speed will make him an average center fielder and he'd be plus in a corner. That's a solid regular, and if you watched him in the playoffs, it's pretty clear there's star upside.

Development Track: Arozarena is only eligible because of the vagaries of the shortened season. He's clearly a present above-average major leaguer and will be an every day outfielder for the 2021 Rays. Arozarena was detained in Mexico in November after domestic violence allegations. His ex-partner declined to press charges.

Variance: Medium. We've seen him make adjustments against major-league breaking stuff as he's gone along, but there's still some hit tool risk. Conversely, if the late-season and playoff performance is real, he's an All-Star.

Mark Barry's Fantasy Take: Arozarena is one of the harder dudes to project heading into 2021, and I wish I knew whether he'd been stuck in a room doing push ups and eating chicken since the World Series. He's likely to hit some homers and steal some bases, and his ultimate fantasy upside will rest with whether he can trim some whiffs from his K-rate, to boost his batting average. His value is already sky high, so while it would be nice to see more, I'm not sure you'll have the chance before making an acquisition.

★ ★ ★ *2021 Top 101 Prospect* **#24** ★ ★ ★

3 **Shane Baz** **RHP**   OFP: 60   ETA: 2022

Born: 06/17/99   Age: 22   Bats: R   Throws: R   Height: 6'2"   Weight: 190   Origin: Round 1, 2017 Draft (#12 overall)

YEAR	TEAM	LVL	AGE	W	L	SV	G	GS	IP	H	HR	BB/9	K/9	K	GB%	BABIP	WHIP	ERA	DRA-	WARP
2018	BRS	ROK	19	4	3	0	10	10	45¹	45	2	4.6	10.7	54	63.0%	.344	1.50	3.97		
2018	PRN	ROK	19	0	2	0	2	2	7	11	1	7.7	6.4	5	48.0%	.417	2.43	7.71		
2019	BG	LO-A	20	3	2	0	17	17	81¹	63	5	4.1	9.6	87	37.1%	.280	1.23	2.99	79	1.2
2021 FS	TB	MLB	22	2	3	0	57	0	50	47	7	6.2	8.2	45	41.4%	.283	1.64	5.50	124	-0.5

Comparables: Casey Crosby, Daniel Norris, Elvin Ramirez

The Report: The third piece in the Chris Archer deal is the only one with prospect eligibility left, and he's a hell of a pitching prospect. Baz has easy plus-plus cheese, sitting in the upper-90s and routinely hitting 100. He pairs the fastball with a plus power slider with good tilt. The change-up flashes but is a work in progres. Although as you might have noted with another pitcher in that trade—Tyler Glasnow—when your top two pitches are this good, you don't need to throw your third one all that much. However, also like Glasnow, Baz can struggle with his command and control at times. It's not quite as effectively wild as Glasnow was as a prospect, but both the command and control are below average and that will need to be ironed out to cement him as a starting pitcher, well as much as the Rays use a traditional starter anyway.

Development Track: Baz has spent all of 80 innings above short-season ball so far. The alternate site work might allow him to start 2021 in Double-A, but he could use a full, normalish, minor league season to really put a stamp on where he is as a pitching prospect right now. The stuff isn't a question, what role it's best utilized in is.

Variance: Medium. Baz may need to tone down the "grip it and rip it" mechanics a little, but he can give back some of the top-end velocity for command and still have plenty of stuff. Of course that trade off can be easier said than done. So relief risk remains.

Mark Barry's Fantasy Take: The Rays of It All does throw a wrench into evaluating a lot of their arms in terms of fantasy. Sure, Glasnow is given a little leash, but many of their starters don't venture into the waters of the dreaded third time through the order. That's fine, it just caps the fantasy ceiling. For Baz, he has definitely displayed a knack for striking dudes out, but I worry he won't be trusted with a ton of volume. I also worry that's a sentiment that will be shared with most Rays pitching prospects.

★ ★ ★ *2021 Top 101 Prospect* **#25** ★ ★ ★

4 **Luis Patiño** **RHP**   OFP: 60   ETA: Debuted in 2020

Born: 10/26/99   Age: 21   Bats: R   Throws: R   Height: 6'1"   Weight: 192   Origin: International Free Agent, 2016

YEAR	TEAM	LVL	AGE	W	L	SV	G	GS	IP	H	HR	BB/9	K/9	K	GB%	BABIP	WHIP	ERA	DRA-	WARP
2018	FW	LO-A	18	6	3	0	17	17	83¹	65	1	2.6	10.6	98	42.1%	.323	1.07	2.16	75	1.7
2019	LE	HI-A	19	6	8	0	18	17	87	61	4	3.5	11.7	113	40.2%	.278	1.09	2.69	55	2.4
2019	AMA	AA	19	0	0	0	2	2	7²	8	0	4.7	11.7	10	19.0%	.381	1.57	1.17	92	0.0
2020	SD	MLB	20	1	0	0	11	1	17¹	18	3	7.3	10.9	21	34.7%	.326	1.85	5.19	110	0.1
2021 FS	TB	MLB	21	9	9	0	26	26	150	138	25	4.3	9.5	158	35.7%	.289	1.40	4.55	104	0.8
2021 DC	TB	MLB	21	4	4	0	40	9	78	71	13	4.3	9.5	82	35.7%	.289	1.40	4.55	104	0.5

Comparables: Jenrry Mejia, Taijuan Walker, Tyler Skaggs

The Report: We are four prospects into this list now and we still can't manage worse than "one of the best pitching prospects in baseball" as an epithet. Patiño projects for four above-average pitches, and not in that "squint to get them to 55" way either. The fastball sits mid-90s with explosive life as a starter, and he can find more velocity when he needs it. The slider is a plus pitch, a power mid-80s breaker that can also show as a 70 grade offering when there's more bottom to it. The curve isn't a mere second breaking ball look, but an above-average offering in its own right with hard, late 11-5 action. The change can be on the firm side, but projects as a potential third plus pitch due to the tumble and fade it can flash. Patiño is on the smaller side, and while he's smoothed out the delivery some as a pro, there's still a big leg kick and he throws across his body some, which can impact his command and control.

Development Track: Patiño was called up to the majors from the alternate site in August to try and bolster a leaky Padres 'pen. He was making the jump to the bis after just a brief Double-A cup of coffee and asked to pitch in a new role on the fly. There were some growing pains, and Patiño struggled badly with his command and control. However, the 20-year-old's stuff looked lively and he missed plenty of major-league bats among his struggles. We do think his 2020 was a slight negative for the overall profile projection, but that's almost all "well, we think the reliever risk is a bit higher until we see command improvements." It's more than a minor quibble, but we aren't all that worried about him.

Variance: Medium. The stuff will play in the majors, the command will determine when, where, and how well. FWIW, If you were going to acquire a high end pitching prospect to use in a similar manner to how the Rays used Snell in order to maximize his in-game impact, Patiño would be among the pitching prospects I think could benefit most from that 30-start, 150-inning type workload.

Mark Barry's Fantasy Take: I like Patiño a little bit more than Baz, personally. I think he carries more strikeout upside and a better chance at logging innings. He also walks a bunch of guys, but I guess nobody's perfect. Also, depending on what the Rays do in terms of service-time manipulation, Patiño could be impactful as quickly as this season.

★ ★ ★ *2021 Top 101 Prospect* **#67** ★ ★ ★

5 **Vidal Bruján** **2B** OFP: 60 ETA: 2021, as needed

Born: 02/09/98 Age: 23 Bats: S Throws: R Height: 5'10" Weight: 180 Origin: International Free Agent, 2014

YEAR	TEAM	LVL	AGE	PA	R	2B	3B	HR	RBI	BB	K	SB	CS	AVG/OBP/SLG	DRC+	BABIP	BRR	FRAA	WARP
2018	BG	LO-A	20	434	86	18	5	5	41	48	53	43	15	.313/.395/.427	140	.351	8.2	2B(87) 4.4	4.0
2018	CHA	HI-A	20	114	26	7	2	4	12	15	15	12	4	.347/.434/.582	164	.380	1.0	2B(24) 4.5	1.4
2019	CHA	HI-A	21	196	28	8	3	1	15	17	26	24	5	.290/.357/.386	131	.333	5.5	2B(29) 0.7, SS(14) 0.7	2.0
2019	MTG	AA	21	233	28	9	4	3	25	20	35	24	8	.266/.336/.391	95	.304	-2.6	2B(33) 2.7, SS(15) -0.1	0.6
2021 FS	TB	MLB	23	600	61	27	5	10	59	44	110	30	12	.247/.310/.371	86	.293	0.9	2B 15, SS 0	2.7
2021 DC	TB	MLB	23	67	6	3	0	1	6	4	12	3	1	.247/.310/.371	86	.293	0.1	2B 2	0.3

Comparables: Steve Lombardozzi, Corban Joseph, Jose Altuve

The Report: Bruján's profile is carried by a plus hit tool and plus-plus speed. The swing is contact-oriented with minimal over-the-fence power, but don't mistake it for slappy, as Bruján has strong wrists that generate plus bat speed from both sides. He can drive the ball into the gaps, which should allow him to run into plenty of doubles and triples, even if the home run pop remains in the single digits. The approach can tend to the aggressive side, but he'll take a walk if given it. The bat is going to be batting-average dependent, but those averages could start with a 3 some years. Defensively, Bruján has split time at the middle infield spits, but is a much better fit for second base as the arm is merely above-average and the hands and actions don't pop quite enough for the 6. His best actual defensive fit might be center field, and he did play there a couple times in the 2019 Arizona Fall League. Bruján could use the defensive flexibility regardless, and the path to middle infield playing time in the Trop is pretty well blocked at the moment.

Development Track: Bruján spent time at the alternate site, the Rays' playoff taxi squad, and then the Dominican Winter League. As 2020 developmental opportunities go, that's not a bad amount of reps. Bruján didn't dominate Double-A the first time of asking in 2019, but assuming some consolidation time in the upper minors in 2021, should be ready for a major league opportunity if and when a spot opens up in Tampa.

Variance: Medium. Bruján can hit a little, run a bunch, and at least stand at all three up-the-middle spots. At worst that's a good 450 PA bench piece, but I think the actual delta here is fairly low and clustered around "solid regular."

Mark Barry's Fantasy Take: He's got LEGS and he knows how to use them—you know, for steals and such. Bruján makes a ton of contact, which I personally adore, and does so with plus speed. His stolen base efficiency has been improving as well, which certainly bodes well for his future green light. There's probably not any power coming, but that's OK. The potential for sweet, sweet steals is enough to keep him in the top-40 for dynasty prospects.

★ ★ ★ *2021 Top 101 Prospect* **#80** ★ ★ ★

6 **Shane McClanahan** **LHP** OFP: 60 ETA: Debuted in 2020, sorta

Born: 04/28/97 Age: 24 Bats: L Throws: L Height: 6'1" Weight: 200 Origin: Round 1, 2018 Draft (#31 overall)

YEAR	TEAM	LVL	AGE	W	L	SV	G	GS	IP	H	HR	BB/9	K/9	K	GB%	BABIP	WHIP	ERA	DRA-	WARP
2018	PRN	ROK	21	0	0	0	2	2	4	2	0	2.2	15.8	7	50.0%	.333	0.75	0.00		
2018	RAY	ROK	21	0	0	0	2	2	3	1	0	0.0	18.0	6	50.0%	.250	0.33	0.00		
2019	BG	LO-A	22	4	4	0	11	10	53	38	3	5.3	12.6	74	47.5%	.304	1.30	3.40	78	0.8
2019	CHA	HI-A	22	6	1	0	9	8	49¹	33	1	1.5	10.8	59	40.7%	.267	0.83	1.46	51	1.5
2019	MTG	AA	22	1	1	0	4	4	18¹	30	3	2.9	10.3	21	39.7%	.450	1.96	8.35	163	-0.7
2021 FS	TB	MLB	24	8	9	0	26	26	150	138	23	4.9	9.4	156	40.5%	.291	1.47	4.78	112	0.1
2021 DC	TB	MLB	24	3	4	0	28	9	63	58	9	4.9	9.4	65	40.5%	.291	1.47	4.78	112	0.2

Comparables: Julio Urías, Brendan McKay, Austin Voth

The Report: McClanahan's fastball is absolutely electric. He sits in the high-90s and hit 100 mph in the playoffs. It's difficult to pick up and it moves around; it's just a tough pitch for batters to deal with. He pairs that with a slurvy low-to-mid-80s breaking ball. It's a knee-buckler when it's right, but he struggles to throw it with consistency and command. We also think it's pretty likely that he's going to end up in the bullpen; our staff opinions on this range from "there's an outside chance he'll start" to "there's very little chance he'll start." His changeup is underdeveloped (he barely threw it in his playoff cameo), his command isn't great, and his delivery is inconsistent. These are all major relief markers.

Development Track: McClanahan was called up for the postseason, and indeed became the first pitcher in major-league history to make his debut in the playoffs, where he pitched low-to-low-medium leverage innings for the Rays on their pennant run. His stuff was nasty and his command was all over the place, so he basically pitched to his report.

Variance: Medium. It's a really good fastball, but our confidence in him ever making 30 starts is low.

Mark Barry's Fantasy Take: I think the Rays tipped their hand for McLanahan's usage pattern, calling on him to make four appearances from the bullpen. Best case scenario, he winds up as a 2+ inning guy or part of the Rays Famous Closer Carousel. Worst case scenario, he winds up as an overqualified version of whatever the modern-day equivalent of a LOOGY is.

--- ★ ★ ★ *2021 Top 101 Prospect* **#93** ★ ★ ★ ---

7 Xavier Edwards SS

OFP: 60   ETA: Late 2021/Early 2022

Born: 08/09/99   Age: 21   Bats: S   Throws: R   Height: 5'10"   Weight: 175   Origin: Round 1, 2018 Draft (#38 overall)

YEAR	TEAM	LVL	AGE	PA	R	2B	3B	HR	RBI	BB	K	SB	CS	AVG/OBP/SLG	DRC+	BABIP	BRR	FRAA	WARP
2018	SD1	ROK	18	88	19	4	1	0	11	13	10	12	1	.384/.471/.466		.438			
2018	TRI	SS	18	107	21	4	0	0	5	18	15	10	0	.314/.438/.360	179	.380	-0.3	SS(19) -1.1, 2B(5) -0.0	0.7
2019	FW	LO-A	19	344	44	13	4	1	30	30	35	20	9	.336/.392/.414	141	.371	0.2	2B(51) 4.1, SS(21) 3.1	3.4
2019	LE	HI-A	19	217	32	5	4	0	13	14	19	14	2	.301/.349/.367	101	.331	3.5	2B(36) 0.2, SS(9) -1.2	0.9
2021 FS	TB	MLB	21	600	54	25	3	5	53	44	114	22	7	.273/.330/.366	93	.335	4.3	2B 5, SS 1	2.6

Comparables: José Ramírez, Jorge Polanco, Asdrúbal Cabrera

The Report: We talk a lot about whether prospects have carrying tools. Edwards has two. His hit tool has received a consistent plus evaluation in our live looks, between his quick hands, his strong bat-to-ball ability, and his excellent plate approach. He's also lightning fast, with 80 grade speed, 70 on his worst days. So it's not hard to come up with the contours of a very good player here, driven by averages around .300 and a ton of speed, mixed in with some defensive versatility. But there's major flaws too. Edwards has basically no present game power—he's hit just one homer in 168 professional games—and he doesn't project to pick a whole lot up later on. We're naturally wary of hit tool projections that are backed up by so little power and haven't been shown to work at the highest levels. His arm probably isn't strong enough for shortstop, so his positional versatility might end up just being second and the outfield (where we assume his speed would play up).

Development Track: Edwards was traded to the Rays last offseason. The team brought him to the alternate site mid-season, and his batted ball data there was exactly as weak as you'd expect given his lack of game power. We had many internal conversations over what that meant—just like we had many conversations over how to project him in 2019—and basically left him his ranking intact in deference to the copious amount of live looks that pointed to a plus hit tool.

Variance: High. We're concerned about the hit tool collapsing at the highest levels, although he has obvious bench/utility fallbacks if things sour given his speed and versatility.

Mark Barry's Fantasy Take: Not sure if you've caught on by now, but it's hard to find steals in standard-roto formats. Edwards is very fast, and has hit for average in the minors, but there's a real threat that no semblance of power will ever come, which leaves him in danger of having a Billy Hamilton (or worse) fantasy future.

8 Cole Wilcox RHP

OFP: 60   ETA: 2023

Born: 07/14/99   Age: 21   Bats: R   Throws: R   Height: 6'5"   Weight: 232   Origin: Round 3, 2020 Draft (#80 overall)

The Report: When Wilcox was included in the Snell trade, some analyses dismissed him as some distant ho-hum third-round pick. That is a gross mischaracterization, as his signing bonus would indicate, receiving essentially what would have been the 20th overall slot. The big righty out of Georgia had some of the best stuff in the draft. His issue(s) were mostly derived from an inefficient delivery that led to below-average control. When dialed-in, it's a heavy fastball that can reach 100 with a sharp slider and sinking power changeup. Early indicators from the spring showed a refined delivery with better control at the cost of a tick less velocity.

Development Track: Reports from Padres instructs prior to the trade had Wilcox up to 97 with many of the same qualities seen during his draft-eligible sophomore year. If you could point to the two organizations that are perhaps best equipped with getting pitchers to harness their elite power arsenal, it would be the Pads and Rays. In either case, he's in good hands and has a very high ceiling.

Variance: High. If it turns out he's more the player he was as a frosh, then he's more likely to be a freak in the 'pen. If the more recent version is closer to his true outcome, it's an easy call as a well above-average starter with star traits. ---Keanan Lamb

Mark Barry's Fantasy Take: Wilcox's profile screams "BULK GUY" in this organization. That's still useful, for sure, but it limits his fantasy upside.

9 Greg Jones SS   OFP: 55   ETA: 2022
Born: 03/07/98   Age: 23   Bats: S   Throws: R   Height: 6'2"   Weight: 175   Origin: Round 1, 2019 Draft (#22 overall)

YEAR	TEAM	LVL	AGE	PA	R	2B	3B	HR	RBI	BB	K	SB	CS	AVG/OBP/SLG	DRC+	BABIP	BRR	FRAA	WARP
2019	HV	SS	21	218	39	13	4	1	24	22	56	19	8	.335/.413/.461	173	.467	4.2	SS(21) 2.2	2.6
2021 FS	TB	MLB	23	600	48	27	3	7	51	37	210	26	12	.222/.278/.326	66	.342	-3.5	SS 4	-0.6

Comparables: Jared Hoying, Chris Shaw, Trey Mancini

The Report: Jones presents one of the more unique profiles you'll find of any top-200 prospect. Drafted as an ultra-fast college shortstop with projection, his physical measurements make you think he'd be this monster with five tool potential. In reality, while his switch-hitting ability might allow him to get on-base at an advanced clip, nothing other than his 70-plus grade speed is clearly above average. It's more line-drive power with plenty of extra-base hits mixed in, and his defense is okay enough to stay up the middle. If he hits anywhere near his first pro foray in short-season he could be a top-of-the-order threat.

Development Track: Jones could end up anywhere on the field. He played some center field at the Cape, some scouts think he's more suited at second base, but in the end it's inconsequential where he plays since he'll be fine. If the hit tool and on-base skills continue trending upward, his speed will allow him to play anywhere the Rays need to shoe-horn him in. Which, in a system as abundant as theirs, having a flexible player like this is incredibly valuable.

Variance: High. At his floor, he's a serviceable bench player with clear skills to be utilized. If the contact rates remain elevated given his speed he should be a good everyday player.

Mark Barry's Fantasy Take: I'd have Jones closer to Bruján in terms of dynasty. He might not have Edwards's wheels, but I think it's more likely that Jones will get on base at a decent clip and could even sock a dinger or two. Perhaps it's splitting hairs, but for me Jones is a top-75 or so fantasy prospect.

10 Josh Lowe CF   OFP: 55   ETA: Late 2021/Early 2022
Born: 02/02/98   Age: 23   Bats: L   Throws: R   Height: 6'4"   Weight: 205   Origin: Round 1, 2016 Draft (#13 overall)

YEAR	TEAM	LVL	AGE	PA	R	2B	3B	HR	RBI	BB	K	SB	CS	AVG/OBP/SLG	DRC+	BABIP	BRR	FRAA	WARP
2018	CHA	HI-A	20	455	62	25	3	6	47	47	117	18	6	.238/.322/.361	95	.318	1.1	CF(102) 4.1	0.8
2019	MTG	AA	21	519	70	23	4	18	62	59	132	30	9	.252/.341/.442	128	.316	5.6	CF(110) -7.0, RF(9) 2.2, LF(1) -0.2	3.3
2021 FS	TB	MLB	23	600	60	26	3	16	64	59	212	13	5	.222/.302/.373	86	.333	0.7	CF -1, RF 0	0.8

Comparables: Michael Saunders, Luis Robert, Chris Young

The Report: Originally drafted as a prep third baseman, the Rays converted Lowe to center field the following season and he's taken to it quite well. His plus speed and arm work well on the grass, and despite only playing the outfield for a few seasons, he projects as an overall above-average defender there. Lowe's plus raw pop would have played fine as a corner infielder, but it makes the bat potentially special in center field. However, hit tool questions remain as Lowe has swing-and-miss issues with spin. But even if he only manages to Xerox his Double-A line further up the ladder, .250 and 20 bombs as an above-average center fielder is a good everyday guy.

Development Track: Lowe spent time at the alternate site and should be in the mix for reps in Tampa at some point in 2021. A Kevin Kiermaier trade might not exactly clear the path right away, but if he gets off to a good start in Triple-A and shows some improvement against higher-quality spin, it will be tough to justify keeping him off the carpet at the Trop.

Variance: Medium. Lowe has had some Double-A success already and the pop, speed, and glove all line up well for at least a fringe starter role, although the potential issues with southpaws and spin might limit the upside.

Mark Barry's Fantasy Take: There must have been a rule about having more than one member of the Lowe family in the lineup, as the Rays shipped out Nate so Josh could fly. Or whatever. Josh Lowe has power, speed, and the ability to work a walk. If he scales back on the swing-and-miss, he could be an impact fantasy option, taken in the first 3-4 rounds for years to come. If he doesn't, then maybe he's Drew Stubbs?

The Prospects You Meet Outside This Top Ten

Several more OFP 55s in somewhat particular order

Blake Hunt   C   Born: 11/10/98   Age: 22   Bats: R   Throws: R   Height: 6'3"   Weight: 215   Origin: Round 2, 2017 Draft (#69 overall)

YEAR	TEAM	LVL	AGE	PA	R	2B	3B	HR	RBI	BB	K	SB	CS	AVG/OBP/SLG	DRC+	BABIP	BRR	FRAA	WARP
2018	TRI	SS	19	245	34	13	0	3	25	27	56	2	1	.271/.371/.377	116	.351	-1.0	C(47) -0.7	0.4
2019	FW	LO-A	20	376	40	21	3	5	39	35	67	4	1	.255/.331/.381	117	.303	-5.2	C(77) -1.0, 1B(9) -0.4	1.6
2021 FS	TB	MLB	22	600	51	27	2	11	56	35	196	1	0	.215/.271/.334	65	.311	0.5	C -2, 1B 0	-0.6

Comparables: Victor Caratini, Francisco Mejía, Tucker Barnhart

The third prospect piece in the Snell deal, Hunt had a bit of a star turn in instructs, showcasing hard contact and advanced defensive skills. He always projected as a plus defensive catcher and showed plus raw pop, but his swing and plate discipline limited how much of it he could get into games. We need to see the new look bat in minor league games before calling this a full breakout, but Hunt looks like he might be the next prep catching prospect made good.

Brendan McKay   LHP   Born: 12/18/95   Age: 25   Bats: L   Throws: L   Height: 6'2"   Weight: 220   Origin: Round 1, 2017 Draft (#4 overall)

YEAR	TEAM	LVL	AGE	PA	R	2B	3B	HR	RBI	BB	K	SB	CS	AVG/OBP/SLG	DRC+	BABIP	BRR	FRAA	WARP
2018	BG	LO-A	22	91	12	2	0	1	16	28	13	0	0	.254/.484/.333	174	.306	-3.1	1B(9) -0.3, P(6) 0.1	0.4
2018	CHA	HI-A	22	139	19	6	1	5	21	16	38	0	0	.210/.317/.403	96	.260	0.5	1B(18) -0.4, P(11) -0.3	-0.2
2019	MTG	AA	23	90	8	2	0	0	8	7	26	0	1	.167/.256/.192	49	.241	0.3	P(8) 0.5	-0.3
2019	DUR	AAA	23	78	11	2	0	5	11	10	24	1	0	.239/.346/.493	93	.289	-0.3	P(7) -0.2	0.0
2019	TB	MLB	23	11	2	0	0	1	1	1	2	0	0	.200/.273/.500	56	.143	-0.1	P(13) -0.1	0.0
2021 FS	TB	MLB	25	600	65	26	2	15	59	69	192	1	0	.219/.319/.366	91	.314	0.4	1B -5	-0.3

YEAR	TEAM	LVL	AGE	W	L	SV	G	GS	IP	H	HR	BB/9	K/9	K	GB%	BABIP	WHIP	ERA	DRA-	WARP
2018	RAY	ROK	22	0	0	0	2	2	6	2	0	1.5	13.5	9	58.3%	.167	0.50	1.50		
2018	BG	LO-A	22	2	0	0	6	6	24²	8	1	0.7	14.6	40	60.5%	.167	0.41	1.09	56	0.8
2018	CHA	HI-A	22	3	2	0	11	9	47²	45	4	2.1	10.2	54	36.8%	.355	1.17	3.21	62	1.2
2019	MTG	AA	23	3	0	0	8	7	41²	25	2	1.9	13.4	62	40.5%	.280	0.82	1.30	51	1.2
2019	DUR	AAA	23	3	0	0	7	6	32	17	1	2.5	11.2	40	45.1%	.232	0.81	0.84	31	1.6
2019	TB	MLB	23	2	4	0	13	11	49	53	8	2.9	10.3	56	35.4%	.333	1.41	5.14	118	0.0
2021 FS	TB	MLB	25	9	8	0	26	26	150	130	22	3.0	10.5	175	39.9%	.292	1.20	3.63	86	2.2
2021 DC	TB	MLB	25	5	5	0	16	16	82	71	12	3.0	10.5	95	39.9%	.292	1.20	3.63	86	1.5

Comparables: Nick Margevicius, Eric Lauer, Tarik Skubal

McKay is in a similar spot to A.J. Puk in the Oakland system: they both had labrum surgery during the season. Given the seriousness of labrum issues, that dropped both of them off the Top 101, but where that drop didn't even move Puk out of the top spot in the A's system, it drops McKay all the way out of the Top 10 here, which is a testament to the extreme system depth. If healthy, McKay's fastball/curveball combo and pitchability should make him a mid-rotation starter very quickly, but until he has a clean bill of health and is throwing well again we can't fully project that out yet.

Ronaldo Hernández   C   Born: 11/11/97   Age: 23   Bats: R   Throws: R   Height: 6'1"   Weight: 230   Origin: International Free Agent, 2014

YEAR	TEAM	LVL	AGE	PA	R	2B	3B	HR	RBI	BB	K	SB	CS	AVG/OBP/SLG	DRC+	BABIP	BRR	FRAA	WARP
2018	BG	LO-A	20	449	68	20	1	21	79	31	69	10	4	.284/.339/.494	132	.292	-0.8	C(85) 1.2	2.8
2019	CHA	HI-A	21	427	43	19	3	9	60	17	65	7	0	.265/.299/.397	105	.290	1.8	C(81) 1.9	2.3
2021 FS	TB	MLB	23	600	64	27	2	18	68	32	133	3	1	.243/.292/.395	87	.289	-0.8	C 0	1.4
2021 DC	TB	MLB	23	67	7	3	0	2	7	3	14	0	0	.243/.292/.395	87	.289	-0.1	C 0	0.2

Comparables: Travis d'Arnaud, Jesús Sucre, John Ryan Murphy

A converted infielder, Hernández has above-average potential as a two-way catcher, but his defense needs to continue to improve, and he needs to tame his approach to get more of his plus raw pop into games against higher level pitching. The exposure to higher level pitching didn't functionally happen outside of the Rays alternate site in 2020, so we'll see where we are next year. He's dropped a little ordinally because of improvements around him in the system, but we think he's the same OFP 55 prospect.

Nick Bitsko RHP Born: 06/16/02   Age: 19   Bats: R   Throws: R   Height: 6'4"   Weight: 225   Origin: Round 1, 2020 Draft (#24 overall)

During the organizing process of putting together this extensive list for the Rays, Bitsko was easily within the top 5-7 prospects as one of the best prep pitchers in last year's draft. However, whenever you talk about injuries to pitchers you specifically want to avoid, it's anything involving the shoulder. After he had surgery to repair his labrum in December, he is questionable to pitch in 2021 after not pitching the spring of his draft year. That would be two full years off from competitive action. The big righty, when healthy, has mid-90's heat with projection for more, although at this juncture we hope for a full recovery to at least get back to where he was before.

Joe Ryan RHP Born: 06/05/96   Age: 25   Bats: R   Throws: R   Height: 6'2"   Weight: 205   Origin: Round 7, 2018 Draft (#210 overall)

YEAR	TEAM	LVL	AGE	W	L	SV	G	GS	IP	H	HR	BB/9	K/9	K	GB%	BABIP	WHIP	ERA	DRA-	WARP
2018	HV	SS	22	2	1	0	12	7	36¹	26	3	3.5	12.6	51	35.4%	.303	1.10	3.72	47	1.3
2019	BG	LO-A	23	2	2	0	6	6	27²	19	2	3.6	15.3	47	28.6%	.315	1.08	2.93	59	0.7
2019	CHA	HI-A	23	7	2	0	15	13	82²	47	3	1.3	12.2	112	36.6%	.246	0.71	1.42	41	3.0
2019	MTG	AA	23	0	0	0	3	3	13¹	11	2	2.7	16.2	24	23.1%	.375	1.12	3.38	85	0.1
2021 FS	TB	MLB	25	9	8	0	26	26	150	126	22	3.8	10.9	181	35.9%	.288	1.26	3.90	97	1.3
2021 DC	TB	MLB	25	2	3	0	20	8	50	42	7	3.8	10.9	60	35.9%	.288	1.26	3.90	97	0.5

Comparables: Alex Reyes, Drew Rasmussen, Brad Mills

After a downright dominant 2019 across three levels, Ryan made our 2020 Rays Top Ten and looked poised to ... well, be 2020's Josh Fleming. I don't know the vagaries of the Rays baseball ops decisions, but you could argue Ryan's stuff isn't quite as good as that gaudy 38 percent K-rate. The fastball and curve are more above-average than true plus, and the cutter and change lag behind them. Ryan does throw all of them in the zone effectively, and there's certainly plenty of room for him on the 2021 Rays' pitching staff nowadays.

Drew Strotman RHP Born: 09/03/96   Age: 24   Bats: R   Throws: R   Height: 6'3"   Weight: 195   Origin: Round 4, 2017 Draft (#109 overall)

YEAR	TEAM	LVL	AGE	W	L	SV	G	GS	IP	H	HR	BB/9	K/9	K	GB%	BABIP	WHIP	ERA	DRA-	WARP
2018	BG	LO-A	21	3	0	0	9	9	46	40	0	3.5	8.4	43	44.8%	.325	1.26	3.52	128	-0.4
2019	RAY	ROK	22	0	1	0	4	4	8	9	0	3.4	11.2	10	56.5%	.375	1.50	3.38		
2019	CHA	HI-A	22	0	2	0	5	5	16	20	3	5.1	7.3	13	43.1%	.354	1.81	5.06	155	-0.5
2021 FS	TB	MLB	24	2	3	0	57	0	50	47	7	4.5	7.3	40	44.9%	.279	1.46	4.67	115	-0.3

Comparables: Carlos Hernández, Corey Oswalt, Locke St. John

Strotman was our 2018 Low Minors Sleeper in this system. I saw him post-draft as a polished four-pitch righty, who touched 96 and had three average-to-above secondaries. He looked like he would fit well as a bulk-innings arm down the line. Well, the bulk part was a problem as he's thrown only 90 innings total since that 2017 season in the Penn League. Tommy John cost him most of 2018 and 2019, but he popped back up this year, healthy and sitting mid-90s. The slider and curve both look above-average, and yeah maybe the Rays still use him as a bulk innings guy given the durability concerns, but it's mid-rotation starter stuff.

Pedro Martinez SS Born: 01/28/01   Age: 20   Bats: S   Throws: R   Height: 5'11"   Weight: 165   Origin: International Free Agent, 2018

YEAR	TEAM	LVL	AGE	PA	R	2B	3B	HR	RBI	BB	K	SB	CS	AVG/OBP/SLG	DRC+	BABIP	BRR	FRAA	WARP
2018	DSL CUBR	ROK	17	228	37	3	5	2	25	26	26	31	9	.310/.398/.406		.349			
2019	CUBB	ROK	18	121	12	6	3	2	17	12	27	8	5	.352/.417/.519		.456			
2019	EUG	SS	18	112	15	2	3	0	7	12	36	11	5	.265/.357/.347	83	.419	1.1	2B(15) 1.7, SS(11) -1.2, 3B(1) 0.3	0.4
2021 FS	TB	MLB	20	600	45	26	4	5	48	34	195	32	13	.218/.267/.314	59	.323	1.1	SS 1, 2B 1	-0.9

Comparables: Edmundo Sosa, Tim Lopes, Alen Hanson

Acquired for 22 Jose Martinez plate appearances, Martinez was the seventh-best prospect in the Cubs' system coming into the season. We have no reason to think he's any worse and he doesn't crack the Rays' Top 15 or so. A speedy, hit-tool driven switch-hitting infielder who could probably play a few different spots competently, he's the platonic ideal of a Rays solid-average position player prospect. He hasn't seen full-season ball yet, but there's potential for more than just solid-average projection if he grows into some power and hits in A-ball.

Seth Johnson RHP Born: 09/19/98 Age: 22 Bats: R Throws: R Height: 6'1" Weight: 200 Origin: Round 1, 2019 Draft (#40 overall)

YEAR	TEAM	LVL	AGE	W	L	SV	G	GS	IP	H	HR	BB/9	K/9	K	GB%	BABIP	WHIP	ERA	DRA-	WARP
2019	RAY	ROK	20	0	0	0	5	5	10	7	0	1.8	6.3	7	43.3%	.233	0.90	0.00		
2019	PRN	ROK+	20	0	1	0	4	4	7	10	0	1.3	11.6	9	40.0%	.500	1.57	5.14		
2021 FS	TB	MLB	22	2	3	0	57	0	50	54	8	4.7	7.0	38	37.3%	.302	1.61	5.75	132	-0.8

Comparables: Brusdar Graterol, Luis Marte, Jesse Litsch

Johnson is an infield convert with a plus-plus fastball, a plus-flashing slider, and significant questions about how he will hold up in the pros under a starter's workload. Obviously those weren't answered in 2020 and he's the highest variance prospect in this tier, non-shoulder-surgery division.

Heriberto Hernandez C Born: 12/16/99 Age: 21 Bats: R Throws: R Height: 6'1" Weight: 180 Origin: International Free Agent, 2017

YEAR	TEAM	LVL	AGE	PA	R	2B	3B	HR	RBI	BB	K	SB	CS	AVG/OBP/SLG	DRC+	BABIP	BRR	FRAA	WARP
2018	DSL RAN2	ROK	18	239	56	15	5	12	49	53	41	5	5	.292/.464/.635		.315			
2019	RAN	ROK	19	224	42	17	4	11	48	27	57	3	3	.344/.433/.646		.440			
2019	SPO	SS	19	10	4	0	0	0	1	2	3	3	0	.375/.500/.375	163	.600	0.7	RF(1) -0.2	0.1
2021 FS	TB	MLB	21	600	47	27	4	8	50	47	211	7	3	.199/.268/.310	59	.306	-0.4	1B -1, C 0	-1.9

Comparables: Austin Meadows, Oswaldo Arcia, Joc Pederson

What if I told you the Rays traded for a player from the Rangers who 90 percent of people didn't know about, but the 10 percent who did cursed under their breath. Probably "Yeah idiot, I already knew about Pete Fairbanks." No, this is the sequel to that hit indie film. Hernandez is a Class-A outfielder with power to burn and development time needed to craft the rest into a functional MLB player. He'd be a great fit in an organization who understands talent maximization and patience for its … well you get the idea. He's a Ray now, which means in three years he'll probably get a clutch hit in a playoff series while most of the country scratches their head and Googles. Not you, dear reader. You will know, and you will be prepared.

Brent Honeywell Jr. RHP Born: 03/31/95 Age: 26 Bats: R Throws: R Height: 6'2" Weight: 195 Origin: Round 2, 2014 Draft (#72 overall)

YEAR	TEAM	LVL	AGE	W	L	SV	G	GS	IP	H	HR	BB/9	K/9	K	GB%	BABIP	WHIP	ERA	DRA-	WARP
2021 FS	TB	MLB	26	9	8	0	26	26	150	134	21	2.9	9.5	157	34.5%	.287	1.22	3.72	94	1.6
2021 DC	TB	MLB	26	3	4	0	12	12	63	56	9	2.9	9.5	66	34.5%	.287	1.22	3.72	94	0.9

Comparables: Mitch Keller, Zack Littell, Stephen Gonsalves

Honeywell underwent his fourth elbow surgery in the last three years in December. Once a three-time Top 25 prospect, now he hasn't officially been on the rubber since the end of the 2017 season, although he's thrown some bullpens at times. In theory he had top-of-the-rotation stuff the last time he saw him and will be back on the mound in 2021, although he's going to be 26 by the time the season starts and we have no idea if his elbow can hold up.

Kevin Padlo 3B Born: 07/15/96 Age: 24 Bats: R Throws: R Height: 6'2" Weight: 210 Origin: Round 5, 2014 Draft (#143 overall)

YEAR	TEAM	LVL	AGE	PA	R	2B	3B	HR	RBI	BB	K	SB	CS	AVG/OBP/SLG	DRC+	BABIP	BRR	FRAA	WARP
2018	CHA	HI-A	21	449	54	26	0	8	54	47	119	5	0	.223/.318/.353	94	.295	-0.1	3B(87) -2.5, 1B(18) -1.0	-0.3
2019	MTG	AA	22	277	39	20	0	12	35	47	70	11	4	.250/.383/.505	166	.299	0.2	3B(57) 7.1, 1B(6) -0.4	3.5
2019	DUR	AAA	22	155	25	11	1	9	27	21	46	1	0	.290/.400/.595	128	.382	1.0	3B(31) 3.5, 1B(3) -0.2, 2B(3) 0.2	1.3
2021 FS	TB	MLB	24	600	70	28	2	22	68	69	197	5	2	.218/.318/.408	100	.303	-1.0	3B 6, 1B 0	1.7
2021 DC	TB	MLB	24	67	7	3	0	2	7	7	22	0	0	.218/.318/.408	100	.303	-0.1	3B 1	0.2

Comparables: Pedro Álvarez, Nick Senzel, Brett Wallace

A swing change at the end of 2019 to maximize his power certainly succeeded as Padlo slugged a career-high .538. But there are never solutions, always tradeoffs. Padlo can pop up a lot of pitches, and with most of the league going to high heaters this can be exploited. While he has above-average arm strength, he is slow footed at third and may be a better fit at first in an everyday role. This is another high-variance prospect in this organization. If it all clicks he is a middle-of-the-order thumper who splits between corner infield positions. If it doesn't, he may end up mashing in Korea.

Neraldo Catalina RHP   Born: 06/21/00   Age: 21   Bats: R   Throws: R   Height: 6'6"   Weight: 202   Origin: International Free Agent, 2018

YEAR	TEAM	LVL	AGE	W	L	SV	G	GS	IP	H	HR	BB/9	K/9	K	GB%	BABIP	WHIP	ERA	DRA-	WARP
2019	RAY	ROK	19	3	3	0	11	1	21	20	0	3.9	9.9	23	60.3%	.357	1.38	2.14		
2021 FS	TB	MLB	21	2	3	0	57	0	50	52	8	5.4	7.8	43	46.8%	.300	1.64	6.05	135	-0.9

Comparables: John Holdzkom, Wander Suero, Domingo Germán

Catalina has plenty of upside and is starting to get to it. He is much more physical now, as he has started to fill out his lean, 6-foot-6 frame. The fastball velocity is among the best in the system, a mid-to-high 90s pitch with quality extension. The curveball velocity has ticked up as well and is now a power pitch with hard downer depth. Given this velocity and power of the breaker, it is difficult to locate at present, often spiked, but can also elicit some bad swings. Catalina needs innings, and could be pushed aggressively to Low-A to start '21.

And now a selection of OFP 50s

Josh Fleming LHP   Born: 05/18/96   Age: 25   Bats: R   Throws: L   Height: 6'2"   Weight: 220   Origin: Round 5, 2017 Draft (#139 overall)

YEAR	TEAM	LVL	AGE	W	L	SV	G	GS	IP	H	HR	BB/9	K/9	K	GB%	BABIP	WHIP	ERA	DRA-	WARP
2018	BG	LO-A	22	6	1	0	10	10	60	41	1	1.5	6.3	42	56.1%	.234	0.85	1.20	77	1.1
2018	CHA	HI-A	22	3	3	0	9	7	50¹	51	4	1.6	6.8	38	44.7%	.301	1.19	4.11	70	1.1
2019	MTG	AA	23	11	4	0	21	17	127²	127	9	1.3	6.5	92	51.6%	.299	1.14	3.31	96	0.3
2019	DUR	AAA	23	1	3	0	4	3	21	24	6	3.4	6.9	16	65.2%	.286	1.52	5.14	107	0.3
2020	TB	MLB	24	5	0	0	7	5	32¹	28	5	1.9	7.0	25	63.9%	.250	1.08	2.78	86	0.5
2021 FS	TB	MLB	25	9	8	0	26	26	150	153	17	2.5	6.7	111	55.2%	.296	1.30	4.06	94	1.6
2021 DC	TB	MLB	25	5	6	0	19	19	93	95	11	2.5	6.7	69	55.2%	.296	1.30	4.06	94	1.3

Comparables: Nick Margevicius, David Peterson, Bernardo Flores Jr.

Speaking of Fleming, the crafty lefty was a bit of a surprise call up given the starting pitching depth in the system, but he pounded the zone with his bowling-ball, low-90s sinker, four or five innings at a time, and kept the ball on the ground and let the Rays' infield defense do it's work. He offers a pretty good sinking change as well to mitigate any platoon issues. I don't know if he can continue to suppress hits to this level, and both DRA and FIP thought the sub-3.00 ERA was unsustainable. But they also both thought he was at least an average arm. Score another one for Tampa's player dev.

Alika Williams   Born: 03/12/99   Age: 22   Bats: R   Throws: R   Height: 6'2"   Weight: 180   Origin: Round CBA, 2020 Draft (#37 overall)

If there is a "type" it seems the Rays have been targeting recently with college players, it's high contact/low strikeout players with track records. A three-year starter at Arizona State, surrounded by the likes of Hunter Bishop, Spencer Torkelson, among others, Williams served as a table-setter and steady defender for the Sun Devils. At present he's more of a glove-first option with confidence he'll stay at shortstop, although less confidence the offense will allow him to start everyday, even if buried at the back of the lineup.

Taylor Walls SS   Born: 07/10/96   Age: 24   Bats: S   Throws: R   Height: 5'10"   Weight: 185   Origin: Round 3, 2017 Draft (#79 overall)

YEAR	TEAM	LVL	AGE	PA	R	2B	3B	HR	RBI	BB	K	SB	CS	AVG/OBP/SLG	DRC+	BABIP	BRR	FRAA	WARP
2018	BG	LO-A	21	540	87	28	6	6	57	66	80	31	12	.304/.393/.428	142	.354	6.5	SS(104) 11.7	5.9
2019	CHA	HI-A	22	180	22	7	2	4	26	19	28	13	6	.269/.339/.417	123	.295	0.7	SS(36) 2.4, 2B(1) 0.1	1.5
2019	MTG	AA	22	243	42	16	5	6	20	26	51	15	9	.270/.346/.479	131	.321	0.4	SS(35) -0.9, 2B(9) 1.1, 3B(6) 0.8	1.9
2021 FS	TB	MLB	24	600	57	27	3	12	60	50	163	19	9	.236/.304/.370	85	.315	-3.4	SS 9, 2B 1	1.5

Comparables: Trevor Story, Erick Mejia, Dansby Swanson

Walls has strong skills, but when looking at the final report he doesn't really stand out for a tool that is above-average. A switch-hitter with quality plate discipline, Walls is a tough out as he has above-average barrel control and works the whole field. A lot of the contact is of the low line drive style, so while he can hit the ball hard, there won't be a lot of home run power. The speed is average home to first, but it's enough to allow him to steal bases and cover ground well defensively. He has played second, short, and third in the minors, but will look to get some outfield work this upcoming season to add even more versatility—the Rays like this sort of thing.

Michael Plassmeyer LHP Born: 11/05/96 Age: 24 Bats: L Throws: L Height: 6'2" Weight: 197 Origin: Round 4, 2018 Draft (#118 overall)

YEAR	TEAM	LVL	AGE	W	L	SV	G	GS	IP	H	HR	BB/9	K/9	K	GB%	BABIP	WHIP	ERA	DRA-	WARP
2018	EVE	SS	21	0	1	0	13	12	24	16	1	1.5	16.5	44	47.7%	.349	0.83	2.25	132	-0.3
2019	BG	LO-A	22	2	1	0	5	5	29^1	21	3	2.1	9.8	32	39.1%	.273	0.95	1.23	66	0.7
2019	CHA	HI-A	22	7	2	0	19	18	101^2	89	5	1.4	6.7	76	46.4%	.281	1.03	2.12	75	1.6
2021 FS	TB	MLB	24	2	3	0	57	0	50	49	7	2.8	7.8	43	42.2%	.290	1.30	4.09	104	0.0

Comparables: David Peterson, Josh Fleming, Brendan McKay

Putting Plassmeyer's measurables on this website doesn't make him stand out as much as if you see him in person. A low-slot lefty who throws strikes, this is a pitcher type that the Rays have had plenty of success with. He has a lot of deception in the delivery, which allows his otherwise mediocre fastball to be extremely effective. Similar to Ryan Yarbrough or Fleming, the changeup is his best offspeed pitch with late diving action that elicits its fair share of weak contact and swings and misses. As an advanced arm with a relatively high floor, Plassmeyer has a strong chance to make a debut this season.

Niko Hulsizer OF Born: 02/01/97 Age: 24 Bats: R Throws: R Height: 6'2" Weight: 225 Origin: Round 18, 2018 Draft (#554 overall)

YEAR	TEAM	LVL	AGE	PA	R	2B	3B	HR	RBI	BB	K	SB	CS	AVG/OBP/SLG	DRC+	BABIP	BRR	FRAA	WARP
2018	OGD	ROK	21	202	47	13	0	9	32	30	52	12	2	.281/.426/.531		.360			
2019	GL	LO-A	22	256	46	17	1	15	49	37	75	4	1	.268/.395/.574	185	.339	-3.3	LF(29) 4.2, RF(4) 1.0	2.9
2019	CHA	HI-A	22	39	4	2	0	1	4	4	11	0	1	.235/.308/.382	95	.304	-0.1	LF(5) 0.1, RF(3) 0.3	0.1
2019	RC	HI-A	22	98	15	6	0	5	18	9	33	3	2	.259/.327/.506	99	.340	1.1	LF(15) 1.6	0.5
2021 FS	TB	MLB	24	600	56	27	1	16	62	46	227	3	2	.195/.273/.346	70	.299	-2.1	LF 4, RF 2	-0.4

Comparables: Kole Calhoun, Jerry Sands, Jesse Winker

A big outfielder with big—read: plus-plus—raw, Hulsizer is a three-true-outcome bat whose swing-and-miss proclivities haven't been truly tested against upper minors pitching yet. The suite of defensive tools are average, so he's spent almost all his time in a corner outfield spot, and left is probably the best fit. So the walks and pop will have to keep showing up in the stat sheet to make him a regular in the bigs.

Top Talents 25 and Under (as of 4/1/2021):

1. Wander Franco, SS
2. Willy Adames, SS
3. Randy Arozarena, OF
4. Austin Meadows, OF
5. Shane Baz, RHP
6. Luis Patiño, RHP
7. Francisco Mejía, C
8. Vidal Bruján, IF
9. Shane McClanahan, LHP
10. Xavier Edwards, SS/2B

Yes, there's even more high-end young talent in the majors. Willy Adames would be ahead of nearly every prospect in baseball, but Franco is the best prospect in baseball. He was our No. 15 prospect himself in 2018, and is just a few points of batting average (or more national exposure) away from being a two-way star. And he's not even the best young shortstop in the system, somehow.

Austin Meadows had a bad 2020 after an All-Star 2019. He battled an oblique injury and missed some time with COVID-19, so we're assuming this is a blip and expecting him to run it back in 2021, where he blasted 33 home runs and a 135 DRC+. When healthy, he's an all-around offensive force.

Francisco Mejía needed a chance of scenery, and it came in the Snell trade. The 2018 No. 5 prospect is only 25, and he was actually fine in part-time duty in 2019. But the Padres just didn't seem to have any faith in him. It was only a few years ago that we saw him as baseball's next star catcher, and Tampa Bay is a very good place for him to try to turn it around.

Texas Rangers

The State of the System:

We tend to like the Rangers' system more than most. But it's maybe not quite as fun/deep as recent vintages.

The Top Ten:

★ ★ ★ *2021 Top 101 Prospect* **#26** ★ ★ ★

1 **Leody Taveras** **CF**   OFP: 60   ETA: Debuted in 2020
Born: 09/08/98 Age: 22 Bats: S Throws: R Height: 6'2" Weight: 195 Origin: International Free Agent, 2015

YEAR	TEAM	LVL	AGE	PA	R	2B	3B	HR	RBI	BB	K	SB	CS	AVG/OBP/SLG	DRC+	BABIP	BRR	FRAA	WARP
2018	DE	HI-A	19	580	65	16	7	5	48	51	96	19	11	.246/.312/.332	90	.292	0.3	CF(123) 7.0, RF(3) 0.0	0.8
2019	DE	HI-A	20	290	44	7	4	2	25	31	62	21	5	.294/.368/.376	123	.378	-0.4	CF(34) -0.6, RF(23) 4.0, LF(7) -0.7	1.7
2019	FRI	AA	20	293	32	12	4	3	31	23	60	11	8	.265/.320/.375	97	.327	0.5	CF(65) 8.1	1.8
2020	TEX	MLB	21	134	20	6	1	4	6	14	43	8	0	.227/.308/.395	84	.319	1.1	CF(33) 0.9	0.4
2021 FS	*TEX*	*MLB*	*22*	*600*	*64*	*23*	*4*	*11*	*47*	*45*	*172*	*13*	*6*	*.228/.288/.351*	*74*	*.311*	*0.1*	*CF 2, LF 0*	*0.1*
2021 DC	*TEX*	*MLB*	*22*	*528*	*56*	*21*	*4*	*9*	*42*	*40*	*151*	*11*	*5*	*.228/.288/.351*	*74*	*.311*	*0.1*	*CF 2*	*0.1*

Comparables: Derrick Robinson, Luis Alexander Basabe, Xavier Avery

The Report: Taveras has long tantalized, flashing all five-tools as a switch-hitting center fielder while never really imposing his will on opposing pitchers at any minor league stop. The defensive tools did more than flash and we were always confident he would at least be a plus center fielder given his high-end plus speed and above-average throwing arm. Taveras would flash plus raw power from both sides, but never slugged over .400 at any level. He was never overmatched at the plate and improved his approach and quality of contact as he moved up levels, always young for his league. Age-relative-to-league only gets you so far—as does noting that Down East is a terrible place to hit and his line there in 2019 was 24 percent better than league average by DRC+—and there were those on staff who saw Taveras and thought he would just be a glove-first, average regular in center field.

Development Track: Well Taveras still hasn't slugged .400 at any level, but he posted a career high .395—with a .168 ISO—after getting handed the everyday center field gig in September for the Rangers. It was the hit tool that actually let him down a bit, as the K-rate ballooned seeing major league offspeed for the first time. It was a big jump for the bat, and there's some positives to take away there going forward. The glove was as-advertised as Taveras immediately looked like a Gold Glove candidate in center field. There isn't as much clarity here as you'd like, and Taveras remains a bit of a Rorsrach test, you can still see the potential All-Star, or the Role-5 glove guy if you stare at his 2020 season.

Variance: Low. Taveras didn't really answer the questions about his bat in the majors, but the glove and speed will keep him manning center in Texas for a while, and he flashed some more of the raw power in games while not being completely overmatched in what was a pretty big jump in difficulty.

Mark Barry's Fantasy Take: Taveras might still be better IRL than in fantasy, but two notable takeaways from his first bout against big-league pitching could portend to future fantasy success: 1) He played great defense in center field, which automatically extends his audition, and 2) He stole eight bases in 33 games without being caught. If he can figure out how to scale back on the strikeouts, the steals alone give him OF3 upside.

★ ★ ★ *2021 Top 101 Prospect* **#56** ★ ★ ★ ────────

2 **Josh Jung** **3B** OFP: 60 ETA: 2021, service time manipulation TBD

Born: 02/12/98 Age: 23 Bats: R Throws: R Height: 6'2" Weight: 215 Origin: Round 1, 2019 Draft (#8 overall)

YEAR	TEAM	LVL	AGE	PA	R	2B	3B	HR	RBI	BB	K	SB	CS	AVG/OBP/SLG	DRC+	BABIP	BRR	FRAA	WARP
2019	RAN	ROK	21	19	5	1	1	1	5	2	3	0	0	.588/.632/.941		.692			
2019	HIC	LO-A	21	179	18	13	0	1	23	16	29	4	1	.287/.363/.389	136	.341	0.6	3B(35) 2.5	1.5
2021 FS	TEX	MLB	23	600	55	27	2	9	54	36	157	3	1	.227/.281/.334	71	.300	0.5	3B 13	0.3
2021 DC	TEX	MLB	23	99	9	4	0	1	8	6	25	0	0	.227/.281/.334	71	.300	0.1	3B 2	0.1

Comparables: Garin Cecchini, Jedd Gyorko, Stephen Piscotty

The Report: You know those posts you keep seeing during these pandemic times from that one really annoying friend about "If you didn't grind you wasted time" or some variant? Jung must have seen one and taken that to heart. Coming into the year, Jung's major concerns were whether he'd hit for enough power to be a top-level corner infield prospect. Working at Texas' alternate site, Jung answered that with a yes. Without major swing changes, Jung began driving the ball more to all fields. There was minimal doubt about his ability to make contact, but the development of real above-average power is a huge add to his toolbox.

Defensively, nothing has changed much. Jung played both shortstop and third base at Texas Tech before moving exclusively to the hot corner post draft. Jung has the range and quickness to handle the position without being anywhere near a liability. Is there some room for improvement? Most likely, but that upward movement would take him from above league average to potential Gold Glove. Whether that is feasible seems difficult to foresee, but with the improvements at the plate the current defensive level is more than palatable.

Development Track: If Jung's power was the $64,000 question, this is the $32,000. Texas has finally said what everyone watching already knew: The rebuild is on. This includes the moving of Gold Glove winner Isiah Kiner-Falefa from third base to shortstop replacing veteran Elvis Andrus. That leaves a large, No. 2-prospect-shaped-hole at the hot corner. Jung is ready to take that spot, Texas is ready for him to do it, but nothing is official yet.

Variance: Medium. Low doesn't feel right post pandemic 2020, but folks who saw Jung pre-2020 saw the potential of what appears to have happened. So, split the difference.

Mark Barry's Fantasy Take: This guy has grown on me. I'm not sure why I came in so "meh" on Jung, but every time I come back to his player card and read reports, I like him a little more each time. I think right now is the last time you'll be able to scoop him up at anything resembling fair market value, and I'd even be willing to pay a slight premium, especially with rumblings that Jung has found a bit of pop.

★ ★ ★ *2021 Top 101 Prospect* **#60** ★ ★ ★ ────────

3 **Dane Dunning** **RHP** OFP: 60 ETA: Debuted in 2020

Born: 12/20/94 Age: 26 Bats: R Throws: R Height: 6'4" Weight: 225 Origin: Round 1, 2016 Draft (#29 overall)

YEAR	TEAM	LVL	AGE	W	L	SV	G	GS	IP	H	HR	BB/9	K/9	K	GB%	BABIP	WHIP	ERA	DRA-	WARP
2018	WS	HI-A	23	1	1	0	4	4	24¹	20	2	1.1	11.5	31	61.3%	.300	0.95	2.59	74	0.5
2018	BIR	AA	23	5	2	0	11	11	62	57	0	3.3	10.0	69	48.8%	.343	1.29	2.76	76	1.3
2020	CHW	MLB	25	2	0	0	7	7	34	25	4	3.4	9.3	35	44.6%	.239	1.12	3.97	91	0.5
2021 FS	TEX	MLB	26	9	8	0	26	26	150	137	21	3.5	9.4	156	43.9%	.291	1.30	4.13	95	1.5
2021 DC	TEX	MLB	26	6	8	0	22	22	115	105	16	3.5	9.4	120	43.9%	.291	1.30	4.13	95	1.5

Comparables: Tyler Wilson, Sean Manaea, Jordan Montgomery

The Report: Before his Tommy John surgery in March 2019, Dunning was knocking on the door of the majors with a solid four-pitch mix headlined by a sinker he could move effectively around the zone and a potential plus changeup. He was a typical mid-rotation starter prospect with a durable frame and better command and change than that profile typically features in Double-A. Conversely Dunning was maybe a little short on the fastball velocity and breaking ball projection. The uncertainty of the surgery knocked him off our national list coming into the season, but there was little reason to believe he wouldn't be an above-average major league starter assuming a normal rehab.

Development Track: Dunning's rehab went well enough that he was moved into the major league rotation down the stretch and made seven, well, above-average starts for the White Sox. He moved his low-90s fastball around the zone well enough, and improvements in both the slider and curve gave him two potential average-or-better breaking ball looks. The change still flashed plus although it was used relatively sparingly in the majors. Dunning should slot right into the 2021 Rangers rotation when he will be two years removed from the surgery. We'll know a lot more by this time next year, but the mid-rotation projection still looks good for now.

Variance: Medium. The command, secondary feel and overall stamina aren't quite all the way back coming off surgery, but we're fairly confident Dunning is at least an average major league starter.

Mark Barry's Fantasy Take: Dunning was one of the biggest surprises and best stories of the 2020 season, for my money, though he doesn't figure to be more than an SP4/5. He struck out over a batter per inning this past season and had a solid swinging-strike rate at 11.4 percent, but he doesn't get many swings outside the strike zone and has middling control numbers. Dunning posted a 4.25 DRA, which speaks to his run-of-the-mill fantasy profile. However, it doesn't seem that fantasy analysts are getting too excited about the right-hander. He sits outside the Top 250 in redraft leagues and outside the Top 400 in dynasty rankings. That seems about right, as it's hard to see too much upside unless his changeup takes a significant step forward.

★ ★ ★ *2021 Top 101 Prospect* **#98** ★ ★ ★

4 Sam Huff C OFP: 60 ETA: Debuted in 2020

Born: 01/14/98 Age: 23 Bats: R Throws: R Height: 6'5" Weight: 240 Origin: Round 7, 2016 Draft (#219 overall)

YEAR	TEAM	LVL	AGE	PA	R	2B	3B	HR	RBI	BB	K	SB	CS	AVG/OBP/SLG	DRC+	BABIP	BRR	FRAA	WARP
2018	HIC	LO-A	20	448	53	22	3	18	55	23	140	9	1	.241/.292/.439	96	.317	-0.1	C(56) 1.9, 1B(11) -0.4	0.4
2019	HIC	LO-A	21	114	22	5	0	15	29	6	37	4	1	.333/.368/.796	216	.375	0.8	C(14) 0.9	1.8
2019	DE	HI-A	21	405	49	17	2	13	43	27	117	2	5	.262/.326/.425	110	.347	-2.7	C(51) 1.9, 1B(4) 0.1	1.5
2020	TEX	MLB	22	33	5	3	0	3	4	2	11	0	0	.355/.394/.742	103	.471	-0.8	C(10) 0.1	0.0
2021 FS	TEX	MLB	23	600	60	25	2	20	67	39	228	3	1	.217/.276/.383	78	.326	-0.5	C -3, 1B 0	0.2
2021 DC	TEX	MLB	23	231	23	9	0	7	25	15	87	1	0	.217/.276/.383	78	.326	-0.2	C -2	0.1

Comparables: Jorge Alfaro, Eric Haase, Tommy Joseph

The Report: In his short stint in the majors following a surprising September call-up, Huff did exactly what he did in the minors: He showed strong power, struck out a decent amount, and didn't walk, while displaying average catcher defense with the potential for more down the road. That's the Huff profile in a nutshell. Off the field is where the work was stacked for the young backstop. The Rangers noted that Huff—and all catchers at the alternate site—were working with coaches daily putting together game plans for the pitching matchups across the street. The goal was to accelerate the mental side of the position, cutting down the learning curve for baseball's most difficult position. There's a good chance the biggest growth in Texas' potential future catcher is something unseen, but something necessary all the same.

Development Track: Huff's growth was described as "steady," which is good. That also means, based on where Huff was pre-pandemic, that major league readiness is still a ways off. Huff needs to be facing age- and level-appropriate competition in real games, something that the alternate site could only simulate. If Huff can go to Double A as the starting catcher in 2021, we'll learn a lot more. There's a chance, albeit a small one, that Huff could be given the backup job behind Jose Trevino in Arlington. That seems less than ideal, barring an extreme playing time split. Huff needs to play every day somewhere, preferably somewhere more representative of his current skills.

Variance: High. Huff's chance of moving off catcher feel less likely than before, but that still means he's going to have to make improvements to be a plus regular. That means fewer strikeouts, higher quality of contact, and continued growth behind the plate. That's a lot to ask of any player, and the various ways the profile could go sideways dictate a high variance designation.

Mark Barry's Fantasy Take: If Huff can maintain the .355/.394/.742 line that he posted upon his debut, he'll have a very bright future as a fantasy catcher. He still struck out a ton, though, so it's more likely that he'll come back to earth and hover in that range of other decent fantasy backstops, spending some seasons in the top 5-10 at the position and others as a streamer, easily replaceable with someone fresh from the wire.

5   Cole Winn   RHP   OFP: 60   ETA: 2022
Born: 11/25/99   Age: 21   Bats: R   Throws: R   Height: 6'2"   Weight: 190   Origin: Round 1, 2018 Draft (#15 overall)

YEAR	TEAM	LVL	AGE	W	L	SV	G	GS	IP	H	HR	BB/9	K/9	K	GB%	BABIP	WHIP	ERA	DRA-	WARP
2019	HIC	LO-A	19	4	4	0	18	18	68²	59	5	5.1	8.5	65	46.6%	.292	1.43	4.46	112	-0.2
2021 FS	TEX	MLB	21	2	3	0	57	0	50	49	8	6.8	7.6	42	41.9%	.285	1.74	6.03	135	-0.8

Comparables: Max Fried, Tyler Chatwood, Luke Jackson

The Report: Winn is a four pitch starting pitching prospect with his fastball checking in as the best pitch in his arsenal along with a changeup, slider, and curveball. He's had an uneven development curve since being drafted, but If Jung had the best alternate site performance, Winn was right alongside him. His ascent this year came for a few reasons. One of the big factors is time: Winn just turned 21 this past November, and more time in the organization has aided his development. Winn better understands what he is and isn't.

Which leads to one of his major improvements: throwing more strikes. Winn previously held a mentality of avoiding contact entirely, and as a result would throw more pitches outside the zone than necessary. Hitters caught up to that some, and as a result would put him in awkward situations that forced him to throw less-than-ideal pitches in the zone. This year, Winn spent time learning how to be more cerebral with his pitch mix along with utilizing his whole arsenal to get more weak contact on those in zone pitches.

Development Track: Winn hasn't pitched above Low-A yet, which matters for a Texas organization that over the last two years has decelerated its upward pitcher movement through the minors. Even a strong alternate site showing probably means Winn is heading to either High-A or Double-A to start 2021, and is likely to spend his entire season below the bigs. That said, his 2020 progress is enough that barring more issues it's not impossible to dream on a 2022 debut for Winn.

Variance: High. So much of this year's results are hard to put in the frame, but Winn's growth is encouraging. He's not risk proof, because no pitcher is. That said, this is probably the best to feel about Winn since he got drafted.

Mark Barry's Fantasy Take: It would be nice if Winn's proclivity to throw more strikes translated into real games, but I don't know if that will necessarily help his fantasy profile. Seems like a pretty clear back-end starter for me.

6   Justin Foscue   2B   OFP: 55   ETA: Late 2022 / Early 2023
Born: 03/02/99   Age: 22   Bats: R   Throws: R   Height: 6'0"   Weight: 203   Origin: Round 1, 2020 Draft (#14 overall)

The Report: As one of the best second basemen in all of college baseball in 2019, it still felt weird to hear Foscue's name called so early in the first round by the Rangers. In a year where certainty was hard to find in the draft, taking a big time producer from the SEC at a position with a low bar for expectations became a valuable commodity for the Rangers. Foscue can probably play some third base or shortstop in a pinch, but the hitting potential might up his value considering the pull power he can get to is seldom found in most of today's second sackers.

Development Track: Another selling point on his draft card has to be the juxtaposition of his baseball maturity (advanced) against his relative youth as a young-for-his-class junior. The latter likely helped buoy his draft stock for algorithmically-inclined teams, which is to say perhaps he has more at the end of his rope while still being ahead of the curve.

Variance: Low. Could he put together an All-Star campaign? Sure, why not. What he offers is a high floor with a modest ceiling, and every team trying to compete needs these guys somewhere on the roster.

Mark Barry's Fantasy Take: Best case scenario, Foscue gives you something like a Cesar Hernandez-y line. Worst case scenario, how do you feel about the Bryson Stott experience in Philadelphia? There might be hits, but there might not be much else.

7   Anderson Tejeda   SS   OFP: 55   ETA: Debuted in 2020
Born: 05/01/98   Age: 23   Bats: S   Throws: R   Height: 6'0"   Weight: 200   Origin: International Free Agent, 2014

YEAR	TEAM	LVL	AGE	PA	R	2B	3B	HR	RBI	BB	K	SB	CS	AVG/OBP/SLG	DRC+	BABIP	BRR	FRAA	WARP
2018	DE	HI-A	20	522	76	17	5	19	74	49	142	11	4	.259/.331/.439	119	.330	3.0	SS(105) 2.9, 2B(12) 1.6	2.9
2019	DE	HI-A	21	181	22	10	1	4	24	17	58	9	4	.234/.315/.386	83	.333	1.3	SS(39) 2.4	0.8
2020	TEX	MLB	22	77	7	4	1	3	8	2	30	4	1	.253/.273/.453	76	.381	0.1	SS(18) -0.2, 2B(4) -0.1	0.0
2021 FS	TEX	MLB	23	600	59	25	5	19	67	33	229	5	2	.218/.265/.390	75	.327	2.7	2B 7, SS 0	1.1
2021 DC	TEX	MLB	23	165	16	7	1	5	18	9	63	1	0	.218/.265/.390	75	.327	0.7	2B 2, SS 0	0.3

Comparables: Junior Lake, Gleyber Torres, Marcus Semien

The Report: What a difference a year makes. Last year, Tejeda was outside the top 10 in part because of a shoulder injury. Now, he's put a major-league debut in his rear view mirror before playing a minor league game above High-A. Tejeda shares a lot of qualities at the plate with Huff: He strikes out a lot, doesn't walk a lot, but can hit the snot out of the ball when he squares it up. The difference for Tejeda is his defense is more advanced. Tejeda is capable of handling second base, shortstop, and probably even third base if given the opportunity. He's an electric defender who uses quickness, athleticism, and a hard to quantify fearlessness to cover anywhere on the infield. The question for Tejeda will be if he can hit for enough power across a full season to cover the approach and contact deficiencies. But if Tejeda is going to be a long term starter and not just a fifth infield type, who can play all over the diamond when called upon, his plate discipline will need to improve.

Development Track: Tejeda's 2020 debut signaled the start of Texas going young. Tejeda now has every opportunity to find his way onto the major league roster full time in 2021. The exact role is cloudy though.

Variance: Medium. The offensive issues for Tejeda are well known, and he's either going to fix them or not. That said, those problems will determine starter versus bench and that's not an insignificant gap.

Mark Barry's Fantasy Take: If Tejeda gets his swing-and-miss under control, he's a sneaky-good power/speed option at MI. If not, I guess he's still a sneaky power/speed option, but not necessarily a good one. Maybe, like, Niko Goodrum with fewer walks? Does that tickle your fancy?

8   Evan Carter   OFP: 55   ETA: 2024
Born: 08/29/02   Age: 18   Bats: L   Throws: R   Height: 6'4"   Weight: 190   Origin: Round 2, 2020 Draft (#50 overall)

The Report: Our focus on the Baseball Prospectus Prospect Team is pro coverage, but we usually at least know of almost everyone picked during Day 1 of the draft. The Rangers' selection of Evan Carter at 50 elicited "who?" from much more embedded amateur evaluators than us. We did manage to source a third-hand report, and while there is always risk in that kind of game of telephone, Carter appeared to be a steal in the second round with a potential plus hit tool driving the profile.

Development Track: No one remains an unknown for long in the prospect world, and Carter crushed the instructional league, standing shoulder to shoulder with other first-round picks with the bat. This ranking feels super aggressive, but I suspect it will look overly conservative by June of 2021.

Variance: Extreme. Carter didn't play like a virtually unknown second rounder at instructs, but even if the Rangers snagged an extra first round talent with the bat, that first round talent is still a prep that hasn't played in a real professional game yet.

Mark Barry's Fantasy Take: Your guess is as good as mine about how Carter's status will be viewed in the dynasty world. At the very least he seems like a great breakout candidate who you should absolutely be ready to pounce on early in the 2021 season.

9 Kyle Cody RHP OFP: 55 ETA: Debuted in 2020

Born: 08/09/94 Age: 26 Bats: R Throws: R Height: 6'7" Weight: 225 Origin: Round 6, 2016 Draft (#189 overall)

YEAR	TEAM	LVL	AGE	W	L	SV	G	GS	IP	H	HR	BB/9	K/9	K	GB%	BABIP	WHIP	ERA	DRA-	WARP
2018	RAN	ROK	23	0	0	0	2	2	5	2	0	1.8	16.2	9	50.0%	.250	0.60	0.00		
2020	TEX	MLB	25	1	1	0	8	5	22²	15	1	5.2	7.1	18	47.5%	.233	1.24	1.59	98	0.2
2021 FS	TEX	MLB	26	8	9	0	26	26	150	143	22	4.5	8.7	145	44.1%	.292	1.45	4.80	106	0.5
2021 DC	TEX	MLB	26	3	5	0	14	14	62	59	9	4.5	8.7	60	44.1%	.292	1.45	4.80	106	0.4

Comparables: Aaron Blair, Alex Meyer, Jordan Montgomery

The Report: Cody was one of our favorite prospects based on 2017 live looks. At the time, he was throwing a bowling ball sinker that got up into the mid-90s, and both his breaking ball and changeup were flashing at least above-average. Tommy John surgery in 2018 wiped out most of his next two seasons, and it was honestly a bit of a surprise when the Rangers added him to the 40-man last offseason given that he was 25 with no experience above A-ball and coming off two lost seasons.

Development Track: He popped up in the majors down the stretch, initially in the bullpen and then stretched out for starts as long as five innings. While his extremely shiny ERA was mostly a mirage, he still posted an above-average DRA. The stuff was largely as I remembered—fastball up to the mid-90s with sink and a flashing breaking ball and change, though the former is more slidery now. He's not going to be a whiff machine and the command needs to tighten, but Cody just might be a decent MLB starting pitcher already.

Variance: Medium. He pretty much is what he is, except for latent durability concerns.

Mark Barry's Fantasy Take: The excitement ends here. Cody is a cool story, but I'm not sure you have to worry about him in a fantasy sense.

10 Tyler Phillips RHP OFP: 55 ETA: 2022

Born: 10/27/97 Age: 23 Bats: R Throws: R Height: 6'5" Weight: 225 Origin: Round 16, 2015 Draft (#468 overall)

YEAR	TEAM	LVL	AGE	W	L	SV	G	GS	IP	H	HR	BB/9	K/9	K	GB%	BABIP	WHIP	ERA	DRA-	WARP
2018	HIC	LO-A	20	11	5	0	22	22	128	117	4	1.0	8.7	124	52.8%	.308	1.02	2.67	64	3.2
2019	DE	HI-A	21	2	2	0	6	6	37²	28	1	1.4	6.7	28	54.3%	.262	0.90	1.19	71	0.7
2019	FRI	AA	21	7	9	0	18	16	93¹	95	15	1.9	7.1	74	50.9%	.292	1.23	4.72	108	-0.4
2021 FS	TEX	MLB	23	2	3	0	57	0	50	49	7	2.6	6.9	38	46.3%	.282	1.28	4.24	102	0.1
2021 DC	TEX	MLB	23	2	3	0	30	6	54	53	8	2.6	6.9	41	46.3%	.282	1.28	4.24	102	0.4

Comparables: Rony García, Gabriel Ynoa, Joe Ross

The Report: Coming into 2020, Phillips was a command first pitcher with good, not great stuff who tended to get knocked around every time the command wobbled. The offseason and alternate site time was dedicated to figuring out why that was. The fastball was a prime offender; Phillips throws a four seam, but the velocity and spin rate made it look like a two-seam. This season, Phillips focused on adding more carry and spin to the pitch. That resulted in more vertical movement, making it harder to hit. This also happened with Phillips' curveball, which was flat at times last year making it a less desirable offering. To pair with all this verticality, Phillips is now throwing a slider as well. The mixture of horizontal and vertical made a big difference for Phillips, who paired this with his already mature approach to show great strides over his inconsistent 2019.

Development Track: Phillips made all these changes, but until he can road test them against real opposition it'll be hard to say more about how effective they are. Phillips probably took a step forward this season, but 2021 will be the proof in the pudding.

Variance: Low. Phillips had a high floor already, and was likely to see a fifth starter-type role even before the changes he made this year. The improvements this year could see an improvement to that projection, but it's more marginal than most.

Mark Barry's Fantasy Take: Another right-handed, potential back-end starter? Sure, why not?

The Prospects You Meet Outside The Top Ten

Top Ten Prospects in a shallower (or literally the White Sox) system

Sherten Apostel 3B Born: 03/11/99 Age: 22 Bats: R Throws: R Height: 6'4" Weight: 235 Origin: International Free Agent, 2018

YEAR	TEAM	LVL	AGE	PA	R	2B	3B	HR	RBI	BB	K	SB	CS	AVG/OBP/SLG	DRC+	BABIP	BRR	FRAA	WARP
2018	BRS	ROK	19	175	28	7	0	7	26	32	42	3	1	.259/.406/.460		.319			
2018	SPO	SS	19	49	7	1	0	1	10	9	8	0	1	.351/.469/.459	201	.400	0.0	3B(8) -0.6	0.4
2019	HIC	LO-A	20	319	38	13	1	15	43	28	71	2	1	.258/.332/.470	119	.290	-3.0	3B(70) 1.6, 1B(12) 0.0	1.4
2019	DE	HI-A	20	159	18	5	1	4	16	23	49	0	0	.237/.352/.378	116	.341	1.6	3B(41) 1.4	1.1
2020	TEX	MLB	21	21	1	1	0	0	0	1	9	0	0	.100/.143/.150	63	.182	-0.1	1B(5) 0.3, 3B(2) -0.2	-0.1
2021 FS	TEX	MLB	22	600	60	24	2	16	61	55	222	2	1	.209/.287/.358	77	.318	-0.2	1B 0, 3B 2	-0.4
2021 DC	TEX	MLB	22	198	19	8	0	5	20	18	73	0	0	.209/.287/.358	77	.318	-0.1	1B 0, 3B 1	-0.2

Comparables: Josh Bell, Will Middlebrooks, Jeimer Candelario

Another who got a look in the big leagues this year, Apostel still hits the ball hard and still shows a surprisingly strong aptitude for defense. Between trades and internal growth, the system grew in strength which forced Apostel down the list some. He'd still be a Top Ten player in most systems, which says more about how Texas improved on the farm this year.

Avery Weems LHP Born: 06/06/97 Age: 24 Bats: R Throws: L Height: 6'2" Weight: 205 Origin: Round 6, 2019 Draft (#170 overall)

YEAR	TEAM	LVL	AGE	W	L	SV	G	GS	IP	H	HR	BB/9	K/9	K	GB%	BABIP	WHIP	ERA	DRA-	WARP
2019	WSX	ROK	22	1	1	0	4	4	13	10	0	2.1	9.7	14	78.1%	.312	1.00	0.69		
2019	GTF	ROK+	22	4	3	0	10	10	47¹	43	1	1.3	11.4	60	65.0%	.353	1.06	2.47		
2021 FS	TEX	MLB	24	2	3	0	57	0	50	49	8	4.3	7.6	42	54.9%	.287	1.48	4.97	118	-0.4

Comparables: Carlos Hernández, Brendan McKay, Brock Burke

The other piece in the Lance Lynn deal, Weems got squeezed out from a spot at the White Sox alternate site but looked unhittable in instructs, showing a bit more velocity than he had in college. He'l be ticketed for full-season ball in 2021 and could be a fast mover if the Rangers choose to make him a full-time reliever immediately. He offers 95 from the left side and an absolutely wipeout breaker.

Prospects to dream on a little

Ricky Vanasco RHP Born: 10/13/98 Age: 22 Bats: R Throws: R Height: 6'3" Weight: 180 Origin: Round 15, 2017 Draft (#464 overall)

YEAR	TEAM	LVL	AGE	W	L	SV	G	GS	IP	H	HR	BB/9	K/9	K	GB%	BABIP	WHIP	ERA	DRA-	WARP
2018	RAN	ROK	19	3	3	0	7	3	24²	25	1	4.7	9.1	25	45.2%	.393	1.54	4.38		
2019	SPO	SS	20	3	1	0	9	9	39	23	2	5.1	13.6	59	50.0%	.292	1.15	1.85	63	1.0
2019	HIC	LO-A	20	0	0	0	2	2	10²	5	0	2.5	13.5	16	47.4%	.263	0.75	1.69	55	0.3
2021 FS	TEX	MLB	22	2	3	0	57	0	50	44	7	6.0	10.3	57	41.2%	.290	1.55	4.97	115	-0.3

Comparables: Demarcus Evans, Jarlin García, Dylan Cease

Vanasco was on his way to a Top Ten spot on the list this season, after an impressive showing at the alternate site. Then in September, Vanasco had Tommy John surgery, which means we won't see if what he did at the alternate site will translate into games until 2022.

Keithron Moss 2B   Born: 08/20/01   Age: 19   Bats: S   Throws: R   Height: 5'11"   Weight: 165   Origin: International Free Agent, 2017

YEAR	TEAM	LVL	AGE	PA	R	2B	3B	HR	RBI	BB	K	SB	CS	AVG/OBP/SLG	DRC+	BABIP	BRR	FRAA	WARP
2018	DSL RGR1	ROK	16	204	29	11	1	0	23	35	62	8	7	.196/.350/.276		.314			
2019	RAN	ROK	17	147	27	4	3	2	14	21	40	8	2	.308/.425/.442		.443			
2021 FS	TEX	MLB	19	600	46	26	3	7	49	41	259	14	6	.207/.269/.304	58	.374	-1.7	2B -5, SS -1	-2.0

Comparables: Sherten Apostel, Lane Thomas, Trevor Story

A Baby Ranger with a lot of hype, Moss continues to be one to watch. His speed is the lead, but improved defense and contact are helping fill out the profile. The second base/shortstop combo is one of many infielder-with-upside types who populate the lowest levels of the system.

Jonathan Ornelas 3B   Born: 05/26/00   Age: 21   Bats: R   Throws: R   Height: 6'1"   Weight: 178   Origin: Round 3, 2018 Draft (#91 overall)

YEAR	TEAM	LVL	AGE	PA	R	2B	3B	HR	RBI	BB	K	SB	CS	AVG/OBP/SLG	DRC+	BABIP	BRR	FRAA	WARP
2018	RAN	ROK	18	202	34	10	4	3	28	25	41	15	4	.298/.386/.456		.366			
2019	HIC	LO-A	19	472	61	24	3	6	38	42	103	13	4	.257/.333/.373	116	.322	-1.7	SS(63) -4.0, 2B(34) -0.3, LF(10) -1.1	1.7
2021 FS	TEX	MLB	21	600	49	26	3	8	52	37	186	11	4	.221/.277/.328	65	.317	1.5	SS -5, 2B 0	-1.3

Comparables: Daniel Robertson, Tim Beckham, Brad Harman

The 21-year-old infielder also has a lot of buzz right now. Ornelas faded down the stretch in 2019, a season in which he got the most playing time of his career. As he matures, his body is filling out particularly in his upper half. In a system overloaded with potential standout infielders, Ornelas is one of the most intriguing prospects in that group and like many of them, can handle himself at three different spots on the dirt.

Ronny Henriquez RHP   Born: 06/20/00   Age: 21   Bats: R   Throws: R   Height: 5'10"   Weight: 155   Origin: International Free Agent, 2017

YEAR	TEAM	LVL	AGE	W	L	SV	G	GS	IP	H	HR	BB/9	K/9	K	GB%	BABIP	WHIP	ERA	DRA-	WARP
2018	DSL RAN2	ROK	18	5	0	0	11	11	58	37	2	1.2	12.3	79	47.7%	.273	0.78	1.55		
2019	HIC	LO-A	19	6	6	0	21	19	82	91	6	3.0	10.8	98	36.8%	.383	1.44	4.50	121	-0.7
2021 FS	TEX	MLB	21	2	2	0	57	0	50	44	7	3.6	9.0	50	37.3%	.279	1.29	3.88	96	0.2

Comparables: Pedro Avila, José Álvarez, Luis Severino

A diminutive dealer, Henriquez is a fastball first pitcher who attacks hitters. Over the last year, Henriquez improved on his changeup while working at the Texas spring training complex. The 20-year-old will need more seasoning, with only 19 starts above the Dominican Summer League. Henriquez does have a high ceiling, low floor profile that could provide an exciting reliever if starting doesn't work out.

MLB arms, but probably relievers

Hans Crouse RHP   Born: 09/15/98   Age: 22   Bats: L   Throws: R   Height: 6'4"   Weight: 180   Origin: Round 2, 2017 Draft (#66 overall)

YEAR	TEAM	LVL	AGE	W	L	SV	G	GS	IP	H	HR	BB/9	K/9	K	GB%	BABIP	WHIP	ERA	DRA-	WARP
2018	SPO	SS	19	5	1	0	8	8	38	25	2	2.6	11.1	47	35.5%	.253	0.95	2.37	91	0.4
2018	HIC	LO-A	19	0	2	0	5	5	16²	18	1	4.3	8.1	15	38.5%	.340	1.56	2.70	135	-0.2
2019	HIC	LO-A	20	6	1	0	19	19	87²	86	12	2.0	7.7	75	31.3%	.295	1.20	4.41	105	0.1
2021 FS	TEX	MLB	22	2	3	0	57	0	50	50	8	4.1	8.0	44	32.6%	.292	1.46	5.05	118	-0.4

Comparables: Joe Ross, Robert Gsellman, Felix Doubront

A lot of factors played into Crouse going from Top Ten stalwart to others receiving vote(s). One was Crouse missed some time near the end of a season that was already going to have limited developmental opportunities. Another is that his home is looking more likely to be the bullpen. Crouse has a military grade arm, but as he continues his journey, it appears that his future could likely resemble that of current reliever Jonathan Hernandez. If that was the case, Texas should still be pleased.

Owen White RHP Born: 08/09/99 Age: 21 Bats: R Throws: R Height: 6'3" Weight: 170 Origin: Round 2, 2018 Draft (#55 overall)

The former second-round pick had Tommy John surgery in 2019, so his future is quite nebulous. That said, White appears ready to go for whatever 2021 will look like. When he does, White will bring a good fastball and slider to the mix. He could be destined for Low-A Down East; that was his likely first stop pre-surgery.

The Bonus Babies

Maximo Acosta SS Born: 10/29/02 Age: 18 Bats: R Throws: R Height: 6'1" Weight: 170 Origin: International Free Agent, 2019

One of a pair of mysteriously intriguing prospects in Texas' system along, Acosta got some field time stateside at the most recent instructional league in Arizona. The 18-year-old looked like a teenager with minimal pro experience. The defense showed positive signs; Acosta is a plus athlete who will build on that profile with age and body maturation. The bat still has a way to go as well, with the more fine skills like pitch recognition still in development.

Bayron Lora RF Born: 09/29/02 Age: 18 Bats: R Throws: R Height: 6'3" Weight: 190 Origin: International Free Agent, 2019

Lora, meanwhile, had a less-than-favorable appearance in Arizona. The bat looked overmatched and lacked the power expected form a 6-foot-5 outfielder. The defensive profile is still a mystery, as is much of what Lora brings to the table. That's not necessarily a warning bell, but more of a caution sign. Young players need time, and in the case of Lora it's best to be patient and watch.

Top Talents 25 and Under (as of 4/1/2021):

1. Leody Taveras, OF
2. Josh Jung, 3B
3. Dane Dunning, RHP
4. Sam Huff, C
5. Cole Winn, RHP
6. Nate Lowe, 1B
7. Justin Foscue, IF
8. Anderson Tejeda, SS
9. Evan Carter, OF
10. Kyle Cody, RHP

Had the Rangers not traded for Nate Lowe, it's possible that they wouldn't have had any non-rookie make this list. With Kolby Allard bombing out as a starter, Jonathan Hernandez would've been the best candidate, and he's a reliever, even if he looks like he might be turning into a good one.

But they did trade for Lowe, and he's pretty clearly worthy ranking somewhere on the 25U. The Rays never gave him a clean opportunity at a full-time job, and he hasn't been stellar in the majors in limited chances. He's a three true outcomes slugger and likely to be a useful power bat for at least the rest of his 20s.

Toronto Blue Jays

The State of the System:

There's still some potential impact talent at the top, but less depth than recent editions.

The Top Ten:

———————————— ★ ★ ★ *2021 Top 101 Prospect* **#22** ★ ★ ★ ————————————

1 **Austin Martin** **SS**   OFP: 60   ETA: 2022
Born: 03/23/99   Age: 22   Bats: R   Throws: R   Height: 6'0"   Weight: 185   Origin: Round 1, 2020 Draft (#5 overall)

The Report: A Swiss Army knife, a jack of all trades, he's basically the Dos Equis guy minus the hyperbolic backstory. Heading into the 2020 college season it appeared to be a two-horse race for the first overall pick between Martin and the eventual selection Spencer Torkelson. The previous year had put Martin squarely on track for the top of the draft: He hit for more power, got on base at a nearly 50 percent clip, was aggressive on the basepaths, and played all over the field defensively. It actually made it difficult when scouting him, knowing he was playing in so many different spots in the field and in the order to accommodate his team that you had to wonder if he was being knee-capped from displaying his true potential.

His spring season started exceptionally well. He rarely swung and missed, let alone struck out. It's a bit of a throwback swing; he keeps his hands low and relaxed at load and allows his body to fire off in sequence a short stride to waist bend that creates natural loft on his swing plane. Bat speed, barrel control, pitch recognition, he's got it all. The funny part about his role at Vanderbilt is that it will likely continue with the Jays, who could plug him in alongside other players who lack the same versatility and athleticism.

Development Track: It remains entirely possible that with young stars already entrenched on the major league roster that Martin could be aggressively pushed to join them while a contention window opens. So long as he handles each level of pitching with nary a challenge, his only real area of focus to develop is wherever he ends up positionally. Maybe the Jays want to keep him flexible, in which case, it's a fluid exercise interdependent of what his best position might be, and how fast the fast-track becomes wholly reliant on how much he hits.

Variance: High. We think he's going to hit, but not unlike Royce Lewis, there are some moving parts to the swing that could be tough to break if there are any hiccups. Without the hit tool and at least average power numbers, he drops to a quality utilityman.

J.P. Breen's Fantasy Take: I'm obviously no scout, but the above description (and pre-draft scouting reports) make Martin sound like an early-career Anthony Rendon—a guy who could play across the infield, hitting .270-.290 with 20 homers and 15 steals. If the average becomes late-career Rendon or his speed allows him to steal 20-plus bases, we're talking a potential elite five-category fantasy producer. He's a top-20 dynasty prospect for me.

★ ★ ★ *2021 Top 101 Prospect* **#35** ★ ★ ★

2 Nate Pearson   RHP

OFP: 60   ETA: Debuted in 2020

Born: 08/20/96   Age: 24   Bats: R   Throws: R   Height: 6'6"   Weight: 250   Origin: Round 1, 2017 Draft (#28 overall)

YEAR	TEAM	LVL	AGE	W	L	SV	G	GS	IP	H	HR	BB/9	K/9	K	GB%	BABIP	WHIP	ERA	DRA-	WARP
2018	DUN	HI-A	21	0	1	0	1	1	1²	5	1	0.0	5.4	1	44.4%	.500	3.00	10.80	40	0.1
2019	DUN	HI-A	22	3	0	0	6	6	21	10	2	1.3	15.0	35	35.1%	.229	0.62	0.86	32	0.9
2019	NH	AA	22	1	4	0	16	16	62²	41	4	3.0	9.9	69	38.8%	.250	0.99	2.59	65	1.4
2019	BUF	AAA	22	1	0	0	3	3	18	12	2	1.5	7.5	15	44.0%	.208	0.83	3.00	74	0.5
2020	TOR	MLB	23	1	0	0	5	4	18	14	5	6.5	8.0	16	38.5%	.191	1.50	6.00	137	-0.2
2021 FS	TOR	MLB	24	9	9	0	26	26	150	137	25	4.4	9.4	157	38.5%	.287	1.41	4.63	103	0.8
2021 DC	TOR	MLB	24	7	8	0	24	24	121	111	20	4.4	9.4	126	38.5%	.287	1.41	4.63	103	1.1

Comparables: Mitch Keller, Marco Gonzales, Tyler Mahle

The Report: Pearson is one of the hardest throwing starting pitchers in baseball, sitting in the upper-90s much of the time and touching triple-digits often; he once hit 104 in the Arizona Fall League Fall Stars Game. He pairs that fastball velocity with a vicious hard slider that is already plus and flashing plus-plus. There aren't many pitch combinations from a starter that good, and Pearson also brings a curveball and changeup as usable additional offerings. His command is decent, although he does sometimes need to dial the velocity back to reach it, and his mechanics are reasonably smooth given the quality of his stuff. Injuries have been a recurring theme for him, dating back to a screw inserted into his elbow in high school, and including a broken pitching arm he suffered when a hard comebacker hit him in 2018.

Development Track: Toronto called Pearson up literally on the exact day they could claw back a year of his service time in July. His stuff was a little less loud and his command a little worse than we expected, and then he ended up missing more than a month with elbow/flexor problems. He came back very late in the season in a relief role, and the velocity ticked back up again airing it out. That might just be where this all ends up, although it won't be for lack of talent.

Variance: High. He's only pitched in one full season (2019) without getting hurt.

J.P. Breen's Fantasy Take: Pearson remains an elite dynasty pitching prospect. He missed fewer bats than expected—particularly in the zone compared to the rest of the league—but it's hard to separate his diminished stuff from his injury troubles. While Pearson has considerable variance in terms of his ultimate role, he should be a top-end arm, whether that's in the rotation or the bullpen. What separates Pearson from someone like A.J. Puk is that Puk suffered a dreaded shoulder injury. Pearson remains a top-20 dynasty prospect and a top-150 overall dynasty player.

★ ★ ★ *2021 Top 101 Prospect* **#41** ★ ★ ★

3 Jordan Groshans   SS

OFP: 60   ETA: 2022/2023

Born: 11/10/99   Age: 21   Bats: R   Throws: R   Height: 6'3"   Weight: 205   Origin: Round 1, 2018 Draft (#12 overall)

YEAR	TEAM	LVL	AGE	PA	R	2B	3B	HR	RBI	BB	K	SB	CS	AVG/OBP/SLG	DRC+	BABIP	BRR	FRAA	WARP
2018	BLU	ROK	18	48	4	1	0	1	4	2	8	0	0	.182/.229/.273		.194			
2018	BLU	ROK	18	159	17	12	0	4	39	13	29	0	0	.331/.390/.500		.387			
2019	LAN	LO-A	19	96	12	6	0	2	13	13	21	1	1	.337/.427/.482	169	.433	-0.4	SS(20) -1.8	0.9
2021 FS	TOR	MLB	21	600	51	26	2	10	55	38	181	1	0	.224/.279/.335	69	.313	-0.6	SS 1, 3B 0	-0.7

Comparables: Carter Kieboom, Corey Seager, Rowdy Tellez

The Report: Groshans was one of the early breakouts of the 2019 campaign. He showed off a plus hit/plus power combination with very high polish for a prep hitter less than a year out from the draft. Then he went down with a foot injury about a month in. After some stops and starts, he never did find his way back to the field. We saw enough to view him as a potential middle-of-the-order bat anyway. Defensively, he's currently a shortstop, but we think he probably profiles best at third base over the long haul.

Development Track: Groshans was at the alternate site last summer getting much-needed reps. It's not quite a substitute for in-game work, and he absolutely needs those reps after missing most of 2019, but he was healthy and getting good work in.

Variance: High. The foot issues are hopefully in the past, but we still need to see in-game production over a full campaign (or as close to it as we'll get in 2021).

J.P. Breen's Fantasy Take: Groshans's combination of hit and power reminds me of Alex Kirilloff from a couple of years ago, except Groshans has more speed and scouts feel more confident in his long-term power production. The foot injury is scary, no doubt, but the 21-year-old is one of the most well-rounded impact hitting prospects in the minors. He's a top-50 guy in all formats.

★ ★ ★ *2021 Top 101 Prospect* **#101** ★ ★ ★

4 Alejandro Kirk C OFP: 55 ETA: Debuted in 2020

Born: 11/06/98 Age: 22 Bats: R Throws: R Height: 5'8" Weight: 265 Origin: International Free Agent, 2016

YEAR	TEAM	LVL	AGE	PA	R	2B	3B	HR	RBI	BB	K	SB	CS	AVG/OBP/SLG	DRC+	BABIP	BRR	FRAA	WARP
2018	BLU	ROK	19	244	31	10	1	10	57	33	21	2	0	.354/.443/.558		.354			
2019	LAN	LO-A	20	96	15	6	1	3	8	18	8	1	0	.299/.427/.519	162	.299	0.9	C(17) 0.1	1.1
2019	DUN	HI-A	20	276	26	25	0	4	36	38	31	2	0	.288/.395/.446	153	.317	-3.4	C(68) 0.8	2.4
2020	TOR	MLB	21	25	4	2	0	1	3	1	4	0	0	.375/.400/.583	96	.421	-0.3	C(7) -0.1	0.0
2021 FS	TOR	MLB	22	600	64	30	2	13	65	53	105	0	0	.257/.329/.395	100	.297	-0.3	C -4	2.1
2021 DC	TOR	MLB	22	134	14	6	0	3	14	12	23	0	0	.257/.329/.395	100	.297	-0.1	C -1	0.3

Comparables: Luis Campusano, Logan Morrison, Chance Sisco

The Report: Kirk's future is all about his hit tool and on-base abilities. He has plus-plus bat-to-ball skills coming out of a compact, direct swing. He pairs that with an excellent plate approach and pitch recognition, and indeed he walked more than he struck out at every minor-league level. We have projected him to this point with the hit tool dragging along the power; he hits the ball hard but without much loft in his swing to get it in the air, with a line-drive oriented approach. If he can start hitting it in the air more, there's a chance some more game power shows up.

Defensively, he's getting there. If you like your catcher frames short and stout, Kirk is the epitome of that. His arm is above-average and his receiving is improving. It was a big vote of confidence in his glove to get playing time behind the plate this year, and we think he's likely to stay at the position.

Development Track: Kirk was called up and got a bit of playing time down the stretch, even making a start at DH in the playoffs. He looked just fine as a 21-year-old catcher with only 151 professional games and none above A-ball, smashing the ball around in a handful of at-bats. That the Blue Jays even felt comfortable bringing him up into the playoff picture with that little experience is an extremely positive sign.

Variance: Medium. We're pretty confident he'll hit some and be able to catch at least part-time, so he has a high floor, but he is a young catcher.

J.P. Breen's Fantasy Take: A couple of years ago, dynasty owners everywhere drooled over the prospect of Willians Astudillo getting regular big-league at-bats. Although it never happened, Kirk could be the next best thing. If he can hit .280 with 10 homers in a good lineup, Kirk could be a top-10 fantasy catcher. He has the bat to do that, too. Fun fact: Only Wilson Ramos hit .280-plus with double-digit home runs among catchers in 2019.

5 Orelvis Martinez SS OFP: 55 ETA: 2023

Born: 11/19/01 Age: 19 Bats: R Throws: R Height: 6'1" Weight: 188 Origin: International Free Agent, 2018

YEAR	TEAM	LVL	AGE	PA	R	2B	3B	HR	RBI	BB	K	SB	CS	AVG/OBP/SLG	DRC+	BABIP	BRR	FRAA	WARP
2019	BLU	ROK	17	163	20	8	5	7	32	14	29	2	0	.275/.352/.549		.296			
2021 FS	TOR	MLB	19	600	43	26	4	7	48	29	187	3	0	.201/.247/.302	49	.287	3.1	SS -3, 3B -1	-2.2

Comparables: Anderson Tejeda, Yu Chang, Corey Seager

The Report: Martinez received the highest bonus of the Jays' J2 class in 2018 and put on a strong debut in 2019 that had the organization buzzing about 2020. Well it didn't really happen for him of course, but the organization still values Martinez very highly. He came to instructs with more physical strength, which was scary given that he was already posting high exit velos as a 17-year-old. This may mean he moves off short sooner rather than later, but the bat will play regardless. The logical position is third base given his plus arm strength and good instincts, as well as his physical stature.

Development Track: 2020 was the year Martinez was set to make his full-season debut, and we will have to wait until this year to see how it looks against better arms. He will play all of 2021 at 19 years old, so age isn't a detriment currently. We need to see him against better sequencing and for further development defensively.

Variance: High, but lower than last year? He is still a teenage prospect who hasn't faced competition outside the complex. The physical gains at such a young age are a concern, as it could mean some loss in athleticism.

J.P. Breen's Fantasy Take: Martinez is a bit less exciting as a dynasty prospect at third base, but it's still potential above-average power with a solid average. He's comfortably a top-100 dynasty prospect. If the power production is loud in full-season ball, or if he carries an elite average, his dynasty ranking might take a step forward. The fact that he won't steal double-digit bases, though, limits his ultimate upside.

6 Simeon Woods Richardson RHP   OFP: 55   ETA: Late 2021/Early 2022

Born: 09/27/00   Age: 20   Bats: R   Throws: R   Height: 6'3"   Weight: 210   Origin: Round 2, 2018 Draft (#48 overall)

YEAR	TEAM	LVL	AGE	W	L	SV	G	GS	IP	H	HR	BB/9	K/9	K	GB%	BABIP	WHIP	ERA	DRA-	WARP
2018	MTS	ROK	17	1	0	1	5	2	11¹	9	0	3.2	11.9	15	50.0%	.321	1.15	0.00		
2018	KNG	ROK	17	0	0	0	2	2	6	6	1	0.0	16.5	11	38.5%	.417	1.00	4.50		
2019	COL	LO-A	18	3	8	0	20	20	78¹	78	5	2.0	11.1	97	49.5%	.358	1.21	4.25	103	0.1
2019	DUN	HI-A	18	3	2	0	6	6	28¹	18	1	2.2	9.2	29	33.8%	.246	0.88	2.54	62	0.7
2021 FS	TOR	MLB	20	2	2	0	57	0	50	44	7	3.4	8.8	48	41.6%	.278	1.27	3.75	96	0.2

Comparables: Noah Syndergaard, Kolby Allard, Julio Urías

The Report: Woods Richardson fired himself off draft boards in 2018 after a velocity bump had him touching the upper-90s. He settled into the low-90s as a pro starter, reaching back for more at times, but the fastball had good late life and despite an uptempo delivery with some effort, Woods Richardson showed excellent body control and repeatability of the mechanics. Thus, strike-throwing has never really been a problem. His out pitch has been a power 12-6, high spin breaker, although he has at times struggled to command it as well as the fastball. It has the most likely plus outcome in the arsenal though. Woods Richardson replicates his arm speed well on the change but the pitch has generally had inconsistent shape and results.

Development Track: Woods Richardson added a slider at the alternate site, rounding out a full four-pitch mix. The fastball velocity was still more in an average band, and the longer he goes without tapping into that extra gear, the more likely the fastball just is what it is. It's enough fastball to start, and he's had no issues getting A-ball hitters out. The upper minors in 2021 will be the last test for the profile.

Variance: Medium. Woods Richardson has never consistently found his draft year pop-up velocity in the pros. He's built a more well-rounded arsenal in the interim, but there might not be that late inning relief fallback without the mid-90s heat. As a starter it's more a collection of average -> above-average stuff which might limit the upside.

J.P. Breen's Fantasy Take: Woods Richardson's dynasty stock remains a bit higher than his current scouting reports justify. Dynasty owners remember his 2018 breakout and won't let it go. At this point, though, the right-hander looks more like a solid mid-rotation starter without impressive strikeout numbers. Maybe the secondary stuff can carry him to SP3 territory. For now, though, you can treat him a bit like, say, Dane Dunning.

7 C.J. Van Eyk   OFP: 50   ETA: 2023

Born: 09/15/98   Age: 22   Bats: R   Throws: R   Height: 6'1"   Weight: 198   Origin: Round 2, 2020 Draft (#42 overall)

The Report: At a baseball powerhouse like Florida State, you expect young players to contribute right away, and then watch further maturation happen right in front of you for two or three years. In the case of Van Eyk, you saw flashes of the potential but always waited for the big breakout that never quite came. He's very much the same pitcher now that he was as a freshman, utilizing a low-to-mid-90s fastball to go along with a hard breaking downer curveball. The strikeouts have never been an issue, it's the command that has been suspect. The delivery could use some tightening up, as it lacks consistency and is often the source of the command issues.

Development Track: Beyond what can be done to help repeat his delivery more regularly, the changeup is mostly a show-me pitch with some arm-side fade that is telegraphed with his arm action. Development of that third pitch would help quell some of the reliever risk fears. Additionally, there's room on the frame to add a few extra pounds which could not only help with an extra tick of velocity, but help some of the core delivery problems as well.

Variance: Medium. After watching essentially the same product for three years, we have to believe he mostly is who he is.

J.P. Breen's Fantasy Take: Potential back-end starters who have issues with both their command and their third pitch are absolutely not my jam. Van Eyk isn't a top-400 dynasty prospect and can be safely avoided in all but the most ludicrous of formats.

8   Alek Manoah   RHP   OFP: 50   ETA: 2023

Born: 01/09/98   Age: 23   Bats: R   Throws: R   Height: 6'6"   Weight: 260   Origin: Round 1, 2019 Draft (#11 overall)

YEAR	TEAM	LVL	AGE	W	L	SV	G	GS	IP	H	HR	BB/9	K/9	K	GB%	BABIP	WHIP	ERA	DRA-	WARP
2019	VAN	SS	21	0	1	0	6	6	17	13	1	2.6	14.3	27	35.3%	.364	1.06	2.65	64	0.4
2021 FS	TOR	MLB	23	2	3	0	57	0	50	47	8	5.0	9.2	51	34.7%	.294	1.51	5.14	120	-0.4

Comparables: Mitch Keller, Humberto Mejía, David Peterson

The Report: Mostly used as a reliever in his first two years in college, it took a breakout summer at the Cape Cod League, followed by a monster draft year at West Virginia, to convince scouts Manoah was worth the first-round grade as a future starter. The lively fastball and wicked slider combo can be very tough pitches to handle as he attacks the zone early and then tries to get chases out of it. The changeup is still M.I.A. which would help alleviate some of the platoon issues he'd face in a major league rotation. However, the main concern regarding his days as a starter possibly being numbered are reports from camp that had his velocity down more in the low 90s.

Development Track: He's always had a notoriously bad body, listed at 260 pounds it isn't weight carried well, showing in his delivery. There's plenty of effort needed to generate the kinetic energy used to drive down the mound, so any further deterioration of his physique will negatively impact all parts of his game. 2020 was a weird year for pitchers though, so perhaps he bounces back with a more normal minor league season.

Variance: Very High. Things are going in the wrong direction for Manoah. He's young and there is still plenty of time to turn it around, but the relief risk has been there since college.

J.P. Breen's Fantasy Take: This might be the first pitching prospect to reportedly have their stuff regress in 2020. The relief risk, the body risk, and the disappointing camp reports all should have him tumbling out of our top-400 dynasty lists. No wonder folks in our experts leagues have been trying to float Manoah on the trade block.

9   Gabriel Moreno   C   OFP: 50   ETA: 2022 or 2023

Born: 02/14/00   Age: 21   Bats: R   Throws: R   Height: 5'11"   Weight: 160   Origin: International Free Agent, 2016

YEAR	TEAM	LVL	AGE	PA	R	2B	3B	HR	RBI	BB	K	SB	CS	AVG/OBP/SLG	DRC+	BABIP	BRR	FRAA	WARP
2018	BLU	ROK	18	66	10	5	0	2	14	3	13	1	0	.279/.303/.459		.312			
2018	BLU	ROK	18	101	14	12	2	2	22	4	7	1	1	.413/.455/.652		.429			
2019	LAN	LO-A	19	341	47	17	5	12	52	22	38	7	1	.280/.337/.485	130	.282	0.4	C(54) 1.0	2.5
2021 FS	TOR	MLB	21	600	54	26	3	14	63	24	113	7	2	.239/.276/.378	78	.274	1.8	C 0	0.9

Comparables: Chance Sisco, John Ryan Murphy, Manuel Margot

The Report: Moreno was sent to the Midwest League as a 19-year-old catcher and more than held his own. It's a hit-over-power profile at present with good bat control, but he already shows an ability to sting the ball despite minimal weight transfer, and he should grow into more strength on what is presently a relatively slight frame for a catcher. The profile is also bat-first as Moreno is inexperienced behind the plate and will need to work on his receiving. He will also need to show he can handle the rigors of a full catching workload up the ladder.

Development Track: Despite the need for extra catchers at any alternate site, Toronto didn't send Moreno to their alternate site in Rochester. I wouldn't read too much into his absence given the relatively stable Blue Jays catching situation and he did get instructs time. Still, that likely keeps him on a relatively conservative time table, with an Advanced-A assignment on tap for 2021 in all likelihood.

Variance: High. There's a fair bit of positive variance here. Moreno could improve enough defensively to where the above-average offensive projection makes him a good starter. He could add enough power that you live with fringy defense. But catchers are weird, and we aren't quite convinced he's a catcher yet.

J.P. Breen's Fantasy Take: Moreno is more interesting in real life than in fantasy baseball. Without monster power or a batting average that annually pushes .290, he doesn't profile as someone who could potentially be a top-10 fantasy catcher in the big leagues. Since that's the case, Moreno would have to be on the cusp of the majors to be worth rostering in most dynasty formats. More interesting low-level catching prospects exist for fantasy purposes, if that's your thing.

10   T.J. Zeuch   RHP   OFP: 50   ETA: Debuted in 2019

Born: 08/01/95   Age: 25   Bats: R   Throws: R   Height: 6'7"   Weight: 245   Origin: Round 1, 2016 Draft (#21 overall)

YEAR	TEAM	LVL	AGE	W	L	SV	G	GS	IP	H	HR	BB/9	K/9	K	GB%	BABIP	WHIP	ERA	DRA-	WARP
2018	DUN	HI-A	22	3	3	0	6	6	36¹	34	4	2.2	5.9	24	61.4%	.275	1.18	3.47	121	-0.2
2018	NH	AA	22	9	5	0	21	21	120	120	7	2.3	6.1	81	55.2%	.299	1.26	3.08	85	1.9
2019	DUN	HI-A	23	0	0	0	2	2	8²	7	0	2.1	12.5	12	59.1%	.318	1.04	4.15	44	0.3
2019	BUF	AAA	23	4	3	0	13	13	78	70	6	3.7	4.5	39	57.8%	.256	1.31	3.69	81	2.1
2019	TOR	MLB	23	1	2	0	5	3	22²	22	2	4.4	7.9	20	48.5%	.303	1.46	4.76	108	0.1
2020	TOR	MLB	24	1	0	0	3	1	11¹	9	1	3.2	2.4	3	62.5%	.205	1.15	1.59	100	0.1
2021 FS	TOR	MLB	25	3	4	0	57	0	50	53	7	3.8	6.2	34	53.1%	.292	1.50	5.34	117	-0.4
2021 DC	TOR	MLB	25	3	4	0	40	6	66	70	10	3.8	6.2	45	53.1%	.292	1.50	5.34	117	-0.1

Comparables: Andrew Miller, Elieser Hernandez, Brandon Woodruff

The Report: I said last year that Zeuch throws a "bushel of average or slightly-above pitches," and that's still what we've got here. Pitch Info has already picked up six distinct offerings—four-seam fastball, sinker, cutter, slider, changeup, and curveball—over his 34 MLB innings. The sinker is the best of them, and it's the above-average one, coming in mostly in the low-90s with quality movement and a good angle given his height. All of the offspeeds are fine, but there's no swing-and-miss pitch here, so there's way less upside than you'd think or hope for from a first-round pitcher. He has advanced pitchability and command.

Development Track: It's a bit surprising that Zeuch wasn't up earlier in the season. The Blue Jays called upon him in mid-September, and he had a couple nice long relief appearances. He got a start in the last week of the season and threw five shutout innings without registering a strikeout or walk. His stuff was pretty much the same as past reports.

Variance: Low. Zeuch is what he is.

J.P. Breen's Fantasy Take: Zeuch is useful enough as a real-life big leaguer, but he's not worth rostering in dynasty leagues. He walks too many guys and doesn't miss enough bats to be interesting.

The Prospects You Meet Outside The Top Ten

Prospects to dream on a little

Leonardo Jimenez   2B   Born: 05/17/01   Age: 20   Bats: R   Throws: R   Height: 5'11"   Weight: 160   Origin: International Free Agent, 2017

YEAR	TEAM	LVL	AGE	PA	R	2B	3B	HR	RBI	BB	K	SB	CS	AVG/OBP/SLG	DRC+	BABIP	BRR	FRAA	WARP
2018	BLU	ROK	17	150	13	8	2	0	19	16	17	0	0	.250/.333/.341		.284			
2019	BLU	ROK+	18	245	34	13	2	0	22	21	42	2	1	.298/.377/.377		.368			
2021 FS	TOR	MLB	20	600	49	26	3	8	53	34	157	1	0	.226/.277/.332	68	.299	1.0	2B -1, SS 0	-0.4

Comparables: Jahmai Jones, Ramón Flores, Maikel Franco

Signed out of Panama in 2017, Jimenez is one of the best defenders in the organization at SS. He has quality hands with a smooth easy arm that rates as above-average. Not a burner but he shows a quick first step and has the instincts one looks for at short. He hasn't shown much power in-game, but came to instructs with more physicality, including hitting a home run (which he has yet to do in an official game). The glove is the noteworthy item here, but with an improving offensive skill set he can become a hidden gem in the org.

Miguel Hiraldo 3B Born: 09/05/00 Age: 20 Bats: R Throws: R Height: 5'11" Weight: 170 Origin: International Free Agent, 2017

YEAR	TEAM	LVL	AGE	PA	R	2B	3B	HR	RBI	BB	K	SB	CS	AVG/OBP/SLG	DRC+	BABIP	BRR	FRAA	WARP
2018	DSL BLJ	ROK	17	239	41	18	3	2	33	23	30	15	6	.313/.381/.453		.355			
2018	BLU	ROK	17	40	3	4	0	0	3	1	12	3	0	.231/.250/.333		.333			
2019	BLU	ROK+	18	256	43	20	1	7	37	14	36	11	3	.300/.348/.481		.328			
2019	LAN	LO-A	18	4	0	0	1	0	0	0	0	0	0	.250/.250/.750	79	.250	0.0	2B(1) 0.0	0.0
2021 FS	TOR	MLB	20	600	45	27	2	7	51	27	162	18	6	.218/.258/.319	55	.291	2.5	SS 3, 3B 0	-1.1

Comparables: J.P. Crawford, Estevan Florial, Ramón Flores

A bat-first infielder, Hiraldo has one of the more notable hit/power combo in the organization, which is what is going to have to carry him going forward. The bat is loud but can be exploited as he is quite pull happy and can loop his hands while loading. But pitcher-beware: when Hiraldo connects it often goes a long way. Hiraldo has filled out more now and has always struggled with his lateral range, so he won't be a shortstop for long and projects as a keystone player.

Eric Pardinho RHP Born: 01/05/01 Age: 20 Bats: R Throws: R Height: 5'10" Weight: 155 Origin: International Free Agent, 2017

YEAR	TEAM	LVL	AGE	W	L	SV	G	GS	IP	H	HR	BB/9	K/9	K	GB%	BABIP	WHIP	ERA	DRA-	WARP
2018	BLU	ROK	17	4	3	0	11	11	50	37	5	2.9	11.5	64	45.1%	.274	1.06	2.88		
2019	LAN	LO-A	18	1	1	0	7	7	33²	29	1	3.5	8.0	30	44.1%	.304	1.25	2.41	96	0.2
2021 FS	TOR	MLB	20	2	3	0	57	0	50	47	7	5.2	8.7	48	39.2%	.288	1.53	5.00	117	-0.3

Comparables: Elvis Luciano, Julio Teheran, Kolby Allard

Pardinho starred for Team Brazil in the 2016 WBC qualifiers as a 15-year-old, and that made him pretty famous for a teenage prospect. He signed for $1.4 million the following summer, and at the beginning of his pro career he was extremely advanced and on the fringes of Top 101 prospect contention; he didn't actually make it owing to his limited projection. Unfortunately, he started dealing with elbow problems in 2019 and had Tommy John surgery last spring. At his best he's got a fastball he can command in the low-to-mid-90s and a plus curve, but we need to see him throw a full season before we're going to be back in substantially.

MLB arms, but probably relievers

Jackson Rees RHP Born: 07/30/94 Age: 26 Bats: R Throws: R Height: 6'4" Weight: 210 Origin: Undrafted Free Agent, 2018

YEAR	TEAM	LVL	AGE	W	L	SV	G	GS	IP	H	HR	BB/9	K/9	K	GB%	BABIP	WHIP	ERA	DRA-	WARP
2018	BLU	ROK	23	2	1	0	8	0	9²	12	1	1.9	10.2	11	51.7%	.393	1.45	5.59		
2018	BLU	ROK	23	0	1	0	8	0	11²	13	1	3.9	9.3	12	39.5%	.324	1.54	4.63		
2019	LAN	LO-A	24	2	0	2	14	0	25¹	13	0	1.4	15.6	44	65.9%	.295	0.67	0.36	36	0.9
2019	DUN	HI-A	24	3	2	7	25	0	36¹	27	1	2.7	10.9	44	59.1%	.299	1.05	0.99	72	0.5
2021 FS	TOR	MLB	26	2	2	0	57	0	50	43	7	3.9	9.9	54	48.9%	.285	1.30	3.87	98	0.2

Comparables: Kodi Whitley, Andrew McKirahan, Paul Sewald

Rees struggled with effectiveness and injuries as an amateur, signing to no fanfare for $1K as an UDFA. I mentioned him as an interesting pop-up arm in 2019 spring training, and he popped up for sure. He finished the year with over 12 Ks per 9, a 0.73 ERA, and earned a spot in the Arizona Fall League. Toronto, recognizing his size, moved his arm slot higher and had him pitching in shorter stints out of the bullpen, which increased his velocity. He is now 95-96 with hard cut and deception, as well as featuring a plus slider that has quality vertical depth. At 26, and turning 27 in July, Rees will be on the fastrack as long as he keeps getting outs.

MLB bats, but less upside than you'd like

Kevin Smith **SS** Born: 07/04/96 Age: 25 Bats: R Throws: R Height: 6'0" Weight: 190 Origin: Round 4, 2017 Draft (#129 overall)

YEAR	TEAM	LVL	AGE	PA	R	2B	3B	HR	RBI	BB	K	SB	CS	AVG/OBP/SLG	DRC+	BABIP	BRR	FRAA	WARP
2018	LAN	LO-A	21	204	36	23	4	7	44	17	33	12	1	.355/.407/.639	189	.397	3.1	SS(24) 1.7, 3B(21) 0.7	3.2
2018	DUN	HI-A	21	371	57	8	2	18	49	23	88	17	5	.274/.332/.468	125	.319	4.6	SS(63) 6.9, 2B(13) 1.0, 3B(6) -0.2	3.0
2019	NH	AA	22	468	49	22	2	19	61	29	151	11	6	.209/.263/.402	91	.269	1.4	SS(87) 0.4, 3B(18) -1.1, 2B(5) -0.9	1.5
2021 FS	TOR	MLB	24	600	59	26	2	21	70	33	205	11	3	.214/.263/.386	72	.295	2.3	SS 8, 3B 0	0.8

Comparables: Junior Lake, Orlando Calixte, Brad Harman

Smith dropped from the 101 long list in 2019, to barely on the Jays' list in 2020. A swing change intended to boost Smith's power instead sapped his whole stat line. He's been working his way back to the old swing in 2020, but fits better as a good bench infielder nowadays.

Top Talents 25 and Under (as of 4/1/2021):

1. Vladimir Guerrero Jr., 1B/3B
2. Bo Bichette, SS
3. Austin Martin, IF
4. Nate Pearson, RHP
5. Cavan Biggio, 2B/3B/OF
6. Jordan Groshans, SS
7. Danny Jansen, C
8. Alejandro Kirk, C
9. Orelvis Martinez, IF
10. CJ Van Eyk, RHP

Yeah, we know Vladdy hasn't actually gotten close to the 8 hit/8 power projection we put on him yet. He's played two MLB seasons, posted a better-than-average DRC+ in both, and he hasn't even turned 22 yet. Give it time.

Bo Bichette has also played two MLB seasons, has also posted a better-than-average DRC+ in both of his MLB seasons, and instead of bouncing between the corners has played an acceptable shortstop. He's a star too, even if he could do with trying to yank it to Mars a few less times a week, and he's closing the gap with Guerrero for the best son of a '90s star in the system.

Incredibly, those two actually have additional competition. Cavan Biggio, who was a much lesser prospect than either, has also posted a better than-average DRC+ in both of his MLB seasons—actually, the best offensive output of any of the three. He's a versatile defender who has some pop and walks a lot, and that's carried his production thus far.

Danny Jansen, our 2019 No. 89 prospect, only hit .183 in 2020, but that belies a 108 DRC+. He's not a star, and as far as I know he's not related to anyone I watched play baseball when I was a kid. But he's looking like a decent starting catching, even if the hit tool is lacking some, and there aren't a lot of those floating around.

Washington Nationals

The State of the System:
Flags fly forever, but that flag is a bit further in the rear view mirror now, and objects ahead aren't as close as they appear.

The Top Ten:

1 **Cade Cavalli** **RHP**   OFP: 60   ETA: 2023
Born: 08/14/98   Age: 22   Bats: R   Throws: R   Height: 6'4"   Weight: 226   Origin: Round 1, 2020 Draft (#22 overall)

The Report: The 2020 draft, for obvious reasons, was one of the most difficult ever to evaluate talent. From small sample sizes to no sample size in some cases, there would be risk no matter what strategy an org employed. The Nationals have been known to roll the dice in recent years when it comes to their first round selections, and rather than play it safe with the added uncertainty in 2020, they pressed on the gas once again with Cavalli. The boxy right hander brings the heat with easy mechanics that make his high-90s fastball look effortless. However, injuries have prevented him from pitching for long stretches, with his summer on the Collegiate National Team and superb spring giving glimpses of the elite stuff he brings to the mound. A nasty breaking ball that can be located in the zone or as a swing-and-miss chase pitch. It complements the heater well, as does a developing changeup.

Development Track: It's all about proving his case as a starter. Can he hold up over the course of a full season? And if not, how quickly is he moved as a reliever where his electric stuff could bolster an often suspect Nats bullpen? The health and reliever risks are real. On the other hand, if his most recent history is indicative of the true potential then you put aside those worries until they're actualized.

Variance: Very High. The difference between a top-half-of-the-rotation guy and high-leverage reliever is a significant gap. Both good on their own, with history suggesting the likelier scenario is the one with less stress on the arm.

J.P. Breen's Fantasy Take: While the value differential between a frontline starter and a high-leverage reliever is massive in real-life baseball, it's much smaller in fantasy. Dominant, high-strikeout relievers—whether they are amassing saves are not—have a home in today's fantasy environment. Unlike many of the potential high-leverage relief prospects that we've covered throughout these Top Ten lists, though, Cavalli has a chance to be an impact starter. The health risks keep him outside the top-200 dynasty prospects, but he's a top-25 guy in supplemental drafts this winter.

2 **Jackson Rutledge** **RHP**   OFP: 60   ETA: Late 2022/2023
Born: 04/01/99   Age: 22   Bats: R   Throws: R   Height: 6'8"   Weight: 250   Origin: Round 1, 2019 Draft (#17 overall)

YEAR	TEAM	LVL	AGE	W	L	SV	G	GS	IP	H	HR	BB/9	K/9	K	GB%	BABIP	WHIP	ERA	DRA-	WARP
2019	NAT	ROK	20	0	0	0	1	1	1	4	0	9.0	18.0	2	80.0%	.800	5.00	27.00		
2019	AUB	SS	20	0	0	0	3	3	9	4	2	3.0	6.0	6	41.7%	.091	0.78	3.00	73	0.2
2019	HAG	LO-A	20	2	0	0	6	6	27¹	14	0	3.6	10.2	31	44.4%	.222	0.91	2.30	70	0.6
2021 FS	WAS	MLB	22	2	3	0	57	0	50	48	8	5.7	8.1	44	40.5%	.286	1.60	5.48	126	-0.6

Comparables: Parker Markel, Mat Latos, Reynaldo López

The Report: Out of the gate, the 2019 first rounder hit the ground running, making it to Low-A Hagerstown after short stints in the Gulf Coast and New York-Penn Leagues. Rutledge pitched well with the Suns over six starts, compiling a 2.30 ERA and 31 strikeouts against 11 walks in 27 ⅓ innings. This past year, Rutledge worked on improving his mechanics to boost his command. His fastball—a plus-plus offering—can get as high as 99 with life up in the zone that makes it a swing-and-miss pitch on its own. Backing the heater is a mid-to-upper-80s slider that can also miss bats due to its late break.

Development Track: The slider is clearly his best secondary, so Rutledge worked on his curveball and changeup this past year with positive results. Honing his command and the development of a second go-to offspeed pitch will dictate Rutledge's time table and ultimate major league role, but there's a lot to like here if everything comes together.

Variance: High. The reports from the alternate site are encouraging, but not enough to lower the variance quite yet. Even though he is athletic on the mound, being 6-foot-8 can be worrisome from a mechanical and injury standpoint. More innings on the bump can alleviate that to some degree. There is also high-leverage reliever possibility with his fastball/slider combination if all else fails. But we're not close to that outcome yet.

J.P. Breen's Fantasy Take: Rutledge was one of my favorite pitchers from the 2019 draft class, so I understand that I'm higher on him than most dynasty analysts. Still, he's a potential No. 2 starter and has shown the ability to throw strikes—though maybe not good strikes yet. I'll take the alternate site improvement stories with a grain of salt, as I have all offseason, but I like high-upside arms who have a safe floor of being a potentially elite reliever. Rutledge is flirting with being a top-100 dynasty prospect.

3. Drew Mendoza 3B   OFP: 50   ETA: 2023
Born: 10/10/97 Age: 23 Bats: L Throws: R Height: 6'5" Weight: 230 Origin: Round 3, 2019 Draft (#94 overall)

YEAR	TEAM	LVL	AGE	PA	R	2B	3B	HR	RBI	BB	K	SB	CS	AVG/OBP/SLG	DRC+	BABIP	BRR	FRAA	WARP
2019	HAG	LO-A	21	239	23	12	0	4	25	34	57	3	0	.264/.377/.383	127	.348	0.8	1B(44) -3.5, 3B(6) 1.2	0.8
2021 FS	WAS	MLB	23	600	49	26	2	10	53	39	196	0	0	.202/.262/.316	59	.291	0.2	1B -6, 3B 1	-2.8

Comparables: Nate Lowe, Tyler Flowers, Ji-Man Choi

The Report: A graduate of Florida State with a Masters degree in three-true-outcomes, Mendoza is still a work in progress when it comes to just about every aspect of his game. He's always shown the potential for hitting the ball hard and over the fence, and over time he's tried everything from opening his stance to closing off, tinkering with hand locations, all in an effort to become a more complete hitter. An admirable quest, to say the least. He was fine as a third baseman in college with a short throwing motion, but he's a big man with limited range and the Nats seem content moving him over to first base without delay.

Development Track: The experimentation continued with reports from camp that he was working to be more aggressive in his approach, not letting too many pitches go by that he falls behind in the count. The fact he has shown an openness to work through so many ideas to better himself is a definite plus.

Variance: High. If he doesn't hit enough, if the TTO becomes two or less outcomes, there isn't much else there. Then again, something like .250/.350/.450 is assuredly possible.

J.P. Breen's Fantasy Take: A three-true-outcome profile at first base is rarely an impact profile. The .250/.350/.450 slash line mentioned above is basically what Christian Walker posted in 2019, which is usable but nothing special. Mendoza has to produce elite power numbers to become a Max Muncy or Matt Olson, who are both posting slugging percentages between .510 and .500. Scouting reports suggest that Mendoza has that kind of raw power, but we're nowhere close to seeing him tap into it in games. I don't have him in my personal top-400 dynasty prospects.

4. Tim Cate LHP   OFP: 50   ETA: Late 2021/Early 2022
Born: 09/30/97 Age: 23 Bats: L Throws: L Height: 6'0" Weight: 185 Origin: Round 2, 2018 Draft (#65 overall)

YEAR	TEAM	LVL	AGE	W	L	SV	G	GS	IP	H	HR	BB/9	K/9	K	GB%	BABIP	WHIP	ERA	DRA-	WARP
2018	AUB	SS	20	2	3	0	9	8	31	34	1	2.9	7.5	26	42.0%	.333	1.42	4.65	208	-1.6
2018	HAG	LO-A	20	0	3	0	4	4	21	23	4	2.6	8.1	19	41.8%	.306	1.38	5.57	140	-0.4
2019	HAG	LO-A	21	4	5	0	13	13	70¹	61	2	1.7	9.3	73	53.4%	.314	1.05	2.82	74	1.3
2019	FBG	HI-A	21	7	4	0	13	13	73¹	71	4	2.3	8.1	66	56.7%	.321	1.23	3.31	108	-0.3
2021 FS	WAS	MLB	23	2	3	0	57	0	50	49	7	3.6	7.1	39	48.8%	.286	1.41	4.48	111	-0.2

Comparables: Patrick Sandoval, Braxton Garrett, Cristian Javier

The Report: Cate had some first-round buzz going into his junior season, due to his very pretty, and very plus curveball. His velocity bounced around early in the season and he was eventually shut down until tourney time, where he came back as a reliever. A possibly balky arm has never scared off the Nats, and Cate tossed more than 140 innings in his first full pro season in 2019. The curve remained far at the head of the arsenal, but there was enough command and cut on the fastball—usually a tick or two either side of 90—to keep righties off the barrel. The profile was on the backend starter side with the fringe fastball and change setting up the hook as a potential out pitch.

Development Track: Cate added a tick or two on the fastball as the alternate site and there were positive change-up developments as well. That bumps the floor as long as the durability issues stay in his rear view mirror. Cate would have started 2020 in Double-A, and may still end up in Harrisburg to open 2021, but I'd also expect him to be in play for major league starts at some point next season as needed. And speaking of durability issues, the Nats rotation has had their fair share recently, so slots might open up.

Variance: Medium. Cate was used heavily at UConn, and his arm paid the price for it. It hasn't lingered as an issue in the pros, but it will be in the back of my mind. Everything else in the profile looks like a fairly safe backend starter. But we will get our one, "also, he's a pitcher" for the year here.

J.P. Breen's Fantasy Take: Potential back-end starters who logged a crap ton of innings in college aren't my jam. Cate might be a waiver-wire pickup in deep leagues if he reaches the majors and gets a few starts in 2021, but he'll struggle to carve out a role that makes him fantasy relevant on a yearly basis.

5 Yasel Antuna SS   OFP: 55   ETA: 2023
Born: 10/26/99   Age: 21   Bats: S   Throws: R   Height: 6'0"   Weight: 170   Origin: International Free Agent, 2016

YEAR	TEAM	LVL	AGE	PA	R	2B	3B	HR	RBI	BB	K	SB	CS	AVG/OBP/SLG	DRC+	BABIP	BRR	FRAA	WARP
2018	HAG	LO-A	18	362	44	14	2	6	27	32	79	8	7	.220/.293/.331	83	.269	-0.6	SS(67) -8.8, 2B(9) 0.2	-0.9
2021 FS	WAS	MLB	21	600	51	26	3	11	56	41	172	8	5	.218/.276/.337	69	.295	-4.9	SS -10, 3B 0	-2.0

Comparables: Andrew Velazquez, Juan Diaz, Delino DeShields

The Report: Our Antuna report is basically stuck in time at this point. He had Tommy John surgery late in 2018, and missed all but a small handful of GCL rehab games in 2019. Dating back to 2018, he showed wide-ranging potential with very little of it actualized yet. He flashed above-average potential on both hit and power, but wasn't getting them into games as he got eaten alive by full-season pitching. His defense at shortstop was inconsistent, and we've never been sure where he was going to land on the infield.

Development Track: We got very strong positive feedback on Antuna's offensive growth at the alternate site and fall instructs. The Nationals weren't in the alternate site share, so take it with appropriate salt, but the system is so weak that it pushed him up substantially anyway. If he comes out and hits at a full-season level in 2021, there isn't exactly a ton standing in his way from the top of the system.

Variance: Extreme. He still hasn't hit in games above complex ball yet.

J.P. Breen's Fantasy Take: Antuna is one for your watch lists, as he has the potential skills to be a corner- or middle-infield depth piece in most dynasty formats. Still, we haven't seen substantive at-bats from him since 2018. And even then, it wasn't pretty.

6 Cole Henry RHP   OFP: 50   ETA: 2023
Born: 07/15/99   Age: 21   Bats: R   Throws: R   Height: 6'4"   Weight: 211   Origin: Round 2, 2020 Draft (#55 overall)

The Report: As a high school senior, Henry was well known for his projectable body and big arm. He was mentioned as a possible early Day 2 pick. With a solid commitment to LSU, he went to college and worked on the glaring issue that plagued his prep days: An out-of-control delivery that led to bouts of erratic performances. Positive strides were clearly made as soon as he stepped on campus, especially quieting a violent head whack. It showed as a freshman and really took off during his short draft-eligible sophomore spring. His mid-90s fastball was located to both sides of the plate, and he improved the command of his curveball and changeup both in and out of the zone.

Development Track: Nobody wants to leave the table when you've got a hot hand, and Henry was among those in 2020 who didn't want their streak to end. As hard as he worked on his delivery and improving his changeup, you hope to see that diligence keep pace as he settles in with the Nationals' system. There is still some room for growth and he's yet to pitch a full season, and with that comes questions of the glass half-full or half-empty variety. Can he sustain it? Or is there more beneath the surface that is still untapped?

Variance: Medium. It's easy to fall in love with the most recent game action. The flags remain and will continue to exist until proven otherwise.

J.P. Breen's Fantasy Take: Henry seems to have more upside than his OFP would indicate, due to his impressive pre-COVID-19 showing at LSU, but the fact that he's, at best, a non-frontline pitching prospect keeps him comfortably outside the purview of most dynasty leagues. If he gets hot in 2021 and looks to move quickly as a usable No. 4 starter, he might be worth an add in deeper leagues. Keep him on your watch list for now.

7 Matt Cronin LHP   OFP: 50   ETA: 2021
Born: 09/20/97   Age: 23   Bats: L   Throws: L   Height: 6'2"   Weight: 195   Origin: Round 4, 2019 Draft (#123 overall)

YEAR	TEAM	LVL	AGE	W	L	SV	G	GS	IP	H	HR	BB/9	K/9	K	GB%	BABIP	WHIP	ERA	DRA-	WARP
2019	HAG	LO-A	21	0	0	1	17	0	22	11	1	4.5	16.8	41	12.5%	.333	1.00	0.82	48	0.6
2021 FS	WAS	MLB	23	2	3	0	57	0	50	45	8	6.2	10.9	60	32.7%	.303	1.61	5.36	123	-0.5

Comparables: Demarcus Evans, Cristian Javier, Patrick Sandoval

The Report: After being selected in the 2019 draft, Cronin quickly made the jump to Low-A Hagerstown and dominated. Over 22 relief innings, the lefty fanned 41 against 11 walks with a 0.82 ERA. Cronin's explosive fastball sits 93-96 and features late hop that plays well up in the zone. His curveball, mid-70s, is a wipeout offering with a high spin rate, which garners plenty of whiffs. He commands both pitches well. The delivery is quite aggressive and requires a lot of effort but it hasn't been an issue so far, as hitters have trouble timing it up and picking up pitches. Cronin will be a quick mover impacting the big league club in the back end of games sooner than later.

Development Track: As mentioned above, Cronin should move really fast. He won't need a lot of innings at each stop to prove that his stuff is lethal and will continue to garner whiffs as he progresses.

Variance: Low. There isn't much to worry about here, but the upside is also limited to late-inning pen work. One could be concerned about the delivery but so far it's been repeatable and durable for him.

J.P. Breen's Fantasy Take: As I've mentioned often in these blurbs, quality relievers are valued more in fantasy than they've ever been. Rightfully so. Still, they're not worth rostering as prospects. There are too many quality non-closing relievers available in the majors to be worried about that.

8 Andry Lara   OFP: 50   ETA: 2025
Born: 01/06/03   Age: 18   Bats: R   Throws: R   Height: 6'4"   Weight: 180   Origin: International Free Agent, 2019

The Report: Lara has yet to make his official pro debut. However, he had a positive 2020 while training stateside. He has a slow and deliberate windup with easy actions that he repeats. Lara has good arm speed which generates his low-to-mid-90s fastball. He already spins his curveball well and is developing a changeup. The right-hander controls the zone and has a sturdy frame with long limbs. Lara is a quick learner and advanced in a lot of areas for a teenager.

Development Track: Lara was stateside for most of 2020, as returning home to Venezuela became difficult during the pandemic. So traditional thinking would have Lara competing in the complex leagues and get more experience against opposing hitters before sending him to an affiliate. Check back in a year, or two.

Variance: Extreme. Lara hasn't thrown in an official game yet, and likely has another season of extended and complex-level ball ahead of him. There's a lot of ways this profile can go in the next couple years, both positive and negative.

J.P. Breen's Fantasy Take: Dynasty owners can't afford to wait on intriguing J2 bats, but they can absolutely afford to be patient with intriguing J2 arms. Don't worry about Lara until he's producing in full-season ball, unless the stuff really becomes special.

9 Sammy Infante   OFP: 50   ETA: 2024
Born: 06/22/01   Age: 20   Bats: R   Throws: R   Height: 6'1"   Weight: 185   Origin: Round 2, 2020 Draft (#71 overall)

The Report: Not the kind of player who would normally be featured in many top ten lists, and yet, here we are. Infante was a surprise over-slot selection when it was believed he would attend The U, where he could get some additional seasoning and return as a draft-eligible sophomore in 2022. The Nats are a clear believer in the bat, which does have some alluring qualities to it. He tracks the ball well and keeps his body in sync with an uphill swing that can be used to get to his power. Listed as a shortstop, it's believed he'll eventually move off the position, though reports from the org suggest he'll start there and see what happens.

Development Track: The minor league realignment to erase short season affiliates likely puts Infante on track to start in extended spring training or the rookie level Gulf Coast League, depending on whenever the minors (hopefully) get going in 2021. There are some building blocks in his foundation, more on the hitting side, with the rest of his game needing all the nurturing he can get.

Variance: Extreme. Too many unknowns to have a clue which direction it goes.

J.P. Breen's Fantasy Take: With more than a few question marks, Infante is best avoided in dynasty leagues. He's unlikely to see full-season ball in 2021, and he's someone who has shown significant contact issues in the past—and that's without the lighttower power potential that we'd need to see to make him worth rostering in dynasty.

10 Mason Denaburg RHP   OFP: 50   ETA: 2023/2024
Born: 08/08/99   Age: 21   Bats: R   Throws: R   Height: 6'4"   Weight: 195   Origin: Round 1, 2018 Draft (#27 overall)

YEAR	TEAM	LVL	AGE	W	L	SV	G	GS	IP	H	HR	BB/9	K/9	K	GB%	BABIP	WHIP	ERA	DRA-	WARP
2019	NAT	ROK	19	1	1	0	7	4	20¹	23	1	6.2	8.4	19	46.8%	.361	1.82	7.52		
2021 FS	WAS	MLB	21	2	3	0	57	0	50	54	8	6.6	7.2	40	39.7%	.303	1.83	6.93	148	-1.2

Comparables: Sugar Ray Marimon, Hunter Cervenka, Keynan Middleton

The Report: Since before the 2018 draft, Denaburg has been plagued by injuries. Thus far in his professional career he has been able to complete only 20 1/3 innings in the Gulf Coast League in 2019, pitching to a 7.52 ERA with 19 strikeouts against 14 walks. So there's plenty of trepidation with how his career has begun. However, Denaburg is healthy again and pitching in live situations. Before the injuries, Denaburg showed promise with above-average command, offering a mid-90s fastball, sluvry curveball and developing changeup.

Development Track: With the injuries, Denaburg hasn't had time to develop pitches or build up his endurance for a full season. If he can stay healthy, 2021 will be a crucial year developmentally for the right-hander to understand where he needs to improve. Keep a long term outlook here.

Variance: High. Although reportedly healthy, Denaburg will need to demonstrate that health in games in 2021. Until the ledger has more innings the variance will remain.

J.P. Breen's Fantasy Take: A potential back-end starter with a significant injury history? At No. 10? Yikes, at least the Nats have a fun major-league squad!

The Prospects You Meet Outside The Top Ten

Prospects to dream on a little

Jeremy De La Rosa OF Born: 01/16/02   Age: 19   Bats: L   Throws: L   Height: 5'11"   Weight: 160   Origin: International Free Agent, 2018

YEAR	TEAM	LVL	AGE	PA	R	2B	3B	HR	RBI	BB	K	SB	CS	AVG/OBP/SLG	DRC+	BABIP	BRR	FRAA	WARP
2019	NAT	ROK	17	99	14	1	2	2	10	12	29	3	2	.232/.343/.366		.321			
2021 FS	WAS	MLB	19	600	44	26	3	6	47	33	245	9	4	.203/.254/.296	50	.348	-0.6	RF -4, LF -1	-2.8

Comparables: Rosell Herrera, Jorge Bonifacio, Nick Williams

Signed for $300,000 by the Nats in July 2019, de la Rosa's profile is highlighted by plus bat speed and barrel control from the left side of the plate. The bat stays through the zone a long time, which helps him drive the ball to all fields, and the power might end up a little above-average. He will likely end up being an average defender in left so the bat will need to reach close to full potential. de la Rosa will be entering his age-19 season in 2021 and his second stint stateside. Long way to go but there's above-average upside.

Roismar Quintana OF Born: 02/06/03   Age: 18   Bats: R   Throws: R   Height: 6'1"   Weight: 175   Origin: International Free Agent, 2019

Signed for $820,000 out of last year's J2 class, Quintana offers potential upside both offensively and defensively. The right-hander has a good feel for the barrel and plus bat speed, showcasing burgeoning power. Quintana has a chance to stick in center with his present defensive aptitude, but may eventually be moved to left as he fills out his already quite physical frame. There isn't a tool that will wow you. However, the 18-year-old has a broad base of tools that are intriguing.

MLB bats, but less upside than you'd like

Jackson Cluff **SS** Born: 12/03/96 Age: 24 Bats: L Throws: R Height: 6'0" Weight: 185 Origin: Round 6, 2019 Draft (#183 overall)

YEAR	TEAM	LVL	AGE	PA	R	2B	3B	HR	RBI	BB	K	SB	CS	AVG/OBP/SLG	DRC+	BABIP	BRR	FRAA	WARP
2019	HAG	LO-A	22	280	33	8	5	5	19	26	63	11	5	.229/.320/.367	93	.284	-1.4	SS(59) 1.8, 2B(1) 0.1	1.0
2021 FS	WAS	MLB	24	600	54	26	4	13	59	38	188	12	6	.219/.279/.353	74	.306	-1.5	SS 6, 2B 0	0.4

Comparables: Zach Vincej, Ryan Schimpf, Kelby Tomlinson

Although an older prospect because he spent two years on a mission while attending Brigham Young University, Ciuff possesses plus defensive skills at shortstop with his range, actions, and arm all grading out as above-average. Seen as a possible super-utility infielder, Cluff is also an above-average to plus runner, swiping 11 bags in 63 games with Low-A Hagerstown in 2019. The lefty in the box has a quick stroke with some pull side pop but is working to stay inside the ball more and lay off pitches out of the zone.

Top Talents 25 and Under (as of 4/1/2021):

1. Juan Soto, OF
2. Victor Robles, OF
3. Carter Kieboom, 3B
4. Luis García, 2B/SS
5. Cade Cavalli, RHP
6. Jackson Rutledge, RHP
7. Drew Mendoza, 3B/1B
8. Tim Cate, LHP
9. Yasel Antuna, IF
10. Cole Henry, RHP

If you have a young star as good as Juan Soto, your farm system being on a downswing hurts a lot less. Soto turned 22 during the World Series. He was, by nearly any metric, one of the best hitters in baseball in 2020. And that's his true talent.

Victor Robles's offensive output has been trending down for three seasons now, which isn't what you want from a young potential star. His average exit velocity dipped to 82.2 mph in 2020, the absolute worst in MLB. Robles never had a lot of power in his profile, but he should have more than that. At least he's still stellar in center field.

Carter Kieboom's hit tool—which we projected as high as plus as a prospect—has deserted him in the majors so far. His power deserted him in 2020 as well, with just one double and zero homers in 122 plate appearances, but he still put up an 86 DRC+ and 0.5 WARP. I don't know where this is going, but it's worth keeping in mind that as bad as he's been in the majors, it's been over just 165 plate appearances in two seasons, and at this time last year he'd been a Top 20 prospect for two years running.

Luis García came up just three months after his 20th birthday, coming off an age-19 season where he struggled mightily at Double-A. He certainly wasn't good—he racked up a -1.3 WARP in only 139 plate appearances—but he still probably did better than you'd expect someone who slashed .257/.280/.337 at Double-A last year to do. Were he a prospect, he might've even made the Top 101.

The Top 101 Dynasty Prospects

by Ben Carsley, Jesse Roche and Bret Sayre

One of the most difficult things about playing in dynasty leagues is staying patient. And there's been no bigger test of our collective patience this century than navigating a year that both saw no minor league games and an abbreviated MLB season under extremely extenuating circumstances. Honestly, it wouldn't have been the worst take to just run last year's list again and shrug away anything that happened over the last 12 months. However, while we don't want to put an incredible amount of stock in 2020, there are some events, observations and reports that have shifted the value propositions of the players below. Mostly they break into three different categories: the 2020 overperformers, the 2020 underperformers and the subjects of whispers from instructs or alternate sites.

Regardless of where the noise comes from, we just have to make sure that too much isn't being read into any of it. That's why even if there are certainly some notable movers due to performances we simply couldn't overlook (yes, we're looking at you Ian Anderson and Randy Arozarena), the list remains relatively steady. Of course that also means that without a year of data, there's going to be a LOT of movement between now and next year's list. But in the meantime, taking big swings on who that will be based on hearsay and speculation isn't going to do anyone any favors, and it's not how we would choose to manage our own fantasy teams.

As always, there are a few list-specific disclaimers to go over before we jump in. These rankings are for fantasy purposes only, and they do not directly take into account things like an outfielder's ability to stick in center or a catcher's pop time. That being said, these factors matter indirectly as they affect a player's ability to either stay in the lineup or maintain eligibility. Additionally, we factor in home parks and organizational strengths, just as when we are talking about a major-league player. We can't pretend that these prospects operate in a vacuum, unaffected by park factors. Of course, there's no guarantee that they will reach the majors with their current organization, so while it is reflected, it's not a heavy ranking factor. Most importantly, the intention of this list is to balance the upside, probability and proximity of these players to an active fantasy lineup.

Within the list below, you'll find important information about each prospect, including their potential fantasy value (in dollars) at their peak and the risk factor associated with reaching their projected output. Also, you will find a fantasy overview, which summarizes the number of categories in which each player will be useful, along with any that carry impact. For this exercise, we defined "impact" as having the potential to be top-20 players in a given category. For instance, impact in home runs roughly equates to the potential to hit 30, impact in steals is 25, and impact for strikeouts is the potential to punch out 200. Then, you'll see a realistic ceiling and floor for each prospect, purely in terms of rotisserie value. Each player's ceiling is labeled as "Don Orsillo Says" in recognition of a great broadcaster who enjoys the sport he covers, while each player's floor is labeled as "John Smoltz Says" for reasons you can likely guess. The comments are brief because we've already written fantasy-specific comments on each of these players in the individual top-10 lists.

Previous Rank correlates to where repeat entrants placed on the 2020 version of the list. The "NR" key means the player was not ranked, while "N/A" means they were not eligible. Ages listed are as of 4/1/2020.

And so it goes. Another year of prospects around the sun:

1. Wander Franco, SS, Tampa Bay Rays (Age: 20, Previous Rank: 2)

Potential Earnings: $35+

  Risk Factor: Low

  Fantasy Overview: Five-category contributor; impact potential in AVG, R, RBI

  Fantasy Impact ETA: 2021

  Don Orsillo Says: José Ramírez at shortstop

  John Smoltz Says: Ozzie Albies

2. Julio Y. Rodríguez, OF, Seattle Mariners (Age: 20, Previous Rank: 5)

Potential Earnings: $35+

  Risk Factor: Medium

  Fantasy Overview: Four-category contributor; impact potential in AVG, HR, RBI, R

  Fantasy Impact ETA: Mid 2021

  Don Orsillo Says: J.D. Martinez

  John Smoltz Says: Michael Conforto, maybe? The floor here is pretty high.

3. Jarred Kelenic, OF, Seattle Mariners (Age: 21, Previous Rank: 6)

Potential Earnings: $30-35

Risk Factor: Low

Fantasy Overview: Five-category contributor; impact potential in AVG, R

Fantasy Impact ETA: 2021

Don Orsillo Says: George Springer with a few more bags

John Smoltz Says: Marcell Ozuna with a few more bags? The floor here is pretty high.

4. Jo Adell, OF, Los Angeles Angels (Age: 21, Previous Rank: 1)

Potential Earnings: $35+

Risk Factor: Medium

Fantasy Overview: Five-category contributor; impact potential in AVG, HR, RBI

Fantasy Impact ETA: 2021

Don Orsillo Says: The last few seasons of Bryce Harper, plus a few more SB

John Smoltz Says: Once upon a time we were warned that prospects will break your heart ...

5. Andrew Vaughn, 1B, Chicago White Sox (Age: 22, Previous Rank: 7)

Potential Earnings: $30-35

Risk Factor: Medium

Fantasy Overview: Four-category contributor; impact potential in AVG, HR, RBI, R

Fantasy Impact ETA: 2021

Don Orsillo Says: Not quite peak Anthony Rizzo, but pretty close

John Smoltz Says: Peak Brandon Belt

6. Spencer Torkelson, 3B/1B, Detroit Tigers (Age: 21, Previous Rank: N/A)

Potential Earnings: $30-35

Risk Factor: Medium

Fantasy Overview: Four-category contributor; impact potential in AVG, HR, RBI, R

Fantasy Impact ETA: 2022

Don Orsillo Says: Not quite peak Freddie Freeman, but pretty close

John Smoltz Says: Peak Brandon Belt

7. Marco Luciano, SS, San Francisco Giants (Age: 19, Previous Rank: 12)

Potential Earnings: $35+

Risk Factor: High

Fantasy Overview: Five-category contributor; Impact potential in AVG, HR, RBI, R

Fantasy Impact ETA: 2023

Don Orsillo Says: The next dude we value like Wander Franco

John Smoltz Says: The next dude we value like Anderson Tejeda

8. CJ Abrams, SS, San Diego Padres (Age: 20, Previous Rank: 19)

Potential Earnings: $35+

Risk Factor: High

Fantasy Overview: Five-category contributor; Impact potential in AVG, R, SB

Fantasy Impact ETA: 2023

Don Orsillo Says: Trea Turner

John Smoltz Says: Amed Rosario

9. Nick Madrigal, 2B, Chicago White Sox (Age: 24, Previous Rank: 15)

Potential Earnings: $20-25

Risk Factor: Low

Fantasy Overview: Three-category contributor; Impact potential in AVG, R, SB

Fantasy Impact ETA: 2020

Don Orsillo Says: Those early Jose Altuve years

John Smoltz Says: David Eckstein with pedigree

10. Adley Rutschman, C, Baltimore Orioles (Age: 23, Previous Rank: 10)

Potential Earnings: $25-30

Risk Factor: Medium

Fantasy Overview: Four-category contributor; Impact potential in AVG, HR

Fantasy Impact ETA: 2022

Don Orsillo Says: Who Matt Wieters was supposed to be

John Smoltz Says: Maybe *this* time we'll learn to stop valuing catching prospects

11. MacKenzie Gore, LHP, San Diego Padres (Age: 22, Previous Rank: 11)

Potential Earnings: $25-30

Risk Factor: Medium

Fantasy Overview: Four-category contributor; Impact potential in W, K, ERA, WHIP

Fantasy Impact ETA: Mid 2021

Don Orsillo Says: Prime Madison Bumgarner

John Smoltz Says: Still pretty damn good ... maybe post-peak Jon Lester?

12. Dylan Carlson, OF, St. Louis Cardinals (Age: 22, Previous Rank: 14)

Potential Earnings: $20-25

Risk Factor: Low

Fantasy Overview: Five-category contributor; Impact potential in AVG, R, RBI

Fantasy Impact ETA: Early 2021

Don Orsillo Says: Healthy Michael Brantley

John Smoltz Says: Solid but not special: think Brian Anderson

13. Bobby Witt Jr., SS, Kansas City Royals (Age: 20, Previous Rank: 28)

Potential Earnings: $30-35

Risk Factor: High

Fantasy Overview: Five-category contributor; Impact potential in R, HR, RBI, SB

Fantasy Impact ETA: 2023

Don Orsillo Says: Corey Seager with more speed

John Smoltz Says: Kyle Seager with more speed

14. Sixto Sánchez, RHP, Miami Marlins (Age: 22, Previous Rank: 45)

Potential Earnings: $20-25

Risk Factor: Low

Fantasy Overview: Four-category contributor; Impact potential in ERA, WHIP

Fantasy Impact ETA: He's already there

Don Orsillo Says: A strong SP3 who should really miss more bats than he does

John Smoltz Says: A strong SP4 who should really miss more bats than he does

15. Randy Arozarena, OF, Tampa Bay Rays (Age: 26, Previous Rank: NR)

Potential Earnings: $20-25

Risk Factor: Low

Fantasy Overview: Five-category contributor; Impact potential in R, RBI

Fantasy Impact ETA: Did you see the playoffs last year?

Don Orsillo Says: Did you SEE the playoffs last year?

John Smoltz Says: The lowest floor of them all: proving Craig right

16. Kristian Robinson, OF, Arizona Diamondbacks (Age: 20, Previous Rank: 9)

Potential Earnings: $30-35

Risk Factor: High

Fantasy Overview: Five-category contributor; Impact potential in R, HR, RBI, SB

Fantasy Impact ETA: 2023

Don Orsillo Says: The next version of who we still think Jo Adell can be

John Smoltz Says: A toolsy OF3/4 who leaves you wanting more

17. Ian Anderson, RHP, Atlanta Braves (Age: 22, Previous Rank: 61)

Potential Earnings: $20-25

Risk Factor: Low

Fantasy Overview: Four-category contributor; Impact potential in W, K, ERA

Fantasy Impact ETA: 2020

Don Orsillo Says: A super steady SP2/3, like Aaron Nola-lite

John Smoltz Says: An overdrafted SP4 more akin to Sonny Gray

18. Drew Waters, OF, Atlanta Braves (Age: 22, Previous Rank: 8)

Potential Earnings: $25-30

Risk Factor: Medium

Fantasy Overview: Five-category contributor; Impact potential in AVG, RBI

Fantasy Impact ETA: Mid 2021

Don Orsillo Says: Ian Desmond as a shortstop, in the outfield

John Smoltz Says: Ian Desmond as an outfielder

19. Royce Lewis, SS, Minnesota Twins (Age: 21, Previous Rank: 16)

Potential Earnings: $25-30

Risk Factor: Medium

Fantasy Overview: Five-category contributor; Impact potential in AVG, R, SB

Fantasy Impact ETA: 2022

Don Orsillo Says: I can't believe we already burned our one Ian Desmond comp

John Smoltz Says: What if Jonathan Villar stole fewer bases?

20. Ryan Mountcastle, OF/1B, Baltimore Orioles (Age: 24, Previous Rank: 39)

Potential Earnings: $20-25

Risk Factor: Low

Fantasy Overview: Four-category contributor; Impact potential in AVG, RBI

Fantasy Impact ETA: Right now

Don Orsillo Says: We'll stop using Nick Castellanos here when it stops being so perfect

John Smoltz Says: More of a .260/25 OF5 type of guy

21. Corbin Carroll, OF, Arizona Diamondbacks (Age: 20, Previous Rank: 52)

Potential Earnings: $25-30

Risk Factor: High

Fantasy Overview: Five-category contributor; Impact potential in AVG, R, SB

Fantasy Impact ETA: 2023

Don Orsillo Says: Healthy Lorenzo Cain

John Smoltz Says: Enough speed and average to be an OF5

22. Austin Martin, OF/3B, Toronto Blue Jays (Age: 22, Previous Rank: N/A)

Potential Earnings: $20-25

Risk Factor: Medium

Fantasy Overview: Five-category contributor; Impact potential in AVG, R, RBI

Fantasy Impact ETA: 2022

Don Orsillo Says: Aston Martin

John Smoltz Says: Richie Martin

23. Alex Kiriloff, OF/1B, Minnesota Twins (Age: 22, Previous Rank: 32)

Potential Earnings: $20-25

Risk Factor: Medium

Fantasy Overview: Four-category contributor; Impact potential in AVG, HR, RBI

Fantasy Impact ETA: 2021

Don Orsillo Says: A more athletic Trey Mancini

John Smoltz Says: A less powerful Brandon Moss

24. Nate Pearson, RHP, Toronto Blue Jays (Age: 24, Previous Rank: 25)

Potential Earnings: $20-25

Risk Factor: Medium

Fantasy Overview: Four-category contributor; Impact potential in W, K, ERA

Fantasy Impact ETA: 2021

Don Orsillo Says: A healthy SP2

John Smoltz Says: An oft-injured closer

25. Casey Mize, RHP, Detroit Tigers (Age: 23, Previous Rank: 22)

Potential Earnings: $20-25

Risk Factor: Medium

Fantasy Overview: Four-category contributor; Impact potential in W, WHIP

Fantasy Impact ETA: 2021

Don Orsillo Says: Trevor Bauer with a normal brain

John Smoltz Says: Forrest Whitley's career path

26. Jasson Dominguez, OF, New York Yankees (Age: 18, Previous Rank: 26)

Potential Earnings: $35+

Risk Factor: Extreme

Fantasy Overview: Five-category contributor; Impact potential in HR, RBI, R, SB

Fantasy Impact ETA: 2024

Don Orsillo Says: The best player in the history of organized baseball

John Smoltz Says: Out of the game by the time he's 25

27. Ke'Bryan Hayes, 3B, Pittsburgh Pirates (Age: 24, Previous Rank: 96)

Potential Earnings: $15-20

Risk Factor: Low

Fantasy Overview: Four-category contributor; Impact potential in AVG, RBI

Fantasy Impact ETA: Did you see him last year?

Don Orsillo Says: Justin Turner with less OBP

John Smoltz Says: Fancy Dog Bill Mueller

28. George Valera, OF, Cleveland (Age: 20, Previous Rank: 27)

Potential Earnings: $25-30

Risk Factor: High

Fantasy Overview: Five-category contributor; Impact potential in AVG, HR, RBI

Fantasy Impact ETA: 2023

Don Orsillo Says: Traded for a middling return once he gets expensive in ~7 years

John Smoltz Says: Bad enough that Cleveland can afford to keep him

29. Vidal Bruján, 2B/SS, Tampa Bay Rays (Age: 23 , Previous Rank: 21)

Potential Earnings: $20-25

Risk Factor: Medium

Fantasy Overview: Three-category contributor; Impact potential in R, SB

Fantasy Impact ETA: 2022

Don Orsillo Says: Elvis Andrus with multi-position eligibility

John Smoltz Says: Danny Santana

30. Nick Gonzales, 2B/SS, Pittsburgh Pirates (Age: 21, Previous Rank: N/A)

Potential Earnings: $20-25

Risk Factor: Medium

Fantasy Overview: Five-category contributor; Impact potential in AVG, R

Fantasy Impact ETA: 2022

Don Orsillo Says: Kolten Wong with inverted power/speed

John Smoltz Says: Adam Frazier 2: Adamer Frazierer

31. Heliot Ramos, OF, San Francisco Giants (Age: 21, Previous Rank: 24)

Potential Earnings: $25-30

Risk Factor: High

Fantasy Overview: Five-category contributor; Impact potential in HR, RBI

Fantasy Impact ETA: 2022

Don Orsillo Says: What we hope Kyle Lewis is

John Smoltz Says: A high pick only in name drafts

32. Alek Thomas, OF, Arizona Diamondbacks (Age: 20, Previous Rank: 35)

Potential Earnings: $20-25

Risk Factor: Medium

Fantasy Overview: Five-category contributor; Impact potential in R

Fantasy Impact ETA: 2022

Don Orsillo Says: 2018 Andrew Benintendi

John Smoltz Says: 2019 Andrew Benintendi

33. Brendan Rodgers, 2B/SS, Colorado Rockies (Age: 24, Previous Rank: 20)

Potential Earnings: $25-30

Risk Factor: High

Fantasy Overview: Four-category contributor; Impact potential in AVG, HR, RBI

Fantasy Impact ETA: It better be 2021

Don Orsillo Says: I can't believe we're doing this again

John Smoltz Says: Hopefully this will be the last time

34. Zac Veen, OF, Colorado Rockies (Age: 19, Previous Rank: N/A)

Potential Earnings: $30-35

Risk Factor: Extreme

Fantasy Overview: Five-category contributor; Impact potential in AVG, HR, RBI, R

Fantasy Impact ETA: 2024

Don Orsillo Says: A spoonerism you associate with brighter days ahead

John Smoltz Says: A spoonerism your Very Online aunt hates

35. Michael Kopech, RHP, Chicago White Sox (Age: 24, Previous Rank: 51)

Potential Earnings: $25-30

Risk Factor: High

Fantasy Overview: Four-category contributor; Impact potential in W, ERA, K

Fantasy Impact ETA: 2021

Don Orsillo Says: We'll have waited a long time for Noah Syndergaard

John Smoltz Says: We'll have waited a long time for Nate Eovaldi

36. Luis Patiño, RHP, Tampa Bay Rays (Age: 21, Previous Rank: 33)

Potential Earnings: $20-25

Risk Factor: Medium

Fantasy Overview: Four-category contributor; Impact potential in ERA, K

Fantasy Impact ETA: 2021

Don Orsillo Says: A should-be SP2, who we wish threw more innings

John Smoltz Says: We swear to god if the Rays use him as an opener …

37. Brennen Davis, OF, Chicago Cubs (Age: 21, Previous Rank: 40)

Potential Earnings: $25-30

Risk Factor: High

Fantasy Overview: Five-category contributor; Impact potential in HR, RBI

Fantasy Impact ETA: 2023

Don Orsillo Says: Tommy Pham, sans a little OBP

John Smoltz Says: Jason Heyward's successor in all the wrong ways

38. Trevor Larnach, OF, Minnesota Twins (Age: 24, Previous Rank: 30)

Potential Earnings: $20-25

Risk Factor: Medium

Fantasy Overview: Four-category contributor; Impact potential in HR, RBI

Fantasy Impact ETA: Late 2021

Don Orsillo Says: Those good Jay Bruce years

John Smoltz Says: Some bum like J.J. Bleday

39. J.J. Bleday, OF, Miami Marlins (Age: 23, Previous Rank: 38)

Potential Earnings: $20-25

Risk Factor: Medium

Fantasy Overview: Four-category contributor; Impact potential in HR, RBI

Fantasy Impact ETA: 2022

Don Orsillo Says: Those good Jay Bruce years

John Smoltz Says: Some bum like Trevor Larnach

40. Noelvi Marte, SS, Seattle Mariners (Age: 19, Previous Rank: 63)

Potential Earnings: $30-35

Risk Factor: Extreme

Fantasy Overview: Five-category contributor; Impact potential in AVG, R, SB

Fantasy Impact ETA: 2023

Don Orsillo Says: The next next Wander Franco

John Smoltz Says: The next next Adrian Rondon

41. Nolan Gorman, 3B, St. Louis Cardinals (Age: 20, Previous Rank: 36)

Potential Earnings: $20-25

Risk Factor: Medium

Fantasy Overview: Three-category contributor; Impact potential in HR, RBI

Fantasy Impact ETA: 2022

Don Orsillo Says: Troy Glaus

John Smoltz Says: Brandon Wood

42. Daulton Varsho, OF/C, Arizona Diamondbacks (Age: 24, Previous Rank: 74)

Potential Earnings: $20-25

Risk Factor: Medium

Fantasy Overview: Five-category contributor

Fantasy Impact ETA: 2021

Don Orsillo Says: Who we wanted Blake Swihart to be

John Smoltz Says: Loses catcher eligibility before he turns 27

43. Jordan Groshans, SS, Toronto Blue Jays (Age: 21, Previous Rank: 46)

Potential Earnings: $20-25

Risk Factor: Medium

Fantasy Overview: Five-category contributor; Impact potential in AVG, RBI

Fantasy Impact ETA: 2022

Don Orsillo Says: A slightly lesser Bo Bichette

John Smoltz Says: A slightly lesser Didi Gregorius

44. Riley Greene, OF, Detroit Tigers (Age: 20, Previous Rank: 50)

Potential Earnings: $25-30

Risk Factor: High

Fantasy Overview: Five-category contributor; Impact potential in AVG, HR, RBI

Fantasy Impact ETA:

Don Orsillo Says: A top-10 dynasty prospect at this time next year

John Smoltz Says: Whither Estevan Florial?

45. Jazz Chisholm, 2B/SS, Miami Marlins (Age: 23, Previous Rank: 43)

Potential Earnings: $20-25

Risk Factor: Medium

Fantasy Overview: Four-category contributor; Impact potential in HR, RBI

Fantasy Impact ETA: Now

Don Orsillo Says: Store brand Javy Báez

John Smoltz Says: Lewis Brinson: Infielder Edition

46. Erick Pena, OF, Kansas City Royals (Age: 18, Previous Rank: 86)

Potential Earnings: $30-35

Risk Factor: Extreme

Fantasy Overview: Five-category contributor; Impact potential in HR, RBI, R

Fantasy Impact ETA: 2024

Don Orsillo Says: The best player in the history of organized baseball

John Smoltz Says: Out of the game by the time he's 25

47. Triston Casas, 1B, Boston Red Sox (Age: 21, Previous Rank: 78)

Potential Earnings: $20-25

Risk Factor: Medium

Fantasy Overview: Three-category contributor; Impact potential in HR, RBI, R

Fantasy Impact ETA: Mid 2021

Don Orsillo Says: 2019 Matt Olson, but every year

John Smoltz Says: 2018 Matt Olson, but every year

48. James Karinchak, RHP, Cleveland (Age: 25, Previous Rank: NR)

Potential Earnings: $20-25

Risk Factor: Medium

Fantasy Overview: Four-category contributor; Impact potential in ERA, SV

Fantasy Impact ETA:

Don Orsillo Says: A dominant closer who stays healthy, like Jonathan Papelbon

John Smoltz Says: A dominant set-up man who doesn't, like Seranthony Dominguez

49. Josh Jung, 3B, Texas Rangers (Age: 23, Previous Rank: 71)

Potential Earnings: $20-25

Risk Factor: Medium

Fantasy Overview: Four-category contributor; Impact potential in AVG, RBI

Fantasy Impact ETA: 2022

Don Orsillo Says: Rounding into Alec Bohm

John Smoltz Says: Rounding into Alec Bohm's predecessor

50. Brandon Marsh, OF, Los Angeles Angels (Age: 23, Previous Rank: 57)

Potential Earnings: $20-25

Risk Factor: Medium

Fantasy Overview: Five-category contributor

Fantasy Impact ETA: 2021

Don Orsillo Says: Oh sweet, they cloned Adam Eaton

John Smoltz Says: Oh my god they cloned Kole Calhoun

51. Deivi García, RHP, New York Yankees (Age: 21, Previous Rank: 54)

Potential Earnings: $20-25

Risk Factor: Medium

Fantasy Overview: Four-category contributor; Impact potential in W, ERA

Fantasy Impact ETA: Hopefully 2021

Don Orsillo Says: What if Marcus Stroman missed more bats?

John Smoltz Says: What if Marcus Stroman pitched at Yankee Stadium?

52. Asa Lacy, LHP, Kansas City Royals (Age: 21, Previous Rank: N/A)

Potential Earnings: $25-30

Risk Factor: High

Fantasy Overview: Four-category contributor; Impact potential in W, ERA, K

Fantasy Impact ETA: 2023

Don Orsillo Says: A "safe" pitching prospect like Ian Anderson

John Smoltz Says: A "safe" pitching prospect like Dylan Bundy

53. Forrest Whitley, RHP, Houston Astros (Age: 23, Previous Rank: 23)

Potential Earnings: $25-30

Risk Factor: High

Fantasy Overview: Four-category contributor; Impact potential in W, ERA, K

Fantasy Impact ETA: Your guess is as good as mine

Don Orsillo Says: Carlos Carrasco

John Smoltz Says: Ryne Stanek

54. Luis Matos, OF, San Francisco Giants (Age: 19, Previous Rank: HM)

Potential Earnings: $30-35

Risk Factor: Extreme

Fantasy Overview: Five-category contributor; Impact potential in AVG, R, SB

Fantasy Impact ETA: 2023

Don Orsillo Says: Peak A.J. Pollock

John Smoltz Says: You won't even remember him in four years

55. Shane Baz, RHP, Tampa Bay Rays (Age: 21, Previous Rank: 55)

Potential Earnings: $25-30

Risk Factor: High

Fantasy Overview: Four-category contributor; Impact potential in W, ERA, K

Fantasy Impact ETA: 2022

Don Orsillo Says: Tyler Glasnow, pretty much

John Smoltz Says: Another argument for the "openers are ruining the game" crowd

56. Cristian Pache, OF, Atlanta Braves (Age: 22, Previous Rank: 31)

Potential Earnings: $10-15

Risk Factor: Low

Fantasy Overview: Four-category contributor

Fantasy Impact ETA: 2021

Don Orsillo Says: Jackie Bradley Jr. with wheels

John Smoltz Says: Fancy Dog Kevin Pillar

57. Garrett Mitchell, OF, Milwaukee Brewers (Age: 22, Previous Rank: N/A)

Potential Earnings: $20-25

Risk Factor: High

Fantasy Overview: Five-category contributor; Impact potential in AVG, R, SB

Fantasy Impact ETA: 2023

Don Orsillo Says: An OF2 in the Lorenzo Cain mold

John Smoltz Says: An OF5 who can swipe you 20 but offers little else

58. Ronny Mauricio, SS, New York Mets (Age: 19, Previous Rank: 49)

Potential Earnings: $20-25

Risk Factor: High

Fantasy Overview: Four-category contributor; Impact potential in HR, RBI

Fantasy Impact ETA: 2023

Don Orsillo Says: A .280-plus average and 25-plus homers from the hot corner

John Smoltz Says: This publication would NEVER overrate a Mets prospect,

59. Matt Manning, RHP, Detroit Tigers (Age: 23, Previous Rank: 47)

Potential Earnings: $15-20

Risk Factor: Medium

Fantasy Overview: Four-category contributor; Impact potential in W, K

Fantasy Impact ETA: 2021

Don Orsillo Says: Keto Lance Lynn

John Smoltz Says: Matt Barnes

60. Ha-Seong Kim, 2B/OF, San Diego Padres (Age: 25, Previous Rank: N/A)

Potential Earnings: $15-20

Risk Factor: Medium

Fantasy Overview: Five-category contributor; Impact potential in AVG, R

Fantasy Impact ETA: They didn't pay him to sit

Don Orsillo Says: What some still think Jurickson Profar can be

John Smoltz Says: What we're worried Jurickson Profar will always be

61. Jordyn Adams, OF, Los Angeles Angels (Age: 21, Previous Rank: 53)

Potential Earnings: $25-30

Risk Factor: Extreme

Fantasy Overview: Five-category contributor; Impact potential in SB

Fantasy Impact ETA: 2023

Don Orsillo Says: Healthy Jacoby Ellsbury (not that near-MVP year though)

John Smoltz Says: Ender Inciarte

62. Hunter Bishop, OF, San Francisco Giants (Age: 22, Previous Rank: 44)

Potential Earnings: $20-25

Risk Factor: High

Fantasy Overview: Four-category contributor; Impact potential in HR, RBI, R

Fantasy Impact ETA: 2022

Don Orsillo Says: Hunter Pence

John Smoltz Says: The Hunted Pence (too soon?)

63. Grayson Rodriguez, RHP, Baltimore Orioles (Age: 21, Previous Rank: 77)

Potential Earnings: $20-25

Risk Factor: High

Fantasy Overview: Four-category contributor; Impact potential in W, ERA, K

Fantasy Impact ETA: 2022

Don Orsillo Says: A top-20 prospect at this time next season

John Smoltz Says: An Orioles pitching project, so pray for him ...

64. Spencer Howard, RHP, Philadelphia Phillies (Age: 24, Previous Rank: 42)

Potential Earnings: $15-20

Risk Factor: Medium

Fantasy Overview: Four-category contributor; Impact potential in W

Fantasy Impact ETA: 2021

Don Orsillo Says: Philly's best Howard since Ryan

John Smoltz Says: RON HOWARD VOICE: He's a reliever

65. Andres Gimenez, SS/2B, Cleveland (Age: 22, Previous Rank: 90)

Potential Earnings: $10-15

Risk Factor: Low

Fantasy Overview: Four-category contributor; Impact potential in SB

Fantasy Impact ETA: Right now

Don Orsillo Says: The last few years of José Iglesias with some steals thrown in

John Smoltz Says: Little more than an AL-Only accumulator

66. Tarik Skubal, LHP, Detroit Tigers (Age: 24, Previous Rank: 84)

Potential Earnings: $15-20

Risk Factor: Medium

Fantasy Overview: Three-category contributor; Impact potential in K

Fantasy Impact ETA: Right now

Don Orsillo Says: A volatile SP3-5 in the mold of Robbie Ray

John Smoltz Says: Staying with "King of Skubals mountain"

67. Heston Kjerstad, OF, Baltimore Orioles (Age: 22, Previous Rank: N/A)

Potential Earnings: $20-25

Risk Factor: High

Fantasy Overview: Four-category contributor; Impact potential in HR, RBI

Fantasy Impact ETA: 2022

Don Orsillo Says: We may come to view him like Alex Kiriloff

John Smoltz Says: We may come to view him like Alex Dickerson

68. Geraldo Perdomo, SS, Arizona Diamondbacks (Age: 21, Previous Rank: 72)

Potential Earnings: $15-20

Risk Factor: Medium

Fantasy Overview: Five-category contributor

Fantasy Impact ETA: 2022

Don Orsillo Says: The absolute best version of Joey Wendle

John Smoltz Says: All average and no oomph, like Miguel Rojas

69. Taylor Trammell, OF, Seattle Mariners (Age: 23, Previous Rank: 34)

Potential Earnings: $20-25

Risk Factor: High

Fantasy Overview: Five-category contributor; Impact potential in R, SB

Fantasy Impact ETA: 2021

Don Orsillo Says: The ceiling still looks like Starling Marte -- you just have to squint to see it

John Smoltz Says: Won't play enough for his speed to matter

70. Logan Gilbert, RHP, Seattle Mariners (Age: 23, Previous Rank: 73)

Potential Earnings: $15-20

Risk Factor: Medium

Fantasy Overview: Four-category contributor; Impact potential in W

Fantasy Impact ETA: 2021

Don Orsillo Says: Another Marco Gonzales, which is weirdly now a compliment

John Smoltz Says: The last starting pitcher you roster in a 12-team league

71. Max Meyer, RHP, Miami Marlins (Age: 22, Previous Rank: N/A)

Potential Earnings: $20-25

Risk Factor: High

Fantasy Overview: Four-category potential. Impact potential in ERA, K

Fantasy Impact ETA: 2022

Don Orsillo Says: About 90 percent of Walker Buehler

John Smoltz Says: About 90 percent of Carson Fulmer

72. Garrett Crochet, LHP, Chicago White Sox (Age: 21, Previous Rank: N/A)

Potential Earnings: $20-25

Risk Factor: High

Fantasy Overview: Four-category contributor; Impact potential in ERA, K

Fantasy Impact ETA: 2022, assuming the Sox eventually let him start

Don Orsillo Says: The Josh Hader we asked our mom for

John Smoltz Says: The A.J. Puk she said we had at home

73. Triston McKenzie, RHP, Cleveland (Age: 23, Previous Rank: NR)

Potential Earnings: $15-20

Risk Factor: Medium

Fantasy Overview: Four-category contributor; Impact potential in WHIP

Fantasy Impact ETA: 2021

Don Orsillo Says: I can't believe we ever took him off this list!

John Smoltz Says: I can't believe we added him back to this list!

74. Jeter Downs, SS/2B, Boston Red Sox (Age: 22, Previous Rank: 65)

Potential Earnings: $15-20

Risk Factor: Medium

Fantasy Overview: Five-category contributor

Fantasy Impact ETA: 2021

Don Orsillo Says: Fancy Dog Cesar Hernandez

John Smoltz Says: A reason for Sox fans to dust off those "Jeter Sucks" t-shirts

75. Nolan Jones, 3B, Cleveland (Age: 22, Previous Rank: 62)

Potential Earnings: $15-20

Risk Factor: Medium

Fantasy Overview: Four-category contributor; Impact potential in R

Fantasy Impact ETA: 2022

Don Orsillo Says: Hunter Dozier

John Smoltz Says: Michael Chavis

76. Orelvis Martinez, SS/3B, Toronto Blue Jays (Age: 20, Previous Rank: 85)

Potential Earnings: $25-30

Risk Factor: Extreme

Fantasy Overview: Five-category contributor; Impact potential in AVG, HR, RBI

Fantasy Impact ETA: 2023

Don Orsillo Says: We said "this year's Marco Luciano" last year so I guess we'll run that back again

John Smoltz Says: Fifty million Orelvis fans can't be wrong

77. Oneil Cruz, "SS," Pittsburgh Pirates (Age: 22, Previous Rank: 48)

Potential Earnings: $20-25

Risk Factor: High

Fantasy Overview: Four-category contributor; Impact potential in HR, RBI

Fantasy Impact ETA: Well, this is complicated..

Don Orsillo Says: What if Jorge Soler had infield eligibility?

John Smoltz Says: Out of organized baseball

78. Austin Hendrick, OF, Cincinnati Reds (Age: 19, Previous Rank: N/A)

Potential Earnings: $20-25

Risk Factor: High

Fantasy Overview: Five-category contributor; Impact potential in HR, RBI, R

Fantasy Impact ETA: 2024

Don Orsillo Says: A 35-homer OF2

John Smoltz Says: Just another windmill

79. Nick Lodolo, LHP, Cincinnati Reds (Age: 23, Previous Rank: HM)

Potential Earnings: $15-20

Risk Factor: Medium

Fantasy Overview: Four-category contributor; Impact potential in W

Fantasy Impact ETA: 2022

Don Orsillo Says: A good enough SP3

John Smoltz Says: Mike Minor, probably

80. Bobby Dalbec, 1B, Boston Red Sox (Age: 25, Previous Rank: HM)

Potential Earnings: $10-15

Risk Factor: Low

Fantasy Overview: Three-category contributor; Impact potential in HR

Fantasy Impact ETA: 2021

Don Orsillo Says: Mark Reynolds in Fenway Park

John Smoltz Says: More swings and misses than a Bob Nightengale tweet

81. Daniel Lynch, LHP, Kansas City Royals (Age: 24, Previous Rank: 87)

Potential Earnings: $15-20

Risk Factor: Medium

Fantasy Overview: Four-category contributor; Impact potential in ERA

Fantasy Impact ETA:

Don Orsillo Says: Funhouse mirror Chris Sale

John Smoltz Says: Store brand Josh Hader

82. Joey Bart, C, San Francisco Giants (Age: 24, Previous Rank: 60)

Potential Earnings: $15-20

Risk Factor: Medium

Fantasy Overview: Four-category contributor

Fantasy Impact ETA: 2022, or a Buster Posey injury

Don Orsillo Says: A 25-dong catcher

John Smoltz Says: A 20-dong catcher

83. Xavier Edwards, 2B/SS, Tampa Bay Rays (Age: 21, Previous Rank: 56)

Potential Earnings: $20-25

Risk Factor: High

Fantasy Overview: Three-category contributor; Impact potential in R, SB

Fantasy Impact ETA: 2023

Don Orsillo Says: Luis Castillo, the hitter

John Smoltz Says: Fancy Dog José Peraza

84. Josiah Gray, RHP, Los Angeles Dodgers (Age: 22, Previous Rank: 76)

Potential Earnings: $15-20

Risk Factor: Medium

Fantasy Overview: Four-category contributor; Impact potential in W

Fantasy Impact ETA: 2021

Don Orsillo Says: The platonic ideal of an SP4

John Smoltz Says: Another SP bust you won't remember because his name is too generic

85. Edward Cabrera, RHP, Miami Marlins (Age: 22, Previous Rank: HM)

Potential Earnings: $15-20

Risk Factor: Medium

Fantasy Overview: Four-category contributor; Impact potential in ERA, WHIP

Fantasy Impact ETA: Mid 2021

Don Orsillo Says: The platonic ideal of an SP4

John Smoltz Says: Another SP bust you won't remember because his name is too generic

86. Robert Hassell III, OF, San Diego Padres (Age: 19, Previous Rank: N/A)

Potential Earnings: $20-25

Risk Factor: High

Fantasy Overview: Five-category contributor; Impact potential in AVG, R

Fantasy Impact ETA: 2023

Don Orsillo Says: Trent Grisham isn't a bad outcome anymore

John Smoltz Says: But it was for a while

87. DL Hall, LHP, Baltimore Orioles (Age: 22, Previous Rank: HM)

Potential Earnings: $15-20

Risk Factor: Medium

Fantasy Overview: Three-category contributor; Impact potential in K

Fantasy Impact ETA: 2021

Don Orsillo Says: Are we really going to compare every wild-ish lefty to Robbie Ray?

John Smoltz Says: He's literally an Orioles pitcher named "DL," so the Mariana Trench?

88. Greg Jones, SS, Tampa Bay Rays (Age: 22, Previous Rank: 70)

Potential Earnings: $20-25

Risk Factor: High

Fantasy Overview: Four-category contributor; Impact potential in SB

Fantasy Impact ETA: 2022

Don Orsillo Says: Jean Segura when he ran

John Smoltz Says: A really good pinch runner

89. Brayan Rocchio, SS/2B, Cleveland (Age: 20, Previous Rank: 94)

Potential Earnings: $15-20

Risk Factor: Medium

Fantasy Overview: Five-category contributor

Fantasy Impact ETA: 2022

Don Orsillo Says: The Nationals Luis García career track

John Smoltz Says: The Phillies Luis Garcia career track

90. Matthew Liberatore, LHP, St. Louis Cardinals (Age: 21, Previous Rank: 95)

Potential Earnings: $15-20

Risk Factor: Medium

Fantasy Overview: Four-category contributor; Impact potential in W, ERA

Fantasy Impact ETA: 2022

Don Orsillo Says: A top-30 pitcher

John Smoltz Says: THIS was the guy we gave up for Arrow's Arena?

91. Emerson Hancock, RHP, Seattle Mariners (Age: 21, Previous Rank: N/A)

Potential Earnings: $15-20

Risk Factor: Medium

Fantasy Overview: Four-category contributor; Impact potential in W, ERA

Fantasy Impact ETA: 2022

Don Orsillo Says: A brand-new Honda Accord

John Smoltz Says: A gently used Toyota Camry (YMMV)

92. Leody Taveras, OF, Texas Rangers (Age: 22, Previous Rank: 82)

Potential Earnings: $10-15

Risk Factor: Low

Fantasy Overview: Five-category contributor

Fantasy Impact ETA: Who else do the Rangers have to play?

Don Orsillo Says: We don't have to rank him anymore

John Smoltz Says: We don't have to worry about where he goes on lists

93. Adrian Morejon, LHP, San Diego Padres (Age: 22, Previous Rank: 88)

Potential Earnings: $15-20

Risk Factor: Medium

Fantasy Overview: Four-category contributor; Impact potential in ERA

Fantasy Impact ETA: Never, if the Padres keep trading for every pitcher

Don Orsillo Says: 120% of Wade Miley

John Smoltz Says: 80% of Wade Miley

94. Khalil Lee, OF, Kansas City Royals (Age: 22, Previous Rank: 89)

Potential Earnings: $10-15

Risk Factor: Low

Fantasy Overview: Four-category contributor

Fantasy Impact ETA: Who else do the Royals have to play?

Don Orsillo Says: Faster Aaron Hicks

John Smoltz Says: Michael A. Taylor

95. Aaron Bracho, 2B, Cleveland (Age: 19, Previous Rank: 97)

Potential Earnings: $20-25

Risk Factor: High

Fantasy Overview: Five-category contributor; Impact potential in AVG, R

Fantasy Impact ETA: 2023

Don Orsillo Says: The Willie Calhoun we wanted

John Smoltz Says: The Willie Calhoun we got

96. A.J. Puk, LHP, Oakland Athletics (Age: 25, Previous Rank: 37)

Potential Earnings: $15-20

Risk Factor: Medium

Fantasy Overview: Three-category contributor; Impact potential in K

Fantasy Impact ETA: 2021

Don Orsillo Says: Healthy

John Smoltz Says: Hurt

97. Clarke Schmidt, RHP, New York Yankees (Age: , Previous Rank: NR)

Potential Earnings: $15-20

Risk Factor: Medium

Fantasy Overview: Four-category contributor; Impact potential in W

Fantasy Impact ETA: 2021

Don Orsillo Says: 120-160 solid innings a year

John Smoltz Says: 60-70 great innings a year

98. Brett Baty, 3B, New York Mets (Age: 21, Previous Rank: 81)

Potential Earnings: $20-25

Risk Factor: High

Fantasy Overview: Four-category contributor; Impact potential in HR, RBI, R

Fantasy Impact ETA: 2023

Don Orsillo Says: Mike Moustakas

John Smoltz Says: It's the Mets, so probably Ike Davis

99. Josh Lowe, OF, Tampa Bay Rays (Age: 23, Previous Rank: NR)

Potential Earnings: $15-20

Risk Factor: Medium

Fantasy Overview: Four-category contributor

Fantasy Impact ETA: 2021

Don Orsillo Says: The good Danny Santana

John Smoltz Says: The other Danny Santana

100. George Kirby, RHP, Seattle Mariners (Age: 23, Previous Rank: HM)

Potential Earnings: $15-20

Risk Factor: Medium

Fantasy Overview: Four-category contributor; Impact potential in WHIP

Fantasy Impact ETA: 2022

Don Orsillo Says: A Kyle Hendricks-esque SP3

John Smoltz Says: Dave Bush

101. Hunter Greene, RHP, Cincinnati Reds (Age: 21, Previous Rank: HM)

Potential Earnings: $20-25

Risk Factor: Extreme

Fantasy Overview: Four-category contributor; Impact potential in ERA, K

Fantasy Impact ETA: 2023

Don Orsillo Says: Trogdor

John Smoltz Says: DARGON

Honorable Mention (in alphabetical order): Matthew Allan, SP, NYM; Francisco Alvarez, C, NYM; Sherten Apostel, 3B, TEX; Jordan Balazovik, RHP, MIN; Alexander Canario, OF, SF; Keoni Cavaco, SS, MIN; Dane Dunning, RHP, TEX; Jarren Duran, OF, BOS; Tyler Freeman, SS, CLE; Jose Garcia, SS, CIN; Brusdar Graterol, RHP, LAD; Kody Hoese, 3B, LAD; Ed Howard, SS, CHC; Alejandro Kirk, C, TOR; Brailyn Marquez, LHP, CHC; Brendan McKay, LHP, TB; Kyle Muller, LHP, ATL; Jesús Sánchez, OF, MIA; Bryson Stott, SS, PHI; Misael Urbina, OF, MIN; Miguel Vargas, 3B, LAD; Devin Williams, RHP, MIL; Simeon Woods Richardson, RHP, TOR.

The Top 50 Fantasy Prospects For 2021 Only

by Mike Gianella

Whether you're a newcomer to fantasy baseball or a seasoned veteran, one of the biggest challenges you face every season is trying to parse prospect lists and figure out how to apply them to your league. While the quality and quantity of information available is unprecedented, most of this information is geared toward the real kind of baseball and not the fantasy variety. This is a good thing overall, but it also means you must make your own rough mental calculations about issues like how much to downgrade a prospect because of his good defense or what kind of weight to put on a catcher's value.

If you only play in redraft leagues, an additional set of challenges makes this exercise even more arduous. How much value should be a placed on a prospect's proximity to the majors versus his ceiling? If a Top 10 overall prospect has a slim chance of making the majors but could be an immediate impact player when he arrives, how do you account for this in your valuation?

The list below is designed specifically for players in one-and-done leagues. Beyond the obvious fact that prospects who are clearly two or more years away aren't listed, you'll also see more rookies who clearly aren't top prospects but have a clear opportunity for playing time in 2021 as we go to press. Your primary goal is to win your league now, not to have a great prospect on your reserve list for six months.

Of course, this list wouldn't exist without the amazing work the Baseball Prospectus prospect team churns out every year, especially their essential Top 10 lists. Their diligent research and top-flight writing are a significant starting point for what you see below. But it is exactly that, a jumping off point, not a final say in these one-and-done rankings.

This list uses MLB's rookie eligibility rules, which is why you won't see Jo Adell, James Karinchak and Brendan Rodgers (among others) below. All three players did not reach MLB's 130-at-bat or 50-inning rookie threshold but are no longer rookies based on MLB's decision that service time accrued on an active roster in September 2020 counts in determining rookie status.

One final note: these rankings assume a standard 5x5 Roto, 15-team mixed league with moderate reserve lists. Your mileage may vary depending on what format your league uses. Nevertheless, we believe the list below is an excellent resource for your league or leagues, and at the very least a solid jumping off point for your own research and preparation.

1. Randy Arozarena, OF, Tampa Bay Rays
The Rays reputation as baseball's prospect Rumpelstiltskin is well deserved, and Arozarena is yet another feather in the team's cap. Seen by most prior to 2020 as a future fourth outfielder who fell into the tweener category, Arozarena busted out, hitting 17 home runs in 161 combined regular season and postseason plate appearances. No one is suggesting Arozarena is the second coming of Mike Trout, but even if he can "only" muster a 25-homer/15-steal season in 2021 he easily makes the top of this 2021-centric list.

2. Ha-seong Kim, 2B/SS, San Diego Padres
Signed away from the KBO with a $25-million, four-year pact, Kim instantly enters the conversation as a potential 2021 NL Rookie of the Year. He's eligible at shortstop based on games played in the KBO but should start at second for the Padres. Projecting Kim's major league output is a near impossible task. His athleticism and tools are unquestioned but moving from a league where 95 on the radar gun is a rarity to a circuit where it is common could lead to a difficult adjustment period. However, Kim is younger and better than any previous KBO imports so assuming he'll similarly slip is foolhardy. Kim should steal 15-20 bases; when and if the power comes and how much of it arrives will determine whether this ranking is too aggressive or dead on.

3. Ian Anderson, RHP, Atlanta Braves

No one doubted Anderson's long-term future as a major league starter when he was a prospect, but questions about his command and change up made some wonder whether that future was going to be as a mid-tier arm or a high-end SP2. Anderson's impressive 2020 debut easily put him in the latter category. This combined with his high strikeout and ground ball rates make Anderson less of a prospect and more of a proven commodity, and you won't be sorry if Anderson's your SP2 in any fantasy format.

4. Ke'Bryan Hayes, 3B, Pittsburgh Pirates

Hayes' prospect reputation was mostly burnished thanks to his superb defensive reputation, so the fact that he came out of the gate hitting was a pleasant surprise. It wasn't a shock, though, as scouts had indicated that the combination of a solid approach at the plate and the lively major league ball could work to Hayes' benefit in the majors. Hayes won't hit .376 (like he did in 2020) or swat 30 bombs but a .280 AVG with 20-25 home runs and 10 steals is a realistic outcome and puts Hayes firmly in our top five.

5. Dylan Carlson, OF, St. Louis Cardinals

It's easy and perhaps lazy to use 2020 as a magic wand to cast away all negativity about poor, small sample size performances. But in Carlson's case, his disappointing big-league debut should be seen in the context of a difficult Cardinals season that saw COVID-19 blow a two-and-a-half-week hole in their schedule and forced them to play 22 doubleheaders. Carlson's raw numbers were unequivocally poor, but his hard-hit percentage and average exit velocity were in the top third among all hitters with at least 50 qualifying events. Carlson will get another opportunity sooner rather than later and the power/speed combination that propelled him to the top of 2020's prospect list makes him a potential fantasy force.

6. Sixto Sánchez, RHP, Florida Marlins

2020's seven start (regular season) sample was a pithy encapsulation of why Sánchez is so highly regarded but also with where the danger lies. He can dial his fastball into triple-digits, but it frequently doesn't have enough movement to fool hitters. His secondary pitches, particularly his change, improved but still don't seem quite as good as you'd expect from an elite prospect. All this nattering about Sánchez's warts gloss over the fact that he's only 22 years old and continued to improve despite the lack of minor league reps in 2020. There is performance and durability risk, but Sánchez's raw ability and ceiling make him one of the better potential rookie buys in 2021.

7. Leody Taveras, OF, Texas Rangers

Taveras showed flashes of what he can do with the bat in his major league debut, hitting four home runs and swiping eight bases in a mere 134 plate appearances. Alas, he also hit .227 and struck out 32 percent of the time, revealing some holes in his game that indicate he might need the time at Triple-A that wasn't available in 2020. If this ranking seems aggressive based on the potential downside, keep in mind that 30-40 steal players are a rarity in today's game, so if Taveras can deliver even a modicum power to go with that game-changing speed, he'll be a dynamic fantasy force.

8. Ryan Mountcastle, 1B/OF, Baltimore Orioles

On a dynasty-centric/long-term prospect list, Mountcastle would rank closer to the bottom of a 50-player list than the top. But for 2021 only, he ranks high because he's locked into a job as the Orioles Opening Day first baseman and is as safe as a rookie can be thanks to a modest, 20-homer floor with a decent batting average. The friendly confines of Camden Yards could push that home run total even higher, and if you're looking to place a prop bet on which rookie could hit 40 bombs, Mountcastle is where your money should go.

9. Nick Madrigal, 2B, Chicago White Sox

There's little doubting Madrigal will be a good major league player. He is already one of the best contact hitters in the game and is excellent defensively. Valuing him for fantasy is difficult, because Madrigal is an extreme ground ball hitter and didn't hit the ball hard in his big-league debut. Power isn't an absolute requirement to be a good fantasy hitter, but without it the margin of error dips considerably. Maybe Madrigal can be a perennial .320 hitter with 20 steals, but if he isn't, he's going to be problematic in shallower mixed leagues. He's still a worthy add in nearly every format and is a top fantasy option for 2021 among rookies because he's all but locked in as the White Sox starting second baseman.

10. Triston McKenzie, RHP, Cleveland Indians

If we could assuredly project McKenzie's 2020 truncated output across 180 innings, he would rank a few slots higher. But while the raw numbers looked great, McKenzie's velocity dropped to 90-92 miles-per-hour by season's end and he was moved to the bullpen for the last week of the regular season and the playoffs. The endurance/durability questions can't be written off solely because of 2020's abbreviated ramp up either, as McKenzie missed large chunks of time in the minors in 2018-2019 as well. There are lots of potential outcomes here, but while the ceiling is high the risk is as well.

11. Alex Kirilloff, OF, Minnesota Twins

The Twins surprising non-tender of Eddie Rosario makes it likely Kirilloff has a slot in Minnesota's Opening Day lineup. He is a polarizing player in the scouting community: an athlete who at times has looked like a future 30-40 home run power threat and at others has battled inconsistency, with his aggressive approach leading to poor results. Split the difference and you're probably going to get a decent but not great hitter who will swat 20 homers with an acceptable batting average. The variance makes Kirilloff a potential bargain but is also why he is one of the few hitters seemingly guaranteed an Opening Day job ranked outside of our Top 10.

12. Bobby Dalbec, 1B, Boston Red Sox

It's tempting to look at Dalbec's 2020 power output, hope he duplicates Pete Alonso's 2019 NL Rookie of the Year campaign and call it a day. But comps are bad for a reason, and Dalbec's considerable swing-and-miss issues, which plagued him even in the minors, cannot be ignored. Dalbec does have a legitimate shot at 30 homers if he sticks with the Red Sox – and perhaps more thanks to the lively ball – but he's going to need to keep that average around .240 to be more than a bench or platoon bat. Dalbec is a fun gamble for fantasy but remember that he is a gamble.

13. Andrew Vaughn, 1B, Chicago White Sox

Vaughn projects as a future perennial All-Star first baseman and with Edwin Encarnación and Nomar Mazara no longer on the roster, there's a clear path to playing time for the University of California product. The minor league numbers in 2019 were underwhelming outside of a solid K/BB rate, but Vaughn's approach suggests that even if he doesn't excel out of the gate, he's unlikely to struggle either. Vaughn is limited to first base defensively, but this is no longer the impediment it was in fantasy it was 8-10 years ago.

14. Wander Franco, SS, Tampa Bay Rays

Will Franco's elite bat carry him to the majors as a 20-year-old in 2021? Regardless of how effusive the press clippings are, there is risk in any 20-year-old rookie making his major league debut, but Franco is a special enough hitter that the fantasy upside cannot be ignored. Don't get too excited about the 36 steals across three minor league levels in 2019; Franco was also thrown out 28 times and even if he curbs his enthusiasm he projects as an average baserunner long term. But it is the bat that will make him special, with the only questions being how soon Franco will be promoted and how quickly will his over-the-fence power develop.

15. Dane Dunning, RHP, Texas Rangers

Although it was only a seven-start sample, Dunning proved he belonged in the majors with a solid debut for the White Sox. Traded to the Rangers for Lance Lynn, Dunning benefits by moving to a more pitcher-friendly venue, although it could be argued that his favorable results were propped up by mostly light-hitting AL and NL Central opponents. Dunning is a reliable option who does a good job mixing up two low 90s heaters with a slider and change, but it's more likely he is a future SP4 or SP5 than a mid-tier arm.

16. Jarred Kelenic, OF, Seattle Mariners

Despite a mere 92 plate appearances in the high minors, there is a distinct possibility Kelenic makes his major league debut in 2021. If we were confident the Mariners were going to be aggressive with Kelenic, he'd easily rank in the top 10 but the loss of a development year means we might not see him until the second half. Kelenic could be an instant 20/20 player. The concern that he might not stick in center field is irrelevant for our purposes. If your one-and-done league has any kind of reserve list, Kelenic should be on it.

17. Ryan Jeffers, C, Minnesota Twins

These rankings assume two-catcher formats; if you play in a one-catcher league, you'll need to downgrade all the backstops on this list accordingly. Jeffers doesn't have the clearest path to playing time thanks to the presence of Mitch Garver, but all Jeffers has done as a professional is hit. He can field his position too, which matters in a version of the game where there are maybe five or six competent offensive catchers at any given moment. There is some short-term playing time risk here, but Jeffers is a better play in a 15-team, two-catcher league than a bad offensive starter with a secure path to playing time.

18. Nate Pearson, RHP, Toronto Blue Jays

If Pearson can prove he's healthy in Spring Training, this ranking will be far too conservative. For now, the barking elbow that sidelined Pearson for a month in mid-August and led to one relief outing after his return is enough of a reason to exercise caution. Pearson's velocity was also lower than his advertised 100 mph, and while a mid-90s heater is nothing to sneeze at, it was frequently too flat and hittable. If this was all health related and Pearson comes back in 2021 looking like the second coming of Noah Syndergaard, then draft him aggressively but otherwise we're advising some caution in the near-term.

19. Michael Kopech, RHP, Chicago White Sox

Stop us if you've heard this one before, but if it weren't for injuries, we'd have this pitching prospect ranked much higher. Kopech voluntarily sat out in 2020 and hasn't thrown a pitch in a competitive game since 2018. When healthy, the high 90s fastball and knee-buckling slider make Kopech a potential stud. What isn't clear is if he'll ever have the durability to be a rotation mainstay or if he'll wind up a long-term bullpen arm. Kopech's ceiling is considerable, but for 2021 alone the ceiling and floor are a gaping chasm.

20. MacKenzie Gore, LHP, San Diego Padres

Gore remains the best fantasy pitching prospect in baseball, but the combination of the lack of a minor league season in 2020 and the Padres loading up on stud starting pitchers could make Gore's inevitable 2021 debut a little less so. When he does arrive, it will be with four pitches that are above average if not better, a rarity for any pitcher, let alone a 20-year-old prep arm. The Padres have been extremely judicious about building up Gore's workload so if there's a concern about him in 2021 drafts, it's that he might only amass 140 innings, with a good chunk of those coming in the minors.

21. Deivi García, RHP, New York Yankees

A 4.98 ERA isn't anything to write home about, but most of that damage came in one lousy outing against the Red Sox in September. García mostly showed why the Yankees have had him on the fast track to the majors, displaying a low 90s fastball with loads of deception and a curve with great spin and command. One question 2020 couldn't answer is how García's small size will play with a full season's workload. It's possible García starts 2021 in the minors, but regardless of when he arrives there's enough to like to make him one of the more promising rookie arms you'll see this season.

22. Adbert Alzolay, RHP, Chicago Cubs

Alzolay's fastball/power curve combination is one of the better two-pitch mixes in the minors and puts him on track for a big-league future. Whether that future is as a starter or a front-line reliever is an open question, and while a slider he added to his pitch mix late in 2020 offers hope, questions about Alzolay's ability to stay healthy and go deep into games remain. He'll have an opportunity on a Cubs team that is suddenly in rebuilding mode and the ceiling is high enough to make him an intriguing risk on draft day.

23. Cristian Pache, OF, Atlanta Braves

Pache's calling card is defense, which cements his future in the majors but is the wet blanket of qualifiers in fantasy. Pache is only 22 years old and has plenty of talent, and if he can translate his speed into stolen bases then there's suddenly much more to like. Because this is a 2021 ranking, it's impossible to count on that happening and while we believe Pache will hold his own if he sticks in the majors, offensively it's a deep league profile in the short term. Pache could initially resemble Nick Markakis, one of the Atlanta outfielders he'd be replacing. That's nothing to sneeze at for a rookie but, again, those aren't game changing numbers outside of NL-only.

24. Tarik Skubal, LHP, Detroit Tigers

It's foolish enough to selectively parse data in a 162-game season, so doing so in an abbreviated 60-game one is particularly dumb. However, while Skubal's overall 2020 stat line is awful, most of that came in two outings against the White Sox and Cardinals. Skubal succeeded when he stopped leaning too heavily on the fastball and mixed in his slider and change more.

Even so, there are questions about whether Skubal can succeed as a starter long-term or if his stuff will play up more in the pen. Short-term, he's the best bet of three Tigers rookie arms to be a success in 2021, although given the early returns that's damning with the faintest of praise.

25. Sam Huff, C, Texas Rangers
Huff might have difficulty staying behind the plate in the long-term (more because of his immense size than due to any defensive deficiencies), but the nice thing about a 2021-centric list is the long-term doesn't matter. Huff's raw power is a true 70 on the scouting scale, and when he connects, he hits the ball a long way. The challenge for Huff is a lack of patience, something even pitchers in the low minors were able to exploit. Jose Trevino isn't the long-term answer for Texas, but it's unlikely Huff will be the short-term one for the Rangers on Opening Day either.

26. Alejandro Kirk, C, Toronto Blue Jays
At any other position, Kirk's lack of significant over-the-fence power or stolen base ability would relegate him to the very bottom of the list. As a catcher-eligible rookie, Kirk is interesting even if the most likely outcome is a .270 hitter with 10-15 home runs. While his physical build looks like a non-starter, Kirk's athleticism is legitimate, and he will get a shot with Toronto. How soon that opportunity comes for a prospect with no experience above High-A prior to 2020 will matter a great deal to fantasy drafters this spring.

27. Casey Mize, RHP, Detroit Tigers
On ceiling alone, Mize is one of the best prospects on this list and if everything works out, he could be a legitimate ace. Unfortunately, that "if" is emblazoned in gold. Mize followed up a second-half 2019 collapse in the minors with a poor 2020 where his command, in-game endurance and velocity all suffered. There's still a lot to like if Mize can get back to where he was two years ago, but the risk is considerably high and as a short-term bet there are other arms more worthy of your consideration.

28. Spencer Howard, RHP, Philadelphia Phillies
The good news: Howard appears to be locked in as the Phillies no. 4 starter for Opening Day. The bad news: almost everything else. Howard's fastball velocity was down, his secondary offerings didn't look nearly as sharp as expected, and the results were bad. Topping off the shit sundae, Howard was placed on the IL in mid-September with shoulder stiffness, ending his season. The potential remains for a future ace, but in the short-term there are too many yellow flags, and there's a legitimate risk that Howard misses significant time in 2021 if the shoulder reemerges as an issue. He's ranked this high because if he is healthy and can put it all back together, the stuff still plays up to an SP2, at least.

29. Trevor Rogers, LHP, Miami Marlins
Rogers took significant strides forward with his stuff in 2020, averaging 94 mph with good spin on his fastball to go along with a plus changeup and developing slider. While his DRA and non-ERA stats suggest a bright future, Rogers' shaky and inconsistent command led to a lot of deep counts and early exits. Rogers only made it past the fourth inning in two of his seven starts and only into the sixth once. The punchout potential makes Rogers enticing, but he's going to need to improve on his 20 pitch per inning average to realize his fantasy – and real life – potential.

30. A.J. Puk, LHP, Oakland Athletics
The Athletics are committed to using Puk in the rotation in 2021 but given his injury history and command issues it's fair to wonder if Oakland would be better served using him as a reliever. Puk throws upper 90s gas and a power slider that can hit 90 but will need a consistent third offering to survive as a starter. He's a fun, high ceiling prospect but if you draft him make sure to have at least one backup plan; even if Puk stays healthy, an innings cap is likely.

31. Tanner Houck, RHP, Boston Red Sox
Not every name on a 2021-only prospect list is going to be an exciting one. Opportunity trumps talent, particularly as you get to the bottom half of this list. Houck is here because the Red Sox are rebuilding, you need five pitchers to fill out a rotation, and their system is thin on arms at the upper levels. Houck was awesome in three starts, but there are major concerns he doesn't have enough of an arsenal to survive as a starter and that his delivery will leave him exposed against left-handed hitters. The ceiling is an SP4 and for all the negatives we've lobbed at him in this space, Houck has earned the opportunity to prove everyone wrong.

32. Tyler Stephenson, C, Cincinnati Reds

An eight-game major league sample isn't enough to draw any sweeping conclusions, but outside of an exceedingly high strikeout rate Stephenson more than held his own during his cup of coffee. The Reds will start the year with Tucker Barnhart at catcher, but it should be Stephenson's job eventually. Despite his size, Stephenson has been more of a contact-oriented hitter, but a .260-.270 hitter with even moderate pop plays behind the plate in all two-catcher formats.

33. Luis Patiño, RHP, Tampa Bay Rays

Traded to the Rays in the Blake Snell deal, Patiño is on track to make his Tampa debut sometime in 2021. He made his big-league entrance for the Padres last year with mixed results, impressing with his high-end fastball velocity but showing inconsistency with command and control. Getting traded to the Rays is a blessing and a curse for a player's fantasy value. Their ability to get the most out of their players is renowned, but so is their reputation for using players in non-traditional and limited roles. Patiño could easily be the Rays Next Big Thing, but that greatness could be limited to a smattering of bullpen innings in 2021.

34. Joey Bart, C, San Francisco Giants

No player's status on his list is tied to more closely to another player's health/durability than Bart's is to Buster Posey's. The Giants legend hasn't exactly fallen off a cliff, but after two meh seasons and opting out of 2020, Posey is now a 34-year-old catcher who hasn't been elite since 2017. Bart could use more seasoning and having Posey back in the fold gives the Giants a nice problem to have, but if Posey falls off the aging catcher cliff, we will see Bart in 2021. You can mostly ignore Bart's 2020 line. With regular reps, he's likely to be a top-10 option behind the dish. We just don't know when those reps will come.

35. Isaac Paredes, 3B, Detroit Tigers

Paredes is arguably the least exciting hitter on this list, but short-term opportunity makes him clearly deserving of a spot on our Top 50. Paredes' lackluster 2020 line makes him a bit of a sleeper, as his potential speaks more to a 20-home run hitter with a .260-.270 average. That's not going to do much for anyone in a standard mixer, but deep league players should keep Paredes in mind in the later rounds. In leagues that put too much stock in ceiling over performance, Paredes is a probable bargain.

36. Jazz Chisholm, 2B/SS, Miami Marlins

Chisholm showed brief flashes of why the Marlins traded Zac Gallen even up for the Bahamian middle infielder, but most of Chisholm's debut showed why he could spend 2021 in the minors putting the finishing touches on his game. Chisholm has loud tools and a path to a perennial 20/20 player, but the swing-and-miss issues are considerable. While his defensive abilities could lead to a long, productive major league career unless Chisholm's plate discipline and contact improve, he could be more of a league average player than a future superstar.

37. Clarke Schmidt, RHP, New York Yankees

Schmidt might not be in the Yankees Opening Day rotation, but he should get first crack at a job when an opening occurs. Schmidt has an intriguing arsenal, but the pitch that gets everyone all hot and bothered is a curveball that looks more like a slider and gives hitters fits. The fastball is nothing to sneeze at either, but Schmidt has the typical inconsistent third pitch/lack of command issues that could make him a future bullpen arm. Schmidt is a decent reserve pick in the hope he gets an opportunity but isn't someone you should hold onto at all costs if he struggles early in the minors.

38. Adley Rutschman, C, Baltimore Orioles

Rutschman is the best catching prospect in baseball (sorry, Joey Bart) and one of the best we've seen the last few years. The scouting reports all point to a hitter with an excellent swing plane, great barrel control, good plate approach and plus power. The problem is that he has all of 155 professional plate appearances, with only 47 of those above rookie/short season ball. Rutschman certainly could be up in 2021, but we're guessing it will be on the later side so he can get more reps to finalize the finishing touches on his game.

39. Kohei Arihara, RHP, Texas Rangers

When "durable" is the first adjective your new team uses to describe you in their press release, it doesn't exactly inspire loads of confidence. Arihara doesn't throw that hard (his fastball clocks in at 92 mph) but he mixes in six pitches for strikes and has great location. One thing that could work to Arihara's benefit is that he logged 47 more innings in Japan than any American pitcher did during major league baseball's truncated 2020. Stable but boring is appealing in a year when innings and health might be hard to come by across the board.

40. Matt Manning, RHP, Detroit Tigers

Manning didn't make his major league debut in 2020 because he was shut down with forearm soreness. This seems minor and he should be ready for 2021, but it's something to watch, nonetheless. His mid-90s heater and power curve looks major league ready but the change needs a little work. The high strikeout potential makes Manning intriguing for fantasy, but the ceiling is closer to a mid-tier SP3 than an ace.

41. Garrett Crochet, LHP, Chicago White Sox

The White Sox short-term plan for Crochet is to use him as a reliever in the majors while developing him as a starter in the long-term. This is a tough needle to thread and makes it tough to predict Crochet's 2021 outcome. If he stays in the majors all year, he could be a dominant reliever who produces double-digit fantasy earnings even if he isn't closing. But he could also be on a strict innings limit and/or go back to the minors if Chicago decides they want to stretch him out as a starter. The ceiling is high regardless of role but for 2021 only your best hope at any return is out of the pen, which caps Crochet's short-term value unless he's closing.

42. Keegan Akin, LHP, Baltimore Orioles

It's understandable if you're skeptical about Akin's 2020, but even a modest eight-game major league sample gives him a leg up on many of the pitchers in our top 50. Akin throws a fastball he can dial into the mid-90s that can overpower hitters and allows him to mix in a change and slider that are unspectacular but have plenty of separation from the heater. It's a back-of-the-rotation arm, but Akin's smooth mechanics and repeatable delivery give him a chance to be a mainstay for Baltimore.

43. Logan Gilbert, RHP, Seattle Mariners

Gilbert is one of the more boring names on this list, but if you're solely looking for a contributor in 2021 that's not necessarily a bad thing. None of Gilbert's four pitches are dominant and his fastball lacks high-end velocity, but he throws all four for strikes and has excellent poise and presence on the mound. There might never be a lot of strikeouts attached to Gilbert's stat line – which is an obvious fantasy drawback – but when Gilbert does arrive, he's attached to less risk than most pitching prospects.

44. Edward Cabrera, RHP, Miami Marlins

You might wonder why a pitcher with such great raw stuff who is close to the majors is so low on this list. Cabrera has a fastball with great movement that sits in the mid-90s and can dial up to 99. His curve and change are plus pitches and his ease-of-delivery and repeatability make Cabrera enticing. But the combination of the Marlins caution with their minor league arms and minor injuries throughout Cabrera's professional career hurt him on a short-term list. Cabrera could get called up early, but given Miami's recent history, a second half debut is more likely…assuming Cabrera doesn't get hurt again.

45. Forrest Whitley, RHP, Houston Astros

If he's healthy, Whitley deserves a much more generous ranking than this one. That's a gigantic if, though, as Whitley had a combined 86 minor league innings in 2018-2019 and couldn't find his way to the majors in 2020 despite the Astros desperate need for arms. There isn't even a great performance track record to look at in those 86 innings. It would be foolish to write Whitley off completely, but we haven't seen even a hint of elite since 2017. Whitley is the epitome of a boom or bust arm, and this ranking is the coward's way of splitting the difference.

46. Jared Oliva, OF, Pittsburgh Pirates

The first thing that jumps out about Oliva's minor league line are the steals, most recently 36 swipes in 46 attempts at Double-A Altoona in 2019. But Oliva's inclusion on this list isn't merely as steals speculation. He was an underrated prospect who has proven himself at every level except the majors and has a shot to log significant time for the Pirates in 2021. The risk is he's a tweener who might wind up as a fourth outfielder and not a regular but being on a thin Pirates team helps Oliva's short-term stock.

47. Taylor Trammell, OF, Seattle Mariners

The Mariners are loaded with outfielders and it is quite possible Trammell gets lapped by Kelenic and Julio Rodríguez in Seattle. But Trammell's speed is legitimate and more importantly has repeatedly translated to stolen bases as a pro, which is why Trammell is still worth watching in fantasy. The bat still needs to take a step forward for Trammell to be more than a future fourth outfielder, but on a team trying to figure out which pieces are going to be part of their future, Trammell has plenty of near-term opportunity.

48. Dean Kremer, RHP, Baltimore Orioles

Kremer ranks higher on the prospect team's Orioles Top 10 than his teammate Akin, but in the short-term Kremer has a few more warts that cap his value. Kremer has a solid fastball and nasty curve that falls off the table, but he needs a consistent third pitch and while he excelled in a four-game sample he's likely to get exposed if that third pitch doesn't come along. There are enough potential strikeouts for a back-of-the-rotation arm, but it's a deep mixed streaming and AL-only profile in the short-term.

49. Drew Waters, OF, Atlanta Braves

A high ceiling/high floor player, Waters could make a significant impact in the majors as soon as 2021. That's a significant if for several reasons though, most notably because of an incredibly aggressive approach that might lead to too many whiffs against major league pitching. Atlanta has no incentive to rush Waters, and with a mere 119 plate appearances at Triple-A in 2019 that's probably where Waters will start again in 2021. He's also more projection than stats in the power department thus far; just be aware that while Waters could be a 20-25 home run hitter, he might not realize that potential immediately.

50. Khalil Lee, OF, Kansas City Royals

If this were a non-fantasy prospect list, Lee might not even sniff the top 100. But this is a fantasy list, Lee is super-fast and he stole 53 at Double-A Northwest Arkansas in 2019. This is a boom or bust pick. Lee isn't close to being a finished product and at the very least needs to make moderate adjustments to make enough contact and capitalize on his power to be a viable major league outfielder. But if it does happen, Lee is a name you'll want to get to know in a hurry in 2021. It certainly helps that Franchy Cordero isn't any kind of real obstacle on the Royals' depth chart.

Thanks for Mark Barry for the additional assistance.

—Mike Gianella is an author of Baseball Prospectus.

Ordinality in an Unordinary Year

by Jeffrey Paternostro, Jarrett Seidler and Keanan Lamb

When we started looking at player development during the pandemic, our first question was: what development even was there? We didn't see a whole lot with our own eyes. There was no minor-league season at all. Spring training was truncated right as players were ramping up.

Select prospects had time at the alternate training site, and teams took wildly different approaches in choosing who was on those rosters. At the extremes, Milwaukee and Oakland loaded up with extremely young talent, including recent draftees and international signees with little to no pro experience, figuring that simulated games against upper-level prospects and minor-league vets were a better developmental experience than nothing at all. Other teams, like the Mets and Astros, went heavy on Quad-A types and added the further-away kids later in the summer (and only a small handful at that). Most teams were somewhere in the middle.

Evaluating tools, skills and overall projection—and how those things change throughout a season—is the foundational aspect of how the Top 101 is assembled. A previous year's work is not torn up when it comes time to create a new one, as track record and trajectory play a substantial part. But why Julio Rodríguez thrived in leagues where he was nearly a half-decade younger than the average player, or why Dylan Carlson went from slugging .390 in A-ball to .542 in the upper-minors is a puzzle that needs to be assembled. The performance exists to be explained—good, bad or indifferent.

Rodríguez was not an unknown entering the 2019 season. He was a seven-figure IFA outfielder who had industry buzz based on his performance in the Dominican Summer League. We tend to be fairly cautious with ranking these prospects—international complex ball has wildly variant competition, and even reliable second-hand looks are hard to come by—and he wasn't one of our Top 101 Prospects entering the season. Rodríguez opened 2019 in the South Atlantic League as an 18-year-old—an extremely aggressive assignment. His arrival in full-season ball allowed our team to get live looks (our most-valued data point), and each one suggested he was among the top prospects in all of baseball: a potential five-tool outfielder with light-tower power. Similarly effervescent reports followed a late-season promotion to High-A and it was clear that Rodríguez had established himself as a 70 OFP prospect—a potential all-star—by our evaluation system. He ranked as the no. 10 prospect in all of baseball going into 2020.

Every minor-league season provides us with new information about prospects. And every season a handful of them have this kind of breakout. Perhaps with Rodríguez it was merely a matter of our team getting eyes on him, but for teammate Jarred Kelenic, there was an obvious swing tweak that unlocked a new level for both his hit and power tools. That moved him from the no. 63 prospect in baseball to no. 7. Dodgers infielder Gavin Lux added loft and power and dominated the high-minors without losing his speed or infield range. The aforementioned Carlson started lifting the ball more consistently and took to center field better than expected.

Young players change rapidly and are reminders that development is not linear. As recently as 10 years ago, the widespread belief in baseball was that the most important thing you could do was identify talent at point of acquisition, whether it be in the draft and international market or through trade and free agency. For amateur talent especially, the idea was that you need to merely water the prospects and they would grow into whatever was preordained. Sure, that skinny Texas prep arm would add a couple miles an hour as he naturally filled out; that was foreseeable, mere extrapolation. But with the sheer amount of data teams now compile on their prospects, with the highly specialized technology that exists to measure every output from every baseball action, identifying what and how much you can change the players in your organization is paramount.

Baseball Prospectus doesn't have access to most of what goes behind the curtain, but we try to be front row when the stage lights go on. The backbone of our work is live looks. We might not know exactly what a team saw in a pitcher's arm stroke, release point and spin axis that suggested a new slider grip, but can evaluate the new pitch and how well it works in games. The end product is what we are both looking for anyway.

Yet whereas our evaluations are usually composed of hundreds and hundreds of live looks, we had a scant few dozen in 2020—some spring training and early-season college action, plus a few scattered amateur showcases in the summer and fall instructional league looks. And we weren't alone. Major League Baseball banned live amateur scouting from March until June, and kept professional scouts working from home all summer, only relenting for fall coverage.

Domestic instructional leagues varied wildly, too, ranging from the Royals running a longer program split between two locations to the Yankees and Cardinals running nothing at all. For many, fall instructs—normally a waystation for minor-leaguers to get in a little extra work and experimentation during informal games—were not just the best opportunity to get updated reports on players, but also the primary source of direct team instruction for the entire year.

So, what were the minor leaguers doing the rest of the time? For starters, they were dealing with the ugly ramifications of a worldwide pandemic. Players got sick. Players got hurt. Players got stuck thousands of miles away from their homes for months on end, at team complexes instead of with their families. Most did the best they could off the radar, working out on their own at home or informal private camps. A few even popped up in indy ball or collegiate summer leagues; Jake Burger and Colin Barber, for example, played well in those conditions and were later added to alternate site rosters. Communication with the team—and even sometimes training sessions—took place over Zoom and FaceTime. In some cases, team sources we talked to didn't even know for sure what their prospects were up to.

In what might sum up the overall weirdness of the season, and the conundrum of ranking players in this moment, *Baseball America* reported that many of the Cubs' top pitching prospects wouldn't be present at the fall instructs after not being assigned to the alternate site because they "accumulated their required innings through a virtual training program."

There were fewer opportunities for players to improve than in a normal year, and while we've concluded that there simply were fewer breakouts this year, it's possible, even likely, that some of them happened in places we couldn't see.

⚾   ⚾   ⚾

Our biggest problem in compiling lists wasn't a *lack* of information, but rather information asymmetry. While we were able to get responses on nearly every player we asked about, the amount of information available varied significantly depending on what the player was doing during the lack of minor-league season.

While the various levels of competition, environmental conditions and org-specific development goals make evaluations complicated to reconcile in a normal year, 2020 put into sharp relief how good we've had it. Some prospects produced an end product by pitching in the majors or in college. Others produced a partial product via alternate site reports and data generation—about two-thirds of the teams participated in the video and data share—or third-party live scouting reports from fall instructs. Still others had teams that didn't participate in data-sharing or reciprocal scouting during instructs, and thus were even more nebulous. Consider the following five prospects, all pitchers ranked within the Top 25 who were born in 1998 or 1999:

- Ian Anderson — Made 10 brilliant major-league starts in the regular season and postseason, with all the video and Statcast data that comes with that.

- Luis Patiño — Thirteen major-league relief appearances and one start as an opener in the regular season and postseason; didn't look so hot, but was adjusting to a different role under difficult circumstances.

- MacKenzie Gore — Pitched all summer at the alternate site without getting called up even though the Padres really could have used him; San Diego was not in the data share, so third-party sources don't have much new information on him.

- Shane Baz — Pitched all summer at the alternate site; the Rays were in the data share, so pro scouts did updated work on him and we were able to get their opinions, and he also threw in televised exhibitions.

- Asa Lacy — Made four starts at Texas A&M before the college season was shut down and ended up at the alternate site and instructs toward the end of the summer; the Royals were also not in the data share.

Those are wildly different levels of information about each player, and it was hard to figure out how to weigh everything against prior reports. We do suspect there were Julio Rodríguezes or Dylan Carlsons making major skill improvements—prospects who should be jumping way up the list. We're pretty confident a few made skills leaps behind closed doors; prospects like Corbin Carroll and Edward Cabrera, but a constant question hung over the entire process like the sword of Damocles: how can we be sure?

A major-league track record provides the highest-confidence information. Anderson, for example, threw 51 innings between the regular season and playoffs. He was absolutely phenomenal in that stretch, and he has clearly surpassed not just his 2019 skill level but his projection as of a year ago. We thought his changeup might have above-average or even plus potential, yet he showed up in the majors with a regular plus-plus *cambio*, fully developed.

Admittedly, we have been bitten in the past by aggressively ranking pitchers based off huge late-season jumps in stuff. But Anderson has been on this list four times before. He was the no. 3 overall pick in the 2016 draft as a prep righty, which is a heck of a starting point. He's been on the edge of a 70 OFP grade for two cycles. Is it really that hard to believe he took a major step with his changeup development and got there in the calendar year we didn't see him?

In a normal season, a half-season of Anderson tormenting Triple-A batters would back up the major-league improvements—if he hadn't been called up earlier and lost prospect eligibility. This year, there is no safety net, no additional context against which to determine whether what was shown in the majors was real; not just on Anderson but also on Sixto Sánchez, Ke'Bryan Hayes, Ryan Mountcastle, Dane Dunning and Triston McKenzie. Similarly, we had to figure out whether Carlson, Casey Mize, Joey Bart, Spencer Howard and Tarik Skubal struggling in the majors were real downward profile shifts or just noise. In a few cases, like Shane McClanahan, Brailyn Marquez and Alex Kirilloff, there is only the tiniest bit of big-league action to try and glean changes off of. If minor-league evaluations and performance provide a safety net for major-league glimpses, 2020 was a Wallenda-level challenge.

Suffice to say, if you flip over a few pages, you'll see that we believe Anderson's changeup development is real, just like we believe that Hayes will sustain at least some of his sudden and similarly unexpected big jump with his in-game power. Both the data and our eyes support those conclusions. We're optimistic Carlson will still play back to his tools, which mostly showed up as expected even as he struggled mightily, but we're relatively less optimistic on Mize, who only flashed brief glimpses of the ace-in-waiting he'd shown prior to his 2019 injury.

⚾ ⚾ ⚾

As complicated as things were on the pro scene, the amateur side was not much better and possibly worse.

The 2020 draft was sliced from its customary 40 rounds down to only five, so there were far fewer players selected, even though 2020 was widely viewed as a strong draft class. Most teams executed pool-manipulation strategies, so the 160 players selected weren't precisely the best 160 players that would've been taken in a normal draft. While much of the scouting work for this past draft was already completed by the time things started shutting down in March, the scouting community surely missed some late risers from the high school and college seasons—Rangers second-rounder Evan Carter, for example, elicited a community reaction of "who is that?" when selected, but later shined during fall instructs. Even the top draft picks, like Lacy, didn't actually play much in their draft year.

The changes will continue rippling. The 2021 draft is likely to be shortened, even though it will have stronger depth than normal because of college players who would've signed in a normal 2020 draft now stampeding towards pro ball. The 2023 draft is likely to have a bumper crop of college talent because of all the preps that didn't have an opportunity to sign last year.

As part of the league's One Baseball initiative, MLB is getting more involved with draft showcases and wood bat summer leagues—and the all-important data output from those events. This funneling helps to filter the manpower needed for team decision-makers to see as many top prospects as possible. Not only is it more convenient, players will face competition closer to their own level, making for an easier assessment when comparing like prospects.

With a new CBA coming and minor-league reorganization reducing the number of players a team can have under contract, it's very possible that there won't be another 40-round draft. The draft process consolidation is already leading to staff reductions in amateur scouting departments, a trend we expect to continue as teams aggressively cut costs. Saying the quiet part out loud: we were already heading this way long before a worldwide pandemic provided a tidy excuse to begin implementation.

⚾ ⚾ ⚾

Baseball tried to look like itself in 2020. We've tried to present a Top 101 Prospects list that at least *looks* like the ones you're accustomed to. If you check under the hood, though, there's less movement than on lists in the past. Where there has been change for non-obvious reasons, there will be an accompanying explanation, be it a change in profile verified by sourcing, or something altogether different.

We will be back at the ballpark at some point, watching baseball from behind home plate in minor leagues that have been transformed by MLB in our absence. Hopefully, next year's 101 will reflect that. ▪

—*Jeffrey Paternostro, Jarrett Seidler and Keanan Lamb are authors of Baseball Prospectus.*

The Fight For, And Plight Of, The Modern Minor Leaguer

by Jen Ramos

There have always been labor issues as it relates to Minor League Baseball. For years, wages have been below the poverty line — *Senne et al v. Kansas City Royals et al*, a class action lawsuit regarding wages, was first filed in 2014 — and working conditions, such as outdated stadium facilities, have been problematic at best.

As the pandemic changed the course of the 2020 minor league season, eventually making it a season that never was, it's become apparent to a larger audience that these labor issues exist. At the end of May, hundreds of minor leaguers were released across all 30 teams. Nonprofits such as Advocates for Minor Leaguers pushed for MLB to continue paying stipends through the end of what would have been the season and More Than Baseball helped with financial assistance if needed.

This has solidified that Major League Baseball, as an entity, and all of its 30 teams do not value minor league labor unless it can be commodified in some way at its highest level. And even in the face of the successful ways in which that's been done, those minor leaguers remain woefully underpaid. It all ends with a majority of minor leaguers — those who could be called "organizational filler" — left in a collectively untenable situation.

Ty Kelly, a co-founder of Advocates for Minor Leaguers and a retired major-league utility player, cited the overall treatment of minor leaguers — from wages, living situations, travel conditions, and how minor leaguers have to get jobs in the offseason to make ends meet. "Clearly the major league organizations are not seeing minor leaguers as future major leaguers. They're seeing them as warm bodies to put in their system and basically just hoping that the cream rises to the crop."

The sentiment that minor leaguers aren't seen as future major leaguers was echoed by Alex King, a 2018 35th-round pick by the Arizona Diamondbacks. He was among the hundreds released in May.

King said he was aware that his role in the organization was as one of those warm bodies to put in their system. In the first month and a half of his professional career, he bounced from short-season Hillsboro to complex ball in the AZL to rookie-level Missoula back to Hillsboro, then back to AZL.

"I was 100% a filler role in my minor league career," King said. "I was basically treated not like a human. I never had a chance to settle in. I lived on a twin air mattress with two other guys in a one-bedroom apartment in Missoula, Montana and I still paid $270 a month for rent. Conditions were not ideal. Going all the way up to [High-A] Visalia, I contributed a lot in the regular season, but when it came time to win in the postseason, I didn't see the field once. That really reassured my role and definitely reassured they did not really care about me in any sense as a human."

In 2018, Congress passed the Save America's Pastime Act, which was meant to exempt minor leaguers from federal labor laws. The act states that "any employee employed to play baseball who is compensated pursuant to a contract that provides for a weekly salary for services performed during the league's championship season (but not Spring Training or the offseason) at a rate that is not less than a weekly salary equal to the minimum wage under section 6(a) for a workweek of 40 hours, irrespective of the number of hours the employee devotes to baseball related activities." Simply because it is law does not mean it is right or just.

"It's cruel," King said. "It's evil to not pay your workers living wage[s] and expect them to put in full effort day in and day out to become an elite athlete and compete at the highest level."

When the act was first introduced in 2016, MLB said in a press release, "Moreover, for the overwhelming majority of individuals, being a Minor League Baseball player is not a career but a short-term seasonal apprenticeship in which the player either advances to the Major Leagues or pursues another career."

The league may consider this a "short-term seasonal apprenticeship," but they never define "seasonal." Ballplayers are expected to stay in condition throughout the offseason without receiving wages or access to resources. They have to find a way to make ends meet until baseball season, as defined by MLB, begins. They're not even paid during Spring Training. This "seasonal apprenticeship" ends up looking more like an unpaid internship.

Ballplayers are putting in work weeks that typically amount to more than 40 hours per week, but they aren't compensated appropriately. Time of play varies and can be anywhere from two hours to four or five; but minor league players get to the park early to train. Batting practice starts 3.5 hours before first pitch is scheduled. Travel times vary depending on the league, but that alone adds many hours related to their employment. Minor league schedules can go every day, and sometimes teams only get one off day in a month. Add that all up and you've got a work week that can come to nearly double the typical 40-hour work week.

"I just think that Major League Baseball and every organization understands what players are going through during the season and in offseason just to survive, just to continue playing baseball, yet they want to consider the minor leagues as seasonal apprenticeships," Kelly said. "They want to continue pushing those ideas and pushing guys into working odd jobs rather than supporting their training and paying for good living conditions."

King said he thinks part of the reason he was never very good at keeping in shape during the offseason is because of a lack of income.

"I never had any income to pay for a membership to a gym, pay for a membership to an indoor facility," King said. "I was milking my way around, trying to find a place that would let me in for free, and half the time I couldn't find a spot."

Similar to how minor leaguers are expected to stay in playing condition during the offseason, they were also expected to do the same through the beginning of the COVID-19 pandemic. Access to equipment and facilities were made far more difficult due to lockdown restrictions, and even when it was safe, it was still unaffordable for many minor leaguers. Most were sent home when camps shut down during Spring Training, so there was no access to team facilities either.

"They were saying, 'Stay ready as much as you can because we don't know what's going to happen,'" Kelly said. "They're trying to be able to not pay them while asking them to do things for their organization, yet they still need to get ready for next year or go to instructs."

Kelly said he doesn't know what would have been possible as far as helping ballplayers train due to the pandemic but thinks that the best thing teams could've done is pay minor leaguers enough so that they could afford to train whenever that was possible.

King thinks MLB teams could have done a better job taking care of its minor leaguers.

"Just to leave guys out to dry, expecting them to train and be at their peak performance level, ready to come back at any given point and not pay them … I know we do it in the offseason, but this is a completely different situation where hardly anybody can find a job and you're not gonna pay your guys and expect them to keep in tip-top shape?" King said. "I think that's just absolutely ridiculous."

Despite all of this, MLB is quick to market top-round draft picks and prospects who are pegged as future All-Stars. They become "must-see" prospects if they come through your nearest minor league town. They're names to watch at the Futures Game during the MLB All-Star weekend. The league earns revenues from doing this while those minor leaguers that they market earn below poverty wages.

What MLB sees here is a very specific forest and none of the trees. Minor leaguers are viewed through the lens of what they can do one day in the future. The present value they have, in the minor leagues, is unquantified because MLB doesn't care about the guys designated as organizational filler — they're not the ones who can bring in that meaningful long-term income.

"They do want to essentially just use the very top stars to sort of mask what is happening in the minor leagues," Kelly says. "[They want] to make it seem like it's all up-and-coming stars and it's very exciting, yet not compensate them for being the next best thing, Because at the end of the day, they don't believe that 99% of those players are going to get called up and be marketable for them."

The idea that minor league labor isn't valued, especially if the labor doesn't provide anything for a major league team, is also apparent when looking at which players get access to the resources MLB teams provide to their farm system. King noticed a difference in how minor leaguers were treated depending on their roles: top prospects versus organizational filler. Top prospects would often be given preferential treatment in situations such as training, practice and access.

"They're the future of the organization," King said. "You only get 25 guys on a big-league roster and they have some of the higher odds to make that 25-man roster. It totally makes sense. But for the other 95% of us that are grinding every day, working our tails off, all of this is hard. It's hard for us because we don't get preferred treatment. We just gotta grind it out and make do with what we got."

The focus on top prospects also erases how there's a number of underdog stories, though. Guys who aren't top draft picks or highly touted prospects do make it to the majors and contribute in significant ways. Take Daniel Nava's story, for example. He went undrafted after being an equipment manager at Santa Clara University, was signed by the Boston Red Sox from the independent league Chico Outlaws, then went on to have 1,977 plate appearances over seven seasons in the majors with a career 6.0 WARP.

"There are so many good players that get drafted after the fifth round, after the 10th round, undrafted free agents, you get those stories all the time," Kelly said. "There's just so many underdog stories. Look at Albert Pujols who's been playing for the last 20 years: 13th rounder. Guys in the playoffs this year who were late rounders or undrafted free agents making an impact. The fact that they want to cut the draft as short as possible, essentially says they're fine with eliminating a lot of those underdog stories to just sort of hope for the best in the draft."

Some examples of unheralded prospects who made an impact in the 2020 postseason include the Tampa Bay Rays' Mike Brosseau, who went undrafted out of Oakland University after his senior year and ended up hitting the game-winning home run to advance the Rays to the ALCS, and the Rays' Diego Castillo, an international free agent who wasn't considered a top prospect and only allowed three runs (two earned) as a reliever throughout the postseason.

It all goes back to the idea that most minor leaguers are not viewed as future major leaguers.

"If they really wanted to treat them like future major leaguers, they would be feeding them well, giving them enough money so that they could afford to sleep in beds and not on air mattresses. Giving them enough money so that don't have to work odd jobs in the offseason, so they can put all their time into training," Kelly said.

For King, he knew this as a minor leaguer. He said the Diamondbacks were great and gave ballplayers everything that was needed, but it was very apparent he was never intended to be a guy for them.

"That's a really hard thing to live with when you're playing as a minor leaguer," King said. "I know I'm not the only one that was like that. Like I said, probably 75-90% of guys on a minor league roster are treated that way. That's no way to treat employees in your company, especially the ones that make you money."

After being released, King retired from playing and got a job with Game Day USA, a youth baseball tournament company. He said he feels like he's giving back to the game that's given him a lot but has his own fears that come with it.

"It's a really good feeling to see kids have intense passion for the game, have lots of skills, and it just pains me to know that if they do make it to the next level, to that pro level, they're going to be greeted with a rude surprise with how Major League Baseball actually operates," King said.

—Jen Ramos is an author of Baseball Prospectus.

Team Codes

CODE	TEAM	LG	AFF	NAME
ABD	Aberdeen	NYP	Orioles	IronBirds
AKR	Akron	EAS	Cleveland	RubberDucks
ABQ	Albuquerque	PCL	Rockies	Isotopes
ALT	Altoona	EAS	Pirates	Curve
AMA	Amarillo	TEX	Padres	Sod Poodles
ARI	Arizona	NL	-	D-backs
ARK	Arkansas	TEX	Mariners	Travelers
ART	Artemisa	CNS	-	-
ASH	Asheville	SAL	Rockies	Tourists
ATL	Atlanta	NL	-	Braves
AUB	Auburn	NYP	Nationals	Doubledays
AUG	Augusta	SAL	Giants	GreenJackets
ANG	AZL Angels	AZL	Angels	-
ASGO	AZL Athletics Gold	AZL	Athletics	-
ASGR	AZL Athletics Green	AZL	Athletics	-
BRB	AZL Brewers Blue	AZL	Brewers	-
BRG	AZL Brewers Gold	AZL	Brewers	-
CLT	AZL Cleveland Blue	AZL	Cleveland	-
CLE	AZL Cleveland Red	AZL	Cleveland	-
CUBB	AZL Cubs 1	AZL	Cubs	-
CUBR	AZL Cubs 2	AZL	Cubs	-
DIA	AZL D-backs	AZL	D-backs	-
DOD1	AZL Dodgers 1	AZL	Dodgers	-
DOD2	AZL Dodgers 2	AZL	Dodgers	-
GIB	AZL Giants Black	AZL	Giants	-
GIO	AZL Giants Orange	AZL	Giants	-
MAR	AZL Mariners	AZL	Mariners	-
SD1	AZL Padres 1	AZL	Padres	-
SD2	AZL Padres 2	AZL	Padres	-
RAN	AZL Rangers	AZL	Rangers	-
RED	AZL Reds	AZL	Reds	-
ROY	AZL Royals	AZL	Royals	-
WSX	AZL White Sox	AZL	White Sox	-
BAL	Baltimore	AL	-	Orioles
BAT	Batavia	NYP	Marlins	Muckdogs
BEL	Beloit	MID	Athletics	Snappers
BIL	Billings	PIO	Reds	Mustangs
BLX	Biloxi	SOU	Brewers	Shuckers
BNG	Binghamtom	EAS	Mets	Rumble Ponies
BIR	Birmingham	SOU	White Sox	Barons
BLU	Bluefield	APP	Blue Jays	Blue Jays
BOI	Boise	NWL	Rockies	Hawks
BOS	Boston	AL	-	Red Sox
BOW	Bowie	EAS	Orioles	Baysox

CODE	TEAM	LG	AFF	NAME
BG	Bowling Green	MID	Rays	Hot Rods
BRD	Bradenton	FSL	Pirates	Marauders
BRS	Bristol	APP	Pirates	Pirates
BRK	Brooklyn	NYP	Mets	Cyclones
BUF	Buffalo	INT	Blue Jays	Bisons
BUR	Burlington	APP	Royals	Royals
BUR	Burlington	MID	Angels	Bees
CAR	Carolina	CAR	Brewers	Mudcats
CR	Cedar Rapids	MID	Twins	Kernels
CSC	Charleston	SAL	Yankees	RiverDogs
CHA	Charlotte	FSL	Rays	Stone Crabs
CHA	Charlotte	INT	White Sox	Knights
CHA	Chattanooga	SOU	Reds	Lookouts
CHB	Chiba Lotte	NPB	-	Marines
CHW	Chicago	AL	-	White Sox
CHC	Chicago	NL	-	Cubs
CHU	Chunichi	NPB	-	Dragons
CFG	Cienfuegos	CNS	-	-
CIN	Cincinnati	NL	-	Reds
CLR	Clearwater	FSL	Phillies	Threshers
CLE	Cleveland	AL	-	-
INDB	Cleveland Blue	AZL	Cleveland	-
INDR	Cleveland Red	AZL	Cleveland	-
CLI	Clinton	MID	Marlins	LumberKings
COL	Columbia	SAL	Mets	Fireflies
COL	Columbus	INT	Cleveland	Clippers
COH	Columbus	INT	Cleveland	Clippers
ONE	Connecticut	NYP	Tigers	Tigers
CC	Corpus Christi	TEX	Astros	Hooks
DAN	Danville	APP	Braves	Braves
DYT	Dayton	MID	Reds	Dragons
DAY	Daytona	FSL	Reds	Tortugas
DEL	Delmarva	SAL	Orioles	Shorebirds
DET	Detroit	AL	-	Tigers
DE	Down East	CAR	Rangers	Wood Ducks
DUN	Dunedin	FSL	Blue Jays	Blue Jays
DUR	Durham	INT	Rays	Bulls
ELP	El Paso	PCL	Padres	Chihuahuas
ELZ	Elizabethton	APP	Twins	Twins
ERI	Erie	EAS	Tigers	SeaWolves
EUG	Eugene	NWL	Cubs	Emeralds
EVE	Everett	NWL	Mariners	AquaSox
FAY	Fayetteville	CAR	Astros	Woodpeckers
BRV	Florida	FSL	Braves	Fire Frogs

CODE	TEAM	LG	AFF	NAME
FTM	Fort Myers	FSL	Twins	Miracle
FW	Fort Wayne	MID	Padres	TinCaps
FRE	Frederick	CAR	Orioles	Keys
FRE	Fresno	PCL	Nationals	Grizzlies
FRI	Frisco	TEX	Rangers	RoughRiders
FKU	Fukuoka	NPB	-	Hawks
AST	GCL Astros	GCL	Astros	-
BLJ	GCL Blue Jays	GCL	Blue Jays	-
BRA	GCL Braves	GCL	Braves	-
CRD	GCL Cardinals	GCL	Cardinals	-
MRL	GCL Marlins	GCL	Marlins	-
MTS	GCL Mets	GCL	Mets	-
NAT	GCL Nationals	GCL	Nationals	-
ORI	GCL Orioles	GCL	Orioles	-
PHE	GCL Phillies East	GCL	Phillies	-
PHW	GCL Phillies West	GCL	Phillies	-
PIR	GCL Pirates	GCL	Pirates	-
RAY	GCL Rays	GCL	Rays	-
RSX	GCL Red Sox	GCL	Red Sox	-
TIG	GCL Tigers East	GCL	Tigers	-
TIW	GCL Tigers West	GCL	Tigers	-
TWI	GCL Twins	GCL	Twins	-
YAE	GCL Yankees East	GCL	Yankees	-
YAW	GCL Yankees West	GCL	Yankees	-
GJ	Grand Junction	PIO	Rockies	Rockies
GTF	Great Falls	PIO	White Sox	Voyagers
GL	Great Lakes	MID	Dodgers	Loons
GRN	Greeneville	APP	Reds	Reds
GBO	Greensboro	SAL	Pirates	Grasshoppers
GVL	Greenville	SAL	Red Sox	Drive
GWN	Gwinnett	INT	Braves	Stripers
HAG	Hagerstown	SAL	Nationals	Suns
HNS	Hanshin	NPB	-	Tigers
HBG	Harrisburg	EAS	Nationals	Senators
HFD	Hartford	EAS	Rockies	Yard Goats
HIC	Hickory	SAL	Rangers	Crawdads
HIL	Hillsboro	NWL	D-backs	Hops
HRO	Hiroshima Toyo	NPB	-	Carp
HOU	Houston	AL	-	Astros
HV	Hudson Valley	NYP	Rays	Renegades
IDF	Idaho Falls	PIO	Royals	Chukars
IND	Indianapolis	INT	Pirates	Indianapolis
IE	Inland Empire	CAL	Angels	66ers
IOW	Iowa	PCL	Cubs	Cubs
JXN	Jackson	SOU	D-backs	Generals
JAX	Jacksonville	SOU	Marlins	Jumbo Shrimp
JC	Johnson City	APP	Cardinals	Cardinals
JUP	Jupiter	FSL	Marlins	Hammerheads
KNC	Kane County	MID	D-backs	Cougars
KAN	Kannapolis	SAL	White Sox	Intimidators
KC	Kansas City	AL	-	Royals
KNG	Kingsport	APP	Mets	Mets
HAB	La Habana	CNS	-	
LC	Lake Country	MID	Cleveland	Captains
LE	Lake Elsinore	CAL	Padres	Storm
LAK	Lakeland	FSL	Tigers	Flying Tigers

CODE	TEAM	LG	AFF	NAME
JS	Lakewood	SAL	Phillies	BlueClaws
LNC	Lancaster	CAL	Rockies	JetHawks
LAN	Lansing	MID	Blue Jays	Lugnuts
LTU	Las Tunas	CNS	-	
LV	Las Vegas	PCL	Athletics	Aviators
LHV	Lehigh Valley	INT	Phillies	IronPigs
LEX	Lexington	SAL	Royals	Legends
LAA	Los Angeles	AL	-	Angels
LAD	Los Angeles	NL	-	Dodgers
LOU	Louisville	INT	Reds	Bats
LOW	Lowell	NYP	Red Sox	Spinners
LYN	Lynchburg	CAR	Cleveland	Hillcats
MV	Mahoning Valley	NYP	Cleveland	Scrappers
MEM	Memphis	PCL	Cardinals	Redbirds
MIA	Miami	NL	-	Marlins
MID	Midland	TEX	Athletics	RockHounds
MIL	Milwaukee	NL	-	Brewers
MIN	Minnesota	AL	-	Twins
MIS	Mississippi	SOU	Braves	Braves
MIS	Missoula	PIO	D-backs	Osprey
MOB	Mobile	SOU	Angels	BayBears
MOD	Modesto	CAL	Mariners	Nuts
MTG	Montgomery	SOU	Rays	Biscuits
MB	Myrtle Beach	CAR	Cubs	Pelicans
NAS	Nashville	PCL	Rangers	Sounds
NH	New Hampsire	EAS	Blue Jays	Fisher Cats
NO	New Orleans	PCL	Marlins	Baby Cakes
NYY	New York	AL	-	Yankees
NYM	New York	NL	-	Mets
NIP	Nippon Ham	NPB	-	Fighters
NOR	Norfolk	INT	Orioles	Tides
NWA	NW Arkansas	TEX	Royals	Naturals
OAK	Oakland	AL	-	Athletics
OGD	Ogden	PIO	Dodgers	Raptors
OKC	Oklahoma City	PCL	Dodgers	Dodgers
OMA	Omaha	PCL	Royals	Storm Chasers
ORM	Orem	PIO	Angels	Owiz
ORX	Orix	NPB	-	Buffaloes
PMB	Palm Beach	FSL	Cardinals	Cardinals
WOR	Pawtucket	INT	Red Sox	Red Sox
PNS	Pensacola	SOU	Twins	Blue Wahoos
PEO	Peoria	MID	Cardinals	Chiefs
PHI	Philadelphia	NL	-	Phillies
PIT	Pittsburgh	NL	-	Pirates
POR	Portland	EAS	Red Sox	Sea Dogs
FBG	Potomac	CAR	Nationals	Nationals
PRN	Princeton	APP	Rays	Rays
PUL	Pulaski	APP	Yankees	Yankees
QC	Quad Cities	MID	Astros	River Bandits
RAK	Rakuten	NPB	-	Golden Eagles
RC	Rancho Cucamongo	CAL	Dodgers	Quakes
REA	Reading	EAS	Phillies	Fightin Phils
RNO	Reno	PCL	D-backs	Aces
RIC	Richmond	EAS	Giants	Flying Squirrels
ROC	Rochester	INT	Twins	Red Wings
COL	Rockies	NL	-	Rockies

CODE	TEAM	LG	AFF	NAME
RMV	Rocky Mountain	PIO	Brewers	Vibes
ROM	Rome	SAL	Braves	Braves
RR	Round Rock	PCL	Astros	Express
SAC	Sacramento	PCL	Giants	River Cats
SAL	Salem	CAR	Red Sox	Red Sox
SK	Salem-Keizer	NWL	Giants	Volcanoes
SL	Salt Lake	PCL	Angels	Bees
SA	San Antonio	PCL	Brewers	Missions
SD	San Diego	NL	-	Padres
SF	San Francisco	NL	-	Giants
SJ	San Jose	CAL	Giants	Giants
SWB	Scranton/WB	INT	Yankees	RailRiders
SEA	Seattle	AL	-	Mariners
SEI	Seibu	NPB	-	Lions
SB	South Bend	MID	Cubs	Cubs
SPO	Spokane	NWL	Rangers	Spokane
SPR	Springfield	TEX	Cardinals	Cardinals
STL	St. Louis	NL	-	Cardinals
SLU	St. Lucie	FSL	Mets	Mets
SCO	State College	NYP	Cardinals	Spikes
SI	Staten Island	NYP	Yankees	Yankees
STK	Stockton	CAL	Athletics	Ports
SYR	Syracuse	INT	Mets	Mets
TAC	Tacoma	PCL	Mariners	Rainiers
TAM	Tampa	FSL	Yankees	Tarpons
TB	Tampa Bay	AL	-	Rays
TNS	Tennessee	SOU	Cubs	Smokies
TEX	Texas	AL	-	Rangers
TOL	Toledo	INT	Tigers	Mud Hens
TOR	Toronto	AL	-	Blue Jays
TRN	Trenton	EAS	Yankees	Thunder
TCV	Tri-City	NYP	Astros	ValleyCats
TRI	Tri-City	NWL	Padres	Dust Devils
TUL	Tulsa	TEX	Dodgers	Drillers
VAN	Vancouver	NWL	Blue Jays	Canadians
VER	Vermont	NYP	Athletics	Lake Monsters
VIS	Visalia	CAL	D-backs	Rawhide
WAS	Washington	NL	-	Nationals
WEV	West Virginia	NYP	Pirates	Black Bears
WV	West Virginia (PIT)	SAL	Mariners	Power
WM	Western Michigan	MID	Tigers	Whitecaps
WIL	Williamsport	NYP	Phillies	Crosscutters
WIL	Wilmington	CAR	Royals	Blue Rocks
WS	Winston-Salem	CAR	White Sox	Dash
WIS	Wisconsin	MID	Brewers	Timber Rattlers
YKL	Yakult	NPB	-	Swallows
YKO	Yokohama DeNa	NPB	-	BayStars
YOM	Yomiuri	NPB	-	Giants

Index of Names